Essays on the history of the American West

P9-DUP-729

Essays on the history of the American West

Edited by

Stephen Salsbury
University of Delaware

The Dryden Press
Hinsdale, Illinois

Preface

Ever since Hollywood the American West has become synonymous with cowboys, Indians, outlaws and dead-eye marshals. America will probably never lose this romantic view, but students of history quickly come to learn there is much more to the West than cowponies, tomahawks, six-shooters, and tin stars. The first problem is the very definition of West. As a third-generation native Californian I grew up thinking that "back East" meant Salt Lake City and Denver as well as Chicago and Philadelphia. And when I moved to Cambridge, Massachusetts, I discovered that the Bostonians considered the Connecticut Valley and Albany "western," not to mention such remote places as Buffalo, St. Louis, and Walla Walla.

Time further complicates the problem. During the colonial period America was little more than a string of settlements hugging the Atlantic. Few people lived beyond the fall line. In colonial times Springfield, Massachusetts and Lancaster, Pennsylvania were western. Even during the Federalist period, the Northwest meant what was to become the states of Ohio, Indiana, Michigan, Illinois, and Wisconsin, while the Southwest meant land later to be part of Alabama, Mississippi, and Louisiana. The westward movement soon turned these areas into the "East," but historians still use the terms Old Northwest and Old Southwest to refer to the Federalist West. For the purpose of this book I have followed Frederick Jackson Turner by defining *West* as the frontier of American civilization. Thus the essays I have selected do not confine themselves to a single geographic region but cover the United States from Dedham, Massachusetts to San Francisco, California (both of which, of course, qualify as western places to my Boston friends).

The main problem facing an editor who would put together an anthology of essays on the westward movement is the vast quantity of material. Frederick Jackson Turner's famous 1893 paper "The Significance of the Frontier in American History" unleashed two generations of intensive scholarship. Although interest in frontier history has waned since 1940, every year still sees a large quantity of new work appear. The first thing, however, that strikes one about the literature is its uneven quality. Some subjects—such as land policy or the West as safety valve, for example—have generated high-quality scholarship. Other topics—for example, mining and water use—remain largely untapped or in the hands of antiquarians. In this volume, I have tried to collect a sample of the best traditional essays together with some of the more provocative modern work. In all cases I have selected work that has been pathbreaking in its interpretation and that attempts to tie western history into the mainstream of America's development.

I would like to thank Professor Ralph Goodwin of East Texas State University for his advice and for permission to print for the first time his essay "Righting the Century of Dishonor: Indian Reform as a Reaffirmation of Conservative Values." In the final analysis, however, I must take full responsibility for the selection of the material in the book and for any errors.

Stephen Salsbury

Newark, Delaware
January, 1974

Contents

Part 1
The frontier and American society: The Turner thesis and its ramifications

The significance of the frontier in American history

Frederick Jackson Turner

In this essay, Frederick Jackson Turner formulated the frontier hypothesis which he thought unlocked the secret of the origins of American democracy. Born in Portage, Wisconsin in 1861, Turner took his bachelor's and master's degrees at the University of Wisconsin. In 1888 he went East to Johns Hopkins University in Baltimore for graduate work. There he studied with Herbert Baxter Adams, a proponent of the germ theory of civilization who traced American institutions, especially democratic government, back to the forests of medieval Germany, inhabited by freedom-loving teutonic tribes. Turner accepted the high standards of scholarship and thought characteristic of Johns Hopkins, but he questioned Adams' explanation for the formation of American institutions. After receiving his doctorate Turner returned home to teach at the University of Wisconsin. He presented his famous paper at a meeting of the American Historical Association held at the Chicago World's Columbian Exposition in July 1893. American democracy derived not from Europe, he argued, but from experiences along the raw frontier, which started with the first settlements of the Virginia Company of 1607 and continued until the census of 1890 announced the end of the frontier. Turner went further: he insisted that nearly all the great developments in American history—economic growth, the constitutional struggle over slavery, the Civil War, the Indian wars, the triumph of nationalism over localism, to name but a few—were directly molded by the frontier.

It took nearly a decade for Turner's views to win wide acceptance, but by 1903 his ideas carried all before them. Turner is significant not for the quantity of his writing, for his output was relatively small, but because of the enormous influence he had on his contemporaries and on serious students of American history. Turner ended his career at Harvard, and after his death in 1932 his ideals were perpetuated by Frederick Merk. Merk trained a devoted band of disciples deeply influenced by Turner's ideas, some of whom (such as Paul Gates and Ray Billington) were destined to become great historians in their own right.

For further reading: Frederick Jackson Turner, *The Frontier in American History* (New York: Henry Holt and Company, 1920)*; Ray Allen Billington, *America's Frontier Heritage* (New York: Holt, Rinehart and Winston, 1966)*; Lee Benson, *Turner and Beard*

Reprinted from the *Annual Report of the American Historical Association* for 1893, pp. 199-227.

(Glencoe, Ill.: Free Press, 1960)*; Fulmer Mood, "The Development of Frederick Jackson Turner as a Historical Thinker," Colonial Society of Massachusetts, *Transactions, 1937-1942,* XXXIV (1943), 283-352; Gilman M. Ostrander, "Turner and the Germ Theory," *Agricultural History*, XXXII (1958), 258-261; Carl Becker, "Frederick Jackson Turner," in Howard W. Odum, ed., *American Masters of Social Science* (New York: Henry Holt and Company, 1927), 273-318; Frederic L. Paxson, "A Generation of the Frontier Hypothesis," *Pacific Historical Review*, II (1933), 34-51; George W. Pierson, "The Frontier and Frontiersman of Turner's Essays," *Pennsylvania Magazine of History and Biography*, XXIV (1940), 449-478; George W. Pierson, "The Frontier and American Institutions: A Criticism of the Turner Theory," *New England Quarterly*, XV (June 1942), 224-255; Gene M. Gressley, "The Turner Thesis—a Problem in Historiography," *Agricultural History*, XXXII (1958), 227-249; Ray A. Billington, *Frederick Jackson Turner* (New York: Oxford University Press, 1973).

*Available in paperback.

In a recent bulletin of the Superintendent of the Census for 1890 appear these significant words: "Up to and including 1880 the country had a frontier of settlement, but at present the unsettled area has been so broken into by isolated bodies of settlement that there can hardly be said to be a frontier line. In the discussion of its extent, its westward movement, etc., it can not, therefore, any longer have a place in the census reports." This brief official statement marks the closing of a great historic movement. Up to our own day American history has been in a large degree the history of the colonization of the Great West. The existence of an area of free land, its continuous recession, and the advance of American settlement westward, explain American development.

Behind institutions, behind constitutional forms and modifications, lie the vital forces that call these organs into life and shape them to meet changing conditions. The peculiarity of American institutions is, the fact that they have been compelled to adapt themselves to the changes of an expanding people—to the changes involved in crossing a continent, in winning a wilderness, and in developing at each area of this progress out of the primitive economic and political conditions of the frontier into the complexity of city life. Said Calhoun in 1817, "We are great, and rapidly—I was about to say fearfully—growing!"[1] So saying, he touched the distinguishing feature of American life. All peoples show development; the germ theory of politics has been sufficiently emphasized. In the case of most nations, however, the development has occurred in a limited area; and if the nation has expanded, it has met other growing peoples whom it has conquered. But in the case of the United States we have a different phenomenon. Limiting our attention to the Atlantic coast, we have the familiar phenomenon of the evolution of institutions in a limited area, such as the rise of representative government; the differentiation of simple colonial governments into complex organs; the progress from primitive industrial society, without division of labor, up to manufacturing civilization. But we have in addition to this a recurrence of the process of evolution in each western area reached in the process of expansion. Thus American development has exhibited not merely advance along a single line, but a return to primitive conditions on a continually advancing frontier line, and a new development for that area. American social development has been continually beginning over again on the frontier. This perennial rebirth, this fluidity of American life, this expansion westward with its new opportunities, its continuous touch with the simplicity of primitive society, furnish the forces dominating American character. The true point of view in the history of this nation is not the Atlantic coast, it is the great West, Even the slavery struggle, which is made so exclusive an object of attention by writers like Prof. von Holst, occupies its important place in American history because of its relation to westward expansion.

In this advance, the frontier is the outer edge of the wave—the meeting point between savagery and civilization. Much has been written about the frontier from the point of view of border warfare and the chase, but as a field for the serious study of the economist and the historian it has been neglected.

The American frontier is sharply distinguished from the European frontier—a fortified boundary line running through dense populations. The most significant thing about the American frontier is, that it lies at the hither edge of free land. In the census reports it is treated as the margin of that settlement which has a density of two or more to the square mile. The term is an elastic one, and for our purposes does not need sharp definition. We shall consider the whole frontier belt, including the Indian country and the outer margin of the "settled area" of the census reports. This paper will make no attempt to treat the subject exhaustively; its aim is simply to call attention to the frontier as a fertile field for investigation, and to suggest some of the problems which arise in connection with it.

In the settlement of America we have to observe how European life entered the continent, and how America modified and developed that life and reacted on Europe. Our early history is the study of European germs developing in an American environment. Too exclusive attention has been paid by institutional students to the Germanic origins, too little to the American factors. The frontier is the line of most rapid and effective Americanization. The wilderness masters the colonist. It finds him a European in dress, industries, tools, modes of travel, and thought. It takes him from the railroad car and puts him in the birch canoe. It strips off the garments of civilization and arrays him in the hunting shirt and the moccasin. It puts him in the log cabin of the Cherokee and Iroquois and runs an Indian palisade around him. Before long he has gone to planting Indian corn and plowing with a sharp stick; he shouts the war cry and takes the scalp in orthodox Indian fashion. In short, at the frontier the environment is at first too strong for the man. He must accept the conditions which it furnishes, or perish, and so he fits himself into the Indian clearings and follows the Indian trails. Little by little he transforms the wilderness, but the outcome is not the old Europe, not simply the development of Germanic germs, any more than the first phenomenon was a case of reversion to the Germanic mark. The fact is, that here is a new product that is American. At first, the frontier was the Atlantic coast. It was the frontier of Europe in a very real sense. Moving westward, the frontier became more and more American. As successive terminal moraines result from successive glaciations, so each frontier leaves its traces behind it, and when it becomes a settled area the region still partakes of the frontier characteristics. Thus the advance of the frontier has meant a steady movement away from the influence of Europe, a steady growth of independence on American lines. And to study this advance, the men who grew up under these conditions, and the political, economic, and social results of it, is to study the really American part of our history.

Stages of Frontier Advance

In the course of the seventeenth century the frontier was advanced up the Atlantic river courses, just beyond the "fall line," and the tidewater region became the settled area. In the first half of the eighteenth century another advance occurred. Traders followed the Delaware and Shawnese Indians to the Ohio as early as the end of the first quarter of the century.[2] Gov. Spotswood, of Virginia, made an expedition in 1714 across the Blue Ridge. The end of the first quarter of the century saw the advance of the Scotch-Irish and the Palatine Germans up the Shenandoah Valley into the western part of Virginia, and along the Piedmont region of the Carolinas.[3] The Germans in New York pushed the frontier of settlement up the Mohawk to German Flats.[4] In Pennsylvania the town of Bedford indicates the line of settlement. Settlements had begun on New River, a branch of the Kanawha, and on the sources of the Yadkin and French Broad.[5] The King attempted to arrest the advance by his proclamation of 1763,[6] forbidding settlements beyond the sources of the rivers flowing into the Atlantic; but in vain. In the period of the Revolution the frontier crossed the Alleghanies into Kentucky and Tennessee, and the upper waters of the Ohio were settled.[7] When the first census was taken in 1790, the continuous settled area was bounded by a line which ran near the coast of Maine, and included New England except a portion of Vermont and New Hampshire, New York along the Hudson and up the Mohawk about Schenectady, eastern and southern Pennsylvania, Virginia well across the Shenandoah Valley, and the Carolinas and eastern Georgia.[8] Beyond this region of continuous settlement were the small settled areas of Kentucky and Tennessee, and the Ohio, with the mountains intervening between them and the Atlantic area, thus giving a new and important character to the frontier. The isolation of the region increased its peculiarly American tendencies, and the need of transportation facilities to connect it with the East called out important schemes of internal improvement, which will be noted farther on. The "West," as a self-conscious section, began to evolve.

From decade to decade distinct advances of the frontier occurred. By the census of 1820[9] the settled area included Ohio, southern Indiana and Illinois, southeastern Missouri, and about one-half of Louisiana. This settled area had surrounded Indian areas, and the management of these tribes became an object of political concern. The frontier region of the time lay along the Great Lakes, where Astor's American Fur Company operated in the Indian trade,[10] and beyond the Mississippi, where Indian traders extended their activity even to the Rocky Mountains; Florida also furnished frontier conditions. The Mississippi River region was the scene of typical frontier settlements.[11]

The rising steam nativation[12] on western waters, the opening of the Erie Canal, and the westward extension of cotton[13] culture added five frontier states to the Union in this period. Grund, writing in 1836, declares: "It appears then that the universal disposition of Americans to emigrate to the western wilderness, in order to enlarge their dominion over inanimate nature, is the actual result of an expansive power which is inherent in them, and which by continually agitating all classes of society is constantly throwing a large portion of the whole population on the extreme confines of the State, in order to gain space for its development. Hardly is a new State or Territory formed before the same principle manifests itself again and gives rise to a further emigration; and so is it destined to go on until a physical barrier must finally obstruct its progress."[14]

In the middle of this century the line indicated by the present eastern boundary of Indian Territory, Nebraska, and Kansas marked the frontier of the Indian country.[15] Minnesota and Wisconsin still exhibited frontier conditions,[16] but the distinctive frontier of the period is found in California, where the gold discoveries had sent a sudden tide of adventurous miners, and in Oregon, and the settlements in Utah.[17] As the frontier has leaped over the Alleghanies, so now is skipped the Great Plains and the Rocky Mountains; and in the same way that the advance of the frontiersmen beyond the Alleghanies had caused the rise of important questions of transportation and internal improvement, so now the settlers beyond the Rocky Mountains needed means of communication with the East, and in the furnishing of these arose the settlement of the Great Plains and the development of still another kind of frontier life. Railroads, fostered by land grants, sent an increasing tide of immigrants into the far West. The United States Army fought a series of Indian wars in Minnesota, Dakota, and the Indian Territory.

By 1880 the settled area had been pushed into northern Michigan, Wisconsin, and Minnesota, along Dakota rivers, and in the Black Hills region, and was ascending the rivers of Kansas and Nebraska. The development of mines in Colorado had drawn isolated frontier settlements into that region, and Montana and Idaho were receiving settlers. The frontier was found in these mining camps and the ranches of the Great Plains. The superintendent of the census for 1890 reports, as previously stated, that the settlements of the West lie so scattered over the region that there can no longer be said to be a frontier line.

In these successive frontiers we find natural boundary lines which have served to mark and to affect the characteristics of the frontiers, namely: The "fall line;" the Alleghany Mountains; the Mississippi; the Missouri, where its direction approximates north and south; the line of the arid lands, approximately the ninety-ninth meridian; and the Rocky Mountains. The fall line marked the frontier of the seventeenth century; the Alleghanies that of the eighteenth; the Mississippi that of the first quarter of the nineteenth; the Missouri that of the middle of this century (omitting the California movement); and the belt of the Rocky Mountains and the arid tract, the present frontier. Each was won by a series of Indian wars.

The Frontier Furnishes a Field for Comparative Study of Social Development

At the Atlantic frontier one can study the germs of processes repeated at each successive frontier. We have the complex European life sharply precipitated by the wilderness into the simplicity of primitive conditions. The first frontier had to meet its Indian question, its question of the disposition of the public domain, of the means of intercourse with older settlements, of the extension of political organization, of religious and educational activity. And the settlement of these and similar questions for one frontier served as a guide for the next. The American student needs not to go to the "prim little townships of Sleswick" for illustrations of the law of continuity and development. For example, he may study the origin of our land policies in the colonial land policy; he may see how the system grew by adapting the statutes to the customs of the successive frontiers.[18] He may see how the mining experience in the lead regions of Wisconsin, Illinois, and Iowa was applied to the mining laws of the Rockies,[19] and how our Indian policy has been a series of experimentations on successive frontiers. Each tier of new States has found in the older ones material for its constitutions.[20] Each frontier has made similar contributions to American character, as will be discussed farther on.

But with all these similarities there are essential differences, due to the place element and the time element. It is evident that the farming frontier of the Mississippi Valley presents different conditions from the mining frontier of the Rocky Mountains. The frontier reached by the Pacific Railroad, surveyed into rectangles, guarded by the United States Army, and recruited by the daily immigrant ship, moves forward at a swifter pace and in a different way than the frontier reached by the birch canoe or the pack horse. The geologist traces patiently the shores of ancient seas, maps their areas, and compares the older and the newer. It would be a work worth the historian's labors to mark these various frontiers and in detail compare one with another. Not only would there result a more adequate conception of American development and characteristics, but invaluable additions would be made to the history of society.

Loria,[21] the Italian economist, has urged the study of colonial life as an aid in understanding the stages of European development, affirming that colonial settlement is for economic science what the mountain is for geology, bringing to light primitive stratifications. "America," he says, "has the key to the historical enigma which Europe has sought for centuries in vain, and the land which has no history reveals luminously the course of universal history." There is much truth in this. The United States lies like a huge page in the history of society. Line by line as we read this continental page from west to east we find the record of social evolution. It begins with the Indian and the hunter; it goes on to tell of the disintegration of savagery by the entrance of the trader, the pathfinder of civilization; we read the annals of the pastoral stage in ranch life; the exploitation of the soil by the raising of unrotated crops of corn and wheat in sparsely settled farming communities; the intensive culture of the denser farm settlement; and finally the manufacturing organization with city and factory system.[22] This page is familiar to the student of census statistics, but how little of it has been used by our historians. Particularly in eastern States this page is a palimpsest. What is now a manufacturing State was in an earlier decade an area of intensive farming. Earlier yet it had been a wheat area, and still earlier the "range" had attracted the cattleherder. Thus Wisconsin, now developing manufacture, is a State with varied agricultural interests. But earlier it was given over to almost exclusive grain-raising, like North Dakota at the present time.

Each of these areas has had an influence in our economic and political history; the evolution of each into a higher stage has worked political transformations. But what constitutional historian has made any adequate attempt to interpret political facts by the light of these social areas and changes?[23]

The Atlantic frontier was compounded of fisherman, fur-trader, miner, cattle-raiser, and farmer. Excepting the fisherman, each type of industry was on the march toward the West, impelled by an irresistible attraction. Each passed in successive waves across the continent. Stand at Cumberland Gap and watch the procession of civilization, marching single file—the buffalo following the trail to the salt springs, the Indian, the fur-trader and hunter, the cattle-raiser, the pioneer farmer—and the frontier has passed by. Stand at South Pass in the Rockies a century later and see the same procession with wider intervals between. The unequal rate of advance compels us to distinguish the frontier into the trader's frontier, the rancher's frontier, or the miner's frontier, and the farmer's frontier. When the mines and the cow pens were still near the fall line the traders' pack trains were tinkling across the Alleghanies, and the French on the Great Lakes were fortifying their posts, alarmed by the British trader's birch canoe. When the trappers scaled the Rockies, the farmer was still near the mouth of the Missouri.

The Indian Trader's Frontier

Why was it that the Indian trader passed so rapidly across the continent? What effects followed from the trader's frontier? The trade was coeval with American discovery. The Norsemen, Vespuccius, Verrazani, Hudson, John Smith, all trafficked for furs. The Plymouth pilgrims settled in Indian cornfields, and their first return cargo was of beaver and lumber. The records of the various New England colonies show how steadily exploration was carried into the wilderness by this trade. What is true for New England is, as would be expected, even plainer for the rest of the colonies. All along the coast from Maine to Georgia the Indian trade opened up the river courses. Steadily the trader passed westward, utilizing the older lines of French trade. The Ohio, the Great Lakes, the Mississippi, the Missouri, and the Platte, the lines of western advance, were ascended by traders. They found the passes in the Rocky Mountains and guided Lewis and Clarke,[24] Fremont, and Bidwell. The explanation of the rapidity of this advance is connected with the effects of the trader on the Indian. The trading post left the unarmed tribes at the mercy of those that had purchased fire-arms—a truth which the Iroquois Indians wrote in blood, and so the remote and unvisited tribes gave eager welcome to the trader. "The savages," wrote LaSalle, "take better care of us French than of their own children; from us only can they get guns and goods." This accounts for the trader's power and the rapidity of his advance. Thus the disintegrating forces of civilization entered the wilderness. Every river valley and Indian trail became a fissure in Indian society, and so that society became honeycombed. Long before the pioneer farmer appeared on the scene, primitive Indian life had passed away. The farmers met Indians armed with guns. The trading frontier, while steadily undermining Indian power by making the tribes ultimately dependent on the whites, yet, through its sale of guns, gave to the Indians increased power of resistance to the farming frontier. French colonization was dominated by its trading frontier; English colonization by its farming frontier. There was an antagonism between the two frontiers as between the two nations. Said Duquesne to the Iroquois, "Are you ignorant of the difference between the king of England and the king of France? Go see the forts that our king has established and you will see that you can still hunt under their very walls. They have been placed for your advantage in places which you frequent. The English, on the contrary, are no sooner in possession of a place than the game is driven away. The forest falls before them as they advance, and the soil is laid bare so that you can scarce find the wherewithal to erect a shelter for the night."

And yet, in spite of this opposition of the interests of the trader and the farmer, the Indian trade pioneered the way for civilization. The buffalo trail became the Indian trail, and this because the trader's "trace;" the trails widened into roads, and the roads into turnpikes, and these in turn were transformed into railroads. The same origin can be shown for the railroads of the South, the far West, and the Dominion of Canada.[25] The trading posts reached by these trails were on the sites of Indian villages which had been placed in positions suggested by nature; and these trading posts, situated so as to command the water systems of the country, have grown into such cities as Albany, Pittsburg, Detroit, Chicago, St. Louis, Council Bluffs, and Kansas City. Thus civilization in America has followed the arteries made by geology, pouring an ever richer tide through them, until at last the slender paths of aboriginal intercourse have been broadened and interwoven into the complex mazes of modern commercial lines; the wilderness has been interpenetrated by lines of civilization growing ever more numerous. It is like the steady growth of a complex nervous system for the originally simple, inert continent. If one would understand why we are to-day one nation, rather than a collection of isolated states, he must study this economic and social consolidation of the country. In this progress from savage conditions lie topics for the evolutionist.[26]

The effect of the Indian frontier as a consolidating agent in our history is important. From the close of the seventeenth century various intercolonial congresses have been called to treat with Indians and establish common measures of defense. Particularism was strongest in colonies with no Indian frontier. This frontier stretched along the western border like a cord of union. The Indian was a common danger, demanding united action. Most celebrated of these conferences was the Albany congress of 1754, called to treat with the Six Nations, and to consider plans of union. Even a cursory reading of the plan proposed by the congress reveals the importance of the frontier. The powers of the general council and the officers were, chiefly, the determination of peace and war with the Indians, the regulation of Indian trade, the purchase of Indian lands, and the creation and government of new settlements as a security against the Indians. It is evident that the unifying tendencies of the Revolutionary period were facilitated by the previous cooperation in the regulation of the frontier. In this connection may be mentioned the importance of the frontier, from that day to this, as a military training school, keeping alive the power of resistance to aggression, and developing the stalwart and rugged qualities of the frontiersman.

The Rancher's Frontier

It would not be possible in the limits of this paper to trace the other frontiers across the continent. Travelers of the eighteenth century found the "cowpens" among the cane-brakes and peavine pastures of the South, and the "cowdrivers" took their droves to Charleston, Philadelphia, and New York.[27] Travelers at the close of the War of 1812 met droves of more than a thousand cattle and swine from the interior of Ohio going to Pennsylvania to fatten for the Philadelphia market.[28] The ranges of the Great Plains, with ranch and cowboy and nomadic life, are things of yesterday and of to-day. The experience of the Carolina cowpens guided the ranchers of Texas. One element favoring the rapid extension of the rancher's frontier is the fact that in a remote country lacking transportation facilities the product must be in small bulk, or must be able to transport itself, and the cattle raiser could easily drive his product to market. The effect of these great ranches on the subsequent agrarian history of the localities in which they existed should be studied.

The Farmer's Frontier

The maps of the census reports show an uneven advance of the farmer's frontier, with tongues of settlement pushed forward and with indentations of wilderness. In part this is due to Indian resistance, in part to the location of river valleys and passes, in part to the unequal force of the centers of frontier attraction. Among the important centers of attraction may be mentioned the following: fertile and favorably situated soils, salt springs, mines, and army posts.

Army Posts

The frontier army post, serving to protect the settlers from the Indians, has also acted as a wedge to open the Indian country, and has been a nucleus for settlement.[29] In this connection mention should also be made of the Government military and exploring expeditions in determining the lines of settlement. But all the more important expeditions were greatly indebted to the earliest pathmakers, the Indian guides, the traders and trappers, and the French voyageurs, who were inevitable parts of governmental expeditions from the days of Lewis and Clarke.[30] Each expedition was an epitome of the previous factors in western advance.

Salt Springs

In an interesting monograph, Victor Hehn[31] has traced the effect of salt upon early European development, and has pointed out how it affected the lines of settlement and the form of administration. A similar study might be made for the salt springs of the United States. The early settlers were tied to the coast by the need of salt, without which they could not preserve their meats or live in comfort. Writing in 1752, Bishop Spangenburg says of a colony for which he was seeking lands in North Carolina, "They will require salt and other necessaries which they can neither manufacture nor raise. Either they must go to Charleston, which is 300 miles distant * * * Or else they must go to Boling's Point in V[a] on a branch of the James and is also 300 miles from here * * * Or else they must go down the Roanoke—I know not how many miles—where salt is brought up from the Cape Fear."[32] This may serve as a typical illustration. An annual pilgrimage to the coast for salt thus became essential. Taking flocks or furs and ginseng root, the early settlers sent their pack trains after seeding time each year to the coast.[33] This proved to be an important educational influence, since it was almost the only way in which the pioneer learned what was going on in the East. But when discovery was made of the salt springs of the Kanawha, and the Holston, and Kentucky, and central New York, the West began to be freed from dependence on the coast. It was in part the effect of finding these salt springs that enabled settlement to cross the mountains.

From the time the mountains rose between the pioneer and the seaboard, a new order of Americanism arose. The West and the East began to get out of touch of each other. The settlements from the sea to the mountains kept connection with the rear and had a certain solidarity. But the overmountain men grew more and more independent. The East took a narrow view of American advance, and nearly lost these men. Kentucky and Tennessee history bears abundant witness to the truth of this statement. The East began to try to hedge and limit westward expansion. Though Webster could declare that there were no Alleghanies in his politics, yet in politics in general they were a very solid factor.

Land

The exploitation of the beasts took hunter and trader to the west, the exploitation of the grasses took the rancher west, and the exploitation of the virgin soil of the river valleys and prairies attracted the farmer. Good soils have been the most continuous attraction to the farmer's frontier. The land hunger of the Virginians drew them down the rivers into Carolina, in early colonial days; the search for soils took the Massachusetts men to Pennsylvania and to New York. As the eastern lands were taken up migration flowed across them to the west. Daniel Boone, the great backwoodsman, who combined the occupations of hunter, trader, cattle-raiser, farmer, and surveyor—learning, probably from the traders, of the fertility of the lands on the upper Yadkin, where the traders were wont to rest as they took their way to the Indians, left his Pennsylvania home with his father, and passed down the Great Valley road to that stream. Learning from a trader whose posts were on the Red River in Kentucky of its game and rich pastures, he pioneered the way for the farmers to that region. Thence he passed to the frontier of Missouri, where his settlement was long a landmark on the frontier. Here again he helped to open the way for civilization, finding salt licks, and trails, and land. His son was among the earliest trappers in the passes of the Rocky Mountains, and his party are said to have been the first to camp on the present site of Denver. His grandson, Col. A. J. Boone, of Colorado, was a power among the Indians of the Rocky Mountains, and was appointed an agent by the Government. Kit Carson's mother was a Boone.[34] Thus this family epitomizes the backwoodsman's advance across the continent.

The farmer's advance came in a distinct series of waves. In Peck's New Guide to the West, published in Boston in 1837, occurs this suggestive passage:

Generally, in all the western settlements, three classes, like the waves of the ocean, have rolled one after the other. First comes the pioneer, who depends for the subsistence of his family chiefly upon the natural growth of vegetation, called the "range," and the proceeds of hunting. His implements of agriculture are rude, chiefly of his own make, and his efforts directed mainly to a crop of corn and a "truck patch." The last is a rude garden for growing cabbage, beans, corn for roasting ears, cucumbers, and potatoes. A log cabin, and, occasionally, a stable and corn-crib, and a field of a dozen acres, the timber girdled or "deadened," and fenced, are enough for his occupancy. It is quite immaterial whether he ever becomes the owner of the soil. He is the occupant for the time being, pays no rent, and feels as independent as the "lord of the manor." With a horse, cow, and one or two breeders of swine, he strikes into the woods with his family, and becomes the founder of a new county, or perhaps state. He builds his cabin, gathers around him a few other families of similar tastes and habits, and occupies till the range is somewhat subdued, and hunting a little precarious, or, which is more frequently the case, till the neighbors crowd around, roads, bridges, and fields annoy him, and he lacks elbow room. The preemption law enables him to dispose of his cabin and cornfield to the next class of emigrants; and, to employ his own figures, he "breaks for the high timber," "clears out for the New Purchase," or migrates to Arkansas or Texas, to work the same process over.

The next class of emigrants purchase the lands, add field to field, clear out the roads, throw rough bridges over the streams, put up hewn log houses with glass windows and brick or stone chimneys, occasionally plant orchards, build mills, schoolhouses, court-houses, etc., and exhibit the picture and forms of plain, frugal, civilized life.

Another wave rolls on. The men of capital and enterprise come. The settler is ready to sell out and take the advantage of the rise in property, push farther into the interior and become, himself, a man of capital and enterprise in turn. The small village rises to a spacious town or city; substantial edifices of brick, extensive fields, orchards, gardens, colleges, and churches are seen. Broadcloths, silks, leghorns, crapes, and all the refinements, luxuries, elegancies, frivolities, and fashions are in vogue. Thus wave after wave is rolling westward; the real Eldorado is still farther on.

A portion of the two first classes remain stationary amidst the general movement, improve their habits and condition, and rise in the scale of society.

The writer has traveled much amongst the first class, the real pioneers. He has lived many years in connection with the second grade; and now the third wave is sweeping over large districts of Indiana, Illinois, and Missouri. Migration has become almost a habit in

*the West. Hundreds of men can be found, not over 50 years of age, who have settled for
the fourth, fifth, or sixth time on a new spot. To sell out and remove only a few hundred
miles makes up a portion of the variety of backwoods life and manners.* [35]

Omitting those of the pioneer farmers who move from the love of adventure, the advance
of the more steady farmer is easy to understand. Obviously the immigrant was attracted
by the cheap lands of the frontier, and even the native farmer felt their influence
strongly. Year by year the farmers who lived on soil whose returns were diminished by
unrotated crops were offered the virgin soil of the frontier at nominal prices. Their
growing families demanded more lands, and these were dear. The competition of the
unexhausted, cheap, and easily tilled prairie lands compelled the farmer either to go west
and continue the exhaustion of the soil on a new frontier, or to adopt intensive culture.
Thus the census of 1890 shows, in the Northwest, many counties in which there is an
absolute or a relative decrease of population. These States have been sending farmers to
advance the frontier on the plains, and have themselves begun to turn to intensive farming
and to manufacture. A decade before this, Ohio had shown the same transition stage.
Thus the demand for land and the love of wilderness freedom drew the frontier ever
onward.

   Having now roughly outlined the various kinds of frontiers, and their modes of advance, chiefly from the point of view of the frontier itself, we may next inquire what
were the influences on the East and on the Old World. A rapid enumeration of some of
the more noteworthy effects is all that I have time for.

Composite Nationality

First, we note that the frontier promoted the formation of a composite nationality for
the American people. The coast was preponderantly English, but the later tides of continental immigration flowed across to the free lands. This was the case from the early
colonial days. The Scotch Irish and the Palatine Germans, or "Pennsylvania Dutch,"
furnished the dominant element in the stock of the colonial frontier. With these peoples
were also the freed indented servants, or redemptioners, who at the expiration of their
time of service passed to the frontier. Governor Spottswood of Virginia writes in 1717,
"The inhabitants of our frontiers are composed generally of such as have been transported hither as servants, and, being out of their time, settle themselves where land is to
be taken up and that will produce the necessarys of life with little labour." [36] Very
generally these redemptioners were of non-English stock. In the crucible of the frontier
the immigrants were Americanized, liberated, and fused into a mixed race, English in
neither nationality or characteristics. The process has gone on from the early days to our
own. Burke and other writers in the middle of the eighteenth century believed that
Pennsylvania [37] was "threatened with the danger of being wholly foreign in language,
manners, and perhaps even inclinations." The German and Scotch-Irish elements in the
frontier of the South were only less great. In the middle of the present century the
German element in Wisconsin was already so considerable that leading publicists looked
to the creation of a German state out of the commonwealth by concentrating their
colonization. [38] Such examples teach us to beware of misinterpreting the fact that there is
a common English speech in America into a belief that the stock is also English.

Industrial Independence

In another way the advance of the frontier decreased our dependence on England. The coast, particularly of the South, lacked diversified industries, and was dependent on England for the bulk of its supplies. In the South there was even a dependence on the Northern colonies for articles of food. Governor Glenn, of South Carolina, writes in the middle of the eighteenth century: "Our trade with New York and Philadelphia was of this sort, draining us of all the little money and bills we could gather from other places for their bread, flour, beer, hams, bacon, and other things of their produce, all which, except beer, our new townships begin to supply us with, which are settled with very industrious and thriving Germans. This no doubt diminishes the number of shipping and the appearance of our trade, but it is far from being a detriment to us."[39] Before long the frontier created a demand for merchants. As it retreated from the coast it became less and less possible for England to bring her supplies directly to the consumer's wharfs, and carry away staple crops, and staple crops began to give way to diversified agriculture for a time. The effect of this phase of the frontier action upon the northern section is perceived when we realize how the advance of the frontier aroused seaboard cities like Boston, New York, and Baltimore, to engage in rivalry for what Washington called "the extensive and valuable trade of a rising empire."

Effects on National Legislation

The legislation which most developed the powers of the National Government, and played the largest part in its activity, was conditioned on the frontier. Writers have discussed the subjects of tariff, land, and internal improvement, as subsidiary to the slavery question. But when American history comes to be rightly viewed it will be seen that the slavery question is an incident. In the period from the end of the first half of the present century to the close of the civil war slavery rose to primary, but far from exclusive, importance. But this does not justify Dr. von Holst (to take an example) in treating our constitutional history in its formative period down to 1828 in a single volume, giving six volumes chiefly to the history of slavery from 1828 to 1861, under the title "Constitutional History of the United States." The growth of nationalism and the evolution of American political institutions were dependent on the advance of the frontier. Even so recent a writer as Rhodes, in his History of the United States since the compromise of 1850, has treated the legislation called out by the western advance as incidental to the slavery struggle.

This is a wrong perspective. The pioneer needed the goods of the coast, and so the grand series of internal improvement and railroad legislation began, with potent nationalizing effects. Over internal improvements occurred great debates, in which grave constitutional questions were discussed. Sectional groupings appear in the votes, profoundly significant for the historian. Loose construction increased as the nation marched westward.[40] But the West was not content with bringing the farm to the factory. Under the lead of Clay—"Harry of the West"—protective tariffs were passed, with the cry of bringing the factory to the farm. The disposition of the public lands was a third important subject of national legislation influenced by the frontier.

The Public Domain

The public domain has been a force of profound importance in the nationalization and development of the Government. The effects of the struggle of the landed and the landless States, and of the ordinance of 1787, need no discussion.[41] Administratively the frontier called out some of the highest and most vitalizing activities of the General Government. The purchase of Louisiana was perhaps the constitutional turning point in the history of the Republic, inasmuch as it afforded both a new area for national legislation and the occasion of the downfall of the policy of strict construction. But the purchase of Louisiana was called out by frontier needs and demands. As frontier States accrued to the Union the national power grew. In a speech on the dedication of the Calhoun monument Mr. Lamar explained: "In 1789 the States were the creators of the Federal Government; in 1861 the Federal Government was the creator of a large majority of the States."

When we consider the public domain from the point of view of the sale and disposal of the public lands we are again brought face to face with the frontier. The policy of the United States in dealing with its lands is in sharp contrast with the European system of scientific administration. Efforts to make this domain a source of revenue, and to withhold it from emigrants in order that settlement might be compact, were in vain. The jealousy and the fears of the East were powerless in the face of the demands of the frontiersmen. John Quincy Adams was obliged to confess: "My own system of administration, which was to make the national domain the inexhaustible fund for progressive and unceasing internal improvement, has failed." The reason is obvious; a system of administration was not what the West demanded; it wanted land. Adams states the situation as follows: "The slave-holders of the South have brought the cooperation of the western country by the bribe of the western lands, abandoning to the new Western States their own proportion of the public property and aiding them in the design of grasping all the lands into their own hands. Thomas H. Benton was the author of this system, which he brought forward as a substitute for the American system of Mr. Clay, and to supplant him as the leading statesman of the West. Mr. Clay, by his tariff compromise with Mr. Calhoun, abandoned his own American system. At the same time he brought forward a plan for distributing among all the States of the Union the proceeds of the sales of the public lands. His bill for that purpose passed both Houses of Congress, but was vetoed by President Jackson, who, in his annual message of December, 1832, formally recommended that all public lands should be gratuitously given away to individual adventurers and to the States in which the lands are situated.[42]

"No subject," said Henry Clay, "which has presented itself to the present, or perhaps any preceding, Congress, is of greater magnitude than that of the public lands." When we consider the far-reaching effects of the Government's land policy upon political, economic, and social aspects of American life, we are disposed to agree with him. But this legislation was framed under frontier influences, and under the lead of Western statesmen like Benton and Jackson. Said Senator Scott of Indiana in 1841: "I consider the pre-emption law merely declaratory of the custom or common law of the settlers."

National Tendencies of the Frontier

It is safe to say that the legislation with regard to land, tariff, and internal improvements —the American system of the nationalizing Whig party—was conditioned on frontier ideas and needs. But it was not merely in legislative action that the frontier worked against the sectionalism of the coast. The economic and social characteristics of the frontier worked against sectionalism. The men of the frontier had closer resemblances to the Middle

region than to either of the other sections. Pennsylvania had been the seed-plot of
frontier emigration, and, although she passed on her settlers along the Great Valley into
the west of Virginia and the Carolinas, yet the industrial society of these Southern
frontiersmen was always more like that of the Middle region than like that of the tidewater portion of the South, which later came to spread its industrial type throughout the
South.

The Middle region, entered by New York harbor, was an open door to all Europe. The
tide-water part of the South represented typical Englishmen, modified by a warm climate
and servile labor, and living in baronial fashion on great plantations; New England stood
for a special English movement—Puritanism. The Middle region was less English than the
other sections. It had a wide mixture of nationalities, a varied society, the mixed town
and county system of local government, a varied economic life, many religious sects. In
short, it was a region mediating between New England and the South, and the East and
the West. It represented that composite nationality which the contemporary United
States exhibits, that juxtaposition of non-English groups, occupying a valley or a little
settlement, and presenting reflections of the map of Europe in their variety. It was
democratic and nonsectional, if not national; "easy, tolerant, and contented;" rooted
strongly in material prosperity. It was typical of the modern United States. It was least
sectional, not only because it lay between North and South, but also because with no
barriers to shut out its frontiers from its settled region, and with a system of connecting
waterways, the Middle region mediated between East and West as well as between North
and South. Thus it became the typically American region. Even the New Englander, who
was shut out from the frontier by the Middle region, tarrying in New York or Pennsylvania on his westward march, lost the acuteness of his sectionalism on the way.[43]

The spread of cotton culture into the interior of the South finally broke down the
contrast between the "tide-water" region and the rest of the State, and based Southern
interests on slavery. Before this process revealed its results the western portion of the
South, which was akin to Pennsylvania in stock, society, and industry, showed tendencies
to fall away from the faith of the fathers into internal improvement legislation and
nationalism. In the Virginia convention of 1829-30, called to revise the constitution, Mr.
Leigh, of Chesterfield, one of the tide-water counties, declared:

*One of the main causes of discontent which led to this convention, that which had the
strongest influence in overcoming our veneration for the work of our fathers, which
taught us to condemn the sentiments of Henry and Mason and Pendleton, which weaned
us from our reverence for the constituted authorities of the State, was an overweening
passion for internal improvement. I say this with perfect knowledge, for it has been
avowed to me by gentlemen from the West over and over again. And let me tell the
gentleman from Albemarle (Mr. Gordon) that it has been another principal object of
those who set this ball of revolution in motion, to overturn the doctrine of State rights,
of which Virginia has been the very pillar, and to remove the barrier she has interposed to
the interference of the Federal Government in that same work of internal improvement,
by so reorganizing the legislature that Virginia, too, may be hitched to the Federal car.*

It was this nationalizing tendency of the West that transformed the democracy of Jefferson into the national republicanism of Monroe and the democracy of Andrew Jackson.
The West of the war of 1812, the West of Clay, and Benton, and Harrison, and Andrew

Jackson, shut off by the Middle States and the mountains from the coast sections, had a solidarity of its own with national tendencies.[44] On the tide of the Father of Waters, North and South met and mingled into a nation. Interstate migration went steadily on—a process of cross-fertilization of ideas and institutions. The fierce struggle of the sections over slavery on the western frontier does not diminish the truth of this statement; it proves the truth of it. Slavery was a sectional trait that would not down, but in the West it could not remain sectional. It was the greatest of frontiersmen who declared: "I believe this Government can not endure permanently half slave and half free. It will become all of one or all of the other." Nothing works for nationalism like intercourse within the nation. Mobility of population is death to localism, and the western frontier worked irresistibly in unsettling population. The effects reached back from the frontier and affected profoundly the Atlantic coast and even the Old World.

Growth of Democracy

But the most important effect of the frontier has been in the promotion of democracy here and in Europe. As has been indicated, the frontier is productive of individualism. Complex society is precipitated by the wilderness into a kind of primitive organization based on the family. The tendency is anti-social. It produces antipathy to control, and particularly to any direct control. The tax-gatherer is viewed as a representative of oppression. Prof. Osgood, in an able article,[45] has pointed out that the frontier conditions prevalent in the colonies are important factors in the explanation of the American Revolution, where individual liberty was sometimes confused with absence of all effective government. The same conditions aid in explaining the difficulty of instituting a strong government in the period of the confederacy. The frontier individualism has from the beginning promoted democracy.

The frontier States that came into the Union in the first quarter of a century of its existence came in with democratic suffrage provisions, and had reactive effects of the highest importance upon the older States whose peoples were being attracted there. An extension of the franchise became essential. It was *western* New York that forced an extension of suffrage in the constitutional convention of that State in 1821; and it was *western* Virginia that compelled the tide-water region to put a more liberal suffrage provision in the constitution framed in 1830, and to give to the frontier region a more nearly proportionate representation with the tide-water aristocracy. The rise of democracy as an effective force in the nation came in with western preponderance under Jackson and William Henry Harrison, and it meant the triumph of the frontier—with all of its good and with all of its evil elements.[46] An interesting illustration of the tone of frontier democracy in 1830 comes from the same debates in the Virginia convention already referred to. A representative from western Virginia declared:

But, sir, it is not the increase of population in the West which this gentleman ought to fear. It is the energy which the mountain breeze and western habits impart to those emigrants. They are regenerated, politically I mean, sir. They soon become working *politicians; and the difference, sir, between a* talking *and a* working *politician is immense. The Old Dominion has long been celebrated for producing great orators; the ablest metaphysicians in policy; men that can split hairs in all abstruse questions of political economy. But at home, or when they return from Congress, they have negroes to fan them asleep. But a Pennsylvania, a New York, an Ohio, or a western Virginia statesman, though far inferior in logic, metaphysics, and rhetoric to an old Virginia statesman, has this advantage, that when he returns home he takes off his coat and takes hold of the plow. This gives him bone and muscle, sir, and preserves his republican principles pure and uncontaminated.*

So long as free land exists, the opportunity for a competency exists, and economic power secures political power. But the democracy born of free land, strong in selfishness and individualism, intolerant of administrative experience and education, and pressing individual liberty beyond its proper bounds, has its dangers as well as its benefits. Individualism in America has allowed a laxity in regard to governmental affairs which has rendered possible the spoils system and all the manifest evils that follow from the lack of a highly developed civic spirit. In this connection may be noted also the influence of frontier conditions in permitting lax business honor, inflated paper currency and wild-cat banking. The colonial and revolutionary frontier was the region whence emanated many of the worst forms of an evil currency.[47] The West in the war of 1812 repeated the phenomenon on the frontier of that day, while the speculation and wild-cat banking of the period of the crisis of 1837 occurred on the new frontier belt of the next tier of States. Thus each one of the periods of lax financial integrity coincides with periods when a new set of frontier communities had arisen, and coincides in area with these successive frontiers, for the most part. The recent Populist agitation is a case in point. Many a State that now declines any connection with the tenets of the Populists, itself adhered to such ideas in an earlier stage of the development of the State. A primitive society can hardly be expected to show the intelligent appreciation of the complexity of business interests in a developed society. The continual recurrence of these areas of paper-money agitation is another evidence that the frontier can be isolated and studied as a factor in American history of the highest importance.[48]

Attempts to Check and Regulate the Frontier

The East has always feared the result of an unregulated advance of the frontier, and has tried to check and guide it. The English authorities would have checked settlement at the headwaters of the Atlantic tributaries and allowed the "savages to enjoy their deserts in quiet lest the peltry trade should decrease." This called out Burke's splendid protest:

If you stopped your grants, what would be the consequence; The people would occupy without grants. They have already so occupied in many places. You can not station garrisons in every part of these deserts. If you drive the people from one place, they will carry on their annual tillage and remove with their flocks and herds to another. Many of the people in the back settlements are already little attached to particular situations. Already they have topped the Appalachian mountains. From thence they behold before them an immense plain, one vast, rich, level meadow; a square of five hundred miles. Over this they would wander without a possibility of restraint; they would change their manners with their habits of life; would soon forget a government by which they were disowned; would become hordes of English Tartars; and, pouring down upon your unfortified frontiers a fierce and irresistible cavalry, become masters of your governors and your counselers, your collectors and comptrollers, and of all the slaves that adhered to them. Such would, and in no long time must, be the effect of attempting to forbid as a crime and to suppress as an evil the command and blessing of Providence, "Increase and multiply." Such would be the happy result of an endeavor to keep as a lair of wild beasts that earth which God, by an express charter, has given to the children of men.

But the English Government was not alone in its desire to limit the advance of the frontier and guide its destinies. Tidewater Virginia[49] and South Carolina[50] gerrymandered those colonies to insure the dominance of the coast in their legislatures. Washington desired to settle a State at a time in the Northwest; Jefferson would reserve from settlement the territory of his Louisiana purchase north of the thirty-second parallel, in order to offer it to the Indians in exchange for their settlements east of the Mississippi. "When we shall be full on this side," he writes, "we may lay off a range of States on the western bank from the head to the mouth, and so range after range, advancing compactly as we multiply." Madison went so far as to argue to the French minister that the United States had no interest in seeing population extend itself on the right bank of the Mississippi, but should rather fear it. When the Oregon question was under debate, in 1824, Smyth, of Virginia, would draw an unchangeable line for the limits of the United States at the outer limit of two tiers of States beyond the Mississippi, complaining that the seaboard States were being drained of the flower of their population by the bringing of too much land into market. Even Thomas Benton, the man of widest views of the destiny of the West, at this stage of his career declared that along the ridge of the Rocky mountains "the western limits of the Republic should be drawn, and the statue of the fabled god Terminus should be raised upon its highest peak, never to be thrown down."[51] But the attempts to limit the boundaries, to restrict land sales and settlement, and to deprive the West of its share of political power were all in vain. Steadily the frontier of settlement advanced and carried with it individualism, democracy, and nationalism, and powerfully affected the East and the Old World.

Missionary Activity

The most effective efforts of the East to regulate the frontier came through its educational and religious activity, exerted by interstate migration and by organized societies. Speaking in 1835, Dr. Lyman Beecher declared: "It is equally plain that the religious and political destiny of our nation is to be decided in the West," and he pointed out that the population of the West "is assembled from all the States of the Union and from all the nations of Europe, and is rushing in like the waters of the flood, demanding for its moral preservation the immediate and universal action of those institutions which discipline the mind and arm the conscience and the heart. And so various are the opinions and habits, and so recent and imperfect is the acquaintance, and so sparse are the settlements of the West, that no homogeneous public sentiment can be formed to legislate immediately into being the requisite institutions. And yet they are all needed immediately in their utmost perfection and power. A nation is being 'born in a day.' * * * But what will become of the West if her prosperity rushes up to such a majesty of power, while those great institutions linger which are necessary to form the mind and the conscience and the heart of that vast world. It must not be permitted. * * * Let no man at the East quiet himself and dream of liberty, whatever may become of the West. * * * Her destiny is our destiny."[52]

With the appeal to the conscience of New England, he adds appeals to her fears lest other religious sects anticipate her own. The New England preacher and school-teacher left their mark on the West. The dread of Western emancipation from New England's political and economic control was paralleled by her fears lest the West cut loose from her religion. Commenting in 1850 on reports that settlement was rapidly extending northward in Wisconsin, the editor of the Home Missionary writes: "We scarcely know whether to rejoice or mourn over this extension of our settlements. While we sympathize in whatever tends to increase the physical resources and prosperity of our country, we can not forget that with all these dispersions into remote and still remoter corners of the land the supply of the means of grace is becoming relatively less and less." Acting in accordance with such ideas, home missions were established and Western colleges were erected. As seaboard cities like Philadelphia, New York, and Baltimore strove from the mastery of Western trade, so the various denominations strove for the possession of the West. Thus an intellectual stream from New England sources fertilized the West. Other sections sent their missionaries; but the real struggle was between sects. The contest for power and the expansive tendency furnished to the various sects by the existence of a moving frontier must have had important results on the character of religious organization in the United States. The multiplication of rival churches in the little frontier towns had deep and lasting social effects. The religious aspects of the frontier make a chapter in our history which needs study.

Intellectual Traits

From the conditions of frontier life came intellectual traits of profound importance. The works of travelers along each frontier from colonial days onward describe certain common traits, and these traits have, while softening down, still persisted as survivals in the place of their origin, even when a higher social organization succeeded. The result is that to the frontier the American intellect owes its striking characteristics. That coarseness and strength combined with acuteness and inquisitiveness; that practical, inventive turn of mind, quick to find expedients; that masterful grasp of material things, lacking in the artistic but powerful to effect great ends; that restless, nervous energy;[53] that dominant individualism, working for good and for evil, and withal that buoyancy and exuberance which comes with freedom—these are traits of the frontier, or traits called out elsewhere because of the existence of the frontier. Since the days when the fleet of Columbus sailed into the waters of the New World, America has been another name for opportunity, and the people of the United States have taken their tone from the incessant expansion which has not only been open but has even been forced upon them. He would be a rash prophet who should assert that the expansive character of American life has now entirely ceased. Movement has been its dominant fact, and, unless this training has no effect upon a people, the American energy will continually demand a wider field for its exercise. But never again will such gifts of free land offer themselves. For a moment, at the frontier, the bonds of custom are broken and unrestraint is triumphant. There is not *tabula rasa*. The stubborn American environment is there with its imperious summons to accept its conditions; the inherited ways of doing things are also there; and yet, in spite of environment, and in spite of custom, each frontier did indeed furnish a new field of opportunity, a gate of escape from the bondage of the past; and freshness, and confidence, and scorn of older society, impatience of its restraints and its ideas, and indifference to its lessons, have accompanied the frontier. What the Mediterranean Sea was to the Greeks, breaking the bond of custom, offering new experiences, calling out new institutions and activities, that, and more, the ever retreating frontier has been to the United States directly, and to the nations of Europe more remotely. And now, four centuries from the discovery of America, at the end of a hundred years of life under the Constitution, the frontier has gone, and with its going has closed the first period of American history.

Notes

Since the meeting of the American Historical Association, this paper has also been given as an address to the State Historical Society of Wisconsin, December 14, 1893. I have to thank the Secretary of the Society, Mr. Reuben G. Thwaites, for securing valuable material for my use in the preparation of the paper.

1. Abridgment of Debates of Congress, v., p. 706.

2. Bancroft (1860 ed.), III, pp. 344, 345, citing Logan MSS.; [Mitchell] Contest in America, etc. (1752), p. 237.

3. Kercheval, History of the Valley; Bernheim, German Settlements in the Carolinas; Winsor, Narrative and Critical History of America, V, p. 304; Colonial Records of North Carolina, IV, p. XX; Weston, Documents Connected with the History of South Carolina, p. 82; Ellis and Evans, History of Lancaster County, Pa., chs. iii, XXVI.

4. Parkman, Pontiac, II; Griffis, Sir William Johnson, p. 6; Simms's Frontiersmen of New York.

5. Monette, Mississippi Valley, I, p. 311.

6. Wis. Hist. Cols., XI, p. 50; Hinsdale, Old Northwest, p. 121; Burke, "Oration on Conciliation," Works (1872 ed.), I, p. 473.

7. Roosevelt, Winning of the West, and citations there given; Cutler's Life of Cutler.

8. Scribner's Statistical Atlas, xxxviii, pl. 13; MacMaster, Hist. of People of U.S., I, pp. 4, 60, 61; Imlay and Filson, Western Territory of America (London, 1793); Rochefoucault-Liancourt, Travels Through the United States of North America (London, 1799); Michaux's "Journal," in Proceedings American Philosophical Society, XXVI, No. 129; Forman, Narrative of a Journey Down the Ohio and Mississippi in 1780-'90 (Cincinnati, 1888); Bartram, Travels Through North Carolina, etc. (London, 1792); Pope, Tour Through the Southern and Western Territories, etc. (Richmond, 1792); Weld, Travels Through the States of North America (London, 1799); Baily, Journal of a Tour in the Unsettled States of North America, 1796-'97 (London, 1856); Pennsylvania Magazine of History, July, 1886; Winsor, Narrative and Critical History of America, VII, pp. 491, 492, citations.

9. Scribner's Statistical Atlas, xxxix.

10. Turner, Character and Influence of the Indian Trade in Wisconsin (Johns Hopkins University Studies, Series IX), pp. 61 ff.

11. Monette, History of the Mississippi Valley, II; Flint, Travels and Residence in Mississippi; Flint, Geography and History of the Western States; Abridgment of Debates of Congress, VII, pp. 397, 398, 404; Holmes, Account of the U.S.; Kingdom, America and the British Colonies (London, 1820); Grund, Americans, II, chs. i, iii, vi (although writing in 1836, he treats of conditions that grew out of western advance from the era of 1820 to that time); Peck, Guide for Emigrants (Boston, 1831); Darby, Emigrants' Guide to Western and Southwestern States and Territories; Dana, Geographical Sketches in the Western Country; Kinzie, Waubun; Keating, Narrative of Long's Expedition; School-

craft, Discovery of the Sources of the Mississippi River, Travels in the Central Portions of the Mississippi Valley, and Lead Mines of the Missouri; Andreas, History of Illinois, I, 86-99; Hurlbut, Chicago Antiquities; McKenney, Tour to the Lakes; Thomas, Travels through the Western Country, etc. (Auburn, N.Y., 1819).

12. Darby, Emigrants' Guide, pp. 272 ff.; Benton, Abridgment of Debates, VII, p. 397.

13. De Bow's Review, IV, p. 254; XVII, p. 428.

14. Grund, Americans, II, p. 8.

15. Peck, New Guide to the West (Cincinnati, 1848), ch. IV; Parkman, Oregon Trail; Hall, The West (Cincinnati, 1848); Pierce, Incidents of Western Travel; Murray, Travels in North America; Lloyd, Steamboat Directory (Cincinnati, 1856); "Forty Days in a Western Hotel" (Chicago), in Putnam's Magazine, December, 1894; Mackay, The Western World, II, ch. II, III; Meeker, Life in the West; Bogen, German in America (Boston, 1851); Olmstead, Texas Journey; Greeley, Recollections of a Busy Life; Schouler, History of the United States, V, 261-267; Peyton, Over the Alleghanies and Across the Prairies (London, 1870); Loughborough, The Pacific Telegraph and Railway (St. Louis, 1849); Whitney, Project for a Railroad to the Pacific (New York, 1849); Peyton, Suggestions on Railroad Communication with the Pacific, and the Trade of China and the Indian Islands; Benton, Highway to the Pacific (a speech delivered in the U.S. Senate, December 16, 1850).

16. A writer in The Home Missionary (1850), p. 239, reporting Wisconsin conditions, exclaims: "Think of this, people of the enlightened East. What an example, to come from the very frontiers of civilization!" But one of the missionaries writes: "In a few years Wisconsin will no longer be considered as the West, or as an outpost of civilization, any more than western New York, or the Western Reserve."

17. Bancroft (H. H.), History of California, History of Oregon, and Popular Tribunals; Shinn, Mining Camps.

18. See the suggestive paper by Prof. Jesse Macy, The Institutional Beginnings of a Western State.

19. Shinn, Mining Camps.

20. Compare Thorpe, in Annals American Academy of Political and Social Science, September, 1891; Bryce, American Commonwealth (1888), II, p. 689.

21. Loria, Analisi della Proprieta Capitalista, II., p. 15.

22. Compare Observations on the North American Land Company, London, 1796, pp. XV, 144; Logan, History of Upper South Carolina, I, pp. 149-151; Turner, Character and Influence of Indian Trade in Wisconsin, p. 18; Peck, New Guide for Emigrants (Boston, 1837), ch. iv; Compendium Eleventh Census, I, p. xl.

23. Illustrations of the political accompaniments of changed industrial conditions are given later in this paper.

24. But Lewis and Clarke were the first to explore the route from the Missouri to the Columbia.

25. Narrative and Critical History of America, VIII, p. 10; Sparks' Washington Works, IX, pp. 303, 327; Logan, History of Upper South Carolina, I; McDonald, Life of Kenton, p. 72; Cong. Record, XXIII, p. 57.

26. On the effect of the fur trade in opening the routes of migration, see the author's Character and Influence of the Indian Trade in Wisconsin.

27. Lodge, English Colonies, p. 152 and citations; Logan, Hist. of Upper South Carolina, I, p 151.

28. Flint, Recollections, p. 9.

29. See Monette, Mississippi Valley, I, p. 344.

30. Coues', Lewis and Clarke's Expedition, I, pp. 2, 253-259; Benton, in Cong. Record, XXIII, p. 57.

31. Hehn, Das Salz (Berlin, 1873).

32. Col. Records of N.C., V, p. 3.

33. Findley, History of the Insurrection in the Four Western Counties of Pennsylvania in the Year 1794 (Philadelphia, 1796), p. 35.

34. Hale, Daniel Boone (pamphlet).

35. Compare Baily, Tour in the Unsettled Parts of North America (London, 1856), pp. 217-219, where a similar analysis is made for 1796. See also Collot, Journey in North America (Paris, 1826), p. 109; Observations on the North American Land Company (London, 1796), pp. XV, 144; Logan, History of Upper South Carolina.

36. "Spottswood Papers," in Collections of Virginia Historical Society, I, II.

37. [Burke], European Settlements, etc. (1765 ed.), II, p. 200.

38. Everest, in Wisconsin Historical Collections, XII, pp. 7 ff.

39. Weston, Documents connected with History of South Carolina, p. 61.

40. See, for example, the speech of Clay, in the House of Representatives, January 30, 1824.

41. See the admirable monograph by Prof. H. B. Adams, Maryland's Influence on the Land Cessions; and also President Welling, in Papers American Historical Association, III, p. 411.

42. Adams Memoirs, IX, pp. 247, 248.

43. Author's article in The Aegis (Madison, Wis.), November 4, 1892.

44. Compare Roosevelt, Thomas Benton, ch. i.

45. Political Science Quarterly, II, p. 457. Compare Sumner, Alexander Hamilton, Chs. ii-vii.

46. Compare Wilson, Division and Reunion, pp. 15, 24.

47. On the relation of frontier conditions to Revolutionary taxation, see Sumner, Alexander Hamilton, Ch. iii.

48. I have refrained from dwelling on the lawless characteristics of the frontier, because they are sufficiently well known. The gambler and desperado, the regulators of the Carolinas and the vigilantes of California, are types of that line of scum that the waves of advancing civilization bore before them, and of the growth of spontaneous organs of authority where legal authority was absent. Compare Barrows, United States of Yesterday and To-morrow; Shinn, Mining Camps; and Bancroft, Popular Tribunals. The humor, bravery, and rude strength, as well as the vices of the frontier in its worst aspect, have left traces on American character, language, and literature, not soon to be effaced.

49. Debates in the Constitutional Convention, 1829-1830.

50. [McCrady] Eminent and Representative Men of the Carolinas, I, p. 43; Calhoun's Works, I, pp. 401-406.

51. Speech in the Senate, March 1, 1825; Register of Debates, I, 721.

52. Plea for the West (Cincinnati, 1835), pp. 11 ff.

53. Colonial travelers agree in remarking on the phlegmatic characteristics of the colonists. It has frequently been asked how such a people could have developed that strained nervous energy now characteristic of them. Compare Sumner, Alexander Hamilton, p. 98, and Adams's History of the United States, I, p. 60; IX, pp. 240, 241. The transition appears to become marked at the close of the war of 1812, a period when interest centered upon the development of the West, and the West was noted for restless energy. Grund, Americans, II., ch. i.

Toward a reorientation of Western history: Continuity and environment

Earl Pomeroy

Any thesis that enjoys widespread acceptance is eventually bound to come under strong attack; Turner's frontier hypothesis is no exception. The onslaught began in the 1930s, coinciding with Turner's death and with the economic collapse of the Great Depression. Criticisms took two main approaches. The first rejected Turner's hypothesis as an analytic device; the second attacked the assumptions on which it was based. Historians George W. Pierson and Richard Hofstadter were representatives of the first group. They argued that Turner's ideas were too vague to permit careful analysis. His very terms—democracy, the West, individualism, the frontier—cried for definitions that Turner never supplied. Were all frontiers the same? Could one equate the slow-moving agricultural West of the 1790s in Kentucky and Tennessee with the rapid-moving settlement line that followed the post-Civil War railroad construction in Kansas, Nebraska, and Wyoming? And when precisely did a frontier cease to be western and join the ranks of the long settled East? Turner's writings produced no consistent answers.

The second main attack focused on Turner's assumptions. The frontier hypothesis carried to its logical conclusion seemed to imply that geography and climate played the major role in shaping American character. This geographic determinism rankled the Marxists and produced a spirited review of Turner's *The Significance of Sections in American History* (1932) by Louis M. Hacker, who asserted that class structure reached across the new nation from settled parts to the edge of the frontier and that it was class divisions that best explained American development.

In the following essay, Earl Pomeroy, Professor of History at the University of Oregon, questions Turner's assumption that the frontier stripped settlers of their cultural heritage. Pomeroy puts in sharp focus the question of geographic determinism versus cultural continuity.

For further reading: George Wilson Pierson, "American Democracy and the Frontier," *Yale Review*, XX (1930), 349-365; Richard Hofstadter, "Turner and the Frontier Myth," *American Scholar*, XVIII (October 1949), 433-443; Louis Hacker, Review of Turner's *The Significance of Sections in American History*, in *The Nation*, 137 (July 26, 1933), 108-110; Everett S. Lee, "The Turner Thesis Re-examined," *American Quarterly*, XIII

Reprinted with permission from *Mississippi Valley Historical Review*, (March 1955), 579-600.

(Spring 1961), 77-83;* David M. Potter, *People of Plenty, Economic Abundance and the American Character* (Chicago: University of Chicago Press, 1954);* Walter Prescott Webb, "Ended: 400 Year Boom, Reflections on the Age of the Frontier," *Harper's Magazine*, CCIII (October 1951), 26-33; Harry C. Allen, "F. J. Turner and the Frontier in American History," in H. C. Allen and C. P. Hill, eds., *British Essays in American History* (London: E. J. Arnold, 1957), 1957), 150-166.

*Available in paperback.

The books we write about the West, a literary critic remarked recently, no longer explain our national history, no longer represent the historical possibilities of the West itself as they once seemed to do in the generation of Theodore Roosevelt and Frederick Jackson Turner.[1] They may explain less because many historians of the West do not write well, and because many have narrowed the limits within which they write, even while investigators in other fields have broadened their inquiries and the West itself has greatly grown and changed. More fundamentally, most of those who write western history seem to assume that physical environment has dominated western life and has made the West rough and radical. Although he may scorn the popular appeal of the "Western" novel and motion picture, the historian has himself often operated within a formula, neglecting the spread and continuity of "Eastern" institutions and ideas.

It may seem sometimes that Turner gained recognition for western history as "a field for the serious study of the economist and the historian"[2] only to open university doors to romanticists and antiquarians, who borrowed Turner's phrases rather than his methods and the range of his imagination. In his time the environmental theory and the radical theme helped to integrate the story of the West into a more convincing pattern. Growing up in the Wisconsin fur-trading country, where Indian and European cultures still merged at the portage, he knew men who personified the impact of the forest. "The wilderness masters the colonist."[3] He did his principal research on the West of the eras of Thomas Jefferson, Henry Clay, and Andrew Jackson, when the West seemed to spawn movements of protest that spread over the whole country. In his popular essays and in the classroom he pointed to the Populists as a contemporary example of western radicalism, once more disturbing and leavening the nation and demanding some new general synthesis or equilibrium that would incorporate some of the frontier into the whole.

The environmental interpretation appealed to Americans in a nationalistic and ostensibly democratic era, even though the nation was visibly becoming more like Europe in its drift to industrial power and an urban orientation of society. It had especial appeal when it elevated a century's romantic fascination with the western horizon, whether as promise or as threat, into the dignity of social science. Thus both Edward Channing[4] and Turner, among other historians, set forth environmental interpretations of American history. Turner made the greater impact in part because of the unconscious assistance of others who were not historians but whose careers seemed to confirm his interpretation: Ignatius Donnelly, William J. Bryan, and Mary E. Lease, and later Robert M. LaFollette, William D. Haywood, and Hiram W. Johnson.

Today the environmental-radical theme in western history has lost much of its appeal. To Turner the frontier was a cause that acted ultimately on the East; but now the effects that he thought he saw seem to have other causes, if they exist at all. American radicalism, such as it is, no longer looks to western centers like Madison, Lincoln, or Terre Haute; and in recent years as historians have turned increasingly to its history, perhaps with some of the nostalgia with which they have looked at the disappearing frontier, the radicalism that they study is chiefly of the twentieth century—urban or at least post-frontier.

Though the old environmental-radical theme no longer seems so relevant to the present as it once did, it tends to govern the limits of western history-writing. While no longer finding (or, for that matter, seeking) the effects of environment that they once thought they found—the elements of western and national character that Turner described—historians still tend to concentrate on those aspects of the West where the impact of environment is clearest and sharpest. In so doing, they forget that they have performed an act of abstraction from a larger scene. They argue the importance of environmental influences in the West while demanding that the West qualify as West by being the place where environment predominates. They have run an irregular boundary line about the historical West that sometimes has to pass down the middle of city streets to avoid men and events that do not fit the formula. The line that they draw coincides with the antiquarian bias for localism, since under the primitive conditions of early settlement the outside world was less accessible than it shortly afterward became, and the immediate problems of subsistence had to find a largely local solution. Such limits prevail more generally among the popular histories and novels than among the works of broader framework noted in this paper, but they are familiar enough on university campuses as well as in the local journals. Courses and textbooks on the history of the West conventionally stop with the 1890s (though Turner extended his own course, History 17, well into the twentieth century); the mid-point of a representative college course in the history of California may be 1848, while miners and vigilantes dominate the "American period"; and in the published histories of western states the last chapters tend to become prim annals.[5]

If we refuse to let another generation, in effect, force its interpretations on us by excluding such data as do not fit them, we may see that conservatism, inheritance, and continuity bulked at least as large in the history of the West as radicalism and environment. The Westerner has been fundamentally imitator rather than innovator, and not merely in the obvious though important sense that his culture was Western European rather than aboriginal. He was often the most ardent of conformists, although in times of imperfect communication he knew local standards better than national standards of conformity. Now it seems only natural that those major instruments of standardization, the motion picture and television studios, should have moved to the Pacific Coast, and that great state university systems as well as politicians who attack the freedom of inquiry that universities live on should flourish most of all in western states.

The colonial everywhere, by virtue of his colonial status, tends to chafe against economic and political bonds, but he remains a colonial, which is to say a cultural transplant, often more traditionalist in attitude than his cousins in the older settlements. Such loyalty is not entirely a function of prosperity. If the emigrant prospered, he was no more interested in institutional change than was any other self-made man—often less interested, since it was so easy to believe that the country had grown up because of him, rather than he with it. In the West more than in the East, failure meant that a man had less contact with new ideas and with other men who might join him as reformers. The Westerner's perennial plea to the traveler to concede that the West had equaled or surpassed the East in schools, hotels, or civic virtue revealed the nature of his ambition. American culture often was diluted on the frontier, but often loyalty to it was strengthened. California, said *Overland Magazine* in 1883, "is in almost every respect an intensification of the American spirit. . . . All this is merely America, 'only more so.' "[6]

Social change, however visible, was relative and irregular; different Wests often lived side by side, on the same street.[7] While the on-rush of settlers seemed sometimes, as Henry R. Schoolcraft said, to tear up the old plan of life,[8] still the raw frontier, which the settlers changed as they enveloped it, usually had been more in flux than the larger West behind it; and the disposition of the settlers was basically to conserve and transport what they had known before. Institutions and values changed less than geography, individual fortunes, and techniques. Even techniques often changed little as transportation improved. Institutional changes might have been greater if the men who led the West had sought a new country more than they sought individual self-realization and self-improvement. In general they were neither refugees nor entirely exiles. New York or Pennsylvania was still a second home. Coming in hope rather than in fear or bitterness, often with some small stake for the new venture, members of a fairly homogeneous culture, they had little in common with Indians moved from their hereditary lands, or with convicts transported from Europe. Seeing the vigor of individual aspiration, historians sometimes have assumed too readily that Westerners wished to cut themselves off from eastern ways, much as historians once exaggerated the antipathy of colonial Puritans to England and the Anglican church. In fact most attempts to illustrate the western spirit by referring to large and purposeful institutional innovations are likely to break down.

In the field of government and politics, most clearly of all, it is evident that western history has been constricted by a local framework that has slighted similarities, antecedents, and outside influences generally. Territorial government, which clearly was the instrument of Congress, has been described with more attention to establishment than to operation, though the operation of government is the more vital field as well as the field in which outside influences are more apparent. Emphasizing the form of the Ordinance of 1787 rather than the evolution of political life under it and under later territorial frameworks, historians have tended to overstress first the liberal side of territorial government and then the autocratic side.[9] They have overlooked the significant extent to which the territorial system, whatever its conception, figured as a channel in the large process of acculturation, transporting American ways from East to West.[10] It performed this channeling function despite the motives of the framers of the Ordinance of 1787, and it may have done so the more effectively because it put Westerners under closer restraints than Jefferson had planned in 1781. The system of restraints—the authority of appointed governors, secretaries, and judges—brought with it eastern personnel and methods, and connections with eastern party systems. Jefferson himself used the territorial system as an instrument of political education and assimilation in Mississippi and Louisiana, though he had spoken of the first stage of territorial government as "a despotic oligarchy without one rational object."[11]

On the other hand, historians of frontier justice in general have drawn less on formal than on informal sources, which tend to sustain the conventional picture of western roughness and independence. Semi-legendary frontier magistrates such as Roy Bean and Three-Legged Willie seem impregnably enshrined as western types alongside Buffalo Bill, Calamity Jane, and Black Bart. Yet between territorial judges, who usually came from the eastern bench and bar, and western lawyers, who as a group were well versed in the law, the practices of the older states persisted. Territorial judges often were unpopular, but the more fundamental grievance was that there were not enough of them.[12] Sometimes vigilantes supplanted them but chiefly when regular government had failed; and it was sometimes as significant that the vigilantes acted to protect property and to maintain some kind of due process as that they acted irregularly, or that property needed protection.[13]

The constitutional history of all the western territories and states remains to be written. The better accounts of the processes of forming new state governments reveal a western dependence on the examples of older states that is suggestively inconsistent with the conventional view of admission to statehood as the climax of antagonism between East and West. But most of these studies are richer in detail than in analysis. There is still no western counterpart to any of the many thorough studies of institutions and functions in seventeenth- and eighteenth-century colonial government, or to Fletcher M. Green's useful survey of *Constitutional Development in the South Atlantic States.*[14]

Constitutional innovations in the West were rare, as Turner himself noted,[15] although in a local framework it is easy to overemphasize manhood suffrage in Vermont, woman suffrage in Wyoming, or the recall of judges in Arizona. Relative to Easterners living under older constitutions, Westerners entering the Union had unusual opportunities to make constitutional changes; but from the time when the founders of the state of Franklin turned down a more democratic system in favor of the North Carolina constitution, pioneers held to the old laws, and to the more conservative laws. John D. Hicks found few new departures, even in the "omnibus states" of 1889-1890, in a time of economic unrest.[16] When Westerners did depart from conventional patterns, it was sometimes because eastern forms were unsuitable or meaningless (for example, a property qualification for the suffrage where either everyone had land or no one had title). Many of the innovations had come close to adoption in older states. There were few "western reforms, in fact, that Westerners had not brought in their baggage of ideas from the East. Sometimes the raw frontier environment itself suggested social change; but on the political-constitutional plane it more often contributed to change by not including factors that had retarded or inhibited change in the older states.[17] Frequently Westerners restricted the suffrage or the rights of Negroes by sizable majorities, while Easterners kept older restrictions only because the restrictions tended to perpetuate themselves in spite of majority opinion.

The legend of unqualified western radicalism has been especially persistent in the history of political parties, where it appears in the persons of Jefferson, Jackson, and Lincoln, to say nothing of Nathaniel Bacon or Hiram Johnson. Likewise, the Populist revolt, which so fascinated Turner and his audience in the 1890s, seems to continue to persuade us, without much more evidence, that western politics were fundamentally radical.[18]

The history of western politics in the middle years of the nineteenth century needs further study and clarification. The figure of Lincoln himself has reached fairly sharp focus (except in some of the textbooks), but his party appears too often as the embodiment of the radical West. Yet political parties were less often media for frontier revolt against other sections than arteries by which policies and personnel moved westward. New and radical parties, unsupported by national patronage or unknown to Westerners when they were last in the East, usually took hold slowly. Beyond the Mississippi,

Westerners were slow to join the Republicans, and when they did they often repudiated the radicalism of the middle-western and eastern branches of the party. Leland Stanford, campaigning in California in 1859, insisted that he preferred a white man's country,[19] and Oregon (where, as in California, only about a third of the popular vote of 1860 was Republican) appeared with a constitution so unfriendly to Negroes and with an electorate so overwhelmingly Democratic that Congress was reluctant to grant statehood.[20] It was not until slavery ceased to be an issue (that is, until the Democratic party was no longer the more conservative party) and until more Easterners moved West that the Far West became Republican. Westerners generally, as Josiah Royce noted of the Californians, were slow to develop new political issues.[21]

The stories of the Federalist and Whig parties in the West of an earlier period likewise have had little interest for historians, and one may suspect that this is so because the facts do not correspond satisfactorily to the environmental-radical interpretation and do not fit easily within the conventionally local framework. We know that the Federalists openly predominated in some parts of the West, as in the Natchez area when it was first occupied.[22] While enemies of dissident Republicans sometimes labeled them as Federalists, it is probable that under territorial government more than a few Westerners used the name Republican only because it was convenient to seem to agree with the party in power in Washington, which had a formidable weapon in the patronage and, under Jefferson, was ready to use it effectively.[23] In a later generation, not only were some western Democrats often impressively conservative, and others of doubtful loyalty, as western Republicans had been, but the Whigs themselves were strong under their own name.[24]

Probably no students of western society have been more active in exploring the relations of East and West than the economic historians. Western radicalism as they have pictured it came less from the physical atmosphere, whether malarial or salubrious, than in reaction to economic concentration in the West analogous to the pressure of wealth and power that simultaneously evoked radicalism in the East. The poor emigrant who found his future on the frontier is an authentic figure, but Paul W. Gates has shown the prevalence of tenancy in the Old Northwest, and Fred A. Shannon has footnoted the darkest pictures of Hamlin Garland, all but proving that west of the Missouri River there could be no westward movement at all, in the traditional sense.[25]

The economic history of even the pre-agricultural frontiers, once a pageant of individual adventure, is coming to rest on the cold facts of investment capital. Even in the early stages, the frontier invited collective exploitation from without, while it disposed frontiersmen to undertake collective action to meet new problems that put too much strain on individual effort.[26] Because large-sized economic units or aggregations were necessary in the West, the West sometimes assumed a more capitalistic shape than the East. It may have retained it more securely because (at least before the 1890s) there was no self-conscious western proletariat to resist frontier capitalism. The masses might not acquire property of their own, but they believed that they might; and in any event the majority of Westerners, scattered and preoccupied with individual tasks and aspirations, could not effectively resist the capitalist or eastern orientation of western economic life.[27] "The real peculiarity of our present Pacific civilization," said *Overland*, "is that it is, perhaps, the most completely realized embodiment of the purely commercial civilization on the face of the earth."[28] Yet romantic biases still dictate the proportions of much of our western economic history. We still know the homesteader better than the landlord, the railroad builder better than the railroad operator. The trapper, the prospector, and the cowboy, moving picturesquely over a background of clean air and great distances, hold us more than the tycoons and corporations that dominated them and the Rocky Mountain country.

The historian's selection of picaresque and romantic characters is particularly clear in most western social history. The indolent backwoodsman—some variant of the Boone stereotype, ever retreating before civilization—typifies frontier degradation. "Is it not time," Frederick Law Olmsted asked in 1859, that "the people of the free West were delivered from the vague reputation of bad temper, recklessness, and lawlessness, under which they suffer?" The general impression of lawless violence in the West, he contended, was "based upon, and entirely sustained by, occurrences which are peculiar to the frontier of the Slave States."[29] Yet the legend prevailed, and today some southern historians insist that Olmsted actually described the West rather than the South when he painted his most unattractive pictures of slaveholding society,[30] and quote his words to illustrate the view of the West that he had rejected.

Local foreign groups have loomed over-large, on the other hand, whether because they were colorful or because they represented a more indigenous and environmental cultural ingredient than the Americans who moved in from the East. The role of Spanish culture in the Southwest has been exaggerated from the day of Helen Hunt Jackson and the Ramona legend to the day of the latest real estate speculator who manufactures Spanish-sounding place names.[31] Actually the native Spanish and Mexican elements in many parts of the West—particularly California, where they are most revered today—were small and uninfluential, often fairly recent arrivals themselves; the typical American settler was ignorant of their language and despised their institutions.

English-speaking aristocracies meanwhile have been less prominent in books on the West.[32] In neglecting prosperous and conservative transplanted elements in the pioneer Southwest, many historians have submitted to a stereotype as readily as those who describe southern ante-bellum society and slavery entirely from the records and prejudices of the great planters and neglect the yeoman farmers. Yet students of the southern frontier have been particularly successful in tracing continuity in social institutions and social stratification.[33]

The educated well-to-do families of the Frankfort area kept up "the ancient customs and fashions of the English," recalled the Reverend James B. Finley.[34] These new planters may have seemed upstarts to their counterparts in the eastern states, who had forgotten their own pioneer past, but often they were equally devoted to tradition. Farther west, though distances from the East were greater, improved transportation and new riches sustained even larger aristocracies. The flourishing commerce of cities such as New Orleans and St. Louis brought in scores of professional businessmen; the mines and cattle ranches of the Far West drew on all classes of society, Easterners becoming more prominent than in the older West. "You will often find some graduate of Yale 'bull-whacking' his own team from the river to the mines, looking as if he had seldom seen soap and water," reported a traveler from Colorado.[35] There were enough gentleman ranchers and miners, rich men with weak lungs, officeholders and lawyers to add substantial cultural leavening, in a West that was quick to demand schools, colleges, and grand opera. That aristocracies existed is unmistakable, but they are so new as subjects of serious historical study that historians have not sufficiently appraised their role in the West or compared them with aristocracies in the East. We know too little about the structure of western society to be sure that it behaved conservatively on occasion because the aristocrats had overawed it or because aristocratic oppression was too slight to arouse sharp class consciousness, because monopoly was too incomplete to make a farce of the western habit of measuring success by material standards.

The Army has suffered striking neglect as a factor in acculturation and as a social ingredient that often seemed more gentlemanly than it does in the folk-images identifying the military with Buffalo Bill, Davy Crockett, and Andrew Jackson the frontiersman (not Jackson the planter). The role of the military in warfare was intermittent; between campaigns it traded and built roads. It carried civilization to the frontier, sometimes dramatically, as when General James Wilkinson's barge appeared on the Ohio with musicians and luxurious foods;[36] but more significantly in the daily contact of garrison and settlement. The frontier military post was bridge as well as barrier between savagery and civilization. The officer class brought in not only a considerable buying power but social prestige and sometimes the refinements of family life. "I met numbers of United States officers," wrote an English visitor who had hunted and traveled with them in the West, "and I always found them the same—gentleman-like and agreeable, and more resembling Englishmen . . . than any other class I met in America."[37] Little of this wider impact of the military appears in the records of exploration and Indian wars, and little enough even in the records of roadbuilding and other civilian activities.

Until recently the image of crudity has persisted especially in pictures of western religion, although religion was a major factor in acculturation. Some entire sects still suffer from picturesque libels. Yet the preachers were in large part responsible for their own reputation. They maligned their rivals and stressed the wickedness of the unconverted in terms so sweeping as to suggest that Westerners generally were immoral and that the western clergy was fanatical and anti-intellectual.[38] In the course of a more sympathetic approach to American religious history generally, this picture has changed, and the circuit riders now appear as a hard-working and relatively literate group, most of them less eccentric than Peter Cartwright if less learned than their Congregationalist and Presbyterian rivals.[39]

The current generation of church historians is coming to describe the western clergy less as promoters of an orgiastic expression of cultural primitivism than as major ties to the older way of life left behind in the East. Still the old preoccupation with the local shape of organized religion—and with the external and cruder side of religious life, in conformance with a tendency to what has been called "decerebrate history"[40] —has left much to do. We need fuller appraisal of spiritual, moral, and cultural conditions of whole communities and their antecedents; of the appeal of evangelical religion and of sectarianism in the West, and in turn of their effects on other aspects of western culture. How irreligious were Westerners before the missionaries came, and how uncultured, in general? "Much has been said, and foolishly said, of Western character," warned the Reverend Rufus Babcock. "Most people in the West formed their characters before they emigrated thither; and they have been slightly or not at all modified by their change of residence."[41]

Similarly, we need a fuller story of western literacy and education, confined within neither the buffoonery of *Hoosier Schoolmaster* types nor the desiccated annalistic and eulogistic framework of most college histories. "I have read in books," recalled a Kansas pioneer, "that the people of the frontier kept moving ever westward to escape civilization. But if my experience counts for anything, such people were the exceptions. So eager were we to keep in touch with civilization that even when we could not afford a shot gun and ammunition to kill rabbits, we subscribed to newspapers and periodicals and bought books."[42] Westerners boasted of their new homes, but they often felt, as Timothy Flint said of his traveling companions, their "love for the dear homes they had left, increasing as they receded from them."[43] The written word bridged the gap as nothing else could, and the western appetite for books and newspapers was prodigious.[44] Granville Stuart, the Montana pioneer, married an Indian wife, but read volumes of Shakespeare and Adam Smith, which he brought three hundred miles through the mountains in winter.[45] Even in the mines, times of enforced idleness often were times to read and study.

Not only has the western historian concentrated on the more physical side of the West, slighting intangible factors, but he has neglected even some physical aspects of western life and culture that do not fit the environmental-radical theme. No one has explored the history of architecture in the West as Easterners have done so fruitfully for the colonies, although visitors to the West often were more impressed with the transplantation of eastern styles than they were with the crudities of cabin and sod house. One can see nostalgia, pretension, and habit in the striking architectural incongruities that Westerners achieved in their new environments: the sham fronts that concealed so little in a treeless, one-street town; the useless Saratoga-style cupolas and gingerbread that they preferred to the awnings and porches needed to cut off the hot western sun; steep roofs to shed snow that never fell; resort hotels straight from the White Mountains.[46]

Perhaps the narrowness of our concern with western culture would have been less unfortunate if it had not coincided with an undiscriminating use of sources, which helped to perpetuate original error, or converted tendency into excess. The sources on the West are in large part literary. Whether because of the enormous volume of material or because of the prestige of hypotheses that have seemed to require only illustration, western historians have been slow to use the techniques of literary criticism.[47]

It is easy, for example, to rely uncritically on travelers' accounts, many of which reflect little more than city dwellers' encounters with canalboats, corduroy roads, strap-hung stagecoaches, and the kinds of citizens likely to seem most conspicuous to strangers without letters of introduction. Few travelers met the cultural elite on the frontier, or realized that men in sod houses might have come from communities like their own; and the West as they saw it seemed at the extremity of a shift from moral to physical purposes. Few of them, moreover, were capable of reporting objectively the undeniable facts of crudity and squalor that they had seen; more often than not their biases disposed them to darken the picture.[48] If they became settlers they saw the contrast between real estate prospectuses and the hard reality of western roads and swamps. The promoter's fine promises may have sprung in part from his preoccupation with eastern standards, but they often made the West seem a sham. New Englanders who inherited their section's belief in frontier depravity sometimes merely excepted themselves when they became frontiersmen.[49]

European travelers often expected laborers to be poorer as well as more respectful of their betters than they were in America; Englishmen might be surprised to find the temper of rural America so different from that of rural England, where aristocracy had its strongest supporters. Most of those who could afford to visit the Far West and had the leisure to write of what they saw were rich men; and being accustomed to a narrow sector of English or eastern society, they "saw people as they are not" and believed the tallest of tales. Richard Cobden complained in 1859 that European "writers and travellers fall into a great unfairness in comparing the middle and upper classes with whom alone the tourists and the book-writing class associate in Europe with the *whole people* whom they meet at the table d'hotes and in the railway cars in the United States."[50]

Belief in western sterotypes was especially easy for travelers who knew the patterns of earlier travelers' accounts and who sensed the popular appeal of color and low comedy in descriptions of the West. By the 1870's a western traveler must keep to the pace of the dime novel as well; he was a poor sort unless he had seen a Mormon wife in distress, a Buffalo Bill, or a Calamity Jane. "It is absolutely essential to a Californian entering London society," reported one who was there, "that he has slain at least one grizzly bear. This is expected and required of him."[51] The European traveler who visited the West and stayed long enough to overcome the literary conventions, on the other hand, sometimes gave a more sober and objective report than the American who, as a prospective settler, shared the settlers' awful preoccupation with the task of making the West into the East and felt oppressed by a sense of personal or national responsibility as he wrote.

An appraisal of western conservatism and continuity, however, must leave ample room for qualification, and not merely exchange new narrowness for old. It would be as easy to exaggerate conservatism in the 1950's as it was to exaggerate radicalism in the 1890's. Sharp distinctions between liberal and conservative factors are sure to be artificial, and they are especially suspect in the history of a transplanted society. In part the conservative West of the nineteenth century was the copy of the East that it tried to be. It contained hierarchies of culture, wealth, and influence in which the upper classes were small but influential beyond their size; it clung to traditional institutional forms and social practices; and it hungered after intellectual and social contact and parity with the East. A large part of western opportunity was the opportunity to imitate an older society. At the same time, realization tended to fall short of aspiration; and both innovations and transplantations were often unfinished business, forced to give priority to the more pressing problems of subsistence. Thus neither the radical nor the conservative could even try to go so far as he might wish to go. A western aristocracy was likely to be newer and more mobile than its counterpart in the East, and generally innocent of any body of ideas or sense of social responsibility comparable to the constructive political philosophy of a John Adams or a Henry L. Stimson. Much western conservatism might as well be called materialism. Yet some such differences were only relative. To an Englishman, the ascent of the Schoenberg-Belmont family within two generations in New York might seem only somewhat less surprising than the ascent and descent of the Tabor family within two decades in Colorado.

The historian of the Pacific Coast states, as of any of the newer wests, must guard especially against forcing the history of the whole West into a new pattern, though thus far much popular Pacific Coast history simply dresses Daniel Boone in *chaparajos* and puts the Mississippi River toughs on horseback. The dude ranch country of the Rocky Mountains may too readily conclude that it is the most western part of the West, as if Wall Street ruled only in the shadows of the skyscrapers; West Texas may too readily conclude that it comprises all of America. But the coast began by being closer to the East than the interior was; and if San Francisco brings the aspirations of the West to focus, so that one cannot understand the Nevada desert without knowing also "the city," the city alone tells little of the desert to one who has not gone there.

Two generations after Turner set forth his environmental interpretation of the American West, it seems to rest more on tradition than on the testimony of recent events. As we move away from his time, our own time alerts us to continuity and conservatism, among other themes. The volume of research on the more recent West increases, even while the pioneer period dominates most courses and textbooks on the history of the West and many western history research libraries. The historian cannot easily ignore the challenge to explain this new present in which he lives and works, a present in which West and East are visibly more alike than they were in Turner's day. Some of Turner's critics, on the other hand, have been moved too much by the atmosphere of their own time and of their own section, and have, in effect, condemned the nineteenth-century West because it is not the twentieth-century East. Both they and those Westerners who achieve a new antiquarianism in a narrow treatment of recent events pass by the larger opportunities of western history.

It may be that the greater stimulus to western history-writing could come from other fields. It would be useful, for instance, for western historians, who in a large sense are colonial historians, to look more closely at our colonial roots. As a group, colonial historians have been far more successful than the Westerners in integrating their story into large regional patterns and in exploring institutions and ideas.[52] The western historian might be more critical of his sources and his premises if he had not tended to drift so far into intellectual isolation from his colleagues. Cultivating selected furrows in a separate patch, he confirms his isolation by retaining to an unusual degree an earlier generation's faith in accumulated information, even though his field is one whose personnel and specific events are so little known that he has an unusual obligation to present them in large patterns and attractive style. Correspondingly, some of the most thoughtful contributions to western history have seemed to be, if not products of intellectual hybridization, at least the work of men who ignore the orthodox limitations of the western historian.

If there is an answer to the complaint against the restricted outlook of western historians, it is not likely to be found in decrying Turner's mistakes and the inspiration of his time, nor in deprecating the reverence that he still commands. It would be no solution to turn western history over to economists, political scientists, and others not conversant with the massive literature of the field, though when they have tried their hand at it as critics of Turner some of them have done embarrassingly well, and Turner's defenders have not clearly done better in the argument.[53] Rather the trouble with western history may be that we are not enough like Turner in his larger qualities: his concern for both analysis and synthesis, his effective English style, and the keenness of his mind. Turner advocated a radical-environmental approach, but it is clear enough from what he said about other forces in the West, including eastern forces, that he did not hold to that approach alone. The prophet was less orthodox than the priesthood. He was a good salesman, and he had other errors to combat in his time, by overemphasis if necessary. He showed clearly where his preference lay between the antiquarians and those who considered western history "in its relations to world-history, not in the spirit of the local historian," appreciating that they were "describing a phase in the general movement of civilization."[54] He taught courses in national as well as regional history; and his students ranged widely into other fields and other interpretations,[55] as he had done in his own university studies and teaching.

What we need most in western history is probably not simply recency in subject-matter but more of the breadth and flexibility of mind that will disregard arbitrary boundaries in time and space, among other boundaries; not a new conservative bias but more freedom from an old radical-environmental bias, among other biases. An anti-intellectual interpretation may have perpetuated itself not only by excluding the evidence that did not sustain it but also by driving out the intellectuals themselves.[56] One might usefully ask also whether enough students are selecting western history as an area of concentration for reasons more consistent with the larger values of their craft than that they may forego fluency in a foreign language, find topics that no one else has "done," publish their work easily in state and local journals, and escape the strenuous demands and criticisms current in the larger and more intellectualized paths of inquiry. Some of us may have abetted such tendencies by regarding the field as a refuge for the flabbier minds among our graduate students, by encouraging factual rather than interpretative studies, by conferring academic dignity on vulgarization, by debasing literature into accumulation. Yet an answer to such criticisms may lie in the bibliographical citations in surveys such as this. Good books on western history still do appear, and few fields present so many subjects for other good books still to be written.

Notes

1. H. L. Davis, "The Elusive Trail to the Old West," *New York Times Book Review*, February 7, 1954, pp. 1, 17.

2. Frederick J. Turner, "The Significance of the Frontier in American History," American Historical Association, *Annual Report*, 1893 (Washington, 1894), 200.

3. Clarence W. Alvord once remarked that Turner might not have generalized as he did if he had known Kentucky and Illinois as well as he knew Wisconsin. *Mississippi Valley Historical Review* (Cedar Rapids), VII (March, 1921), 406-407.

4. Edward Channing, *Town and County Government in the English Colonies* (Baltimore, 1884). Like some other Easterners, Channing later was unwilling to ascribe to western environment the same force that he saw in eastern environment. By the 1920's and 1930's, some Easterners found frontier influences a convenient explanation of Babbittry rather than of individualism.

5. For a notable exception see Henry C. Hubbart, *The Older Middle West, 1840-1880* (New York, 1936), an impressive study of post-frontier society in the Old Northwest. There is still no satisfactory history of a western state in the Populist period. The conventional justification for cutting off western history in the 1890's—that thereafter the social laboratory of the frontier ceases to provide standard conditions of social temperature and pressure and the West is no longer separate, but a part of the nation—is simply argument by definition, or experimentation without control. It would be more convincing if those who rested on it could point to any time when standard conditions did prevail on the frontier, or to any Westerner or western institution conceived and delivered *in vitro*.

6. *Overland* (San Francisco), Second Series, II (December, 1883), 658.

7. A visitor described Helena, Montana, in 1883 as "typical of this Western life. Luxury and rudeness jostle each other; frontier barbarisms mingle with the latest fashions from 'the States'; the cowboy and the drummer . . . eat at the same table, and perchance sleep in the same bed." Almon Gunnison, *Rambles Overland* (Boston, 1884), 86.

8. Henry R. Schoolcraft, *Personal Memoir of a Residence of Thirty Years with the Indian Tribes* (Philadelphia, 1851), 590.

9. For recent views of the authors of the Ordinance of 1787 as architects of reaction, see Merrill Jensen, *The New Nation* (New York, 1950), and Francis S. Philbrick, "Introduction," *The Laws of*

Illinois Territory, 1809-1818 ([Illinois State Historical Library, *Collections*, Vol. XXV], Springfield, 1950), lv-cccclxxvii.

10. Dorothy O. Johansen, "A Tentative Appraisal of Territorial Government in Oregon," *Pacific Historical Review* (Berkeley), XVIII (November, 1949), 485-99.

11. Thomas Jefferson to Harry Innes, January 23, 1800, Paul L. Ford (ed.), *The Writings of Thomas Jefferson* (10 vols., New York, 1892-1899), IX, 100. See also James Wilkinson to James Madison, August 24, 1805, Clarence E. Carter (ed.), *Territorial Papers of the United States* (20 vols. to date, Washington, 1934-   ), XIII (1948), *The Territory of Louisiana-Missouri, 1803-1806*, p. 189; Jefferson to Samuel Smith, May 4, 1806, *ibid.*, 504; Jefferson to Albert Gallatin, November 9, 1803, *ibid.*, IX (1940), *The Territory of Orleans*, 100-101.

12. Curtis Nettels, "The Mississippi Valley and the Federal Judiciary, 1807-1837," *Mississippi Valley Historical Review*, XII (September, 1925), 202-26. See also William Francis English, *The Pioneer Lawyer and Jurist in Missouri* (Columbia, Mo., 1947). Justices Stephen J. Field and George Sutherland well represent the conservative western lawyer type.

13. Both Turner and Charles H. Shinn (*Mining Camps* [New York, 1885]) were unduly brusque with the vigilantes. For Turner "the forest," for Shinn the environment of the mines and the spirit of the race tended to overshadow transplanted ideas of property and government. On the record of crime in frontier Colorado, see Lynn I. Perrigo, "Law and Order in Early Colorado Mining Camps," *Mississippi Valley Historical Review*, XXVIII (June, 1941), 61.

14. (Chapel Hill, 1930). But see also John D. Hicks, *The Constitutions of the Northwest States* (Lincoln, 1923), and Bayrd Still, "State Constitutional Development in the United States, 1829-1851" (Ph.D. Dissertation, University of Wisconsin, 1933).

15. Fulmer Mood (ed.), *The Early Writings of Frederick Jackson Turner* (Madison, 1938), 38. Cf. Benjamin F. Wright, "American Democracy and the Frontier," *Yale Review* (New Haven), XX (December, 1930), 349-65, and Chester McA. Destler, "Western Radicalism, 1865-1901; Concepts and Origins," *Mississippi Valley Historical Review*, XXXI (December, 1944), 335-68. Lord Bryce cites a western legislature whose members told him (1881 or 1883) "that the political point of view—the fact that they were the founders of new commonwealths . . .—had not crossed their minds. . . . The arrangements of his government lie in the dim background of the picture which fills the western eye. In the foreground he sees ploughs and sawmills, ore-crushers and railway locomotives." James Bryce, *The American Commonwealth* (New ed., 2 vols., New York, 1910), II, 900.

16. Hicks, *Constitutions of the Northwest States*.

17. "All the advanced forms of thought upon education and woman's rights have been imported direct from the New England States," wrote a visitor to Kansas in 1867, "and have quickly developed in this virgin soil to an extent hitherto unprecedented." William A. Bell, *New Tracks in North America* (2 vols., London, 1869), I, 15. The need to make a new western state constitution upon admission, like the need to draw up new southern state constitutions after the Civil War, often released movements for change more easily suppressed or ignored in older states. See Howard K. Beale, "On Rewriting Reconstruction History," *American Historical Review* (New York), XLV (July, 1940), 807-27.

18. While the Populist period in the Middle West and the South has attracted some of the ablest historians of American political movements, it is noteworthy that very little has been done on Populism in the Far West.

19. George T. Clark, *Leland Stanford* (Stanford University, 1931), 83.

20. Henry H. Simms, "The Controversy over the Admission of the State of Oregon," *Mississippi Valley Historical Review*, XXXII (December, 1945), 355-74. Anti-Negro provisions in their state

constitutions also delayed the admission of Colorado and Nebraska, following the enabling acts of 1864. "Our new Territories in their early history show wonderful uniformity," wrote a traveler. "At its first election each invariably votes the democratic ticket." Albert D. Richardson, *Beyond the Mississippi* (Hartford, 1867), 502.

21. Josiah Royce, *California from the Conquest in 1846 to the Second Vigilance Committee* (Boston, 1886), 492-94, 498.

22. Arthur P. Whitaker, *The Mississippi Question, 1795-1803* (New York, 1934), 61-63. Governor William C. C. Claiborne said that "As federal influence declines in the States, the remote Territories will naturally become Asylums for that Party." Claiborne to Jefferson, August 30, 1804, Carter (ed.), *Territorial Papers*, IX, 286. Later there were similar explanations of Democratic strength on the west coast. "When President Taylor was elected in 1848," said the New York *Herald*, "all the democratic politicians in the United States were thrown out of employment; and gold being discovered simultaneously in California, they went off there. . . . They introduced the New York system of politics into San Francisco." Quoted in San Francisco *Daily Alta California*, July 16, 1856. On conservatism in Kentucky, see Whitaker, *Mississippi Question*, 25, 226, and Thomas P. Abernethy, *Three Virginia Frontiers* (Baton Rouge, 1940), 76-77.

23. "Men whose whole lives have been devoted to the abuse of Mr. Jefferson and republicanism here declare that they belong to our party." James Brown to John Breckinridge, January 22, 1805, Carter (ed.), *Territorial Papers*, IX, 380. On Jefferson's use of the patronage to check Federalism, see Jefferson to Governor Robert Williams, April 28 and July 6, 1805, *ibid.*, V (1937), *The Territory of Mississippi*, 400, 413, and Caleb Wallace to Madison, February 22, 1805, *ibid.*, XIII, 91.

24. "The first Delegate from the Territory [of Wisconsin] was understood to be a Whig, when elected; but the administration . . . being of the Democratic party, it was deemed prudent by himself and his friends to change his political character." Alfred Brunson, "Thomas P. Burnett," State Historical Society of Wisconsin, *Collections* (Madison), II (1865), 312. Yet the Whigs sent two delegates to Congress from Michigan and one from Wisconsin while Democratic presidents sat in the White House. While the territorial West elected only four Republicans in nine elections during the Buchanan administration, it elected seven Democrats along with fourteen Republicans during the Lincoln administration. Statisticians and compilers have neglected the territories.

25. See, for example, Paul W. Gates, *Frontier Landlords and Pioneer Tenants* (Ithaca, 1945), and "The Homestead Law in an Incongruous Land System," *American Historical Review* (New York), XLI (July, 1936), 652-81; Fred A. Shannon, "The Homestead Act and the Labor Surplus," *ibid.*, 637-51, and "A Post Mortem on the Labor-Safety-Valve Theory," *Agricultural History* (Washington), XIX (January, 1945), 31-37. See also Senate Committee on Education and Labor, "Report upon the Relations between Labor and Capital," *Senate Reports*, No. 1262, 48 Cong., 2 Sess. (5 vols., Washington, 1885), II, 572-73 and *passim*.

26. Currin V. Shields, "The American Tradition of Empirical Collectivism," *American Political Science Review* (Menasha, Wis.), XLVI (March, 1952), 107-108; Guy S. Callender, "Early Transportation and Banking Enterprises of the States in Relation to the Growth of Corporations," *Quarterly Journal of Economics* (Boston), XVII (November, 1902), 111-62.

27. The Western Federation of Miners and the Industrial Workers of the World, while representing the impact of large-scale enterprise in the later West, drew most heavily on recent arrivals from older states. Citing the lack of apologies for the Leadville strikers in 1896, G. W. Steevens remarked that "In a land where you may be a pauper today and a millionaire tomorrow . . . a man looks upon the wealth of others as held in trust for himself, and will suffer no diminution of its sanctity." *The Land of the Dollar* (Edinburgh, 1897), 204-205.

28. *Overland*, Second Series, II (December, 1883), 657.

29. Frederick L. Olmsted, *A Journey Through Texas; or, A Saddle-trip on the Southwestern Frontier* (New York, 1859), xix n. Turner attributed the backwardness of education among the pioneers to poverty and to "the traditions of the southern interior from which they so largely came." "The Colonization of the West," *American Historical Review*, XI (January, 1906), 326. James F. Rusling, among other travelers, emphasized the Missouri influence in the more backward parts of the West. "Outside of Portland . . . the Oregonians appeared . . . to have retained many of their old Missouri and so-called 'conservative' ideas still. . . . 'The left wing of Price's army is still encamped in this region.' " *Across America: or the Great West and the Pacific Coast* (New York, 1875), 267.

30. Frank L. Owsley, *Plain Folk of the Old South* (Baton Rouge, 1949), 36.

31. For a brief appraisal see John D. Hicks, "The California Background—Spanish or American?" *The Westerners Brand Book* (Winnetka, Ill.), V (June, 1948), 21-23, 26-28. Carey McWilliams, *California: The Great Exception* (New York, 1949), traces recent social tensions to the Spanish and Mexican labor systems. On the Creole in New Orleans, see Joseph G. Tregle, "Early New Orleans Society: A Reappraisal," *Journal of Southern History* (Baton Rouge), XVIII (February, 1952), 20-36.

32. Exceptions are such romantic exiles from civilization as Dr. John McLoughlin and Harman Blennerhassett (rather significantly, neither an American) whose estates, before their ultimate and almost inevitable downfalls, contrasted sharply with the hovels of their pioneer neighbors.

33. Thomas P. Abernethy, "Democracy and the Southern Frontier," *Journal of Southern History*, IV (February, 1938), 3-13; William C. Binkley, "The South and the West," *ibid.*, XVII (February, 1951), 5-22; John D. Barnhart, "The Southern Element in the Leadership of the Old Northwest," *ibid.*, I (May, 1935), 186-97; William B. Hamilton, "The Southwestern Frontier, 1795-1817; An Essay in Social History," *ibid.*, X (November, 1944), 389-403; Frank L. Owsley, "The Pattern of Migration and Settlement on the Southern Frontier," *ibid.*, XI (May, 1945), 147-76; and other studies. Western society needs more analysis in the spirit of L. B. Namier, whose work in British history seems more Turnerian than the work most Turnerians in this country have done.

34. James B. Finley, *Autobiography* (Cincinnati, 1853), 97.

35. Alexander K. McClure, *Three Thousand Miles through the Rocky Mountains* (Philadelphia, 1869), 102. The Far West became notoriously overstocked with lawyers. Noting that there were five hundred in San Francisco, one writer remarked: "The *gentleman* is out of place . . . unless he can be furnishing aid in the shape of money towards the development of resources." T. H. Rearden, "Over-Crowded Professions on the Pacific Coast," *Overland*, I (September, 1868), 251.

36. Henry M. Brackenridge, *Recollections of Persons and Places in the West* (Philadelphia, 1834), 48. Recent descriptions of the Army's contribution include Francis P. Prucha, *Broadax and Bayonet: The Role of the United States Army in the Development of the Northwest, 1815-1860* (Madison, 1953), W. Turrentine Jackson, *Wagon Roads West* (Berkeley, 1952), and W. N. Davis, "Post Trading in the West," *Explorations in Entrepreneurial History* (Cambridge), VI (October, 1953), 30-40.

37. Edward Sullivan, *Rambles and Scrambles in North and South America* (London, 1852), 162-163.

38. See, for example, Finley, *Autobiography*, and William P. Strickland (ed.), *Autobiography of Peter Cartwright* (New York, 1856). For a protest against the prevailing notion that western preachers were "mostly uncultivated, ignorant persons from the lower classes," see Nils W. Olsson (ed.), *A Pioneer in Northwest America, 1841-1858: The Memoirs of Gustaf Unonius* (Minneapolis, 1950), 337-38.

39. Charles A. Johnson, "The Frontier Camp Meeting: Contemporary and Historical Appraisals, 1805-1840," *Mississippi Valley Historical Review*, XXXVII (June, 1950), 91-110. Thomas P. Abernethy, *From Frontier to Plantation in Tennessee* (Chapel Hill, 1932), 219-20, points out that the evangelists

came to dominate the South only after the frontier had passed. See also Niels H. Sonne, *Liberal Kentucky, 1780-1828* (New York, 1939).

40. Henry Nash Smith, "The West as an Image of the American Past," *University of Kansas City Review* (Kansas City), XVIII (Autumn, 1951), 39.

41. Rufus Babcock (ed.), *Forty Years of Pioneer Life: Memoir of John Mason Peck* (Philadelphia, 1864), 347 n. While western religion sometimes is interpreted as an expression of equality in social, economic, and political conditions, it is clear that such equality was not universal. Elizabeth K. Nottingham, *Methodism and the Frontier: Indiana Proving Ground* (New York, 1941), attributes the appeal of evangelical religion to resentment against the inequities of this world—the prosperity of gamblers, speculators, and tavern-keepers who flourished while the righteous labored.

42. Elise D. Isely, *Sunbonnet Days* (Caldwell, Idaho, 1935), 180. There are suggestive accounts of opposition to western school taxes in Isaiah Bowman, *The Pioneer Fringe* (New York, 1931), 22, 31-32, 122, and Lloyd P. Jorgensen, "The Origins of Public Education in Wisconsin," *Wisconsin Magazine of History* (Madison), XXXIII (September, 1949), 15-27.

43. Timothy Flint, *Recollections of the Last Ten Years* (Boston, 1826), 7. According to Henry R. Schoolcraft (1823), a "long . . . exclusion from the ordinary sources of information has the effect to increase the appetite for this kind of intellectual food [newspapers], and the circumstance probably leads us to give up more time to it than we should were we not subject to these periodical exclusions." *Personal Memoir of Residence with Indian Tribes*, 158.

44. Western coverage of eastern news was comparable to the colonial press's coverage of English and European news. Newspapers like the Denver *Rocky Mountain News* in the 1860's and 1870's gave their readers more complete coverage than do many local newspapers today.

45. Granville Stuart, *Forty Years on the Frontier* (2 vols., Cleveland, 1925), I, 159-60, 206.

46. Horace A. Vachell, *Life and Sport on the Pacific Slope* (London, 1900), 175, 180. Westerners often "built not in harmony with their new surroundings, but in memory of the old ones they left behind them." Mary H. Foote, "A Sea-Port on the Pacific," *Scribner's Monthly* (New York), XVI (August, 1878), 459. On early western architecture, see Rexford Newcomb, *Architecture of the Old Northwest Territory* (Chicago, 1950), and *Architecture of Old Kentucky* (Urbana, 1953).

47. Henry Nash Smith, *Virgin Land: The American West as Symbol and Myth* (Cambridge, 1950), has most impressively broken new ground.

48. Timothy Flint pointed out that the better classes of settlers were not in the main river settlements but off the lateral streams, where travelers were less likely to penetrate. John E. Kirkpatrick, *Timothy Flint, Pioneer, Missionary, Author, Editor, 1780-1840* (Cleveland, 1911), 78. For similar observations, see James Hall, *Sketches of History, Life, and Manners in the West* (2 vols., Philadelphia, 1835), II, 71, and John H. Beadle, *The Undeveloped West* (Philadelphia, 1873), 371-72.

49. See, for example, Clarence King, *Mountaineering in the Sierra Nevada* (Boston, 1872), 28, 111, 115, 287.

50. Elizabeth H. Cawley (ed.), *The American Diaries of Richard Cobden* (Princeton, 1952), 208. See also William A. Baillie-Grohman, *Camps in the Rockies* (London, 1882), 9, 10, 25, for similar comments at a later date; and for British impressions in general, Robert G. Athearn, *Westward the Briton* (New York, 1953).

51. Prentice Mulford, "Justifiable Fiction," *Overland*, XI (July, 1873), 39. See Mody C. Boatright, *Folk Laughter on the American Frontier* (New York, 1949), 2-11, on the folklore of frontier backwardness and crass materialism.

52. See, for example, Charles M. Andrews, "Conservative Factors in Colonial History," Harvard Tercentenary Conference of Arts and Sciences, *Authority and the Individual* (4 vols., Cambridge, 1936-1937), II, 154-69; or the chapter on "The Back Settlements," in Carl Bridenbaugh, *Myths and Realities: Societies of the Colonial South* (Baton Rouge, 1952), 119-96. Among western regional studies, William J. Trimble, *The Mining Advance into the Inland Empire* (Madison, 1914), and Walter P. Webb, *The Great Plains* (Boston, 1931), are still unsurpassed for the areas covered. In Webb's case, reviewers paid tribute by debating whether he had written history, or sociology, or geography. See especially Social Science Research Council, *Critiques of Research in the Social Sciences*: III, *An Appraisal of Walter Prescott Webb's* The Great Plains (Bulletin 46: New York, 1940).

53. The critics might have made a greater contribution if they had not (as was quite natural for outsiders working largely in eastern materials) concentrated on minimizing the West as a force in the making of the nation rather than on analyzing the forces that made the West.

54. See especially Turner's essay, "Dominant Forces in Western Life," *Atlantic Monthly* (Boston), LXXIX (April, 1897), reprinted in *The Frontier in American History* (New York, 1920), Chap. VIII; and note his reviews of books by Theodore Roosevelt and Justin Winsor, *American Historical Review*, II (October, 1896), 171-76, and III (April, 1898), 556-61; *The Nation* (New York), LX (March 28, 1895), 240-42; and *Dial* (Chicago), X (August, 1889), 71-73.

55. Evident in such names as Carl L. Becker, Herbert E. Bolton, Homer C. Hockett, William S. Robertson, Joseph Schafer, and George M. Stephenson from the Wisconsin period; and Lois K. Mathews, Colin B. Goodykoontz, Thomas P. Abernethy, Merle Curti, and Arthur P. Whitaker from Harvard.

56. It seems significant, for example, that none of the participants in the stimulating panel at the American Historical Association meeting of 1933, whose essays were later published in Dixon Ryan Fox (ed.), *Sources of Culture in the Middle West* (New York, 1934), has continued to work in frontier history.

The mission as a frontier institution in the Spanish-American colonies

Herbert E. Bolton

Frederick Jackson Turner and his followers have examined the impact of the frontier upon pioneers of European stock in the American wilderness. Others, such as Earl Pomeroy, have reversed the Turner idea, stressing that imported cultural traits shaped frontier life. In either case the emphasis has always been on a European migration. Spain's frontier experience does not fit the Turner model. Spanish migration to the New World was relatively slight, and when it did take place, its purpose was seldom to supplant or destroy Indian culture. In most cases Spain counted upon using the native populations as part of its grand imperial scheme. Unlike the English colonies, where the aborigines were quickly pushed aside, the Spanish colonies emerged as a unique blend of European and native cultures. What is surprising, however, is the large success that a small number of Spaniards had in reshaping Indian culture. Herbert E. Bolton was born in Wisconsin in 1870. In the mid-1890's he studied at the University of Wisconsin, where he was exposed to Turner's ideas. He then went East, and in 1899 he received his doctorate from the University of Pennsylvania. Bolton soon emerged as a historian of the southwestern frontier. He spent most of his career at the University of California, Berkeley. In the following essay Bolton examines how Spain molded the southwestern frontier in its own image.

For further reading: Herbert E. Bolton, *The Spanish Borderlands* (New Haven: Yale University Press, 1921); Herbert E. Bolton, *Rim of Christendom: A Biography of Eusebio Francisco Kino, Pacific Coast Pioneer* (New York: Macmillan, 1936); Peter Masten Dunne, *Pioneer Black Robes on the West Coast* (Berkeley: University of California Press, 1940); Lewis Hanke, *Bartolomé de las Casas: Bookman, Scholar, and Propagandist* (Philadelphia: University of Pennsylvania Press, 1952); Lewis Hanke, ed., *Do the Americas Have a Common History? A Critique of the Bolton Theory* (New York: Knopf, 1964); C. H. Haring, *The Spanish Empire in America* (New York: Oxford University Press, 1947)*; Lesley Byrd Simpson, *Many Mexicos* (Berkeley: University of California

Reprinted with permission from *American Historical Review*, XXIII (October 1917), 42-61.

Press, 1941)*; Lesley Byrd Simpson, *The Encomienda in New Spain: The Beginning of Spanish Mexico*, rev. and enl. ed. (Berkeley: University of California Press, 1966).

*Available in paperback.

Of the missions in Spanish America, particularly those in California, much has been written. But most of what has been produced consists of chronicles of the deeds of the Fathers, polemic discussions by sectarian partizans, or sentimental effusions with literary, edifying, or financial intent. They deal with the heroic exploits of individuals, with mooted questions of belief and practice, or with the romance that hovers round the mission ruins. All this is very well, and not to be ridiculed, but it is none the less true that little has been said of these missions in their relation to the general Spanish colonial policy, of which they were an integral and a most important part. Father Engelhardt's learned books are a notable exception, but his view is confined closely to California, whereas the mission, in the Spanish colonies, was an almost universal establishment.

One of the marvels in the history of the modern world is the way in which that little Iberian nation, Spain, when most of her blood and treasure were absorbed in European wars, with a handful of men took possession of the Caribbean archipelago, and by rapid yet steady advance spread her culture, her religion, her law, and her language over more than half of the two American continents, where they still are dominant and still are secure—in South America, Central America, and a large fraction of North America, for fifty million people in America to-day are tinged with Spanish blood, still speak the Spanish language, still worship at the altar set up by the Catholic kings, still live under laws essentially Spanish, and still possess a culture largely inherited from Spain.

These results are an index of the vigor and the virility of Spain's frontier forces; they should give pause to those who glibly speak of Spain's failure as a colonizing nation; and they suggest the importance of a thoughtful study of Spain's frontier institutions and methods. Professor Turner has devoted his life to a study of the Anglo-American frontier, and rich has been his reward. Scarcely less conspicuous in the history of the Western world than the advance of the Anglo-American frontier has been the spread of Spanish culture, and for him who interprets, with Turner's insight, the methods and the significance of the Spanish-American frontier, there awaits a recognition not less marked or less deserved.

Whoever essays this task, whoever undertakes to interpret the forces by which Spain extended her rule, her language, her law, and her traditions, over the frontiers of her vast American possessions, must give close attention to the missions, for in that work they constituted a primary agency. Each of the colonizing nations in America had its peculiar frontier institutions and classes. In the French colonies the pioneers of pioneers were the fur-trader and the missionary. Penetrating the innermost wilds of the continent, one in search of the beaver, the other in quest of souls to save, together they extended the French domains, and brought the savage tribes into friendly relations with the French government, and into profitable relations with the French outposts. In the English colonies the fur-trader blazed the way and opened new trails, but it was the backwoods settler who hewed down the forest, and step by step drove back the Indian with whom he did not readily mingle. In the Spanish colonies the men to whom fell the task of extending and holding the frontiers were the *conquistador*, the presidial soldier, and the missionary.

All of these agents were important; but in my study of frontier institutions in general, and in my endeavor in particular to understand the methods and forces by which Spain's frontiers were extended, held, and developed, I have been more and more impressed with the importance of the mission as a pioneering agency. Taking for granted for the moment its very obvious religious aspects, I shall here devote my attention more especially to the mission's political and social meaning. My point of view embraces all of New Spain—all of the Spanish colonies, indeed—but more particularly the northern provinces, from Sinaloa to Texas, from Florida to California. My conclusions are based on the study of documents, unprinted for the most part, which have been gathered mainly from the archives of Mexico and Spain.

The functions of the mission, from the political standpoint, will be better understood if it is considered in its historical relations. The central interest around which the mission was built was the Indian. In respect to the native, the Spanish sovereigns, from the outset, had three fundamental purposes. They desired to convert him, to civilize him, and to exploit him. To serve these three purposes, there was devised, out of the experience of the early conquerors, the *encomienda* system. It was soon found that if the savage were to be converted, or disciplined, or exploited, he must be put under control. To provide such control, the land and the people were distributed among Spaniards, who held them in trust, or in *encomienda*. The trustee, or *encomendero*, as he was called, was strictly charged by the sovereign, as a condition of his grant, to provide for the protection, the conversion, and the civilization of the aborigines. In return he was empowered to exploit their labor, sharing the profits with the king. To provide the spiritual instruction and to conduct schools for the natives—for Indian schools were actually prescribed and maintained—the *encomenderos* were required to support the necessary friars, by whom the instruction was given. Thus great monasteries were established in the conquered districts.

But the native had his own notions, especially about being exploited, and he sometimes fled to the woods. It was soon discovered, therefore, that in order properly to convert, instruct, and exploit the Indian, he must be kept in a fixed place of residence. This need was early reported to the sovereigns by *encomenderos* and friars alike, and it soon became a law that Indians must be congregated in pueblos, and made to stay there, by force if necessary. The pueblos were modelled on the Spanish towns, and were designed not alone as a means of control, but as schools in self-control as well.

Thus, during the early years of the conquest, the natives were largely in the hands of the *encomenderos*, mainly secular landholders. The friars, and afterward the Jesuit priests, came in great numbers, to preach and teach, but they lacked the authority of later days. In 1574 there were in the conquered districts of Spanish America nearly nine thousand Indian towns, containing about one and a half million adult males, representing some five million people, subject to tribute. These nine thousand towns were *encomiendas* of the king and some four thousand *encomenderos*.

The *encomienda* system then, by intention, was benevolent. It was designed for the conversion and the civilization of the native, as well as for the exploitation of his labor. But the flesh is weak, and the system was abused. The obligations to protect, convert, and civilize were forgotten, and the right to exploit was perverted into license. Practical slavery soon resulted, and the *encomienda* system became the black spot in the Spanish-

American code. Philanthropists, led by Las Casas, begged for reform; abuses were checked, and *encomiendas* were gradually, though slowly, abolished.

This improvement was made easier by the decreasing attractiveness of *encomiendas*, as the conquest proceeded to the outlying districts. The semi-civilized Indians of central Mexico and Peru had been fairly docile, had had a steady food supply and fixed homes, were accustomed to labor, and were worth exploiting. The wilder tribes encountered later—the Chichimecos, as they were called—were hostile, had few crops, were unused to labor, had no fixed villages, would not stand still to be exploited, and were hardly worth the candle. Colonists were no longer so eager for *encomiendas*, and were willing to escape the obligation to protect and civilize the wild tribes, which were as uncomfortable burdens, sometimes, as cub-tigers in a sack. Moreover, the sovereigns, with increasing emphasis, forbade the old-time abuses of exploitation, but as strongly as before adhered to the ideal of conversion and civilization. Here, then, was a larger opening for the missionary, and to him was entrusted, or upon him was thrust, consciously or unconsciously, not only the old work of conversion, but a larger and larger element of responsibility and control. On the northern frontier, therefore, among the roving tribes, the place of the discredited *encomendero* was largely taken by the missionary, and that of the *encomienda* by the mission, the design being to check the evils of exploitation, and at the same time to realize the ideal of conversion, protection, and civilization.

These missionaries became a veritable corps of Indian agents, serving both Church and State. The double capacity in which they served was made easier and more natural by the close union between Church and State in Spanish America, where the king exercised the *real patronato*, and where the viceroys were sometimes archbishops as well.

Under these conditions, in the seventeenth and eighteenth centuries, on the expanding frontiers of Spanish America, missions became well-nigh universal. In South America the outstanding examples were the Jesuit missions in Paraguay. Conspicuous in North America were the great Franciscan establishments in Alta California, the last of Spain's conquests. Not here alone, however, but everywhere on the northern frontier they played their part—in Sinaloa, Sonora, and Lower California; in Chihuahua, Coahuila, Nuevo León, and Nuevo Santander; in Florida, New Mexico, Texas, and Arizona. If there were twenty-one missions in California, there were as many in Texas, more in Florida, and twice as many in New Mexico. At one time the California missions had over thirty thousand Indians under instruction; but a century and a half earlier the missions of Florida and New Mexico each had an equal number.

The missionary work on the northern frontier of New Spain was conducted chiefly by Franciscans, Jesuits, and Dominicans. The northeastern field fell chiefly to the Franciscans, who entered Coahuila, Nuevo León, Nuevo Santander, New Mexico, Texas, and Florida. To the Northwest came the Jesuits, who, after withdrawing from Florida, worked especially in Sinaloa, Sonora, Chihuahua, Lower California, and Arizona. In 1767 the Jesuits were expelled from all Spanish America, and their places taken by the other orders. To Lower California came the Dominicans, to Alta California the Franciscans of the College of San Fernando, in the City of Mexico.

The missions, then, like the presidios, or garrisons, were characteristically and designedly frontier institutions, and it is as pioneer agencies that they must be studied. This is true whether they be considered from the religious, the political, or the social standpoint. As religious institutions they were designed to introduce the Faith among the heathen.

Having done this, their function was to cease. Being designed for the frontier, they were intended to be temporary. As soon as his work was finished on one frontier, the missionary was expected to move on to another. In the theory of the law, within ten years each mission must be turned over to the secular clergy, and the common mission lands distributed among the Indians. But this law had been based on experience with the more advanced tribes of Mexico, Central America, and Peru. On the northern frontier, among the barbarian tribes, a longer period of tutelage was always found necessary.

The result, almost without fail, was a struggle over secularization, such as occurred in California. So long as the Indians were under the missionaries, their lands were secure from the land-grabber. The land-grabber always, therefore, urged the fulfillment of the ten-year law, just as the "squatters", the "sooners", and the "boomers" have always urged the opening of our Indian reservations. But the missionaries always knew the danger, and they always resisted secularization until their work was finished. Sooner or later, however, with the disappearance of frontier conditions, the missionary was expected to move on. His religious task was beside the soldier, *entre infieles*, in the outposts of civilization.

But the missionaries were not alone religious agents. Designedly in part, and incidentally in part, they were political and civilizing agents of a very positive sort, and as such they constituted a vital feature of Spain's pioneering system. From the standpoint of the Church, and as viewed by themselves, their principal work was to spread the Faith, first, last, and always. To doubt this is to confess complete and disqualifying ignorance of the great mass of existing missionary correspondence, printed and unprinted, so fraught with unmistakable proofs of the religious zeal and devotion of the vast majority of the missionaries. It is quite true, as Engelhardt says, that they "came not as scientists, as geographers, as school-masters, nor as philanthropists, eager to uplift the people in a worldly sense, to the exclusion or neglect of the religious duties pointed out by Christ". But it is equally true, and greatly to their credit, that, incidentally from their own standpoint and designedly from that of the government, they were all these and more, and that to all these and other services they frequently and justly made claim, when they asked for government aid.

The missions, then, were agencies of the State as well as of the Church. They served not alone to Christianize the frontier, but also to aid in extending, holding, and civilizing it. Since Christianity was the basic element of European civilization, and since it was the acknowledged duty of the State to extend the Faith, the first task of the missionary, from the standpoint of both State and Church, was to convert the heathen. But neither the State nor the Church—nor the missionary himself—in Spanish dominions, considered the work of the mission as ending here. If the Indian were to become either a worthy Christian or a desirable subject, he must be disciplined in the rudiments of civilized life. The task of giving the discipline was likewise turned over to the missionary. Hence, the missions were designed to be not only Christian seminaries, but in addition were outposts for the control and training schools for the civilizing of the frontier.

Since they served the State, the missions were supported by the State. It is a patent fact, and scarcely needs demonstrating, that they were maintained to a very considerable extent by the royal treasury. The Franciscan missions of New Spain in the eighteenth century had four principal means of support. The annual stipends of the missionaries (the *sínodos*) were usually paid by the government. These *sínodos* varied in amount according to the remoteness of the missions, and on the northernmost frontier were usually $450 for each missionary. In 1758, for example, the treasury of New Spain was annually paying *sínodos* for twelve Querétaran friars in Coahuila and Texas, six Jaliscans in Coahuila, eleven Zacatecans in Texas, ten Fernandinos in the Sierra Gorda, six Jaliscans in Nayarit, twenty-two Zacatecans in Nuevo León and Nueva Vizcaya, seventeen Zacatecans in Nuevo Santander, five San Diegans in Sierra Gorda, and thirty-four friars of the Provincia del Santo Evangelio in New Mexico, or, in all, 123 friars, at an average of about 350 *pesos* each. This report did not include the Provincia de Campeche or the Yslas de Barlovento, for which separate reports had been asked. Other appropriations were made for missionaries in the Marianas and the Philippine Islands, dependencies of New Spain.

Besides the *sínodos*, the government regularly furnished the missionaries with military protection, by detaching from the near-by presidios from two to half a dozen or more soldiers for each mission. In addition, the royal treasury usually made an initial grant (*ayuda de costa*) of $1000 to each mission, to pay for bells, vestments, tools, and other expenses of the founding, and in cases of emergency it frequently made special grants for building or other purposes.

These government subsidies did not preclude private gifts, or alms, which were often sought and secured. In the founding of new missions the older establishments were expected to give aid, and if able they did respond in liberal measure. And then there were endowments. The classic examples of private endowments on the northern frontier were the gifts of Don Pedro de Terreros, later Conde de Regla, who offered $150,000 to found Apache missions in Coahuila and Texas, and the Jesuit Fondo Piadoso, or Pious Fund, of California. This latter fund, begun in 1697, grew by a variety of gifts to such an amount that the missions of Lower California were largely supported by the increase alone. With the expulsion of the Jesuits in 1767 the fund was taken over by the government, and became the principal means of support of the new Franciscan missions of Alta California, besides being devoted in part to secular purposes. Even in Alta California, however, the royal treasury paid the wages (*sueldos*) of the mission guards, and gave other financial aid.

Finally, the Indians of the missions were expected soon to become self-supporting, and, indeed, in many cases they did acquire large wealth through stock-raising and agricultural pursuits. But not a penny of this belonged to the missionaries, and the annual *sínodos*, or salaries, continued to be paid from other sources, from the Pious Fund in California, and from the royal treasury generally elsewhere.

While it is thus true that the missions were supported to a very considerable degree by the royal treasury, it is just as plain that the amount of government aid, and the ease with which it was secured, depended largely upon the extent to which political ends could be combined with religious purposes.

The importance of political necessity in loosening the royal purse-strings is seen at every turn in the history of Spanish North America. Knowing the strength of a political appeal, the friars always made use of it in their requests for permission and aid. While the monarchs ever used pious phrases, and praised the work of the padres—without hypocrisy no doubt—the royal pocketbook was not readily opened to found new missions unless there was an important political as well as a religious object to be gained.

Striking examples of this fact are found in the histories of Texas and California. The missionaries of the northern frontier had long had their eyes on the "Kingdom of the Texas" as a promising field of labor, and had even appealed to the government for aid in cultivating it. But in vain, till La Salle planted a French colony at Matagorda Bay. Then the royal treasury was opened, and funds were provided for missions in eastern Texas.

The French danger passed for the moment, and the missions were withdrawn. Then for another decade Father Hidalgo appealed in vain for funds and permission to re-establish the missions. But when St. Denis, agent of the French governor of Louisiana, intruded himself into Coahuila, the Spanish government at once gave liberal support for the re-founding of the missions, to aid in restraining the French.

The case was the same for California. Since the time of Vizcaíno the missionaries had clamored for aid and for permission to found missions at San Diego and Monterey. In 1620 Father Ascensión, who had been with Vizcaíno eighteen years before, wrote, "I do not know what security His Majesty can have in his conscience for delaying so long to send ministers of the Gospel to this realm of California", and, during the next century and a half, a hundred others echoed this admonition. But all to no purpose till the Russian Bear began to amble or to threaten to amble down the Pacific Coast. Then money was forthcoming—partly from the confiscated Pious Fund, it is true—and then missionaries were sent to help hold the country for the crown. On this point Father Engelhardt correctly remarks:

The missionaries, who generally offered to undergo any hardships in order to convert the Indians, appear to have been enlisted merely for the purpose of securing the territory for the Spanish king . . . [and] the Spanish government would not have sent ships and troops to the northwest if the Russians had not crept down the Pacific coast. . . . .

The men who presumed to guide the destinies of Spain then, and, as a rule ever since, cared not for the success of Religion or the welfare of its ministers except in so far as both could be used to promote political schemes.

In this last, I think, Father Engelhardt is too hard on the Spanish monarchs. Their pious professions were not pure hypocrisy. They were truly desirous of spreading the Faith. But they were terribly "hard up", and they had little means to support religious projects unless they served both political and religious ends.

The value of the missionaries as frontier agents was thus clearly recognized, and their services were thus consciously utilized by the government. In the first place, they were often the most useful of explorers and diplomatic agents. The unattended missionary could sometimes go unmolested, and without arousing suspicion and hostility, into districts where the soldier was not welcome, while by their education and their trained habits of thought they were the class best fitted to record what they saw and to report what should be done. For this reason they were often sent alone to explore new frontiers, or as peace emissaries to hostile tribes, or as chroniclers of expeditions led by others. Hence it is that the best of the diaries of early exploration in the Southwest—and, indeed, in most of America—were written by the missionaries.

As illustrations of this kind of frontier service on the part of the missionaries we have but to recall the example of Friar Marcos, who was sent by Viceroy Mendoza to seek the rumored "Seven Cities" in New Mexico; the rediscovery of that province, under the viceroy's patronage, by the party led by Fray Agustín Rodríguez; the expeditions of Father Larios, unattended, into Coahuila; the forty or more journeys of Father Kino across the deserts of Sonora, and his demonstration that California was a peninsula, not an island, as most men had thought; the part played by Kino in pacifying the revolt of the Pimas in 1695, and in making the frontier safe for settlers; the diplomatic errands of Fathers Calahorra and Ramírez, sent by the governors of Texas to the hostile northern tribes; the lone travels of Father Garcés, of two thousand miles or more, over the untrod trails, in Arizona, California, and New Mexico, seeking a better route to California; and the expedition of Fathers Dominguez and Escalante, pathfinders for an equal distance in and about the Great Basin between the Rockies and the Sierras.

The missions served also as a means of defense to the king's dominions. This explains why the government was more willing to support missions when the frontier needed defending than at other times, as in the cases, already cited, of Texas and California. It is significant, too, in this connection, that the Real Hacienda, or Royal Fisc, charged the expenses for presidios and missions both to the same account, the Ramo de Guerra, or "War Fund". In a report for New Spain made in 1758 a treasury official casually remarked,

Presidios are erected and missions founded in tierra firme *whenever it is necessary to defend conquered districts from the hostilities and invasions of warlike, barbarian tribes, and to plant and extend our Holy Faith, for which purposes* juntas de guerra y hacienda *are held.*

It is indeed true that appropriations for missions were usually made and that permission to found missions was usually given in councils of war and finance.

The missionaries counteracted foreign influence among their neophytes, deterred them from molesting the interior settlements, and secured their aid in holding back more distant tribes. Nearly every army that was led from San Antonio, Texas, in the eighteenth century, against the hostile Apaches and Comanches, contained a strong contingent of mission Indians, who fought side by side with the Spaniards. Father Kino was relied upon by the military leaders of Sonora to obtain the aid of the Pimas, his beloved neophytes, in defense of the Sonora settlements. When he was assigned to California, in company with Salvatierra, the authorities of Sonora protested, on the ground that, through his influence over the natives, he was a better means of protection to the province than a whole company of soldiers. When a Spanish expedition was organized to attack the Apaches, Kino was sent ahead to arouse and enlist the Pima allies. When the Pimas put the Apaches to flight, it was Kino to whom they sent the count of the enemy's dead, recorded by notches on a pole; on the same occasion it was Kino who received the thanks of citizens and officials of the province; and, when doubt was expressed as to what the Pimas had accomplished, it was Kino who rode a hundred miles or more to count the scalps of the vanquished foe, as evidence with which to vindicate his Pima friends.

The very mission plants were even built and often served as fortresses, not alone for padres and neophytes, but for near-by settlers, too. Every well-built mission was ranged round a great court or patio, protected on all sides by the buildings, whose walls were sometimes eight feet thick. In hostile countries these buildings were themselves enclosed within massive protecting walls. In 1740 President Santa Ana wrote that Mission Valero, at San Antonio, Texas, was better able to withstand a siege than any of the three presidios of the province. This of course was only a relative excellence. Twenty-two years later the same mission was surrounded by a wall, and over the gate was a tower, equipped with muskets, ammunition, and three cannon. At the same time the mission of San José (Texas) was called "a castle" which more than once has been proof against the Apaches.

Not only were the missionaries consciously utilized as political agents to hold the frontier but they often served, on their own motion, or with the co-operation of the secular authority, as "promoters" of the unoccupied districts. They sent home reports of the outlying tribes, of the advantages of obtaining their friendship, of the danger of foreign incursions, of the wealth and attractions of the country, and of the opportunities to extend the king's dominion. Frequently, indeed, they were called to Mexico, or even to Spain, to sit in the royal councils, where their expert opinions often furnished the primary basis of a decision to occupy a new outpost. As examples of this, near at home, we have but to recall Escobar, Benavides, and Ayeta of New Mexico, Massanet, Hidalgo, and Santa Ana of Texas, Kino of Lower California, and Serra of Alta California. Thus consciously or unconsciously, directly or indirectly, with or without secular initiative, the missionaries served as most active promoters, one might even call them "boosters", of the frontier.

But the missionaries helped not only to extend and hold and promote the frontier; more significantly still, they helped to civilize it. And this is the keynote of my theme. Spain possessed high ideals, but she had peculiar difficulties to contend with. She laid claim to the lion's share of the two Americas, but her population was small and little of it could be spared to people the New World. On the other hand, her colonial policy, equalled in humanitarian principles by that of no other country, perhaps, looked to the preservation of the natives, and to their elevation to at least a limited citizenship. Lacking Spaniards to colonize the frontier, she would colonize it with the aborigines. Such an ideal called not only for the subjugation and control of the natives, but for their civilization as well. To bring this end about the rulers of Spain again made use of the religious and humanitarian zeal of the missionaries, choosing them to be to the Indians not only preachers, but also teachers and disciplinarians. To the extent that this work succeeded it became possible to people the frontier with civilized natives, and thus to supply the lack of colonists. This desire was quite in harmony with the religious aims of the friars, who found temporal discipline indispensable to the best work of Christianization.

Hence it is that in the Spanish system—as distinguished from the French, for example—the essence of the mission was the *discipline*, religious, moral, social, and industrial, which it afforded. The very physical arrangement of the mission was determined with a view to discipline. The central feature of every successful mission was the Indian village, or pueblo. The settled tribes, such as the Pueblo Indians of New Mexico, or the Pimas of Arizona, could be instructed in their native towns, but wandering and scattered tribes must be assembled and established in pueblos, and kept there, by force if necessary. The reason why the missions of eastern Texas failed was that the Indians refused to settle in pueblos, and without more soldiers than were available it was impossible to control them. It was on this question that Father Serra split with Governor Neve regarding the Santa Barbara Indians in California. To save expense for soldiers, Neve urged that the friars should minister to the Indians in their native rancherías. But the missionaries protested that by this arrangement the Indians could not be disciplined. The plan was given up therefore, and instead the Indians were congregated in great pueblos at San Buenaventura and Santa Barbara. Thus, the pueblo was essential to the mission, as it had been to the *encomienda*.

Discipline called for control, and this was placed largely in the hands of the missionaries. The rule was two friars for each mission, but in many instances there was only one. The need of more was often urged.

As a symbol of force, and to afford protection for missionaries and mission Indians, as well as to hold the frontier against savages and foreigners, presidios, or garrisons, were established near by. And thus, across the continent, from San Agustín to San Francisco, stretched a long and slender line of presidios—San Agustín, Apalache, Pensacola, Los Adaes, La Bahia, San Antonio, San Juan Bautista, Rio Grande, San Sabá, El Paso, Santa Fé, Janos, Fronteras, Terrenate, Tubac, Altár, San Diego, Santa Barbara, Monterey, and San Francisco—a line more than twice as long as the Rhine-Danube frontier held by the Romans, from whom Spain learned her lesson in frontier defense.

To assist the missionaries in their work of disciplining and instructing the neophytes, each mission was usually provided with two or more soldiers from the nearest presidio. To help in recovering runaways—for the Indians frequently did abscond—special detachments of soldiers were furnished. The impression is often given that the missionaries objected to the presence of soldiers at the missions, but as a rule the case was quite the contrary. What they did object to was unsuitable soldiers, and outside interference in the selection and control of the guard. It is true, indeed, that immoral or insubordinate soldiers were deemed a nuisance, and that since the presidials were largely half-breeds— mestizoes or mulattoes—and often jailbirds at that, this type was all too common. But in general military aid was demanded, and complaint of its inadequacy was constantly made. On this point the testimony of Fray Romualdo Cartagena, guardian of the College of Santa Cruz de Querétaro, is valid. In a report made in 1772, still in manuscript, he wrote,

What gives these missions their permanency is the aid which they receive from the Catholic arms. Without them pueblos are frequently abandoned, and ministers are murdered by the barbarians. It is seen every day that in missions where there are no soldiers there is no success, for the Indians, being children of fear, are more strongly appealed to by the glistening of the sword than by the voice of five missionaries. Soldiers are necessary to defend the Indians from the enemy, and to keep an eye on the mission Indians, now to encourage them, now to carry news to the nearest presidio in case of trouble. For the spiritual and temporal progress of the missions two soldiers are needed, for the Indians cannot be trusted, especially in new conversions.

This is the testimony of missionaries themselves. That protection was indeed necessary is shown by the martyrdom of missionaries on nearly every frontier—of Father Segura and his entire band of Jesuits in Virginia in 1570; of Father Saeta in Sonora; of Fathers Ganzábal, Silva, Terreros, and Santiesteban in Texas; of Fathers Carranco and Tamaral in Lower California; of Father Luis Jayme at San Diego (Alta California); of Father Garcés and his three companions at Yuma, on the Colorado; and of the twenty-one Franciscans in the single uprising in New Mexico in 1680. But these martyrdoms were only occasional, and the principal business of the soldiers was to assist the missionaries in disciplining and civilizing the savages.

As teachers, and as an example to new converts, it was the custom to place in each new mission three Indian families from the older missions. After a time the families might return to their homes. As Father Romualdo remarked: "It is all the better if these families be related to the new, for this insures the permanence of the latter in the missions, while if they do flee it is easier to recover them by means of their relatives than through strangers."

Notable among the Indians utilized as teachers and colonists in the northern missions were the Tlascaltecans, of Tlascala, the native city of Mexico made famous by Prescott. Having been subdued by Cortés, the Tlascaltecans became the most trusted supporters of the Spaniards, as they had been the most obstinate foes of the "Triple Alliance", and, after playing an important part in the conquest of the Valley of Mexico, they became a regular factor in the extension of Spanish rule over the north country. Thus, when San Luis Potosí had been conquered, colonies of Tlascaltecans were set to teach the more barbarous natives of that district both loyalty to the Spaniards and the elements of civilization. In Saltillo a large colony of Tlascaltecans was established by Urdiñola at the end of the sixteenth century, and became the mother colony from which numerous offshoots were planted at the new missions and villages further north. At one time a hundred families of Tlascaltecans were ordered sent to Pensacola; in 1755 they figured in the plans for a missionary colony on the Trinity River, in Texas; two years later a little band of them were sent to the San Sabá mission in western Texas to assist in civilizing the Apaches; and twenty years afterward it was suggested that a settlement, with these people as a nucleus, be established far to the north, on the upper Red River, among the Wichita Indians of Texas and Oklahoma. To help in civilizing the mission Indians of Jalisco, Sinaloa, and Sonora, the Tarascans of Michoacán were utilized; further north, the Opatas, of southern Sonora, were sent into Arizona as teachers of the Pimas; to help in civilizing the Indians of California, Serra brought mission Indians from the Peninsula.

Discipline and the elements of European civilization were imparted at the missions through religious instruction, through industrial training, and, among more advanced natives, by means of rudimentary teaching in arts and letters.

Every mission was, in the first place, a Christian seminary, designed to give religious discipline. Religious instruction, of the elementary sort suited to the occasion, was imparted by a definite routine, based on long experience, and administered with much practical sense and regard for local conditions.

Aside from the fundamental cultural concepts involved in Christianity, this religious instruction in itself involved a most important means of assimilation. By the laws of the Indies the missionaries were enjoined to instruct the neophytes in their native tongues, and in the colleges and seminaries professorships were established to teach them. But it was found that, just as the natives lacked the concepts, the Indian languages lacked the terms in which properly to convey the meaning of the Christian doctrine. Moreover, on some frontiers there were so many dialects that it was impossible for the friars to learn them. This was pre-eminently true of the lower Rio Grande region, where there were over two hundred dialects, more than twenty of which were quite distinct. On this point Father Ortiz wrote in 1745:

The ministers who have learned some language of the Indians of these missions assert that it is impossible to compose a catechism in their idiom, because of the lack of terms in which to explain matters of Faith, and the best informed interpreters say the same. There are as many languages as there are tribes, which in these missions aggregate more than two hundred. . . . Although they mingle and understand each other to some extent, there are twenty languages used commonly by the greater number of the tribes. And since they are new to us, and there are no schools in which to learn them, and since the Fathers are occupied with ministering to the spiritual and temporal needs of the Indians, and in recovering those who flee, the Fathers can hardly be held blameworthy for not learning the native languages.

For these reasons, on the northern frontier instruction was usually given in Spanish, through interpreters at first, and directly as soon as the Indians learned the language of the friars. In the case of children, who were the chief consideration, this was quickly done. And thus incidentally a long step toward assimilation was accomplished, for we all know the importance of language in the fusing of races and cultures. The firmness of the hold of the Spanish language upon any land touched by Spain, however lightly, has often been noted. It was partly, or even largely, due to this teaching of the native children at the missions.

The routine of religious discipline established by the Franciscans in the missions taken over from the Jesuits in Sonora, in 1767, was typical of all the Franciscan missions, and was not essentially different from that of the other orders. It was described by Father Reyes, later Bishop Reyes, as follows:

Every day at sunrise the bells call the Indians to Mass. An old Indian, commonly called mador, *and two* fiscales, *go through the whole pueblo, requiring all children and unmarried persons to go to the church, to take part in the devotion and silence of the Mass. This over, they repeat in concert, in Spanish, with the minister, the prayers and the Creed. At sunset this exercise is repeated at the door of the church, and is concluded with saying the rosary and chanting the* salve *or the* alavado. *The* mador *and the* fiscales *are charged, on Sundays and feast days, to take care to require all men, women, and children to be present at Mass, with their poor clothes clean, and all washed and combed.*

The very act of going to church, then, involved a lesson in the amenities of civilization. There was virtue then as now in putting on one's "Sunday clothes".

On these days [Father Reyes continues] Mass is chanted with harps, violins [all played by the natives], and a choir of from four to six [native] men and women. In Lent all have been required to go to Mass daily. . . .

 *On Palm Sunday, at the head missions (*cabeceras*), that feast is observed with an image and processions. After Easter, censuses are made to ascertain what ones have complied with the Church. In the first years it seemed impossible to us missionaries to vanquish the rudeness of the Indians, and the difficulties of making them confess, and of administering communion. But lately all the young men and some of the old have confessed. In the principal pueblos, where the missionaries reside, many attend the sacraments on feast days. On the Day of Santa Maria the rosary is sung through the pueblo. On other occasions they are permitted to have balls, diversions, and innocent games. But because they have attempted to prohibit superstitious balls and the scalp dance, the missionaries have encountered strong opposition from the [secular] superiors of the province, who desire to let the Indians continue these excesses.*

They contributed, no doubt, to the war spirit, and thus to the defense of the province against the Apaches.

If the mission was a Christian seminary, it was scarcely less an industrial training school. Father Engelhardt writes:

It must be remembered that the friars came to California as messengers of Christ. They were not farmers, mechanics, or stock breeders. Those who, perhaps, had been engaged in such pursuits, had abandoned them for the higher occupation of the priest of God, and they had no desire to be further entangled in worldly business. In California, however [and he might have added, quite generally] the messengers of the Gospel had to introduce, teach, and supervise those very arts, trades, and occupations, before they could expect to make any headway with the truths of salvation. . . . As an absolutely necessary means to win the souls of the savages, these unworldly men accepted the disagreeable task of conducting huge farms, teaching and supervising various mechanical trades, having an eye on the livestock and herders, and making ends meet generally.

The civilizing function of the typical Spanish mission, where the missionaries had charge of the temporalities as well as of the spiritualities, was evident from the very nature of the mission plant. While the Church was ever the centre of the establishment, and the particular object of the minister's pride and care, it was by no means the larger part. Each fully developed mission was a great industrial school, of which the largest, as in California, sometimes managed more than 2000 Indians. There were weaving rooms, blacksmith shop, tannery, wine-press, and warehouses; there were irrigating ditches, vegetable gardens, and grain fields; and on the ranges roamed thousands of horses, cattle, sheep, and goats. Training in the care of fields and stock not only made the neophytes self-supporting, but afforded the discipline necessary for the rudiments of civilized life. The women were taught to cook, sew, spin, and weave; the men to fell the forest, build, run the forge, tan leather, make ditches, tend cattle, and shear sheep.

Even in New Mexico, where the missionaries were not in charge of the temporalities—that is, of the economic interests of the Indians—and where the Indians had a well-established native agriculture, the friars were charged with their instruction in the arts and crafts, as well as with their religious education. And when the custodian, Father Benavides—later Bishop of Goa—wrote in 1630, after three decades of effort by the friars in that province, he was able to report fourteen monasteries, serving fifty-odd pueblos, each with its school, where the Indians were all taught not only to sing, play musical instruments, read, and write, but, as Benavides puts it, "all the trades and polite deportment", all imparted by "the great industry of the Religious who converted them".

In controlling, supervising, and teaching the Indians, the friars were assisted by the soldier guards, who served as *mayor domos* of the fields, of the cattle and horse herds, of the sheep and goat ranches, and of the shops. In the older missions, even among the most backward tribes, it sometimes became possible to dispense with this service, as at San Antonio, Texas, where, it was reported in 1772, the Indians, once naked savages who lived on cactus apples and cotton-tail rabbits, had become so skilled and trustworthy that "without the aid of the Spaniards they harvest, from irrigated fields, maize, beans, and cotton in plenty, and Castilian corn for sugar. There are cattle, sheep, and goats in abundance", all being the product of the care and labor of the natives.

The results of this industrial training at the missions were to be seen in the imposing structures that were built, the fertile farms that were tilled, and the great stock ranches that were tended, by erstwhile barbarians, civilized under the patient discipline of the missionaries, assisted by soldier guards and imported Indian teachers, not in our Southwest alone, but on nearly every frontier of Spanish America.

The missionaries transplanted to the frontiers and made known to the natives almost every conceivable domestic plant and animal of Europe. By requiring the Indians to work three days a week at community tasks, the Jesuits in Pimería Alta—to give a particular illustration—established at all the missions flourishing ranches of horses, cattle, sheep, and goats, and opened fields and gardens for the cultivation of a vast variety of food plants. Kino wrote in 1710 of the Jesuit missions of Sonora and Arizona,

*There are already thrifty and abundant fields . . . of wheat, maize, frijoles, chickpeas, beans, lentils, bastard chickpeas (*garabanzas*), etc. There are orchards, and in them vineyards for wine for the Masses; and fields of sweet cane for syrup and panocha, and with the favor of Heaven, before long, for sugar. There are many Castilian fruit trees, such as figs, quinces, oranges, pomegranates, peaches, apricots, pears, apples, mulberries, etc., and all sorts of garden stuff, such as cabbage, lettuce, onions, garlic, anise, pepper, mustard, mint, etc.*

Other temporal means [he continues] are the plentiful ranches, which are already stocked with cattle, sheep, and goats, many droves of mares, horses, and pack animals, mules as well as horses, for transportation and commerce, and very fat sheep, producing much tallow, suet, and soap, which is already manufactured in abundance.

An illustration of some of the more moderate material results is to be had in the following description of the four Querétaran missions in Texas, based on an official report made in 1762.

Besides the church, each mission had its *convento*, or monastery, including cells for the friars, porter's lodge, refectory, kitchen, offices, workshops, and granary, usually all under a common roof and ranged round a *patio*. At San Antonio de Valero the *convento* was a two-story structure fifty *varas* square with two *patios* and with arched cloisters above and below. The others were similar.

An important part of each mission was the workshop, for here the neophytes not only helped to supply their economic needs, but got an important part of their training for civilized life. At each of these four missions the Indians manufactured *mantas, terlingas, sayales, rebozos, frezadas,* and other common fabrics of wool and cotton. At Mission San Antonio the workshop contained four looms, and two store-rooms with cotton, wool, cards, spindles, etc. At Concepción and San Francisco there were three looms each.

The neophytes of each mission lived in an Indian village, or pueblo, closely connected with the church and monastery. Of those of the four Querétaran missions we have the fullest description of the pueblo at Mission San Antonio de Valero. It consisted of seven rows of houses built of stone, with arched porticoes, doors, and windows. There was a plaza through which ran a water-ditch, grown with willows and fruit trees. Within the plaza was a curbed well, to supply water in case of a siege by the enemy. The pueblo was surrounded by a wall, and over the gate was a tower, with embrasures, and equipped with three cannon, firearms, and ammunition. The houses were furnished with high beds, chests, metates, pots, kettles, and other domestic utensils. The pueblo of San Antonio was typical of all.

Agricultural and stock-raising activities had increased since 1745. At the four Querétaran missions there were now grazing 4897 head of cattle, 12,000 sheep and goats, and about 1600 horses, and each mission had from thirty-seven to fifty yoke of working oxen. Of the four missions San Francisco raised the most stock, having 2262 head of cattle and 4000 sheep and goats. Each mission had its ranch, some distance away, where the stock was kept, with one or more stone houses, occupied by the families of the overseers; the necessary corrals, farming implements, and carts; and tools for carpentry, masonry, and blacksmithing. Each mission had well-tilled fields, fenced in and watered by good irrigating ditches, with stone dams. In these fields maize, chile, beans, and cotton were raised in abundance, and in the *huertas* a large variety of garden truck.

This picture of the Texas missions is interesting, but in magnitude the establishments described are not to be compared with those in Paraguay or even in California, where, in 1834, on the eve of the destruction of the missions, 31,000 mission Indians at twenty-one missions herded 396,000 cattle, 62,000 horses, and 321,000 hogs, sheep, and goats, and harvested 123,000 bushels of grain, and where corresponding skill and industry were shown by the neophytes in orchard, garden, wine-press, loom, shop, and forge.

The laws of the Indies even prescribed and the missions provided a school for self-government, elementary and limited, it is true, but germane and potential nevertheless. This was effected by organizing the Indians of the missions into a pueblo, with civil and military officers, modelled upon the Spanish administration. When the mission was founded the secular head of the district—governor, captain, or alcalde—as representative of the king, formally organized the pueblo, appointed the native officers, and gave title to the four-league grant of land. In constituting the native government, wisdom dictated that use should be made of the existing Indian organization, natives of prestige being given the important offices. Thereafter the civil officers were chosen by a form of native election, under the supervision of the missionary, and approved by the secular head of the jurisdiction.

The civil officers were usually a governor, captain, alcaldes, and alguacil, who by law constituted a cabildo, or council. The military officers were a captain or a *teniente*, and subalterns, and were appointed by the secular head, or by a native captain-general subject to approval by the secular head. The military officers had their own insignia, and, to give them prestige, separate benches were placed in the churches for the governor, alcalde, and council. In Sonora there was a *topil*, whose duty was to care for the community houses—a sort of free hostelry, open to all travellers, which seems to have been of native rather than of Spanish origin. The Indians had their own jail, and inflicted minor punishments, prescribed by the minister. Indian overseers kept the laborers at their work and, indeed, much of the task of controlling the Indians was effected through Indian officers themselves. Of course it was the directing force of the padres and the restraining force of the near-by presidio which furnished the ultimate pressure.

This pueblo government was established among the more advanced tribes everywhere, and it succeeded in varying degrees. It was often a cause for conflict of jurisdiction, and in California, where the natives were of the most barbarous, it was strongly opposed by the missionaries. It has been called a farce, but it certainly was not so intended. It was not self-government any more than is student government in a primary school. But it was a means of control, and was a step toward self-government. It is one of the things, moreover, which help to explain how two missionaries and three or four soldiers could make an orderly town out of two or three thousand savages recently assembled from divers and sometimes mutually hostile tribes. So deeply was it impressed upon the Indians of New Mexico that some of them yet maintain their Spanish pueblo organization, and by it still govern themselves, extra-legally. And, I am told, in some places even in California, the descendants of the mission Indians still keep up the pueblo organization as a sort of fraternity, or secret society.

In these ways, then, did the missions serve as frontier agencies of Spain. As their first and primary task, the missionaries spread the Faith. But in addition, designedly or incidentally, they explored the frontiers, promoted their occupation, defended them and the interior settlements, taught the Indians the Spanish language, and disciplined them in good manners, in the rudiments of European crafts, of agriculture, and even of self-government. Moreover, the missions were a force which made for the preservation of the Indians, as opposed to their destruction, so characteristic of the Anglo-American frontier. In the English colonies the only good Indians were dead Indians. In the Spanish colonies it was thought worth while to improve the natives for this life as well as for the next. Perhaps the missions did not, in every respect, represent a twentieth-century ideal. Sometimes, and to some degree, they failed, as has every human institution. Nevertheless, it must not be forgotten that of the millions of half-castes living south of us, the grandparents, in a large proportion of cases, at some generation removed, on one side or the other, were once mission Indians, and as such learned the elements of Spanish civilization. For these reasons, as well as for unfeigned religious motives, the missions received the royal support. They were a conspicuous feature of Spain's frontiering genius.

Land, population and the evolution of New England society 1630-1790

Kenneth Lockridge

Almost all of Turner's disciples and critics have examined his thesis by analyzing conditions on the actual frontier. Few have examined what happened to a region once the frontier era was over. The process of transforming a pioneer agricultural society into a mature one requires careful study. Yet until recently colonial historians, for example, have emphasized the founding of the colonies or of key crisis periods such as Indian wars, rebellions, and religious revivals. The less exciting but equally important year-by-year evolution through which settlements achieved political and economic maturity has remained largely hidden from historical view. Unfortunately, some historians, such as Robert E. Brown, have postulated that the colonies were a static society dominated by middle-class farmers who made up the vast majority of the population. Brown's studies have assumed that land was always plentiful and readily available to settlers.

In the following essay, Kenneth Lockridge, who teaches history at the University of Michigan, throws new light on the nature of economic and social development in colonial New England. His ideas are based on an analysis of Dedham, Massachusetts and on studies of other New England towns by other scholars. Lockridge questions whether land was indeed abundant in much of New England during the late colonial period. He suggests that by 1790 New England experienced serious overcrowding, which led to social and political class divisions, making the social structure of New England increasingly resemble that of Old England. Lockridge's analysis powerfully supports Turner's contention that an area of free or cheap land on the western frontier played a vital role in shaping the development of American democracy.

For further reading: Robert E. Brown, *Middle-Class Democracy and the Revolution in Massachusetts, 1691-1780* (Ithaca, N.Y.: Cornell University Press, 1955)*; Robert E. and B. Katherine Brown, *Virginia 1705-1786: Democracy or Aristocracy?* (East Lansing: Michigan State University Press, 1964); Jackson Turner Main, *The Social Structure of Revolutionary America* (Princeton: Princeton University Press, 1965)*; Kenneth A. Lockridge, *A New England Town: The First Hundred Years, Dedham, Massachusetts,*

1636-1736 (New York: Norton, 1970)*; John Demos, *A Little Commonwealth: Family Life in Plymouth Colony* (New York: Oxford University Press, 1970)*; Charles S. Grant, *Democracy in the Connecticut Frontier Town of Kent* (New York: Columbia University Press, 1961)*; Philip Greven, Jr., *Four Generations: Population, Land, and Family in Colonial Andover, Massachusetts* (Ithaca, N.Y.: Cornell University Press, 1970).*

*Available in paperback.

I

Was early America an overcrowded society? Though the idea seems absurd on the face of it, there is evidence in its favour.

American society began with a few men set down in the midst of a vast and fruitful wilderness. From this beginning until late in the nineteenth century there was no time at which the country was without a frontier in the literal sense of the word. Whatever it was or whatever it has meant to those seeking the origins of the American character, the frontier has had one meaning upon which all men, colonial speculators, genteel visitors from abroad and modern historians alike, could agree. That meaning is room. Land was always available. If some did not take it up or if others found themselves holding bad land, still others, millions and generations of others who might never have had the opportunity had they lived in another country, did take up acres of good land and throve on those acres.

Yet at first Americans moved only slowly out into the wilderness. For most of the two hundred years preceding 1800 they clustered near the eastern coastline. Particularly in the later eighteenth century, even as Daniel Boone and Ethan Allen led settlers into what were to become the states of Kentucky and Vermont, a variety of circumstances held most would-be settlers back of the Appalachian mountains. Behind the mountains, this side of the war zones of the interior, there had developed by the end of the eighteenth century a society in some respects old, stable, concentrated.

Some historians have been led to reflect on the precocious maturity of late colonial and early national society and to weigh the possibility that the society might have become less than comfortable for some of its inhabitants.[1] But the prevailing tendency has been to treat early American society as a relatively fixed conception, trimmed at either end by periods of "settlement" and "early nationhood", a conception in which the powerful influence of the frontier and the widespread existence of opportunity are not seriously questioned.[2] Certainly no historian has yet come to grips with the quantitative problems posed by the maturation and relative containment of early American society. What does it signify that, by 1790, Americans were not entirely a new or a restless people, or that some counties in Virginia or Maryland and some towns in New England could trace their histories back through a century and a half? How much had the conditions of life changed with time? Was it everywhere, always, necessarily, the America of room and opportunity?

Land and time must be the touchstones of any enquiry into the social evolution of early America: land because the economy was overwhelmingly agricultural and because land has been both the symbol and the essence of American opportunity; time because there was so much of it, so much time in which evolution might have taken place. How much land was available to the typical farmer and how were this and other characteristics of the society changing with time? As a beginning, these questions will be asked of early New England at large and in particular of the agricultural towns of eastern Massachusetts in the years 1630-1790.[3]

II

The only authoritative work on agriculture in colonial New England is a *History of Agriculture in the Northern United States, 1620-1860* by P. W. Bidwell and J. I. Falconer. In discussing the average area of land holdings in early seventeenth century New England they offer a figure of 25 to 50 acres. But, as the authors freely admit, the evidence from which this figure is drawn is extremely weak. Nearly every one of the several hundred cases upon which they base their estimate is rendered valueless by the circumstances under which it was recorded.[4] But, if casting doubt on the 25-50 acre figure of Bidwell and Falconer is a simple matter, putting a new estimate in its place is not so simple. The best source of information on landholdings in these years should be the public records of land grants made by the various towns.[5] These would show how much land the typical early settler could expect to receive in his lifetime.[6] The trouble with using New England town records as a source is that few are precise in recording the number and area of dividends granted. In spite of this difficulty, enough bits and pieces of evidence exist to replace Bidwell and Falconer's several hundred suspect cases with several hundred other, better examples. Drawn chiefly from the records of older communities in eastern Massachusetts, these cases show that the usual early settler received a good deal more than 25 to 50 acres.

A thorough investigation has been made of the system of land allotment in Dedham, Massachusetts.[7] Complete records of land acquisitions both public and private can be compiled for thirty-two of the first fifty men to settle in the town. They averaged no less than 210 acres apiece in grants and purchases during lifetimes which ended between 1650 and 1690. From the record of public land divisions alone (of which there were from ten to thirteen between the founding of Dedham in 1636 and the year 1660) it is clear that *any* man in town by 1640 and still alive in 1660 could have expected town grants of between 100 and 200 acres. Some men who died before 1660 and missed the large divisions of the 1650s received less than this, but others who lived long and prominent lives were granted public lands up to a total of 400 acres. Since the divisions continued into the first decade of the eighteenth century, the second generation likewise drew large totals of land. Altogether, there were not fewer than 200 individuals each of whom lived for more than three decades as an adult in the town between 1636 and 1690. The typical man among them received an average of 150 acres from the common lands of Dedham.

The records of neighbouring Watertown include land records which give a complete survey of landholdings in the 1630s.[8] For the 160 men listed at this time the average landholding was 126 acres. This average may exclude a few unlisted men who held no land, but it also excludes whatever lands those who were listed held in other towns or were granted in the several subsequent general divisions. Specifically, it does not take cognizance of the fact that the men who held only tiny "homelots" when this record was made were soon after granted farms of respectable acreage. With Dedham, Watertown gives from 300 to 400 cases averaging from 125 to 150 acres.

In six other towns of the immediate region there are indications that the seventeenth-century settlers found that America had plenty of land to offer. Medfield split off from Dedham in 1651; during the first two decades of its existence it made at least six general divisions of land. A man who lived in the town for these two decades would have received roughly 150 acres. The division of 1659 alone ranged from 50 to 150 acres per man.[9] A recent study of Sudbury, Massachusetts implies that any men who lived in that town from its founding in 1638 until 1658 must have been granted approximately 150 acres apiece.[10] The original proprietors of Milford, near Dedham in south-eastern Massachusetts, resolved in 1662 "that the divisions of land . . . shall be by these ensuing rules: that to one hundred pounds estate be granted one hundred and fifty acres of land". Since an estate of twice one hundred pounds was average, the forty original proprietor-settlers must have planned on very large individual holdings.[11] The fifty-five founders of Billerica, north of Cambridge, started off with 115 acres each.[12] A survey of the sixty men living in one section of Concord, Massachusetts in 1665 revealed that each of them held on the average 250 acres.[13] In nearby Andover, "four successive divisions of town land [between 1646 and 1662], together with additional divisions of meadow and swampland, provided each of the inhabitants with at least one hundred acres of land for farming, and as much as six hundred acres".[14] With the information from Dedham and Watertown, these references make it seem that an estimate of 150 acres for the typical early inhabitant of an eastern Massachusetts town is a reasonable figure. Scattered evidence from early communities elsewhere in New England re-enforces this assumption.[15]

In 1786 the Revolution was over. America was now an independent nation. Dedham had been founded exactly a century and a half before; Watertown was older still; Milford, Medfield and the other towns not quite so old. By 1786 Dedham was a town of some 2,000 souls; Watertown had grown more slowly but contained nearly 1,000 inhabitants; there were more than 775 persons in Medfield, close to 1,500 in Billerica, nearly 2,000 in Concord and more than 2,000 in Sudbury.[16] These were no longer tiny villages, but were now towns of a respectable population for an agricultural society. In 1786 the Commonwealth of Massachusetts enacted a law which required every community in the state to complete a detailed questionnaire on the basis of which taxes were to be assessed. Among other items to be filled in were the number of male polls (males over sixteen) and the acreage of every type of land within the town. This last is of the utmost importance. Included under it were "tillage", "English upland and mowing", "fresh meadow", "salt-marsh", "pasture", "woodlands", "other unimproved land", and "unimprovable land". No type of land was left out. By dividing the number of adult males in a given town (polls minus a quarter yields a rough estimate of the number of males over twenty-one)[17] into the total acreage of the town, one may arrive at the average number of acres per man.[18]

In what had been the "Puritan Village" of Sudbury, there were now 56 acres for each man, and in Medfield and Dedham 44 and 38 acres respectively. Even though town lands and worn lands are indiscriminately included, this represents a shrinkage to less than one-third of the landholdings of the first generation. The shrinkage was greater in Watertown, where the average had fallen to a mere 17 acres per man—less than one-seventh of what it had been in the 1630s! But whether one-third or one-seventh, the change was substantial in each of these old towns. The same might be said of all the towns of the area, almost without exception. The truth is that for the whole of Suffolk County the land area per adult male now averaged no more than 43 acres. If the average rose to 71 acres in Chelsea, it fell to 22 acres next door in Roxbury; if to the south in Wrentham the imaginary "typical" man had 70 acres, to the east in Hingham he had but 32 acres.[19]

If time and the growth that time brought were essential factors in the decrease in the average area of landholdings, the oldest towns in the county should have had the lowest average acreages per man. This was exactly the situation. Twelve towns of Suffolk County were founded between 1630 and 1673.[20] In 1786, their adult males would have had but 37 acres apiece had all the land in these towns been parcelled out equally. The seven newer towns founded between 1705 and 1739 contained in 1786 some 55 acres for every adult male residing within their bounds—an average holding significantly above that found in the older towns, if still substantially below the average of the first generation of New England farmers.[21] Moreover, there is evidence that pressure on the land supply was most severe in the older towns. "Woodlands" and "unimproved" lands totalled 25 acres per man in the towns begun since 1705 but only 13 acres in those begun before 1673. The older towns had half as much uncultivated land per capita because the need for farm land had become most intense in these towns and was pushing men to put poor land under the plough.

More sharply diminished landholdings and a greater cultivation of marginal lands in the older towns are two indications of a mounting pressure on the land supply. A third index is the level of land prices. If there was a disproportionate demand for land, land prices, and probably food prices as well, should have risen more than the prices of most other commodities through the colonial period. A perusal of hundreds of inventories of estates for all of the rural towns of Suffolk County in the years 1660-1760 reveals that land values easily doubled and often tripled over the century throughout the region. By contrast, there was a remarkable long-term stability in items of personal estate, such as furniture, tools, and even clothing. Though a systematic enquiry might refine this contrast, it seems to have been a general phenomenon.

A similar decline in average landholdings may have prevailed elsewhere in New England, and may elsewhere have reached the point at which many towns were becoming "crowded", with waste land turned to crops and the cost of land soaring. A striking study of one particular Connecticut town follows the fortunes of local families through three generations, from 1740 to 1800. Family lands were divided and divided again to accommodate the increasing numbers of young men in the families, young men who did not seem to want to try their fortunes elsewhere. Ultimately, in Kent, Connecticut, "economic opportunity, which had been exceptionally bright from 1740 to 1777, was darkened . . . by the pressure of population . . . against a limited supply of land".[22] Speaking of the whole of late eighteenth century Connecticut, Albert Laverne Olson observed, "Contemporaries were well aware of the decline of Connecticut agriculture and the exhaustion of its soil". It was plain to several of these observers that the population, which had grown fourfold from 1715 to 1756, had become too great for the countryside to support. Land values were rising sharply and marginal lands were being turned into farmland.[23]

The "why" of the process, whether in eastern Massachusetts or in Connecticut, is fairly obvious. In Suffolk County as in Kent, Connecticut the pressure of population against a limited supply of land was the critical mechanism. Boston and a few suburbs aside, Suffolk County was a predominantly agricultural area. Farmers, "yeoman" or "husbandman" or "gentleman" farmers were the solid main stock of inhabitants.[24] Land was the essence of life throughout the region; a sufficiency of land was a vital concern of the great majority of men. Yet, despite the simultaneous settlement of scores of towns to the west, the estimates of the population of eastern Massachusetts reveal the same inexorable growth which was characteristic of Connecticut.[25] Up until 1765, and for most towns even after, an increase of from one to five per cent a year was a normal condition of life. Accompanying this growth, again as in Connecticut, was a pattern of inheritance in which partible descent dominated. Virtually no men left their lands intact to any one son. A double share of the whole estate for the eldest son with equal shares going to all other children (sons and daughters alike) was the standard set by the law for cases of intestacy. Even the minority of men who left wills followed this standard with very few deviations. Since emigration was not sufficient to relieve the situation, the consequence was a process of division and re-division of landholdings.

The process was a product of the fundamental conditions of existence in New England, and its operation could be perceived long before its effects became serious. As early as 1721, "Amicus Patriae" observed that "many of our old towns are too full of inhabitants for husbandry; many of them living upon small shares of land, and generally all are husbandmen. . . . And also many of our people are slow in marrying for want of settlements: . . .".[26] Had "Amicus Patriae" returned in 1790, he might well have redoubled his lamentations.

There is a paradox involved in considering that thousands of farmers in late eighteenth-century New England held on the average little over 40 acres of land apiece. It is the paradox of a land full of opportunity and with room to spare which in practice was coming to support an agricultural society reminiscent of that in the old, more limited nations of Europe. Nor is this just so much verbiage. The English yeoman of the previous century had farmed lands ranging in area from 25 to 200 acres.[27] In terms of land, many "yeomen" or "husbandmen" in this section of late eighteenth-century America were not perceptibly better off as a result of the long-ago emigration of their great-great-grandfathers.[28] In terms of the future, in terms of the sons of these American farmers and of the amount of land which each son could hope to inherit, America was no longer the land of opportunity.

III

Further evidence drawn from eastern Massachusetts brings to light the possibility that the process which was causing the decrease in average landholdings might have been accompanied by, and perhaps have been leading to, alterations in the structure of the society.

A study of the distribution of estates from the agricultural villages of Suffolk County has been undertaken to see if the pattern in which wealth was distributed in the society could have been changing with time.[29] For the several years on either side of 1660, 300 inventories have been distributed according to their size in £100 increments and the same has been done for 310 inventories from the years adjoining 1765. A process of economic polarization was under way. In 1660 there were only 13 of 300 men whose estates surpassed £900 and only three of these were worth more than £1,500. By 1765 there were 53 out of 310 men worth more than £900 and 19 of them had estates which ranged above £1,500, averaging £2,200. The average estate in 1660 was worth £315; the average in 1765 was £525. This difference came about not because of any long-term inflation or because of any true increase in the individual wealth of most men (land prices went up, but landholdings fell); it is the huge estates of the fifty-four rich men which caused nearly all of the increased size of the "average" estate in the sample of 1765! If there were more very rich men, there were also more distinctly poor individuals among those sampled in

1765. In 1660, fifty-seven men had left estates worth less than £100. In 1765, in spite of the greater aggregate wealth represented in this later sample, seventy-two men had estates in the lowest category. Moreover, the distance between the poor and the rest of society was growing. In 1660 the better-off 80 per cent of the sample had an average wealth 7·6 times as great as the average wealth of the lowest 20 per cent. By 1765 the bulk of society had estates which averaged 13·75 times the size of the estates of the poorest one-fifth. Not only were the rich becoming more numerous and relatively more rich, but the poor were becoming more numerous and relatively poorer.

Before 1700, it has been rare for an inhabitant of a Suffolk County town to call himself "gentleman" or "Esquire" when the time came for him to write his will. This, too, changed as America approached the revolution and in one more small way this change hints at an evolving society. For by the 1750s no less than 12.5 per cent of some 150 men from the farming towns had appropriated these titles of distinction. This becomes more impressive when one considers that the corresponding figure for the great metropolis of Boston was only 13·5 per cent.[30] Perhaps some sort of landed gentry was arising here in the hallowed home of the New England yeoman!

An American pauper class may also have been developing at the same time and for the same reasons. In Dedham the number of vagabonds warned out of town increased sixfold in the first three decades of the eighteenth century, reaching the point where three strangers had to be moved along in the typical year.[31] There was a parallel increase in Watertown.[32] In Rehoboth, the warnings-out increased steadily from one a year (1724-33) to 3·8 (1734-43) to 4·5 (1744-53) to 6·25 (1754-7—where the record ends).[33] In all three towns in the previous century it had been an unusual year which had seen the selectmen have to bestir themselves to ask anyone to move along. By the middle 1700s the wandering poor had become a part of the landscape in this part of New England.

If the town of Dedham has been cited from time to time as an example, it is because this is the only town in the immediate area for which an intensive analysis has been made.[34] Though that analysis has been carried in detail only to 1736, it has uncovered more bits and pieces of evidence indicating social change. Almost every development thus far suggested may be seen in microcosm in Dedham. To run through these quickly. The population grew steadily and few sons emigrated. "Worn land" appears in the inventories of Dedham estates after 1700. In the tax assessment surveys of the 1760s, 70s, and 80s a rich "loaner class" appears in the town, men with large amounts out at interest, men for whom very few seventeenth-century counterparts can be found to have existed. Not only do the numbers of vagabonds warned out increase but the numbers of indigenous poor also rise sharply after 1700. After 1710 the collective and very English term "the poor" comes into use in this town; contributions are taken under this heading almost yearly. As in the 610 Suffolk inventories, so in Dedham the pyramid of wealth derived from tax and proprietors' lists changes in such a way as to put a greater percentage of men in the lower brackets. The numbers of men with no taxable land increase from less than 5 per cent around 1700 to 12 per cent by 1736. Not fully developed in 1736, projected over another half-century these trends must have had a powerful effect on the nature of life in Dedham. Similar trends most certainly had a great effect on the society of Kent, Connecticut.[35]

In all of this there is (as there is in the study of Kent) an assumption of some degree of cause-and-effect relationship between the process which was causing a shrinkage in land-holdings and these indications of social polarization—the two together going to make up what has been labelled an "overcrowded" society. Various linkages are possible. The most obvious would run as follows. In the intensifying competition for land, some men would lose out through ill luck or a lack of business sense. Since competition would be pushing land prices up, a loser would find recovery ever more difficult, a family with little land would have a hard time acquiring more. By the same token those men and families who somehow had acquired large amounts of land would prosper as its value rose with rising demand. In such a process, the pressure would be greater at the lower end of the spectrum. There the continuing division by inheritance would reduce ever greater numbers of young men to dependence upon other sources of income, sources from which to supplement the insufficient profits from their small plots of land, sources which might or might not be available.

IV

Clearly there were evolutionary patterns present within the society of early New England, patterns which reflect most significantly on the direction in which that society was heading. To repeat the hypothesis, the trends which existed in New England were essentially those first isolated in Kent by Charles Grant: [36]

Economic opportunity, bright in 1751, had turned relatively dark by 1796 . . . society, predominantly middle class in 1751, included a growing class of propertyless men by 1796 . . . increased poverty stemmed from the pressure of a population swollen by a fantastic birthrate against a limited amount of land.

A finite supply of land and a growing population, a population notably reluctant to emigrate, were combining to fragment and reduce landholdings, bringing marginal lands increasingly into cultivation and raising land prices. Ultimately, the collision of land and population may have been polarizing the structure of society, creating an agricultural "proletariat" and perhaps even a corresponding rural "gentry". As it was in Kent, so, our evidence has suggested, it could have been throughout much of eastern Massachusetts and implicitly throughout much of New England.

What might such a process mean for our understanding of the history of early America? Charles Grant saw one of the major implications of the process which had turned his "frontier town" of Kent into a crowded and poverty-stricken backwater within fifty years. Since 1955 Robert E. Brown has been insisting that colonial society can best be characterized as a "middle-class democracy". He depicts a prosperous, satisfied society in which room and opportunity were available to nearly all, a society in which land and wealth were distributed widely and in which the suffrage was accordingly broad (since the suffrage was tied to a property qualification). The era of the American Revolution, in Brown's view, involved little internal social antagonism. The colonists simply defended their "middle-class democracy", by throwing off British rule and writing the Federal Constitution.[37] Brown musters impressive evidence to support his analysis of the society, yet his critics and other analysts of the society have found scattered evidence to the contrary, evidence which argues for poverty, for a relative lack of opportunity, for a narrower suffrage than he claims prevailed, and for bitter social conflicts in the Revolutionary era.[38] The real issue, as Grant perceived, may not be "who is right?" but "from what period of time does each side draw its evidence?" Thus:

If Kent were established as typical, then Brown's "middle-class democracy" would be characteristic of the early stages of a new settlement . . . On the other hand, Brown's prosperity would disappear, and the depressed conditions described by a Nettels or an Adams would creep in [together with a reduction in the numbers of men qualified to vote] at a later date. Such conditions . . . would emerge mainly from the pressure of population on a limited supply of land.[39]

In short, as the century wears on Brown's thesis loses validity. In so far as the level of the suffrage is one (and to Brown the chief) element in political democracy, the overcrowding which was becoming a part of the social evolution of so many New England towns must have contributed to a reduction in democratic expression in the society by the time of the American Revolution or shortly after. As the numbers of landless or near-landless men rose, the numbers of men qualified to participate in the political process fell. The men of the Suffolk County town of Dorchester demonstrated their awareness of the political dimensions of the social change which was taking place when, in objecting to the suffrage qualifications written into the Massachusetts Constitution of 1780, they observed that even a low property qualification "infringes upon the Rights and Liberties of a number of useful and Respectable members of Society; which number we believe is daily increasing and possibly may increase in such proportion that one half the people of this Commonwealth will have no choice in any branch of the General Court".[40]

But the most important issue is not whether social changes were reducing the level of the suffrage in early America. Even when *Kent* appeared in 1961, most historians were a bit weary of the battle over Brown's definition of political "democracy". Most were and are more occupied with political democracy as a matter of social attitudes and political traditions than as the difference between a suffrage of 90 per cent and one of 60 per cent.[41] What is of greatest consequence is not that the society was becoming less "democratic" in the sense of a narrowing suffrage, but that it was becoming less "middle-class". Brown treated eighteenth-century colonial society as relatively static, but the evolutionary hypothesis derived from Kent and from eastern Massachusetts shows the flaw in this conception and points to a society moving from decades of rosy "middle-class" existence toward years of economic polarization and potential class conflict.

Further, the evolutionary patterns which threatened to erode the "middle-class" society described by Brown may have shaped the thinking of many of America's Revolutionary leaders. Recent work suggests that a number of American clergymen and politicians of the later eighteenth century were dissatisfied with the condition of their society. That society was certainly not as stratified, oppressive and corrupt as the society of England had become, but it seemed to some men that it was moving in that direction. The fear of a gradual "Europeanization" of American society, a fear given ground by the tendencies outlined here, probably lent a special energy to their Revolutionary rhetoric. Thus, the leaders of the Revolution adopted Enlightenment ideas with such speed and fervor not merely because these ideas described the egalitarian, "middle-class" society which was the distinctive feature of life in the American colonies, but also because independence and the reforms engendered by Enlightenment ideas would guarantee that happy society against the changes which even then were bringing it closer to the Old World model. The radical ideas of European intellectuals would restore and protect, as well as "complete, formalize, systematize and symbolize", the unique American social order which was the pride of the Revolutionary generation.[42]

If the evolutionary hypothesis advanced here poses problems for one controversialist, it resurrects another. Frederick Jackson Turner was convinced that the frontier—and by this he meant above all the expansive frontier of the nineteenth century—had a great rôle in shaping an energetic, egalitarian and optimistic American character. His speculations have lent energy to several generations of undergraduate lecture courses, but they have most often served as targets for historians who have been more cautious if usually less interesting.[43] Most of these critics have attacked Turner on the basis that conditions on the frontier either were not what he said they were or did not have the effect on men that he claimed they did, or both. A question which might better be asked is: Where would we have been without Turner's frontier? The trend to an overcrowded society sketched in the previous pages throws a new light on this question. Without the emigration that followed 1790, New England society would have become ever more crowded at a rapid rate. If already by 1790 many towns were experiencing an excessive demand for land and the attendant consequences of that demand, what would conditions have been twenty or thirty years later? The most important point to make about the mass exodus to the frontier of the nineteenth century may be that it rescued America as the land of mobility and opportunity at a time when it was beginning to lack both and was beginning to undergo major social changes as a result.[44] ·

V

Regardless of one's view of the evidence and speculations presented here, it should be clear that historians' understanding of the evolution of early American society is not at all adequate.

For example, a decline in landholdings, even if it was general, need not have meant an overcrowded society. There are at least four interrelated propositions whose validity would render a substantial decline in landholdings meaningless in terms of "negative" social and economic effects. The validity of several of these propositions would open the possibility that any decline in landholdings could actually have been accompanied by an improvement in productivity and in the overall social and economic situation—the evidence offered above notwithstanding. First, agricultural methods might have improved to a substantial degree and, in company with the more favourable man-land ratio which could have resulted from a decrease in the land-area per man, this improvement would have meant that 40-odd acres in 1786 were far more productive than 150-odd acres *circa* 1660. Second, better transportation coupled with the growth of urban areas might have so improved the market situation that a given quantity of agricultural produce in 1786 was worth more than that same quantity *circa* 1660. Third, non-farm occupations (presumably crafts and manufacturing) might have increased in the period under consideration, offering lucrative alternatives to men who chose to or had to leave the land. Finally, 40-odd acres, even though it included "worn" or waste lands, might still have been ample with which to support a large family. The point which must be made is that there is available virtually no evidence in favour of any of these propositions—probably because they are not valid, but also and most significantly because no one has cared to try to find the evidence. What evidence does exist argues that propositions one, two, and probably three are not valid.[45] The only enquiry into the question of subsistence sets the total landholdings required for the support of a farm family at between 40 and 89 acres,[46] indicating that Suffolk County had reached a critical point by 1786.

Papers calling for "further study" have become one of the clichés of the historical profession. Yet the unavoidable conclusion is that the impact of this paper must reside not so much in its evidence and speculations as in a long list of specific questions. Was the decline in landholdings general? Was it always accompanied by the use of marginal lands and by a relative rise in the price of land?[47] How much of the land farmed in the late eighteenth century was "worn" land? Was there an improvement in agricultural techniques and in the man-land ratio? Was there an improvement in access to markets?[48] Did non-farm occupations offer alternate sources of income?[49] Why did sons not leave the crowded towns, towns like Kent, Connecticut and Watertown, Massachusetts, to take advantage of the room which the frontier seemed to offer? Was it fear of Indians or the traditional inertia of rural society or something not yet considered?[50] Was 40 acres enough to support a large family, and exactly how large were families in this period?[51] Was the distribution of wealth in the society changing with time? How reliable are inventories of estates in determining this? Are tax lists better sources for this purpose? Did the numbers of vagabonds and paupers increase with time? Was the increase, if any, greater than the mere rise in population would account for? Did the appropriation of titles of social distinction increase similarly? Who appropriated these titles and why? How did all these factors come together in the history of a single town? The studies of Kent, Connecticut and Dedham, Massachusetts are the only long-term local case histories presently available. We need more of them.[52] Finally, what were the attitudes of thoughtful men of the time regarding the state of their society? Was there a universal awareness of change?

Until this work is begun, the irritating hypothesis that much of New England was becoming seriously "overcrowded" by 1790 will have to stand. Instead of being the land of opportunity, this part of America was rapidly becoming more and more an old world society; old world in the sense of the size of farms, old world in the sense of an increasingly wide and articulated social hierarchy, old world in that "the poor" were ever present and in increasing numbers. The word "becoming" is carefully selected. The fact of independence and the egalitarian ideas broadcast by the Revolution, together with the great exodus to the west after 1790, quickly made it ridiculous to speak of this or any part of America as an old world society. Yet this had been the tendency in much of New England for decades. Had it been allowed, by some miraculous suspension of subsequent events, to continue unchecked—who can say what might have been the result? This part of America might soon have come to resemble the Anglicized society dreamed of by some arch-Federalists more than the vigorous, expansive society which has since been a characteristic feature of our national history.

Notes

Professors Peter Coleman, Jackson T. Main, Darrett Rutman, Philip Greven, Jr., and Van Beck Hall have rendered invaluable assistance in the preparation of this paper. Any remaining errors are, of course, the author's responsibility.

1. Rowland Berthoff, "The American Social Order: A Conservative Hypothesis", *Amer. Hist. Rev.*, lxv (April, 1960), pp. 495-514, particularly p. 501; see also, Lois Kimball Mathews, *The Expansion of New England* (Boston, 1909), and Percy Wells Bidwell and John I. Falconer, *History of Agriculture in the Northern United States, 1620-1860* (Washington, 1925).

2. Stuart Bruchey, *The Roots of American Economic Growth, 1607-1861* (New York, 1965); though sensitive to hints of change, Bruchey is forced by sheer lack of evidence to accept the prevailing assumptions of continuity and opportunity. Jackson Turner Main, *The Social Structure of Revolutionary America* (Princeton, 1965), has made the first systematic attempt to study the structure of early American society. Main's conception is fundamentally static, covering only the decades encompassing the Revolution (1760s-1780s), but he is the first to recognize the need for further, long range studies.

3. The questions at hand could just as well be put to the southern colonies. See Robert E. and B. Katherine Brown, *Virginia 1705-1786: Democracy or Aristocracy?* (East Lansing, 1964). The Browns assert that room and opportunity were prevailing characteristics, but no long-range statistical studies exist which would either support or weaken their view. As will be seen, there are indications that a contrary argument could be offered.

4. Percy Wells Bidwell and John I. Falconer, *History of Agriculture in the Northern United States 1620-1860* (Washington, 1925), pp. 37-8, 53-4. Two major flaws may be noted. In the cases drawn from the towns of Dorchester, Hartford and New Haven, the acreage-per-individual is merely that granted in a single public division of town land. As is well known and as will become evident below, a settler in most early towns could expect roughly three to ten such divisions to be made during his lifetime. Secondly, the figures for several towns on Long Island are only for taxable land. In the Long Island towns the figures "do not include pasture land which was largely held in common" and which was a major component of a man's land-rights. Had this been included, the average acreage would have been "much larger". This circumstance may also have prevailed near Boston; in any event Muddy River was an area assigned to Boston's poor—hardly a fair test-area!

5. The early estate inventories are unreliable.

6. He might sell these lands as fast as they were granted him but on the other hand he might buy more land privately. Neither action, given a fairly self-contained local land market, would affect the average area of landholdings per man.

7. Published town records have been cross-checked against manuscript land records in the Town Hall. Samples of each of the first two generations have been taken and their wills, inventories and deeds co-ordinated with the local records. A full exposition of the methods and results of this work may be found in K. A. Lockridge, *Dedham, 1636-1736: The Anatomy of a Puritan Utopia* (unpublished Ph.D. dissertation, Princeton University, 1965). See also the *Early Records of the Town of Dedham* (Dedham, 1866-1936), i-vi, ed. Don Gleason Hill (i-v) and Julius H. Tuttle (vi). The deeds are in manuscript in the Dedham Historical Society and in the Registry of Deeds in the Suffolk County Courthouse in Boston. There is no indication that more than a very few (if any) landless adult males have escaped inclusion in the averages.

8. *Watertown Records* (Watertown, 1894-1939), i-viii. Volumes i and ii have been used. The editorial warnings on the use of these records have been observed.

9. William S. Tilden, *History of the Town of Medfield, Massachusetts* (Boston, 1887); and inventories and wills for the period in the Suffolk County Courthouse.

10. Sumner Chilton Powell, *Puritan Village* (Middletown, Connecticut, 1963), pp. 118, 122, 191, and Plate xi. The 130-acre farms spoken of on page 191 are the chief component of the total. Sudbury is north of Dedham, a few miles east of Boston. Nearby Marlborough, in deliberately retarding the process of division and keeping most land in common for some time (see Charles Hudson, *History of the Town of Marlborough* [Boston, 1862]) seems to have been the exception to the rule set by Watertown and Sudbury.

11. A. Ballou, *History of the Town of Milford* (Boston, 1882), pp. 5, 33; also inventories for Suffolk County.

12. Henry Hazen, *History of Billerica, Massachusetts* (Boston, 1883).

13. Lemuel Shattuck, *History of the Town of Concord* (Boston, 1835), pp. 36-7.

14. Philip J. Greven, Jr. "Family Structure in Seventeenth-Century Andover, Massachusetts", *William and Mary Quarterly*, 3rd ser., xxiii (1966), pp. 234-56.

15. To the evidence of Massachusetts' towns should be added that of Rehoboth, then a part of Plymouth Colony. Here there were some fifteen divisions of land between 1643 and 1713. Richard Le Baron Bowen, *Early Rehoboth* (Rehoboth, 1945-50), 4 vols., iv, pp. 1-21. Another bit of evidence on early land holdings may be drawn from Bidwell and Falconer, one of whose larger samples was based upon the records of New Haven in Connecticut. There 123 persons were found to have averaged a mere 44 acres each. But, as has been pointed out, a single division accounted for the acreage held by these individuals. A few pages later, in another context, the authors reveal that a second division in New Haven in the very same year had the effect of raising the average holding to 110 acres; Bidwell and Falconer, *History of Agriculture*, pp. 37, 54. In nearby Milford, Connecticut, there were four divisions in addition to an initial distribution of homelots between the founding of the town in 1639 and 1657. The process of division continued through the seventeenth century, including a large division ranging from roughly 50 to 200 acres in 1687; Leonard W. Labaree, *Milford, Connecticut, the Early Development of a Town as Shown in its Land Records* (New Haven, 1933), no. 13 in a series of pamphlets sponsored by the Tercentenary Commission of the State of Connecticut.

16. E. V. Greene and V. Harrington, *American Population before the Federal Census of 1790* (New York, 1932), pp. 19-40.

17. By comparing information available in volumes i and vi of the *Early records of . . . Dedham*, it is possible to find out how many males included in the typical tax list were not of age; K. A. Lockridge, "The Population of Dedham, Massachusetts, 1636-1736", *Econ. Hist. Rev.*, 2nd ser., xix (1966), pp. 318-44. The estimate that one-fourth of all males over 16 years of age were in the 16-21 group is a conservative one, judging from an article by James A. Henretta on the "Social Structure of Colonial Boston", *William and Mary Quarterly*, 3rd ser., xxii (1965), pp. 75-92.

18. The discussion which follows is based upon uncatalogued documents in the Archives of the State of Massachusetts. They are in microfilm in volume clxiii. The resultant figures do not include lands held in other towns, but what evidence exists argues that it was not usual for a man to hold more than trifling amounts of land in towns other than his own. Further, the results make no distinction between good and worn land. Since over a century of rather unsophisticated New World farming must have produced worn land in many towns, an acre in 1786 was likely to have been less productive than an acre in 1636. Lockridge, *Dedham*, chaps. vi and vii; the Suffolk inventories also bear out this assertion. Finally, residual public (town) lands seem to be included in the total, though these were not in the possession of individual farmers. Subsequent computer analysis of the 1786 lists by Professor Van Beck Hall of the University of Pittsburgh indicates that the estimates derived here are in every respect conservative and that the *arable* land per adult male in the older areas of Massachusetts probably fell below five acres. Professor Hall is now engaged in work which will make these revealing documents yield a full picture of the economy and society of Massachusetts at the end of the eighteenth century.

19. The narrowness of the range from top to bottom is significant. The average of 43 acres for Suffolk County was not produced by a few impossibly crowded towns pulling down the average of a more comfortable, well-endowed majority. The figures for each town begin with Roxbury's 22 acres and rise through averages of 25, 32, 32, 36, 38, 42, 44, 44, 47, 51, 52, 60, 68 and 70 acres to the peak of 71. As the years passed many of the inventories of estates on file in the Suffolk County Courthouse became quite specific as to landholdings. A sample of 300 of these for the years 1765-75 confirms the average-landholding figure derived from the assessment lists of 1786. The average rural estate included 65 acres of land. There are good reasons why this earlier figure is a little above the 43 acres average of

1786. For one thing, these are acreages at death. A man is likely to have held more land at the end of his life than he held on the average throughout that life. There is a second way in which they reflect success. Though there are inventories for men who held no land whatsoever (and 17 per cent of the 300 had no land at death, confirming the indications of the assessment lists that the suffrage could not possibly have been above 90 per cent), inventories for servants and paupers who had virtually no real or personal estate are extremely rare—almost nonexistent. Evidence will be presented below to show that such persons must have existed. Their exclusion from the sample of inventories naturally raises the average landholdings attributed to those who were included. With these adjustments made, it may be seen that the inventories describe much the same situation with regard to landholdings as was described in the town assessment lists of 1786. And, as would be expected, the inventories of estates from the older towns tend to include less land than those based on estates in towns more recently established.

20. Watertown is included as one of the twelve, though it later came under the jurisdiction of Middlesex County. As it was only the eleventh largest of the nineteen towns considered, its inclusion does not greatly weight the results.

21. Brookline, Needham, Medway, Bellingham, Walpole, Stoughton and Chelsea. No towns were incorporated between 1673 and 1705.

22. Charles S. Grant, *Democracy in the Connecticut Frontier Town of Kent* (New York, 1961), p. 170.

23. Albert Laverne Olson, *Agricultural Economy and the Population in Eighteenth Century Connecticut* (New Haven, 1935), no. 40 in a series of pamphlets sponsored by the Tercentenary Commission of the State of Connecticut.

24. See Lockridge, *Dedham, 1636-1736*. Also, wills and inventories of estates for all of Suffolk and parts of Middlesex and Essex Counties may be found in the Probate Office of the Suffolk County Courthouse in Boston; several thousand of these have been surveyed. For one example, of 142 men who died in Suffolk County towns outside Boston from 1750 to 1759, 71 per cent were "yeomen" or "husbandmen", and roughly a third of the remaining 29 per cent held over half of their estates in the form of land.

25. See E. V. Greene and V. Harrington, *American Population Before the Federal Census of 1790*. One of these eastern towns, Dedham, has been studied as a demographic test case, and confirms the broad outlines above. The curve of Dedham's population follows that of the colony as a whole, rising slowly in the seventeenth century, surging and hesitating between 1690 and 1730, rising steadily thereafter—but never declining. Growth of a little less than three per cent a year was average. Natural increase seems to have accounted for the growth, as immigration was negligible until 1736 and probably thereafter. As in Kent, there was no general exodus to new western towns, though the population rose from less than 400 in 1645 to nearly 2,000 in 1765. K. A. Lockridge, "The Population of Dedham, Massachusetts, 1636-1736".

26. A. P. (John Wise?), *A Word of Comfort to a Melancholy Country* (Boston, 1721), in A. M. Davis, ed., *Colonial Currency Reprints*, ii (Boston, 1911), p. 189.

27. Mildred Campbell, *The English Yeoman Under Elizabeth and the Early Stuarts* (New Haven, 1942), pp. 74-100. A remarkably similar process of crowding was experienced in this same period by the English village of Wilston Magna; see W. G. Hoskins, *The Midland Peasant* (London, 1957).

28. For hints of similar changes in the southern colonies, see V. J. Wyckoff, "The Sizes of Plantations in Seventeenth-Century Maryland", *Maryland Historical Magazine*, xxxii (1937), pp. 331-9; and Jackson T. Main, "The Hundred", *William and Mary Quarterly*, xi (1955), pp. 354-84.

29. The inventories of these estates may be found in the Probate Office in the Suffolk County Courthouse in Boston. The sample taken represents over 50 per cent of the existing inventories for the towns studied in the years for which the sample was taken.

30. This is based on a study of 350 wills in connection with an investigation into charitable bequests. The wills are in the Suffolk County Probate Office.

31. Lockridge, *Dedham*, 98; the figures are from the *Early Records of . . . Dedham*, vols. iii-vi.

32. *Watertown Records*, vols. i and ii.

33. Bowen, *Rehoboth*, ii, pp. 139 ff.

34. Lockridge, *Dedham*.

35. Grant, in *Kent*, observes that a similar evolutionary process had created an agricultural "proletariat" by 1800: *Kent*, p. 97. Main's *Social Structure of Revolutionary America* confirms these indications. Using tax lists and inventories from many towns, he finds that at least 20 per cent of men in late eighteenth century New England lived a marginal existence, with little, if any, land.

36. The following excerpts are from Grant, *Kent*, pp. 83-103.

37. Robert E. Brown, *Middle Class Democracy and the Revolution in Massachusetts* (Ithaca, 1955); see also Robert E. and B. Katherine Brown, *Virginia 1705-1786* (cited above, note 3).

38. See James Truslow Adams, *Provincial Society* (New York, 1948); Curtis P. Nettels, *Roots of American Civilization* (New York, 1940); and Robert Taylor's review of Brown's book on Massachusetts in the *Mississippi Valley Hist. Rev.*, lxiii (1956).

39. Grant, *Kent*, pp. 102-3.

40. Massachusetts Archives, cclxxvii, p. 67; quoted in Robert J. Taylor, ed., *Massachusetts, Colony to Commonwealth* (Chapel Hill, 1961), p. 155.

41. J. R. Pole, "Historians and the Problem of Early American Democracy", *Amer. Hist. Rev.*, lxvii (1962), pp. 626-646. (It might, however, be noted that the reduction in the suffrage caused by "overcrowding" might have been as great as the difference between a suffrage of 90 per cent and one of 60 per cent. The tax surveys of 1786 reveal that at least 20 per cent of the men in the towns of Suffolk County had not enough real or personal property to qualify as voters. See also Grant, *Kent*, p. 140 for evidence of a similar decline.) It is only fair to add that Brown himself has broadened his definition of "democracy" and increased the subtlety of his argument; see Brown, *Virginia*.

42. The relevant works are Alan Heimert, *Religion and the American Mind from the Great Awakening to the Revolution* (Cambridge, Massachusetts, 1966); and Gordon S. Wood, "Republicanism as Revolutionary Ideology" (Paper delivered at the Organization of American Historians meeting in Chicago in April, 1967) and "Rhetoric and Reality in the American Revolution", *William and Mary Quarterly*, 3rd ser., xxiii (1966). The view that Enlightenment ideas served chiefly to "complete, formalize, systematize and symbolize" the American national spirit is that of Bernard Bailyn, "Political Experience and Enlightenment Ideas in Eighteenth Century America", *Amer. Hist. Rev.*, lxvii (1962), p. 351; Bailyn's analysis rests in large part upon an acceptance of Brown's thesis.

43. Among those both cautious and interesting have been Paul W. Gates, "Frontier Estate Builders and Farm Laborers", *The Frontier in Perspective* (Madison, Wisconsin, 1957), pp. 143-63; and Page Smith, *As a City upon a Hill: the Town in American History* (New York, 1966).

44. The hypothesis likewise reflects on the background of the exodus of 1790-1830. If conditions were tending in the directions depicted, it may be that the waves of New Englanders heading west after 1790 were more "pushed" west by the difficulties of life in Old New England than "pulled" west by the attraction of better land. Lois Mathews felt that this was the case, but even she does not seem to have realized how great the difficulties caused by a dense population might have become by 1790: *Expansion of New England*, pp. 99 ff.

45. Bruchey's basic argument, in his *Roots of American Economic Growth*, rests on the substantial invalidity of propositions one, two, and possibly of proposition three, in the period preceding 1790. Bidwell and Falconer, in their *History of Agriculture*, pp. 84 ff., 142, are skeptical about proposition one and have little to say about propositions two and three.

46. Grant, *Kent*, pp. 36-8. Only a fraction of this total would be under cultivation—the rest serving as woodlot and pasture or lying fallow, but being nonetheless essential.

47. For the theoretical basis of the study of differential price increases, see E. Phelps-Brown and S. Hopkins, "Wage-Rates and Prices: Evidence for Population Pressure in the Sixteenth Century", *Economics*, vii (1967).

48. Inventories of estates could provide answers to these questions, since they list tools, crops as well as debts and credits resulting from commercial transactions. They also list "worn" lands in many instances.

49. It would be possible to do a long-term census based on records of land transactions in the Registries of Deeds in each county. Men's occupations and ranks are listed with great consistency in these documents.

50. See Grant, *Kent*, p. 102; Lockridge, "The Population of Dedham"; Greven, "Family Structure in Andover" for various explanations of inertia. This is an essential question, since, as this enquiry shows, the real problem may have been not so much the lack of a viable frontier as the relative failure to take advantage of that frontier.

51. On the uses of historical demography, American scholars could learn a great deal from the work of their French and English colleagues. See E. A. Wrigley, ed., *An Introduction to English Historical Demography* (London, 1966).

52. At the Iowa University Conference on Early American History in March of 1967, Professor John M. Bumsted of Simon Fraser University (now of McMaster University) delivered a paper on "Religion, Finance, and Democracy in Massachusetts; the Town of Norton as a Case Study"; Norton, like Kent, Connecticut was a relatively new town which within three generations began to experience many of the characteristic difficulties of overcrowding; here, as elsewhere, there was a reluctance to emigrate. A recent and excellent study of Andover, Massachusetts (Philip Greven, Jr., "Family Structure in . . . Andover", "Four Generations: a Study of Family Structure, Inheritance, and Mobility in Andover, Massachusetts, 1630-1750" [Ph.D. dissertation, Harvard University, 1965]) confirms the trends depicted here, but also supports the possibility that these trends may have called forth a contemporaneous response. Emigration increased during the third and fourth generations, while the use of partible inheritance declined. When and where such responses operated, they could have done much to mitigate the effects of the trend to overcrowding.

Part II
The frontier and the American Indian

Indian cultural adjustment to European civilization

Nancy Oestreich Lurie

The Red Man's civilization posed vexing problems for white colonizers. No Spanish, French, or English frontiersman could ignore his Indian neighbors, and much has been written about the white man's view of the native American. Comparatively little, however, is known about what the Indians thought of the first English settlers. There are good reasons for this. The Indians left no written records. Furthermore, the tribes that the English first encountered in Virginia and Massachusetts were destroyed during the first seven decades of settlement. Thus there were few, if any, eastern Indians to preserve even an oral tradition. Archeological remains are equally scant. Therefore, much of what we know about the Indian comes from English records. But these sources are problematical. As newcomers in a strange world the British often misunderstood or failed to perceive the Indian civilizations as they really were. Yet there are many important questions that can only be answered by attempting to reconstruct the Indian view of the English. For example, did the Red Man, as some have asserted, hate the whites from the very beginning? Why didn't the Indians drive white settlers from the continent while the newcomers were weak and vulnerable? Did the Indians see much of value in English culture, and if so, what?

In the following essay Nancy Lurie, a curator of the Milwaukee, Wisconsin, Public Museum, addresses herself to these and other questions that help explain why Indian-English relations developed as they did. The essay also throws light on what happens when two widely different cultures confront each other for the first time.

For further reading: Lewis Hanke, *Aristotle and the American Indians* (Chicago: Regnery, 1959); Alfred L. Kroeber, *Cultural and Natural Areas of Native North America,* (University of California Publications in American Archaeology and Ethnology, Vol. XXXVIII (Berkeley, 1939); Maurice A. Mook, "The Anthropological Position of the Indian Tribes of Tidewater Virginia," *William and Mary Quarterly*, 2d series, XXIII (1943), 27-40; Verne F. Ray, ed., *Proceedings of the 1957 Annual Spring Meeting of the American Ethnological Society* (1957); Social Science Research Council Summer Seminar

Reprinted with permission from the Institute of Early American History and Culture, Williamsburg, from James M. Smith, *Seventeenth-Century America: Essays in Colonial History* (Chapel Hill: University of North Carolina Press, 1959), pp. 33-60.

in Acculturation, 1953, "Acculturation, an Exploratory Formulation," *American Anthropologist*, 56 (1954), 973-1005; Frank G. Speck, *Penobscot Man: The Life History of a Forest Tribe in Maine* (Philadelphia: University of Pennsylvania Press, 1940); Ruth Murray Underhill, *Red Man's America: A History of Indians in the United States* (Chicago: University of Chicago Press, 1953).

In 1907, on the 300th anniversary of the beginning of English colonization in America, James Mooney made the brief observation that the Jamestown settlers "landed among a people who already knew and hated whites." In effect, this remark summed up the accepted anthropological explanation for the Indians' unpredictable behavior; it indicated why they alternated elaborate expressions and actions of good will with apparent treachery. Mooney implied that the Indians' attitudes and behavior were more than justified by the demonstrated greed and aggressiveness of the whites.[1]

Little work was done in the succeeding years to explore the complete significance of Mooney's remark or to probe more deeply into underlying motivations for the Indians' actions. This neglect was inevitable, since attention had to be devoted to a more fundamental problem. Before achieving an understanding of Indian reaction to the effects of contact with Europeans, it was necessary to establish a valid and cohesive picture of aboriginal culture.[2] Thanks to the labors of such scholars as Mooney, Frank G. Speck, David I. Bushnell, John R. Swanton, Maurice A. Mook, and others, the fragmentary data relating to native life have been gathered into comprehensive and analytical accounts concerned with such problems as Indian demography, the cultural and linguistic identity of given tribes, tribal locations, and the prehistoric diffusion and changes in Indian cultures.

Likewise, in the past fifty years, general theoretical techniques of ethnological interpretation have been refined through field research in observable situations of culture contact. These acculturational studies, which are an invaluable aid in the interpretation of historical data, have investigated the reasons why some groups lose their cultural identity in a situation of culture contact while other groups continue to preserve ethnic integrity despite widespread alterations of purely native patterns.[3] With this backlog of necessary information and analysis, anthropologists have begun a more intensive consideration of the dynamics of culture contact in ethnohistorical terms.

Turning to Mooney's contention, there is evidence that the Virginia Indians had several opportunities to form opinions about Europeans both in terms of direct experience and of information communicated to them. Direct knowledge of Europeans may have occurred as early as the first quarter of the sixteenth century, when Giovanni de Verrazano and Estevan Gomez are believed to have made observations in the Chesapeake Bay region.[4] Of somewhat greater significance is the alleged founding of a Spanish Jesuit mission on the York River in 1570. According to this theory, the missionaries were killed by Indians under the leadership of a native known as Don Luis de Velasco, who had lived in Spain, where he was educated and converted to Christianity. The Spaniards had hoped that he would act as guide and model in the proselytizing of his people, but it appears that the effects of his early life negated his later training. In 1572 a punitive expedition under Pedro Menendez de Aviles attacked and defeated the Indians responsible for the destruction of the mission; in succeeding years Menendez made other forays into the region. A recent study insists that this area must have been along the Virginia coast.[5]

Whether or not the case for a sixteenth-century mission in Virginia has been proved is problematical. Many details are uncertain: the precise location of the mission on the York River, the tribal affiliations of Don Luis, the extent of his leadership, his age at the time he lived in Spain, and his possible genealogical affiliations with the ruling hierarchy of the Virginia Indians of the seventeenth century. However, historical investigation leaves no doubt of Spanish activity at this time, and these ventures must have occurred between St. Augustine and the Potomac River. The natives of Virginia, who borrowed cultural traits from neighboring tribes along the coast and further inland, could have received news of European explorations to the south and west by the same routes that carried purely native ideas. Generalized impressions of Europeans were doubtless prevalent in the Virginia area long before 1607.

The Spaniards came to America primarily as adventurers and fortune seekers. Although they attempted to found settlements their efforts usually met with failure. They plundered Indian villages but did not remain long in any one region; they were frequently routed by angry Indians or by their own inability to subsist in a strange terrain. After 1520, raids were conducted along the Gulf and southern Atlantic coast to obtain slaves for shipment to the West Indies. News of these incursions may have reached Virginia via the various coast tribes, and similarly Virginia natives may have heard of De Soto's hapless wanderings to the south and west. Even though the Spaniards later achieved success in colonization in Florida through the use of missionaries, the first hostile impressions had been made.

The French entered the scene to the south of Virginia in 1562. Because of lack of supplies and Spanish aggression, they failed in their attempts to establish a foothold in the region. However, the interests of France as well as of Britain were served by unknown numbers of piratical freebooters from the Caribbean area who touched along the coast of the Carolinas and intrigued with the Indians. Not until 1580 was Spain able to dislodge foreign intruders and punish recalcitrant Indians. Even then, Spanish dominion remained precarious, although the Spanish Franciscans continued to extend their missions up the coast. Finally, in 1597, a general uprising among the Carolina tribes destroyed these religious outposts and forced Spain again to concentrate most of her forces in Florida.

Thus, during much of the sixteenth century Europeans were active in regions immediately adjacent to Virginia and possibly in Virginia itself. Their activity was often associated with violence, and there was sufficient time for rumors concerning them to have reached the Virginia natives before any direct contacts were made. By the time the English attempted to found colonies on the east coast toward the close of the sixteenth century, they encountered difficulties which may have been more than the simple result of European inexperience in developing techniques for survival in the New World. Raleigh's enterprise, for example, may have been singularly ill-timed. A general unrest in Indian-white relationships marked the period from 1577 to 1597 in the Carolina region where Raleigh's followers chose to remain. Pemisipan, a Secotan chief who attempted to organize opposition to the British in 1585, could hardly have been blamed if he saw a curious similarity to accounts he may have heard concerning the Spanish when, for the trifling matter of the theft of a silver cup, the English burned the corn and destroyed the buildings at his village of Aquascogoc.[6]

The later events at Cape Henry, the first landfall of the Jamestown colonists, suggest that the immediate hostility expressed by the Indians was inspired by fear of reprisals for the fate of Raleigh's colony. The Indians who attacked the English belonged to the

Chesapeake tribe, immediately adjacent to the tribes with whom Pemisipan conspired.[7] It is also possible, as Mooney implies, that by 1607 the Virginia Indians evaluated any sudden appearance of Europeans as evil and took immediate measures to repel them. However, this view oversimplifies several important factors. Long before any Europeans arrived at Jamestown, the Indians had been fighting over matters of principle importance to them, such as possession of land and tribal leadership. If they were aware of the fate of other Indians at the hands of Europeans, there was no reason for them to assume that their fate would be similar; they were not necessarily allied with the beleaguered tribes, nor did they share a sense of racial kinship. Sharp cultural differences and even sharper linguistic differences separated the various Indian societies. While there was reason to fear and hate the Europeans as invaders who made indiscriminate war on all Indians, the fear was only that of being taken unawares and the hate could be modified if the tribes which had fallen victim thus far were strangers or even enemies. If the Indians of Virginia had any knowledge of Europeans, they must have been aware that the white men were fundamentally outnumbered, frequently unable to support themselves in an environment which the Indians found eminently satisfactory, and that European settlements were usually short lived. The appearance of the English was probably far less alarming than 350 years of hindsight indicate ought to have been the case.

This is demonstrated by the fact that the Virginia Indians under the leadership of Powhatan seem to have made their first adjustments to Europeans in terms of existing native conditions.[8] Primary among these conditions were Powhatan's efforts to gain firmer control over his subject tribes and to fight tribes traditionally at enmity with his followers. It was expedient to help the settlers stay alive, for they could be useful allies in his established plans; but at the same time he could not allow them to gain ascendancy. The situation was complicated by factionalism in Powhatan's ranks and lack of accord among the settlers. However, recognition of the fundamental aboriginal situation makes the early events at Jamestown understandable on a rational basis. It offers a logical foundation for subsequent developments in Indian-white relationships and Indian adjustments to European civilization as the result of something more than barbaric cupidity and a thirst for the white man's blood.

Certainly a wary sensitivity to any sign of hostility or treachery characterized the behavior of both whites and Indians at the outset of settlement at Jamestown. The Europeans were still seriously concerned about the probable fate of Raleigh's colony and they had already been attacked by the Indians at Cape Henry. The Indians, in turn, may well have possessed information concerning the alarmingly retributive temperament of Europeans, at least in terms of the incident at nearby Aquascogoc, if not through generalized opinions derived from the long history of intermittent European contact along the east coast.

Nevertheless, the party of Europeans that set out on exploration of the country about Jamestown encountered a welcome at the various Indian villages different from the greetings offered at Cape Henry. Except for one cold but not overtly hostile reception in the Weanoc country, the white men were feted, fed, and flattered. At the same time a suggestion of the uncertainty of the next years occurred before the exploring party had even returned to their headquarters—at Jamestown the remaining colonists were attacked by a party of local Indians.[9] Events of this nature as well as the general observations recorded during the first two years at Jamestown are particularly instructive in any attempt to understand Indian motivations and policy regarding the British.

The narratives are difficult to follow because of the variety of orthographies employed for Indian words. Certain features remain speculative because initial communication between whites and Indians was limited to the use of signs and the few native words that could be learned readily.[10] However, it is possible to see native culture in terms of regularities and consistencies which were not obvious to the colonists. Likewise, the apparent inconsistencies on the part of the natives, recounted by the settlers as innate savage treachery, indicate that the aboriginal culture was in a process of growth, elaboration, and internal change. These phases of culture, which included both extensive tendencies of intertribal confederation and divisive reactions expressed by individual tribes, were interrupted and redirected but not initiated by the arrival of Europeans in 1607.

From the viewpoint of the twentieth century, it is difficult to realize that the material differences between the Indians and the European colonists, who lived before the full development of the industrial revolution, were equalled if not outweighed by the similarities of culture. This was especially true in Virginia, where a local florescence of culture and a demonstrated ability to prevail over other tribes gave the Indians a sense of strength which blinded them to the enormity of the threat posed by the presence of Europeans. There was actually little in the Europeans' imported bag of tricks which the Indians could not syncretize with their own experience. Metal was not unknown to them: they used native copper, brought in from the West, for decorative purposes. Metal weapons and domestic utensils were simply new and effective forms of familiar objects to accomplish familiar tasks. Even guns were readily mastered after the noise, which evoked astonishment at first, was understood as necessary to their operation. Likewise, fabrics and articles of personal adornment were part of Indian technology. Many utilitarian objects such as nets, weirs, and gardening implements were very similar in both Indian and European culture. European ships were simply larger and different, as was fitting for a people interested in traveling greater distances by open water than the Indians had ever cared to do.

Expansive accounts of the size and permanence of the great European cities could easily have been likened by the natives to the impressive aboriginal developments in the lower Mississippi Valley; archeological evidence suggests that knowledge of this cultural complex was widespread.[11] Even if these Indian models of nascent urbanization are discounted, the statements made by Europeans about their country and king may well have sounded like the exaggerations of outnumbered strangers endeavoring to buttress their weaknesses with talk of powerful but distant brothers. This explanation is admittedly conjectural, although we find ample documentation of the Indians' disinclination to admit any significant superiority in white culture at a somewhat later period. During the early nineteenth century, when the industrial revolution was underway and the eastern United States was heavily populated by whites, Indian visitors were brought from the West in the hope that they would be cowed by the white man's power and cease resistance to the forces of civilization. The Indians remained singularly unimpressed.[12] Furthermore, at the time Jamestown was founded in the seventeenth century, the only knowledge Indians possessed concerning Europeans indicated that Indians were well able to oppose white settlement. Raleigh's ill-fated colony was a clear reminder of the Europeans' mortality.

Although the early accounts tend to take a patronizing view of the Indians, the points on which the Europeans felt superior had little meaning for the aborigines: literacy, different sexual mores, ideas of modesty, good taste in dress and personal adornment, and

Christian religious beliefs. The argument of technological superiority at that time was a weak one; despite guns and large ships the Europeans could not wrest a living from a terrain which, by Indian standards, supported an exceptionally large population. Scientific knowledge of generally predictable group reactions thus suggests that the degree of ethnocentrism was probably equal on both sides of the contact between Indians and Europeans in Virginia. Recognition of the Indians' self-appraisal is necessary for a clear understanding of their basis of motivation and consequent behavior in relation to Europeans.

Moreover, it was evident to the colonists that they were dealing with a fairly complex society, exhibiting many characteristics of leadership, social classes, occupational specialization, social control, and economic concepts that were eminently comprehensible in European terms. If the exploring parties overstated the case when they translated *weroance* as "king" and likened tribal territories to European kingdoms, they at least had a truer understanding of the nature of things than did the democratic Jefferson, who first designated the Virginia tribes as the "Powhatan Confederacy."[13] Since the term "Confederacy" is so firmly entrenched in the literature, it will be retained here as a matter of convenience; but, in reality, Powhatan was in the process of building something that approximated an empire. By 1607 it was not an accomplished fact, but the outlines were apparent and the process was sufficiently advanced to allow a geographical description of the extent of Powhatan's domain.

Powhatan's influence, if not his undisputed control, extended over some thirty Algonkian-speaking tribes along the entire length of the present Virginia coast, including the Accohannoc and Accomac of the Eastern Shore. The nucleus of this domain consisted of six tribes which were centrally located in the region drained by the James, Pamunkey, and Mattaponi rivers. These tribes were the Powhatan, Arrohattoc, Pamunkey, Youghtanund, Appomattoc, and Mattaponi, with Powhatan's own tribe, the Pamunkey, consistently referred to in the early narratives as the largest and most powerful.[14] The Confederacy was bounded to the north and south by other Algonkian tribes. Except on the basis of their declared political allegiance, the uniformity of language and culture in the region makes it difficult to differentiate between the tribes within the Confederacy and even between the Confederacy and neighboring Maryland and Carolina groups.

It is generally accepted that these Algonkian peoples moved into the lower coastal region from the north. According to their own account this had occurred about three hundred years before Jamestown was settled, although recent archeological investigations suggest a longer occupation.[15] Once arrived, the Algonkians acquired numerous cultural traits from the Southeast culture area and developed many similarities to the interior Muskhogean-speaking groups. Some of these new elements were in turn transferred to the more northerly Algonkians, but they never existed there in the cohesive complexity found in the tidelands.[16]

Powhatan inherited the six central tribes as an already unified intertribal organization and extended his domain by conquest from the south bank of the Potomac to the Norfolk region. The Chesapeake Indians are included in the Confederacy, but this southernmost group was not fully under Powhatan's control at the time the settlers arrived. Their attack on the colonists at Cape Henry gave Powhatan the opportunity to gain favor with the English by swiftly avenging the hostile action. Although some historians have implied that Powhatan destroyed the entire tribe, it is far more likely that he simply killed the leaders and placed trusted kinsmen in these positions.[17]

Powhatan's method of fighting and his policy of expanding political control combined a reasoned plan of action with quick ferocity and a minimum of bloodshed. Indian warfare was generally limited to surprise attacks and sniping from cover. Constant replacements of fighting men kept the enemy occupied and wore down their resistance, while actual casualties were relatively limited in number. Accounts of Powhatan's conquests and the occurrences observed after 1607 point to a carefully devised method of establishing his control over a wide territory. Entire communities might be killed if they proved exceptionally obstinate in rendering homage and paying tribute, but in most cases Powhatan simply defeated groups of questionable loyalty and upon their surrender moved them to areas where he could keep better watch over them. Trusted members of the Confederacy were then sent to occupy the vacated regions, while Powhatan's relatives were distributed throughout the tribes in positions of leadership.[18] Mook's studies indicate that the degree of Powhatan's leadership decreased in almost direct proportion to the increase in geographical distance between the Pamunkey and the location of a given tribe.[19] Throughout the entire region, however, the combination of ample sustenance, effective techniques of production, provident habits of food storage, and distribution of supplies through exchange offset shortcomings in the political framework connecting the tribes and helped to cement social ties and produce a commonality of culture.

Despite certain internal dissensions the Confederacy can be seen as a unified bloc, distinct from neighboring tribes. To the north were numerous small Algonkian-speaking tribes, either friendly or representing no serious danger to Powhatan. They tended to shade off in cultural characteristics toward the more northern Algonkian types to be found along the coast into New England. The best known of these tribes was the Nanticoke in eastern Maryland and Delaware. North of the Potomac lived the Conoy (Piscataway), Tocwough, Ozinie, and others, about whom little is recorded. At a later date the tribes in this region were known collectively as the "Doeg" Indians. Beyond the Conoy and up into the present state of Pennsylvania were the Susquehanna, in Captain John Smith's judgment a powerful and impressive group, distinguished from the Virginia tribes in both language and culture.[20] However, they seem to have felt closer ties of friendship with the Algonkians than they did with their Iroquoian linguistic affiliates to the north. The Nansemond and Chesapeake tribes formed the southern terminus of the Confederacy, and beyond them in the Carolina region were a number of linguistically and culturally similar tribes extending along the coast to the Neuse River. The Roanoke narratives and particularly the illustrations of John White provide somewhat fuller documentation for the southerly neighbors of the Confederacy than is available for the northern Algonkian groups.[21]

The western border, formed by the fall line and paralleling the coast, was characterized by greater cultural and linguistic differences than those observed to the north and south of the Confederacy; it also represented a definite danger area for Powhatan. Virtually all Indian occupation ended somewhat east of the falls, however, allowing a strip of land a mile to ten or twelve miles wide as a safe margin between the Powhattan tribes and their nearest neighbors, who were also their deadliest enemies, the tribes of the Virginia piedmont region. These peoples have long been designated as Siouan-speaking but a recent study casts doubt on this identification. It is now suggested that these groups spoke a highly divergent and extremely old dialect of the basic Algonkian language stock.[22] Except for linguistic distinctiveness little is known about these piedmont people. This is most unfortunate, since they appear to figure as a key to much of Powhatan's policy toward the English and helped to influence the course of Indian adjustment to European settlement.[23] A few of these tribes are known by name, but they are usually considered as having comprised two major confederacies, comparable in some measure to the groupings associated with Powhatan. These were the Manahoac on the upper Rappahannock and surrounding region, and the Monacan along the upper James and its tributary streams. Both were aggressive groups, and their incursions were a constant threat to the tidelands Indians. Powhatan's desire to subdue these westerly tribes as a matter of protection was underscored by another consideration: copper, highly prized by the Virginia Confederacy, came from the West, and the enemy tribes formed an obstacle to trade for that commodity.[24]

Thus, at the outset of colonization in 1607 Powhatan's policies can best be understood in relation to circumstances antedating the arrival of the Jamestown settlers. Powhatan saw the whites in his territory as potential allies and as a source of new and deadly weapons to be used in furthering his own plans for maintaining control over his Confederacy and protecting the Confederacy as a whole against the threat posed by the alien tribes of the piedmont region. Likewise, existing concepts of intertribal trade in foodstuffs and other commodities were extended to include trade with the newly arrived whites. It is worth noting that European novelties, apart from weapons, were of far less interest to Powhatan than the fact that the British possessed copper, an object vested with traditional native values and heretofore obtained with great difficulty.[25]

In the initial stages of contact between the Indians and the whites, therefore, it is hardly surprising that Powhatan and his people felt at least equal to the English. The chieftain could appreciate the foreigners as allies in the familiar business of warfare and trade, but in general there seemed little to emulate in European culture and much to dislike about the white men. However, even in the most difficult phases of their early relationship, Powhatan did not indulge in a full-scale attack against the settlers. At that time he was still engaged in strengthening his Confederacy and perhaps he could not risk extensive Indian defection to the side of the whites. But there is an equal likelihood that Powhatan's primary motivation was the desire to control and use the whites for his own purposes rather than to annihilate them.

At the time Jamestown was founded, native civilization was enjoying a period of expansion, and Powhatan had ample reason for sometimes considering the English as more an annoyance than a serious danger. The unusually rich natural environment and the security offered by the Confederacy stimulated the growth of social institutions and cultural refinements. In addition, the Virginia Indians were exceptionally powerful and, by aboriginal standards, their population was large: the entire Confederacy numbered some 8,500 to 9,000 people, or a density of approximately one person to every square mile.[26] The Indians lived according to a well-ordered and impressively complex system of government. They dwelled in secure villages, had substantial houses and extensive gardens, and had a notable assemblage of artifacts for utilitarian, religious, and decorative purposes.

The Indians won the grudging respect of the colonists for their advanced technology, but the Europeans were contemptuous of their seemingly hopeless commitment to superstition, while their ceremonialism appeared to the whites a ridiculous presumption of dignity.[27] A typical bias of communication between Europeans and Indians is seen in Smith's account of the Quiyoughcohannock chief who begged the settlers to pray to the Christian God for rain because their own deities had not fulfilled the Indians' requests.

Smith asserted that the Indians appealed to the whites because they believed the Europeans' God superior to their own, just as the Europeans' guns were superior to bows and arrows. Yet Smith notes with some wonder that the Quiyoughcohannock chief, despite his cordiality and interest in the Christian deity, could not be prevailed upon to "forsake his false Gods."[28] Actually this chief of one of the lesser tribes of the Confederacy illustrated the common logic of polytheistic people who often have no objection to adding foreign deities to their pantheon if it seems to assure more efficient control of the natural universe. The chief was not interested in changing his religious customs in emulation of the Europeans; he merely wished to improve his own culture by judicious borrowing—a gun at one time, a supernatural being at another.

Nor would the chief have dared respond to a new religion in its entirety, even if such an unlikely idea had occurred to him. The whole structure of tribal life relied upon controlling the mysterious aspects of the world by a traditional body of beliefs which required the use of religious functionaries, temples, idols, and rituals. These were awesome arrangements and not to be treated lightly, although improvement by minor innovations might be permitted.[29]

The geopolitical sophistication of the Virginia tribes is reflected in the secular hierarchy of leadership which extended in orderly and expanding fashion from the villages, through the separate tribes, up to Powhatan as head of the entire Confederacy. A gauge of the complexity of government is the fact that the Confederacy shared with the Europeans such niceties of civilization as capital punishment.[30] In small societies having a precarious economy, indemnities in goods or services are usually preferred to taking the life of a culprit even in crimes as serious as murder. However, where the life of the offender or one of his kinsmen is exacted for the life of the victim, punishment is the concern of the particular families involved; the rest of the group merely signifies approval of the process as a means of restoring social equilibrium after an offense is committed. Powhatan's government, however, was much closer to that of the English than it was to many of the tribes of North America. Punishment was meted out by a designated executioner for an offense against the society as the society was symbolized in the person of the leader.

Nevertheless, despite its elaborate civil structure, the Confederacy exhibited a universal rule of any society: a complex theory of government does not necessarily assure complete success in application. Powhatan not only had unruly subjects to deal with, but entire tribes in his domain could not be trusted. Relations between whites and Indians therefore were always uncertain, largely because of political developments within the Confederacy. When the colonists were supported by Powhatan, they were in mortal danger from those dissatisfied tribes of the Confederacy which had the foresight to realize that the English might one day assist Powhatan to enforce his authority. When Powhatan and his closest associates turned upon the settlers, the less dependable tribes became friendly to the whites.

In view of this morass of political allegiances, it is little wonder that early accounts of the settlers are replete with material which seems to prove the innate treachery of the Indians. Yet the militant phases of Indian activity, as illustrated by the initial attack on Jamestown and Powhatan's vengeance on the offending Chesapeake tribe, must be seen as part of a larger policy involving alternative methods of settling inter-group differences. Although the settlers knew that dissatisfaction among Powhatan's followers offered a means of preventing a coordinated Indian attack, they also discovered that established mechanisms of diplomacy existed among the Indians that could be employed for their benefit. For example, the Jamestown settlement was located in the territory of the Paspehegh tribe, and relations with this tribe frequently became strained. The Powhatan forces represented by the leaders of the Pamunkey, Arrohattoc, Youghtanund, and Mattaponi offered to act as intermediaries in negotiating peace with the Paspehegh and other hostile tribes or, if necessary, to join forces with the settlers in an armed assault on mutual enemies.[31]

If the Europeans found it difficult to live among the Indians, the Europeans seemed equally unpredictable to the Indians. Early in his relationship with the English, Powhatan was promised five hundred men and supplies for a march on the Monacan and Manahoac; but instead of finding wholehearted support among his allies for this campaign, Powhatan discovered that the whites were helpless to support themselves in the New World. As time wore on and they became increasingly desperate for food, the Europeans were less careful in the difficult business of trying to distinguish friends from enemies. They extorted supplies promiscuously, driving hard bargains by the expedient of burning villages and canoes.[32]

It is problematical whether, as Smith implies, Powhatan was actually unable to destroy the handful of English because he could not organize his tribes for a full-scale offensive or whether he was biding his time in the hope of eventually establishing a clear-cut power structure in which the colonists would be allowed to survive but remain subservient to his designs in native warfare. At any rate, after two years of English occupation at Jamestown, Powhatan moved from his traditional home on the Pamunkey River some fifteen miles from the Europeans and settled in a more remote village upstream on the Chickahominy River. Violence flared periodically during these early years: colonists were frequently killed and often captured. Sometimes, being far from united in their allegiance, they fled to the Indian villages, where they were usually well treated. Captives and runaways were exchanged as hostages when one side or the other found it convenient. However, if Powhatan was willing to take advantage of dissident feeling among the whites, he was no fool and he finally put to death two colonists who seemed to be traitors to both sides at the same time. The execution was much to Smith's satisfaction, for it saved him from performing the task and assured a far more brutal punishment than he would have been able to inflict upon the renegades.[33]

Throughout the period from 1607 to 1609, the chronicles include a complexity of half-told tales involving alliances and enmities and mutual suspicions, of Indians living among settlers and settlers living among Indians. Although this interaction was of an individual nature, the two groups learned something of each other; yet each side maintained its own values and traditions as a social entity. The Indians were primarily concerned with obtaining new material goods. By theft, trade, and the occupation of European artisans in their villages, they increased their supply of armaments and metal work. With the use of Indian guides and informants, the settlers became familiar with the geography of the region, and they also learned the secrets of exploiting their new environment through techniques of native gardening. For the most part, however, conscious efforts to bridge the cultural gap were unavailing. There was one amusing attempt to syncretize concepts of Indian and European monarchy and thereby bring about closer communication, when Powhatan was treated to an elaborate "coronation." The chief *weroance* was only made more vain by the ceremonies; he was by no means transformed into a loyal subject of the English sovereign, as the white settlers had intended.[34]

An increasing number of settlers arrived in Virginia and, with the help of Indians who by this time had ample reason to let the whites perish, managed to weather the hazards of the "starving time." As the whites became more firmly established, competition between Europeans and Indians took on the familiar form of a struggle for land. Armed clashes occurred frequently, but there were no organized hostilities, and the Indians continued to trade with the English. A peace which was formally established in 1614 and lasted until 1622 is often attributed to a refinement of Powhatan's sensibilities because of the marriage of Pocahontas and John Rolfe. Although Pocahontas was indeed the favorite child of Powhatan, it is likely that the chieftain's interest in her marriage was not entirely paternal. This strengthening of the social bond between Indians and Europeans helped solidify Powhatan's power and prestige among the confederated tribes, as he was thus enduringly allied with the whites.

Continuation of harmony between Indians and whites for a period of eight years was doubtless rendered possible because enough land still remained in Virginia for both settlers and Indians to live according to their accustomed habits. The seriousness of the loss of Indian land along the James River was lessened by the existence of a strip of virtually unoccupied territory just east of the fall line which ran the length of the Confederacy's holdings. If properly armed and not disturbed by internal dissensions and skirmishes with the English, the Powhatan tribes could afford to settle at the doorstep of their piedmont neighbors and even hope to expand into enemy territory. Hostilities require weapons, and peaceful trade with the English meant easier access to arms which the Confederacy could turn against the Monacan and Manahoac. It is also possible that by this time Powhatan realized the vast strength of the English across the sea and was persuaded to keep the settlers as friends. Knowledge of Europe would have been available to the chieftain through such Indians as Machumps, described by William Strachey as having spent "somtym in England" as well as moving "to and fro amongst us as he dares and as Powhatan gives him leave."[35]

Whatever were Powhatan's reasons for accepting the peace, it appears that he utilized the lull in hostilities to unify the Confederacy and deal with his traditional enemies. We have no direct evidence of activities against the piedmont tribes, for there is little historical data regarding the western area at this time. However, by the time the fur trade became important in the West the Monacan and Manahoac had lost the power which had once inspired fear among the tribes of the Confederacy. In view of Powhatan's years of scheming and the probable closer proximity of the Confederacy to the piedmont region after 1614, it may be conjectured that the Virginia chieftain and his people took some part in the downfall of the Monacan and Manahoac.[36]

When Powhatan died in 1618, his brother Opechancanough succeeded him as leader of the Confederacy.[37] Opechancanough continued to observe Powhatan's policy of peace for four years, although relations between Indians and Europeans were again degenerating. The Indians' natural resources were threatened as the increasing tobacco crops encroached on land where berries had grown in abundance and game had once been hunted. In the face of European advance, the Indians became restive and complained of the settlers' activities; but these signs went unnoticed by the colonists.[38] Opechancanough was aware that the real danger to the Confederacy arose from neither internal dissensions nor traditional Indian enemies but from the inexorable growth of European society in Virginia. He was apparently able to convince all the member tribes of this fact, if they had not already drawn their own conclusions. The subsequent uprising of 1622 was a well-planned shock to the English; it was alarming not so much for the destruction wrought, since by that time the Europeans could sustain the loss of several hundred people, but for the fact that the Confederacy could now operate as a unified fighting organization. This was a solidarity which Powhatan either had been unable or was disinclined to achieve.

Doubtless Opechancanough expected reprisals, but he was totally unprepared for the unprecedented and utter devastation of his lands and the wholesale slaughter of his people. The tribes were scattered, some far beyond the traditional boundaries of their lands, and several of the smaller groups simply ceased to exist as definable entities. Gradually as the fury of revenge died down, the remnants of the Confederacy regrouped and began to return to their homelands. However, the settlers were no longer complacent about their Indian neighbors. In addition to campaigning against the natives, they erected a string of fortifications between Chesiac and Jamestown, and they tended to settle Virginia in the south rather than toward the north and west.[39] In effect, therefore, Opechancanough accomplished a limited objective; a line was established between Indians and Europeans, but the line was only temporary and the Indians paid a terrible price.

Moreover, the cultural gap widened during the ensuing years. Following the period of reprisals the Indians were left to make a living and manage their affairs as best they could. Many old grievances seemed to be forgotten, and the natives gave the appearance of accepting their defeat for all time. Opechancanough, who had eluded capture immediately after the attack of 1622, remained at large, but the Europeans attempted to win tribes away ʻfrom his influence rather than hunt him down at the risk of inflaming his followers. Finally, white settlement once more began to spread beyond the safety of concentrated colonial population. Tensions were re-created on the frontier, and there were minor skirmishes; the Indians complained to the English, but they also continued their trading activities. Thus matters continued for more than twenty years until large-scale hostilities again broke out.[40]

The uprising of 1644 was surprisingly effective. It is generally known that in both the 1622 and the 1644 uprisings the percentage of Indians killed in relation to the total Indian population was far greater than the percentage of settlers killed in relation to the total white population. Yet with far fewer Indians to do the fighting, Opechancanough managed to kill at least as many Europeans in the second attack as he had in the first.[41] The uprising is another proof that the Indians' method of adjusting to changes wrought by the Europeans continued to be an attempt to prevail over or remove the source of anxiety—the settlers—rather than to adapt themselves to the foreign culture. Certainly the Indians never felt that their difficulties would be resolved by assimilation among the whites, a solution which the colonists at times hoped to effect through the adoption of Indian children, intermarriage, and Indian servitude.[42]

Hopeless though the uprising appears in retrospect, it was entirely logical within Opechancanough's own cultural frame of reasoning. It is impossible to determine whether the Indians were aware of the futility of their action, nor do we know enough about the psychology of these people to ascribe to them such a grim fatalism that they would prefer a quick and honorable death to the indignities of living in subjection to the whites. But there is something impressive about Opechancanough, an old and enfeebled man, being carried on a litter to the scene of battle. Whatever the outcome his days were numbered. His young warriors, however, knew of the horrible reprisals of 1622 and they understood the cost of being defeated by the white man. Yet they too were willing to risk an all-out attack.

There is little doubt that Opechancanough realized the danger inherent in rebellion. He was a shrewd strategist and a respected leader. It is entirely possible that he hoped for assistance from forces outside the Confederacy. Tension had existed between the whites of Virginia and Maryland for a number of years, and in one instance the Virginians had hoped to incite the Confederacy against their neighbors. Maryland had been settled only ten years before the second uprising, and although hostile incidents between whites and Indians had occurred, her Indian policy had been more just and humane than Virginia's. If Opechancanough did expect military assistance from whites for his uprising against whites, he had historical precedent to inspire him. Powhatan had exploited factionalism among the Jamestown settlers, and it may be that the tension between Virginia and Maryland suggested an extension of his policy to Opechancanough. Whatever the motivations behind Opechancanough's design for rebellion, the second uprising attested to the strength of the old Confederacy and indicated clearly the stubborn resistance of the Indians to cultural annihilation.

Although the usual revenge followed the attack of 1644, Virginia's Indian policy was beginning to change. The Powhatan tribes were too seriously reduced in numbers to benefit greatly by the progress, but their treatment at the hands of the colonists following the uprising marked a new development in Indian-white relations, one which eventually culminated in the modern reservation system. In 1646 a formal treaty was signed with the Powhatan Confederacy establishing a line between Indian and white lands and promising the Indians certain rights and protection in their holdings. While their movements were to be strictly regulated, the natives were guaranteed recognition for redress of wrongs before the law. There were two particularly important features of the treaty. First, the Indians were to act as scouts and allies against the possibility of outside tribes' invading the colony; this policy was in contrast to the earlier device of attempting to win the friendship of peripheral tribes to enforce order among the local Indians.[43] Second, and consistent with the growing importance of the fur trade in colonial economics, the Indians were to pay a tribute each year in beaver skins. During the following years various legislative acts were adopted to protect the Indians in their rights and establish mutual responsibilities with the tribes.[44]

As the treaty of 1646 symbolized the establishment of new policies in dealing with the Indians, so did the circumstances surrounding Bacon's Rebellion afford a glimpse of other future developments. Within the tangled events of the Rebellion was an indication of the later effects of the frontier on many Indian groups. The Rebellion reflected the heretofore traditional rivalry between Indians and whites; its outcome marked the final defeat of the Virginia Indians and the complete demise of some tribes. But in the records of Bacon's Rebellion appears a new element which was to have continuing influence in Indian adjustment to Europeans. By 1675 Indian-white relations were no longer highly localized. The English began to appreciate the need for greater unity among their scattered colonies—the struggle of European countries to establish sovereignty over all of North America had begun—and they recognized the value of the Indians as allies rather than opponents in the design of an empire.

The turmoil of international rivalry delayed the movement of settlement inland, and the development of the fur trade also promoted isolation of the West. The fur traders strongly opposed pioneer settlement, in order to protect the natural habitat of the beaver —and incidentally the status quo of the Indians who engaged in the actual business of hunting and trapping the animals. Thus circumstances combined to give the Indians of the inland tribes a vital delay. From the beginning of contact, the western natives had an opportunity to meet the white man on equal terms, and they came to accept the presence of Europeans as a permanent and in many ways a desirable phenomenon. They developed policies of negotiation, diplomacy, and warfare, and distinguished one European group from another as ally or enemy as seemed most expedient to their own interests. This was in sharp contrast to the coastal situation, where hostilities represented a more clear-cut contest between Indians and whites for supremacy.[45]

The events of Bacon's Rebellion in Virginia contributed to the final ruin of both the tidelands and the piedmont tribes, but the complications of alliances of interest groups illustrate the changing situation of the frontier as it affected the Indians. Initially the Rebellion involved the border settlers of Virginia and Maryland, and the Susquehanna, Seneca, and "Doeg" Indians. The Susquehanna had enjoyed friendly relations with the French as early as 1615, but, living on the Susquehanna River, they were too far removed from French outposts to benefit by the association.[46] To the north were their traditional enemies, the Seneca, a member tribe of the powerful league of the Iroquois. The Seneca, however, appeared as a threat to the colonists of Maryland, and the settlers in that area therefore allied themselves with the Susquehanna and supplied the tribe with arms. Later Maryland, an English colony, arranged a pact of peace with the Seneca in accordance with the general alliance of the Iroquois league with the English at that time. The Susquehanna, nominally allied with the French, were left without arms or nearby allies and were thus forced by the new alliance to retreat from their homeland. In the face of armed action they took up residence north of the Potomac among the Algonkian-speaking tribes, although they were themselves of Iroquoian linguistic affiliation. Shifts of tribal residence and inter-Indian campaigns involved Iroquoian tribes of the Carolina region as well as certain so-called Siouan groups such as the Tutelo and Occaneechi, who were enemies of the Seneca.

Meanwhile white settlement had penetrated west and north to the extent that skirmishes between whites and the Indians occurred. The memories of the uprisings of 1622 and 1644 had not died easily among the English, and when protection furnished by Governor Berkeley seemed inadequate, an unofficial campaign against the natives was initiated by the border settlers of the once competitive Virginia and Maryland. Although the causes of Bacon's Rebellion were also deeply rooted in internal disputes among the colonists, its results were catastrophic for the Virginia Indians. Bacon's followers showed no disposition to distinguish Indians as friends or enemies; they made indiscriminate war on all natives. After Bacon's forces had decimated the Susquehanna and Algonkians, they turned upon the Occaneechi, who had long been allied with the English as middlemen in the fur trade between the coastal settlements and the tribes located farther inland. The final action was against the Pamunkey, peacefully residing on lands secured to them by the treaty of 1646.[47] The Pamunkey king had been killed some ten years after the treaty of 1646 while serving with the colonists against a presumed invasion of the colony by a group of strange Indians known as Richeharians.[48] Thus his people were considered doubly wronged, for they were not only at peace with the colonists, but they had made common cause with the English against Indian enemies.[49]

Peace was finally affirmed officially with the Virginia tribes in a treaty signed in 1677. However, the effects of the Rebellion had been devastating, and after their long history of war and defeat, the Indians of the tidelands and piedmont regions found it increasingly difficult to preserve their accustomed habits of existence. This was equally true of the Susquehanna and Algonkian tribes north of the Potomac.

Nevertheless, several tribes of the Powhatan Confederacy are represented today by groups preserving a sense of social distinctiveness, based largely on historical and racial origins rather than any cultural characteristics. These tribes are the Pamunkey, Rappahannock, Mattaponi, Chickahominy, and Nansemond.[50] The story of their survival is uncertain in its details. Often it appeared that these tribes had been swept away by the rush of history, but each time after an interval the names reappeared on contemporary documents. For example, the signatory tribes of the Confederacy in the treaty of 1677 included the Pamunkey, Appomattoc, Weanoc, Nansemond, Nantaughtacund, and Portobacco—the last a collective term for the tribes of the Eastern Shore. Also signatory to the treaty were the Iroquoian-speaking tribes of the piedmont, the Nottaway and Meherrin, as well as Powhatan's old enemies, the Monacan. Undoubtedly the Pamunkey, the largest tribe of the Confederacy, had temporarily subsumed the unlisted Chickahominy, Mattaponi, and Rappahannock.[51]

In a similarly complex process of development, many of the piedmont tribes which were still extant in the latter seventeenth century regrouped permanently under different names. The Nottaway, Meherrin, and Monacan, for example, were signatory to the treaty of 1677, but only the Nottaway and Meherrin signed the Treaty of Albany in 1722. However, the Christanna were named in the 1722 treaty, and this group had come to include remnant Monacan and other piedmont tribes as well as recent migrants from the Algonkian, Iroquoian, and Siouan groups of North Carolina. Governor Spotswood of Virginia gathered these tribes together in 1715 and settled them at Fort Christanna near the Carolina border in southwestern Virginia.[52]

The condition of the Indians toward the end of the seventeenth century is illustrated in many contemporary documents. A letter from the Reverend Mr. Clayton provides a detailed and well-organized summary.[53] It is worth special attention for its factual data and as an illustration that both whites and Indians continued to view each other from their own culture's frame of logic, without any real understanding. Describing the populational degeneration which had resulted largely from disease, deprivation, and malnutrition, the letter states:

This is very certain that the Indian inhabitants of Virginia are now very inconsiderable as to their numbers and seem insensibly to decay though they live under the English protection and have no violence offered them. They are undoubtedly no great breeders.

Clayton, like many white observers imbued with Christian concepts of proselytization, appeared surprised that one of the most striking retentions of native patterns was the cultural aspect of religion. He noted that special structures were still set aside for temples and that the shaman or *wichiost* enjoyed a degree of prestige which was secondary only to that accorded to their "King and to their great War-Captain." The retention of this prestige illustrates secular authority distinguished from the sacred sway of the *wichiost* and shows a continuity of concepts regarding social structure. The king remained the center of authority and continued to receive homage and tribute in the form of personal services performed by other members of the tribe. Apparently the ruling position was still hereditary within a line of descent recognized as that of the chief family. None of the records are clear on this point, for lines of chieftainship are confused in the documents by the indiscriminate use of such titles as "King" and "Queen." Hereditary leadership occasionally did devolve on women, and Archer noted such a case in 1607 when he described the Queen of Appomattoc, who held her rank by virtue of some now obscure genealogical reckoning. Leadership was inherited first by the surviving male siblings and then female siblings, and evidently passed on to the next generation only with the death of all members of the preceding generation.[54] In later years the Queen of Pamunkey was so designated by the whites because her husband, the hereditary Pamunkey ruler, had been killed in 1656 while fighting for the British. The settlers paid his widow the honor of the title, but it is questionable whether she exercised any traditional authority within her own group, although she was their recognized representative in dealings with the colonists.

The role of the ordinary Indian woman generally receives little notice in acculturational descriptions by untrained observers, and the Clayton letter is no exception. A brief sentence notes gardening, cooking, pottery making, and the weaving of mats. The domestic phase of Indian life was easily overlooked although it changed less than other aspects. Actually, the domesticity of the whites and Indians differed only slightly. Kingdoms might rise and fall, but housekeeping, child care, cooking, and garment making had to be regularly performed in both cultures. Like many European observers, Clayton describes hunting, a principal occupation of the Indian male, as "Exercise." This error probably contributed to an early and persistent stereotype of the Indian: the industrious, overburdened woman, the slothful, pleasure-seeking man. Like all stereotypes, it is worthy of examination and it is an especially interesting example of adjustment to change. The traditional division of labor was approximately equal, the men hunting, the women gardening. These two activities supplied the principal subsistence. The English depended on the hunt in the early stages of settlement, but as soon as it ceased to have great economic importance they reverted to the European tradition of categorizing it as sport. The Indians also had their tradition: both men and women considered agriculture to be an unmanly task. When game diminished and gardening became the primary productive activity, they found it extremely difficult to make appropriate changes in the socioeconomic role of the male.

Clayton's references to the material culture of the Indians may be augmented from many sources, as this was the most easily discerned aspect of Indian life. The natives frequently observed traditional habits of dress. They continued to use indigenous material such as deerskin for clothing, but they prized European textiles, being especially fond of linen goods and a heavy woolen cloth, called a "matchcoat," which they often used instead of fur or feather mantles. Certain changes in style, if not modesty, may be noted in the matter of dress. When the Queen of Appomattoc greeted the Europeans in 1607, she wore only a skirt and a great amount of jewelry, but "all ells was naked";[55] but the Queen of Pamunkey was clad in Indian finery from neck to ankles for an occasion of state in 1677.[56]

Although the blue and white shell beads known as "wampum" probably originated as a currency through the trade with the New England tribes, they were manufactured in great quantities by Europeans for use in the fur trade and by 1687 figured as a quasi currency as far south as Virginia. The Indian shaman who also acted in the capacity of physician was paid by the natives in wampum as well as in skins and other commodities. When he treated English settlers, the *wichiost* usually received his remuneration in matchcoats or rum. Further details from Clayton's letter reveal that metal armaments, tools, and utensils were in common usage by the end of the century, although the bow and arrow and native pottery continued to be available.

From Clayton's observations and comparable data it is evident that Indian adjustment to European civilization in the late seventeenth century continued to take the form of resistance whenever there remained any possibility of retaining essential elements of the old culture. Specific items were accepted, as they fitted into existing patterns and represented elaboration or improvement of familiar features. In-group recognition of the danger posed for their traditional ways is illustrated in a fragment of folklore included in Clayton's account. There was supposedly an ancient prophecy, made long before the Europeans arrived, that "bearded men . . . should come and take away their country and that there should none of the original Indians be left within a certain number of years, I think it was an hundred and fifty." This rationalization of history is a recurrent myth found among many Indian groups. It helps to preserve a degree of dignity and pride by saying in effect, "We knew it all along, but we put up an admirable fight anyway."

The cultural disorganization noted in 1687 was to be a continuing process. The prophecy of destruction has now been fulfilled, to the extent that the Indians have ceased to exist as a culturally definable entity, although remnant groups maintain their social identities and tribal names. Throughout the seventeenth and eighteenth centuries the tribes which had temporarily resided with the Pamunkey wandered back to their original territories, leaving only the Pamunkey and part of the Mattaponi on lands secured to them by colonial treaties and guaranteed today by the state of Virginia. Traditional habits were generally abandoned as it became ever more difficult to exist in the white man's world. Eventually, the only effective economic system was that practiced by the surrounding Europeans; the Indians who were not located on reservations tended to settle in neighborhoods and acquire land on an individual basis. The destruction of the native social and religious mores, almost a predictable consequence of the disastrous wars and scattering of tribes, was virtually accomplished. A civil and religious structure which had been designed to accommodate the needs and activities of thirty tribes, almost nine thousand people, was impossibly cumbersome when the population had dwindled to one thousand people who were not in regular communication with one another and who were at any rate overwhelmingly occupied with the problem of sheer physical survival. The Indians in time found social and religious satisfaction in the traditions of their white neighbors; but they remained socially distinct from them.

Despite the loss of their own culture, many Indians remain aware of their historical origins. Beginning in 1908 with the Chickahominy, the various non-reservation natives of Virginia obtained official recognition as Indian tribes from the state government. In 1923 they formed an organization known as the "Powhatan Confederacy" and included the Nanticoke, recognized by Delaware as non-reservation Indians but otherwise not historically eligible for inclusion in the Confederacy. Showing Caucasoid and Negroid ancestry, the Nanticoke are the most racially heterogeneous of the modern confederated tribes, although a blending of racial characteristics may be seen to a lesser extent in the reservation Pamunkey and Mattaponi and the non-reservation Mattaponi, Rappahannock, Chickahominy, and Nansemond. In cultural terms the modern Virginia Indians retain little more of their heritage than tribal names and a sense of common origin.[57] The value of Indian identity has been increased by the social isolation of dark-skinned peoples in American life, since Indians in contrast to other racial minorities have generally enjoyed a degree of prestige in the opinion of the dominant group. In the tidewater region this may well be due to the influence of socially prominent Virginians who trace their ancestry to Pocahontas; she was, after all, a "Princess."

The end result of European contact in the piedmont region presents a somewhat different picture. Along the western border of Virginia and in the adjoining regions there are well-defined groups who claim Indian descent but no longer recall any particular tribal affiliations. They are known locally as Ramps, Melungeons, Brown People, Issues, and other terms. In order to avoid the social disabilities of classification with Negroes, they cling to their unofficial classification as Indians and remain rooted in regions where their peculiar status is known.[58] Some of these people may very well be descendants of the historic piedmont tribes of Virginia which vanished as identifiable tribal entities. Although much research remains to be done on this point, it is probable that their almost complete loss of identity, in contrast to the tidelands tribes, which at least recall their tribal origins, may be traced to the fact that they experienced disorganizing defeats at the hands of other Indians before the tidelands groups were ultimately conquered by the Europeans. The coastal Indians were in possession of European weapons at an earlier date and in all likelihood turned them against traditional enemies in the piedmont region before they found the need to use them primarily in forays against the white settlers. Thus the piedmont groups suffered a military disadvantage almost at the outset of European contact. By the time the whites penetrated to the piedmont region these tribes had already lost much of their former power. Furthermore, by the late seventeenth century they were also harassed by native enemies to the rear.[59] Unlike the tribes further inland, the piedmont peoples did not have time to regroup effectively and take advantage of the fur trade as a means of survival by adaptation to the presence of whites. Throughout the latter part of the seventeenth century they were in the path of westward movement by the whites, northward migrations of dispossessed Carolina tribes, and southern invasions by the Seneca on warlike campaigns. Their only hope for survival was in intertribal mixture and intermarriage with racially alien populations, both Negro and white.

Although the Virginia Indians were utterly defeated by the close of the seventeenth century, the experience of that period laid the foundations for modern adjustment to the white man's culture. As a result of stubborn opposition to amalgamation, some tribes have survived into the mid-twentieth century as populational entities, although they have been unable to retain a distinctive culture. Their primary technique of adjustment to European civilization, at least as documented in the Virginia tidelands region, was, with few exceptions, one of rigid resistance to alien ways which held no particular attractions, except for disparate items. Their culture simply disintegrated under the strain of continued pressure placed upon it. In contrast, the tribes further inland, by their more flexible adaptation to Europeans, achieved a social and cultural continuity which is still impressive despite many material innovations from European and American civilization.

Notes

1. James Mooney, "The Powahatan Confederacy, Past and Present," *Amer. Anthropologist*, 9 (1907), 129 and 120-52 *passim*. This Jamestown anniversary issue featured articles dealing with the Virginia Indians.

2. It must be noted that while the concept of culture can be and often is treated as an abstraction with an existence almost unto itself, this is no more than a semantic devise. Human ideas and

reasoning underlie culture and cultural change. Whenever possible, I have devoted attention to the factors of human motivations which give overt expression to observable cultural characteristics. The terms Indian culture and European civilization merely indicate that comparisons are made of two cultures having distinct origins and historical traditions, differing only in the local expressions of certain universal aspects of culture.

3. Two valuable publications dealing with the general topic of acculturation are: The Social Science Research Council Summer Seminar in Acculturation, 1953, "Acculturation, An Exploratory Formulation," *Amer. Anthropologist*, 56 (1954), 973-1005; and Verne F. Ray, ed., *Proceedings of the 1957 Annual Spring Meeting of the American Ethnological Society* (Seattle, 1957). The latter discusses cultural change and stability.

4. For a good brief account, see John Bartlett Brebner, *The Explorers of North America, 1492-1806*, reprint edn. (New York, 1955).

5. Clifford M. Lewis, S.J., and Albert J. Loomie, S.J., *The Spanish Jesuit Mission in Virginia, 1570-1572* (Chapel Hill, 1953), is an exhaustive study, but the Indian data are treated so summarily throughout that they neither help to substantiate the argument nor cast much light on the influence of the mission among the Indians, wherever it was established.

6. Maurice A. Mook, "Algonkian Ethnohistory of the Carolina Sound," *Jour. of The Washington Academy of Sciences*, 34 (1944), 185-86, quotes and discusses the journal of 1585, usually attributed to Sir Richard Grenville, regarding this incident and also establishes the location of Aquasogoc in North Carolina.

7. [George Percy], "Observations gathered out of *A Discourse of the Plantation of the Southerne Colonie in Virginia by the English, 1606*: written by that Honorable Gentleman, Master George Percy," in Edward Arber, ed., *Captain John Smith . . . Works, 1608-1631* (Birmingham, Eng., 1884), xxl-li.

8. There are many data to indicate that in culture contact situations, generally regular processes of cultural acceptance and rejection can be traced to the formulation of analogies between innovations and existing phenomena on the part of the recipient culture. See Melville J. Herskovits, *Man and His Works* (New York, 1950), 553-58, for a discussion of the processes of reinterpretation and syncretism; Ralph Linton, *The Study of Man* (New York, 1936), 317-18, and Homer G. Barnett, "Cultural Processes," *Amer. Anthropologist,* 42 (1940), 21-48, give similar but independent analyses of analogy formulation on the basis of form, function, meaning, and use or principle of given traits.

9. [Captain Gabriel Archer], "A Relayton of the Discovery &c. 21 May-22 June, 1607," in Arber, ed., *Works of John Smith*, li-lii. It is worth noting that news of the attack was apparently communicated to the Indians who were entertaining the exploring party, but that Powhatan had either been unable to prevent the attack or had not known of the plan until it was accomplished.

10. Throughout the present study, spelling of Indian words, apart from direct quotations, has been regularized according to the pattern of Mook's publications.

11. Paul Martin, George Quimby, and Donald Collier, *Indians Before Columbus* (Chicago, 1947), offer useful illustrations for the far-flung continental diffusion of cultural traits in prehistoric times, although dates assigned have been reassessed during the last ten years.

12. See Katherine C. Turner, *Red Men Calling on the Great White Father* (Norman, Okla., 1951), which presents a series of essays on such visits. Although the Indians considered their trips as entertaining educational experiences, their quoted remarks in the main reveal opinions that the white man had an unnecessarily complex and burdensome way of life at the expense of the finer one enjoyed by the Indians.

13. John Smith observed that "one as Emperour ruleth over many kings or governours." *A Map of*

Virginia with a Description of the Countrey . . . and *The General Historie of Virginia . . .* , in Arber, ed., *Works of John Smith,* 79, 375. Mook, "Aboriginal Population of Tidewater Virginia," *Amer. Anthropologist,* 44 (1944), 197, attributes the first use of the term "Powhatan Confederacy" to Jefferson.

14. Mooney, "Powhatan Confederacy," *Amer. Anthropologist,* 9 (1907), 135-36, notes the possible inclusion of the Werowocomoco and Chiskiac in the nuclear group of tribes inherited by Powhatan. Mook, "Aboriginal Population," *ibid.,* 44 (1944), 194 ff., lists thirty tribes as the largest number in the Confederation at any one time.

15. The Indian informants of the seventeenth century may have referred merely to the period of development of the distinctive social and political characteristics of the region rather than to original occupation. Frank G. Speck, "The Ethnic Position of the Southeastern Algonkian," *Amer. Anthropologist,* 26 (1924), 194, substantially agrees with the Indian accounts. Professor James B. Griffin, University Museum, University of Michigan, stated in a personal communication that unpublished data regarding a site near Washington, D.C., indicate an Algonkian intrusion into the southern area long before 1300.

16. Speck, "Southeastern Algonkian," *Amer. Anthropologist,* 26 (1924), 198, and 184-200 *passim,* sets forth this view of populational migration and cultural diffusion. Alfred L. Kroeber, *Cultural and Natural Areas of Native North America* (Berkeley, Calif., 1939), 94, disagrees with Speck as to the influence of southeastern Muskhogean peoples. Mook, "The Anthropological Position of the Indian Tribes of Tidewater Virginia," *Wm. and Mary College Qtly.,* 2nd ser., 23 (1943), 27-40, defends Speck's reconstruction with further evidence to substantiate the Muskhogean traits, and may be taken as the final word on the matter to date.

17. [Archer], "Relayton," Arber, ed., *Works of John Smith,* xliv; William Strachey, *The Historie of Travaile into Virginia Britannia,* Hakluyt Society edn. (London, 1849), 101, 105; Mooney, "Powhatan Confederacy," *Amer. Anthropologist,* 9 (1907), 130.

18. Mooney, "Powhatan Confederacy," *Amer. Anthropologist,* 9 (1907), 136.

19. Mook, "Virginia Ethnology from an Early Relation," *Wm. and Mary College Qtly.,* 2nd ser., 23 (1943), 115.

20. Mooney, "Powhatan Confederacy," *Amer. Anthropologist,* 9 (1907), 140, tentatively identifies the "Doeg" as the Nanticoke. A review of materials relating to Bacon's Rebellion as well as the accounts of the local tribes presented in Kroeber, *Cultural Areas,* 91, 93-94, suggests that "Doeg" was applied to the Nanticoke and other Algonkian groups north of the Potomac. For John Smith's discussion of the Susquehanna, see Arber, ed., *Works of John Smith,* 77, 367.

21. Reproductions of White's original works may be found in David I. Bushnell, "John White—The First English Artist to Visit America, 1585," *Va. Mag. of Hist. and Biog.,* 35 (1927), 419-30, and 36 (1928), 17-26, 124-34. Although less well known, these illustrations are preferable to DeBry's familiar engravings and the work of other copyists in representing the Carolina tribes to augment textual descriptions in the Roanoke accounts.

22. Carl F. Miller, "Revaluation of the Eastern Siouan Problem with Particular Emphasis on the Virginia Branches—The Occaneechi, the Saponi, and the Tutelo," Bureau of American Ethnology, Smithsonian Institution Bulletin 164, *Anthropological Papers,* No. 52 (Washington, D.C., 1957), 115-211, discusses the origin of the conjecture that Siouan dialects were spoken in the piedmont area and indicates why such reasoning may be erroneous. However, the traditional view is far from abandoned; see William C. Sturtevant, "Siouan Languages in the East," *Amer. Anthropologist,* 60 (1958), 138-43, for a specific refutation of Miller's argument.

23. Ethnologists have long been aware of the significance of the so-called Siouans in Powhatan's

actions, although the point is usually mentioned as a side issue in connection with village locations, population size, and tribal distributions. See Bushnell, "The Five Monacan Towns in Virginia," Smithsonian Institution, *Miscellaneous Collections*, 82 (1930), 1-38; "The Manahoac Tribes in Virginia," *ibid.*, 94 (1935), 1-56; John R. Swanton, "Early History of the Eastern Siouan Tribes," in *Essays in Anthropology Presented to A. L. Kroeber* (Berkeley, Calif., 1936), 371-81.

24. John Smith lists the locations and names of subsidiary tribes of the Monacan and Manahoac. Arber, ed., *Works of John Smith*, 71, 366-67.

25. "Their manner of trading is for copper, beads, and such like, for which they giue such commodities as they haue, as skins, fowle, fish, flech, and their country corne." *Ibid.*, 74, 369. Smith reported that Powhatan requested him to abandon the settlement among the Paspehegh and move to his own country: "Hee promised to giue me Corne, Venison, or what I wanted to feede vs: Hatchets and Copper wee should make him, and none should disturb vs." *Ibid.*, 20.

26. Mook, "Aboriginal Population," *Amer. Anthropologist*, 44 (1944), 201, 208.

27. [Archer], "Relayton," Arber, ed., *Works of John Smith*, I, provides a characteristic response of the colonists in his description of Opechancanough, who "so set his Countenance stryving to be stately, as to our seeming he became a fool."

28. Arber, ed., *Works of John Smith*, 79, 374.

29. For a general account of religion derived from the basic sources, see Charles C. Willoughby, "The Virginia Indians of the Seventeenth Century," *Amer. Anthropologist*, 9 (1907), 61-63. The most complete single account in the early narratives based on firsthand observation is included in Henry Spelman, "Relation of Virginea," 1613, in Arber, ed., *Works of John Smith*, cv-cvi.

30. Arber, ed., *Works of John Smith*, 81-82, 377-78; Spelman, "Relation," *ibid.*, cxi.

31. [Archer], "Relayton," *ibid.*, lv.

32. See Mooney, "Powhatan Confederacy," *Amer. Anthropologist*, 9 (1907), 136-39, for an exhaustive review of instances illustrating the ever harsher measures taken by the colonists in coercing the Indians. In his indignation, Mooney scarcely notes that the Indians took measures of revenge by killing whites so that the process of hostilities increased over a period of time, with each side intent on settling some score with the other side.

33. Smith admitted that Powhatan's move to the village of Orapaks was simply to get away from the settlers. Arber, ed., *Works of John Smith*, 20, 70-71, 366-67; for the execution, see *ibid.*, 487.

34. *Ibid.*, 124-25, 434-35. Smith's disgust was aroused by the coronation because it not only made Powhatan conceited, but it threatened to disrupt the trade in copper. Powhatan had been willing to exchange huge amounts of corn for a pittance, and Smith feared he would be spoiled by the rich coronation gifts.

35. Strachey, *Historie of Travaile into Virginia*, 54.

36. Throughout the accounts of 1607-8 there are references to aiding Powhatan in dealing with the piedmont Siouans and Powhatan's satisfaction in the promises. Arber, ed., *Works of John Smith*, 20, 70-71, 366-67; [Archer], "Relayton," *ibid.*, xlvii. As relations between Powhatan and the settlers became strained, Powhatan discouraged the settlers from going to the Monacan, fearing that the whites might ally themselves with his enemies. Smith quotes Powhatan: "As for the *Monacans*, I can revenge my own iniuries." *Ibid.*, 124, and see 482-83. For the subsequent decline of the Monacan, see the journal of Batt's expedition reprinted from the British Museum manuscript in Bushnell, "Discoveries Beyond the Appalachian Mountains in September, 1671," *Amer. Anthropologist*, 9 (1907), 46-53.

37. Arber, ed., *Works of John Smith*, 451; Robert Beverley, *The History and Present State of Virginia*, ed. by Louis B. Wright (Chapel Hill, 1947), 61.

38. Edward D. Neill, *History of the Virginia Company of London* (Albany, N.Y., 1869), 317-19, cites references which suggest that the Indians expressed excessive protestations of kindness and friendship in order to lull the settlers' suspicions in 1622. Shortly after Powhatan's death, however, fear of the Indians was so intense that Captain Spelman was harshly dealt with on the belief that he was engaged in inciting the Indians to hostile acts.

39. Mook, "Aboriginal Population," *Amer. Anthropologist*, 44 (1944), 204-5, discusses shifts in Indian tribal populations as a response to European movements after 1622.

40. Edward D. Neill, *Virginia Calororum; The Colony under the Rule of Charles the First and Second, A.D. 1625-A.D. 1685* (Albany, N.Y., 1886), 60-61.

41. Mooney, "Powhatan Confederacy," *Amer. Anthropologist*, 9 (1907), 138-39, discusses reductions in Indian population. Opechancanough's secrecy inspires wonder, but the success of the attack is indicative of the degree of separation that marked the lives of the colonists and the Indians by 1644.

42. Neill, *Virginia Calororum*, 74.

43. As early as 1609, the instructions given Thomas Gates as acting governor of the colony indicate the initial policy decided upon: "If you make friendship with any of thiese nations as you must doe, choose to do it with those that are farthest from you & enemies unto those amongst whom you dwell for you shall have least occasion to have differences with them, and by that means a surer league of amity." The entire text of Gates's instructions as they related to the Indians is quoted in Bushnell, "Virginia From Early Records," *Amer. Anthropologist*, 9 (1907), 35.

44. See Wesley Frank Craven, *The Southern Colonies in the Seventeenth Century, 1607-1689* (Baton Rouge, La., 1949), 361-66, for a discussion of changes in Virginia's Indian policy.

45. These facts, central to the theoretical propositions underlying the initial research in the present study, doubtless contributed to continuing adaptability of the more inland tribes. It is possible to see striking destruction of coastal or peripheral tribes along both the Atlantic and the Pacific oceans in North America, while the groups somewhat inland have been able to preserve a greater degree of cultural integrity. The Plains area, however, represents a third zone in the effects of the frontier on Indian cultures; the absence of white allies and of a social symbiosis between whites and Indians based on the fur trade explains in large part the rapid cultural disorganization when the tide turned against the Indians.

46. Brebner, *Explorers*, 144-49, discusses the "Andastes" Indians, but they are easily identified by internal evidence as the Susquehanna.

47. See Wilcomb E. Washburn, *The Governor and the Rebel, A History of Bacon's Rebellion in Virginia* (Chapel Hill, 1957), for a recent analysis of Bacon's Rebellion which devotes special attention to the complications of the Indian problem. Washburn notes that there is no evidence that Bacon's followers killed any really hostile Indians; instead, they attacked tribes which were neutral in the border disputes or nominally friendly to the whites.

48. Mooney, "Powhatan Confederacy," *Amer. Anthropologist*, 9 (1907), 141, tentatively identifies the Richeharians as Cherokee. Although this view has been questioned by other scholars, there is no agreement on any alternative identification. The Richeharians defeated the attacking party of whites and allied Indians, and the incident is worthy of notice in regard to the later events of Bacon's Rebellion as a gauge of the insecurity felt by the border settlers as early as 1656. An investigation of the affair indicated that the Richeharians probably only wanted to trade but that hostilities began before the intentions of these strange Indians were determined.

49. [The Royal Commissioners], "A True Narrative of the Late Rebellion in Virginia," in Charles M. Andrews, ed., *Narratives of the Insurrections, 1675-1690* (New York, 1915), 123 and 127; [Thomas Mathew], "The Beginning, Progress and Conclusion of Bacon's Rebellion, 1675-1676," *ibid.*, 26.

50. William H. Gilbert, "Surviving Indian Groups in the Eastern United States," in Smithsonian Institution, *Annual Reports of the Board of Regents* (Washington, D.C., 1948), 417-18.

51. Mooney, "Powhatan Confederacy," *Amer. Anthropologist*, 9 (1907), 141-47, traces the course of affiliations and residence of piedmont and tidelands Indians between 1677-1722 on the basis of the two treaties and intervening documents.

52. *Ibid.*, 144-52; see also J. C. Householder, "Virginia's Indian Neighbors in 1712," Indiana Academy of Science, *Proceedings,* 55 (1946), 23-25, for a discussion of Governor Spotswood's administration of Indian affairs.

53. Bushnell, "Virginia From Early Records," *Amer. Anthropologist*, 9 (1907), 41-44, prints the entire text of the letter from the original in the records of the British Museum, "A Letter from the Rev. Mr. John Clayton, afterwards Dean of Kildare in Ireland, to Dr. Green in answer to several qurys sent to him . . . A.D. 1687. . . ." All references to the condition of the Indians in this period are from Clayton unless otherwise noted.

54. Arber, ed., *Works of John Smith*, 451.

55. [Archer], "Relayton," *ibid.*, I.

56. [Mathew], "Bacon's Rebellion," Andrews, ed., *Narratives of the Insurrections, 1675-1690*, 25-56; [Royal Commissioners], "Late Rebellion," *ibid.*, 126-27.

57. Gilbert, "Surviving Indian Groups," Smithsonian Institution, *Annual Reports of the Board of Regents*, 418-19.

58. *Ibid.*, 419.

59. Mooney, "Siouan Tribes of the East," Bureau of American Ethnology, Smithsonian Institution, *Bulletin 22* (Washington, D.C., 1894), 28, notes that the Monacan were "directly in the path of the Richahecrian (Rickohockan, Cherokee)," who ostensibly invaded the Virginia area in 1656. Thus, Mooney suggested that the Monacan may have been victims of attacks by tribes to their west.

Pequots and Puritans: The causes of the War of 1637

Alden T. Vaughan

Almost from the beginning, tragic Indian wars ravaged the American frontier. At first, whites in Virginia had friendly relations with Powhatan and his confederacy of tribes; but Powhatan's successor, Chief Opechancanough, launched a ten-year war with the bloody massacre of 1622. Nearly everywhere it was the same. No matter what Indian policy was devised by the individual colonies, periods of peaceful relations gave way to brutal conflict. And no matter how much the white man suffered, the Indian suffered more. In many instances whole tribes vanished. In the twentieth century, American historians have come to have a deep appreciation and sympathy for the diverse Indian cultures and a sense of guilt about their passing. Much attention has been focused on the causes of the wars which were so much a part of the Indians' decline.

In 1965 Alden Vaughan, a professor at Columbia University, published a major reinterpretation of Puritan Indian policy from the founding of Plymouth to the start of the disastrous King Philip's War in 1675. Professor Vaughan, a defender of the Puritans, rejects simplistic explanations for colonial Indian wars. In common with Nancy Lurie in the previous article, Vaughan stresses that the American Indians were sorely divided among themselves. He sees little if any racism operating among either the Indians or the Puritans. Nor does he accept the view that conflict arose over land; he maintains there was plenty to sustain both cultures. Rather Vaughan attributes the ultimate Indian defeat to the terrible ravages of disease and intertribal conflict. He sees Indian culture as technologically backward, unprogressive, and self-satisfied. With the Indians divided and weak and the Puritans strong and unified, the outcome was inevitable. In this essay, Professor Vaughan attempts to fix the blame for the first major New England conflict.

For further reading: James Truslow Adams, *The Founding of New England* (Boston: Little, Brown,1921), Chapters VIII, XIV;* Verner W. Crane, *The Southern Frontier, 1670-1732* (Durham, N.C.: Duke University Press, 1928);* G. T. Hunt, *The Wars of the Iroquois* (Madison: University of Wisconsin Press, 1940);* Douglas Edward Leach, *Flintlock and Tomahawk: New England in King Philip's War* (1st ed. 1958; New York: Norton, 1966);* Francis Parkman, *The Conspiracy of Pontiac* (1st ed. 1851, revised

Reprinted with permission from *William and Mary Quarterly*, 3rd Series, XXI, no. 2 (April 1964), 256-269.

1870; New York: Collier Books, 1962);* Howard H. Peckham, *Pontiac and the Indian Uprising* (Chicago: University of Chicago Press, 1947);* William S. Powell, "Aftermath of the Massacre, the First Indian War, 1622-1632," *Virginia Magazine of History and Biography*, 66 (1958), 44-75; Alden T. Vaughan, *New England Frontier, Puritans and Indians 1620-1675* (Boston: Little, Brown, 1965);* Wilcomb E. Washburn, "The Moral and Legal Justification for Dispossessing the Indians," in James M. Smith, ed., *Seventeenth-Century America: Essays on Colonial History*, (Chapel Hill: University of North Carolina Press, 1959).*

* Available in paperback.

The war of 1637 between the Puritans and the Pequot Indians was one of the most dramatic episodes in early New England history, possessing an intensity and a significance deserving of far more attention than it has usually been accorded. While more limited in scope than King Philip's War, and less tied to controversial issues than the Antinomian crisis or the banishment of Roger Williams, the Pequot War had unique elements which made it memorable in its own right. It resulted in the extermination of the most powerful tribe in New England, it witnessed one of the most sanguinary battles of all Indian wars—when some five hundred Pequot men, women, and children were burned to death in the Puritans' attack on Mystic Fort—and it opened southern New England to rapid English colonization. The war was not soon forgotten by the other tribes in the northeast, nor by the English who memorialized the victory in prose and poetry.[1] It even found its way into *Moby Dick* when Herman Melville chose the name of the vanquished tribe for Captain Ahab's ill-fated whaling vessel.[2]

As in the case of most wars, the conflict between the Pequot Indians and the Puritans of New England raises for its historian the twin problems of cause and responsibility. Involved is the whole question of Indian-white relations during the first century of English settlement in New England, the basic nature of the Puritan experiment, and the justice and humanity of the participants. Writers in eighteenth-century New England tended to side with their ancestors and view the conflict as a defensive maneuver on the part of the righteous forces of Puritanism prodded into action by the Pequot hordes, or, as Puritan rhetoric would have it, by Satan himself. Later historians sharing a popular antipathy toward Puritanism and all its works concluded that the war was a simple case of Puritan aggression and Pequot retaliation. Others would have us believe that it was fundamentally a manifestation of English land-hunger with the Pequots fighting for their lands as well as their lives.[3] The well-established facts seem to indicate that the proper explanation lies in none of these interpretations alone, but in a blend of the first two, modified by a radical restatement of the third.

Although the early history of the Pequot tribe is shrouded in obscurity, it is generally accepted that prior to the tribe's arrival in southern New England, it had inhabited lands in northern New Netherland close to the Mohawk Indians. For reasons that will probably always remain uncertain, the Pequot tribe, then called Mohegan, migrated into west central New England in the early seventeenth century and then turned southward until it reached the shores of the Atlantic Ocean. Unlike the Pilgrims who were exploring and settling Plymouth harbor at about the same time, the Mohegans gained their territory by force of arms. Along the route of their journey they made innumerable enemies and incurred such a reputation for brutality that they became known as "Pequots," the Algonquin word for "destroyers of men."[4] Animosity toward the Pequots was particularly strong among the small tribes of the Connecticut Valley who were forced to acknowledge the suzerainty of the intruders and to pay them annual tribute. Equally unfriendly were the Narragansetts, the Pequots' nearest neighbors to the east, who resented the presence of a militarily superior tribe and refused to be cowed by it. The result was almost constant warfare between the Narragansetts and the Pequots, the final campaign of which was one phase of the Pequot War of 1637.

Not only were the Pequots unable to live peacefully with their Indian neighbors, they alienated the adjacent European settlers as well.[5] In 1634 the Pequots were at war with both Dutch New Netherland and the Narragansetts. In the same year they made their first hostile move against the English with the assassination of Captain John Stone of Virginia and eight other Englishmen. Friendly Indians informed the Massachusetts authorities that the Pequots had assassinated the ship captain while he was sleeping in his bunk, had murdered the rest of his crew, and plundered his vessel. The Puritans could hardly let the murder of nine colonists go unchallenged if they intended to maintain their precarious foothold in a land where the natives vastly outnumbered them.

With the English demanding revenge for the murder of John Stone, the Pequots decided that this was one enemy too many, and late in October 1634 they sent ambassadors to Massachusetts to treat for peace and commerce, reinforcing their appeal with gifts of wampum.[6] The Puritan authorities, after consulting with some of the clergy, demanded Stone's assassins as a prelude to negotiations. The Pequots replied with an account of Stone's death that differed markedly from the colonists' version. Stone, the Indians contended, had seized and bound two braves who had boarded his ship to trade. It was after this, they said, that several of the braves' friends ambushed the captain when he came ashore. They also insisted that the sachem responsible for the ambush had since been killed by the Dutch and all but two of his henchmen had fallen victim to the pox.

The Pequots told their story "with such confidence and gravity" that the English were inclined to accept it, and after several days of negotiations the Pequots and the Bay Colony signed a treaty on November 1, 1634. By its terms the Indians agreed to hand over the two remaining assassins when sent for and "to yield up Connecticut," by which they probably meant as much of the valley as the English desired for settlement. In addition, the Pequots promised to pay an indemnity of four hundred fathoms of wampum, forty beaver and thirty otter skins. Commercial relations were projected by an agreement that Massachusetts would send a trading vessel to the Pequots in the near future. Peace was thus maintained in New England. Commerce between the Bay Colony and the Pequots did not materialize, however. When John Oldham took his trading ship into Pequot territory the next spring, he found them "a very false people" and disinclined to amicable trade.[7]

Peace between the Bay Colony and the Pequots lasted until the fall of 1636, but those two years witnessed a rapid deterioration of the relations between the two. The Pequots failed to surrender the remaining assassins of Stone, the indemnity was paid only in part, and reports of further Pequot disingenuousness began to drift into Boston. By midsummer of 1636, Massachusetts had lost patience and commissioned John Winthrop, Jr., then in Connecticut, to demand that Chief Sassacus of the Pequots surrender at once the assassins of Captain Stone and reply to several other charges of bad faith. Should the

Pequots fail to meet these demands, the Bay Colony threatened to terminate the league of amity and to "revenge the blood of our Countrimen as occasion shall serve."[8] But before Winthrop could fulfill his mission, an event occurred that put an end to all peaceful dealings with the Pequot tribe.

Late in July, John Callop, en route by sea to Long Island, spied near Block Island John Oldham's pinnace, its deck crowded with Indians and no sign of a white man. When no one answered his hail, Gallop tried to board to investigate; a frenzied battle followed in which Gallop routed the Indians. On board he found the naked and mutilated body of Oldham.[9]

At first it appeared that the Narragansetts were responsible for Oldham's murder. The Block Island tribe was subservient to them, and according to one report, all the Narragansett sachems except Canonicus and Miantonomo (the two leading chiefs) had conspired with the Block Islanders against Oldham because of his attempts to trade with the Pequots the previous year. The Massachusetts leaders contemplated war with the Narragansetts and warned Roger Williams "to look to himself." But Canonicus and Miantonomo speedily regained the confidence of the English by returning Oldham's two boys and his remaining goods from Block Island, and by assuring the Bay Colony, through Roger Williams, that most of the culprits had been killed by Gallop. Meanwhile the few surviving assassins sought refuge with the Pequots.[10]

The upshot of all this was a punitive expedition of ninety Massachusetts volunteers under magistrate John Endicott against Block Island. The troops were also ordered to visit Pequot territory to secure the remaining murderers of Stone and Oldham and assurances of future good behavior on the part of the Pequots. But when in early September the expedition made contact with the tribe, the Pequot spokesmen obstinately refused to comply with Puritan demands, first offering a new version of the killing of Stone that absolved them of any blame, then claiming that their leading chiefs were on Long Island, and finally insisting that they were still trying to discover who the culprits were. After a few hours of futile negotiations, the English became convinced that the delay was a camouflage for ambush, particularly when they observed the Pequots "convey away their wives and children, and bury their chiefest goods." A brief clash ensued in which a few Pequots were slain, several wounded, and much Pequot property seized or destroyed by the Massachusetts troops.[11]

The Pequots retaliated by torturing and slaying every Englishman they could find. Fort Saybrook at the mouth of the Connecticut River was put under virtual seige, and several of its garrison were ambushed during the next few months. English traders entering the Connecticut River fell victim to Pequot raiding parties. When reinforcements arrived from Massachusetts in the spring of 1637, the Pequots shifted their attacks to the unprotected plantations farther up the river.[12] Early on the morning of April 23, 1637, two hundred howling Pequot braves descended on a small group of colonists at work in a meadow near Wethersfield, Connecticut. Nine of the English were slain, including a woman and child; and the Pequots carried to their stronghold two young women whom the sachems hoped could make gunpowder for the tribe's few firearms. With some thirty Englishmen dead at Pequot hands, the New England colonies had no alternatives but to wage war. Massachusetts Bay had in fact already declared war two weeks before the Wethersfield raid but had done nothing to stop the pattern of massacres. Connecticut could wait no longer, and on May 1, 1637, its General Court declared "that there shalbe an offensive warr against the Pequoitt."[13] Settlers as well as Pequots had engaged in the series of attacks, retaliations, and counter-retaliations preceding the formal declaration, but the wantonness, scope, and cruelty of the Indian raids cast upon them a very heavy burden of responsibility for the war that followed.

The reaction of the other Indian tribes to the outbreak of war reveals much about the nature of the conflict. The Narragansetts, thanks to some last-minute diplomacy by Roger Williams, had already made an offensive alliance with Massachusetts.[14] The Mohegans, a secessionist faction of the Pequot tribe that had revived the old tribal name and separated from Chief Sassacus the year before, also fought on the English side, against their blood brothers. The small valley tribes along the Connecticut River enthusiastically backed the Puritans, whom they had encouraged to settle in the valley as early as 1631 in hope of gaining protection against the Pequots.[15] Connecticut's declaration of war was, in fact, partly due to the urging of these tribes. "The Indians here our friends," wrote Thomas Hooker from Hartford, "were so importunate with us to make warr presently that unlesse we had attempted some thing we had delivered our persons unto contempt of base feare and cowardise, and caused them to turne enemyes agaynst us."[16] Of the hundreds of casualties the Pequots suffered, scores were inflicted by the Indians of southern New England and Long Island. As Captain John Mason, leader of the Connecticut forces observed, "Happy were they that could bring in their Heads to the English: Of which there came almost daily to Winsor, or Hartford."[17] And the greatest prize of all, the head of Chief Sassacus, was delivered by the Mohawks. Sassacus had sought asylum with his former neighbors, but afraid of the Englishmen's "hot-mouthed weapons," the Mohawks seized him and forty of his warriors, cut off their heads and hands, and confiscated their wampum.[18] The Pequots, for their part, were unable to find any important allies among the Indians. Clearly, this was no racial conflict between white man and red. Rather, the Pequot War saw the English colonies, eagerly assisted by several Indian tribes, take punitive action against the one New England tribe that was hated and feared by Indian and white alike.

The short career of the Pequots in history, then, was of a people apparently incapable of maintaining the trust and forbearance of any of their neighbors, red or white, English or Dutch. A prima facie case exists for the claims of Puritan apologists, and its partial validity is undeniable. Unfortunately, it is not the whole story.

The weightiest criticism of Puritan policy, and the one stressed most often by scholars hostile to the New Englanders, is that the conduct of the settlers was incessantly heavy-handed and provocative. It can even be argued that long before the Endicott expedition the English had treated the Pequots with something less than equity. For example, the character of Captain John Stone was such as to lend an air of plausibility to the Pequot version of his death.

Captain Stone, it seems, had piloted a shipload of cattle from Virginia to Boston in 1634. At each stop along the way he managed so to embroil himself with the local authorities that he was soon *persona non grata* in every community north of the Hudson. His first escapade was in New Amsterdam, where he attempted to steal a Plymouth bark and was thwarted only at the last minute by some Dutch seamen. Later, in Plymouth, he almost stabbed Governor Thomas Prence. He acted little better in Massachusetts Bay where he "spake contemptuously of [the] magistrates, and carried it lewdly in his conversation," in particular calling Judge Roger Ludlow "a just as." On top of this he was charged with excessive drinking and adultery. He was tried and acquitted for lack of evidence on the major charge, but his lesser indiscretions earned him a suspended fine of one hundred pounds and banishment from the colony under penalty of death.[19] Stone was on his way back to Virginia, accompanied by Captain Walter Norton and crew, when he stopped off to explore the trading prospects of the Connecticut River and there met his death. As might be expected, news of his fate did not elicit universal mourning: some of the English, secure in their piety, concluded with Roger Clap that "thus did God destroy him that so proudly threatened to ruin us."[20]

These circumstances perhaps explain why no military action was taken against the Pequots in 1634. It should be noted, however, that the treaty the Puritans extracted from the Pequots later that year was hardly a lenient one. Still, hostilities did not break out until the Bay Colony dispatched the Endicott expedition in 1636 to avenge the death of John Oldham. And here again, the Puritans' conception of just retribution was stern indeed. Endicott's instructions were to kill all Indian men on Block Island, seize the women and children, and take possession of the island. He was then to proceed to the Pequot territory and demand the murderers of Stone and Oldham, one thousand fathoms of wampum, and some Pequot children as hostages. Should the Pequots refuse to comply with the terms of this ultimatum, the expedition was to impose them by force.[21] And Endicott vigorously complied with these instructions. He secured a beachhead on Block Island in the face of brief resistance, routed the defenders, and devastated the island. While the Indians of Block Island sought refuge in the swamps, the Massachusetts troops burned wigwams, destroyed cornfields, and smashed canoes. Dissatisfied by the small number of Indian casualties, the English soldiers heartlessly "destroyed some of their dogs instead of men." After two busy days of destruction, the expedition set sail for Pequot territory.[22]

Four days later Endicott's fleet entered Pequot Harbor. The Indians greeted the fleet's appearance with "doleful and woful cries," for it was obvious to the Pequots that this was no friendly mission. And whatever chance there may have been for peaceful negotiations rapidly vanished. When the Pequots refused to meet his demands and began their annoying delays, Endicott landed his troops and took station on a commanding hilltop.[23] Some of the Indians' excuses for delay may have been legitimate, but the English rejected them, and Endicott interpreted a final Pequot suggestion that both sides lay down their arms as a dastardly ruse. "We rather chose to beat up the drum and bid them battle," recorded Captain John Underhill. A volley from the musketeers sent the Pequot warriors scurrying for shelter, and the pattern established on Block Island was repeated. The colonists spent the next two days in rampant destruction and looting. In deference to English firepower, the Indians kept a respectful distance.[24]

By the fourteenth of September, less than three weeks after their departure from Boston, the Massachusetts troops were back in the Bay Colony with but two casualties, neither fatal. The Pequots were mourning far greater losses: several killed and a score or more wounded in addition to the destruction of their property. Ironically, the first Pequot life may well have been taken by Chief Cutshamekin of the Massachusetts Indians, who had joined Endicott as an interpreter and guide.[25] In any event, harsh Puritan "justice" had been imposed; harsh Pequot retaliation soon followed.

The Endicott attack spurred the Pequots to seek retribution. Although the Pequots had suffered few casualties, it was inconceivable that this proud tribe would not insist on revenge. Its land had been invaded, its chief subjected to arrogant demands, and its tribesmen assaulted. The other Puritan colonies were quick to blame the Bay Colony for the massacres that ensued. Spokesmen for Plymouth, Connecticut, and Fort Saybrook (then under separate government) all condemned the Endicott expedition, and even Governor Winthrop later tacitly admitted that Massachusetts had provoked hostilities. Lion Gardiner, commander of the Saybrook garrison, expressed the prevalent opinion even before the Endicott expedition reached Pequot soil. "You come hither," he protested, "to raise these wasps about my ears, and then you will take wing and flee away." [26] His prophecy was accurate; Endicott upset the nest, but the stings were first felt by the few hundred settlers of Connecticut and Fort Saybrook.

There remains the question of why the Bay Colony had resorted to coercive action after having tolerated the crimes attributed to the Pequots prior to their harboring of Oldham's assassins. The explanation may be threefold. In the first place, the Bay Colony, now considering herself the dominant authority in New England, was determined strictly to enforce the peace, a policy more easily undertaken since she was the least likely to feel the brunt of any retaliation. Secondly, shortly before the Endicott expedition was formed Roger Williams had reported a heady boast of the Pequots that they could by witchcraft defeat any English expedition, a challenge hardly designed to soothe Puritan tempers. [27] Finally, Massachusetts was then in the throes of civil and religious controversy. Roger Williams had been ousted but a few months earlier for "divers dangerous opinions," the Crown had recently instituted quo warranto proceedings against the colony's charter, and the first rumblings of the Antinomian movement were faintly audible. If frustration is a prime cause of aggression, the Bay Colony had been overripe for Endicott's blow at Satan's horde.

Added to Pequot perfidy, then, was the harshness of Massachusetts's remedial action. Both contributed to the outbreak of the war.

That the war was a product of English land hunger and Pequot defense of its tribal territory, finds little documentation. It seems doubtful that in 1636 English settlers wanted land with which the Indians were unwilling to part. The Connecticut Valley tribes were welcoming the English and encouraging their settlement there. Neither the Narragansetts nor the Mohegans seem to have been disturbed by colonial expansion; the former had made sizable grants to Roger Williams, and the latter were to make the most vigorous Indian contribution to the downfall of the Pequots. Nor is there any evidence that the Pequots themselves feared immediate English encroachment on their tribal lands. It is true that the Pequots did try to gain Narragansett aid against Massachusetts Bay by raising the specter of future Indian extermination at the hands of the English, but they did not argue that the present danger of dispossession was great. [28] By the treaty of November 1634, the Pequots themselves had granted the Bay Colony the right to settle in Connecticut, though of course the local valley tribes would have denied the right of the Pequots to make such a grant. The English settlement nearest to Pequot territory was at Saybrook, which had a garrison of only twenty men. It was situated, in fact, in the Mohegans' territory after their secession in 1636.

A few historians have attempted to find evidence of a ravenous Puritan land hunger in the rhetoric of Puritan theology, [29] but the evidence presented in support of such a view appears to consist for the most part of theological generalizations—in many cases uttered by Puritan leaders before embarking for the New World—concerning the holiness of their venture and the certainty that God had laid aside for them the lands necessary for its fulfillment. It is far more germane to establish how the Puritans, once settled in New

England and confronted with its realities, went about the mundane business of evolving and administering a practicable land policy. The records clearly demonstrate that the bulk of the settlers proceeded upon the assumption that the Indian—heathen or not—had legal title to the lands upon which he lived, a title that could be changed only through the civilized conventions of sale and formal transfer.[30] Only two instances exist in which the New Englanders acquired any substantial amounts of land from the Indians by means other than treaties. One was the Pequot War of 1637, the other King Philip's War of 1675-76; neither can reasonably be explained as campaigns for territorial expansion.

In seeking to identify the causes of the war and apportion responsibility for its outbreak, one must begin with the fact established by the testimony of all the whites and most Indians that the Pequots were blatantly and persistently provocative and aggressive. Perhaps brilliant diplomacy could have prevented the intransigence of the Pequots from leading to open warfare; but even Roger Williams, the most likely man for the role of arbiter, had no influence upon the Pequots. On the other hand, it is undeniable that Puritan severity in the Endicott campaign provided the spark that set off the ultimate conflagration. Although the harshness of the Bay Colony's policy in the summer of 1636 is understandable, it cannot be excused.

While land as such was plainly not at issue, the Endicott expedition may well have represented something even more fundamental at stake here—the struggle between Puritans and Pequots for ultimate jurisdiction over the region both inhabited. The Puritans, determined to prevent Indian actions that might in any way threaten the New World Zion, had assumed through their governments responsibility for maintaining law and order among all inhabitants, Indian and white. The Plymouth magistrates had accepted this responsibility to the full limit of their resources, and had labored to curb both Indian and English when either threatened the peace. Massachusetts Bay, at first too weak to exert its authority beyond its immediate area of settlement, was by 1636 ready to enforce its fiat on all Indians in southern New England. Prior to the formation of the Confederation of New England in 1643, each colony endeavored to exercise full authority over natives as well as its own people within its own borders; yet Massachusetts, in its dealings with the Narragansetts and Pequots, was obviously assuming jurisdiction over areas outside its charter limits. It did so for the simple reason that otherwise Indians could molest white men, and vice versa, with impunity.

At bottom it was the English assumption of the right to discipline neighboring Indians that led to war in 1637. The Endicott expedition of 1636 was sent primarily to act as a police force, with orders to inflict punishment upon Block Island and obtain sureties of good behavior from the Pequots. The Pequots naturally resented the interference of Massachusetts in an area over which they had but recently acquired hegemony, and rejected the Bay Colony's assumption of the right to impose authority. The result was war. It may be the Puritans of Massachusetts were begging for trouble by extending their authority beyond their chartered territory; but the other tribes of New England not only submitted to the exertion of authority by Massachusetts Bay to keep the peace but even appeared at times to invite it. As the alternative was anarchy outside the settled areas, it is difficult to condemn the policy of Massachusetts, except in its application by Endicott. In short, the Pequot War, like most wars, cannot be attributed to the unmitigated bellicosity of one side and the righteous response of the other. Persistent aggression by the Pequot tribe, the desire for autonomy from or revenge against the Pequots by various other tribes, the harshness of the Endicott campaign, and divergent concepts as to the Englishman's jurisdiction all contributed to the outbreak of New England's first Indian war.

The war itself was brief, brutal, and its outcome thoroughly satisfying to the English and their Indian allies. The toll in human life was extremely high and makes the Pequot War one of the most regrettable episodes in early New England history. Still, it is small, though real, consolation that the blame lies somewhat more heavily upon the Pequots than the Puritans. It may also be hoped that the troubled conscience with which the modern American historian often views our past relations with the Indians can find some balm in contemplating an episode in which the white man groped for workable formulas of friendship and justice, and in which he was not solely responsible for their ultimate failure.

Notes

Mr. Vaughan is a member of the Department of History, Columbia University.

1. See, for examples, Timothy Dwight, *Greenfied Hill: A Poem in Seven Parts* (New York, 1794), Bk. IV, and Samuel G. Drake, *The Book of the Indians*, 9th ed. (Boston, 1845), Bk. ii, 106-107.

2. For an explanation of Melville's familiarity with the history of the Pequot War and his reasons for employing the name of the tribe see the edition by Luther S. Mansfield and Howard P. Vincent (New York, 1952), 68, 631-633.

3. For a representative of the first view, see Benjamin Trumbull, *A Complete History of Connecticut . . .* (New Haven, 1818), I, chap. 5. The second viewpoint, prevalent among non-New England authors in the 19th century and among 20th-century historians regardless of locale, can be found in John R. Brodhead, *History of the State of New York*, I (New York, 1853), 237-273; William C. MacLeod, *The American Indian Frontier* (New York, 1928), 209-219; and William T. Hagan, *American Indians* (Chicago, 1961), 12-14. The latter two also see the Puritans coveting Indian lands; they thus have much in common with the third school of interpretation, which finds its most articulate presentation in Roy Harvey Pearce, *The Savages of America* (Baltimore, 1953), 19-35.

4. Roger Williams, "A Key into the Language of America . . . ," in Narragansett Club, *Publications*, I (Providence, 1866), 22*n*, 203.

5. See Brodhead, *History of New York*, I, 242; James Kendall Hosmer, ed., *Winthrop's Journal, "History of New England," 1630-1649* (New York, 1908), I, 79, 139.

6. The details of these negotiations can be found in *Winthrop's Journal*, I, 138-140; Winthrop to John Winthrop, Jr., Dec. 12, 1634, in Allyn Bailey Forbes, ed., *Winthrop Papers*, III (Boston, 1943), 177; and Winthrop to William Bradford, n.d., in William Bradford, *Of Plymouth Plantation, 1620-1647*, ed. Samuel E. Morison (New York, 1952), 291.

7. *Winthrop's Journal*, I, 139-140; Winthrop to Bradford, Mar. 12, 1635, in Bradford, *Of Plymouth Plantation*, 291-292.

8. Jonathan Brewster to John Winthrop, Jr., June 18, 1636, in *Winthrop Papers*, III, 270-271; Colony of Massachusetts Bay to John Winthrop, Jr., July 4, 1636, *ibid.*, 284-285.

9. *Winthrop's Journal*, I, 183-184; Thomas Cobbet, "A Narrative of New England's Deliverances," *New England Historical and Genealogical Register*, VII (1853), 211-212.

10. *Winthrop's Journal*, I, 184-185; Bradford, *Of Plymouth Plantation*, 292; William Hubbard, *The*

History of the Indian Wars in New England . . . , ed. Samuel G. Drake (Roxbury, Mass., 1865), II, 11.

11. John Underhill, "News from America . . . ," in Massachusetts Historical Society, *Collections*, 3d Ser., VI (Boston, 1837), 4-10, is the only eyewitness account of the Endicott expedition. See also *Winthrop's Journal*, I, 187-189; and Lion Gardiner, *A History of the Pequot War* . . . (Cincinnati, 1860), 12-13.

12. Gardiner, *History of the Pequot War*, 14-21; *Winthrop's Journal*, I, 191-192, 194, 208, 212; Lion Gardiner to John Winthrop, Jr., Mar. 23, 1637, in *Winthrop Papers*, III, 381-382.

13. Underhill, "News from America," 12; J. Franklin Jameson, ed., *Johnson's Wonder-Working Providence, 1628-1651* (New York, 1910), 149; Nathaniel B. Shurtleff, ed., *Records of the Governor and Company of the Massachusetts Bay in New England*, I (Boston, 1853), 192; J. Hammond Trumbull, ed., *The Public Records of the Colony of Connecticut*, I (Hartford, 1850), 9.

14. Williams to John Mason, June 22, 1670, in Narragansett Club, *Publs.*, VI (Providence, 1874), 338; *Winthrop's Journal*, I, 192-194.

15. *Winthrop's Journal*, I, 62; Bradford, *Of Plymouth Plantation*, 258.

16. Hooker to John Winthrop, spring 1637, in *Winthrop Papers*, III, 407.

17. John Mason, "A Brief History of the Pequot War . . . ," in Mass. Hist. Soc., *Colls.*, 2d Ser., VIII (Boston, 1819), 148.

18. Philip Vincent, "*A True* Relation of the Late Battell Fought in *New-England*, between the English and the Pequet Salvages . . ." in Mass. Hist. Soc., *Colls.*, 3d Ser., VI (Boston, 1837), 40. *Winthrop's Journal*, I, 229.

19. *Winthrop's Journal*, I, 102-108; Bradford, *Of Plymouth Plantation*, 268-269; Roger Clap, "Memoirs of Capt. Roger Clap," in Alexander Young, *Chronicles of the First Planters of the Colony of Massachusetts Bay, from 1623 to 1636* (Boston, 1846), 363; *Records of Massachusetts Bay*, I, 108.

20. Bradford, *Of Plymouth Plantation*, 269-271; *Winthrop's Journal*, I, 118; Clap, "Memoirs," in Young, *Chronicles of the First Planters*, 363.

21. *Winthrop's Journal*, I, 186.

22. Underhill, "News from America," 7. Underhill reported that 14 Indians were killed and 40 wounded on Block Island. The Narragansetts later informed the English that there had been only one Indian fatality. (*Winthrop's Journal*, I, 189-190.) In any event, since the island was under the jurisdiction of the Narragansetts, this phase of the Endicott expedition was not considered as an attack on the Pequots; rather, it was a vengeful retaliation for the murder of Oldham.

23. Underhill, "News from America," 7.

24. *Ibid.*, 7-10; *Winthrop's Journal*, I, 188-189.

25. *Winthrop's Journal*, I, 189-190; Gardiner, *History of the Pequot War*, 13; Underhill, "News from America," 11. Gardiner claimed that only one Pequot had been killed, and that Cutshamekin was the slayer. Winthrop reports two killed, while Underhill referred to "certain numbers of theirs slain, and many wounded." The Narragansetts later told Winthrop that 13 Pequots had been killed and 40 wounded. While there is no way of knowing which of these figures is most accurate, it is interesting to note that the two earliest historians of the war accept the lowest figure, but do not place the blame on Cutshamekin. Hubbard, *History of the Indian Wars in New England*, II, 15; Increase Mather, *A Relation of the Troubles which have hapned in New-England, By reason of the Indians*

there . . . , ed. Samuel G. Drake under the title, *Early History of New England* . . . (Boston, 1864), 162.

26. *Winthrop's Journal*, II, 115-116; Gardiner, *History of the Pequot War*, 23-24; Jameson, ed., *Johnson's Wonder-Working Providence*, 164. Although there is no record of Roger Williams's opinion, he undoubtedly was appalled by the severity of the attacks on the Block Islanders and Pequots.

27. Williams to John Winthrop, ca. Sept. 1636, *Winthrop Papers*, III, 298. The text of the letter strongly suggests that it is misdated in the published collection; it was probably written in early Aug.

28. Bradford, *Of Plymouth Plantation*, 294.

29. For example, see Pearce, *Savages of America*, 20.

30. As the Commissioners of the United Colonies put it in 1653, "The English . . . did generally purchase to themselves from the Indians the true propriators a Just Right and title to the lands they ment to Improve if they found not the place a Vacuum Domicilium." Nathaniel B. Shurtleff and David Pulsifer, eds., *Records of the Colony of New Plymouth, in New England* (Boston, 1855-61), X, 13. While there existed, of course, much room for dispute over what land was occupied and what was *vacuum domicilium*, the Indians rarely seem to have felt aggrieved. See also *ibid.*, IV, 19; IX, 11, 112; *Records of Connecticut*, I, 19; *Records of Massachusetts Bay*, III, 281-282; Charles J. Hoadley, ed., *Records of the Colony of Jurisdiction of New Haven* . . . (Hartford, 1858), 518, 593-594; *Winthrop's Journal*, I, 294. Unpublished evidence can be found in such depositories as Massachusetts Archives (vol. XXX), State House, Boston; Connecticut Archives (Indians, vols. I and II), State Library, Hartford; Mass. Hist. Soc. (Miscellaneous Bound Manuscripts, vols. I and II), Boston. For a different interpretation see Chester E. Eisinger, "The Puritans' Justification for Taking the Land," *Essex Institute Historical Collections*, LXXXIV (Salem, Mass., 1948), 131-143, and Wilcomb E. Washburn, "The Moral and Legal Justifications for Dispossessing the Indians," in James Morton Smith, ed., *Seventeenth-Century America: Essays in Colonial History* (Chapel Hill, 1959), 15-32.

Indian removal and land allotment: The civilized tribes and Jacksonian justice

Mary E. Young

There are a few more painful chapters in American history than the removal of the civilized tribes from their homes in Georgia and Alabama, and Mississippi to Oklahoma. The episode brought into clear focus problems in federal Indian policy. Ever since George Washington, the United States had followed the colonial precedent of treating Indian tribes as "nations." This might have been practical when tribes occupied land beyond white governmental jurisdiction. But what happened when the Indians resided inside the boundary of a duly constituted state? Could tribal organizations remain separate and occupy enclaves in which the government's writs could not run? Or did state laws bind the Indians as other people living within a commonwealth? At the heart of the matter was a question that has vexed every civilized society that has encountered a primitive people, whether in the United States, Canada, Australia, South Africa, or South America: Should the primitive society be left alone to develop in its own way and on its own terms, or should it be forced to adopt the culture of the technologically advanced state? Americans have never been able to answer this question, and national policies toward the Indians have gone in both directions, often at the same time.

Mary Young, who teaches history at the University of Rochester, in this essay demonstrates the problems confronting Georgians and their neighbors in Alabama and Mississippi in the Jacksonian era.

For further reading: Henry T. Malone, *Cherokees of the Old South: A People in Transition* (Athens: University of Georgia Press, 1956); Arthur H. DeRosier, Jr., *The Removal of the Choctaw Indians* (Knoxville: University of Tennessee Press, 1970)*; Angie Debo, *The Rise and Fall of the Choctaw Republic* (Norman: University of Oklahoma Press, 1934); Angie Debo, *The Road to Disappearance* (Norman: University of Oklahoma Press, 1941); Grant Foreman, *Indian Removal: The Emigration of the Five Civilized Tribes of Indians* (Norman: University of Oklahoma Press, 1953); Thurman Gabriel, *Elias Boudinot* (Norman: University of Oklahoma Press, 1941); Mary E. Young, *Redskins, Ruffleshirts, and Rednecks: Indian Allotments in Alabama and Mississippi, 1830-1860* (Norman: University of Oklahoma Press, 1961)

*Available in paperback.

Reprinted with permission from *American Historical Review*, LXIV (October 1958), 31-45.

By the year 1830, the vanguard of the southern frontier had crossed the Mississippi and was pressing through Louisiana, Arkansas, and Missouri. But the line of settlement was by no means as solid as frontier lines were classically supposed to be. East of the Mississippi, white occupancy was limited by Indian tenure of northeastern Georgia, enclaves in western North Carolina and southern Tennessee, eastern Alabama, and the northern two thirds of Mississippi. In this twenty-five-million-acre domain lived nearly 60,000 Cherokees, Creeks, Choctaws, and Chickasaws.[1]

The Jackson administration sought to correct this anomaly by removing the tribes beyond the reach of white settlements, west of the Mississippi. As the President demanded of Congress in December, 1830: "What good man would prefer a country covered with forests and ranged by a few thousand savages to our extensive Republic, studded with cities, towns, and prosperous farms, embellished with all the improvements which art can devise or industry execute, occupied by more than 12,000,000 happy people, and filled with all the blessings of liberty, civilization, and religion?"[2]

The President's justification of Indian removal was the one usually applied to the displacement of the Indians by newer Americans—the superiority of a farming to a hunting culture, and of Anglo-American "liberty, civilization, and religion" to the strange and barbarous way of the red man. The superior capacity of the farmer to exploit the gifts of nature and of nature's God was one of the principal warranties of the triumph of westward-moving "civilization."[3]

Such a rationalization had one serious weakness as an instrument of policy. The farmer's right of eminent domain over the lands of the savage could be asserted consistently only so long as the tribes involved were "savage." The southeastern tribes, however, were agriculturists as well as hunters. For two or three generations prior to 1830, farmers among them fenced their plantations and "mixed their labor with the soil," making it their private property according to accepted definitions of natural law. White traders who settled among the Indians in the mid-eighteenth century gave original impetus to this imitation of Anglo-American agricultural methods. Later, agents of the United States encouraged the traders and mechanics, their half-breed descendants, and their fullblood imitators who settled out from tribal villages, fenced their farms, used the plow, and cultivated cotton and corn for the market. In the decade following the War of 1812, missionaries of various Protestant denominations worked among the Cherokees, Choctaws, and Chickasaws, training hundreds of Indian children in the agricultural, mechanical, and household arts and introducing both children and parents to the further blessings of literacy and Christianity.[4]

The "civilization" of a portion of these tribes embarassed United States policy in more ways than one. Long-term contact between the southeastern tribes and white traders, missionaries, and government officials created and trained numerous half-breeds. The half-breed men acted as intermediaries between the less sophisticated Indians and the white Americans. Acquiring direct or indirect control of tribal politics, they often determined the outcome of treaty negotiations. Since they proved to be skillful bargainers, it became common practice to win their assistance by thinly veiled bribery. The rise of the half-breeds to power, the rewards they received, and their efforts on behalf of tribal reform gave rise to bitter opposition. By the mid-1820's, this opposition made it dangerous for them to sell tribal lands. Furthermore, many of the new leaders had valuable plantations, mills, and trading establishments on these lands. Particularly among the Cherokees and Choctaws, they took pride in their achievements and those of their people in assimilating the trappings of civilization. As "founding Fathers," they prized the political and territorial integrity of the newly organized Indian "nations." These interests and convictions gave birth to a fixed determination, embodied in tribal laws and inter-tribal agreements, that no more cessions of land should be made. The tribes must be permitted to develop their new way of life in what was left of their ancient domain.[5]

Today it is a commonplace of studies in culture contact that the assimilation of alien habits affects different individuals and social strata in different ways and that their levels of acculturation vary considerably. Among the American Indian tribes, it is most often the families with white or half-breed models who most readily adopt the Anglo-American way of life. It is not surprising that half-breeds and whites living among the Indians should use their position as go-betweens to improve their status and power among the natives. Their access to influence and their efforts toward reform combine with pressures from outside to disturb old life ways, old securities, and established prerogatives. Re-sistance to their leadership and to the cultural alternatives they espouse is a fertile source of intratribal factions.[6]

To Jacksonian officials, however, the tactics of the half-breeds and the struggles among tribal factions seemed to reflect a diabolical plot. Treaty negotiators saw the poverty and "depravity" of the common Indian, who suffered from the scarcity of game, the mission-ary attacks on his accustomed habits and ceremonies, and the ravages of "demon rum" and who failed to find solace in the values of Christian and commercial civilization. Not unreasonably, they concluded that it was to the interest of the tribesman to remove west of the Mississippi. There, sheltered from the intruder and the whisky merchant, he could lose his savagery while improving his nobility. Since this seemed so obviously to the Indian's interest, the negotiators conveniently concluded that it was also his desire. What, then, deterred emigration? Only the rapacity of the half-breeds, who were unwilling to give up their extensive properties and their exalted position.[7]

These observers recognized that the government's difficulties were in part of its own making. The United States had pursued an essentially contradictory policy toward the Indians, encouraging both segregation and assimilation. Since Jefferson's administration, the government had tried periodically to secure the emigration of the eastern tribes across the Mississippi. At the same time, it had paid agents and subsidized missionaries who encouraged the Indian to follow in the white man's way. Thus it had helped create the class of tribesmen skilled in agriculture, pecuniary accumulation, and political leadership. Furthermore, by encouraging the southeastern Indians to become cultivators and Chris-tians, the government had undermined its own moral claim to eminent domain over tribal lands. The people it now hoped to displace could by no stretch of dialectic be classed as mere wandering savages.[8]

By the time Jackson became President, then, the situation of the United States vis-à-vis the southeastern tribes was superficially that of irresistible force and immovable object. But the President, together with such close advisers as Secretary of War John H. Eaton and General John Coffee, viewed the problem in a more encouraging perspective. They believed that the government faced not the intent of whole tribes to remain near the bones of their ancestors but the selfish determination of a few quasi Indian leaders to retain their riches and their ill-used power. Besides, the moral right of the civilized tribes to their lands was a claim not on their whole domain but rather on the part cultivated by individuals. Both the Indian's natural right to his land and his political capacity for keeping it were products of his imitation of white "civilization." Both might be eliminated by a rigorous application of the principle that to treat an Indian fairly was to treat him like a white man. Treaty negotiations by the tried methods of purchase and selective bribery had failed. The use of naked force without the form of voluntary agreement was forbidden by custom, by conscience, and by fear that the administration's opponents would exploit religious sentiment which cherished the rights of the red man. But within the confines of legality and the formulas of voluntarism it was still possible to acquire the much coveted domain of the civilized tribes.

The technique used to effect this object was simple: the entire population of the tribes was forced to deal with white men on terms familiar only to the most acculturated portion of them. If the Indian is civilized, he can behave like a white man. Then let him take for his own as much land as he can cultivate, become a citizen of the state where he lives, and accept the burdens which citizenship entails. If he is not capable of living like this, he should be liberated from the tyranny of his chiefs and allowed to follow his own best interest by emigrating beyond the farthest frontiers of white settlement. By the restriction of the civilized to the lands they cultivate and by the emigration of the savages millions of acres will be opened to white settlement.

The first step dictated by this line of reasoning was the extension of state laws over the Indian tribes. Beginning soon after Jackson's election, Georgia, Alabama, Mississippi, and Tennessee gradually brought the Indians inside their borders under their jurisdiction. Thus an Indian could be sued for trespass or debt, though only in Mississippi and Tennessee was his testimony invariably acceptable in a court of law. In Mississippi, the tribesmen were further harassed by subjection—or the threat of subjection—to such duties as mustering with the militia, working on roads, and paying taxes. State laws establishing county governments within the tribal domains and, in some cases, giving legal protection to purchasers of Indian improvements encouraged the intrusion of white settlers on Indian lands. The laws nullified the legal force of Indian customs, except those relating to marriage. They provided heavy penalties for anyone who might enact or enforce tribal law. Finally, they threatened punishment to any person who might attempt to deter another from signing a removal treaty or enrolling for emigration. The object of these laws was to destroy the tribal governments and to thrust upon individual Indians the uncongenial alternative of adjusting to the burdens of citizenship or removing beyond state jurisdiction.[9]

The alternative was not offered on the unenlightened supposition that the Indians generally were capable of managing their affairs unaided in a white man's world. Governor Gayle of Alabama, addressing the "former chiefs and headmen of the Creek Indians" in June of 1834 urged them to remove from the state on the grounds that

you speak a different language from ours. You do not understand our laws and from your habits, cannot be brought to understand them. You are ignorant of the arts of civilized life. You have not like your white neighbors been raised in habits of industry and economy, the only means by which anyone can live, in settled countries, in even tolerable comfort. You know nothing of the skill of the white man in trading and making bargains, and cannot be guarded against the artful contrivances which dishonest men will resort to, to obtain your property under forms of contracts. In all these respects you are unequal to the white men, and if your people remain where they are, you will soon behold them in a miserable, degraded, and destitute condition. [10]

The intentions of federal officials who favored the extension of state laws are revealed in a letter written to Jackson by General Coffee. Referring to the Cherokees, Coffee remarked:

Deprive the chiefs of the power they now possess, take from them their own code of laws, and reduce them to plain citizenship . . . and they will soon determine to move, and then there will be no difficulty in getting the poor Indians to give their consent. All this will be done by the State of Georgia if the U. States do not interfere with her law– . . . This will of course silence those in our country who constantly seek for causes to complain–It may indeed turn them loose upon Georgia, but that matters not, it is Georgia who clamors for the Indian lands, and she alone is entitled to the blame if any there be. [11]

Even before the laws were extended, the threat of state jurisdiction was used in confidential "talks" to the chiefs. After the states had acted, the secretary of war instructed each Indian agent to explain to his charges the meaning of state jurisdiction and to inform them that the President could not protect them against the enforcement of the laws. [12] Although the Supreme Court, in *Worcester* vs. *Georgia*, decided that the state had no right to extend its laws over the Cherokee nation, the Indian tribes being "domestic dependent nations" with limits defined by treaty, the President refused to enforce this decision. [13] There was only one means by which the government might have made "John Marshall's decision" effective–directing federal troops to exclude state officials and other intruders from the Indian domain. In January, 1832, the President informed an Alabama congressman that the United States government no longer assumed the right to remove citizens of Alabama from the Indian country. By this time, the soldiers who had protected the territory of the southeastern tribes against intruders had been withdrawn. In their unwearying efforts to pressure the Indians into ceding their land, federal negotiators emphasized the terrors of state jurisdiction. [14]

Congress in May, 1830, complemented the efforts of the states by appropriating $500,000 and authorizing the President to negotiate removal treaties with all the tribes east of the Mississippi. [15] The vote on this bill was close in both houses. By skillful use of pamphlets, petitions, and lobbyists, missionary organizations had enlisted leading congressmen in their campaign against the administration's attempt to force the tribes to emigrate. [16] In the congressional debates, opponents of the bill agreed that savage tribes were duty-bound to relinquish their hunting grounds to the agriculturist, but they argued that the southeastern tribes were no longer savage. In any case, such relinquishment must be made in a freely contracted treaty. The extension of state laws over the Indian country was coercion; this made the negotiation of a free contract impossible. Both supporters and opponents of the bill agreed on one cardinal point–the Indian's moral right to keep his land depended on his actual cultivation of it. [17]

A logical corollary of vesting rights in land in proportion to cultivation was the reservation to individuals of as much land as they had improved at the time a treaty was signed. In 1816, Secretary of War William H. Crawford had proposed such reservations, or allotments, as a means of accommodating the removal policy to the program of assimilation. According to Crawford's plan, individual Indians who had demonstrated their capacity for civilization by establishing farms and who were willing to become citizens should be given the option of keeping their cultivated lands, by fee simple title, rather than emigrating. This offer was expected to reconcile the property-loving half-breeds to the policy of emigration. It also recognized their superior claim, as cultivators, on the regard and generosity of the government. The proposal was based on the assumption that few of the Indians were sufficiently civilized to want to become full-time farmers or state citizens. [18]

The Crawford policy was applied in the Cherokee treaties of 1817 and 1819 and the Choctaw treaty of 1820. These agreements offered fee simple allotments to heads of Indian families having improved lands within the areas ceded to the government. Only 311 Cherokees and eight Choctaws took advantage of the offer. This seemed to bear out the assumption that only a minority of the tribesmen would care to take allotments. Actually, these experiments were not reliable. In both cases, the tribes ceded only a fraction of their holdings. Comparatively few took allotments; but on the other hand, few emigrated. The majority simply remained within the diminished tribal territories east of the Mississippi. [19]

The offer of fee simple allotments was an important feature of the negotiations with the tribes in the 1820's. When the extension of state laws made removal of the tribes imperative, it was to be expected that allotments would comprise part of the consideration offered for the ceded lands. Both the ideology which rationalized the removal policy and the conclusions erroneously drawn from experience with the earlier allotment treaties led government negotiators to assume that a few hundred allotments at most would be required.

The Choctaws were the first to cede their eastern lands. The treaty of Dancing Rabbit Creek, signed in September, 1830, provided for several types of allotment. Special reservations were given to the chiefs and their numerous family connections; a possible 1,600 allotments of 80 to 480 acres, in proportion to the size of the beneficiary's farm, were offered others who intended to emigrate. These were intended for sale to private persons or to the government, so that the Indian might get the maximum price for his improvements. The fourteenth article of the treaty offered any head of an Indian family who did not plan to emigrate the right to take up a quantity of land proportional to the number of his dependents. At the end of five years' residence those who recived these allotments were to have fee simple title to their lands and become citizens. It was expected that approximately two hundred persons would take land under this article. [20]

The Creeks refused to sign any agreements promising to emigrate, but their chiefs were persuaded that the only way to put an end to intrusions on their lands was to sign an allotment treaty. [21] In March, 1832, a Creek delegation in Washington signed a treaty calling for the allotment of 320 acres to each head of a family, the granting of certain supplementary lands to the chiefs and to orphans, and the cession of the remaining territory to the United States. If the Indian owners remained on their allotments for five years, they were to receive fee simple titles and become citizens. [22] Returning to Alabama, the chiefs informed their people that they had not actually sold the tribal lands but "had only made each individual their own guardian, that they might take care of their own possessions, and act as agents for themselves. [23]

Unlike the Creeks, the Chickasaws were willing to admit the inevitability of removal. But they needed land east of the Mississippi on which they might live until they acquired a home in the west. The Chickasaw treaty of May, 1832, therefore, provided generous allotments for heads of families, ranging from 640 to 3,200 acres, depending on the size of the family and the number of its slaves. These allotments were to be auctioned publicly when the tribe emigrated and the owners compensated for their improvements out of the proceeds.[24] Although the fullblood Chickasaws apparently approved of the plan for a collective sale of the allotments, the half-breeds, abetted by white traders and planters, persuaded the government to allow those who held allotments to sell them individually.[25] An amended treaty of 1834 complied with the half-breeds' proposals. It further stipulated that leading half-breeds and the old chiefs of the tribe comprise a committee to determine the competence of individual Chickasaws to manage their property. Since the committee itself disposed of the lands of the "incompetents," this gave both protection to the unsophisticated and additional advantage to the half-breeds.[26]

Widespread intrusion on Indian lands began with the extension of state laws over the tribal domains. In the treaties of cession, the government promised to remove intruders, but its policy in this respect was vacillating and ineffective. Indians whose allotments covered valuable plantations proved anxious to promote the sale of their property by allowing buyers to enter the ceded territory as soon as possible. Once this group of whites was admitted, it became difficult to discriminate against others. Thus a large number of intruders settled among the Indians with the passive connivance of the War Department and the tribal leaders. The task of removing them was so formidable that after making a few gestures the government generally evaded its obligation. The misery of the common Indians, surrounded by intruders and confused by the disruption of tribal authority, was so acute that any method for securing their removal seemed worth trying. Furthermore, their emigration would serve the interest of white settlers, land speculators, and their representatives in Washington. The government therefore chose to facilitate the sale of allotments even before the Indians received fee simple title to them.[27]

The right to sell his allotment was useful to the sophisticated tribesman with a large plantation. Such men were accustomed to selling their crops and hiring labor. Through their experience in treaty negotiations, they had learned to bargain over the price of lands. Many of them received handsome payment for their allotments. Some kept part of their holdings and remained in Alabama and Mississippi as planters—like others planters, practicing as land speculators on the side.[28] Nearly all the Indians had some experience in trade, but to most of them the conception of land as a salable commodity was foreign. They had little notion of the exact meaning of an "acre" or the probable value of their allotments.[29] The government confused them still further by parceling out the lands according to Anglo-American, rather than aboriginal notions of family structure and land ownership. Officials insisted, for example, that the "father" rather than the "mother" must be defined as head of the family and righteously refused to take cognizance of the fact that many of the "fathers" had "a plurality of wives."[30]

Under these conditions, it is not surprising the the common Indian's legal freedom of contract in selling his allotment did not necessarily lead him to make the best bargain possible in terms of his pecuniary interests. Nor did the proceeds of the sales transform each seller into an emigrant of large independent means. A right of property and freedom to contract for its sale did not automatically invest the Indian owner with habits, values, and skills of a sober land speculator. His acquisition of property and freedom actually increased his dependence on those who traditionally mediated for him in contractual relations with white Americans.

Prominent among these mediators were white men with Indian wives who made their living as planters and traders in the Indian nations, men from nearby settlements who traded with the leading Indians or performed legal services for them, and interpreters. In the past, such individuals had been appropriately compensated for using their influence in favor of land cessions. It is likely that their speculative foresight was in part responsible for the allotment features in the treaties of the 1830's. When the process of allotting lands to individuals began, these speculative gentlemen made loans of whisky, muslin, horses, slaves, and other useful commodities to the new property-owner. They received in return the Indian's written promise to sell his allotment to them as soon as its boundaries were defined. Generally they were on hand to help him locate it on "desirable" lands. They, in turn, sold their "interest" in lands to men of capital. Government agents encouraged the enterprising investor, since it was in the Indian's interest and the government's policy that the lands be sold and the tribes emigrate.[31] Unfortunately, the community of interest among the government, the speculator, and the Indian proved largely fictitious. The speculator's interest in Indian lands led to frauds which impoverished the Indians, soiled the reputation of the government, and retarded the emigration of the tribes.

An important factor in this series of complications was the government's fallacious assumption that most of the "real Indians" were anxious to emigrate. Under the Choctaw treaty, for example, registration for fee simple allotments was optional, the government expecting no more than two hundred registrants. When several hundred full-bloods applied for lands, the Choctaw agent assumed that they were being led astray by "designing men" and told them they must emigrate. Attorneys took up the Choctaw claims, located thousands of allotments in hopes that Congress would confirm them, and supported their clients in Mississippi for twelve to fifteen years while the government debated and acted on the validity of the claims. There was good reason for this delay. Settlers and rival speculators, opposing confirmation of the claims, advanced numerous depositions asserting that the attorneys, in their enterprising search for clients, had materially increased the number of claimants.[32] Among the Creeks, the Upper Towns, traditionally the conservative faction of the tribe, refused to sell their allotments. Since the Lower Towns proved more compliant, speculators hired willing Indians from the Lower Towns to impersonate the unwilling owners. They then bought the land from the impersonators. The government judiciously conducted several investigations of these frauds, but in the end the speculators outmaneuvered the investigators. Meanwhile, the speculators kept the Indians from emigrating until their contracts were approved. Only the outbreak of fighting between starving Creeks and their settler neighbors enabled the government, under pretext of a pacification, to remove the tribe.[33]

Besides embarrassing the government, the speculators contributed to the demoralization of the Indians. Universal complaint held that after paying the tribesman for his land they often borrowed back the money without serious intent of repaying it, or recovered it in return for overpriced goods, of which a popular article was whisky. Apprised of this situation, Secretary of War Lewis Cass replied that once the Indian had been paid for his land, the War Department had no authority to circumscribe his freedom to do what he wished with the proceeds.[34]

Nevertheless, within their conception of the proper role of government, officials who dealt with the tribes tried to be helpful. Although the Indian must be left free to contract for the sale of his lands, the United States sent agents to determine the validity of the contracts. These agents sometimes refused to approve a contract that did not specify a fair price for the land in question. They also refused official sanction when it could not be shown that the Indian owner had at some time been in possession of the sum stipulated.[35] This protective action on the part of the government, together with its several investigations into frauds in the sale of Indian lands, apparently did secure the payment of more money than the tribesmen might otherwise have had. But the effort was seriously hampered by the near impossibility of obtaining disinterested testimony.

In dealing with the Chickasaws, the government managed to avoid most of the vexing problems which had arisen in executing the allotment program among their southeastern neighbors. This was due in part to the improvement of administrative procedures, in part to the methods adopted by speculators in Chickasaw allotments, and probably most of all to the inflated value of cotton lands during the period in which the Chickasaw territory was sold. Both the government and the Chickasaws recognized that the lands granted individuals under the treaty were generally to be sold, not settled. They therefore concentrated on provisions for supervising sales and safeguarding the proceeds.[36] Speculators in Chickasaw lands, having abundant resources, paid an average price of $1.70 per acre. The Chickasaws thereby received a better return than the government did at its own auctions. The buyers' generosity may be attributed to their belief that the Chickasaw lands represented the last first-rate cotton country within what were then the boundaries of the public domain. In their pursuit of a secure title, untainted by fraud, the capitalists operating in the Chickasaw cession established a speculators' claim association which settled disputes among rival purchasers. Thus they avoided the plots, counterplots, and mutual recriminations which had hampered both speculators and government in their dealings with the Creeks and Choctaws.[37]

A superficially ironic consequence of the allotment policy as a method of acquiring land for white settlers was the fact that it facilitated the engrossment of land by speculators. With their superior command of capital and the influence it would buy, speculators acquired 80 to 90 per cent of the lands allotted to the southeastern tribesmen.[38]

For most of the Indian beneficiaries of the policy, its most important consequence was to leave them landless. After selling their allotment, or a claim to it, they might take to the swamp, live for a while on the bounty of a still hopeful speculator, or scavenge on their settler neighbors. But ultimately most of them faced the alternative of emigration or destitution, and chose to emigrate. The machinations of the speculators and the hopes they nurtured that the Indians might somehow be able to keep a part of their allotted lands made the timing of removals less predictable than it might otherwise have been. This unpredictability compounded the evils inherent in a mass migration managed by a government committed to economy and unversed in the arts of economic planning. The result was the "Trail of Tears."[39]

The spectacular frauds committed among the Choctaws and Creeks, the administrative complications they created and the impression they gave that certain self-styled champions of the people were consorting with the avaricious speculator gave the allotment policy a bad reputation. The administration rejected it in dealing with the Cherokees,[40] and the policy was not revived on any considerable scale until 1854, when it was applied, with similar consequences, to the Indians of Kansas.[41] In the 1880's, when allotment in severalty became a basic feature of American Indian policy, the "civilized tribes," then in Oklahoma, strenuously resisted its application to them. They cited their memories of the 1830's as an important reason for their intransigence.[42]

The allotment treaties of the 1830's represent an attempt to apply Anglo-American notions of justice, which enshrined private property in land and freedom of contract as virtually absolute values, to Indian tribes whose tastes and traditions were otherwise. Their history illustrates the limitations of intercultural application of the Golden Rule. In a more practical sense, the treaties typified an effort to force on the Indians the alternative of complete assimiliation or complete segregation by placing individuals of varying levels of sophistication in situations where they must use the skills of businessmen or lose their means of livelihood. This policy secured tribal lands while preserving the forms of respect for property rights and freedom of contract, but it proved costly to both the government and the Indians.

How lightly that cost was reckoned, and how enduring the motives and rationalizations that gave rise to it, may be gathered from the subsequent experience of the southeastern tribes in Oklahoma. There, early in the twentieth century, the allotment policy was again enforced, with safeguards hardly more helpful to the unsophisticated than those of the 1830's. Once more, tribal land changed owners for the greater glory of liberty, civilization, and profit.[43]

Notes

This article, in slightly different form, was delivered as a paper at the joint meeting of the Southern Historical Association and the American Historical Association in New York City, December 29, 1957.

1. Ellen C. Semple, *American History and Its Geographic Conditions* (Boston, Mass., 1933), p. 160; Charles C. Royce, "Indian Land Cessions in the United States," Bureau of American Ethnology, *Eighteenth Annual Report, 1896-1897* (2 vols., Washington, D. C., 1899), II, Plates 1, 2, 15, 48, 54-56.

2. James Richardson, *A Compilation of the Messages and Papers of the Presidents of the United States* (New York, 1897), III, 1084.

3. Roy H. Pearce, *The Savages of America: A Study of the Indian and the Idea of Civilization* (Baltimore, Md., 1953), p. 70; *House Report* 227, 21 Cong., 1 sess., pp. 4-5.

4. Moravian missionaries were in contact with the Cherokees as early as the 1750's. Henry T. Malone, *Cherokees of the Old South: A People in Transition* (Athens, Ga., 1956), p. 92. There is a voluminous literature on the "civilization" of the civilized tribes. Among secondary sources, the following contain especially useful information: Malone, *Cherokees*; Marion Starkey, *The Cherokee Nation* (New York, 1946); Angie Debo, *The Rise and Fall of the Choctaw Republic* (Norman, Okla., 1934) and *The Road to Disappearance* (Norman, Okla., 1941); Grant Foreman, *Indian Removal: The Emigration of the Five Civilized Tribes of Indians* (2d ed., Norman, Okla., 1953); Robert S. Cotterill, *The Southern Indians: The Story of the Civilized Tribes before Removal* (Norman, Okla., 1954); Merrit B. Pound, *Benjamin Hawkins, Indian Agent* (Athens, Ga., 1951). Among the richest source material for tracing the agricultural development of the tribes are the published writings of the Creek agent, Benjamin Hawkins: *Letters of Benjamin Hawkins, 1796-1806* in Georgia Historical Society *Collections, IX* (Savannah, 1916), and *Sketch of the Creek Country in the Years 1798 and 1799* in Georgia Historical Society *Publications*, III, (Americus, 1938). For the Choctaws and Cherokees, there is much information in the incoming correspondence of the American Board of Commissioners for Foreign Missions, Houghton Library, Harvard University. On the Chickasaws, see James Hull, "A Brief History of the Mississippi Territory," Mississippi Historical Society *Publications*, IX, (Jackson, 1906).

5. Paul W. Gates, "Introduction," *The John Tipton Papers* (3 vols., Indianapolis, Inc., 1942), I, 3-53; A. L. Kroeber, *Cultural and Natural Areas of Native North America* (Berkeley, Calif., 1939), pp. 62-63; John Terrell to General John Coffee, Sept. 15, 1829, Coffee Papers, Alabama Dept. of Archives and History; Campbell and Merriwether to Creek Chiefs, Dec. 9, 1824, *American State Papers: Indian Affairs*, II, 570; Clark, Hinds, and Coffee to James Barbour, Nov. 19, 1826, *ibid.*, p. 709.

6. See for example, Edward M. Bruner, "Primary Group Experience and the Processes of Acculturation," *American Anthropologist,* LVIII (Aug., 1956), 605-23; SSRC Summer Seminar on Acculturation, "Acculturation: An Exploratory Formulation," *American Anthropologist,* LVI (Dec., 1954), esp. pp. 980-86; Alexander Spoehr, "Changing Kinship Systems: A Study in the Acculturation of the Creeks, Cherokee, and Choctaw," Field Museum of Natural History, *Anthropological Series,* XXXIII, no. 4, esp. pp. 216-26.

7. Wilson Lumpkin, *The Removal of the Cherokee Indians from Georgia* (2 vols., New York, 1907), I, 61-77; Thomas L. McKenney to James Barbour, Dec. 27, 1826, *House Doc.* 28, 19 Cong., 2 sess., pp. 5-13; Andrew Jackson to Colonel Robert Butler, June 21, 1817, *Correspondence of Andrew Jackson,* ed. John Spencer Bassett (6 vols., Washington, D. C., 1926-28), II, 299.

8. For brief analyses of government policy, see Annie H. Abel, "The History of Events Resulting in Indian Consolidation West of the Mississippi," *Annual Report of the American Historical Association for the Year 1907* (2 vols., Washington, D. C., 1908), I, 233-450; George D. Harmon, *Sixty Years of Indian Affairs, 1789-1850* (Chapel Hill, N. Car., 1941).

9. Georgia, *Acts,* Dec. 12, 1828; Dec. 19, 1829; Alabama, *Acts,* Jan. 27, 1829; Dec. 31, 1831; Jan. 16, 1832; Dec. 18, 1832; Mississippi, *Acts,* Feb. 4, 1829; Jan. 19, 1830; Feb. 12, 1830; Dec. 9, 1831; Oct. 26, 1832; Tennessee, *Acts,* Nov. 8, 1833; George R. Gilmer to Augustus S. Clayton, June 7, 1830, Governor's Letterbook, 1829-31, p. 36, Georgia Dept. of Archives and History.

10. Governor John Gayle to former chiefs and headmen of the Creek Indians, June 16, 1834, Miscellaneous Letters to and from Governor Gayle, Alabama Dept. of Archives and History.

11. Feb. 3, 1830, Jackson Papers, Library of Congress.

12. John H. Eaton to John Crowell, Mar. 27, 1829, Office of Indian Affairs, Letters Sent, V, 372-73, Records of the Bureau of Indian Affairs, National Archives; Middleton Mackey to John H. Eaton, Nov. 27, 1829, Choctaw Emigration File III, *ibid.*; Andrew Jackson to Major David Haley, Oct. 10, 1829, Jackson Papers.

13. 6 *Peters,* 515-97.

14. Wiley Thompson to Messrs. Drew and Reese, Jan. 18, 1832, Indian Letters, 1782-1839, pp. 173-74, Georgia Dept. of Archives and History; John H. Eaton to Jackson, Feb. 21, 1831, *Sen. Doc.* 65, 21 Cong., 2 sess., p. 6; Cyrus Kingsbury to Jeremiah Evarts, Aug. 11, 1830, American Board of Commissioners for Foreign Missions Manuscripts; Tuskeneha to the President, May 21, 1831, Creek File 176, Records of the Bureau of Indian Affairs; Journal of the Commissioners for the Treaty of Dancing Rabbit Creek, *Sen. Doc.* 512, 23 Cong., 1 sess., p. 257.

15. 4 *Statutes-at-Large,* 411-12.

16. J. Orin Oliphant, ed., *Through the South and West with Jeremiah Evarts in 1826* (Lewisburg, Pa., 1956), pp. 47-61; Jeremiah Evarts to Rev. William Weisner, Nov. 27, 1829, American Board of Commissioners for Foreign Missions Manuscripts; *Sen. Docs.* 56, 59, 66, 73, 74, 76, 77, 92, 96, 21 Cong., 1 sess.

17. Gales and Seaton, *Register of Debates in Congress,* VI, 311, 312, 320, 357, 361, 1022, 1024, 1039, 1061, 1110, 1135.

18. *American State Papers: Indian Affairs,* II, 27. A general history of the allotment policy is Jay P. Kinney, *A Continent Lost—A Civilization Won: Indian Land Tenure in America* (Baltimore, Md., 1937).

19. 7 *Statutes-at-Large,* 156-60, 195-200, 210-14; Cherokee Reservation Book, Records of the Bureau

of Indian Affairs; Special Reserve Book A, *ibid.*; James Barbour to the Speaker of the House, Jan. 23, 1828, *American State Papers: Public Lands*, V, 396-97.

20. 7 *Statutes-at-Large*, 334-41; manuscript records of negotiations are in Choctaw File 112, Records of the Bureau of Indian Affairs.

21. John Crowell to Lewis Cass, Jan. 25, 1832, Creek File 178, Records of the Bureau of Indian Affairs.

22. 7 *Statutes-at-Large*, 366-68.

23. John Scott to Lewis Cass, Nov. 12, 1835, Creek File 193, Records of the Bureau of Indian Affairs.

24. 7 *Statutes-at-Large*, 381-89.

25. John Terrell to Henry Cook, Oct. 29, 1832 (copy), John D. Terrell Papers, Alabama Dept. of Archives and History; Benjamin Reynolds to John Coffee, Dec. 12, 1832, Chickasaw File 83, Records of the Bureau of Indian Affairs; Terrell to John Tyler, Feb. 26, 1841 (draft), Terrell Papers; G. W. Long to John Coffee, Dec. 15, 1832, Coffee Papers; Rev. T. C. Stuart to Daniel Green, Oct. 14, 1833, American Board of Commissioners for Foreign Missions Manuscripts.

26. 7 *Statutes-at-Large*, 450-57.

27. William Ward to Secretary of War, Oct. 22, 1831, Choctaw Reserve File 133; Mushulatubbee to Lewis Cass, Feb. 9, 1832, Choctaw File 113; W. S. Colquhoun to General George S. Gibson, Apr. 20, 1832, Choctaw Emigration File 121; A. Campbell to Secretary of War, Aug. 5, 1832, Choctaw File 113; John Kurtz to Benjamin Reynolds, Aug. 9, 1833, Office of Indian Affairs, Letters Sent, XI, 74; S. C. Barton to Elbert Herring, Nov. 11, 1833, Choctaw File 113; William M. Gwin to Lewis Cass, Apr. 8, 1834, Choctaw File 84, Records of the Bureau of Indian Affairs; Mary E. Young, "The Creek Frauds: A Study in Conscience and Corruption," *Mississippi Valley Historical Review*, XLVII (Dec., 1955), 415-19.

28. Benjamin Reynolds to Lewis Cass, Dec. 9, 1832, Apr. 29, 1835, Chickasaw File 83, 85, Records of the Bureau of Indian Affairs; David Haley to Jackson, Apr. 15, 1831, *Sen. Doc.* 512, 23 Cong., I sess., p. 426; Elbert Herring to George W. Elliott, Jan. 23, 1833, Office of Indian Affairs, Letters Sent, IX, 516, Records of the Bureau of Indian Affairs; J. J. Albert to J. R. Poinsett, July 19, 1839, Creek File 220, *ibid.* See Special Reserve Books and Special Reserve Files A and C, and William Carroll's List of Certified Contracts for the Sale of Chickasaw Reservations, Special File, Chickasaw, Records of the Bureau of Indian Affairs, and compare Chickasaw Location Book, Records of the Bureau of Land Management, National Archives.

29. George S. Snyderman, "Concepts of Land Ownership among the Iroquois and their Neighbors," in *Symposium on Local Variations in Iroquois Culture*, ed. William N. Fenton, Bureau of American Ethnology *Bulletin 149* (Washington, D. C., 1951), pp. 16-26; Petition of Choctaw Chiefs and Headmen, Mar. 2, 1832, Choctaw Reserve File 133; James Colbert to Lewis Cass, June 5, 1835, Chickasaw File 84; Benjamin Reynolds to Elbert Herring, Mar. 11, 1835, Chickasaw File 85, Records of the Bureau of Indian Affairs.

30. Memorial of Chickasaw Chiefs to the President, Nov. 25, 1835, Chickasaw File 84; Thomas J. Abbott and E. Parsons, Sept. 7, 1832, *Sen. Doc.* 512, 23 Cong., I sess., pp. 443-44; Elbert Herring to E. Parsons, B. S. Parsons, and John Crowell, Oct. 10, 1832, *ibid.*, p. 524; Leonard Tarrant to E. Herring, May 15, 1833, Creek File 202, Records of the Bureau of Indian Affairs; Alexander Spoehr, "Kinship Systems," pp. 201-31; John R. Swanton, *Indians of the Southeastern United States*, Bureau of American Ethnology *Bulletin 137* (Washington, D. C., 1946).

31. John Coffee to Andrew Jackson, July 10, 1830, Creek File 192, Records of the Bureau of Indian Affairs; John Crowell to John H. Eaton, Aug. 8, 1830, Creek File 175, *ibid.*, John H. Brodnax to

Lewis Cass, Mar. 12, 1832, *Sen. Doc.* 512, 23 Cong., I sess., III, 258-59; John Terrell to General John Coffee, Sept. 15 1829, Coffee Papers; J. J. Abert to [Lewis Cass], June 13, 1833, Creek File 202, Records of the Bureau of Indian Affairs; contract between Daniel Wright and Mingo Mushulatubbee, Oct. 7, 1830, *American State Papers: Public Lands*, VII, 19; W. S. Colquhoun to Lewis Cass, Sept. 20, 1833, *ibid.*, p. 13; Chapman Levy to Joel R. Poinsett, June 19, 1837, Choctaw Reserve File 139, Records of the Bureau of Indian Affairs; James Colbert to Lewis Cass, June 5, 1835, Chickasaw File 84, *ibid*; Chancery Court, Northern District of Mississippi, Final Record A, III, M, 235-37, Courthouse, Holly Springs, Mississippi.

32. Mary E. Young, "Indian Land Allotments in Alabama and Mississippi, 1830-1860" (manuscript doctoral dissertation, Cornell University, 1955), pp. 70-82; Franklin L. Riley, "The Choctaw Land Claims," Mississippi Historical Society *Publications*, VIII (1904), 370-82; Harmon, *Indian Affairs*, pp. 226-59.

33. Young, "Creek Frauds," pp. 411-37.

34. Lewis Cass to Return J. Meigs, Oct. 31, 1834, *Sen. Doc.* 428, 24 Cong., I sess., p. 23.

35. Lewis Cass, "Regulations," for certifying Creek contracts, Nov. 28, 1833, *Sen. Doc.* 276, 24 Cong., I sess., pp. 88-89; *id.*, "Regulations," Feb. 8, 1836, Chickasaw Letterbook A, 76-78, Records of the Bureau of Indian Affairs; Secretary of War to the President, June 27, 1836, Choctaw Reserve File 136, *ibid*. For adjudications based on the above regulations, see Special Reserve Files A and C and Choctaw, Creek, and Chickasaw Reserve Files, Records of the Bureau of Indian Affairs, *passim*.

36. "Memorial of the Creek Nation . . . ," Jan. 29, 1883, *House Misc. Doc.* 18, 47 Cong., 2 sess.

37. Average price paid for Chickasaw lands computed from William Carroll's List of Certified Contracts, Special Reserve File, Chickasaw, Records of the Bureau of Indian Affairs; Young, "Indian Allotments," 154-67.

38. See calculations in Young, "Indian Allotments," 141-42, 163-64. No system of estimating percentages of land purchased for speculation from figures of sales is foolproof. The assumption used in this estimate was that all those who bought 2,000 acres or more might be defined as speculators. Compare James W. Silver, "Land Speculation Profits in the Chickasaw Cession," *Journal of Southern History*, X (Feb., 1944), 84-92.

39. For the story of emigration, see Foreman, *Indian Removal*; Debo, *Road to Disappearance*, pp. 103-107 and *Choctaw Republic*, pp. 55-57. Relations between speculation and emigration can be traced in the Creek, Choctaw, and Chickasaw Emigration and Reserve Files, Records of the Bureau of Indian Affairs.

40. Hon. R. Chapman to Lewis Cass, Jan. 25, 1835, Cherokee File 7, Records of the Bureau of Indian Affairs; Lewis Cass to Commissioners Carroll and Schermerhorn, Apr. 2, 1835, Office of Indian Affairs, Letters Sent, XV, 261, *ibid.*; "Journal of the Proceedings at the Council held at New Echota . . . ," Cherokee File 7, *ibid.*; Joint Memorial of the Legislature of the State of Alabama . . . , Jan. 9, 1836, *ibid.*; William Gilmer to Andrew Jackson, Feb. 9, 1835, Jackson Papers; 7 *Statutes-at-Large*, 483-84, 488-89.

41. Paul W. Gates, *Fifty Million Acres: Conflicts over Kansas Land Policy, 1854-1890* (Ithaca, N. Y., 1954), pp. 11-48.

42. Memorial of the Creek Nation on the Subject of Lands in Severalty Among the Several Indian Tribes," Jan. 29, 1883, *House Misc. Doc.* 18, 47 Cong., 2 sess.

43. Compare Angie Debo, *The Five Civilized Tribes of Oklahoma: Report on Social and Economic Conditions* (Philadelphia, Pa., 1951) and Kinney, *Indian Land Tenure*, pp. 243-44.

Righting the century of dishonor: Indian reform as a reaffirmation of conservative values

Ralph W. Goodwin

Mary E. Young, in the final paragraph of her essay on the removal of the civilized tribes from the Southeast, refers to the allotment policy which deprived the same tribes of their western lands in the years following the passage of the Dawes Act of 1887. "Once more," she concludes "tribal land changed owners for the greater glory of liberty, civilization and profit." No one can deny that there were people with selfish motives who wanted Indian land. Railroad builders, homesteaders, and speculators all stood to gain. The issue, however, is not so simple. Almost all students of the land allotment movement have found that the policy received the enthusiastic support of men who operated from the highest motives and from sincere concern for the Indians. Many of these men considered themselves liberal reformers, and they derived no possible economic advantage from the allotment of tribal lands. At the same time some of the strongest defenders of the Indian tribes (such as some cattle ranchers) cared little for reform but took their position because their economic interest lay with preserving tribal control over vast grazing areas.

Ralph Goodwin, Professor of History at East Texas State University, in an essay published here for the first time, examines in detail the support behind Indian "reform" leading to the passage of the Dawes Act. He departs from those who see narrow economic motives controlling the actions of men. Professor Goodwin demonstrates that late nineteenth century Indian reform was made primarily in the East by easterners. His essay is particularly significant because it relates the Dawes Act to the great reform movements of the nineteenth century, such as the fight to abolish slavery. Goodwin makes clear how high principle and base motives combined to produce an act that doomed many western tribes by destroying forever any possibility that their cultural identity might be preserved.

For further reading: Robert F. Berkhofer, Jr., *Salvation and the Savage: An Analysis of Protestant Missions and American Indian Response, 1787-1862* (Lexington: University of Kentucky Press, 1965);* Angie Debo, *And Still the Waters Run* (Princeton: Princeton University Press, 1940); Vine Deloria, Jr., ed., *Of Utmost Good Faith* (San Francisco: Straight Arrow Books, 1971); Harold E. Fey and D'Arcy McNickle, *Indians and Other Americans: Two Ways of Life Meet* (New York: Harper and Brothers, 1959); Henry L. Fritz, *The Movement for Indian Assimilation* (Philadelphia: University of Pennsylvania

An original essay printed with permission of Ralph W. Goodwin.

Press, 1963); William T. Hagan, *American Indians* (Chicago: University of Chicago Press, 1961);* Helen Hunt Jackson, *A Century of Dishonor* (New York: Harper and Brothers, 1881);* Alvin M. Josephy, Jr., *The Indian Heritage of America* (New York: Knopf, 1968); Roy Harvey Pearce, *The Savages of America: A Study of the Indian and the Idea of Civilization* (Baltimore: John Hopkins Press, 1953); Loring Benson Priest, *Uncle Sam:s Stepchildren: The Reformation of United States Indian Policy, 1865-1887* (New Brunswick, N.J.: Rutgers University Press, 1942);* Robert M. Utley, *The Last Days of the Sioux Nation* (New Haven: Yale University Press, 1963).

*Available in paperback.

The presence of the American Indian, loosely occupying but often fiercely defending his lands against white encroachment, has been throughout our history both a major obstacle to the settlement of the frontier and a burden upon the conscience of the American people. That the Indian should be forced to accommodate his way of life to the demands of modern civilization and open his lands and hunting ranges to settlement has never been seriously questioned. Even the staunchest advocates of Indian rights have generally recognized this both as a pragmatic and as a moral necessity. How the process of appropriating tribal lands for this purpose could be justified in terms of the white man's own sense of moral duty and legal obligation however, has been quite another matter.

Actual settlers and enterprisers eager to move in and possess Indian lands, of course, usually found little difficulty in devising reasons to justify even the most ruthless methods of expropriation. Reaching far back into colonial times, for example, the fiction that Indian tribes were in some manner "nations" fully capable of negotiating treaties to cede away their "occupancy titles" to the land long would provide a most useful conceptual device to mask, as much for the white man's own moral satisfaction as for any other reason, the process of forced expropriation behind the facade of convenient legal forms.[1] As long as room remained to which defeated tribes could be removed, what came to be called the "treaty system" in Indian affairs worked effectively to the white man's satisfaction and, given the realistic alternatives at the time, with at least a minimal recognition of the Indian's right to survive.

To most frontier Americans there was never any serious doubt but that this outcome was justified. "That a few naked wandering barbarians should stay the march of civilization and improvement," suggested one highly influential spokesman for the prevailing viewpoint in 1827, "and hold in a state of perpetual unproductiveness, immense regions formed by Providence to support millions of human beings" was unthinkable.[2] The "treaty system" thus proved its effectiveness in opening vast new tracts of Indian lands as the area of settlement swept rapidly into the interior during the opening years of the nineteenth century. Under an elaborate system of treaties, supplementing the general provisions of the Indian Removal Act of 1830, defeated eastern tribes and tribal remnants were transplanted to reservations set aside for them east of the Mississippi or on lands acquired for them by treaty from other tribes across the river along the edge of the western plains. The struggle had been complex and difficult, but the Indian problem, it appeared, had now been solved for the foreseeable future. Except in local frontier areas the question receded from the national consciousness during the 1850s as men turned their attention to another, far vaster conflict.

With the coming of peace at the close of the American Civil War, however, ambitions and energies long dammed up by sectional conflict found release. And since so many of these energies turned toward the West the change would be reflected almost immediately in the development of Indian policy. It was at this point that vigorous new demands emerged once again for opening to settlement the very Indian reservations which had been set aside so solemnly by treaty as final homes for the defeated tribes. In fact, even during the 1850s, with the push of settlement into Kansas and Nebraska, this process had already begun. Thus the nation now became aware once again of what had long been called "the Indian problem." Whether men at the time were fully aware of it or not, a sharp break with the guiding preconceptions of the past had become necessary, yet nothing is more difficult for civilized or primitive men alike than to change abruptly the fundamental conceptions governing their relations with one another. No longer, however, was there further room to which the Indians could retreat. This time the problem posed peculiar difficulties not merely in subduing the yet unconquered tribes of the plains, mounted, hard-fighting, and elusive, but in devising a new rationale to justify breaking open the reservation system itself, the product of some two centuries or more of histori-cal development rooted in deep-seated moral and legal commitments as the basis for a proper relationship between civilized and tribal societies.

The result was a vigorous new Indian reform movement during the 1870s and early 1880s. Gradually, as pressures mounted for breaking open the remaining large reserva-tions in the West, this movement gathered strength among supporters of the missionary societies and private philanthropic agencies concerned for the plight of the Indian; its culmination and final triumph would come in 1887 with passage of the Dawes Severalty Act, "American's Magna Charta for the Indian," authorizing division of reservation lands into individual family tracts for the Indians with sale of the remaining "surplus" lands for white occupancy. Thus the final phase of the process by which the Indian was dis-possessed of his landed heritage began. It was the ancient treaty system itself, the advo-cates for this "new departure" in Indian policy now argued, which had been primarily responsible from the beginning for the whole tragic story of the nation's past treatment of the Indian. To permit such a pathetic and dependent people to continue to be cyni-cally manipulated piecemeal in this way by such convenient legal fictions was beneath the honor of a civilized nation. What was now required, the reformers insisted, was an enlightened new policy which would confer on each Indian a recognition of his right as an individual to be secure in the possession of his own property just as the white man was secure. After all, private property was universally acknowledged as the essential foundation for all civilized society; and it was this above everything else that the treaty system had consistently denied by dealing with Indians only through their ineffective and easily manipulated tribal organizations, thus in effect strengthening rather than weakening the hold which their savage customs held over them.

The movement for reform began with a new emphasis upon an old idea, the nation's responsibility of "wardship" over the Indians. "There is not a man in America who ever gave an hour's calm reflection to this subject, who does not know that our Indian system is an organized system of robbery," charged the angry young Protestant Episcopal bishop of Minnesota, Henry B. Whipple, soon to become a major leader in the movement for Indian reform. In an open letter to President Lincoln, Bishop Whipple protested fervently against the conditions which had produced the fearful Sioux uprising of 1862 in Minne-sota. It was high time, he declared, that the American people should understand "that it is impolitic for our Government to treat a heathen community within our borders as an independent nation, but that they ought to be regarded as our wards."[3] Thus the essential theme of the new reform movement was sounded; again and again over the years ahead it would be repeated in the developing argument for a "new departure" in Indian policy. "The Indians are now in a new relation to the white race, no longer to be forced back into unbroken wilderness," affirmed another leading reform advocate after the movement had gained its principal momentum. "The advancing host of native and immigrant people press the reservations on all sides, and the question of the civilization of the Indians and of their absorption into the body politic cannot be postponed but must be met."[4]

What this "new relation" and the doctrine of wardship now required was a vigorous program of cultural absorption, overriding if necessary even the obligation of treaties, "to break down the [reservation] barriers and let in the flood-tide of Christian civilization."[5] The Indian as a "ward of the nation" must be induced to surrender the separate tribal status which held him apart, and learn to settle down on limited tracts of land as a self-supporting farmer. This, as the essential first step in the transition from savage to civilized life, now became the single central objective of the Indian reform movement. The seeds for the new reform program lay, of course, within the prevailing American dream of an ideal social order based on widely diffused private ownership of property. The means for its accomplishment would be a new program of allotting Indian lands in severalty, destroying the very basis of the old tribal system by partitioning the reservations into separate farm-sized tracts under titles of individual ownership.

This remedy, however, was not as new as its advocates in the late nineteenth century seemed to think. Even before the Civil War, in fact, the adjustment in general policy had begun with the negotiation of a new series of treaties in 1854; these extended to the resettled tribes, who occupied reservations blocking settlement in Kansas and Nebraska, the benefits of allotting their lands into individual family tracts.[6] Once this had been accomplished, the remaining "surplus" lands were sold under the provisions of the new treaties to white settlers for the announced purpose of increasing the funds available for education and tribal improvement while at the same time encouraging the more rapid "adjustment of the races" through closer contact. The Indians themselves, it was assumed, could only benefit from the redeeming effects of private ownership of their lands; very quickly they would abandon their old communal tribal ways, seize the new opportunities for personal improvement now opened to them, and be absorbed into the general body of hard-working, responsible American citizens.[7] Thus, almost in one stroke, by simply extending to the Indian "his natural right because he is a *Man*—not a *red* man or a *white* man, or [even] an *American* man"[8] the Indian problem could be quickly and justly resolved. Such at least was the humanitarian rationale advanced to justify the change. The practical result was something quite different, as anyone familiar with the working of similar allotment provisions in even earlier removal treaties of the 1820s and 1830s might well have foreseen.[9]

As a means for clearing the tribes from their reservations, while at the same time satisfying the requirements of legal form, the allotment treaties of 1854 proved remarkably successful, for the tribal culture of the Indians left them hopelessly unfamiliar with the white man's concept of private property in land.[10] In the words of one recent historian recounting the events which followed the allotment of the Kickapoo lands in Kansas during this period, a veritable "human wolf pack—speculators, bankers, railroad promoters, and United States senators—sensing easy prey, moved in for the kill."[11] Stripped of the protection of his tribal identity, the individual full blood could quite easily be cajoled or bribed by a few trinkets and perhaps a little whiskey into "signing" instruments of sale he had no means of understanding. It was already an old, old story. Frequently, in fact, since with allotment went the extension of the white man's courts and laws over the Indians, not even this was necessary. Any Indian "signature" properly attested might do, or perhaps none at all, for there was also the avenue of landsales for nonpayment of taxes; the possibilities for collusion between speculators and friendly territorial and landoffice officials proved almost inexhaustible, particularly in the political confusion of the 1850s.[12]

But as a means of elevating the Indian to acceptance into American society, which had been at least ostensibly the philanthropic purpose for imposing the change, allotment in the 1850s proved once again unqualifiedly disastrous. Even Commissioner of Indian Affairs George W. Manypenny, who negotiated the allotment treaties in 1854 in good faith as a hopeful humanitarian experiment, would be forced to acknowledge the extent of their failure. "Had I known then, as I now know, what would result from these treaties," he later wrote, warning against further extension of the allotment policy, "I should be compelled to admit that I had committed a high crime."[13] Well intended projects of inexperienced reformers, whether within the Indian service or outside it, often proved as disastrous to the Indians as the shifting designs of the political spoilsmen themselves. The result was a quick flurry of land transactions, strikingly reminiscent of the "flush times" for land speculators following the earlier removal treaties east of the Mississippi, and soon the reservations were dotted with rude farms and booming little crossroads towns, occupied exclusively by white settlers.

Meanwhile, the beaten and pathetic tribal remnants from these reservations, stripped of their lands, sought refuge among the hospitable but better protected "civilized tribes" south of Kansas, whose wary and often well educated mixed-blood chiefs saw demonstrated once again the calamity which allotment and tribal dissolution would bring upon their people. Wherever allotment was adopted in the future it came as a reform thrust upon the Indians from without through force or cajolery and frequently without tribal consent entirely. Educated Indian spokesmen, and there were more of these particularly among the civilized tribes of the Indian Territory than students of Indian policy have been willing to credit, were by this time fully aware of what was at stake.[14] The hard-pressed and bewildered tribes of the plains and the far West, fearful of any concessions which the untrustworthy white man might require, remained simply unable to comprehend what was being asked of them.

The evidence seemed overwhelming that allotment again and again had served only to remove Indians from their lands, disrupting the slow process of acculturation steadily at work wherever tribes gained the protection of a reservation sufficiently isolated from the path of frontier settlement.[15] Yet once again the new Indian reform movement now emerged to insist that the only way by which the injustices of the nation's past treatment of the Indians could be remedied would be through destroying their tribal culture and extending the benefits of private ownership of land, "the rule of law," and ultimately the full privileges of citizenship to Indians as individuals.[16] And again also this demand came not from those experienced in Indian affairs but from a new generation of reformers untroubled by personal contact with actual conditions among the tribes but utterly convinced of the righteousness of their own intentions and the universal validity of the remedy they proposed. It was the reservation system itself, established simply for the white man's convenience in shoving the Indians out of the way, the reformers now insisted, which held the Indian to the bondage of his tribal ways, unwilling and indeed unable to progress further. Justice demanded that the Indian, whether he wished it or not, should be liberated as an individual and allowed to take his place in the great melting pot of peoples that was America.

To middle-class Americans, isolated from the frontier and reared in traditions of personal freedom and individual responsibility, the idea was, and in fact still is, most persuasive. As late as 1963 a leading student of the problem of Indian assimilation concluded that there had been "much wisdom" in the program of the allotment reformers and that its failure "was rather a case of meritorious assimilation measures being out of harmony with the selfish desires of white citizens."[17] In view of the nation's long experience with the results of allotting Indian lands, well before the Civil War, it seems difficult to believe that at least certain white citizens were not fully aware of what they were doing. What is truly difficult to understand is that the strongest voices demanding allotment for the Indian during this period came not from the frontier or even from the West but from determined and well-organized reform groups centering largely in the cities of the northeastern seaboard, most of whose members had no direct association with the problems of the frontier and certainly no immediate prospects for personal gain in the opening of Indian reservations.

That such reformers were genuinely dedicated in their intention to benefit the Indians their work leaves little doubt; it is this very quality which has set many students of Indian policy in this period off balance.[18] Yet men may be both sincere and dedicated and at the same time wrong. Like many convinced enthusiasts, committed in their hearts to truths they know in advance to be right, the supporters of the Indian reform movement of the late nineteenth century saw and heard only what they wanted to; and, like spokesmen for symbolic causes in other times, they early developed a most remarkable capacity to explain away or ignore arguments or evidence tending to discredit the solutions they proposed. To them Indian reform was a matter not merely of theoretical obligation but of driving moral urgency. To understand why such a cause could become so important to the representatives of the comfortably established urban elite who formed the backbone of the Indian reform movement requires first a consideration of the special position in society from which these groups sought to cope with forces swiftly altering the pace and complexity of American life in the late nineteenth century.

For many Americans this was a time of triumph and moral vindication. The sectional stalemate which for so many years consumed and stifled the creative energies of a whole people now had been broken, and the nation surged forward into an era of unprecedented internal development and industrial growth. Flushed with an exhilirating sense that their faith in human freedom as the key to human progress had met successfully its most searing and ultimate test, Americans of comfortable respectability began, however, to look askance at the jostling, raucous society growing up around them.[19] Something—just *what* they could not be sure—was going wrong. The dream of a happy, well ordered society in which each man dealt with every other on a basis of honest equality, assured by the certain working of the laws of individual responsibility, was being lost in the confusion of bewildering new social forces. Powerful new leaders of finance and industry, many of them far from gentlemen in either their origins or outlook, were rising up overnight to seize control of the nation's business and politics by methods exhibiting little enough of the traditional values long cherished by an older America. Material rewards which by earlier standards almost staggered the imagination went not to the industrious and responsible but to the cunning and cynically ruthless, while sprawling new city slums, born of Europe's misery and the demands of industrialism, filled with discontented masses of immigrants threatening to overturn completely the individualistic rural-based patterns of life which Americans had always taken for granted.

At first only dimly aware even of their own dissatisfaction, middle- and upper-class Americans, particularly in the eastern cities where the problem was most evident, began groping for means to cope with a situation they were unprepared either by their experience or their intellectual preconceptions to understand. Some, among the most venturesome and indignant, turned early to the hope of direct political or social action, though the remedies advanced by these "gentle reformers" of the later nineteenth century,[20] however justified for their own sake, seem today almost pathetically inadequate in the face of the concerns that gave them birth. The reform impulse of the late nineteenth century can be understood, however, only in relation to its place in the aftermath of the abolitionist crusade; the very success of this crusade had been a reaffirmation of traditional individualistic values, and was a response to the forces reshaping American life which uneasy men of conservative temper yearned vaguely but nonetheless earnestly to see brought under control.

Always, of course, there remained that strong undercurrent of humanitarian concern for the handicapped and underprivileged so characteristic of middle-class American society in the nineteenth century, which expressed itself in a wide variety of reform enthusiasms—prison reform, women's rights, child labor regulation, special care for the blind and for crippled children, improvement in treatment of the insane and the indigent, as well as the sustained missionary crusade of the churches to bring spiritual salvation and physical melioration to the unfortunate wherever they might be found. It is noteworthy that virtually all the philanthropic ventures that won sustained support in the late nineteenth century shared a common concern for equipping the individual to stand on his own feet in the world as it was, rather than for attacking human problems as products of an imperfect social order.[21] There seemed to be almost no awareness among these nineteenth century reformers that American society itself, now that the burden of slavery had been lifted, might harbor any further basic inadequacies; rather what they sought was a cleansing and a reaffirmation. After all, with personal freedom the sovereign remedy for the ills of mankind, what more should be required?

Not all, by far, of the representative old-line American middle and upper classes, however, were willing to go even so far as such politically active reformers. Comfortably isolated as many were by wealth or inherited social position, well-to-do gentlemen could take refuge in a protective social and moral snobbery. Henry Adams illustrates perhaps the quintessence of the type. Protected and aloof from direct involvement in the real forces shaping the world around them, they found solace in a sense of moral superiority enabling them to deplore the vulgarity and callous greed of a predatory business society yet with no sense of personal obligation to do much more than offer convenient amounts of time or money to charity and public service. Human beings, after all, will seek comfort and self-satisfaction if they can; and only the most stubborn or iron-willed, once their own security is assured, will go very far to propose social remedies that might jeopardize that very security. Still, the New England conscience and the belief in the social responsibilities of gentlemen were yet very much alive and required channels for expression. For men of property and social standing like Henry Spackman Pancoast, J. Rodman Paul, or Philip C. Garrett of Philadelphia to set aside substantial amounts of time from business and professional careers to devote themselves to a cause like Indian reform, or to other projects of community and social service, was well within what one writer has described as the "spartan-puritan" tradition of America's urban elite.[22] This cautious sense of social obligation perhaps helps to explain the wide diffusion of reform and philanthropic activity among conservative and well-to-do Americans of the time. Some of these efforts would of course prove better conceived and more constructive than others; but among most middle- and upper-class Americans, particularly in the urban East, it almost seemed as though anyone with pretense to social recognition was expected to have at least one reform hobby or public service enthusiasm, often the more exotic and irrelevant the better, ranging from the Chinese bronzes of the late George Apley[23] to the verbose but soul-satisfying activities of the Ladies' Missionary Society.[24]

Of all these reform enthusiasms, perhaps the most difficult at first glance to understand was the fervent concern which some of the most respectable elements of eastern society would devote to the cause of Indian reform. What indeed could have been more foreign or distant from upper-class life in cities like Boston or Philadelphia than the fate of some 250,000 pathetic savages scattered widely across the country on isolated reservations or fighting desperately against the inevitable tide of settlement on the western plains, particularly at a time when on their very doorsteps these cities offered far more immediate problems of slum squalor, civic corruption, and industrial injustice? The question, I would suggest, contains its own answer. It was the very distance and isolation of the Indian, like that of the heathen Chinese or the far away peoples of Africa and India, which gave the "Indian question" its fascination. The nineteenth century, for all the forces of rapid change which swept across it, was yet an age of romanticism and genteel sentimentality. Things seemed so much clearer and simpler when one gave thought to the problems of unfortunate peoples in faraway places; and the reports that came back from the missionaries and philanthropic agents sent out to help them were so much more hopeful and encouraging than what one saw in the seething discontent of the slums or the complex realities of political corruption and corporate irresponsibility at home.[25]

There was more to it, of course, than this. Indian reform was not just a diversionary tactic for the comfortably well-to-do unwilling to face up to the disagreeable realities of their own society. The Indian was and always had been, after all, an American problem; and his fate would be in a very real sense a judgment upon American life. That he even remained a definable social or political problem, whether abandoned in hopeless isolation on reservations or ranging still untamed across the plains, was itself a standing reproach. Clearly the cause of his plight, as in the case of the oppressed Negro, lay in the nation's ruthless denial of its own fundamental traditions; and just as surely as slavery had been wrong so this was wrong.[26] Consistently throughout its history the nation had withheld from the Indian, by fraud and pretext, those opportunities he both needed and deserved to take his place as a free man in a free society. Like the arriving immigrant, confused and baffled by the new society surrounding him, the Indian must now be offered these opportunities.[27] In the case of the Indian, the burden of the nation's guilt demanded both repentance and honest restitution insofar as this might still be possible. It made no difference that the Indian, like the immigrant, resisted change and cherished his old barbaric ways; he at least could not be held accountable, for had he not been kept almost as a matter of national policy in a state of ignorance and savagery? Whether he wished the "blessings of civilization" or not, like any stubborn child he must have them thrust upon him for his own good and that of his descendants. They at least would understand.

Part of the reason lay also in the nature of the reform goal itself; for what the reformers seemed to envisage for the Indian, once redeemed from the blighting effects of tribalism and national indifference, was an almost ideal preindustrial society following the traditional American pattern of settlement in scattered family farms. This, the reformers seemed fully confident, was what would inevitably follow upon completion of the work of allotment. That it had not happened during earlier experiments with allotment seemed not to deter them, for the previous attempts had been administered by speculators and dishonest politicians. This time it would be different. At last free to stand "as a man" on his own feet, the Indian would quickly respond by erecting for himself with a minimum of outside help the fundamental institutions of home, church, and school upon which every sound society must inevitably rest.[28]

Students of other aspects of nineteenth century reform in America have often commented on the widely prevalent "predisposition" among reformers "to solve the social problem in the dimensions of the small community";[29] certainly the work of the Indian reformers adds support to this observation. The dream was one of yearning for reaffirmation of the values of an earlier, stabler time. What better way might there be to demonstrate that the old virtues of personal independence and integrity still applied than to see them effectively at work in visibly transforming oppressed savages into hard-working farmers and responsible citizens within, in all probability, less than a generation? And what better way to demonstrate the perfectibility of all men and their common equality as brothers under the same beneficent Father? This, incredibly naive as it now seems, was the limited but honest faith that guided the Indian reformers.

The one voice to become most closely associated politically with the cause of Indian reform was that of the senior United States senator from Massachusetts, Henry Laurens Dawes. And perhaps no one better represented the essentially conservative impulse underlying the movement. There could hardly have been greater contrast than between Dawes and his predecessor and former rival, the flamboyantly moralistic Charles Sumner.[30] A quiet, almost colorless spokesman for the manufacturing interests of Massachusetts, "very popular and influential," Dawes was not the kind of man normally envisaged as a reform leader. He was "not the cultivated man" one might expect to find representing his state, wrote one senatorial colleague of many years with surprising candor, "neither would I say he was a man of strong and independent character."[31] Active from his political base in Berkshire County as an "exponent of republican principles in the westernmost district of Massachusetts" since before the Civil War, Dawes had served as a representative in Congress since 1857. Following the death of Sumner, he had secured election to the Senate in 1875 through cautious political bargaining. He "goes into the Senate with the smooch of Ben Butler on him," a disgruntled John D. Long recorded somewhat unfairly in his diary at the time.[32] Dawes never attained a position of independent power within his state and would always be regarded as occupying "a fringe position in the Senate," yet he proved highly skilled in serving the interests he represented and held his position in the Senate against determined efforts by the "youth" of the party to unseat him, until 1893 when the rising Henry Cabot Lodge at length succeeded.[33]

Dawes spoke, perhaps more effectively than any politician of the day, for what one historian has called the "sprawling rotten borough of Republicanism" that was New England during the decades following the Civil War.[34] "There was in every factory village in Massachusetts some man of influence and ability and wealth," wrote George F. Hoar, for many years his admiring junior colleague from Massachusetts in the Senate, "frequently a large employer of labor, who had been in the habit of depending on Mr. Dawes for the security of his most important interests. . . . They knew him and they knew that he knew them, and their power when they chose to exert it could not be resisted."[35] Yet curiously it would be Dawes who devoted one of the major efforts of his career, even before he entered the Senate in 1875, to the cause of Indian reform. "Let us make a home for the Indian in severalty, and hold it in trust for him, it may be for years in the future," Dawes had proposed during a debate in the House of Representatives in 1871, "but at least let each one of them know that this spot is his, to be defended by him, to be protected by him, and next to be adorned and beautified by him and cultivated, and in that cultivation cultivating himself and his family. Through that civilization comes."[36] Over the years this argument, the bucolic image, even the very language, would scarcely change at all, and in his final canvass for reelection to the Senate in 1886 the need to see that Dawes returned to complete his work in Washington on behalf of the Indians would be one of the arguments used in his support. In some way the cause was one which moved the interests in New England he served and represented.[37]

Slowly, almost imperceptibly, the ground was thus prepared for reception of a vigorous new crusade for Indian rights. Closely linked with the vaguely emerging sense of conservative alienation at home was the growing uneasiness many easterners felt toward the reckless and burgeoning West. It was in the West that all the corrupting influences, the alarming social and economic instability, the exuberant materialism and pervasive moral hypocrisy so disturbing to the security and order of life at home seemed most vigorously at work. That much of this recklessness had received enthusiastic support from financial interests in the East hardly seemed relevant; but the effects of the Panic of 1873 stung hard, particularly within the enclaves of eastern social respectability. Almost all the literature of Indian reform would be filled with denunciations of the short-sighted selfishness and immorality of western interests, the "cattle barons, land-grabbers, and dishonest speculators" held to be primarily responsible for the plight of the Indian.[38] The fate of the Indian thus offered a unique test of the fundamental values now threatened by vast impersonal forces difficult even to discern. And at the same time it presented a neat package of issues through which mounting but uncertain resentments against these forces could be gratified, if only symbolically, without disrupting unduly one's sense of social stability and conservative respectability at home.

This is not to say, of course, that the humanitarian concern of the Indian reformers was not genuine; but it seems striking that those most actively involved in the crusade for allotment of lands, destruction of the reservations and immediate citizenship for the Indians were men and women with little direct experience in Indian affairs, while those who did know the Indian "as he was" from personal and official contact frequently opposed these very efforts with a fervency and vigor most baffling to the reformers.[39] The opposition of selfish western interests was something the reform associations could understand, but this they never found a completely satisfactory way to account for. It was indeed "very strange," wrote Senator Dawes, to find such "excellent men" opposing the cause of allotment who were unquestionably well-intentioned, "having some notions about Indians which seem kind, but on the contrary making trouble and mischief with everybody who is trying to help that people."[40]

The campaign to liberate the Indian from the bonds of national indifference and official policy believed to be holding him in a state of hopeless depression was thus championed by determined bands of eastern amateurs, having little immediate experience in Indian affairs[41] but utterly convinced that private property, suitable training in farming and manual labor skills, and above all the recognition through total destruction of "tribalism" of each individual's personal dignity "as a man among us" would transform the Indian within less than a generation into the "useful and influential citizen" that all men have the potential within them to become. It would be, in a sense, a demonstration of all the values that nineteenth century respectability most deeply cherished. Even the most cautious of the reformers remained willing to accept Senator Dawes' estimate that, with only a few exceptions, the essential process should require no longer than a generation.[42] Others were far more sanguine in their expectations. "We evangelical ministers believe in immediate repentance," declared Lyman Abbott, editor of the *Christian Union*, in addressing a conference of Indian reformers in 1885.

I hold to immediate repentance as a national duty. Cease to do evil, cease instantly, abruptly, immediately. I hold that the reservation barriers should be cast down and the land given to the Indians in severalty; that every Indian should be protected in his right to his home, and in his right to free intercourse and free trade, are his individual, personal rights, which no tribe has the right to take from him, and no nation the right to sanction the robbery of. . . . I would begin at once a process for the survey and allotment of land to individuals in severalty. I would take the Indian and give him the rights of manhood with this great American people; and if there are any tribes so wild and barbaric that this cannot be done with them, I would put them under close surveillance, and would bring them under a compulsory educative process.[43]

So spoke the voice of impatient conviction summarizing in one paragraph a whole complex of attitudes and concerns undergirding the cause of Indian reform. Convinced of their own good intentions, the reformers seemed at times oblivious even to the claims of consistency. "The Indians are wards of the nation," declared a future commissioner of Indian affairs, "and they must, until they are emancipated from this evil paternal system, be compelled to be good to themselves, if such compulsion can be resorted to, without doing violence to any of their treaty rights."[44] As for the treaties, the reformers argued, there should be no qualms about ignoring the assumptions of tribal autonomy on which they rested; these had been mere "devices of expediency" in the first place. Besides, strictly speaking, they were not really treaties at all, but agreements between a sovereign power and its dependents revocable at any time, the Supreme Court had determined, by subsequent acts of Congress.[45] "The faith of every binding treaty must be observed," the reformers agreed; this was undeniably a moral, if not a legal, obligation. Yet "if there are any which, while called treaties, are not binding, the Indians ought not be allowed to suffer by their continuance." What determined whether a treaty should be considered "binding" seemed to be whether or not it served the Indians' own "best interests" as the reformers defined them. There was, after all, "a higher law." "We have no right to do a wrong because we have covenanted to."[46]

Perhaps most striking among the common characteristics linking the men and women who would dedicate so much effort to Indian reform lay in their almost universally inpeccable social credentials. The petitions and membership lists of the various Indian reform associations soon abounded with the names of Thayer, Biddle, Hemenway, Paul,

Chew, Wistar, Goddard, Wolcott, and Houghton, of eminent clergymen and bishops of the church, presidents and professors of the nation's prestigious colleges and universities,[47] as well as businessmen and political leaders with perhaps more immediate reasons to be interested in the destruction of western Indian reservations.[48] "I would be glad if your entire Executive Committee with their magnificent array of names, indicating great friendship for the Indian, could be present," wrote the chairman of the Board of Indian Commissioners in 1886, inviting Herbert Welsh of the Indian Rights Association of Philadelphia to a special conference in Washington.[49] Curiously, few of the individuals involved in the allotment crusade for the Indians appear to have had backgrounds of active support for the cause of abolitionism. Many had been in fact too young to have seen active involvement in the conflicts leading up to the Civil War; and few of the leading reformers other than Samuel G. Armstrong or Richard Henry Pratt, in any case only tangentially associated with the movement for Indian citizenship and allotment of lands, had records of active military service in the war.[50] Though all expressed sympathy for the plight of the Negro, it was taken for granted that everything that could be done for him had already been done; his fate in the future was now where it should be, in his own hands.[51] The most notable of the remaining abolitionist champions would either, like Wendell Phillips and Thomas Wentworth Higginson, offer only occasional verbal support to the allotment cause or, like Samuel F. Tappan, break off angrily with the work of the Indian reform associations well before the movement gathered its full momentum.[52] Tappan, as well as former Commissioner Manypenny, would be among those "excellent men" working so inexplicably to oppose the cause of allotment and immediate citizenship for the Indians.[53]

The reformers seemed, on the whole, to be thoroughly conservative in social outlook and cautious in their political concerns. Many of the most dedicated were men and women long active in the work of the church mission societies or in other ways as much concerned for the conversion and personal salvation of Indians as for their social redemption. Even the reformers occasionally commented good-naturedly on the evangelical flavor of their movement, noting that their conference often seemed more like "meetings of the Missionary Board" than hard-headed sessions for planning political and public relations strategy.[54] Often the sessions began with prayer and ended with the singing of hymns, while many of the petitions and addresses issued to the public would, like the speech of Lyman Abbott in 1884, ring with phrases strongly suggestive of this underlying religious concern. Historians of the missionary movement have often commented on the totality of cultural response which the experience of "salvation" was expected to evoke among native peoples. Certainly this had long been true of Protestant missionary efforts among the American Indians.[55] Though the orientation now became less denominational and perhaps somewhat more secular, the ultimate goal, including religious conversion, would remain the same. "No matter what we may do in Congress, no matter what I may do, no matter what may be done for the education of the Indian," declared President Cleveland, reportedly with tears in his eyes, in speaking to a delegation from the Lake Mohonk Conference of Friends of the Indian in 1885, "there is nothing like the Gospel, after all, to elevate the race."[56]

Since human nature was, after all, universally the same, and cultural differences only superficial, there seemed to be no doubt in the minds of the reformers that their goals could be achieved quite readily once the oppressive hand of bureaucratic interference and speculative legerdemain that had imposed the reservation system upon the tribes in the first place was lifted. The transformation, like religious conversion, would be both rapid and contagious. In 1870, while proposing immediate programs of allotment on the Omaha, Winnebago, and Santee Sioux reservations in Minnesota and Nebraska, a convention of Quakers declared:

When these Indians become civilized and enlightened, as we believe, upon the plan proposed, they will in a comparatively few years," be made powerful auxiliaries in aid of the civilization and enlightenment of the Tribes beyond them, so that instead of the few persons now engaged in the work, the numbers will be augmented year by year, in the benevolent and elevating engagement of drawing their Red Brethren into habits of industry, self-reliance and support, the recognition of their individual manhood and social and family rights, civilization, enlightenment, and ultimately citizenship, with Peace and Love, and their multiplied blessings. [57]

What finer demonstration of the transforming and regenerative powers of individual responsibility and freedom could there be? Like almost all nineteenth century Americans the advocates of Indian reform did not hesitate on occasion to speak of "the irrepressible conflict between a superior and an inferior race when brought in the presence of each other," [58] yet they must not be considered racist as later generations have come to understand that term. Their hopes and aspirations were those of an earlier, pre-Darwinian time. Race, to them, was not the unalterable biological fact it would appear to later generations of Americans, but a matter of almost entirely superficial group and tribal characteristics that humane and enlightened policies might soon wipe away. Looking as they did for an early and rapid merging of the Indians into the general population, the reformers in fact explicitly denied the assumptions that would give importance to race as a factor in human relationships. One of the most hopeful signs of progress among the Sioux, a missionary spokesman pointed out in a report in 1877 revealing a most interesting conjuncture of attitudes, was

the growing evidence that the more civilized and Christianized portions of our Dakota [i.e., Sioux] people are coming more and more into contact with the better class of white people. Many families and individuals are becoming detached from their own people and merged with the whites. . . . This is not miscegenation, but a proper and desirable mixture of the races, the inferior being elevated and finally absorbed and lost in the superior." [59]

Thus the ultimate goal of missionary and Indian reformer alike was to be a single harmonious society from which all significant vestiges of the original native culture, including racial identity itself, had been eliminated.

Clearly in an age of universal progress and improvement, the reformers argued, barbarism had no right to stand as an obstacle to the advance of civilization. And clearly, too, the Indian must be prepared, and quickly, for survival in a society hostile in almost every respect to the communal and tribal pattern of life he knew and cherished. Yet the very insistence on observance of legal forms and proprieties, once so useful in the earlier phases of Indian relations, now created an impasse in conscience and in law which all the ingenuity of the nineteenth century would fail ultimately to resolve to its own satisfaction. For men of integrity and honest purpose like Philip Garrett, "the existence of hundreds of alleged treaties, which imply the perpetual existence of the tribes" posed "a vast and complicated network of difficulties" for which there seemed to be no easy resolution. [60] Above all, the reformers had long insisted, let us for once keep faith with the Indian, for only then can he enjoy the security so necessary for the transition he must inevitably undergo.[61] Meanwhile the frontier pushed relentlessly forward, while the primary objective of the reformers themselves demanded a ruthless cultural transformation imposed from without and which no people would have been able to accept. Ultimately the argument of the reformers became that of historical necessity. "It means that if the Indians refuse all overtures in meeting the inevitable growth of the country," explained Samuel C. Armstrong, "then going to the reservations and taking such lands as we find unoccupied, giving them a full value therefor. It means that, at the rate civilization is advancing, with its ragged, rough edge" there was no choice. One way or another, the reservations would be opened; allotment offered the only means by which at least some portion of the Indian's right to an inheritance could be protected. "We must save them from themselves. If it were not for this imminent, terrible fact, that things cannot stay as they are, it would not be so. It is the spirit of the country—of its inevitable growth."[62]

There was not to be, in fact there could not be, a period of grace in which the natural adjustments so necessary to the process of acculturation might be made; indeed the reformers rejected the idea that such a thing should even be required. Suggestions to this effect seemed to them merely the selfish delaying tactics of an unprincipled opposition or a weak-minded concession to the natural Indian reluctance to surrender the ancient practices and prejudices which imprisoned them.[63] Thus even the transitional institutions—the "courts of Indian offenses," the elected tribal councils, the agency schools and mission churches—were to be designed and imposed from without;[64] meanwhile everything associated with the old tribal ways—the ancient festivals and dances, the customs of hospitality, the traditional mythology, and especially what was denounced as "the rule of the chiefs"—was to be deliberately ignored and suppressed.[65] For the uncomprehending tribes of the plains in particular there would remain nothing familiar to cling to, only an abrupt choice between patterns they were simply unequipped culturally to understand or a pathetic turning back into a mystical reactionism, best illustrated by the famous "ghost dance" movement which swept the plains in the 1880s, leaving them only that much more unprepared to adjust and survive.[66]

With passage of the Dawes Act in 1887, authorizing a general program of allotment for most of the remaining reservations, the opportunity came at last to translate the program of the reformers into reality. And the result, despite every effort to provide safeguards protecting the Indian in his new rights, was a vigorous renewal of the same old game of dispossession under only slightly different rules. The great reservations which once had blocked settlement of large remaining areas of the West now passed quickly from the scene. By the opening of the twentieth century the era of the famous homesteader "runs" and land lotteries by which large tracts of unsettled Indian lands were opened was over; but the process of dispossession in other ways, through one convenient legal device or another, continued. Most of the lands allotted to individual Indians passed swiftly into white hands as the ingenuity of the speculator kept well ahead of the regulations designed to head him off.[67]

Ironic as it may now seem, the very requirements of legal form and Christian morality, which the reformers insisted upon, set the framework for the tragedy that was to follow. And through it all the dogmatic enthusiasm of the Indian reformers hid from their own eyes the true effects of what they were demanding.[68] When the unfolding of events at last made this clear, the eastern reformers, of all people, reacted with the greatest shock and indignation. It must be recorded to their credit that when this happened they and their successors launched a determined fight to reverse the trend of events and to right the wrong that had been done, but by then it was too late. History seldom offers even the well-intentioned a second chance.

Notes

The author wishes to acknowledge financial support made possible by a fellowship from the Charles Warren Center for Studies in American History and to thank Oscar Handlin for his critical advice and encouragement.

1. "It is not easy to reconcile avarice with honor or force with voluntarism, but the Jacksonians tried it. For if they were avaricious, they were also 'all honorable men,' " comments Professor Mary E. Young in discussing the moral dilemma facing the negotiators of Indian land cessions during the 1830s. Young, *Redskins, Ruffleshirts, and Rednecks: Indian Allotments in Alabama and Mississippi, 1830-1860* (Norman, Okla., 1961), pp. 3-5, 45-46, 97, 192-193. Ralph K. Andrist, *The Long Death: The Last Days of the Plains Indian* (New York, 1964), p. 8, comments also on the "pleasant fiction" which undergirded the Indian treaty system. Note especially the article by Wilcomb E. Washburn, "The Moral and Legal Justifications for Dispossessing the Indians," in James Morton Smith, ed., *Seventeenth-Century America: Essays in Colonial History* (Chapel Hill, N. C., 1959), pp. 15-32.

2. Lewis Cass, "Service of Indians in Civilized Warfare," *North American Review*, XXIV (April 1827), 392, cited by Francis Paul Prucha, *Lewis Cass and American Indian Policy*, (Lewis Cass Lecture for 1966, Detroit Historical Society), p. 13. "Cass had no qualms about this process at all," comments Father Prucha, "so long as the Indians were justly reimbursed for whatever possessory right they had in the land and so long as the agreements made in the treaties with the Indians were faithfully fulfilled."

3. Henry B. Whipple, *Plea for the Red Man* (printed pamphlet, n.p., 1863).

4. Remarks of Dr. James E. Rhoads, October 7, 1885, Lake Mohonk Conference of Friends of the Indian, *Proceedings*, 1885, pp. 6-7.

5. Remarks of Lyman Abbott, October 9, 1885, *ibid.*, p. 52.

6. Jay P. Kinney, *A Continent Lost—A Civilization Won: Indian Land Tenure in the United States* (Baltimore, 1937), pp. 112-113. Former Commissioner of Indian Affairs George W. Manypenny discusses the allotment treaties of 1854 from the viewpoint of the official primarily responsible for their negotiation in his book *Our Indian Wards* (Cincinnati, 1880), pp. 115-133. The best study of the land conflicts in Kansas which followed these treaties is Paul Wallace Gates, *Fifty Million Acres: Conflicts over Kansas Land Policy, 1854-1890* (Ithaca, N. Y., 1954).

7. 33 Cong. 1 sess. (1853-54) *S. Ex. Doc. 1*, part 1, pp. 247-252; 33 Cong. 2 sess. (1854-55) *H. Ex. Doc. 1*, part 1, pp. 213-215; Commissioner of Indian Affairs, *Annual Report*, 1855, pp. 17-18. The real reason for the treaties, of course, had been to open the territories to settlement under the Kansas-Nebraska Act. See James C. Malin, *Indian Policy and Westward Expansion* (Lawrence, Kans., 1921), pp. 96-104.

8. Theodore Parker as quoted by Barbara Miller Solomon, *Ancestors and Immigrants: A Changing New England Tradition* (Cambridge, Mass., 1956), p. 6.

9. A copy of an early manuscript of Lewis Cass in the Ayer Collection of the Newberry Library, edited for publication by Donald F. Carmony and Francis Paul Prucha, was recently brought to my attention through the kindness of Father Prucha. The argument of this paper illustrates clearly that the hope of teaching Indians the value of private ownership of land had long been an acknowledged objective of Indian policy. "The first step in the progress of improvement," wrote Cass in 1816, "is to

convert the wandering savage into a settled man by giving him notions of private property, and by ensuring to him the enjoyment of it." A similar rationale would be used to justify the large-scale experiments which allotment in the Indian removal treaties of the 1830s. The suspicion remains strong, however, that for most Americans of the removal period such arguments went little beyond the realm of convenient self-deception. See especially Young, *Redskins, Ruffleshirts, and Rednecks*, p. 45.

10. See Harold E. Driver, *Indians of North America*, (New York, 1961), pp. 246-261, 600-604.

11. Arrell M. Gibson, *The Kickapoos: Lords of the Middle Border* (Norman, Okla., 1963), p. 120.

12. Gates, *Fifty Million Acres*, pp. 15-47.

13. George W. Manypenny, "Shall We Persist in a Policy That Has Failed?" *Council Fire*, VIII (November 1885), 156.

14. Memorial of the Cherokee and Creek delegates, April 3, 1872, National Archives, Records of the United States Senate, pp. 42A-H16. A report of the Associated Executive Committee of Friends on Indian Affairs in 1878, though urging ultimate allotment of Indian lands, cautioned against awarding of "unrestricted fee simple titles" to the Indians, citing the disastrous consequences of the 1854 treaties. *Need of Law on the Indian Reservations* (Philadelphia, 1878), pp. 46-52. Note also the warning of the Quaker spokesman Stanley Pumphrey in 1877 to the same effect. Pumphrey, *Indian Civilization: A Lecture* (Philadelphia, 1877), p. 32.

15. Driver, *Indians of North America*, pp. 603-610. See especially John Gulick, *Cherokees at the Crossroads* (Chapel Hill, N. C., 1960) and Gordon Macgregor, *Warriors without Weapons: A Study of the Society and Personality Development of the Pine Ridge Sioux* (Chicago, 1946).

16. A useful summation statement of the late nineteenth century Indian reform program will be found in the resolutions of the second Lake Mohonk Conference of Friends of the Indians in September of 1884. Lake Mohonk Conference, *Annual Address*, 1884, pp. 6-7, 13-16, 20-22.

17. Henry E. Fritz, *The Movement for Indian Assimilation, 1860-1890* (Philadelphia, 1963), p. 221. Carl F. Kraenzel's condemnation of the reservation system as the root of many of the modern Indian's difficulties also reflects this point of view, though he points out the dangers of withdrawing the protection of the Indian's special status too abruptly. Kraenzel, *The Great Plains in Transition* (Norman, Okla., 1955), pp. 238-242.

18. Note, for example, the somewhat puzzling ambivalence of scholars like Loring B. Priest and Henry E. Fritz toward the work of the allotment reformers. "Overconfidence in Indian ability," writes Priest, "caused certain friends to recommend a plan [allotment] which was advocated with equal enthusiasm by selfish whites." Priest, *Uncle Sam's Stepchildren: The Reformation of United States Indian Policy, 1865-1887* (New Brunswick, N. J., 1942), p. 120. Professor Fritz, while remarking that allotment "virtually condemned reservation Indians to poverty for many generations," considers "the unwillingness of Congress to carry it through" as "perhaps . . . the most important reason why a policy intent upon the acculturation" of the Indians failed. Fritz, *Movement for Indian Assimilation*, pp. 213, 221.

19. This entire paper is of course very much indebted to the concept of the nineteenth century "status revolution" most notably developed in a larger context by the work of Richard Hofstadter, Arthur Mann, Barbara Miller Solomon, Geoffrey Blodgett, and other scholars who comment on the clash of new conditions and old ideals during the decades following the Civil War, particularly among the middle and upper classes of the northeastern seaboard. It was among representatives of these very groups that the Indian reform movement gained its most effective strength; after considerable investigation of the literature of the late nineteenth century Indian reform movement I am convinced that the concept applies here especially.

20. Geoffrey Blodgett, *The Gentle Reformers: Massachusetts Democrats in the Cleveland Era* (Cambridge, Mass., 1966).

21. Arthur Mann, *Yankee Reformers in an Urban Age* (Cambridge, Mass., 1954), pp. 76-80. On the "legalistic inheritance" of many New England reformers see Blodgett, *Gentle Reformers*, pp. 139-140.

22. E. Digby Baltzell, *Philadelphia Gentlemen: The Making of a National Upper-Class*, (Glencoe, Ill., 1958), p. 57.

23. "As you know, for a number of years I have been making a collection of Chinese bronzes," Apley wrote to his son John. "I have not done this because I particularly like these bronzes. As a matter of fact, I think many of my best ones are overdecorated and look inappropriate in the Hillcrest library. I have made this collection out of duty rather than out of predilection, from the conviction that everyone in a certain position owes it to the community to collect something. In this way, industries are stimulated and scholars are given definite occupations. In the end the public will be the gainer." "It would be difficult to find a more accurate expression of the sentiment which has actuated so many individuals in our group," comments Marquand's narrator approvingly. John P. Marquand, *The Late George Apley: A Novel in the Form of a Memoir* (Boston, 1931), pp. 162-163.

24. Note the anecdote involving the conservative habits of one of the leading Indian reformers, J. Rodman Paul of Philadelphia, in Baltzell, *Philadelphia Gentlemen*, p. 58. Paul's father, Dr. John Rodman Paul, is cited by Nathaniel Burt as an example of the "non-practicing doctor" so characteristic of Philadelphia's elite in the nineteenth century. Dr. Paul retired from active practice as a physician at the age of forty to assume the role of a "busy boardsman," serving a wide range of charitable and philanthropic activities. "Much more common," Burt continues, "is the non-practicing lawyer, and it is almost routine for a gifted young man, especially one with literary tastes, to study law, practice a year or two, then go into whatever he pleases, his duty done. But at least a gesture towards work, and preferably towards the two Sacred Professions [law and medicine] is mandatory." Burt, *The Perennial Philadelphians: The Anatomy of an American Aristocracy* (Boston, 1963) pp. 100-101. Burt nowhere cites the name, but he could almost have had in mind one of the most untiring spokesmen for the Indian reform movement, Henry Spackman Pancoast who, though educated as a lawyer, engaged only briefly in his profession and would later become one of the nation's leading nonacademic literary scholars, publishing some of the most widely-used anthologies in English and American literature at the turn of the century. Philip Cope Garrett, another leading Indian reformer, retired early from an active career in textile manufacturing to serve for many years as president of the Pennsylvania Board of Public Charities and as a member and later chairman of the United States Board of Indian Commissioners. Herbert Welsh, with Pancoast a founder and moving spirit of the Indian Rights Association, was the son of the eminent Philadelphia merchant John Welsh and a nephew of William Welsh, the first chairman of the Board of Indian Commissioners. After studying aboard and in Philadelphia as an artist, Herbert Welsh devoted perhaps the greatest effort of his career to the Indian Rights Association and during his later years to civic reform through publication of *City and State*, a weekly devoted to the advancement of good government, which he sponsored and edited.

25. Geoffrey Blodgett identifies a similar motive behind the concern for tariff reform among many conservative New Englanders. "The drive for lower tariffs," he comments, "enabled Massachusetts Democrats to regard themselves as reformers while simultaneously giving them a rationale for economic orthodoxy during years of mounting unrest among industrial workers." *Gentle Reformers*, pp. viii-ix, 72-73, 79-80.

26. Samuel C. Armstrong to Albert K. Smiley, October 6, 1886, Lake Mohonk Conference, *Proceedings*, 1886, pp. 26-28.

27. Note especially the remarks of retired United States Supreme Court justice William Strong comparing the position of the Indian to that of the immigrant, *ibid.*, 1885, p. 32, and the pamphlet of the Indian Rights Association in 1890 proposing that the ultimate solution for the Indian problem lay in "ceasing to grow savages and substituting for a generation of turbulent aliens [*sic*] a new generation of

English-speaking, industrious, thrifty young Americans, educated in American schools." Indian Rights Association, *The Present Need of the Indian School Service*, (Philadelphia, 1890), p. 3.

28. The published *Annual Address* and *Proceedings* of the Lake Mohonk Conference of Friends of the Indian, a yearly gathering of leading spokesmen for the Indian reform movement which met each fall beginning in 1884 at the Lake Mohonk Mountain Lodge near Poughkeepsie, New York, and the papers and extensive collections of published pamphlets of the Indian Rights Association held by the Historical Society of Pennsylvania, Philadelphia, the Harvard University Library, and the Library of Congress contain abundant examples of speeches and statements enunciating the essential themes of the Indian reform credo.

29. Blodgett, *Gentle Reformers*, pp. 118-119. Mann, *Yankee Reformers*, p. 17. See especially Robert F. Berkhofer, Jr., *Salvation and the Savage: An Analysis of Protestant Missions and American Indian Response* (Lexington, Ky., 1965), pp. 10, 70-88.

30. David Donald, *Charles Sumner and the Coming of the Civil War* (New York, 1960), p. 364.

31. Frederick H. Gillett, *George Frisbie Hoar* (Boston, 1934), p. 29. Shelby M. Cullom, *Fifty Years of Public Service* (Chicago, 1911), p. 214.

32. J. E. A. Smith, *The History of Pittsfield (Berkshire County), Massachusetts, from the Year 1800 to the Year 1876* (Springfield, Mass., 1876), p. 661. Margaret Long, ed., *The Journal of John D. Long* (Rindge, N.H. 1956), p. 132. Gillett, *Hoar*, p. 94.

33. David J. Rothman, *Politics and Power: The United States Senate, 1869-1901* (Cambridge, Mass., 1966), p. 154. John A. Garraty, *Henry Cabot Lodge: A Biography* (New York, 1953), pp. 90-94, 129-132.

34. Blodgett, *Gentle Reformers*, p. 2.

35. George F. Hoar, *Autobiography of Seventy Years* (2 vols., New York, 1903), I, 228-229.

36. 41 Cong., 3 sess. (1870-71) *Cong. Globe*, p. 735.

37. Anna L. Dawes to Herbert Welsh, August 31 and November 4, 1886, and Charles C. Painter to Herbert Welsh, September 24, 1886, Papers of the Indian Rights Association, Historical Society of Pennsylvania, Philadelphia. Samuel C. Armstrong to Albert K. Smiley, October 6, 1886, Lake Mohonk Conference, *Proceedings*, 1886, p. 27. "That Dawes was a front man for national organizations and that he was, at least in part, prompted to assume that role because of the popularity of Indian reform among his constituents, is an inescapable conclusion," comments Henry E. Fritz, *Movement for Indian Assimilation*, pp. 211-212.

38. For interesting comment on "the resentments growing out of New England's isolation from the postwar boom beyond the Hudson," particularly following collapse of the western land boom in 1887, see Blodgett, *Gentle Reformers*, pp. 74-75, 96, 175-176.

39. Prominent opponents of the allotment reform program for the Indians included James W. Denver, George W. Manypenny, and Francis A. Walker, all former commissioners of Indian affairs; Enoch Hoag, who had served as superintendent of Indian affairs for the Central Superintendency during the period of the Grant "peace policy"; Alfred B. Meacham, former superintendent of Indian affairs for Oregon; Samuel F. Tappan, superintendent of the government Indian school at Genoa, Nebraska, and a former member of the celebrated Indian Peace Commission to the plains tribes in 1867-68; E. John Ellis, former Louisiana congressman who had been chairman of the House subcommittee on Indian appropriations; Amiel J. Willard, former chief justice of South Carolina now active as an attorney in Washington; and Dr. Thomas A. Bland, editor of the *Council Fire and Arbitrator*, a monthly published in Washington after 1878 dedicated to defending the reservation policy. Note also the anti-allotment

testimony of veteran Indian missionaries like William S. Robertson and Henry F. Buckner, 45 Cong. 3 sess. (1878-79) *S. Rep. 744*, pp. 672-677, and *S. Mis. Doc. 53*, pp. 13-15. It seemed almost as though only those missionaries "comparatively new in the field" could be trusted to be "free from prejudice," commented one irritated member of the Massachusetts Indian Association in Boston. "It seems to me almost impossible for any old agent or missionary to look at matters as we do; there is great hope in fresh eyes & fresh workers, in men and women who have not got used to the cheating and petty oppression of Indians." Martha Le Baron Goddard to Herbert Welsh, August 2, 1886, Papers of the Indian Rights Association.

40. Letter of Henry L. Dawes, August 5, 1884, Springfield, Massachusetts, *Republican*, August 7, 1884.

41. Leading Indian reformers like Henry S. Pancoast, Herbert Welsh, and Charles C. Painter did make occasional flying trips to investigate conditions on the reservations. Their attitudes, however, often seem condescendingly superficial. Note, for example, the remarks of Eliphalet Whittlesey, secretary of the Board of Indian Commissioners, and Charles C. Painter, field representative for the Indian Rights Association, at the Lake Mohonk Conference of 1885. Lake Mohonk Conference, *Proceedings*, 1885, pp. 15, 29.

42. Remarks of Henry L. Dawes, October 8, 1885, *ibid*., pp. 37-38. An editorial in the New York *Tribune* on January 7, 1885, for example, predicted that if the Dawes severalty bill were passed "in less than a generation the Indian problem would be solved, and the whole cumbersome array of treaties, reservations, special agencies, etc., would be swept away."

43. Lake Mohonk Conference, *Proceedings*, 1885, p. 53. "I should like to see the allotment compulsory instead of voluntary, prompt instead of gradual," Abbott wrote privately to Senator Dawes. This was necessary to protect Indians and white settlers alike, he insisted, "because we cannot guard against corruption, or incompetence, or both, in the Government itself; and the consequence is that honest and law-abiding citizens are kept out of the reservations, while scamps and rascals and cowboys get in." Abbott to Dawes, July 20, 1885, Library of Congress Manuscripts Division, Papers of Henry L. Dawes, box 27. Abbott "never visited a reservation and never met more than a dozen Indians during his entire life," his biographer comments. "His knowledge of Indian affairs was entirely second-hand, yet he played a significant role in molding and expressing public opinion in that field." Ira V. Brown, *Lyman Abbott, Christian Evolutionist: A Study in Religious Liberalism* (Cambridge, Mass., 1953), pp. 89-98.

44. Address of John H. Oberly, October 9, 1885, Lake Mohonk Conference, *Proceedings*, 1885, p. 51.

45. Charles C. Painter, "Our Indian Policy as Related to the Civilization of the Indian," *ibid.*, 1886, p. 19. Cherokee Tobacco Case, December, 1870, 11 Wallace 612-622.

46. Philip C. Garrett, "Indian Citizenship," Lake Mohonk Conference, *Proceedings*, 1886, p. 10. Remarks of Lyman Abbott, October 9, 1885, *ibid*., 1885, p. 51.

47. Among those who gave considerably more than mere verbal support to the movement in Philadelphia were of course the Welshes, Paul, Garrett, and Henry S. Pancoast (see note 24 above), and in Boston William H. Lincoln, Thomas Talbot, Frederick O. Prince, Joshua W. Davis, Frank Wood, Henry O. Houghton, and J. Evarts Greene. The list of prominent clergymen supporting the cause of Indian reform was weighted heavily with the names of Episcopal bishops and the secretaries of the major Protestant missionary societies as well as many leading pastors and parish ministers. Principal spokesmen for the American academic community who contributed their influence to the movement included Dr. James E. Rhoads, another Philadelphia "non-practicing doctor" who served as the first president of Bryn Mawr College, Professors James B. Thayer of the Harvard Law School and Francis G. Peabody of the Harvard Divinity School, as well as the presidents or former presidents of Rutgers, Amherst, Princeton, Swarthmore, Vassar, and Johns Hopkins. Such men attended the conferences and participated actively in the work of the reform associations; but on occasion, when it seemed neces-

sary, even more impressive rosters of names could be mustered. Note the resolution of a special meeting at Bar Harbor, Maine, in the summer of 1897 called by the Indian Rights Association to protest the dismissal of a reform movement representative as superintendent of Indian schools. *Answers to Charges Made against Wm. N. Hailmann, Superintendent of Indian Schools, Submitting Quotations from His Writings, Etc.*, Indian Rights Association pamphlet no. 46, second series (Philadelphia, 1898).

48. Clinton B. Fisk, long a strong supporter of the Indian reform movement who as chairman of the Board of Indian Commissioners presided over the meetings of the annual Lake Mohonk Conference of Friends of the Indians, was a New York businessman active in railroad promotion and in fact treasurer for a time of one of the railroad companies most persistently interested in the acquisition of Indian Territory land grants. Ira G. Clark, *Then Came the Railroads: The Century from Steam to Diesel in the Southwest* (Norman, Okla., 1958), p. 67. Angie Debo, *The Road to Disappearance* (Norman, Okla., 1941), p. 209. Fisk's report to President Grant on February 7, 1877, urging further consolidation of Indian reservations followed by allotment of tribal lands offers one particularly interesting suggestion: "If adopted, this policy will not only put the Indian question in a way for speedy settlement, but it will throw much valuable land in the market, which will find a ready sale, and greatly reduce the present expensive method of managing the Indian Department of the Government." Board of Indian Commissioners, *Annual Report*, 1877, p. 6. Henry S. Pancoast, as chairman of the committee on laws of the Indian Rights Association, would declare in a special report on October 9, 1884, that "it is neither wise nor right to let these great, solid blocks of reservations stand in the way of traffic and settlement." Lake Mohonk Conference, *Annual Address*, 1884, p. 12. Whether directly involved in railroad and real estate developments or not, the reformers showed considerable sympathy for the eastern investor's point of view, if not that of the western "land grabber" and "cattle baron."

49. Clinton B. Fisk to Herbert Welsh, December 19, 1886, Papers of the Indian Rights Association.

50. Among the principal spokesmen for the Indian Rights Association Henry S. Pancoast, J. Rodman Paul, Merrill E. Gates, and Herbert Welsh were yet under military age in 1865. Other leading Indian reformers, like James B. Thayer, J. Evarts Greene, Henry O. Houghton, and William H. Lincoln, though somewhat older, apparently lacked records of military service in the Civil War. Several, like James E. Rhoads, Philip C. Garrett, and Clement M. Biddle, were Quakers, and one biographical sketch of Biddle does indicate that "as a young man he worked for the abolition of slavery." *National Cyclopedia of American Biography*, XXII, 107.

51. Barbara Miller Solomon comments that "few Brahmins supported Negro rights unequivocally. They made their moral stand against slavery; the fiascos of Reconstruction made them wonder how far their ideals applied." *Ancestors and Immigrants*, pp. 13-14. Most, however, would resolve this quandary by adopting the doctrine that, except for the help of private philanthropic and educational programs, the Negro must now be left to stand on his own feet and work out his own future. There seemed to be little real interest in further efforts to protect Negro rights through political action in the South; "paternalism" whether for the Indian or the Negro was in fact the very thing the reformers objected to most strongly. Note the remarks of Henry L. Dawes, October 8, and Lyman Abbott, October 9, 1885, Lake Mohonk Conference, *Proceedings*, 1885, pp. 37, 53-54, and Garrett, "Indian Citizenship," p. 10.

52. Robert W. Mardock's "The Humanitarians and Post-Civil War Indian Policy" (Ph.D. thesis, University of Colorado, 1958), pp. 339-348, stresses greater continuity between the abolition reform tradition and later allotment crusade for the Indians than I have been able to discern. Particularly with the founding of the Indian Rights Association in Philadelphia in 1882 and the inauguration of the annual Lake Mohonk Conference of Friends of the Indian in 1883 the goal of the new generation of Indian reformers became much more narrowly focused upon the central issue of allotment and destruction of the reservations. Wendell Phillips, it is true, until his death in 1884 spoke occasionally at public meetings on behalf of the Indian reform movement in Boston, and Thomas Wentworth Higginson befriended and encouraged Helen Hunt Jackson; neither, however, participated actively as leaders of the allotment reform movement itself. Perhaps more directly involved was Edward Everett

Hale, who opened the pages of his reform journal *Lend a Hand* to the Indian reformers, wrote occasional editorials on their behalf, and attended the Lake Mohonk Conference in 1890, but took little part in the more general work of the movement.

53. As the allotment reform movement gathered force following organization of the Indian Rights Association in Philadelphia, December 13, 1882, a rival organization, the National Indian Defence Association, was established in Washington on November 28, 1885, to muster support for maintaining the reservation system. Most of the leading opponents of the allotment program (see note 39 above) were associated with this organization. The National Indian Defence Association never of course gained the widespread support which the Indian Rights Association and other allotment reform organizations enjoyed throughout the East, but it did prove effective enough to cause concern to the Indian reformers. See especially Herbert Welsh, *The Indian Problem: Secretary Welsh of the Indian Rights Association Reviews and Criticizes Dr. Bland's Recent Statements* (Philadelphia, 1886) and *Defense of the Dawes Indian Severalty Bill: A Member of the Indian Rights Association Takes Exception to the Position of the Indian Defense Association* (Philadelphia, 1887).

54. Comment of Thomas L. Riggs, October 10, 1890, Lake Mohonk Conference, *Proceedings*, 1890, p. 138.

55. Berkhofer, *Salvation and the Savage*, pp. 10-11, 70-88. Roy Harvey Pearce, *The Savages of America: A Study of the Indian and the Idea of Civilization* (Baltimore, 1853), pp. 136-150. Christianity often seemed a remarkably all-embracing concept to many nineteenth century Americans. It should not be considered "merely a thing of churches and school-houses," remarked Lyman Abbott at the Lake Mohonk Conference of 1885. "The postoffice is a Christianizing institution; the railroad, with all its corruptions, is a Christianizing power, and will do more to teach the people punctuality than schoolmaster or preacher can." Lake Mohonk Conference, *Proceedings*, 1885, p. 62.

56. As recounted by Clinton B. Fisk, October 12, 1886, *ibid.*, 1886, p. 1, and by Charles W. Shelton, September 28, 1887, *ibid.*, 1887, p. 32.

57. *Letter and Memorial of a Convention of Friends, of Baltimore, Philadelphia, New York and Indiana Yearly Meetings, Connected with the Indians in the Northern Superintendency, State of Nebraska, in Relation to Those Indians* (Washington, 1870). Compare, for example, the address of Amelia Stone Quinton, president of the Women's National Indian Association, October 10, 1890, Lake Mohonk Conference, *Proceedings*, 1890, pp. 98-101, and the letter of Sara T. Kinney, president of the Connecticut Indian Association, *ibid.*, 1891, pp. 80-81.

58. 39 Cong. 2 sess. (1865-66) *S. Rep. 156*, quoted by Fritz, *Movement for Indian Assimilation*, p. 30.

59. Stephen R. Riggs to John Eaton, U. S. Commissioner of Education, August 27, 1877, in S. N. Clark, *Are the Indians Dying Out? Preliminary Observations Relating to Indian Civilization and Education* (Washington, 1877), p. 37. See also Garrett, "Indian Citizenship," p. 9.

60. *Ibid.*, pp. 10-11.

61. See, for example, the petition of the Indian Treaty-Keeping and Protective Association of Philadelphia presented by Senator Dawes, January 19, 1881, 46 Cong. 3 sess. (1880-81) *Cong. Record*, p. 954.

62. Remarks of Samuel C. Armstrong, October 8, 1885, Lake Mohonk Conference, *Proceedings*, 1885, p. 29.

63. The first resolution to be adopted by the Lake Mohonk Conference of 1884, for example, called explicitly for "the disintegration of all tribal organizations." Lake Mohonk Conference, *Annual Address*, 1884, p. 6.

64. See William T. Hagan, *Indian Police and Judges: Experiments in Acculturation and Control* (New Haven, Conn., 1966).

65. "If a postponement for fifty years is likely to cause the destruction of the red man by the inexorable Juggernaut of Western progress, guided by hatred, by inhumanity and party spirit," declared Philip Garrett in a burst of rhetoric, "and if an act of emancipation will buy them life, manhood, civilization, and Christianity, at the sacrifice of a few chieftain's feathers, a few worthless bits of parchment, the cohesion of the tribal relation, and the traditions of their race; then, in the name of all that is really worth having, let us shed the few tears necessary to embalm these relics of the past, and have done with them; and, with fraternal cordiality, let us welcome to the bosom of the nation this brother whom we have wronged long enough." Garrett, "Indian Citizenship," p. 11.

66. Robert M. Utley, *The Last Days of the Sioux Nation* (New Haven, Conn., 1963), pp. 6-39, contains an excellent summary of the causes of the "ghost dance" movement.

67. For a careful study of the impact of allotment on the tribes of the Indian Territory see Angie Debo, *And Still the Waters Run* (Princeton, N. J., 1940).

68. Henry L. Dawes, "Have We Failed the Indian?" *Atlantic Monthly*, LXXXIV (August 1899), 280-285.

Part III
The West as safety valve

Farm-making costs and the "safety valve": 1850-60

Clarence H. Danhof

One of the most important concepts that lay behind Frederick Jackson Turner's frontier hypothesis was that of the "safety valve." In its most stark form the safety-valve thesis postulated that an abundance of free or nearly free western land offered urban workers an escape from low wages or unemployment and hence prevented the rise of a discontented proletariat. Turner did not invent the concept. He merely gave voice to an idea that permeated American thought throughout the nineteenth century. Writing as early as 1829 Edward Everett asserted that the West served as an escape for workers victimized by depressions or changing technology. It was not until Carter Goodrich and Sol Davison wrote "The Wage-Earner in the Westward Movement" in the mid-1930s that scholars began to raise serious objections to the safety-valve concept. Goodrich and Davison assumed that if the West had indeed provided a safety valve, migration would have reached a peak in periods of hard times and unemployment in the industrial economy. Their statistics demonstrated the opposite to be true. Westward migration peaked in prosperous times and waned during depressions. One of Turner's staunchest disciples, Joseph Schafer, answered these articles.

In the following essay Clarence H. Danhof, Professor of Economics at George Washington University, examines another facet of the problem—the cost of western farm-making. In a subsequent book *Change in Agriculture: The Northern United States 1820-1870* (1969) Danhof compiled the best and most comprehensive data to determine the cost of becoming a mid-nineteenth-century farmer in both the East and the West. He analyzes the way in which men of little capital could overcome the obstacles to farm ownership. In addition Danhof's work traces in detail the manner in which land passed from the federal government into the hands of small farmers and the steps which these men had to take to turn their land into productive farms.

For further reading: Clarence H. Danhof, *Change in Agriculture: The Northern United States 1820-1870* (Cambridge, Mass.: Harvard University Press, 1969); Edward Everett, "Flint's Geography and History" (review article), *North American Review*, XXVIII (1829), 80-103; Carter Goodrich and Sol Davison, "The Wage-Earner in the Westward

Reprinted from *Journal of Political Economy*, XLIX (June 1941), 317-359, by permission of the University of Chicago Press. ©1941

Movement," *Political Science Quarterly,* L (1935), 161-185, and LI (1936), 61-116; Murray Kane, "Some Considerations on the Safety Valve Doctrine," *Mississippi Valley Historical Review,* XXIII (1936), 169-188; Joseph Schafer, "Concerning the Frontier as Safety Valve," *Political Science Quarterly,* LII (1937), 407-420; Joseph Schafer, "Was the West a Safety Valve for Labor?" *Mississippi Valley Historical Review,* XXIV (1937), 299-314; Rufus S. Tucker, "The Frontier as an Outlet for Surplus Labor," *Southern Economic Journal,* VII, (1940), 158-186.

The fundamental importance to American economic development of the settlement of the federal landed domain is among the axiomatic propositions of economic history. The recognition of this relationship of land to the economic development of the United States has encouraged widespread acceptance of the more specific dictum that the opportunities provided by the easily available western lands strongly influenced, if they did not actually determine, the course of development of the American wage-earning classes. The theory has been widely accepted that the western lands drew off eastern labor whenever eastern industrial conditions were unsatisfactory, and in this way western lands performed the function of a safety valve for socio-economic conflict. Recent debate indicates that this interpretation remains an unproved hypothesis.[1] Particular importance attaches to this view because the disappearance of this alleged safety valve, as a result of the settlement of the public domain, is often considered a turning-point in the industrial history of the United States and is occasionally used to buttress arguments favoring the adoption of economic reforms.

The assumptions upon which the safety-valve theory rests are few and simple. It is assumed, in the first place, that under certain conditions such as those of depression and unemployment, onerous working conditions, and unsatisfactory wages, labor found it desirable to take advantage of the opportunities afforded by the cheap western lands; in the second place, that wage labor could if it so wished participate with little difficulty in the exploitation of this land; and, third, that labor acted upon this opportunity in significant numbers. The present study proposes to examine the validity of the second of these assumptions by an examination of the costs of farm-making as well as of the ability of wage labor to meet such costs. Our study is confined to the conditions existing in the decade 1850-1860—a decade in which agriculture, particularly in the northern states, under the impact of a spreading network of railroad communications and the rapid introduction of new agricultural implements, emerged entirely from its earlier self-sufficiency into a maturely capitalistic, profit-seeking, and market-focused system.[2]

I

At the outset we must appreciate that the economic aspects of pioneering and its relations to the larger economic life of the nation are not to be understood without adequate analysis of the costs which the farmer and farm-maker faced. The editor of the *New England Cultivator* in 1852 succinctly indicated a factor in the agriculture of his period that the economic historian may not safely overlook: "No error is more universal than for Tyros in farming operations to suppose that the business of farming may be pursued without means and that first crops may be obtained from the soil without additions."[3] Farm-making in the 1850's, whether carried out on the prairie or in forested areas, in the North or in the South, at the frontier of settlement or in well-settled regions, involved a variety of costs which were definite and inescapable. To a degree these costs might be met by the labor and sacrifice of the farm-maker and his family, but this was less possible in the fifties than it had been in the preceding decades. The would-be farm-maker had to acquire land and then prepare it for cultivation, which involved fencing and clearing or breaking; he had to possess draft animals and livestock, seed, and implements with which to conduct farming operations; he had to procure transportation to the West; and he had to build a shelter for his family and to support them through the waiting period until the first crops were harvested. Certain if not all of these were costs which had to be met with money outlays, and any would-be farm-maker consequently found the possession of some capital essential.

The fact that capital was required as a preliminary condition for undertaking agriculture is reiterated continuously in the agricultural literature of the period.[4] Condemnation of the futility of acquiring land without the possession of capital adequate to work it constantly recurs.[5] Though a distinction was commonly made between "farming" and "making farms," the necessity for capital was fully recognized in either case. The sums considered necessary to carry on farming operations were surprisingly large.[6] Similarly, though the numerous writers describing the opportunities of the West generally addressed their observations to the "poor man," examination of their meaning reveals that their remarks were clearly not directed at the impoverished; they wrote in terms of persons of limited or moderate means,[7] and their discussions invariably took for granted the possession of some capital.[8] Large sums of capital actually did accompany immigrants to the farm-making frontiers.[9] Individuals who lacked what these writers considered adequate funds were singled out for special attention. It was pointed out to them that the West offered opportunities for employment and savings which might eventually lead to the ownership of a farm. Foreign immigrants in particular were told that agricultural wage employment in the West provided them an opportunity for learning American methods as well as for accumulating funds. It was suggested to farmers that they could rent improved farm lands on shares and, after four or five years, proceed to purchase their own lands with their savings.[10] They might alternatively contract to improve, on a share arrangement, wild lands owned by someone else[11] or might bid for the lease of state-owned lands.[12] In any case they could accept agricultural employment for wages.[13] Wage employment in the rapidly growing western towns and cities was frequently pictured to eastern mechanics as providing excellent opportunities to share in the growth of the West, since labor was in demand and wages were high.[14] Even schoolteaching was suggested as a method by which the propertyless person might gain a foothold in the West.[15]

Considerable information regarding the amount of capital which was considered necessary to the undertaking of western farm-making is to be had from contemporary sources. Nathan Parker, an Iowa land agent and author of a series of western guidebooks, quotes with approval an estimate that a capital of at least $1,000 was necessary to equip an 80-acre western farm, exclusive of the land.[16] Another observer wrote with reference to Illinois that "any man who wants to commence farming on the prairies must be possessed of means and energy, and not expect to make a fortune too easy. A section of land requires about $5,000 cash to commence profitably, while it will require all of the half of that sum to farm a quarter section as it should be done."[17] Fred Gerhard cites a number of instances of 80-acre Illinois farms which required investments of from $785 to $2,127 to produce first crops.[18] It was asserted with reference to Texas that "any man with $500 can become an independent farmer. . . ."[19] though such a capital was certainly a

£1 = $5

minimum figure; and Frederick Law Olmsted wrote, in contrast, that "a labouring man, who has not one thousand dollars at command will probably find his account in first accumulating that sum by working for others." [20] Elsewhere it was pointed out, also with reference to Texas, that "for success as a cattle raiser the emigrant needs from six to ten thousand dollars." [21] The editor of the *Country Gentleman*, in reply to an inquiry, advised several young mechanics who possessed capitals of from $700 to $1,400 each against buying new lands to farm. [22]

Among foreign travelers reporting on this matter, Stirling suggested to his English countrymen that £200 would secure a start in Iowa; more might permit settlement in Illinois or possibly in Ohio. [23] Cunynghame advised a capital of £300 for transportation to an establishment of an 80-acre farm in the Des Moines valley of Iowa. [24] It was estimated by still another writer that $955 would buy a 200-acre farm, break and fence 60 acres, and build a log cabin and other small buildings. [25] Regan considered the sum of $550 an absolute minimum for an English immigrant designing to settle in the West. [26] An English traveler whose interest was specifically in American lands wrote that "an intelligent, prudent man, with five hundred pounds in his pocket, may rely on finding that sum sufficient to start him successfully on 320 acres of prairie land, if he avails himself of this credit system," land purchase not being provided for in this sum. He goes on to note that "a man with his wife and four children could not transport himself and them from this country to Illinois and place himself comfortably even on a forty acre farm for less than £100." [27] The estimates here quoted as well as others are itemized in Table 1. [28]

The estimates included in Table 1 indicate clearly that substantial amounts of capital were considered necessary to farm-making by contemporary observers. The conditions assumed in these calculations vary widely, however, and the computations likewise differ in their content and inclusiveness. The costs noted, moreover, are at variance in their requirements for liquid capital. Certain items could sometimes be met through the use of credit, others could be provided by labor or sacrifice, and money outlays could sometimes be avoided if the needed property were held. We may profitably consider in detail the individual items in the farm-maker's cost prospect and the possibilities of escaping capital investment in each case.

II

Land acquisition was the basic factor in the farm-maker's problem, and we may begin with an examination of the land market. This market was a complex one; the situation is not described by reference to federal lands at $1.25 per acre, despite the fact that the federal government was the original owner of most of the available lands. [29] From the point of view of the farm-maker there were actually five major sources from which lands could be obtained: the federal government; the state governments; land-grant corporations; private speculators; and private holders of partially improved lands.

The principal method of land sale employed by the federal government was that of auction. Lands offered at auction were held for a minimum price of $1.25 per acre, that price applying also to lands sold to pre-emptors and lands sold privately after having failed to sell at auction. The federal government also sold to private individuals after 1854, at reduced, graduated prices, certain lands which had been on the market for various periods of years. Transfers of land by the federal government to individuals

Table 1
Estimated Costs of Farm-Making: 1850-60
(Contemporary Observers)

Location	Total Cost	Size Acres	Land Cost	Break-ing	Fenc-ing	Seed-ing	Har-vest-ing	Live-stock	Pro-visions	Build-ings	Other
California[a]	$ 2,000	640	$ 800	$ †	$ 600	$ †	$ †	$ 500	$100	$ *	$ †
California[b]	3,000	40	400	†	1,400	200	†	700	†	†	300
Illinois[c]	550	40	50	†	100	20	†	140	50	20	170
Illinois[d]	785	80	100	130	320	40	195	†	†	†	†
Illinois[e]	896	34	170	87	100	468	71	†	†	†	†
Illinois[f]	920	200	320	†	173	†	†	†	†	100	27
Illinois[g]	930	45	500	†	†	20	†	140	50	†	220
Illinois[h]	1,411	80	360	150	400	145	456	†	†	†	†
Illinois[i]	2,100	160	1,000	400	400	†	†	†	†	300	†
Illinois[j]	2,127	80	1,200	175	320	236	196	†	†	†	†
Illinois[k]	2,290	320	240	1,500	†	*	*	†	†	*	550
Illinois[l]	2,750	160	1,600	225	400	†	†	†	†	500	25
Illinois[m]	2,800	100	1,000	1,250	*	*	*	†	†	†	550
Illinois[n]	12,200	640	6,400	1,300	1,200	800	2,500	†	†	†	†
Iowa[o]	440	40	50	80	160	†	†	†	†	†	150
Iowa[p]	850	160	200	320	320	†	†	†	†	†	†
Iowa[q]	1,034	80	†	†	†	†	†	310	†	450	374
Iowa[r]	1,500	80	250	75	75	75	†	200	100	100	550
Iowa[s]	2,650	160	200	600	600	150	200	†	†	650	250
Iowa[t]	3,000	400	1,400	180	300	†	†	305	†	150	665
Michigan[u]	277	40	†	220	40	17	†	†	†	†	†
Michigan[v]	2,475	160	225	1,012	*	*	338	†	†	900	†
Minnesota[w]	705	160	200	†	†	†	†	315	73	†	117
Texas[x]	500	100	200	†	50	†	†	50	100	50	50
Texas[y]	715	50	150	†	60	150	†	260	25	65	†
Texas[z]	1,000	160	400	†	†	†	†	150	150	150	150
Texas[aa]	7,800	160	400	*	600	†	†	4,450	†	750	1,600
Texas[bb]	9,000	1,000	2,500	*	500	†	†	5,250	†	750	†
Wisconsin[cc]	1,690	200	250	480	400	160	400	†	†	†	†
Wisconsin[dd]	2,000	640	800	100	200	†	†	350	150	*	400
Wisconsin[ee]	2,500	100	1,600	*	*	†	†	560	100	*	250

An asterisk (*) indicates that the item is included in the first preceding figure; a dagger (†) indicates that the item is not included in the estimate.

[a] Ernest Seyd, *California and Its Resources* (1858), p. 141. The estimate assumes that 90 acres are fenced. Seed is included with provisions, implements with livestock, and buildings with fencing.

[b] Franklin Langworthy, *Scenery of the Plains, Mountains and Mines* (1855), pp. 195-96. The "Other" item includes $100 for implements.

[c] John Regan, *The Emigrant's Guide to the Western States of America* (1852), p. 353. "Other" includes $50 for furniture and $120 for implements.

[d] Fred Gerhard, *Illinois as It Is* (1857), p. 294.

[e] *Prairie Farmer*, XV (1855), 344.

[f] Josiah T. Marshall, *The Farmer's and Emigrant's Hand-Book* (1852), pp. 402-3. The estimate includes 160 acres of land at $1.25 per acre and 40 acres of timberland at $5.00 per acre. "Other"

includes $15 for a well. The estimate applies to prairie lands in general and not to Illinois specifically. A very similar estimate by an English writer appears in *Working Farmer*, II (1850), 270.

g Regan, *op. cit.*, pp. 356-57. The estimate includes the purchase of 40 acres of improved land—fenced, broken, and including buildings; also of 5 acres of timbered land at $20 per acre. "Other" includes $100 for furniture and $120 for implements.

h Gerhard, *op. cit.*, p. 294.

i *Country Gentleman*, V (1855), 141. Provisions for a year are specified in addition.

j Gerhard, *op. cit.*, p. 295.

k James Caird, *Prairie Farming in America* (1859), p. 91. Includes 100 acres broken, fenced, sown, and harvested; also buildings. "Other" includes horses, implements, and harness.

l Gerhard, *op. cit.*, p. 299.

m Caird, *op. cit.*, p. 89. The item of $1,250 is for breaking, fencing, and harvesting the first crop, as well as for buildings. The "Other" item is for hired labor.

n *Ibid.*, p. 55. Original figures in sterling. Includes entire area fenced and cultivated.

o *Connecticut Valley Farmer and Mechanic*, I (1854), 153.

p *Northern Farmer*, I (1854), 290-91.

q Nathan Parker, *Iowa Handbook for 1856* (1856), pp. 159-60.

r A. Cunynghame, *Glimpse of the Great Western Republic*, (1851), pp. 103-6 and 108. "Other" includes $350 for passage from Great Britain to Iowa and $200 for miscellaneous and surplus. Implements included with seed. Original figures in sterling.

s *Iowa Farmer and Horticulturist*, V (1857), 102.

t *Rural New Yorker*, V (1854), 222. Includes the breaking and cultivation of 80 acres only.

u *Michigan Farmer*, VIII (1850), 265. This is an estimate of capital required for undertaking farm-making on a share basis, the land being owned by a second party with whom the produce is equally divided. Half the required seed is included.

v Sidney Smith, *The Settler's New Home* (1850), p. 91 (citing William Ferguson).

w *New Hampshire Journal of Agriculture*, April 14, 1859. Includes $90 for transportation from New England.

x *DeBow's Commercial Review*, X (1851), 640-41. Includes $50 for transportation.

y *Southern Cultivator*, XIII (1855), 125.

z Frederick Law Olmsted, *Journey through Texas* (1860), p. 460. The "Other" item includes wages, tools, and working cattle.

aa J. De Cordova, *Texas, Her Resources and Her Public Men* (1858), p. 55. The "Other" item includes $900 for wages for agricultural labor and $700 interest on capital for the first year.

bb Olmsted, *op. cit.*, p. 205. The estimate is for a stock farm in western Texas. Fifty acres are assumed fenced and broken. The stock includes 200 head of cattle and 650 sheep. Olmsted gives another estimate involving the same total for a cotton plantation in the same area which includes 70 acres broken, $800 for livestock and implements, and $6,400 for slaves (p. 206).

cc *Working Farmer*, II (1850), 270.

dd Seyd, *op. cit.*, p. 139. Assumes 20 acres cleared. Costs of log house included in fencing. "Other" item of $400 is for implements.

ee *Wisconsin Farmer*, VIII (1856), 440-41. Specifies 50 acres broken. Includes $150 for implements. "If one's means are moderate, one-half of that sum can be made to answer every purpose, by going to the newer portions of the State, and purchasing as good but cheaper land—by substituting two yoke of oxen for the horses and harness, and starting with three cows instead of five. . . ."

totaled almost 50,000,000 acres during the decade. Of this total, 43 per cent was sold at prices below $1.25 per acre.[30] Only 24 per cent of the total land area alienated by the federal government during this decade was disposed of by sale, and only 13 per cent was sold at or above the $1.25 minimum price. As important as land sales were the federal government's grants of lands to individuals. Under the military land-grant acts of 1847 and subsequent years, the government presented, to more than half a million individuals, tracts of lands varying from 40 to 160 acres each and totaling more than 57,000,000 acres.[31] These lands came on the market after the warrants granting them were made assignable in 1852, and an active market was conducted in them with prices substantially below the federal minimum.[32]

The federal government assigned to individuals by these two methods—sale and grant— about 57 per cent of its total land transfers made during the decade. The remaining land conveyances were made as grants to the states, in the form of school, university, internal improvement, and swampland grants, and to canal and railroad corporations. In making these grants the federal government established new sources from which the farm-maker could purchase his land. In most cases the government exercised no regulation as to the price or the method of disposition of these lands. There was no uniformity of policy on the part of the various states with regard to their lands, but the eventual result was in most cases that the lands were thrown on the market for quick sale. Lands not thus sold were then placed open to private sale, often at much lower prices. The prices realized by the states from such sales varied greatly, ranging from as little as 10 cents per acre to as much as $10.

The guidebooks describing the western states and addressed to the prospective immigrant rarely failed to warn him that he must not expect to buy desirable lands at $1.25 per acre. "The immigrant must not come here, as many do, expecting to find first rate land, with timber and water, all spread out before him, very near to some city or town for $1.25 an acre; it is not to be had."[33] Complaints that good lands were not available at government price to the settler were numerous; in order to obtain lands at $1.25 per acre, location had to be made far on the outskirts of settlement if not beyond, or else on poor lands in undesirable locations where communications were difficult and markets distant.

The enthusiasm of the authors of these guidebooks focused upon the "secondhand" lands—virgin lands no longer owned by state or federal government but held by railroad and canal corporations and by private speculators. Such lands were available in large acreages in every state in which farms were being made at prices two to ten times the federal minimum. These lands generally included, wherever settlement was under way, the remaining choice, fertile, and well-located sites. It was frequently pointed out that the differences in prices of these lands as compared with their desirability made them better values than federal minimum-price lands.[34] The most important of the corporation lands on the market during the fifties were those of the Illinois Central Railroad. The prices obtained for these lands ranged substantially above those realized from government sales.[35] More significant were the holdings of virgin lands in the hands of private speculators. Of the importance of the speculator in the land markets of the 1850's, particularly in the northern states, there can be no doubt.[36] In the case of Iowa, which was the most popular immigrant state of the decade, the state census for 1862 reported that some 15,000,000 acres, more than half the privately owned lands in the state, were owned by nonresidents, and commented: "Most of these lands are doubtless held, where they are located very eligibly for speculation."[37] Lands held by speculators were usually priced at upward of $3.00 per acre.

The fifth land market to be considered was that in improved lands—lands on which some breaking, some fencing and building, and possibly some cropping had been done. The supply of such lands came to a large degree from a distinct and well-defined type of farm-maker or speculator who carried out the preliminary tasks of farm-making on purchased or pre-empted lands and who was satisfied to sell out after a few years, taking as his reward the increase in the price of the land which his labor and the increase in surrounding population had produced.[38] These specialists in farm-making were replaced by a more permanent population which itself had been, and indeed continued to be, subject to the similar temptation to sell—to convert the increments in the value of their lands into a cash profit.[39] The supply of such cleared and semicleared farms was contributed to by the California, Pikes Peak, and Oregon migrations.[40] Such lands were sometimes sold as low as $3.00 per acre but were generally valued at from $7.00 to $10.00 and frequently higher.[41] Advice to immigrants regarding such lands was conflicting. Some observers pointed out the profitability of buying such farms which were ready to farm. They argued that improvements could frequently be purchased cheaper than they could be made and that such lands possessed the advantages of civilization, such as neighbors and schools, and were frequently located where markets were cheaply accessible.[42] Others argued that such lands might be seriously injured by crude and careless cultivation and might for that reason be unwise purchases.[43]

The wide choice of sellers which the prospective farm-maker found available was paralleled by the variety of the terms of sale. The federal government sold its lands only for cash or federal land warrants. State lands, however, were frequently sold on credit terms,[44] and credit was usually given by the landed corporations and by private speculators. The period over which credit was given was rarely long, ranging from a year or two to the six years offered by the Illinois Central Railroad. On the other hand, full title to lands might be obtained without investment in certain areas. The states of Maine and Arkansas offered lands to actual settlers, the purchase price to be paid in land script which was issued to these settlers as payment for labor performed in a road-making and drainage.[45] Arkansas and Michigan gave outright donations of certain lands to actual settlers,[46] and Texas, after 1853, gave homesteads to settlers upon payment of office fees and surveying costs.[47]

An important form of land credit was the common practice of laying claim to federal lands beyond the area proclaimed for sale, such lands being put to use without investment of any kind. Such "squatters" or pre-emptors enjoyed the opportunity to improve their claims with the hope that they could make sufficient from the cultivation of the land to pay for it when it was proclaimed for sale. If unfortunate in that respect, they were protected in the value of their improvements by claim associations which guaranteed that, should others desire their claims, they would receive compensation for their improvements.[48] In any case the squatter could with little effort at agriculture or improvement hope for a speculative profit in selling desirable claims to later settlers.[49] The squatter was not, however, the typical farm-maker. He was rather a distinct and well-defined type who undertook a limited number of the operations of farm-making without possessing adequate capital. The great migrations which converted the wild forests and prairies into farms were not composed of squatters; that class had preceded it. The great migrations occurred after federal survey and proclamation of its lands. The typical settler came looking for fertile agricultural land, well located, with a little timber if it were prairie land, close to markets and neighbors.[50]

III

Land was the raw material from which farms were made, but it was nevertheless only one of the factors involved. James Caird, an English observer, pointed out that the "price of land is the least consideration that a British emigrant need take into his calculations"[51] —a caution that was frequently repeated and applicable to the native farm-maker as well as to the foreign immigrant.[52] Following the purchase of the land, began a process which was expensive of labor, capital, and time. The initial task was that of preparing the soil for the seeding of the first crop. In the case of forested lands the timber had to be cleared away; in the case of prairie, the sod had to be broken and rotted. In each case it was possible for the farm-maker to carry out the task by his own labor, but the differences between the two tasks and also the differing character of the period in which forest-clearing predominated from that in which prairie-breaking was typical revealed themselves in the fact that forest-clearing was most generally done by the farm-maker himself while prairie-breaking was very frequently performed by professional breakers on contract.

The cost of clearing timbered land varied from $5.00 to $20.00 and upward per acre.[53] What was considered one of the cheapest and, frequently, also the best method of clearing forest land required that the trees be girdled and then permitted to stand from four to six years, cattle being fed on the land during this period to keep down the underbrush. At the end of the period the timber would be thoroughly dried and could be easily cut and burned. This method was estimated to cost from $5.00 to $8.00 per acre.[54] Though crops might be sown among the dead trees, falling limbs and trunks were a cause of considerable damage.

It was, of course, desirable to hasten the process; this could be done only at increased labor and cost and frequently involved delay in total area cleared and also resulted in a poorer quality of clearing.[55] One of the most common methods of forest-clearing involved the cutting of timber and brush into windrows during the winter, after which the timber lay about two years, and then those parts suitable for rails were removed and the remainder burned. This method was estimated to cost about $10 per acre.[56] The quickest method consisted of chopping the timber in the spring, preferably after the trees had been girdled the previous fall, the logs being burned during the first dry weather; then the ground was harrowed and sown to some crop such as corn or potatoes, which was followed by wheat in the fall.[57] The costs of this method were estimated at $14 or $15 an acre,[58] and the results were less satisfactory than other more time-consuming methods, since the land remained incumbered for many years with green stumps which continued to sprout, defying removal and remaining obstacles to plowing for some years longer than did the roots of girdled trees.[59] Oak openings and brushlands were special problems, since they had both to be cleared and broken. The tough roots present in the soils of such areas made breaking a particularly difficult task. After the timber had been removed from the oak openings of Michigan, a difficult task in itself, the contract cost of breaking the soil, ranging from $3.50 to $5.00 per acre, remained to be met.[60] Brushland was very general along the timbered edges of the prairies and was commonly grubbed at a cost of $10 to $12 per acre, although it was also sometimes merely plowed roughly and seeded, the shrubs, saplings, and roots being destroyed by burning.[61]

The task of preparing the open prairie lands for cultivation was quite different. Once the sod was turned under, little further labor was required and immediate seeding of a crop was possible. A period of waiting for the sod to decay ensued, but the period required was measured in months and not in years. In any case the task was far lighter than that of clearing forested lands, but it was a task unfamiliar to the immigrant from the East, and it involved difficulties and required special tools and skills. The plow used was commonly a heavy, specialized, prairie-breaker, pulled by three to eight yoke of oxen.[62] The skill derived of experience in breaking was a valuable asset, particularly since a poorly broken field in which part of the sod escaped uninjured was a serious handicap for many subsequent years, much as a "bad burn" handicapped the forest-clearer.[63] Timing was also important, the best period for breaking being a short one of about two months in the spring after the sod had sprung up and before it had ceased its early rapid growth.[64] If broken earlier the grass was liable to reappear, while if broken after this period the sod would not rot well and might interfere with the production of a satisfactory crop the following year. It was possible to produce a crop of sod corn on the earliest breaking, but it was very common for the farm-maker to spend an entire summer in breaking, with little or no effort made to get in a crop until wheat was sown in the fall or until the following spring.[65]

Despite these considerations the task of breaking was within the abilities of the average prairie farm maker.[66] Yet, and in contrast to the custom in forest-clearing, the practice of contracting out the breaking of prairie sod to specialists for a money payment was a very common one.[67] The costs of breaking the sod by contract varied somewhat with the region and the character of the work. A commonly quoted price was $2.50 per acre, prices ranging from $1.50 to more than $5.00.[68] The general practice of breaking by contract was based upon important considerations aside from those of skill and specialized implements suggested above. The whole tempo of farm-making as conducted on the prairies was far more rapid than had been the case earlier when the forest had been the farm-maker's problem. Instead of attempting to clear a 40-acre tract in ten or fifteen years, the prairie farm-maker usually thought in terms of clearing his 80 or 160 acres in two to four years.[69] The amount of land which could be placed in crops was limited by no serious problems of decay but only by the area broken. The availability of profitable markets made it desirable to get as much land into crops as possible. Furthermore, no individual could break enough land in the short period available each year and at the same time carry out the many other tasks facing him. Obviously the farm-maker with capital was able to get his land into production far more rapidly than the settler who was forced to do his own breaking. No one could afford to forgo breaking services if they were within his means, particularly as the possibility existed that the first crop would return the entire investment.[70]

Fencing was, next to breaking, the most important farm-making task and was an essential part of the first farm-making operations.[71] The wild, uncultivated lands were the free range of livestock which were always a threat to growing crops. No farmer could afford the risk of even a partial loss of crops from the depredations of such animals. Adequate fences were required under the laws of most of the states in case reimbursement was to be sought for damages inflicted by animals belonging to another. In very sparsely settled areas broken fields were sometimes seeded before they could be fenced.[72] This practice was recognized as bad management, and numerous reports occur of crops lost for this reason.[73] Though it was possible to postpone until farm profits provided the capital all or part of the investment in fencing by vigilance in turning cattle away from cultivated fields or by local agreement to inclose the animals,[74] common practice seems to have regarded fencing as the earliest task of the farm-maker, equal in importance with breaking, and to be completed at the first opportunity. The fact that the area under fence in Iowa in 1862 exceeded the area under cultivation is evidence of the importance attached to fencing in the farm-making process.[75] Throughout the nation, and not only in the farm-making regions, fencing was looked upon as a serious problem and a heavy financial burden, and a solution was eagerly sought in hedging and in wire-fencing.[76] It was pointed out that "fences are to a prairie farm one-third its value."[77] It was certainly a rare farm-maker who had not to invest more capital—or its equivalent in labor in the case of forested areas—in his fence than in land.[78] Where timber was to be had for the taking, the Virginia rail fence was the easiest and cheapest to build. The labor cost involved was estimated at from 35 to 70 cents a rod, which meant that the 320 rods required to fence a 40-acre field involved a cost of from $112 to twice that sum. A 160-acre field requires 640 rods of fence, and thus its cost of fencing was twice that of the 40-acre area. In any case the costs were heavy. Where timber was scarce as on the prairies, liquid capital was necessary with which to purchase local or imported timber or a near-by woodland.[79] Since economy of timber was required under such conditions, the post and rail fence was standard in these areas. Its cost was, however, substantially higher than that of the Virginia rail fence—from $1.00 a rod up, depending upon the value of lumber. A fence around a 40-acre field cost at least $320; a farm of 160 acres broken into four fields required an investment considerably in excess of $1,000 for fences alone.[80]

IV

Clearing and fencing prepared the soil for the farming operations which were to follow. Capital was again required for implements, seed, and livestock. It was no doubt possible for a farm-maker to be possessed of no implements other than a cheap shovel plow, hoe, scythe, spade, harness, and wagon, but such a list represented an investment of perhaps $100. In the South the investment in implements per worker was much smaller, but this list of implements was very inadequate for the West. There the plows used could not be confined to a single type of cast iron but were of numerous varieties and made preferably of the more expensive steel.[81] If corn was cultivated in Iowa in the fifties it was generally done with the horse-drawn cultivator and not with the hoe. The use of the seed drill was beginning to be considered desirable, though its use in the fifties was largely confined to the regions east of the Mississippi.[82] It was the wheat crop which called for the heaviest investment in agricultural implements. The tasks of reaping and harvesting far exceeded the capacity of the western labor supply, and the purchase or hire of both machines was essential to maximize returns from the land.[83] Though thrashing was commonly done on contract, the reaper was usually purchased; and though it was possible to buy 100 acres of land at government price for approximately the price of a mower or reaper, the land had little but speculative value without the machine to make possible its profitable cultivation.

The reaper and drill were not essential implements to the farm-maker, though the advantages to be obtained from their use were so great as to require their acquisition at the earliest opportunity. Excluding these instruments, the common 100-acre wheat-corn farm required an investment of at least $100 in implements and tools. An estimate for a 100-acre Wisconsin farm allocated $150 for plow, drag, cultivator, and small tools to start with.[84] The new machines, however, were frequently considered indispensable.[85] Parker gives a breaking plow, a common plow, a reaper, and a thrasher as a very mimimum of implements, representing an investment of at least $375, without mentioning small tools, cultivators, harrows, rollers, or drills.[86] A 160-acre farm in Illinois was estimated to require among other equipment a breaking plow, two common plows, two cultivators, harness for four horses, a reaper, and a thrashing machine, which would require more than $700.[87] Certainly a minimum of $100 had to be set aside for implements. The value of the implements of the farms of the western states as revealed by the census of 1860 averaged $156 per each 100 acres in farms, compared with a national average of $150 and an average for the farms of New England of $134.[88]

Since the possessors of capital invested much more readily in lands than in animals, livestock was relatively scarce on the farm-making frontiers, though the desirability of animals to take advantage of the pasturage freely afforded on the prairies was well recognized.[89] Draft animals were, nevertheless, essential in farming operations, and hogs were indispensable as a source of food as well as providing a marketable crop which matured quickly and required little capital. The draft animals might be a team of horses, themselves as expensive as a quarter-section of government land; less likely a yoke of cheaper oxen.[90] A minimum investment in draft animals, a few hogs, and some poultry involved from $150 to $200.[91] A well-stocked farm included a small herd of cattle which might well increase the investment required to, or above, $500.[92] Sheep were uncommon in farm-making areas.[93] Capital was also required for the purchase of seed. In the north where wheat was the common initial cash crop the necessity for $1.00 to $2.00 per acre for seed was a significant capital requirement.[94] Corn required a smaller investment, while cotton seed was virtually without value in the South.

Farm-making involved an interval of waiting after the initial investment had been made for the first returns to come in—a period of from six to eighteen months or more.[95] During this interval the maintenance of the family had to be provided for from the farm-maker's capital or credit resources. The period between the beginnings of production and its reward might be reduced to six months if corn and hogs were produced in sufficient quantity the first year to give adequate support.[96] This could be done, however, only if the farm-maker arrived at his new homestead very early in the spring, which was obviously difficult in partially or entirely unsettled country lacking adequate roads. In such case prairie-breaking almost certainly had to be contracted out or, if not, the farm-maker had to content himself with a very limited area planted in crops. Arrival in the late summer and early fall in time to build adequate housing and to collect wild hay to winter the animals involved the longer waiting period but was common and was considered the most desirable.[97] Though the period in which family maintenance had to be supplied from capital was thereby lengthened, arrival at such a time permitted the work of housing and fencing to be completed by spring so that the problem of breaking and seeding could be given uninterrupted attention.

With good fortune the farm-maker could raise within the first year or year and a half enough corn, potatoes, and pork to feed his family. Capital to maintain the family for at least a year was highly desirable. The sod corn was at best an uncertain crop, under any conditions yielding only moderately and frequently producing nothing but cattle fodder.[98] Moreover, it was considered by some to be desirable to permit the breaking to lie without a crop of any kind, since the sod decayed more thoroughly.[99] The wheat sown on land broken the previous summer as well as on land bearing the sod-corn crop provided the first important marketable crop the following spring.[100] Clearly, the advantages were all in favor of the longer waiting period. The sum of $100 was estimated as the cost of the first year's maintenance for a family.[101] That there actually did exist a considerable degree of dependence on the part of new farm-makers upon the purchase of food supplies is indicated by the fact that the earliest settlers in an area ordinarily considered the later arrivals as excellent markets for their produce.[102]

Little generalization is possible regarding travel costs. Emigrants from areas bordering on the farm-making frontier probably traveled with their stock and equipment, and to them the chief costs were time and subsistence. Emigrants from the east coast could travel by water to New Orleans, by canal, lake, and railroad, or entirely by rail, to the Mississippi. The railroad fare from Boston to St. Louis in 1855 was about $29 first class, $13 emigrant class.[103] The expenses of travel are not to be dismissed as trivial, as they were a large item to the eastern immigrant.[104]

Housing was still another necessity which called for some capital in the hands of the farm-maker. In forested areas house, barns, and outbuildings did not present acute problems, since lumber was cheap and log houses could always be temporarily utilized if better could not be afforded. The board shanty or cottage was, however, more easily erected and more desirable than the log house and was built whenever possible. In prairie areas board houses were standard, though substitutes such as log cabins, sod houses, and even tents were used. The costs of housing varied widely of course. Log cabins were estimated to cost from $25 to $100.[105] The cost of a four-room cottage, which was perhaps the most common form, varied from $245 to $450.[106] The materials for a small two-room house could be obtained for as little as $150 on the Illinois prairies, while larger houses cost as much as $1,000. Barns and similar buildings appear in few estimates; they were scarce in any area where farms were still in the making and were among the last items into which capital was placed.

V

No doubt farm-making was frequently undertaken by individuals possessing capital of less than $1,000. In view of the facts presented, however, that sum must be considered as the minimum required for western prairie farm-making under the conditions as they existed in the 1850's. Such a sum permitted the breaking and fencing of 40 acres of land, but not of its purchase, and would supply the minimum required of implements, livestock, and subsistence.[107] This figure was particularly applicable to the prairie areas from Texas to Minnesota—those regions upon which were focused the migrations of the decade. Elsewhere, in forested areas and at the fringes of settlement, somewhat smaller capital might have sufficed. In any case the farm-maker's wealth could not fall much short of $1,000; to the degree that it did, the farm-maker was inevitably forced to undertake farm-making in some round-about fashion, perhaps working part of his time for wages (which implies the possession of capital on the part of the employing farmer) and taking a longer period to develop his farm than the individual who did possess the suggested sum. He would, moreover, suffer correspondingly greater risks and discomforts, the added burden of borrowing capital at the high rates of the West, and probably had to accept smaller and less certain returns.[108]

It is altogether clear that the West of the 1850's cannot be regarded as offering great agricultural opportunities for the poor and poverty-stricken. Cheap land there was in abundance to be sure, but it was raw land, not capable of furnishing an immediate livelihood. It was but the bare surface, requiring much labor and capital before its fertility could be elicited. [109] In contrast we cannot doubt that the possession of a moderate capital such as has been suggested opened the opportunity to develop in a very short time valuable and profitable farm properties.

The sources of the farm-maker's capital were either cash savings or the proceeds from the sale of property. The liquidation of property was, of course, the common method of eastern farmers of raising cash capital for westward removal; such property was purchased by others, and thus, ultimately, the capital taken West came from savings. Such savings were sums brought from abroad by foreign immigrants or they were accumulations derived from wages, profits, or property incomes. It is doubtful if immigrants from abroad brought any large sums into the United States, [110] and it seems certain that far the larger part of the capital that was invested in western farm-making had its origin in the savings of agriculturists or of wage and salary earners in the East. Ultimately, it was thus the profitability of eastern agriculture [111] and the ability of a rapidly growing and profitable eastern industry to pay high wages that made possible the movement of capital to the West.

It is not to be implied that the necessary capitals were easily come by. Common wages for ordinary labor in the fifties did not reach $1.00 per day. [112] Agricultural labor, the class certainly most directly concerned with western opportunities, generally received about $150 per year, besides board and room. [113] From such wages it is unreasonable to expect that savings could greatly exceed $50 a year. [114] The accumulation of a fund adequate for western migration was thus no mean undertaking for the individual and was made doubly difficult, no doubt, by the unsatisfactory banking structure. Certainly the notion that a dissatisfied wage earner could, within a year or two of his decision to go West to undertake the making of a farm, pack up and do so is completely fallacious. Equally certain is it that the West offered no desirable escape at a time of financial crisis or depression when accumulated savings might be lost or difficult to liquidate, when credit was difficult or impossible to secure, and when the attractiveness of western agricultural profits had vanished along with the profits of industry and the security of an industrial wage.

Given a class of men who moved West with adequate capital, it was possible for others lacking such capital to emigrate also. Western development was not exclusively agricultural; it included the development of towns and cities as well as of trade, transportation, and local industries; in fact, all the varied parts of a complex economic structure. [115] Those who wished to emigrate but lacked capital for agricultural enterprise or who had no wish to undertake farming could go West, nevertheless, as laborers on the railroads, in lumber camps, and elsewhere, as tradesmen, and as skilled mechanics, finding economic opportunity in those towns and cities the growth of which paralleled that of agriculture. Wages were higher in the West than in the East, since the supply of labor, particularly of skilled mechanical labor, was smaller, relative to the opportunities for their employment. Cheap land exercised in this way an indirect influence, marked though immeasurable, upon the status and wage of the eastern laborer.

The relationship of the farm-making frontier to eastern economic society was, of course, not simple. The scarcity of capital in the East was at all times a serious deterrent to eastern industrial development, and any movement of capital westward must have accentuated this scarcity and thus must have had a detrimental effect upon the demand for labor and hence upon wages. On the other hand, the western farm-making frontier unquestionably favorably influenced the position of the eastern wage earner. Even though eastern mechanics themselves participated in the migration only on a small scale, [116] they were nevertheless favorably affected if population were drawn West which might alternatively have been drawn into industry and thus increased the eastern labor supply. The movement of native population out of eastern agriculture in the 1850's was in fact not into surrounding industry but rather largely to the West. [117] To the extent, moreover, that foreign immigrants moved westward or replaced emigrating eastern agricultural population, the effect of foreign immigration upon the eastern wage earner was less serious than might otherwise have been the case. The development of the West expanded the largest market open to the industrial East and thus stimulated the demand for the products of eastern wage labor. The fact that the West exported agricultural staples abroad was likewise a favorable factor, since the capital supply open to the East was thus increased.

In view of the costs of farm-making in the West it is clearly an error to consider western farm-making opportunities as directly determinate of the status of eastern wage labor. To the degree that the eastern wage earner actually entered western migration, this was possible only as a result of the high wages being paid in the East. The agricultural population moving westward did so also in large part because of the possibility of selling its eastern property and transferring the necessary capital to the West. Without a prosperous development of industry the East could not have settled the West (the cotton South excepted) with anything approaching the rapidity actually achieved. The ability of that young eastern industrial economy to continue to develop rapidly in the face of the transfer of large sums of wealth to the new agricultural West testified to the fact that fundamentally the productivity and profitability of eastern industry made high wages possible. Rapid growth guaranteed that such wages would actually be paid since industry was under the necessity of attracting sufficient numbers of new wage earners for its expanding needs. Such new wage earners came from eastern agricultural populations and foreign immigrants as well as from the natural increase of the wage-labor populations. No doubt the western frontier might have functioned to prevent serious exploitation had such exploitation been at all possible, and doubtless on occasion eastern industry faced competition from the West for labor, since the wages received by labor in some cases at least permitted the wage earner to accumulate funds for emigration. Such influences were, however, certainly and distinctly secondary.

Notes

1. Notably, on the one hand, Carter Goodrich and Sol Davison, "The Wage-Earner in the Westward Movement," *Political Science Quarterly*, L (1935), 161-85; LI (1936), 61-116; and, on the other, Joseph Schafer, "Concerning the Frontier as Safety Valve," *ibid.*, LII (1937), 407-20. See also Joseph Schafer, "Some Facts Bearing on the Safety-Valve Theory," *Wisconsin Magazine of History*, XX (1936), 216-32; Murray Kane, "Some Considerations of the Safety-Valve Doctrine," *Mississippi Valley Historical Review*, XXIII (1936), 169-88, and "Some Considerations on the Frontier Concept of Frederick Jackson Turner," *ibid.*, XXVII (1940), 379-400; Rufus S. Tucker, "The Frontier as an Outlet for Surplus Labor," *Southern Economic Journal*, VII (1940), 158-86; Fred A. Shannon, "The Homestead Act and the Labor Surplus," *American Historical Review*, XLI (1936), 637-51. For a

general bibliography on the safety-valve doctrine see E. E. Edwards, "References on the Significance of the Frontier in American History," *U.S. Department of Agriculture, Library, Bibliographical Contributions*, No. 25 (1935).

2. Horatio Seymour in an address before the New York State Agricultural Society distinguished between the "old" self-sufficient agriculture and the "new" agriculture of the 1850's, focused upon profits and markets (*Transactions*, XII [1852], 26-30).

3. *New England Cultivator*, I (1852), 201.

4. "No error is more common than to suppose that the farmer does not require Capital" (*Working Farmer*, XI [1859], 148). "To be something before-handed in worldly goods is essential before settling upon a farm; a little ready cash, besides paying for land and stock of cattle is absolutely indispensable if we should farm it ready and have farming pleasant and successful" (*Homestead*, V [1860], 310). "A certain amount of capital is necessary and indispensable to success in farming" (*Rural New Yorker*, V [1854], 261). "The want of capital is a serious obstacle in the way of most young men, which induces them to go into other business in preference to farming. The farmer is under the necessity, about here, of possessing a few thousands of capital to be able to work his farm to advantage" (*New England Farmer*, IV [1852], 478; IX [1857], 148).

5. "A farmer with five or ten thousand dollars is much more likely to invest the whole of it in acres, than in the materials to work his acres with profitably. Unused acres do not pay the taxes on them, and yet they would think it the straight road to ruin to sell an acre" (*Connecticut Valley Farmer and Mechanic*, II [1854], 98). "They almost invariably purchase or hire too much land, and thereby exhaust their resources at once, leaving nothing but their manual labor and a precarious credit to turn the use of this land to good account" (*American Agriculturist*, XV [1856], 127). "They forget that the ownership of this very unimproved land will be sure to prevent their ever having the means to improve it. They don't reflect that the interest upon the value of this unimproved land and the taxes upon it, would buy the land twice over at the end of ten years" (*Iowa Farmer and Horticulturist*, I [1853], 3). "We will suppose a man to come in possession of a farm of fifty acres of land, with the necessary buildings for farming purposes and one thousand dollars in cash. Now do I not state a fact when I say that instead of keeping the $1000 as a capital to conduct the business of the farm with profit and success, seven men out of the nine would seek at once to buy more land, investing the $1000 in this way and perhaps even buying so much more land as to run in debt $1000. . . . " (*Albany Cultivator*, cited in *Colman's Rural World or Valley Farmer*, II [1850], 254). Cf. *American Agriculturist*, IX (1851), 256; X (1852), 92; XII (1854), 387; XV (1856), 65; *American Farmer*, XIII (new ser., 1857), 86-87; *Carolina Cultivator*, II (1856), 205; *Colman's Rural World*, II (1850), 109; III (1851), 58; *Connecticut Valley Farmer and Mechanic*, I (1853), 7; *Genesee Farmer*, XVIII (1857), 193; *Homestead*, I (1855), 753, 786; III (1858), 763; IV (1859), 138, 171; V (1860), 51, 310; *Iowa Farmer and Horticulturist*, IV (1856), 3, 130-31; *Journal of Agriculture*, II (1852), 361; *Northern Farmer*, II (1855), 266; *Plough, Loom and Anvil*, IV (1852), 723; *Rural New Yorker*, V (1854), 364; *Western Agriculturist*, I (1852), 55; *Working Farmer*, VIII (1856), 220; Massachusetts Board of Agriculture, *Annual Report of the Secretary*, IX (1861), 107; Ohio Board of Agriculture, *Annual Report* IV (1849), 55; U.S. Patent Office, *Annual Report: Agriculture*, (1852), p. 134; James Caird, *Prairie Farming in America* (1859), pp. 52-54; John Gregory, *Industrial Resources of Wisconsin* (1855), pp. 61-62.

6. A detailed estimate of the equipment required on a farm of 100 improved acres in New York is presented in the *Illustrated Register of Rural Affairs* (1855), pp. 323-25 (also in *Country Gentleman*, V [1855], 213, cf. p. 278). The items included had an estimated value of $2,009.50, of which $1,010 was allocated to stock, $75 for seed for the first year, $400 for animal food until the first harvest, $350 for hired help, and $424.50 for implements. The latter item did not include seed drills, mower, reaper, thrasher, or horsepower, all of which could be rented. Costs of land and the support of the family during the first year are not included in the total.

Another estimate for a farm of similar size in the same state provided $870 for stock, $437 for implements, $63 for seed, $320 for labor, and $142 for maintenance of animals, a total of $1,832 (quoted with approval by Edwin F. Freedley, in *Practical Treatise on Business* [1852], pp. 65-71, from a New York State Agricultural Society Premium Essay on Farm Management). For similar lists see *Genesee Farmer*, XIX (1858), 213; *Rural Affairs and Cultivator Almanac* (1858), p. 131; *New England Farmer*, V (1853), 568.

The question raised as to the use of $1,000 on a 200-acre Pennsylvania farm led to the conclusion that such capital was inadequate and that at least $2,000 was required on a farm of that size (Pennsylvania Agricultural Society, *Annual Report*, V [1859], 277). The editor of the *Soil of the South* in reply to the query, "Can I, with a capital of $1,000, purchase and work a small farm and make a comfortable living out of it. . . . " says: "From such an investment for farming purposes, a *support*, may be very certainly expected but not very large gains." He suggested a very modest farm of 30-50 acres, a horse, a cow, a sow, and crops such as roots, fruits, and vegetables (*Soil of the South*, VI [1856], 11).

7. Some of the phrases used in referring to those who were evidently considered desirable prospects included: "man of moderate means" (*Rural New Yorker*, VI [1855], 202); "man of slender means" (*ibid.*, p. 302); "a small capital" (*ibid.*, p. 14); "small means" (*ibid.*, VII [1856], 69-70); "A young man with steady, frugal, industrious habits, with $200 or $300 (more is not objectionable)" (*ibid.*, IX [1858], 198); "young men, and women, too, of limited means" (*ibid.*, V [1854], 317); "The immigrants are principally men of small means" (*American Agriculturist*, XII [1854], 128); "limited means" (*Cultivator*, VIII [new ser., 1851], 355); "The good, honest, upright settlers. . . . who with their industry and their capital will make the natural prairie look like an old farm in one year's time" (*Rural New Yorker*, V [1854], 286); "those who have only a small or moderate capital" (*Genesee Farmer*, XVI [1855], 27); "A man with small means" (Fred Gerhard, *Illinois as It Is* [1857], pp. 289-90, 445). A writer who states that "the west is the refuge of the poor and those of very limited means" carried on his discussion in terms of $1,000 and more as the capital required (*Ohio Cultivator*, VIII [1852], 258-59).

8. "For a man to take a family there with barely money enough to defray expenses of the journey, it is worse than foolishness; better work here for $120 a year or even $100" (*New Hampshire Journal of Agriculture*, December 1, 1860). The writer was referring to Minnesota and considered $1,000 as a minimum capital for a man with a family. "You cannot build a house, fence and break your 160 acres, and cultivate it all with $2,000, and I advise you not to attempt it. But despite all I have written you can build a small house, fence and break 40 acres to begin with and live comfortable and make a little money perhaps" (*Rural Register*, II [1860], 356). "It is questionable policy for a man who has reached middle life to cut himself loose from old ties and go to new places in search of fortune. But to the young man of robust constitution and some capital, the younger States undoubtedly afford more abundant opportunities for the profitable use of his energy and capital, than the older states, and to the man of capital, they offer inducements that are exceedingly attractive" (Freedley, *op. cit.*, p. 257).

The secretary of the New England Emigrant Aid Company wrote: "As already suggested the Company *advises no one, entirely destitute of means, to go out, at this early period;* individuals who can command the requisite funds, (which indeed are but small,) to sustain them the first year, in other words until a crop is raised, or employment is sure, can go in perfect safety, and unquestionably *should* better their condition by going; others *may* find sufficient work to supply means, but it is premature for a very large number of such to go although thus far the supply of laborers has not kept pace with the demand; . . . . " (Thomas H. Webb, *Information for Kanzas Immigrants* [1855], p. 16).

Cf. James R. Beste, *The Wabash or Adventures of an English Gentleman's Family in the Interior of America*, I (1856), 281-83; Vol. II, chap. xi; Horace Greeley, *An Overland Journey from New York to San Francisco in the Summer of 1859* (1860), pp. 67-68; Nathan Parker, *Missouri Handbook* (1865), p. 44; *North-Western Review*, I, No. 6 (1857), 2; *Wisconsin and Iowa Farmer*, VII (1855), 10-11; VIII (1856), 54.

9. "Inasmuch as every immigrant comes provided with the means for entering land and defraying expenses till he can make a crop, money has been in freer circulation here than in any other part of the country" (Parker, *Iowa as It Is in 1855* [1855], p. 57). "From one town in New Hampshire, two hundred Mechanics have gone West this Spring, carrying with them at least $100,000" (*Western Farm*

Journal, II [1857], 221). "Every emigrant must take some three hundred dollars with him and thus the State is drained not only of muscle but money" (*Maine Farmer*, February 12, 1852). Another writer in similar vein states that the three hundred thousand men who, it was estimated, would emigrate in 1857 would take $20,000,000 with them (*Western Farm Journal*, II [1857], 197). "The exodus from New England in population and wealth will be equivalent to the removal of the whole city of Boston, men, women and children" (*Working Farmer*, IX [1858], 142, citing the *Chemung County Republican*); cf. *Ohio Farmer*, VIII (1859), 409.

In an address on the state of New Hampshire farming, the comment is made: "Thousands of our young and most energetic men, whom we were least able to spare, have left our borders. Nor have these gone empty handed. It were vain to attempt an estimate of the value of the intelligence and industry in this manner lost to us; but consider for a moment, the pecuniary capital thus abstracted. Many have been persons of wealth. Nearly all have had something. This although of uncertain amount, has left us and gone to swell the inventories of other states" (*New Hampshire Journal of Agriculture*, November 10, 1859).

10. A Wisconsin correspondent of the *Rural New Yorker* wrote in reply to a query regarding the attractiveness of the terms of renting farms in the West: "Although he applies his inquiries only to Illinois and Iowa, they are applied by others to Wisconsin. The renting of farms is much more common in the Southern part of the State than in either of the others named. The customary terms are as follows: The land alone draws one-third, the renter furnishing his own team, tools, house, etc. Where the owner finds team, tools, house-rent, fire-wood, etc., and half the seed, he receives one-half in the half-bushel. This gives the man who has no capital as good a chance as he can ask. . . . Surely such a prospect offers strong inducements to a poor man; for, if he is industrious and economical, in a short time he can purchase a farm of his own" (VI [1855], 230). Cf. Caird, *op. cit.,* pp. 50 and 93; Gerhard, *op. cit.,* p. 404; *New England Farmer*, XII (1852), 258; *Working Farmer*, II (1850), 270; *Farmer and Mechanic*, V (new ser., 1850), 46. Tenancy in the West was by no means uncommon. Cf. Paul Wallace Gates, "Large Scale Farming in Illinois," *Agricultural History*, VI (1932), 20-21, and the descriptions of the methods of large landowners such as Jacob Strawn in Indiana and Illinois (*Genesee Farmer*, XX [1859], 173-74 and 205; *Illinois Farmer*, III [1858], 213; V [1860], 117; *Farmer and Mechanic*, V [new ser., 1851]; 46; *Pennsylvania Farm Journal*, V [1855], 292).

Farming on shares did not entirely eliminate the need for capital as the citation given above indicates. Funds were required for the purchase of family provisions until the first crops were harvested and in many cases for the purchase of seed, implements, and animals. Credit for such items was frequently available, but interest rates were high. For a pessimistic description of tenancy see *Ohio Cultivator*, XIII (1857), 164-65.

11. "Many of our citizens have wild lands that they will lease for improvements. A man with a family may go on such land, clear and fence it, and have the use of it for five years, for the labor of clearing and fencing it, and during that time make money enough to buy a farm of his own" (*Western Agriculturist*, I [1851], 121). See also Caird, *op. cit.*, p. 93; Gerhard, *op. cit.*, p. 404; Parker, *Iowa as It Is in 1855* (1855), p. 67; *Country Gentleman*, XI (1858), 33.

12. State-owned school lands were leased to the highest bidders in Illinois, Indiana, Minnesota, and Texas. Cf. G. W. Knight, "History and Management of Land Grants for Education in the Northwest Territory," *American Historical Association Papers*, I, No. 3 (1895), 44-49, 64, 80-81.

13. "If they have not the required capital to take a farm at once, three or four years will probably place him in funds to commence his career as a proprietor of the soil" (George T. Borrett, *Out West: A Series of Letters from Canada and the United States* [1866]], p. 129). "Very few of the original settlers brought any property with them; consequently, it has been very general for a man disposed to locate himself to begin by working out for a season, to enable him to provision himself for the first year and buy a team; these are by far the most successful" (*Plough, Loom and Anvil*, IV [1852], 687-88). "The laboring man in Ohio can, with suitable economy in one or two years, save enough for a farm to support himself and family, during life and have a home of his own" (*Western Agriculturist*, I [1852], 121). "Many a poor Eastern boy, who has gone West with but a small balance of funds in his pocket, has hired out to work the first year on the farm. The proceeds of this enables him to work a

farm on shares the second and third years, and by the end of the fourth year would enable him to purchase a farm of his own" ("Commencing on the Prairies," *Rural American*, I [1856], 130). It was pointed out that the immigrant who stops in a city as a day laborer will always be that, but "he who hastens to the country and hires out upon a farm will in a few years be able to purchase and stock a farm in the west, with skill to work it profitably. . . . " (*Colman's Rural World or Valley Farmer*, II [1850], 274-75). Cf. *Rural New Yorker*, VI (1855), 126; *Farmer's Journal*, III (Raleigh, 1854), 204; James S. Ritchie, *Wisconsin and Its Resources* (1857), p. 168; Ernest Seyd, *California and Its Resources* (1858), pp. 146 and 156 ff.; Sidney Smith, *The Settler's New Home* (1850), pp. 43-44; Jacob Strawn commonly employed two to three hundred men in cultivating his farms in Indiana and Illinois (*Colman's Rural World or Valley Farmer*, XI [1859], 145).

14. "I have said that Kanzas was not suited to the poor man; I only intended to refer to those who design to till the ground. But to the poor mechanic it offers great inducements. To all carpenters especially and to stone and brick masons it will give constant employment and high wages. The rudest beginner receives $1.50 per day; good workmen, as journeymen receive in regular employment from $2.00 to $3.00 per day. Their expenses are light, the cost of living being low" (quoted in Webb, *op. cit.*, p. 19; also in C. W. Dana, *The Great West* [1859], p. 215; and *Northern Farmer*, III [1856], 168). Cf. C. C. Andrews, *Minnesota and Dacotah* (1857), pp. 130-31; Samuel Freeman, *The Emigrant's Hand Book and Guide to Wisconsin* (1851), p. 95; Gerhard, *op. cit.*, p. 446; Parker, *Iowa as It Is in 1855* (1855), p. 190; *Iowa Handbook for 1856* (1856), pp. 154-55; John Regan, *The Emigrant's Guide to the Western States of America* (1852), pp. 351-52.

15. Gerhard, *op. cit.*, p. 450; *New Hampshire Journal of Agriculture*, December 1, 1860.

16. Parker, *Iowa Handbook for 1856* (1856), pp. 158-60.

17. *American Agriculturist*, XVI (1857), 252.

18. *Op. cit.*, pp. 292-307 and 409-12.

19. J. D. B. DeBow, *DeBow's Commercial Review*, X (1851), 640-41.

20. *Journey through Texas* (1860), p. 460.

21. "Otherwise he must go to the extreme frontier and shift his stock from place to place, as settlements crowd upon him. He has to depend for protection against the Indians upon his rifle and revolver, and leads a life of constant danger and hardship, without neighbors, and debarred the necessaries and comforts enjoyed by the negro on one of our poorest Southern plantations" (correspondent of *New York Evening Post*, cited in *New England Farmer*, XII [1860], 554). Cf. Olmsted, *op. cit.*, p. 205.

22. "Our opinion is, that most of those accustomed to regular mechanical employment only, with a capital of only about one thousand dollars, would find it difficult to buy a farm with buildings, stock it with animals, furnish wagons, carts, and implements generally, and food until a return is made in crops. We would never advise such persons to buy *new* lands but whether they settle west or east, to procure a place even if quite small already under cultivation and with at least some buildings.

"It will be some time before the *most skillful* will receive an amount equal to *two* dollars a day; and we would therefore advise all mechanics, not already well versed in the practical operations of farming, to endeavor to retain for themselves, at some wages, mechanical employment during the most leisure portion of the year—to begin in a small way, to avoid running into debt, and to *feel their way* before engaging in any considerable expenditures" (*Country Gentleman*, V [1855], 8).

23. James Stirling, *Letters from the Slave States* (1857), pp. 19-20.

24. Arthur Cunynghame, *Glimpse of the Great Western Republic* (1851), pp. 103-6.

25. *Working Farmer*, II (1850), 270.

26. *Op. cit.*, p. 353. "Thus for $550 or about £110 sterling, may a man make a promising beginning, and not for less. Those who cannot command this small capital must not think of commencing to operate with land, except indeed it be as renters, in which case a man who has been accustomed to farming may make a beginning on almost nothing; and even with the aforesaid capital, a man must have some ingenuity to carry him through the difficulties of a beginning. I have repeatedly seen in guide books the sum of £100 set down as sufficient to establish a man on 80 acres either in Illinois, Iowa or Wisconsin. This might do were the settler to begin with oxen and fence but a few acres at first. Mr. Newhall, who is considered no mean authority, says, indeed, that the cost of a house, implements, stock and eighty acres of land may be set down at £80! An estimate in which I am unable to concur because I would rather not incur the responsibility of misleading any one" (*ibid.*, pp. 353-54). The reference to Newhall is to J. B. Newhall, *The British Emigrant's Handbook and Guide to the Western States of America* (1844), pp. 61-63. Regan also points out that the frequently cited estimate of Solon Robinson of $200 for prairie farm-making assumes that the farm-maker rents a farm for two or more years and that he possesses in addition to his $200 capital the necessary livestock, implements, and food (*op. cit.*, pp. 360-65).

27. Caird, *op. cit.*, pp. 91, 93. "I cannot, therefore, advise men who are unable to scrape more together than will merely pay their traveling expenses to go to Illinois. And far less can I advise them to go farther west. Suppose they could obtain land in Iowa or Minnesota, 400 miles farther away, at only half the price, the saving of *1s. 6d.* an acre in their deposit, would never compensate even the cost of travel for the additional distance, while every article which they require to purchase must bear an enhanced price from the same cause" (p. 93).

28. All the estimates cited refer to the period 1850-60. Similar estimates are available for earlier dates: e.g., Anon., *Illinois in 1837: A Sketch* (1837), pp. 14 and 70; Richard Baird, *View of the Valley of the Mississippi or the Emigrant's and Traveller's Guide to the West* (1834), pp. 231-32; W. J. A. Bradford, *Notes on the Northwest* (1846), pp. 146-47; S. H. Collins, *The Emigrant's Guide to the United States of America* (1829), p. 101; Henry W. Ellsworth, *Valley of the Upper Wabash* (1838), pp. 49-60 and 65-68; James Hall, *Statistics of the West at the Close of the Year 1836* (1836), pp. 203-4; A. D. Jones, *Illinois and the West* (1838), 140-64; P. Shirreff, *A Tour through North America* (1835). See also Theodore C. Blegen, "Ole Rynning's True Account of America," *Minnesota History Bulletin*, I (1917-18), 248-55 and 260-62; William Cobbett, *The Emigrant's Guide in Ten Letters* (1830), p. 46; J. Pickering, *Inquiries of an Emigrant* (1832).

29. The exceptions were the state-owned lands of Texas and Maine, which were never ceded to the federal government. These lands were on the market in the 1850's.

30. During the calendar years 1850-59, 207,000,000 acres of federal lands were alienated. Of this total, 50,000,000 acres were sold; 52,000,000 acres were granted to individuals; 76,000,000 acres were granted to states; and 28,000,000 acres were granted to corporations. Of the lands sold from 1854 to 1860, 22,000,000 acres went at graduated prices.

Since much attention will be paid in this study to farm-making conditions in Iowa, it should be pointed out that Iowa was by far the most popular state in the Union for land purchasers. During the decade more than 12,000,000 acres were sold in that state, all at or above the $1.25 minimum, though much of this was purchased with land warrants. This acreage was about 34 per cent of the state's area. Next largest sales were made in Missouri, where 7,500,000 acres were sold, and in Alabama, where 4,750,000 acres were transferred. In both these states the large sales were stimulated by the low prices under the graduation act. More than half the 2,500,000 acres sold in Mississippi were sold at these lowered prices. Almost 15 per cent of the area of Arkansas was sold, two-thirds of it at graduated prices. Sales were relatively small in Louisiana and Florida. Among the northern states, aside from Iowa, more than 2,000,000 acres were sold in Michigan and only slightly smaller quantities in Illinois and Minnesota. Data compiled from United States Commissioner of the Land Office, *Annual Reports* (1850-60).

31. Under the Military Bounty Land Grants of 1847, 1850, 1852, and 1855, 530,479 warrants were issued involving 57,781,570 acres of land. Up to September 30, 1860, a total of 49,584,990 acres had been located (United States Commissioner of the Land Office, *Annual Report* [1860], p. 47).

32. The warrants "could be secured from brokerage houses in New York and Washington in unlimited quantities," at prices of from 50 cents to $1.15 per acre, the larger acreages bringing the lower prices (*New York Tribune*, February 5, 1852). Cf. *ibid.*, March 11, 1852. Prices of warrants were frequently quoted in the *New York Journal of Commerce*. See also *Hunt's Merchants' Magazine*, XXXIX (1858), 65; XLII (1860), 427; *Rural New Yorker*, III (1852), 159; IV (1853), 51; *Ohio Cultivator*, VIII (1852), 175; *North-western Review*, I, No. 3 (1857), 13; *Michigan Farmer*, XII (1854), 96; *Rural Register*, II (1860), 176.

33. Parker, *Iowa as It Is in 1855* (1855), p. 68. "Strangers coming to Wisconsin are not to be deceived by supposing that they can get land in any part they please at government price" (Gregory, *op. cit.*, p. 310). "Let me correct an erroneous idea, which many of our Eastern friends entertain in regard to the prices of land here at the West. Let no one think that good land can be procured for a trifling sum. All the unimproved lands in the older counties have been taken up by speculators who demand a higher price for them in proportion to their value, than that of improved farms" (*Northern Farmer*, III [1856], 171. The reference is to Wisconsin). Cf. *Rural New Yorker*, V (1854), 366; *New England Farmer*, VII (1855), 140; Robert Baird, *Impressions and Experiences of the West Indies and North America* (1850), p. 336.

34. The emigrant "must be especially careful not to tempt himself too far from the market, by a cheap bargain, and never to forget that in an inverse ratio from what it is at home, here the first price of the land is by no means the weightiest part of the investment" (Cunynghame, *op. cit.*, p. 102). Cf. Parker, *Iowa Handbook for 1856*, p. 102; *Northwestern Farmer*, II (1858), 127; *Rural New Yorker*, VII (1856), 118; *Genesee Farmer*, XVII (1856), 116.

35. The lands of the Illinois Central came on the market in 1854, and, by 1860, 1,279,382 acres had been sold at an average price of $11.50 per acre on terms of up to six years' credit (Paul Wallace Gates, *The Illinois Central Railroad and Its Colonization Work* [1934], pp. 159 and 260-62). The Hannibal & St. Joseph Rail Road placed some of its lands on the market in 1858, priced at from $5.00 to $20.00 per acre, with nine years' credit (Hannibal & St. Joseph Rail Road, *Farms and Homes in Northern Missouri* [1857], p. 17). Lands of the Illinois and Michigan Canal were sold in small quantities during the decade at prices of from $4.50 to $12.50 per acre (Gates, *op. cit.*, p. 156; *Hunt's Merchants' Magazine*, XXVIII [1853], 277-79; *Rural New Yorker*, IV [1853], 170). Lands of the Des Moines Navigation Company were also offered (*Iowa Farmer*, IV [1856], 187).

36. The federal land office asserted that speculative purchasing was relatively unimportant. The 1857 *Annual Report* estimated that three-quarters of the land located and sold was taken for actual settlement (Commissioner of the Land Office, *Annual Report* [1857], p. 80). The 1859 *Report* said, "We have the fact that our whole operations, sale and locations, have generally been for actual settlement and cultivation, and not for speculation" (*ibid.* [1859], p. 171). President Buchanan in his *Annual Message* in 1857 expressed a contrary opinion. "Speculation has of late years prevailed to a great extent in the public lands. The consequence has been that large portions of them have become the property of individuals and companies, and thus the price is greatly enhanced to those who desire to purchase for actual settlement" (*Annual Message of the President* [35th Cong., 1st sess]., p. 31).
　　The land office claim no doubt possessed some truth as applied to the sales of land at graduated prices, but with regard to other sales all the evidence available confirms President Buchanan's opinion. From the Des Moines Land Office came the report of "men entering land by wholesale, without ever going to see it, staking a quarter section here and another there, shrewdly guessing that genuine hard working men will come after and pick up the vacant lots and soon want *their* lots at $5 to $10 per acre" (*Country Gentleman*, IV [1854], 45). Similar conditions were reported from the Dubuque and Decorah offices (*Iowa Farmer*, III [1855], 178). In southwestern Michigan there remained much unoccupied land, "mostly owned by Eastern speculators, and held at from $3 to $5 per acre" (*Farmer's Companion and Horticultural Gazette*, III [1854], 184). An Illinois observer wrote that "there are such shoals of 'land sharks' (so-called here) or speculators that they absorb *all* the best claims as soon as the lands are offered for sale, that a large proportion of actual settlers have to buy their lands of dealers, at double and many times, more than double, the usual cost at government price" (*Genesee Farmer*, XVII [1856], 116). The Janesville *Free Press* opposed the issuance of land warrants for military service on the ground that nine-tenths would be in the hands of speculators who

got the best lands, increased prices, prevented men with small capitals from coming in, or placed them at the mercy of eastern capitalists (cited in *Colman's Rural World or Valley Farmer*, V [1853], 177). In Minnesota, speculators were said to have located a great many land warrants as well as having purchased much of the best land—"a great curse to a new country" and a disadvantage to the actual settler (Andrews, *op. cit.*, pp. 129-30). Emigrants were reported returning from Kansas in 1856 because "all the locations on which there is timber or water are in the hands of claimants or speculators" (*Wisconsin and Iowa Farmer*, VII [1856], 186). Speculation was not absent in the South (*Southern Cultivator*, XI [1853], 276).

Such speculation could not fail to make itself felt in the East. "In 1857, it is probable that upwards of eight hundred millions of dollars were invested in idle Western lands, and lots in proposed cities, which had been paid for to the extent of one-fourth, the remainder continually being paid in installments" (D. W. Mitchell, *Ten Years in the United States* [1862], p. 328). "In all parts of the East, and here in New York as well as elsewhere there prevails a great inclination to emigrate westward. There is also a continuous stream of money, issuing from those who remain behind, that goes westward to be invested in new lands. The country banks here, which usually hold large deposits of money belonging to the rich agricultural community around, all complain of their deposits being completely drawn away" (*Ohio Valley Farmer*, II [1857], 74). "We are told that a certain bank, in a certain dairy county in the centre of this State had on deposit, in the spring of 1856, the sum of $455,000, money of the farmers. Week before last its deposit account footed up only some $25,000, and the farmers of that county were borrowing money for their spring's operations. The deposits in the bank had been drawn down for investment in the far West. A portion went directly into lands to be held for a rise. The residue and the larger part was transmitted to be loaned at three, four, five and six percent a month, on real estate security and legal assurance of unlimited usury laws. We have also been informed that the surplus moneys of very many counties of this State have gone the same way as the deposited earnings of the dairy district mentioned" (*Albany Evening Journal*, cited in *Western Farm Journal*, I [1856], 148 *Maine Farmer*, May 28, 1857).

It is of interest to note that speculation was not confined to the West. There was during the fifties, for example, much speculation in lands around New York City. Cincinnati mechanics were reported as having invested in lots in villages around that city (*American Agriculturist*, XII [1854], 322). Cf. *American Agriculturist*, XII (1854), 128; X (1856), 63; *Iowa Farmer*, V (1857), 98; *Maine Farmer*, April 30. 1857; *Northwestern Farmer*, IV (1859), 277; *Ohio Cultivator*, VIII (1852), 334; *Prairie Farmer*, XIV (1854), 217; *Rural New Yorker*, VII (1856), 242 and 358; *Wisconsin Farmer*, VIII (1856), 487; Gates, *op. cit.*, chap. vi; Benjamin Horace Hibbard, *History of the Public Land Policies* (1924), pp. 220-25; Addison E. Sheldon, *Land System and Land Policies in Nebraska* ("Publications of the Nebraska State Historical Society," Vol. XXII [1936]), pp. 39-46.

37. The census reported 28,336,345 acres assessed for tax purposes of which 4,170,496 acres were improved and 4,784,886 acres were attached to farms but unimproved (*Census Returns of the Different Counties of the State of Iowa for the Year 1862*) [1863], pp. 61-64). With regard to these figures W. D. Wilson (*Description of Iowa and Its Resources* [1865], p. 82) says: "Of the taxable lands, it is very probable that not less than 15,000,000 acres are owned by non-residents." And further: "Yet the most of them can be obtained for from $2.50 to $5.00 per acre, even in the older settled counties, and from five to ten miles from railroads in, or soon to be in operation." Paul Wallace Gates estimated that 9,000,000 acres in Illinois were in the hands of speculators in 1856. ("The Disposal of the Public Domain in Illinois, 1848-1856," *Journal of Economic and Business History*, III [1931], 321).

38. Speaking of farms being established in the West, one observer commented: "Of the whole number thus commenced, the owners of about *one-half* remain on these new places as permanent residents. The other half consists of a nomad class, that is wandering, but never satisfied in any one place. They either enter Government land, or buy from some railroad or other company at a moderate price, commence farming operations by putting up a shanty and a few rods of fence, and breaking from ten to forty acres of land. They raise a sod crop of corn and sometimes a wheat crop and then a fit of restlessness takes possession of them, and thinking they are making money when they are able to get $5 per acre more for their land than what they gave for it, they sell out, and make a new purchase either in the same State or farther West" (*American Agriculturist*, XVI [1857], 277). Another wrote:

"They are a class by themselves. They never have a home for ten years in a place. They 'settle' as they call it—on the outskirts of civilization—remain a few years in clearing up and 'bringing to' a patch of land. Sometimes they own it and sometimes not. As soon as society begins to thicken inconveniently around them, they get discontented, pull up stakes, and hie off to another wild, unsettled region. A better class comes in, buys out their investments for a trifle and settle themselves permanently on their squattings" (*ibid.*,XV [1836], 224). Cf. *American Farmer's Magazine*, VIII (1858), 212; *Indiana Farmer*, IV (1854-55), 146; *Plough, Loom and Anvil*, VI (1854), 594; *Prairie Farmer*, XII (1852), 378; *Rural New Yorker*, VII (1856), 122; New York State Agricultural Society, *Annual Report*, XXI (1852), 682-83; Andrews, *op. cit.*, p. 115; Smith, *op. cit.*, p. 101.

39. "For the last ten years there has been a vast migration to Illinois, Iowa, Minnesota and Nebraska. This has uniformly been the case with all the states where lands come to $30 or $50 per acre and is caused simply by the fact that it then becomes a speculation for farmers to sell out and commence new farms at government prices" (*Journal of Commerce* [New York, February 11, 1857], quoting the *Cincinnati Gazette*). The prominence of Ohioans among westward migrants was explained thus: "Here soil is too rich and dear to retain a dense population. A poor man can earn enough from a three years' lease on his neighbor's farm to move West, buy a quarter or half section and set up free-holder for himself. A farmer with a few acres of land can sell it to his richer neighbor, go West, and purchase a large farm.

"The temptation is too powerful to be resisted. Thus the large farms are becoming larger and the small free holds are becoming absorbed in them" (*Iowa Farmer*, II [1854], 87-88). A similar analysis is applied to emigration from Illinois: "Many of the land owners of this region are the worthy pioneers who settled it when it belonged to the United States, and have since purchased it. As soon as the Nebraska bill passed many of them thought earnestly of emigrating thither. They saw that land was rising so much above $1.25 per acre, that with their limited means they should not be able to give each of their children 160 acres of prairie and 40 of timber as they always hoped to do and had for their older children. Now that this unprecedented drought has come upon us, many of them are determined to emigrate soon. They are determined to sell their farms at some price" (*Prairie Farmer*, XIV [1854], 346).

40. "For the benefit of those preferring improved lands, I would say that the Oregon and California fevers are continually seizing our oldest pioneer settlers and often others, and they consider it quite a treat to be 'bought out.' These improved lands sell for $8 to $15, and sometimes $20 per acre; are not much injured by culture, and are very desirable spots for the exact farmer, who can bear to have his farm bounded by other cultivated lands instead of the open wilds; in other words, for those who can bear the restraints of civilization." The reference is to Illinois (*Prairie Farmer*, XII [1852], 378). Cf. *Rural New Yorker*, VII (1856), 58, 122; *Farmer's Companion and Horticultural Gazette*, III (1853), 184; *Iowa Farmer*, I (1853), 216.

41. In western Missouri: "Choice tracts of wild land are now selling for from $3 to $5 per acre. Improved lands from $4 to $8. The improvements consist of log houses, and stables, and more or less land plowed and fenced, with now and then a peach orchard" (*North-western Review*, I, No. 7 [1857], 35, cited in *Rural New Yorker*, VIII [1857], 382). In Illinois "a fair average for unimproved farms would be from three to eight dollars per acre, for improved farms from five to twenty-five dollars, depending upon the location with reference to a village and the value of the improvements upon them" (G. W. Hawes, *Illinois State Gazetteer and Business Directory, 1858-1859*, p. xxxiii). Prices are very commonly quoted. See *Illinois Farmer*, II (1857), 184-85; *New England Farmer*, VIII (1856), 260-61; *Northern Farmer*, III (1856), 209; *Ohio Cultivator*, XI (1855), 170; *Prairie Farmer*, XIV (1854), 217, 241, 346; *Rural New Yorker*, V (1854), 294; Gerhard, *op. cit.*, pp. 401-5.

42. "This, usually, is the better way for emigrants from old farms because they thus procure farms where improvements are begun and some land is already prepared for crops, and it has a habitable tenement for their families, until they have time to prepare a better one. We believe the very best bargains, and many of the best locations for permanent homes are made in buying out these pioneers" (*American Agriculturist*, XV [1856], 224). "There is here a great deal of government land not taken up in the Northwestern counties [the reference is to Iowa], but there are thousands of farms for sale,

now in first or second hands, from $2 to $10 an acre, that are cheaper in the end than to purchase government lands at $1.25. We mean by this, that as a man has but one lease of life, if he can command a few hundred dollars, he had better pay $5 an acre for his farm where it is already settled than $1.25 for that where it is a desolate wilderness" (*Northern Farmer*, III [1856], 395). "You can buy an improved farm cheaper than you can buy wild land and improve it" (*Iowa Farmer*, I [1853], 192-93). Cf. William and Robert Chamber, *The Emigrant's Manual* (1851), pp. 119-21; Freeman, *op. cit.*, p. 95; Regan, *op. cit.*, pp. 353 and 356; Smith, *op. cit.*, pp. 81, 85, 105.

There were also arguments against the purchase of "second-hand" land. "The emigrant who has only a small capital to start with, will naturally seek the cheapest method of getting a home, and among the many farms offered for sale, and the rich prairies inviting the farmer to labor, he will be in doubt as to what he should buy. A careful comparison of the cost of making the usual improvements on a western farm, with the cost of wild prairie, convinces us that the latter is decidedly the cheapest. A man who has not calculated the difference will pay $15 an acre for an improved farm—as it is called—when he could get the same quality of unimproved land close to hand for $5 an acre. A house ready to go into with his family and fields already enclosed are tempting baits to the weary emigrants, but a simple calculation will convince him that the improvements have cost him twice as much as they are worth. Often in their purchase the emigrant must take from one to two hundred acres of unimproved land with the farm, and for which he pays the full price of unimproved lands. . . . " (*North-western Review*, I, No. 6 [1857], 4-5). Cf. *Illinois Farmer*, I (1856), 26; *New England Farmer*, VII (1855), 554; Gregory, *op. cit.*, p. 310.

43. *Cultivator*, IX (new ser., 1852), 67; *Ohio Cultivator*, IX (1853), 338-39; Thomas Mooney, *Nine Years in America* (1850), pp. 20-21.

44. Knight, *op. cit.*, pp. 80-81.

45. Maine: Maine State Land Office, *Circular from the Land Office Descriptive of the Public Lands of Maine* (1858), p. 4; Maine Land Agent, *Annual Report* (1853), pp. 6-7; Maine, *Governor's Annual Message* (1860), pp. 10-11; Maine Board of Agriculture, *Annual Report*, IV (1859), 180; *Maine Farmer*, September 26, 1850; April 21, 1853; August 11, 1853; August 3, 1854; March 5, 1859; August 25, 1859; October 5, 1859.

Arkansas: Arkansas, *Report of the Swamp Land Secretary Made to the Governor for 1859-1860* (1860); *Scientific American*, III (1860), 389.

46. *American Agriculturist*, XVIII (1859), 271 and 315; James M. Lewis, *Arkansas Commissioner of Immigration and State Land: Natural Resources of the State of Arkansas* (1869).

47. Alden S. Lang, *Financial History of the Public Lands of Texas* (Baylor University Bull., Vol. XXXV [1932]), pp. 46-48; Reuben McKitrick, *The Public Land System of Texas* (University of Wisconsin Bull., "Economics and Political Science Series," Vol. IX [1918]), pp. 49-52.

48. E. W. Farnham, *Life in Prairie Land* (1855), pp. 328-29; Mooney, *op. cit.*, p. 19; Parker, *Kansas and Nebraska Handbook* (1857), pp. 66-68; Jacob Ferris, *The Great West* (1856), p. 319; *Maine Farmer*, May 26, 1853; B. O. Shambaugh, "Frontier Land Clubs or Claim Associations," *American Historical Association Reports*, I (1901), 69-84; C. J. Ritchey, "Claim Associations and Pioneer Democracy in Early Minnesota," *Minnesota History*, IX (1928), 89-95.

49. Horace Greeley wrote: "I am confident there is not at this hour any kind of a house or other sign of improvement on one-fourth of the quarter-sections throughout Kansas which have been secured by preemption. The squatter who thus establishes a 'claim' sells it out, so soon as practicable, to some speculator, who follows in his wake, getting from $50 to $300 for that which the future bona-fide settler will be required to pay $250 to $1,500 for. . . . To see a man squatted on a quarter-section in a cabin which would make a fair hog-pen, but is unfit for a human habitation, and there living from hand to mouth by a little of this and a little of that, with hardly an acre of prairie broken (sometimes without a fence up), with no garden, no fruit-trees, 'no nothing'—waiting for some one to come along and buy out his Claim and let him move on to repeat the operation somewhere else—this is enough to

give a cheerful man the horrors" (*An Overland Journey from New York to San Francisco* [1860], pp. 65, 70).

50. The farm-making frontiers of the 1850's were not confined to the frontier of settlement but were rather vary broad. They included parts of Maine, Georgia, Florida, New York, Pennsylvania, western Virginia, besides the major belt: Michigan west into Minnesota, Indiana into Nebraska, Missouri, and Kansas, Alabama into western Texas.

51. *Op. cit.*, p. 92.

52. The comment of the Maine State Land Office directed at western lands that "cheapness ends with the price of land" was universally applicable (*Circular from the Land Office Descriptive of the Public Lands of Maine* [1858], p. 13).

53. Lands in Aroostook County, Maine, which could be purchased for 50 cents per acre required $15 per acre for clearing (*Maine Farmer*, August 3, 1854; Maine Board of Agriculture, *Annual Report*, V [1860], p. 205; New York State Agricultural Society, *Annual Report*, XI [1851], 681). The cost of clearing Michigan woodlands was estimated at $10 per acre (E. H. Thomson, *Emigrant's Guide to the State of Michigan* [1849], p. 11), and the cost of clearing and fencing Minnesota timbered lands was given as from $18 to $30 per acre (Parker, *Minnesota Handbook for 1856-57* [1857], p. 131; cf. Parker, *Missouri Handbook*, p. 131; Wisconsin State Agricultural Society, *Transactions* [1851], pp. 243-46).

54. *Michigan Farmer*, VIII (1850), 275; IX (1851), 70-71; *Ohio Cultivator*, XV (1859), 36 and 119; *Southern Cultivator*, XI (1854), 209. In the South the "almost universal practice" was to girdle the trees and let them stand to rot in the moist climate four or five years (*American Agriculturist*, XIX [1860], 32).

55. *Ohio Cultivator*, XV (1859), 2-3.

56. *Michigan Farmer*, IX (1851), 70-71; VIII (1850), 265 and 374; XIII (1855), 365; *New Jersey Farmer*, III (1857), 216.

57. *Michigan Farmer*, VIII (1850), 11; XII (1854), 231-32; *Northern Farmer*, I (1854), 261; *Ohio Cultivator*, XV (1859), 54.

58. *Michigan Farmer*, IX (1851), 70-71; VIII (1850), 275; XII (1854), 297; *Rural New Yorker*, X (1859), 262; Marshall, *op. cit.*, pp. 18 and 21.

59. *Michigan Farmer*, IX (1851), 71; XIII (1855), 365-66; VIII (1850), 374; *Southern Cultivator*, XI (1854), 209.

60. *Michigan Farmer*, VIII (1850), 265.

61. *Northwestern Farmer and Horticultural Journal*, II (1857), 216; *Cultivator*, IX (new ser., 1852), 67; *Prairie Farmer*, XI (1851), 151.

62. *Illinois Farmer*, V (1860), 150; *Plough, Loom and Anvil*, VI (1854), 519-20; Parker, *Iowa as It Is in 1855*, p. 72; Franklin Langworthy, *Scenery of the Plains, Mountains and Mines* (1855), p. 273.

63. "If there is anything that should be well done on a farm, it is this breaking up of virgin sod" (*Prairie Farmer*, III [new ser., 1859], 339). A poorly broken field might require to be entirely broken again and, in any case, would cause serious difficulties in working the soil (*Rural New Yorker*, X [1859], 204).

64. This period is stated as from May 1 to June 30 in Illinois (*Rural New Yorker*, III [1852], 358;

Prairie Farmer, III [new ser., 1859], 339; Gerhard, *op. cit.*, p. 311); May 10 to July 10 in Wisconsin (*Wisconsin Cultivator*, VIII [1851], 277-78); May 15 to July 15 in Minnesota (*Northwestern Farmer and Horticultural Journal*, V [1860], 352-53); May 1 to July 15 in Kansas (Dana, *op. cit.*, p. 214); May 1 to August 1 in Iowa (*Genesee Farmer*, XVIII [1857], 141). Cf. Marshall, *op. cit.*, pp. 399-402.

65. "In Kansas where we have much land to spare, the sod is generally turned under during the summer and allowed to decay till the next spring, and then when plowed over again, yields enormously" (*New England Farmer*, XII [1860], 250-51). Cf. *Prairie Farmer*, II (new ser., 1858), 312; *Cultivator*, VII (new ser., 1850), 277-78; Dana, *op. cit.*, p. 214.

66. *Illinois Farmer*, II (1857), 151; *Prairie Farmer*, XIV (1854), 361-62.

67. "It is a very common practice throughout the entire western prairie country to get the sod broken by contract at a given price per acre, which ranges from $1.50 to $2.50 according to contract, according to the character of the work and the local influences governing the value of labor" (*Cultivator*, IX [new ser., 1852], 67). "Many thousands of acres are thus broken up" (*American Agriculturist*, XVI [1857], 252). "The cost of breaking prairie is from two to three dollars an acre; it is principally done by men who keep teams for the purpose and do their work by the job. A three horse team will break two acres per day, and a heavy ox team with a 36 inch plough will break three acres per day" (Gerhard, *op. cit.*, p. 311). Cf. Ferris, *op. cit.*, p. 210; Parker, *Kansas and Nebraska Handbook*, p. 36; Stirling, *op. cit.*, pp. 18-19; *Genesee Farmer*, XVII (1856), 84-85; *Northwestern Farmer*, I (1856), 128; *Plough, Loom and Anvil*, V (1853), 519-20.

68. Costs of breaking by contract are very frequently quoted—e.g., Illinois: $2.00 (*Ohio Cultivator*, IX [1853], 338-39; $2.50 and board (*Genesee Farmer*, XVII [1856], 84-85); $2.00-$2.50 (*Northwestern Farmer*, I [1856], 128); $1.50-$2.50 (Gerhard, *op. cit.*, pp. 294-300 and 412); $2.50-$3.00 (*American Agriculturist*, XVI [1857], 252). Iowa: $3.00 (*Prairie Farmer*, XV [1855], 159); $1.50-$2.50 (*Cultivator*, IX [new ser., 1852], 67); $2.25-$2.50 (Parker, *Iowa Handbook for 1855*, pp. 67, 72). Kansas: $3.00 (*Maine Farmer*, September 2, 1858); $3.50-$5.00 (*New England Farmer*, XII [1860], 89); $2.50-$4.00 (Parker, *Kansas and Nebraska Handbook*, p. 36); $3.00 (Dana, *op. cit.*, p. 214). Minnesota: $8.00-$12.00 (Rodney C. Loehr, *Minnesota Farmer's Diaries* [1939], p. 15); $4.50-$7.00 (Parker, *Minnesota Handbook*, p. 131). Missouri: $2.50-$3.00 (*North-western Review*, I, No. 7 [1857], 35). Wisconsin: $1.75-$2.00 (*Cultivator*, VII [new ser., 1850], 277-78); $3.00 (Wisconsin State Agricultural Society, *Transactions*, I [1851], 243-46).

69. "The first summer is usually spent in breaking, the fall in building, and the winter in getting out fence. . . . In subsequent years, the proceedings are much the same as in older countries, except that in many cases the fence is incomplete the second year." The reference is to Minnesota (*Plough, Loom and Anvil*, IV [1852], 687-88). Cf. Parker, *Iowa as It Is in 1855*, pp. 73 and 80.

70. *Ohio Cultivator*, IX (1853), 338-39; *Northern Farmer*, I (1854), 290-91; *Plough, Loom and Anvil*, VI (1854), 519-20; *Prairie Farmer*, XV (1855), 344; *Working Farmer*, VIII (1856), 35; Gerhard, *op. cit.*, pp. 293-307 and 412.

71. "In order to farm successfully, even on the fertile prairies of the 'Great West' the first consideration, after all, is to be able to fence. . . . " (*Prairie Farmer*, XIV [1856], 146). "Our fence is the heaviest matter we have to attend to, but one that cannot be neglected" (*Colmen's Rural World and Valley Farmer*, II [1850], 74). In Minnesota "the first winter is usually spent in getting out rails and fencing stuff to enclose the ground he purposes to cultivate the next season" (*American Agriculturist*, XII [1854], 128). Cf. *Cultivator*, VII (new ser., 1854), 277-78; *Carolina Cultivator*, I (1856), 163-64; *Farmer's Journal*, III (Raleigh, N. C., 1854), 204; *Genesee Farmer*, XVII (1856), 84-85; *Plough, Loom and Anvil*, IV (1852), 687-88; *Rural American*, I (1856), 130; *Michigan Farmer*, XIV (1856), 68-69; *U. S. Economist*, II (1853), 2; *Tippecanoe Farmer*, I (1854-55), 6; Loehr, *op. cit.*, p. 15.

72. "A large proportion of the prairie farms are cultivated without a fence to protect the first year's crops" (*Rural American*, I [1856], 130). "It is several years, usually, before the whole farm gets

enclosed" (*American Agriculturist*, XII [1854], 128). "But few farms are well fenced" (*Plough, Loom and Anvil*, VI [1854], 328-29). Cf. *American Agriculturist*, XV (1856), 74; *Michigan Farmer*, XIV (1856), 68-69; *New Hampshire Journal of Agriculture*, October 20, 1860, referring to Illinois; *Plough, Loom and Anvil*, IV (1854), 687-88; VIII (1858), 212; *Rural New Yorker*, VIII (1857), 269; referring to Illinois; *Rural Register*, II (1860), 356; Beste, *op. cit.*, I, 165; Caird, *op. cit.*, p. 50; Regan, *op. cit.*, p. 349.

73. *Prairie Farmer*, XI (1851), 164; *Carolina Cultivator*, I (1855), 226; *Country Gentleman*, VI (1855), 368; *Colman's Rural World or Valley Farmer*, II (1850), 125; U. S. Patent Office, *Report: Agriculture* (1851), p. 390.

74. *Prairie Farmer*, XII (1852), 199-200.

75. According to the census, the area under cultivation was 4,170,496 acres, that under fence 4,784,886 acres, and that attached to farms but unimproved 4,135,613 acres (Wilson, *op. cit.*, p. 82).

76. Few subjects received more attention in the agricultural press than did that of fencing; scarcely a number of any of the journals failed to discuss the costs of fencing or the desirability of securing some substitute for the wood fence. See *Rural New Yorker*, VI (1855), 221 ff.; *Indiana Farmer*, V (1856), 344 and 361-62.

77. *American Agriculturist*, XVI (1852), 278; American Institute of the City of New York, *Reports* (1859-60), pp. 151-53.

78. It was estimated that the amount expended in building fencing in the largely forested state of Wisconsin exceeded the original cost of all the enclosed land in the state (*Prairie Farmer*, XIV [1854], 324). The costs of fencing were particularly heavy in Texas and California. In Texas, "the expense of fencing a farm is two or three times greater than the first cost of the farm itself" (*Plough, Loom and Anvil* VII [1855], 417). Langworthy thought that it would cost $1,400 to fence a 40-acre field in California (*op. cit.*, p. 195). Other estimates place the cost of fencing in California at from $300 to $600 per mile (J. S. Hittel, *Resources of California* [1863], p. 165; *Rural New Yorker*, IX [1858], 110). The costs of the fences were said to exceed the selling value of many New England farms (*American Farmer*, I [new ser., 1861], 52). Cf. Freedley, *op. cit.*, p. 74.

79. Large areas in Illinois were reported fenced with timber from northern Wisconsin and Minnesota (Indiana State Board of Agriculture, *Annual Report* [1854-55], p. 231). One of the benefits expected of the building of the Illinois Central Railroad was that it would furnish the prairies with cheap lumber (Ferris, *op. cit.*, p. 209).

80. The editor of the *Indiana Farmer* wrote with reference to his state: "The man who owns a farm of 80 acres and has two-thirds of it enclosed, and divided into fields of convenient size, has about 1200 rods of fencing. This at a fair estimate is worth about 75 cents per rod, making a total of $900 as the prime cost of his fences, which is equal to nearly $17.00 per acre for all the land enclosed" (*Indiana Farmer*, V [1856], 344). Each 120 acres in farms in Wisconsin was estimated to represent an investment of $1,000 for fencing (*Wisconsin Farmer and Northwestern Cultivator*, IX [1857], 116). Estimates for 40-acre fields fenced with post and board are given as $506 by Gerhard for Illinois (*op. cit.*, p. 312); and as high as $620 for Minnesota (*Western Journal and Civilian*, III [1850], 339). Cf. *American Agriculturist*, XVIII (1859), 175; *Colman's Rural World or Valley Farmer*, I (1849), 31; *Prairie Farmer*, IV (1854), 67; Gerhard, *op. cit.*, pp. 294-99 and 412; Dana, *op. cit.*, p. 217.

These cost estimates compare closely with those of the older states. The cost of fencing was estimated to average $250 per mile throughout Ohio (Ohio Board of Agriculture, *Annual Report*, X [1855], 18 and 275; IX [1854], 192). The average costs of fencing per farm in Maine, Pennsylvania, and Massachusetts where the average farm included less than 100 acres was estimated at $700, and in New York and New Jersey at $900 (American Institute, *Transactions* [1851], pp. 186-87). Cf. Massachusetts Board of Agriculture, *Annual Report*, IX (1861), 89-90; *Pennsylvania Farm Journal*, II (1852-53), 359; Solon Robinson, *Facts for Farmers* (1856), p. 861.

81. Of the plows recommended by the *Valley Farmer*, as good for the West, the Peoria and Moline Steel plows varied in price according to size from $8.00 to $28.00. In contrast, the Phoenix, Jewett, and Eagle plows which were cast iron varied in price from $3.00 to $20.00 with the more common sizes priced at about $6.00 to $7.50 (*Colman's Rural World or Valley Farmer*, IV [1854], 266; Ohio State Board of Agriculture, *Annual Report*, X [1855], 528-29). The steel plow was standard in the West by the middle of the decade, though its relatively high cost prevented it from entirely displacing the cast-iron implement (Gerhard, *op. cit.*, p. 317). The Deere plow works at Moline produced 1,600 plows in 1850 and ten years later had reached an annual output of 10,000 (Robert L. Ardrey, *American Agricultural Implements* [1894], p. 176).

82. Broadcast sowing of wheat remained the most common method throughout Iowa during the decade (Iowa State Agricultural Society, *Annual Report*, VI [1859], 323-24, 376, 378, 402; VII [1860], 390 and 433). Drills seem to have been introduced first in 1851 in Lee County (United States Patent Office, *Annual Reports: Agriculture* [1851], p. 450), but the editor of the *Iowa Farmer* knew of only one in Burlington County up to 1853 (*Iowa Farmer*, I [1853], 4). By 1857 both Pennock's and Moore's drills were being manufactured in the state (*ibid.*, V [1855], 44 and 125), and their use was spreading (United States Patent Office, *Annual Report: Agriculture* [1853], p. 136; *Valley Farmer*, IX [1857], 121 and 147; VIII [1856], 101). In 1865 they remained, however, little known (Missouri State Board of Agriculture, *Annual Report* [1865], p. 101).

83. "All grain is here cut by machine. Cradles are out of the question. . . . If grain be too badly lodged to be so gathered, it is quietly left alone." And, "You observe that this work done by machinery is not very much cheaper than it could be done by hand—but the great question is—where are the hands to come from?" The reference is to Illinois (*Iowa Farmer* V [1857], 139). "We must purchase or hire a reaper; if we purchase one of McCormick's the price is $130.00 cost and freight; if we hire the price is from fifty to seventy-five cents per acre which is about half the cost of harvesting. In thrashing we must do the same way—purchase or hire, which will cost five cents per bushel for wheat, and three for oats" (United States Patent Office, *Annual Report: Agriculture* [1852], p. 396).

84. *Wisconsin Farmer and Northwestern Cultivator*, VIII (1856), 440-41. Marshall (*op. cit.*, p. 16), suggests $254 as necessary on timbered land.

85. The rate of adoption of the reaper during the fifties would seem to indicate that it was. In 1849 there were 2,800 McCormick's, 180 Easterley headers, and "say 100" of all other machines combined in the hands of users, mostly located in the East (*Prairie Farmer*, cited in *Genesee Farmer*, X [1849], 255). McCormick estimated that 73,000 reapers were in operation in the West (west of the Alleghanies) by 1859 (*Country Gentleman*, XIII [1859], 259-60, cited by Leo Rogin, *The Introduction of Farm Machinery in Its Relation to the Productivity of Labor In Agriculture during the Nineteenth Century* ["University of California Publications in Economics," Vol. IX (1931)], p. 78); and Flint considered that the two-horse reapers in operation by 1861 performed the work of a million men (Charles L. Flint, "A Hundred Year's Progress," U. S. Department of Agriculture, *Report* [1872], p. 286).

86. Parker, *Iowa Handbook for 1856*, pp. 159-60.

87. *Rural American*, I (1856), 114.

88. *Eighth Census of the United States, 1860: Agriculture*, p. x. The southern states averaged $148 per each 100 acres in farms; the middle states, $207.

89. It was for lack of capital and not because of greater profits that wheat-farming was typical of farm-making areas in the North. "Today the production of grain for export is the most precarious and worst paid direction which the farmer of Illinois or Iowa can give to his labor. The same amount of effort devoted to the production of Horses, Cattle, Hogs or Sheep, will pay twice as well. But the poor cannot await slow returns and the labor invested in growing Spring wheat or planting Corn can be turned into Cash in the course of six months, while the stock grower must wait three or four years for his reward; so Grain will be grown and shipped, at least until the farmers of the Northwest shall be less

generally harrassed by debt" (*Working Farmer*, XI [1859], 39). Cf. *American Agriculturist*, X (1852), 117; *Iowa Farmer*, I (1853), 254; *Prairie Farmer*, X (1850), 299; *Rural New Yorker*, II (1851), 403; *Wisconsin and Iowa Farmer*, II (1850), 254; *Wisconsin and Iowa Farmer and Northwestern Cultivator*, IV (1852), 58-59.

90. Farm horses were valued at from $100 to $150 each in the northern farm-making regions; oxen at $80 to $100 per yoke; mules $100-$200 (Parker, *Kansas and Nebraska Handbook*, p. 36).

91. In Minnesota, an investment of $315 was suggested to include a yoke of oxen, two cows, one horse, swine, and young stock (*New Hampshire Journal of Agriculture*, April 14, 1859). Gerhard thought that "a pair of good horses, a wagon, one cow, a couple of pigs, several domestic fowls. . . . are all that is necessary for a beginning" (*op. cit.*, p. 446), the group requiring probably about $300. In Texas, where livestock was very cheap, two yoke of oxen, a cart, one hoe, five cows, calves, and a supply of hogs and poultry were estimated to require $260 (*Southern Cultivator*, XIII [1856], 125). Cf. *Rural New Yorker*, V (1854), 222.

92. "An investment of $560 was suggested to include a "good substantial low-priced horse team, wagon and harness, five cows, pigs and poultry" (*Wisconsin Farmer and Northwestern Cultivator*, VIII [1856], 440-41).

93. "If we only had the money to buy them with" (*New Hampshire Journal of Agriculture*, June 2, 1860). Cf. *Prairie Farmer*, XIV (1854), 165-66.

94. Gerhard, *op. cit.*, pp. 294-303; Parker, *Kansas and Nebraska Handbook*, p. 37.

95. "It will be seen that the cost of 'breaking' must be advanced about fifteen months before any returns can be obtained from the land. There are very many who cannot make the advance. It is, in fact, a serious impediment to the advancement of all farmers, even after they have obtained a fair beginning" (*Wisconsin Farmer and Northwestern Cultivator*, IX [1857], 122). Cf. *Plough, Loom and Anvil*, VII (1855), 493; Loehr, *op. cit.*, p. 15; n. 63 above.

96. "Any farmer of ordinary capacity having his team and tools, and being on the ground by the first of April, will be able to raise enough food to keep his family through the winter till another harvest" (Parker, *Kansas and Nebraska Handbook*, p. 24).

97. *Northern Farmer*, I (1854), 440; *New Hampshire Journal of Agriculture*, April 14, 1859; Smith, *op. cit.*, p. 103.

98. "Half a crop" (*Cultivator*, VII [1850], 277-78). "I have raised partial crops of 'sod corn,' on my earliest breaking. . . . but of course, only partial crops" (*Rural New Yorker*, VI [1855], 358). "Indian corn is frequently sown as the first grain on newly broken lands; but as there is no reliance to be placed upon sod-corn many farmers prefer to leave the broken land lying fallow, until September, when it is sown with wheat" (Gerhard, *op. cit.*, p. 323). "Of course, every farmer knows that newly-plowed ground never yields a great crop the first season" (*New England Farmer*, XII [1860], 250-51). Cf. *American Agriculturist*, XII (1850), 128; *DeBow's Commercial Review*, XXI (1856), 96-97; *Genesee Farmer*, XVII (1856), 84-85; XVIII (1857), 141; *Plough, Loom and Anvil*, VI (1854), 519-20.

99. *Rural New Yorker* X (1859), 204.

100. *Indiana Farmer*, III (1853), 292.

101. Cunynghame, *op. cit.*, pp. 103-6; *DeBow's Commercial Review*, X (1851), 640-41; XXI (1856), 96-97; *Rural Register*, I (1859), 9; *Wisconsin Farmer*, VIII (1856), 440-41; Smith, *op. cit.*, 106.

102. "The emigration itself furnishes him a local market and by the time that fails, railways will secure him a more permanent though perhaps less profitable market" (Stirling, *op. cit.*, pp. 18-19).

"The immigrant for the first year is a purchaser and consumer, and of course creates a temporary home demand for our produce" (Iowa State Agricultural Society, *Annual Report*, II [1854], 38). "Already with thousands of emigrants coming into our territory who necessarily have to be sustained for at least twelve months before their labors aid in swelling the common fund, and with other thousands passing through bound for the Pacific coast with their herds and flocks, consuming as they go vast quantities of grain, the amount of produce shipped from our river towns is very great" (*Iowa Farmer*, I [1853], 33). The references are to Iowa. A resident of Wisconsin wrote: "Corn we raise in large quantities, but consume it principally at home. . . . Small quantities only have been hitherto exported; as besides the uses first mentioned, we have had a large influx of hungry Germans and other emigrants to feed, who have consumed no small amount of our marketable grain, while they were preparing the means to live themselves and afford the staff of life to others" (*American Agriculturist*, IX [1851], 15). The rapid growth of Minnesota was ascribed to the "ready market which is found in the limits of the territory for everything which can be raised from a generous soil. . . . This arises from extensive emigration" (Israel D. Andrews, *Report on the Trade and Commerce of the British North American Colonies and upon the Trade of the Great Lakes and Rivers* [1853], p. 171). "Multitudes have rushed from the farm to the building of railroads, from cultivating the soil to speculating in land, from homes in the East where on a harden soil, they were producing a little more than they consumed, to homes in the more fertile West, where, of course, they produce for a year or two, at first, less than they consume" (*American Farmer's Magazine*, X [1858], 193-94). "The probability is that we shall have food enough for our needs, which has not been the case previously since the settlement of the territory" (*American Agriculturist*, XIX [1860], 15, referring to Nebraska). A similar comment is made with reference to Sheboygan County, Wisconsin, concluding that enough will be produced to support its permanent and transient population "something that the best counties in the state cannot boast of" (*Wisconsin and Iowa Farmer and Northwest Cultivator*, III [1851], 145). Cf. *Colman's Rural World or Valley Farmer*, IX (1857), 335; *American Agriculturist*, XII (1854), 128; *Ohio Farmer*, VIII (1859), 386 and 409; *Wisconsin and Iowa Farmer*, VII (1854), 41.

103. Dana, *op. cit.*, p. 394. The cost of the trip from New York to Nebraska by rail or rail and water was about $45 (James M. Woolworth, *Nebraska in 1857* [1857], p. 9). Cf. F. W. Bogen, *The German in America* (1851), p. 49; Joseph H. Colton, *The Emigrant's Handbook* (1848), p. 134; Regan, *op. cit.*, pp. 403-4.

104. "Land in the far West at only $1.25 per acre is sometimes practically almost as remote and inaccessible to citizens of the United States as to the good people of Amsterdam and Harlem themselves. . . ." (U.S. Patent Office, *Reports: Agriculture* [1855], p. 128). "The fertile farms of Iowa and Minnesota, the rich plains of Kansas and Nebraska, the gold and silver of Montana, Colorado and California, are all his—if he can only get to them. It is only to 'go West.' But a poor man with a family finds it as difficult to get from his one room tenement house in New York to a farm beyond the Mississippi as a Londoner in Bethnal Green would to transport himself to Australia" (T.L. Nichols, *Forty Years of American Life* [1937 ed.], p. 414).

105. *Country Gentleman*, IV (1854), 157; *Northern Farmer*, I (1854), 440; *Southern Cultivator*, XIII (1856), 125; C. B. Boynton and T. B. Mason, *Journey through Kansas: With Sketches of Nebraska* (1855), pp. 68-69; Parker, *Kansas and Nebraska Handbook*, p. 37; Dana, *op. cit.*, p. 213; Webb, *op. cit.*, p. 17; Regan, *op. cit.*, pp. 189 and 401.

106. In Illinois, though the figure is applicable to the prairie regions in general (*Rural American*, I [1856], 114). A two-room house, 14 by 26 feet, was quoted at $225-$250; a five-room house, 16 by 28 feet, one and a half floors, at $400-$425. Caird estimates the cost of a three-room house, 18 by 24 feet, at $200 (*op. cit.*, p. 50). Parker quotes with approval the observation that a four-room house, 24 by 24 feet, could be built for $300-$350; a five-room, 20 by 28, one and a half stories, for $450-$500 (*Iowa Handbook for 1856*, pp. 159-60). The Illinois Central Railroad advertised its willingness to supply purchasers of its land with the materials for houses ready to set up at a cost of $150 for a two-room house, $400 for a four-room house, and $500 for five rooms (*Northwestern Farmer, and Horticultural Journal*, I [1856], 128). Cf. *American Agriculturist*, XVI (1857), 252; Dana, *op. cit.*, pp. 213-14; Marshall, *op. cit.*, chap. iv; Regan, *op. cit.*, pp. 300 ff.; Smith, *op. cit.*, pp. 17, 43, 79.

107. The items include the breaking of 40 acres of prairie on contract at $2.50 per acre, or $100; fencing this 40 acres, $320; seed and implements, $100; which is a low figure; livestock, $250; maintenance, $100; housing, $250. This total of $1,120 includes no provision for land or for travel expenses. The land was obtainable on credit or by squatting on the federal domain; its purchase required from $100 to $1,000 more. Though the figure for fencing may be considered somewhat high, it cannot reasonably be reduced, nor can any of the other of the other items be cut to bring the capital required below $1,000, though credit might be obtained for part.

108. In defense of the safety-valve doctrine, descriptions of farm-making involving less capital than we have suggested may easily be obtained. Such accounts commonly ignore various elements of the farm-making process and are generally stamped with the extreme optimism characteristic of the speculative atmosphere of the frontier. The following is an illustration:

"We will suppose a blacksmith, a carpenter or some one who has been supporting a family and saving a very little by his daily labor in the eastern and middle states, makes up his mind in April or May to come to the state of Illinois. He can count when he gets here, all told, say $150, perhaps twice as much, or at most four times that amount. He locates or to use the classical language of the country, 'squats' near a grove on the border of some fine prairie. Not an acre is 'fenced in' for miles around. In a week or two.... he has a log cabin built and his wife and their children.... are safely housed. ... He has taken care, after he makes his location, to find who owns the land he is on. If it belongs to the government, he takes out a preemption, or enters it at $1.25 per acre; if it belongs to some individual, he has got a bond for a deed, at from three to five dollars per acre, payable 'one quarter down,' the balance in one, two and three years, or longer. A few days finds half an acre fenced in and the garden seeds are all planted. Twenty acres are at once plowed, the corn is planted. Then hurrah for the fence while it is coming up. Drive the cattle off on the prairie for a week or two, if the fence don't get done in time, and as for the venerable, matronly old porker, with her numerous family, she must be kept in the yard till the corn is ripe. Fall finds him with six or eight hundred bushels of corn, potatoes and pork enough for his family for the winter, and three or four fine hogs to spare, hay enough for his cattle, cut wherever he pleased on the prairies, and his corn ground sown with winter wheat" (Hawes, *op. cit.*, p. xxxiii). Cf. n. 26.

109. "In the business of squatting on the public lands, there is a deal of delusion. The settlers are too apt to think that, having got a claim to a hundred and sixty acres of land, they have got a farm; whereas all they have got is a part of the raw material out of which, with labor and expense, patient waiting, and the investment of capital a farm may be made" (*Maine Farmer*, May 5, 1859).

110. The census of 1860 estimated that the 4,000,000 foreign-born enumerated in 1860 had brought not less than $400,000,000 into the country. A record kept of third-class passengers (immigrants) arriving at Castle Garden, the immigrant depot of New York City, by the Commissioners of Immigration of the State of New York, revealed an average of $65 brought in per passenger. Other estimates ranged from $60 to $180 per passenger (*U.S. Eighth Census: Population 1860*, p. xxiv). William Hayes Lord wrote: "I have known hundreds of German families who have taken out with them from 10,000 to 40,000 florins each family—from $5,000 to $20,000. It may be admitted as a fact that out of twenty German emigrants, nineteen take out with them the means to establish themselves in the inland states" (*A Tract for the Times* [1855], p. 25). On the other hand, it was believed that "nearly three-fourths of the whole expense of emigration from Ireland is being defrayed by remittances made by previous emigrants" (Baird, *op. cit.*, p. 340). The U. S. Census of 1860 reported that from 1850 to 1860 some $50,000,000 was remitted by private individuals from the United States to Great Britain through large banking and mercantile firms (*Population*, p. xxiv; cf. *Rural New Yorker*, IV [1853], 18). The best study of this problem is that of Marcus Lee Hansen, *The Atlantic Migration, 1607-1860* (1940), pp. 243 f.

111. High land prices in the East were observed to stimulate agricultural emigration to the West (*Rural New Yorker*, V [1854], 317). The English agriculturist, Johnston, pointed out that "speaking generally, every farm from Eastport in Maine to Buffalo on Lake Erie, is for sale. The owner has already fixed a price in his mind for which he would be willing, and even hopes to sell, believing that, with the same money, he could do better for himself and his family by going still farther West"

(James F. W. Johnston, *Notes on North America: Agricultural, Economic and Social*, I [1851], 162-63).

112. Edward Young, *Labor in Europe and America* (1876), p. 743. Skilled labor received from $1.50 to $2.00 per day (*ibid.*, p. 745).

113. *Ibid.*, pp. 739-42.

114. "If a young man saves $52 a year he is doing well" (*New Hampshire Journal of Agriculture*, December 17, 1859). The observation was made of New England farm operators that they "do not average saving one hundred dollars yearly, each" (*Homestead*, III [1858], 221). "Is not a farmer who saves this amount [$100] doing well?" (*New Hampshire Journal of Agriculture*, December 24, 1859). Cf. *New England Farmer*, VII (1855), 454.

115. Emigrants were urged to form groups in the East which would include all the necessary trades in the desirable proportions (*The West as It Is: The Chicago Magazine*, I [1857], 341-44). The suggested occupational distribution of such a group is given in Daniel S. Curtiss, *Western Portraiture, and Emigrant's Guide* (1852), pp. 292-93.

116. There is no doubt that some mechanics emigrated, but there is considerable question as to how many. This is the issue between Goodrich and Davison, on the one hand, and Schafer, on the other. See n. 1 above.

117. Tucker, *op. cit.*, p. 176.

A post mortem on the labor-safety-valve theory

Fred A. Shannon

By the 1940s the research of scholars such as Carter Goodrich, Sol Davison, and Clarence Danhof had demolished the idea that the frontier had been a direct safety valve. Not only did the West fail to attract when times were bad, but as Danhof so forcefully demonstrated in the previous essay, the cost of farm-making ruled out any direct acquisition of land by poor urban workers. The safety-valve thesis did not lack defenders. They argued that if there was not a direct safety valve, certainly there was an indirect one. For example, prior to the Civil War thousands of eastern farmers abandoned marginal lands and moved westward to virgin acreage in western New York and the states of the Old Northwest. The West also attracted the sons of prosperous eastern farmers. This flow, argued the safety valvers, minimized rural discontent in the East and also assured that displaced eastern farmers and their sons did not flood into the cities and depress the labor market there. Ray Allen Billington in *America's Frontier Heritage* (1966) maintains that such a safety valve did indeed operate prior to 1860.

In the following essay the late Fred A. Shannon, Professor of History at the University of Illinois from 1939 until his retirement in 1961, analyzed the arguments of the indirect safety valvers, especially for the period between 1860 and 1900. Professor Shannon, whose book *The Farmer's Last Frontier* (1945)* placed him in the forefront of historians of agriculture on the post-Civil War great plains, found that cities rather than farms provided key economic opportunities.

For further reading: Ray Allen Billington, *America's Frontier Heritage* (New York: Holt, Rinehart and Winston, 1966), Chapter 2; Stephen Salsbury, *The State, the Investor, and the Railroad: The Boston & Albany 1825-1867* (Cambridge, Mass.: Harvard University Press, 1967), Chapter 1; Carl N. Degler, "The West as a Solution to Urban Unemployment," *New York History*, XXXVI (January 1955), 63-85; Anne Bezanson, "Some Historical Aspects of Labor Turnover," in *Facts and Factors in Economic History Articles by Former Students of Edwin Francis Gay* (Cambridge, Mass.: Harvard University Press, 1932), pp. 692-708; Clarence H. Danhof, "Economic Validity of the

Reprinted with permission from *Agricultural History*, (January 1945), 31-37.

Safety-Valve Doctrine," *Journal of Economic History Supplement* (December 1941), pp. 96-106.

*Available in paperback.

Since 1935 there has been a growing suspicion among historians that the venerable theory of free land as a safety valve for industrial labor is dead. Out of respect for the departed one even the newer textbooks on American history have begun to maintain silence on the subject. For generations the hypothesis had such a remarkable vitality that a dwindling remnant of the old guard still profess that they observe some stirrings of life in the assumed cadaver. Consequently, it seems that the time has arrived for the reluctant pathologist to don his gas mask and, regardless of the memphitis, analyze the contents of the internal organs. Are the stirrings in the body an evidence of continued animation, or merely of gaseous and helminthic activity; Before the corpse is given a respectable burial this fact must be ascertained beyond any possible doubt.

There can be no question as to the venerable age of the decedent. Thomas Skidmore foretold him as early as 1829 in *The Rights of Man to Property!* George Henry Evans and his fellow agrarians of the 1840s labored often and long in eulogy of the virtues of the safety valve they were trying to bring into existence. The *Working Man's Advocate* of July 6, 1844, demanded the realization of "the right of the people to the soil" and said:

That once effected, let an outlet be formed that will carry off our superabundant labor to the salubrious and fertile West. In those regions thousands, and tens of thousands, who are now languishing in hopeless poverty, will find a certain and a speedy independence. The labor market will be thus eased of the present distressing competition; and those who remain, as well as those who emigrate, will have the opportunity of realizing a comfortable living. [1]

Long before Frederick Jackson Turner tacitly admitted the validity of the theory,[2] even the name "safety valve" had become a middle-class aphorism. The idea was so old and so generally held that it was commonly repeated without question. The Republican Party had so long made political capital of the Homestead Act and its feeble accomplishments that the benefit to the industrial laborer had become an axiom of American thought. Turner, himself, made only incidental use of the theory as a further illustration of his general philosophy concerning the West. Apparently he made no effort to examine the basis of the safety-valve assumption. Had he done so, no doubt the theory would have been declared dead forty or fifty years ago, and the present autopsy would have been made unnecessary. It was some of the followers of Turner who made a fetish of the assumption, but in recent years few if any have gone so far as to say that Eastern laborers in large numbers actually succeeded as homesteaders.

The approach has been shifted. An early variation of the theme was that the West as a whole, if not free land alone, provided the safety valve.[3] This, as will be seen, was no more valid than the original theory. Another idea, sometimes expressed but apparently not yet reduced to a reasoned hypothesis, is that land, in its widest definition (that is, total natural resources), constituted a safety valve. This is merely one way of begging the question by proposing a new one. Besides, it is easy to demonstrate that as new natural resources were discovered the world population multiplied to take advantage of them and that the old problems were quickly transplanted to a new locality. It can readily be shown that the monopolization of these resources prevented their widest social utilization and that the pressure of labor difficulties was no less intense in new communities than in the old. Witness the Coeur D'Alene strike in Idaho in the same year as the Homestead strike in Pennsylvania. But the natural-resources-safety-valve theory will require a thorough statement and exposition by one of its adherents before an examination can be made. The manufacture of such a hypothesis will be a tough problem, in view of the fact that, ever since the development of the factory system in America, labor unrest has resulted in violently explosive strikes rather than a gentle pop-off of steam through any supposed safety valve. The question will have to be answered: If any safety valve existed why did it not work? Since it did not work, how can it by any twist of the imagination be called a valve at all?

Another turn of the argument is a revival of the supposition of Carter Goodrich and Sol Davison (further expounded) that while no great number of industrial laborers became homesteaders, yet the safety valve existed, because it drained off the surplus of the Eastern farm population that otherwise would have gone to the cities for factory jobs. So, free land was a safety valve because it drew *potential* industrial labor to the West.[4]

Again, the question immediately arises: Why did this potential safety valve not work? Was it really a safety valve at all or was it merely a "whistle on a peanut roaster"? There can be no confusion of definitions involved. There is only one definition of the term: "An automatic escape or relief valve for a steam boiler, hydraulic system, etc." Under the catch-all "etc." one may just as well include "labor unrest." Obviously the safety valve is not for the benefit of the steam, water, or labor that escapes from the boiler, hydraulic system, or factory. It is to prevent the accumulation of pressure that might cause an explosion.

A safety valve is of use only when pressure reaches the danger point. This is where the trouble comes with the labor safety valve in all of its interpretations. It certainly was not working at the time of the Panic of 1837, or in the depression following the Panic of 1873, when over a million unemployed workmen paced the streets and knew that free lands were beyond their reach. It was rusted solid and immovable during the bloody railroad strikes of 1877 and the great labor upheaval of the 1880s. When the old-time Mississippi River steamboat captain "hung a nigger" on the arm of the safety valve when running a race, it can be positively asserted that his safety valve as such did not exist. This belief would doubtless be shared by the possible lone survivor picked maimed and scalded off a sycamore limb after the explosion.

No responsible person has ever tried to deny that at all times in America some few of the more fortunate laborers could and did take up land. But this seepage of steam which went on almost constantly did not prevent the pressure from rising when too much fuel was put under the boiler, and the seepage almost stopped entirely whenever the pressure got dangerously high. It was not till the 1830s, when the factory system in America began to bloom and the labor gangs were recruited for the building of canals and railroads, that any situation arose which would call for a safety valve. The shoemaker or carpenter of colonial days who turned to farming did not do so as a release from an ironclad wage system, as millions between 1830 and 1900 would have liked to do if they could. It was an era of slipshod economy and easy readjustment, where no great obstacle was put in the way of misfits. Even if one admits that a scarcity of free labor for hire was one of the minor reasons for the late development of a factory system, and that the choice of close and cheap land kept down the supply, yet a far greater reason was the scarcity of manufacturing capital. When the factory system began, it was easy to import shiploads of immigrant laborers. The same could have been done a generation or two earlier if there had been the demand.

But perhaps a more substantial argument is needed to answer so attractive a hypothesis as that of the potential safety valve. At first glance this new idea has some charm. Certainly the Western farms did not create their own population by spontaneous generation. If not Eastern industrial laborers, then undoubtedly Eastern farmers must have supplied the initial impulse, and each Eastern farmer who went west drained the Eastern potential labor market by one. But the question is: Did *all* the migration from East to West amount to enough to constitute a safety valve for Eastern labor? Did not the promise of free land, and such migration as actually occurred, simply lure millions of Europeans to American shores, seeking farms or industrial jobs, the bulk of the newcomers remaining in the East to make possible a worse labor congestion than would have existed if everything west of the Mississippi River had been nonexistent? The answer is so simple that it can be evolved from census data alone. The post mortem can now be held. If a sufficient domestic migration did take place with the desired results, then there *was* a safety valve, and there is no corpse of a theory to examine. If not, then the theory is dead and the body can be laid to rest.

The first question to be answered is: How large a surplus of farm population developed and where did it settle between 1860 (just before the Homestead Act) and 1900 (by which date the last gasp of steam is admitted to have escaped from the safety valve)? Here close estimates must substitute for an actual count, for before 1920 the census did not distinguish between actual farm and nonfarm residence. But the census officials did gather and publish figures on the numbers of persons employed for gain in the different occupations, and, wherever comparisons can be made, it is noticeable that the ratio of farm workers to all other persons receiving incomes has always been relatively close to the ratio between total farm and nonfarm population. On this basis of calculation (the only one available and accurate enough for all ordinary needs), in forty years the farm population only expanded from 19,000,000 to 28,000,000, while the nonfarm element grew from somewhat over 12,000,000 to 48,000,000, or almost fourfold. Villages, towns, and cities gained about 18,000,000 above the average rate of growth for the Nation as a whole, while the farm increase lagged by the same amount below the average. These figures are derived from a careful analytical study of occupations, based on census reports, which shows the number of income receivers engaged in agriculture creeping from 6,287,000 to 10,699,000, while those in nonfarm occupations soared from 4,244,000 to 18,374,000.[5]

Small as was the growth of agricultural population, it must be noted further that over 35 percent of the farms in 1900 were tenant-operated,[6] and 43 percent of all farm-income receivers were wage laborers.[7] This leaves only 22 percent as owner operators. But even though 25 percent is conceded, this would allow only 7,000,000 people in 1900 living on farms owned by their families, except for some sons who were also wage laborers or tenants. But the total national population increase was nearly 45,000,000 in forty years. Though the zealot may choose to ignore the fact that at least *some* of the farm workers owned their own land even in 1860 and may accept the figure for 1900 as growth alone, yet he has put but a small fraction of the increased population of the United States on such farms anywhere in the Nation, and hardly enough to consider in the West. This is not the way safety valves are constructed.

A further analysis of the data reveals that only 3,653,000 farms in 1900 were operated, even in part, by their owners. But at the same time at least 21,000,000 farm people were tenants and wage laborers and their families on the total of 5,737,000 farms in the Nation.[8] These laborers were rarely any better off financially (often worse) than the toiling multitudes in the cities. These were not persons who had found release either from the farms or the cities of the East on land of their own in the West. The bulk of them were still east of the Mississippi River. These were not *potential* competitors of the city workers. They were *actual* competitors, for the hard living conditions of each group had a depressing effect on the economic status of the other. Neither element had the opportunity, the finances, the experience, or the heart to try their luck in the West.

These incontestable facts and figures play havoc with the assumption that "perhaps most" of the Eastern boys who left their "ancestral acres" migrated "to the West to acquire and develop a tract of virgin soil."[9] There just was not that much of an increase in the number of farms between 1860 and 1900. Only 3,737,000 units were added to the 2,000,000 of the earlier year, and 2,000,000 of the total in 1900 were tenant-operated.[10] How large a proportion of the Eastern boys who left their fathers' farms could have become by any possibility the owners of the fraction of the increase in farms that lay in the West?

Here the potential-safety-valve advocates spoil their own argument. One of them stresses the great fecundity of Eastern farmers, "a dozen children being hardly exceptional."[11] At only the average rate of breeding for the whole Nation, the 19,000,000 farm population of 1860, with their descendants and immigrant additions, would have numbered about 46,000,000 by 1900. But barely 60 percent of that number were on farms anywhere in the country at the later date, and only 7,000,000 could have been on farms owned by themselves or their families. If farmers were as philoprogenitive as just quoted, then by 1900 the number of persons of farm ancestry must have been closer to 60,000,000 than 46,000,000, and the increase alone would amount to at least 40,000,000. But the growth of farm population was only 9,000,000, and, of these, little more than 2,000,000 could have been on farms owned by their families. If it could be assumed that all the augmentation in farm population had been by migrating native farmers, by 1900 there would have been 31,000,000 of farm background (as of 1860) residing in the villages, towns, and cities; 9,000,000 would have been on new farms or subdivisions of old ones; of these, nearly 7,000,000 would have been tenants or hired laborers and their families, depressing industrial labor by their threat of competition; and about 2,000,000 would have been on their own farms, whether "virgin soil" of the West or marginal tracts in the East. But it would be taking advantage of the opponent's slip of the pen to trace this phantasy further. The law of averages is enough in itself to annihilate the safety valvers' contention. By the use of this conservative tool alone it will be realized that at least twenty farmers moved to town for each industrial laborer who moved to the land, and ten sons of farmers went to the city for each one who became the owner of a new farm anywhere in the Nation.

As to the farms west of the Mississippi River, it is well known that many of them were settled by aliens (witness the West North Central States with their large numbers of

Scandinavians). Here is a theme that might well be expanded. The latest exponent of the potential-labor-safety-valve theory declares that "potential labor was drained out of the country, and to secure it for his fast expanding industrial enterprise, the manufacturer must import labor from Europe.[12] Anyone must admit that a fraction of the surplus farm labor of the East went on new farms. But how does this additional immigrant stream into the cities affect the safety valve? The immigrants may not really have increased the industrial population. It has often been contended that, instead, the resulting competition restricted the native birth rate in equal proportion to the numbers of the newcomers. Apparently this must remain in the realm of speculation. Be this as it may, the immigrants, with their background of cheap living, acted as a drag on wages, thus making the lot of the city laborer all the harder. This is not the way that even a *potential* safety valve should work.

But, returning to the West, there is a further fact to be considered. The total population west of the Mississippi River in 1860 was about 4,500,000. In 1900 it was just under 21,000,000.[13] Surely the "fecund" Westerners must have multiplied their own stock to about 12,000,000 by the latter date. In the same forty years some 14,000,000 immigrants came to America.[14] By 1900, with their descendants, they must have numbered half again as many, or 21,000,000, for it has not been contended that immigrant competition lowered the immigrant birth rate. On this point the census data are not altogether satisfying. Foreign-born persons and their American-born children (counting only half of the children of mixed American and alien parentage) numbered 23,673,000. No doubt the survivors of the foreign-born counted in the Census of 1860, together with their later children, would reduce the alien accretion since 1860 to the 21,000,000 estimate. If anyone can prove that this should be cut still a few more million, he will not greatly change the estimates that follow.

The Western States, in proportion to their total population, had proved amazingly attractive to the immigrants. Though over 19,087,000 of the 1900 count (including those with only one foreign-born parent) lived east of the Mississippi River, 7,112,000 were in the States (including Louisiana and Minnesota) to the west of the same line. In the eleven Mountain and Pacific States they were 47.6 percent of the total population, the figure reaching 61.2 in Utah, 57.3 in Montana, and 54.9 in California. Nevada also had a majority. Kansas and Missouri alone of the West North Central group had less than 40 percent of alien parentage, while the percentage in North Dakota was 77.5, in Minnesota 74.9, and in South Dakota was 61.1. In round numbers Minnesota had 1,312,000, Iowa 958,000, California 815,000, Missouri 741,000, Nebraska 503,000, Texas 472,000, and Kansas 403,000. Aside from Texas the numbers, as well as the percentages, in the West South Central States were low.[15]

In 1860 the trans-Mississippi West contained 653,000 persons of foreign birth,[16] but the number of their American-born children was not given. Even if the survivors and the children numbered over a million, by 1900 those twenty-two States still had 6,000,000 of post-1860 immigrant stock. If the estimate for the increase of the pre-1860 element is too low, so, it can be countered, were the totals of the Census of 1900. Grandchildren were not counted, and mature immigrants of the 1860s could have had a lot of grandchildren by 1900. All the descendants of the pre-1860 immigrants were included in the estimate of 12,000,000 for the increase of the inhabitants of 1860, whereas all after the first descent are excluded from the post-1860 immigrant posterity. On the other hand let it be conceded that 12,000,000 by internal expansion and 6,000,000 by immigration, or

18,000,000 in all, is too much. This would leave only 3,000,000 of the West in 1900, or one-seventh of the total, accounted for by migration from the Eastern States. The calculator can afford to be generous. Subtract two million from the internal expansion and another million from the alien stock, and add these to the migrants from the Eastern States. Suppose, then, that 6,000,000 of the West's population of 1900 was of pre-1860 Eastern United States origin, and three times that many foreigners and their children had come into the East to replace them. It all simmers down to the fact that the West acted as a lure to prospective European immigrants, either to take up lands, to occupy vacated city jobs, or to supply the demands of a growing industry. In any case the effect was just exactly the opposite of a safety valve, actual or potential.

Now the question is in order as to how many of those Eastern boys who left their "ancestral acres" and migrated "to the West" actually were able "to acquire and develop a tract of virgin soil." As will soon be demonstrated, only 47.1 percent of the Western population of 1900 lived on farms. By the same ratio, a mere 2,826,000 of the exaggerated number of the Eastern stock (as listed above) were farm residents. There were barely more than 2,000,000 farms west of the Mississippi in 1900.[17] If two-sevenths of the population was Eastern in origin, it may be assumed that the same proportion of the farming was done by them. This would give them less than 572,000 units to operate as owners, managers, tenants, or hired laborers. But in the West, as in the Nation as a whole, the ratio of tenants and hired laborers to all farmers was very high. A full 35 percent of all Western farms were occupied by tenants. The high ratio in the West South Central region affects the average for all somewhat, but there were several other States that approximated the worst conditions. The percentage in Nebraska was 35.5, in Kansas 33.9, in Iowa 33.6, in Missouri 30.6, and in South Dakota 21.9.[18] But, also, slightly over 40 percent of all Western farm-income receivers were wage laborers.[19] If these same ratios apply to total population on the farms, then well over 1,130,000 of the Eastern element in the West were wage laborers' families; more than 989,000 were on tenant holdings; and less than 707,000 occupied farms owned by themselves. This means that there was only one person on such a family possession for each twenty-five who left the farms of the Nation in the preceding forty years. But perhaps this number is a little too small. No doubt a good number of the hired laborers were also the sons of the owners. Also, though many of the wage workers in the West lived with their families in separate huts on the farms, another considerable number were single men (or detached from their families) who boarded with the owner. How much this situation affected the given figures is uncertain. But here is something more substantial. Only 65 percent of the farms, or less than 372,000 in all, were owner-operated. Here, then, is the number of those tracts of "virgin soil" taken up and kept—one for each forty-eight persons who left their "ancestral acres" in the East, or possibly one family farm for each ten families. What a showing for the potential safety valve!

One point remains: Urban development in its relation to safety-valve theories. Between 1790 and 1860 the percentage of persons in cities of 8,000 or more inhabitants grew from 3.3 to 16.1; the number of such places from 6 to 141; and their population from 131,000 to 5,000,000. Over half of this growth took place after 1840. The city was already draining the country. But this was only the curtain raiser for the act to follow. In the next forty years the number of cities was multiplied to 547, their inhabitants to 25,000,000, and their percentage of the total population to 32.9. They had grown more than twice as fast as the Nation at large.[20] The same rule applies to all municipalities of

2,500 and over, as their population expanded from 6,500,000 to 30,400,000.[21] The cities may have bred pestilence, poverty, crime, and corruption, but there is no evidence that they bred population that rapidly. Immigration alone cannot explain the phenomenon, for, if the entire number of immigrants after 1860 is subtracted from the nonfarm population of 1900, the remainder still represents twice the rate of growth of farm population.

It is conceded that the bulk of the immigrants settled in urban localities, and it has been demonstrated that the great bulk of the surplus of farm population did the same. For that matter, outside the Cotton Belt, the majority of the westward-moving population did not settle on farms. When the Eastern city laborer managed to pay his fare or "ride the rods" westward, he, like the migrating farmer, was likely to establish himself in a mining camp, town, or city, where, as in the Coeur d'Alene region of Idaho, he found that he had exchanged drudgery in an Eastern factory for equally ill-paid drudgery (considering living costs) in a Western factory or mine. The urbanized proportion of the population west of the Mississippi River, where 1,725,000 new farms had been created,[22] very nearly kept pace with the national average. In 1900, when almost half (47.1 percent) of America's people were living in incorporated towns and cities, the ratio west of the Mississippi River was over three-eighths (38.1 percent). Minnesota exceeded, while Missouri, Iowa, and Nebraska nearly equaled the national ratio. The combined eleven Mountain and Pacific States rated even higher than Minnesota, with 50.6 percent of their population in incorporated places. It was only the Dakotas and the West South Central States that were so overwhelmingly rural as to keep the trans-Mississippi West below the national ratio.[23] On the basis of the gainfully employed, always a better measure, the West showed a still higher proportion of nonfarm population. The census figures for 1870, 1890, and 1900 are used in the accompanying table to illustrate this point.[24]

In each decade, the Far-Western regions were well below the national ratio of agricultural to town and city labor, and to 1890 they were far below. In 1870, outside the West South Central States and Iowa, the figure averaged 44.3 percent for seventeen Western States compared with 47.4 percent for the United States. In the next twenty years, when free land was presumed to be the greatest lure of the West, the towns gained on the farms till the latter included only 46.5 percent of the Western total in spite of the still preponderantly rural character of the West South Central division. Then in 1890, according to the legend, the gate to free land flew shut with a bang, and the urban-labor safety valve rusted tight forever. Yet, the increase in agricultural population in the next ten years was nearly a fourth larger than the average for the preceding decades. Whereas the city had been draining labor from the farm before 1890, now that the theoretical safety valve was gone the Western farm was gaining on the Western city. Good land—free, cheap, or at speculators' prices—undoubtedly was more abundant before 1890 than afterward. Before that date, without cavil, this land had helped keep down *rural* discontent and unrest. A small percentage of surplus farmers, and a few other discontented ones in periods of hard times, had been able to go west and take up new farms, but many times that number had sought refuges, however tenuous, in the cities. Whether this cityward migration left the more intelligent and energetic or the duller and more indolent back on the farm is relatively immaterial so far as the release of pressure is concerned. Such evidence as has been uncovered shows no decided weight one way or the other.

This much is certain. The industrial labor troubles of the 1870s and 1880s, when this *potential* safety valve was supposed to be working, were among the most violent ever experienced in the Nation's history. Steam escaped by explosion and not through a safety valve of free land. On the other hand, down to 1890 the flow of excess farmers to the industrial centers was incessant and accelerated. When hard times settled down on the farms of the Middle West, as in the 1870s, Grangers could organize, antimonopoly parties arise, and greenbackers flourish; but the pressure was eased largely by the flow of excess population to the towns. No doubt the migrants would have done better to stay at home and create an explosion. Instead, they went to town to add to the explosive force there. Farm agitation died down when a few reforms were secured, and the continued cityward movement retarded its revival.

Persons Ten Years of Age and Over Gainfully Employed in the West, 1870, 1890, and 1900

Area	1870 Total Thousands	1870 Agriculture Thousands	1870 Agriculture Percent	1890 Total Thousands	1890 Agriculture Thousands	1890 Agriculture Percent	1900 Total Thousands	1900 Agriculture Thousands	1900 Agriculture Percent
United States	12,506	5,922	47.4	22,736	8,466	37.2	29,286	10,438	35.7
Trans-Miss. West	2,199	1,170	53.2	5,811	2,703	46.5	7,717	3,642	47.1
W.N. Central	1,157	648	56.0	2,988	1,432	47.9	3,693	1,707	46.2
W.S. Central	628	417	66.4	1,487	933	62.7	2,322	1,472	63.4
Mountain	134	50	29.9	501	127	25.3	663	192	28.8
Pacific	280	65	23.2	836	212	25.4	1,039	271	26.1

However, after 1890 this release for rural discontent began to fail. The cities were approaching a static condition and were losing their attraction for farmers. This condition continued until between 1930 and 1940 there was virtually no net shift of population between town and country.[25] In the 1890s when the city safety valve for rural discontent was beginning to fail, the baffled farmer was at bay. Drought in the farther West and congestion in the cities left him no direction to go. He must stay on his freehold or tenant farm and fight. Populism in the 1890s was not to be as easily diverted or sidetracked by feeble concessions as had been Grangerism in the 1870s. In the forty years after 1890, the farmers, balked increasingly in their cityward yearnings, began to take far greater risks than ever before in their efforts to conquer the arid regions. Four times as much land was homesteaded as in the preceding decades.[26] Great things were accomplished in the way of irrigation and dry farming; but also great distress was encountered, great dust bowls were created, and great national problems of farm relief were fostered.

Generalization alone does not establish a thesis, but already there is a substantial body of facts to support an argument for the city safety valve for rural discontent. Nevertheless old stereotypes of thought die hard. Quite often they expire only with their devotees. It has been proved time after time that since 1880, at least, the old idea of the agricultural ladder has worked in reverse. Instead of tenancy being a ladder up which workers could climb to farm ownership, in reality the freeholder more often climbed down the ladder to tenancy. Yet there are people in abundance who still nourish the illusion that their old friend remains alive. There is no reason for assuming that in the present instance the truth will be any more welcome than it has proved to be in the past. There never was a free-land or even a Western safety valve for industrial labor. There never was one even of the potential sort. So far did such a valve fail to exist that the exact opposite is seen. The rapid growth of industry and commerce in the cities provided a release from surplus farm population. The safety valve that actually existed worked in entirely the opposite direction from the one so often extolled. Perhaps the growth of urban economy also, on occasion, was rapid and smooth enough to absorb most of the growing population without explosive effect. Once the people concentrated in the cities, there was no safety valve whatever that could prevent violent eruptions in depression periods. Of this, the diehards also will remain unconvinced. The persons who mournfully sing that "The old gray mare, she ain't what she used to be" seldom are ready to admit that she never did amount to much.

The post mortem on the theory of a free-land safety valve for industrial labor is at an end. For a century it was fed on nothing more sustaining than unsupported rationalization. Its ethereal body was able to survive on this slender nourishment as long as the supply lasted. But when the food was diluted to a "potential" consistency, it was no longer strong enough to maintain life. Death came from inanition. The body may now be sealed in its coffin and laid to rest. Let those who will consult the spirit rappers to bring forth its ghost.

Notes

1. John R. Commons and others, eds., *A Documentary History of American Industrial Society*, 7:301 (Cleveland, 1910).

2. Frederick Jackson Turner, *The Frontier in American History*, 259, 275 (New York, 1920).

3. Joseph Schafer, "Was the West a Safety Valve for Labor?" *Mississippi Valley Historical Review*, 24:299-314 (1937).

4. Edward Everett Dale, "Memories of Frederick Jackson Turner," *Mississippi Valley Historical Review*, 30:356 (1943). See also Carter Goodrich and Sol Davison, "The Wage-Earner in the Westward Movement," *Political Science Quarterly*, 51:115 (1936), where the expression "*potential* wage-earners" is first, or at least previously, used.

5. P. K. Whelpton, "Occupational Groups in the United States, 1820-1920," American Statistical Association, *Journal*, 21:339-340 (1926).

6. U. S. Bureau of Foreign and Domestic Commerce, *Statistical Abstract of the United States*, 1931, p. 647.

7. George K. Holmes, "Supply of Farm Labor," U. S. Dept. of Agriculture, Bureau of Statistics, *Bulletin 94*, p. 14-15 (Washington, 1912).

8. *Statistical Abstract*, 1931, p. 647.

9. Dale, "Memories of F. J. Turner," 356.

10. U. S. Census Office, Eighth Census, 1860, *Agriculture*, 222; *Statistical Abstract*, 1931, p. 647.

11. Dale, "Memories of F. J. Turner," 356.

12. *Ibid.*

13. *Statistical Abstract*, 1931, p. 8-9.

14. *Ibid.*, 95.

15. Twelfth Census, 1900, *Population*, 1:clxxxii.

16. Eighth Census, 1860, *Population*, 623.

17. *Statistical Abstract*, 1931, p. 646.

18. Twelfth Census, 1900, *Agriculture*, 1:lxix.

19. Holmes, "Supply of Farm Labor," 17, 19.

20. *Statistical Abstract*, 1941, p. 6.

21. U. S. National Resources Committee, *Population Statistics: 3, Urban Data*, 8 (Washington, 1937).

22. There were 319,335 farms in the West in 1860, out of a national total of 2,044,077. Ninth Census, 1870, *Wealth and Industry*, 340.

23. Twelfth Census, 1900, *Population*, 1:lxii.

24. Calculated from Ninth Census, 1870, *Population and Social Statistics*, 670-671; Eleventh Census, 1890, *Population*, 2:306-337; Twelfth Census, 1900, *Population*, 2:cxxxv.

25. *Statistical Abstract*, 1941, p. 671.

26. *Ibid*, 1931, p. 134.

Part IV
Manifest destiny

Jacksonian liberalism and Spanish law in early Texas

Gerald Ashford

The relationship between the American settlement of Texas and Manifest Destiny has always been controversial. Most historians writing after the Civil War had a northern viewpoint and linked American penetration of Texas with the slave-power conspiracy. These writers assumed that southerners, fearful of the growing political imbalance between free and slave states, encouraged rapid settlement of new land suitable for the South's peculiar institution. If one accepts that premise, then the subsequent Texan revolution against Mexico and the Lone Star State's ultimate annexation by the United States follow as a matter of course. It is true that from the point of view of geography the extension of cotton culture from the lower South to the Texas plains was natural. It may also be true that certain southern leaders desired new lands for slavery. But these factors by themselves do not explain the settlement of Texas or its significance. The only way this can be accomplished is by an examination of the men who undertook the colonization.

If this is done, certain vital facts stand out. First, during the period of American migration into Mexican-controlled Texas (1820-1835) there was no need for a prospective cotton planter to travel to such a distant frontier. There was plenty of richer land in Alabama and Mississippi, and those states had the even greater advantage of good water transportation from plantation to market. What rational slaveholder would have elected Texas under those conditions? The second disturbing fact is the undoubted loyalty of many of the Texan settlers to the government of Mexico. This was demonstrated dramatically when Stephen Austin and his followers helped the Mexican authorities put down Haden and Benjamin Edwards' Fredonian Revolt of 1826. There is in fact considerable evidence that many who moved to Texas sincerely renounced their American citizenship and expected to remain indefinitely citizens of their adopted Mexico. This has always bothered historians, who, in agreement with Leslie Bird Simpson, have stressed the basic conflicts between the Mexican and American political, legal, and social systems.

In the following essay Gerald Ashford, a retired newspaper writer and editor who makes his home in San Antonio, Texas, explains why certain aspects of the Spanish and

From *Southwestern Historical Quarterly*, LVII (July 1953), 1-37. This article is reproduced by permission of the Texas State Historical Association.

Mexican legal system seemed in the eyes of American settlers superior to the traditions of their homeland. Ashford rejects the concept that the American settlement of Texas was part of the slave-power conspiracy as well as the idea that Americans who went to Texas thought that they were extending the benefits of democracy and liberalism to a culturally and politically inferior people.

For further reading: Mattie A. Hatcher, *The Opening of Texas to Foreign Settlements, 1801-1821* (Austin: University of Texas, 1927); Leslie Bird Simpson, *Many Mexicos* (Berkeley: University of California Press, 1941), especially Chapter 20;* Eugene C. Barker, *Life of Stephen Austin*, (origin. ed. 1925; Austin Texas State Historical Association, 1949); William C. Binkley, *The Texas Revolution* (Baton Rouge: Louisiana State University Press, 1952); Samuel H. Lowrie, *Culture Conflict in Texas, 1821-1835* (New York: Columbia University Press, 1932); Ohland Morton, *Terán and Texas: A Chapter in Texas-Mexican Relations* (Austin: Texas State Historical Association, 1948); Justin H. Smith, *The Annexation of Texas*, (orig. ed. 1911; corrected ed., New York: Barnes & Noble, 1941); Joseph W. Schmitz, *Texas Statecraft, 1836-1845* (San Antonio: Naylor, 1941).

*Available in paperback.

The reasons for the revolt of Texas in 1835-1836 are still so obscure that hardly any two scholars will be found to agree on what was the predominant motivation of the colonists during the conflict with the Mexican government which culminated in the Declaration of Independence. Slavery, expansionism, land speculation, cultural incompatibility, racial disharmony, oppression, dictatorship, governmental instability, centralism, religious intolerance, and other factors have been put forward as causes of the revolution, but none of these has gained unanimous acceptance as more than a contributing factor.

There is, however, a common denominator which has not received proper attention and which, if carefully studied, may explain not only the revolt but also the first American settlement of Texas, the long loyalty of the colonists to the Mexican government, the politics of the Republic of Texas, the annexation movement, and in fact a good part of the history of the state to the present time. For a clear understanding of this principle, it would be best to delay its precise definition until a proper foundation in history has been laid.

First, it is necessary to consider the political character of the American settlers in Texas. Although emigrants from the United States did not come in really significant numbers until Stephen F. Austin had received and advertised his empresario grant in 1821, there were a few who migrated during the last years of the eighteenth century and many more between 1803 and 1820. In giving their reasons to the Spanish authorities for wishing to settle in the King's dominion, these migrants usually expressed dissatisfaction with the government and policies of the United States. One Daniel Boone, for example, said to be a nephew of the Kentucky frontiersman, told the Spaniards that the government of the United States did not "suit" him.[1] Such protestations, although questionable, do contain a modicum of truth. Certainly these people must have been dissatisfied with something in the United States, or they would never have taken the trouble to migrate to Texas and take up residence under a radically different form of government.

As early as 1806 Moses Austin, then living in Missouri, reported to a friend in the East that widespread dissatisfaction had been stirred by the United States government's refusal to recognize many land grants made by Spanish authorities shortly before the cession of Louisiana. These complaints, Austin said, were aggravated by the arbitrary rules established by General James Wilkinson, then military governor of the territory, relative to the surveying of claims.[2]

Of the colonists who moved into Texas after 1821, about three-fourths came from the states west of the Alleghenies and south of the Ohio and Missouri rivers, including the state of Missouri.[3] The inhabitants of this region were Andrew Jackson's people, many of whom were Scotch-Irish, "the contentious Calvinistic advocates of liberty," as Frederick Jackson Turner called them.[4]

The region from which the Texas colonists came was in the later stages of development from a frontier to a fully-settled region. Vast tracts of Indian country separated the areas of white settlement, and while a Virginia-style plantation might adorn the banks of a river, pioneer cabins were still being built at the forks of the creek in the near-by hills. According to Turner, "the simplicity of life in this region and these years, together with the vast extent of unoccupied land and unexploited resources, made it easy for this upcountry democrat to conceive of equality and competitive individualism as consistent elements of democracy." The pioneer society, Turner points out, has seemed to its socialist critics not so much a democracy as a society of expectant capitalists. "And this, indeed," responds Turner, "is a part of its character. It was based upon the idea of the fair chance for all men, not on the conception of leveling by arbitrary methods and especially by law."[5] Turner further states:

The section's Western quality is illustrated by the varied origin and aggressive temper of its public men. The youth of the section; its bold, ardent, adventurous, imperialistic qualities; its will-power, sometimes domineering and usually exhibiting the demand for direct action; the common feeling in the Lower South against any restraints upon the right of the slave-holder to participate on equal terms in the opening of new territories. . . . The spirit of the western half [of the Southern people] was that of the eastern half, but infused with the greater recklessness, initiative, energy, and will-power of the West, and more suffused with feeling.[6]

As if in anticipation of these descriptive remarks by the historian, Stephen F. Austin wrote in 1834:

There has been too much of the ardent, impatient, and inflamatory [sic] impetuosity of passion for the last three years in Texas. The people of the U.S. are ardent in everything, it is their national character, and what has raised that country to the unparaleled [sic] prosperity it enjoys, and Americans carry the same ardor and enterprise and love of freedom wherever they go.[7]

Austin was evidently judging "the people of the U.S." by those he knew best; that is, the people of the western South, whom Turner later described in almost the same words.

The democracy of early Americans received its most energetic development on the frontier, the Atlantic coast having been the frontier when the first English colonists landed. As conditions became more settled, economic and social stratification was re-established. In the United States generally, the half-century following the Declaration of Independence was a period of political struggle between the Federalists, who believed with Alexander Hamilton that government rightfully belongs to the rich and well-born, and the followers of Thomas Jefferson, eventually to become the Democratic party, who favored a more broadly based rule of the people. The Democrats predominated in the West, where, as Arthur M. Schlesinger, Jr., says, "orthodox federalism had never discovered a social basis."[8] Schlesinger adds that radicalism in the West was mainly an unconscious process and that there is plenty of evidence that the backwoodsmen assimilated more democracy than they knew. They were deficient in ideology, but the dominant ideas of the time trickled down to them through the stump, the press, and the pulpit, sometimes with a rapidity that seems surprising in those days of slow communications. The sources of these ideas lay, first, in political traditions stretching back to the American Revolution and before, and, second, in a group of radical writers and speakers who flowered in the Jackson administration in much the same way that similar thinkers, not necessarily approved by the administration, burst into bloom during the days of the New Deal a century later.

One of the predecessors of Jackson's "kitchen cabinet" of intellectuals was John Taylor, who played an important part in developing the sometimes naive early ideas of Jefferson to a point where they corresponded to the realities of a society that was growing more and more industrial. Taylor believed:

Wealth, like suffrage, must be considerably distributed, to sustain a democratic republic; and hence, whatever draws a considerable portion of either into a few hands, will destroy it. As power follows wealth, the majority must have wealth or lose power.

He argued in favor of measures to prevent the privileged orders from preying on the people.[9]

In the hard times that followed the Panic of 1819, the new mood of radicalism, as it will do at such times, turned its attention to various subjects. Abolitionism was one of these, although it was mainly confined to the North and was not too popular there. Much the same can be said of socialism, which appeared in a pre-Marxian and idealistic form. Among more moderate proposals, revision of the old common law through statutory action was a live issue in the United States during the period of Anglo-American colonization of Texas. The influence of the clergy in government, another issue, was as widely deplored as it was hotly defended. Imprisonment for debt, still practiced in most of the states in the 1820's, was also a target of the reformers. The right to vote, meanwhile, was only gradually being extended to propertyless men.

To its opponents [according to Schlesinger] the common law seemed an infinite mass of judicial precedents which would always result practically in "judge-made" law; and it is true that in the hands of judges like Peter Oxenbridge Thacher the common law became a bottomless reservoir of reasons why no one should do anything. The democratic movement to revise and codify the laws thus produced another heated battle line. [10]

The anticlerical movement, although it dated back at least to the Constitution with its ban on an established church, became especially active in the 1820's as a reaction to an attempt by the General Union for Promoting the Observance of the Christian Sabbath to have the federal government prohibit the delivery of mail on Sunday. The editor of a fanatically anticlerical semi-monthly charged that there existed "among the leaders of a proud and aspiring priesthood, a determination to establish an *Ecclesiastical Hierarchy*, and to reduce us to worse than Egyptian bondage."[11]

The flow of petitions for a ban on Sunday mail deliveries was routed to a Senate committee headed by Colonel Richard M. Johnson, which answered with a thundering statement in favor of "religious liberty." A House of Representatives report along similar lines became so popular that it was printed on satin, framed, and hung in front parlors, barrooms, and stage offices across the nation. Colonel Johnson, who had been a leader in proposing a law to expunge imprisonment for debt from the federal statute books, now had also become a champion of religious liberty. He was eventually elected vice-president.[12]

Meanwhile the settlers in what was then called the Southwest had special problems of their own. For one thing, the expansion of the cotton-growing industry in the South was not a blessing to everyone in that region. According to H. Hale Bellot, summarizing the recent research in this field,

The increased demand for cotton, consequent first upon the growth of the English cotton industry and then upon that of New England, coupled with the introduction of the cotton gin making profitable the growth of the short-staple variety of cotton that alone could be produced on the uplands, led to rapid extension of the cotton area and the extrusion of small farmers by the planters.[13]

For those forced out of their former holdings, there were not too many places to go, for, although the public land was immense, its distribution was tied up in a huge complex of national policy. The more influential representatives of the South opposed a liberal land policy because their own westward expansion was cut off by Texas and the Indian country of Oklahoma. The available lands were more likely to be settled by a majority of nonslaveholding farmers from the North, eventually creating more free states to upset the balance of power in Congress. Capital in the North, on the other hand, opposed free land because it might lead to a labor shortage and higher wages in the northeastern industrial centers.

The general discontent which followed the Panic of 1819 was heightened by a feeling that the collapse had been brought about by contraction on the part of that great private monopoly, the Bank of the United States, as well as by the action of the government itself in requiring that settlers must pay for public lands in cash, even though the basic price was at the same time lowered from $2.00 to $1.25 an acre.[14] This price, although it seems small today, presented real difficulties to the prospective settler who not only had to pay for his land but also had to find money with which to purchase equipment, transport his family to the frontier, and maintain himself for a year or so until the first produce could be marketed. According to Schlesinger, "The new Western states [in the 1820's] felt their development hampered and thwarted by economic and political institutions too much under Eastern control."[15]

The change in the law was mainly responsible for a decline in government land sales from five million acres in 1819 to three quarters of a million acres in 1821. By 1825, the *Missouri Advocate* could angrily declare that the immigration to Texas was due to the difference between "a republic which gives first-class land gratis and a republic which will not sell inferior land for what it is worth."[16] Not until 1862 did the United States government give land free for the asking, and by that time the frontier had receded so far into the regions of little rainfall that it was increasingly difficult for a settler to make a living.[17]

One clue to the reason why the Texas colonists failed to see the inevitability of their absorption into the United States may be found in a letter which Austin wrote in 1830:

If that [the United States] Govt should get hold of us and introduce its land system etc., etc., thousands who are now on the move and who have not yet secured their titles, would be totally ruined. The greatest misfortune that could befall Texas at this moment would be a sudden change by which many of the emigrants would be thrown upon the liberality of the Congress of the United States of the North—theirs would be a most forlorn hope.[18]

Thus the land policy of the United States loomed as a barrier far more formidable than the Sabine River between the Texans and their motherland. The eventual solution of this problem, arrived at by Texas against its will when it retained the disposition of its own public lands in the agreement of annexation, was foreshadowed in some of the events in the United States in 1827 and 1828. In December, 1828, Governor Ninian Edwards of Illinois presented to his legislature the claim that the public lands within a state were the property of the state rather than of the federal government and that they should, therefore, be ceded to the state. Duff Green, who was then promoting John C. Calhoun's candidacy for the presidency, commended Edwards on his attitude. "Your position in relation to the public lands," Green wrote, "brings you into company with the South and West and in direct conflict with the East."[19]

The rush for free land in Texas began as soon as Austin's modestly-worded announcements appeared in the newspapers of the United States. Americans who were already supplied with unencumbered land, however, generally were not attracted to the new frontier. The principle at work here had been noted long ago by Hector St. John Crêvecoeur, who wrote in 1759, "the rich stay in Europe; it is only the middling and poor that emigrate."[20] Austin similarly wrote in 1828 that the majority of the immigrants to Texas owe debts in the country from which they came, having migrated with the hope of being able, with time and industry, to accumulate sufficient capital to pay their debts. Both Moses and Stephen F. Austin, themselves, had failed in business.[21]

Mary Austin Holley, Stephen F. Austin's cousin and a sympathetic observer of the Texas scene, wrote in her book published in 1836:

Though there are a few who may be styled nabobs, *as far as wealth is concerned, and others who are worthless and wretched: yet, as a general remark, there are no poor people here, and none rich; that is, none who have much money. The poor and the rich, to use the correlatives where distinction there is none, get the same quantity of land on arrival; and if they do not continue equal, it is for want of good management on the one part, or superior industry and sagacity on the other.*[22]

This sweet expression of early nineteenth century liberalism may be partially discounted on the ground that Mrs. Holley was writing to attract settlers, but the evidence for the relative poverty of the Texas colonists, as compared with those who remained in the United States, is ample. Even the nabobs, those who had many slaves, were said to owe large debts at home.

By 1824, Stephen F. Austin began a movement for the relief of Texas colonists who were threatened with suits over debts that they owed before migration. Traditionally, the laws of Spain and Mexico had been far more favorable to debtors than were the laws of either the United States or England. As late as 1830 it was said that five-sixths of the inhabitants of jails in New England had been placed there for debt, although most of them owed less than twenty dollars. The first bill to abolish imprisonment for debt was introduced by Martin Van Buren in the New York Legislature in 1817, but the process was not expunged from federal law until 1832 or from that of most of the states until 1842.[23]

In Spain as early as 1476 a decree of Ferdinand and Isabella forbade the seizure of oxen, other work animals, or tools belonging to farm laborers, except for debts due the King, overlord, or owner of the land. A century later the exemption was extended to the cultivated land occupied by the tenant, excepting crown dues, rent to the landlord, or advances made by the landlord to produce the crop. Plough animals were totally exempt from seizure in every case. Similar protection was extended to the tools of urban work-men by new laws in 1683 and 1786. It does not appear that there was any special legislation to prevent these laws from being applicable to the dominions of the King in the Americas.[24]

Having heard of the old Spanish law, Austin proposed in 1824 that the Mexican congress extend similar protection to the Texas colonists. He wrote, "They will however be able by Cultivating Cotton to pay all their Debts if time is given them, but if their Land and property can be taken for those debts it will ruin them and be of more injury to the improvement of this Country than any thing that could happen."[25]

Austin did not immediately press the point, for as head of the local government in his colony he had, in effect, the power to prevent suits for the collection of debts. Four years later, however, he advocated specifically a law forbidding the forcible collection of foreign debts in the colonies of Texas until 1840 and providing only for the collection of the principal after that date. The prevalence of such debts is indicated by the fact that notes executed by the Texas colonists before their migration were a popular item of merchandise among speculators.

Austin's views met no resistance, but rather general approval, and the law he desired was passed by the legislature of Coahuila and Texas in January, 1829.[26] Protecting lands, farming implements, and tools used in a trade, the law was more favorable to the debtor than Austin had requested, according to Eugene C. Barker, because in practice the vague provision that payment could only be exacted "in a manner not to affect their attention to their families, to the husbandry or art they possess" would probably have outlawed the debt altogether. The essentials of this homestead exemption law, proposed by Austin and based on a decree of Ferdinand and Isabella, were continued in effect under the Constitution of the Republic of Texas and were superseded on February 5, 1840, by an act of Lamar's administration.[27] The principle is still bodied forth in the Constitution of 1876 and in statutes now in effect and has been adopted by the legislatures of many other states. Texas has gone even farther in the same direction with a law which prohibits the garnishment of wages.[28]

Austin even played with the idea of carrying exemption of property from execution for debt to its logical extreme. He wrote to Edward Livingston in 1832,

By changing the old laws so as to base the credit system upon moral character alone, and not upon wealth and coersive [sic] means—or, in other words, to place the whole credit system upon good faith, and annul all laws (avoiding unjust retroactive effects) for the coersive collection of debts, all landed or personal securities, all imprisonment or process against the person or property for debts.[29]

Such a change in the laws would have been revolutionary indeed. Doubtless, upon further reflection, Austin must have become convinced that the proper evaluation of "moral character alone" was a task beyond human power.

Of even more general and positive importance than the protection of debtors, however, was the Spanish-Mexican policy of allotting land in generous quantities for settlement. As compared with the policy in the United States at any time either in the British colonial or the American national period, the Spanish-Mexican policy was more generous, more consistent, wiser, and more realistic. In contrast to the confused policies of the British colonial administration,[30] it was generally true under the Spanish laws of the Indies that, although the policy varied to some extent from time to time and place to place, land was ordinarily granted directly to the ultimate user by the sovereign who owed his title to the highest theological sanctions.[31] Certainly this was true of Texas from the first formal civilian settlement in 1731 to the end of the Spanish regime, and the policy was continued in its essentials by the Mexican government.[32] Under the realistic policy developed during centuries of experience in the semiarid regions of Mexico, and in sharp contrast to the practice of the United States then and later,[33] the Texas colonists were given land in sufficient amounts to carry on profitable farming or ranching under conditions of low rainfall, and the only costs were a nominal tax, deferred for six years, and a service charge of 12½ cents an acre, well earned by the empresario for his services as a co-ordinator. The first settlers were each granted "a league and a labor of land," the league amounting to 4,428.4 acres and the labor to 177.14 acres. In a typical instance, the smaller acreage would be well watered, or accessible to irrigation, and suitable for more intensive farming, while the league might be fit only for a cattle ranch.[34]

In countries as dry as Spain, Mexico, and Texas, water for irrigation gave value to land that would otherwise be worthless. Therefore, although both the Spanish and the English laws of flowing waters were derived from the Roman, the Spanish code held that water, when present, was an integral part of the owner's rights in his land. In humid England, where irrigation was rarely if ever practiced, it was held to be only an "artificial" use, like manufacturing, in distinction from the "natural" use of water for drinking, household needs, and the watering of stock. While the Spanish law preserved the old Roman distinction, it extended the concept of "natural" or indispensable uses to include irrigation. The "reasonable" use of water from a stream for irrigation thus became a vested right of the owner of riparian land, just as much as the title to the land itself.[35]

Spanish and Mexican land grants are the basis of title to 26,280,000 acres of Texas real estate,[36] amounting to approximately one-seventh of the state's land area and having a value in 1952 of several billion dollars; it includes, in addition to valuable farm and ranch lands, oil properties, the entire extent of the fertile, irrigated Lower Rio Grande Valley, and the city of San Antonio as well as many other urban communities. The Spanish royal grants, alone, are estimated at ten million acres.[37]

Titles in these lands are supported by laws reaching back in a direct chain of legal tradition to the ancient Romans. The Roman laws were codified in the sixth century in the *Corpus Juris Civilis* (also called the *Codes and Pandects*) of the Emperor Justinian. This *Corpus Juris* was the principal basis of *Las Siete Partidas*, the codification of Spanish law which was accomplished under Alfonso XI (the Wise) in the thirteenth century.[38] This code remained the fundamental law of Spain and the Spanish empire until modern times, being supplemented by various decrees of the successive monarchs. The decrees which had special application to the overseas colonies were collected under the general title of *The Laws of the Indies*.

Land grants made under these laws generally included the following elements: (1) Title was dependent upon the performance of certain conditions, which usually included use and occupancy for a term of years. (2) Mineral rights were theoretically retained by the king, although in practice the landowner was encouraged to take out gold, silver, and other minerals on payment of the "royal fifth." (3) The grantee received full riparian rights to the use of water adjoining or running through his property, including the right to use water for irrigation to a "reasonable" extent. Even if a piece of property were not contiguous to water, the landowner would command water rights if he had a legal means of access, as by an easement for an irrigation ditch.[39]

The Spanish law remained in effect with no fundamental changes after the revolution of 1821, although the grants were made by the Mexican states rather than by the central government. The greater part of the area of Texas was under the jurisdiction of the combined state of Coahuila and Texas, but the region between the Nueces River and the Rio Grande belonged to the state of Tamaulipas, successor to the Spanish province of Nuevo Santander.

Colonization laws, adopted by the Mexican nation and the states, established liberal provisions for populating Texas. Henderson Yoakum remarks that since the Mexicans regarded the land as without value, they were willing enough to give it away.[40] As was pointed out by John Locke, the father of liberalism, more than a century before, "what would a man value ten thousand or a hundred thousand acres of excellent land, ready cultivated, and well stocked too with cattle, in the middle of the inland parts of America, where he had no hopes of commerce with other parts of the world, to draw money to him by the sale of the product?"[41] It was Locke, also, who stated that labor gives value to land. "Nay, the extent of ground is of so little value without labour that I have heard it affirmed that in Spain itself a man may be permitted to plough, sow, and reap, without being disturbed, upon land he has no other title to, but only his making use of it."[42] If this custom prevailed in Spain when Locke wrote, about 1690, it may be safe to assume that it was a practice of immemorial age, which gave the most respectable antecedent for the Spanish-Mexican policy in Texas. At any rate, the Mexicans can hardly be convicted of unwisdom in liberally giving away land which, by that very fact, would eventually become valuable. Austin recognized this when he told an audience in Louisville, Kentucky, on March 7, 1836, that "the Mexican government have at last discovered that the enterprising people who were induced to remove to Texas by certain promises and guaranties, have by their labors given value to Texas and its lands."[43] The Mexicans, however, had also read Locke and there is no reason to believe that their land policy was a piece of inadvertence. Even without Locke, the old Spanish tradition for bringing in *probladores* would have been enough to account for the policy.

Henderson Yoakum illustrates the Spanish procedure in issuing land titles by reference to a typical grant issuedto José Luis de la Bega in 1792. Captain Juan Cótes, lieutenant governor at that time, had announced that he would donate lands to all who had not received them. De la Bega then presented his petition, asking title to a place called Las Castañas where he had a herd of mules. The lieutenant governor passed the petition to the *procurador*, who granted De la Bega possession in due written legal form. The three papers—petition, order, and act of possession—constituted De la Bega's title. They were filed in the archives, but the owner could have a certified copy. In another case the *procurador* stated in his possessory act that he had led the grantee by hand to the property, and at each corner of the land, "as a sign of possession, he drove stakes, pulled up weeds and threw stones."[44]

Later, as the country around the few towns in Texas grew more crowded with grants, it became necessary to make investigations or surveys in order to prevent conflict before titles were issued. Later still, under the Mexican colonial system, while the increasing number of colonists and the extent of granted land led to the abandonment of such formalities as leading by the hand, the essentials of the Spanish system were preserved. Conditions established by the colonization law were inserted in the decree which became part of the title. Such conditions would typically include setting up permanent landmarks at the corners within one year, the cultivation of the lands, and the payment of the nominal government dues within six years. The three parts of the title were entered into a book, according to their date, and a certified copy (*testimonio*) with a map was delivered to the colonist as his title.[45]

The simple Spanish-Mexican system of land distribution, though it served well in both the slow-paced development of Texas before 1821 and the rapid settlement by Anglo-Americans after that date, did not, of course, work out perfectly at all times, but its imperfections in practice were due largely to personalities and to a circle of mutual suspicion which grew out of language difficulties and cultural differences. Harbert Davenport, basing his opinion on long experience in the legal examination of old land titles, says that the Spanish-Mexican records can be favorably compared with those kept in the southern American states at the same period.[46] It is true, however, that many American settlers filed on land covered by older Spanish grants, either in ignorance of the existence of these grants or on the supposition that they had been forfeited by non-performance of the conditions. The informality in the method of settlement, breaking all the bounds of formal rules, contributed to confusion in this regard.

The results of this confusion are discussed in a letter dated June 30, 1828, from Manuel Mier y Terán to Mexican President Guadalupe Victoria:

. . . the incoming stream of new settlers is unceasing; the first news of these comes by discovering them on land already under cultivation, where they have been located for many months; the old inhabitants set up a claim to the property, basing their titles of doubtful priority, and for which there are not records, on a law of the Spanish government; and thus arises a lawsuit in which the alcalde *has a chance to come out with some money.*[47]

Stephen F. Austin's own policy, from beginning to end, was one of single-minded devotion to whatever he considered to be the best interests of his colonies. In this he was followed by all of the more cool-headed and responsible of the colonists. An unfriendly critic, reading the record too hastily, might accuse Austin of being ruled by expediency to the exclusion of all principle, but such an accusation would be unfair. Austin was thoroughly American in his political philosophy and maintained the highest standard of personal honor, but he subordinated matters of theory to the great enterprise of building a new commonwealth.

It is true that his shifts were sometimes remarkable. In November, 1822, when Emperor Agustin de Iturbide had just come into power, Austin wrote to a friend;

. . . . you must not be frightened at the name of an Imperial government, you like myself have lived under a Monarchy, when Louisiana belonged to Spain and I think we lived as happy then as under the government of the United States–The Emperor has his enemies and in the United States the Democrats will abuse him no doubt, but he is doing the best for his country. These people will not do for a Republic nothing but a Monarchy can save them from Anarchy. [48]

It became evident later, however, that Austin's acceptance of the revolutionary emperor was based on the expectation that Iturbide would provide the stable government which Austin needed for the building of a colony. After Iturbide's fall, Austin wrote in a different tone:

The Emperor has deceived us all–I thought he would have adhered to his oath, and governd according to law–but on the contrary he has violated the one, and trampled on the other–nothing therefore is more just, and more magnanimous than the spirit of indignation and resentment which the nation have manifested and the result I hope and confidently believe will be a Confederated Republic very similar to that of the United States. [49]

From various indications, it is evident that Austin's conception of a "Confederated Republic" leaned toward a southern concept of state's rights.

In the same letter, Austin, writing from Mexico, advised a relative in Texas that

. . . if any questions are asked them [the colonists] as to their opinion of the Govt etc. they ought to answer that they moved here to live under the government which the nation may establish they can do themselves no good by meddling in politics and at such a time as this when the Govt is not yet settled and the nation in a state of political fermentation it is embarking on a doubtfull voyage to embrace any party–as foreigners we have a good excuse for remaining neutral without being lyable to suspicions and this is the safe course. [50]

Security of title in the land was one of the continuing cares with which Austin had to deal as the empresario of his colony. Soon after his arrival in Texas, he had found it advisable to go to Mexico and have the elder Austin's Spanish grant confirmed, so that there would be no question as to the validity of titles, although the local Mexican officials in Texas were permitting the allotment of land under the original arrangement. Agustín de Iturbide fell from power, and Austin did not get his grant finally and definitely confirmed until April 14, 1823. On his return he found that many of the colonists, discouraged by his long absence, had gone back to the United States, and others who had planned to come to Texas had not done so.[51] He promptly reassured the remaining settlers that their titles were now "perfect and complete for ever." In appealing to the colonists to pay him their empresario fees of 12½ cents an acre, which he would accept either in cash or in goods, he went into considerable detail to show that he had spared neither labor nor expense to complete the titles in a way which would render them safe unless the settlers failed to comply with conditions in regard to occupancy and improvement of the land.[52]

Although Austin was not wholly convinced of the rightness of slavery, he was inclined to regard it as essential to the success of his colony.[53] Certainly the use of slaves was considered by the southern whites of that period as an inseparable part of their right to work the land without molestation. In spite of his private reservations, Austin headed a committee which addressed a petition to the Mexican government, asking that the three hundred families to be admitted to the colony should be exempted permanently from the operation of an emancipation law which had been passed. The petition declared: "... many of them [the colonists] brought their negro slaves with them as also all their property intending to establish themselves permanently in this Province."[54]

At the same period Austin showed an especially keen interest in learning the details of certain laws of which he had not received copies. He inquired particularly with regard to the laws on settlement of estates, transfer of property between settlers, punishment of criminals, and collection of debts contracted outside of Texas. In a first draft of this letter of inquiry, Austin had also mentioned religious freedom and the possibility of appointing a *juez de letras* to hear appeals from the *alcaldes*. Both of these subjects were dropped before the letter was sent, and a marginal note in Austin's draft indicates that he decided the first subject, at least, was too difficult to handle.[55] It does not appear, in any case, that the denial of recognition to any but the Catholic church was greatly resented by the colonists. They had gone to Texas deliberately, in full awareness of the law, and those Protestants who felt strongly in sectarian matters had stayed at home in the United States.

Austin's interest in obtaining copies of the laws, though natural to a man in his position, may have been heightened by the fact that he was being criticized severely by some of the colonists for alleged arbitrariness in allotting land and for other actions as a Mexican official. He replied to this criticism frankly in moderate terms, as was his habit, and he added, "I approve of the principle that every public officer is amendable [*sic*] to the law for his official acts.—It is the only solid basis upon which free institutions can rest."[56]

Austin himself had become temporarily a victim of the often fatal weakness of personalism in government, which Mexico inherited from Spain. The ideal in which he believed was "a government not of men but of laws." But Austin himself, as an official left with too much discretion, had been compelled to use that discretion to the displeasure of some of his colonists. In the cases of officials less conscientious and less wise than Austin, this was precisely the situation that piled up a structure of insecurity for the colonists and eventually drove them to revolt.

A premonitory rumble was the Fredonian Rebellion of 1826-1827 when a small number of American colonists—not connected with Austin—rose in revolt at Nacagdoches because of their dissatisfaction with the manner in which the authorities had settled their title disputes with earlier settlers.[57] Whatever may have been the rights and wrongs of this dispute, it is evident that the local Mexican authorities had acted under wide discretionary powers which left neither side any means of determining what rights of theirs would be recognized.

Two of the leaders of the revolt wrote in a manifesto:

We were enticed from our native country under the promise of important advantages to our families, and by a guarantee of our rights and liberties. We have been basely deceived in all these promises, and we know not now, that we have a valid title to one foot of land in the province of Texas. Lands have been granted and taken away at the mere will and pleasure of a corrupt and prejudiced Governor without any regard to the forms of justice or the rights of the Judicial Department of this Government.[58]

While Austin offered his militia to the Mexican government to suppress his countrymen's rebellion, the people of DeWitt's Colony adopted resolutions of loyalty, in the first one of which they declared . . . "that the people of this Colony came to, and settled in the Mexican Nation, by the benign influence of her laws: that as adopted children [they] have full confidence and faith in the equity, justice and liberality in the Federal and State Governments of their new parent."[59] Although these two statements are opposite in spirit as regards the issue of the moment when they appeared, they are firmly in agreement that the signers were brought to Texas by the expectation of being secure in the rights and liberties granted by the laws of Mexico, which for the most part were the laws of Spain as they continued in effect after the political revolution.

More trouble occurred in February, 1831, when a special land commissioner, J. Francisco Madero, reached the lower Trinity River bearing instructions from the governor to issue land titles to the settlers there and farther east, between Nacogdoches and the United States boundary at the Sabine. These people, though they had come as squatters, had made valuable improvements on the lands they occupied. Madero was prevented from carrying out his mission, however, by the violent opposition of the Mexican military commander in the region, the American-born Colonel John Davis Bradburn, who insisted that the issuance of titles would be a violation of the Act of April 6, 1830, which forbade further American immigration into Texas. Mexican officials, other than Bradburn, generally ignored the innumerable violations of this law.[60]

In a speech at Brazoria on September 8, 1835, less than a month before the first battle of the Texas Revolution, Austin looked back to the time when "under the Spanish government, Texas was a separate and distinct local organization." The union with Coahuila, he declared, was only provisional and was always subject to the vested rights of Texas. He continued:

The state, therefore, cannot relinquish those vested rights, by agreeing to the change of government, or by any other act, unless expressly authorized by the people of Texas to do so; neither can the general government of Mexico legally deprive Texas of them without the consent of this people. . . . Texas needs peace, and a local government: its inhabitants are farmers, and they need a calm and quiet life.[61]

As a legal brief, Austin's argument might easily be open to question. During the Spanish regime, of course, Texas was merely a province—an administrative division with no existence as a political entity. It had not been a separate state, and even if it had been, it is doubtful whether a state can be said to have vested rights as the term is used in law, where it is applied to the existing rights of persons as against any contemplated change in the statutes. This utterance by Austin, however, doubtless expressed the thoughts and feelings of the American colonists, and it helps to explain the occurrence of the term, "vested rights," in a different context in the first constitution of the state of Texas in 1845.[62]

Since land was virtually the only form of wealth among the colonists who in 1835 began to break away from Mexico, it is not surprising that the plan of government unanimously signed by the members of the Consultation at Washington-on-the-Brazos on November 13, 1835, implicitly recognized the validity of Mexican and Spanish land titles and continued in effect the laws of Coahuila and Texas.[63] Soon, however, the Texans felt themselves compelled to drop their plan for a new state in the Mexican union and turn to independence as the only solution of their problems.

Immediately after the Declaration of Independence, in March, 1836, the first steps toward establishing a system of law for the new Republic of Texas were taken at a constitutional convention at Washington-on-the-Brazos. The constitution adopted was similar in its main outlines to the Constitution of the United States, insofar as the provisions of that Constitution could be made applicable to a unitary nation which did not have to deal with questions of states' rights. In spite of this large omission, the Constitution of Texas was much longer and more detailed than that of the United States. It is in its miscellaneous departures from the United States pattern that the best clues are found as to what was in the minds of the leaders of early Texas as they set about giving laws to the people of the Republic. No record of the debates at the convention are extant, but the provisions of the Constitution speak for themselves.[64]

Article IV, Section 13, provides:

The Congress shall, as early as practicable, introduce, by statute, the common law of England, with such modifications as our circumstances, in their judgment may require, and in all criminal cases the common law shall be the rule of decision.

The Congress finally found it practicable to reduce this provision to statute nearly four years later in the Act of January 20, 1840. From the provisions of that law and from the importance of Spanish laws relating to land tenure, it may safely be assumed that the makers of the Constitution were aware of the modifications of the common law which would be required by the conditions prevailing in Texas. The requirement relating that the common law be applied in criminal cases was designed to avoid the abuses of Mexican law on this subject, especially the denial of trial by jury. This right, however, had been granted to the Texas colonists by special legislation.

A direct piece of evidence on the prevalence of American liberal ideas in Texas is provided by Article V, Section 1, which reads as follows:

Ministers of the gospel being, by their profession, dedicated to God and the care of souls, ought not to be diverted from the great duties of their functions, therefore, no minister of the gospel or priest of any denomination whatever shall be eligible to the office of the Executive of the Republic, nor to a seat of either branch of the Congress of the same.

Both from the wording of this section and from the debate which occurred when a similar provision was proposed for the first state constitution in 1845,[65] it is evident that this ban was directed at Protestant ministers as well as at Catholic priests, whom the colonists associated with the arbitrary political power against which they had revolted. The colonists, however, had had practically no firsthand experience with Catholic priests, and Protestant ministers also were few in number. The fact that it occurred to the constitution makers to insert such a provision can only be attributed to the popularity of anticlerical ideas in Andrew Jackson's United States.

Manhood suffrage, which was a new thing in the United States at that time, was secured to Texas by Article VI, Section 11:

Every citizen of the Republic who has attained the age of twenty-one years, and shall have resided six months within the district or county where the election is held, shall be entitled to vote for members of the General Congress.

The term "citizen" excluded Negroes, whether slave or free. The extension of suffrage even to all white men, without regard to property qualifications, was, nevertheless, an advanced proposal at the time and had not yet penetrated to all the states of the Union. It is an odd and seldom realized fact that the Constitution of the United States even now, while it prohibits denial of the franchise on grounds of race, color, sex, or previous condition of servitude, does not prohibit Congress or the state legislatures from setting up property qualifications for the vote. In fact, such qualifications are still established, in Texas and elsewhere, for certain types of elections, such as those in which the voters are asked to approve a bond issue.

The transition from Spanish-Mexican law to Texan law with Spanish modifications was cushioned by Section 1 of the Schedule of the Constitution of the Republic which provided:

That no inconvenience may arise from the adoption of this Constitution, it is declared by this Convention that all laws now in force in Texas, and not inconsistent with this Constitution, shall remain in full force until declared void, repealed, altered, or expire by their own limitation.

This is a direct reference to the Spanish-Mexican laws, which had hitherto been kept in force by the plan of the Constitution. A similar provision was included in the first state constitution in 1845. Section 7 of the General Provisions of the 1836 Constitution required:

So soon as convenience will permit, there shall be a penal code formed on principles of reformation, and not of vindictive justice, and the civil and criminal laws shall be revised, digested, and arranged under different heads; and all laws relating to land titles shall be translated, revised, and promulgated.

Revision of the criminal law was a gradual process. The most thorough revision of the criminal law took place pursuant to a legislative act of February 11, 1854, and was carried out, under considerable influence from Spanish law, by a commission composed of John W. Harris, O. J. Hartley, and James Willie, with the task of revising the criminal portion of the law assigned mainly to Willie. The drafts proposed by the commission were adopted by the legislature in 1856.[66]

Continuity of land titles under the new Republic was taken so much for granted by the makers of the Constitution that it was affirmed only by specifying a list of exceptions to the implied rule. The first of these exceptions occurs in Section 8 of the General Provisions, which prescribes:

All persons who shall leave the country for the purpose of evading a participation in the present struggle, or shall refuse to participate in it, or shall give aid or assistance to the present enemy, shall forfeit all rights of citizenship and such lands as they may hold in the Republic.

It is worthy of note that this phraseology includes a virtual equation between citizenship and the ownership of land. This equation is clearly stated in Section 10, where it is provided that:

. . . All citizens now living in Texas, who have not received their portion of land, in like manner as colonists, shall be entitled to their land in the following proportion and manner: Every head of a family shall be entitled to one league and "labour" of land, and every single man of the age of seventeen and upwards, shall be entitled to the third part of one league of land.

This was probably the only time in the history of the world that the opportunity to gain possession of land had been recognized as a right to which people are entitled. The principle thus enunciated was a direct outgrowth of the policy followed by the Spaniards.

Returning to the question of continuity of titles under the changed government, the validity of Spanish-Mexican grants was again given implied recognition in another portion of Section 10 of the General Provisions, which provided:

In all cases the actual settler and occupant of the soil shall be entitled, in locating his land, to include his improvement, in preference to all other claims not acquired previous to his settlement, according to the law of the land and this Constitution.

The law of the land, here referred to, was the law of Mexico and of the state of Coahuila and Texas, which remained in effect.

The Constitution gives further evidence of the importance of the land question in another paragraph of Section 10:

And whereas the protection of the public domain from unjust and fraudulent claims, and quieting of the People in the enjoyment of their lands, is one of the great duties of this Convention . . . .

The Constitution then goes on specifically to annul several large grants, said to amount to a total of 1,100 leagues, which had been given to John T. Mason and others by special acts of the legislature of Coahuila and Texas in 1834 and 1835. These acts were annulled by the Texas constitutional convention on the expressed ground that they were contrary to certain laws passed by the Mexican Congress in 1824. The same section of the constitution voided all surveys, locations, and titles to land made while the land offices were closed during the confusion of the Texas Revolution, when many prior holders of land, being away at the wars, were unable to prevent acts of possession by newcomers.

The Texan Declaration of Rights, which was placed at the end of the Constitution, went a step farther than the United States Bill of Rights in insuring the separation of church and state. Section 1 of Article V barred clergymen from Congress and the presidency of the Republic. The Declaration of Rights, Article 3, further provided:

No preference shall be given by law to any religious denomination or mode of worship over another, but every person shall be permitted to worship God according to the dictates of his own conscience.

This language is much more restrictive than the United States provision that "Congress shall make no law respecting an establishment of religion, or prohibiting the free exercise thereof."

Imprisonment for debt, still prevalent in the United States in 1836, was kept out of Texas by Section 12 of the Declaration of Rights, which provided: "No person shall be imprisoned for debt in consequence of inability to pay." It seems probable that this section was motivated by the popularity of such ideas in the United States at the time, by the high proportion of debtors in the Texas population, and by the tradition of lenience toward debtors which had been handed down in Spanish law since Ferdinand and Isabella.

Two other liberal provisions, not found in the Constitution of the United States, are combined in Section 17 of the Texas Declaration of Rights:

Perpetuities or monopolies are contrary to the genius of a free government, and shall not be allowed; nor shall the law of primogeniture or entailments ever be in force in this Republic.

All forms of entail had been abolished by the Spanish liberal Cortes in 1820 and by the Mexican Congress in 1823. They had also been gradually abolished by the individual states.[67]

The Constitution of the Republic of Texas, although built on a framework of traditional American ideas, contains important modifications derived from the popular advanced thinking of the Jacksonian period and the Mexican tradition of Spanish law. These departures, as well as the more conventional provisions, were, of course, made effective by acts of the Congress. Later they were generally incorporated in the Constitution and laws of the state of Texas.

While the Republic still existed, an Act of January 20, 1840,[68] brought about the adoption of the Anglo-American common law in all matters except those relating to land tenure, which were actually the most numerous and weighty questions dealt with by the courts for many years. A technical analysis of the differences between Spanish and English law would be of little interest, but the Spanish system, besides being bound up to a great extent with the existing property rights of the Texans, was believed to promote justice by its simplicity in theory and practice. It was not case-law, or "judge-made law," but a concise code, which called for no wearisome study of precedents. In the words of Dudley Wooten,

The government had it in its power to establish and maintain a simple and direct method of real-estate tenures, deriving their validity and incidents immediately from the sovereign political power and burdened with none of the restrictions, technicalities, and legal niceties of the feudal and baronial servitudes of the common-law titles to realty, instead of complicating our landed system with the black-letter learning of English courts and statutes. [69]

The land law included the Spanish law of waters. In any event the climate of a large part of Texas would have dictated the adoption of a more realistic policy than that handed down from the English common law. Other arid and semiarid western states struggled for a generation with wholesale violations of statutes that were based on the narrow English doctrine, until that doctrine was modified by the courts or the legislatures in eight of those states and abrogated by eight others in favor of the new "arid region doctrine of prior appropriation," which gives paramount rights to the first user of any source of water. [70]

The climate also led the Texans to imitate Spanish liberality in granting tracts of land large enough to support a ranching establishment on the semiarid plains. Under the Republic, individual or family grants ranged from 640 to 4,605 acres, [71] the latter figure being the equivalent of the Spanish league and labor. At annexation, by the insistence of the United States Congress, Texas retained the right to dispose of its own public lands instead of giving them to the federal government. The later land policy of the state continued the tradition of liberality which had been established by the old Spanish government. [72]

With regard to the titles which had their origin in Spanish and Mexican grants, there was great uneasiness in the years following separation from Mexico. [73] In the case of McMullen v. Hodge, Justice Abner Smith Lipscomb explained the pertinent principles at length and in a manner which indicated that he was writing for public reassurance as much as for the record of the case. Beginning with a discussion of the different kinds of revolutions, he concluded that the revolution in Texas was simply a change of political control, and he stated emphatically: "This court has repeatedly held, that private rights were not destroyed by the change of government." [74] He quoted Chief Justice John Marshall, of the United States Supreme Court, who said in a case arising in Florida after the annexation of that one-time Spanish territory, "It may be worthy of remark that it is very unusual, even in cases of conquest, for the conqueror to do more than displace the sovereign and assume dominion of the country." Marshall, in turn, had cited early English decisions in support of his opinion that private rights could not be affected by a change of sovereignty. [75] As late as 1859, however, Chief Justice Royal T. Wheeler of Texas felt called upon to reaffirm: "There is no more firmly settled or universally approved principle of law, than that a revolution works no change in previously vested rights of property." [76]

Aside from strictly legal considerations, the motives of the early Texas lawmakers in confirming Spanish and Mexican land titles need little discussion. As the courts have stated, the revolt that led to independence in Texas was no social revolution, and there was no reason or intention to interfere with established property relations. Moreover, the men who carried out that revolution were the ones who held most of the privately owned land in Texas. At the date of independence, in fact, almost every citizen of Texas held land under a Spanish or Mexican grant.

Even without court decisions, the continuity of these titles would appear to be sufficiently secured by a section of the first state constitution, adopted in 1845, which became a part of the agreement of annexation between Texas and the United States. This section was copied in succeeding constitutions, including that of 1876 now in effect, where it forms Section 18 of Article XVI, as follows: "Vested rights.—The rights of property and of action, which have been acquired under the Constitution and laws of the Republic and State, shall not be divested. . . ."[77]

Since the rights acquired under Spanish and Mexican land grants and through other operations of Spanish-Mexican law were clearly recognized by the constitutions and laws of the republic and state, it would seem clear that they are fully confirmed by this section of the Constitution as it now stands. And, in the wildly improbable event that Texas should wish to "divest" these rights, the United States Supreme Court could be asked to intervene on the ground that the guarantee in the Constitution of 1845, through its inclusion in the annexation agreement, has become the supreme law of the United States under Article VI of the federal Constitution.

The recognition of Spanish law has worked both ways. Where the original grant depended on conditions which were not fulfilled by the grantee, such as occupancy for a stated term of years, the Texas courts have held the title forfeited.[78] It is such questions concerning the circumstances surrounding the original grant, and not any question as to the general validity of such grants, that have led to prolonged litigation in numerous cases. In the long-fought Padre Island case, decided as recently as 1945, the Texas Supreme Court upheld the claim of the Balli heirs to an area larger than the original grant, which had been augmented by the gradual piling up of sand from the Gulf against the low, tide-washed island.[79] The Texas attorney general thereupon appealed to the United States Supreme Court on the ground that the local court was depriving the state of its property without due process of law, but the highest court refused his appeal. According to Harbert Davenport and J. T. Canales,

This is probably the only instance on record where a State, suing as sovereign proprietor in its own courts, has refused to abide by a decision of its own highest tribunal, or has sought, on alleged "constitutional" grounds to overturn a solemn judgment of its own Supreme Court.[80]

This case was closely involved in the complicated legal question of the status of lands situated between the Nueces and the Rio Grande, which were formerly part of the Mexican state of Tamaulipas and never belonged to the combined state of Coahuila and Texas. On December 19, 1836, the Congress of the Republic of Texas annexed this area by a legislative act which it lacked the power to enforce. The Texan claim to this region was not made good until General Zachary Taylor's United States Army crossed the Nueces in 1846 at the outset of the Mexican War and after Texas had become a state in the Union. Thereafter, while both state and federal courts held that the Treaty of Guadalupe Hidalgo, which protects the property rights of Mexican nationals in the territory annexed in 1848, does not apply to lands situated in the former Republic of Texas, the state Supreme Court has held that the treaty does apply to the region between the Nueces River and the Rio Grande. In the words of Harbert Davenport, of Brownsville:

The one line of decisions applies to Texas as it existed, prior to 1836, as a member of the Mexican Confederation of States; the other to the area between the Nueces and the Rio Grande, to which Texas first asserted claim by the Act of December 19, 1836, which claim was not admitted by Mexico until the Treaty of Guadalupe Hidalgo of February 2, 1848. The courts of Texas disposed of this technical problem by holding: (a) that from and after December 19, 1836, Texas' claim to the trans-Nueces area was good "de jure"; that is, as a matter of law, but that Mexico was in control of the greater portion of this area; and (b) that, as between private individuals, the acts of Mexico and of the Mexican State of Tamaulipas were the acts of the government de facto. The same rule was applied to grants of land. The Texas courts refused to recognize grants of land made by Mexico in this area which originated *after December 19, 1836; but where proceedings for a grant had been begun by a private individual prior to December 19, 1836; and had progressed to the point where the title would have been perfected, but for the change in sovereignty, under the laws of Tamaulipas; vested private rights had been created which, under the Treaty of Guadalupe Hidalgo, were binding upon the courts as well as upon the political authorities of the State.* [81]

It took several acts of the legislature, known as the Relinquishment Acts, to quiet the titles to land between the Nueces River and the Rio Grande. Even then, because of the unsettled condition of the country, not all of the property owners had been able to take advantage of their rights by 1876, and the new Constitution of that date granted them an additional four years in which to validate their titles. [82] Even then, the uncertainties of the law kept some of the Tamaulipas grants in the courts until recently.

Spanish units of measurement are still used in determining the metes and bounds of landed property in Texas. These units exhibited some variability, the length of the basic vara or Spanish yard having ranged from 32.8748 inches to 35 inches. It was not until 1919 that the legislature fixed the legal length of the vara in Texas at 33-1/3 standard inches. [83] On this basis the labor, 1,000 varas square, becomes 177.14 acres; the league, 5,000 varas square, becomes 4,428.4 acres. [84]

The principle now known as community property regulates the rights of married persons in several western states under laws derived from the Spanish codes, which were much more favorable to women than was the English common law which inspired the statutes of most American states. The origin of the Texas law in particular is clearly stated by Chief Justice John Hemphill, who declared in 1857, "Our laws on marital rights are in substance but a continuation of the rules of Spanish jurisprudence on the same subject matter." [85]

Under the common law and its statutory offshoots, all property owned by a woman prior to her marriage becomes the property of her husband, as does any wealth accumulated by the couple after their marriage, the wife retaining only a dower right which usually amounts to one-third of the lands acquired after marriage. Under the Spanish and Texan law, the wife's own property is counted as her contribution to the common capital of marriage. Property acquired after marriage, though subject to the husband's management, is owned equally by husband and wife. [86] As recently as 1948, the existence of such laws in a minority of the states moved Congress to amend the federal income tax law so as to place the residents of all states on a community property basis for income tax purposes, thereby giving them the same advantage that taxpayers in the community property states had enjoyed in being able to divide their incomes when computing the tax.[87]

In spite of the advantage to the Texas wife in being able to claim a greater share of property, the Texas League of Women Voters has found fault with certain provisions of the community property law which place married women in a state of virtual guardianship with regard to the management of property.[88] Just how much these provisions owe to Spanish precedent is a subject of specialized study.

Again adapting Spanish laws of ancient respectability, the Texas legislature formulated statutes of descent and distribution which deny the right of a parent to disinherit his children for any cause except a violent attack on the parent or an attempt to defame him by imputing offenses punishable by law.[89]

The distinction between law and equity, which had originated as a progressive step in early English law but had later degenerated into a plaything of formalism, was abolished in Texas in 1840 when the legislature approved an adaptation of the simple Spanish system of pleading cases in court. According to Davenport,

procedure at common law was based on a series of technical "writs" and "pleas," which lawyers moved about like chessmen in an effort to plead their cases into a single issue of law and fact. Under the common law system of pleading, the more clever lawyer, rather than right and justice, was favored to prevail. [90]

Under the Spanish system, on the other hand, the plaintiff was required only to tell his troubles to the court in plain and concise language. This single system, since its adoption in Texas, had been almost universally introduced in American and even English courts.

Rights to minerals on or under the ground remained vested in the state of Texas under laws which remained in effect for twenty years after annexation, although the state exacted only a 5 per cent royalty instead of the 20 per cent demanded by the King of Spain. In 1866, however, an article in the new constitution of that year, ostensibly designed to aid the owners of certain saline deposits, was so worded that it became applicable to all minerals on privately owned lands, including vast petroleum deposits.[91] It has been estimated that this legislation, by careless wording, cost the state of Texas a billion dollars.[92] Careless or not, the new provision, relinquishing the state's right to underground wealth on private property, was reaffirmed in the Constitution of 1876.

Even the boundaries of Texas to this day are determined by statutes and agreements relating to Spanish precedents, which have been duly invoked when disputes occurred. In the most recent question of this kind, a strip of Oklahoma along the 100th meridian, 132 miles long and containing 28,000 acres, was annexed to Texas pursuant to a decision of the United States Supreme Court in 1931. The line as described in the Adams-Oñís treaty of 1819 was also disputed by Texas and the United States government in the Greer County case in the 1890's and by Texas and New Mexico in 1929.[93]

Although some of the laws formed in early Texas by adapting the principles of the Siete Partidas and the Laws of the Indies have been superseded in later years, all of these laws have gone into the making of a body of legal tradition which is still at work in the state. In addition to the vested rights section, numerous other provisions related to Spanish law are embodied in the Constitution of 1876, which is now in effect. This constitution contains eight distinct sections dealing with questions arising directly out of Spanish and Mexican land titles. It also prescribes the general provisions of the community property laws and the exemption of homesteads and certain personal property from execution for debt. The spirit, if not the letter, of the Spanish laws for the protection of debtors can be seen in a constitutional ban on garnishment of wages.

What were the motives of the founders of the Republic of Texas in adopting so much of their law from the cast-off governments of Spain and Mexico? To some extent, it is true, they followed the line of least resistance, in that it was simpler to take over the old laws bodily than to arrange a transition to a system adopted in its entirety from the Anglo-American tradition. This retention of Spanish law, however, was not necessary. Even where the doctrine of vested rights decreed confirmation of the acts of the former governments, the future working out of these rights could have been subjected to an altogether different system of law. The vested rights principle affected only those rights which had existed before the change of government.

It is significant that the Republic chose to make certain possible changes and rejected others. Adoption of the Spanish-Mexican law was quite selective. Jury trial and freedom of religion, to cite only two examples out of many, were taken over from American law at the same time that the provisions described were taken from the Mexican law. A way to change over to all-American laws could certainly have been found if these Spanish-Mexican laws had been repugnant to the people and their legislators. Evidently they were not repugnant but were gladly accepted, in spite of the Texans' hostile feeling toward the government which had formerly administered these laws. The inadequacies of the English common law having been recognized at that time, the people of the Republic of Texas, in forming their first constitution and the framework of their statutory law, chose to follow Spanish-Mexican rules in many matters—especially those relating to land tenure—rather than the American laws to which they had been long accustomed before their migration.

Their reasons for making this choice are clear. Having an Anglo-American background, the framers of Texas laws were attracted inevitably to the political and economic doctrines that were prevalent in the United States at the time, with preference, perhaps, because of their frontier experience and relative poverty, for the more radical of these doctrines. This *a priori* expectation is confirmed by the actual adoption of some of the more advanced American proposals of the time in the constitution and laws of the Republic of Texas.

The prevalent radicalism was mainly channeled, however, into a desire for freedom and security in the acquisition and undisturbed possession of free land. To the Texas colonists, land was the philosopher's stone, the universal solvent, and the answer to all problems. Where there were such vast expanses of good land to be had for the asking, there was little need for the social reforms on which the rest of mankind might lean for security. The reforms that were made in early Texas, for the most part, had to do with control of land. It is probable that these changes, made by simply adopting large portions of the Spanish-Mexican law, represented in their context as advanced a liberalism as had been shown by any government in the world at that time, even though the text of the changes was derived from the edicts of a paternalistic autocracy.

Under the fortunate circumstance of an apparently unlimited supply of unoccupied land, these laws certainly went farther than any measures adopted in the United States, before or since, to promote the independence of the "little man." The Texan statesmen were not great theorists, and their political philosophy was mainly implicit in their actions; but, whether consciously or not, they reduced to reality a far-reaching ideal of favoring the small enterpriser which would have gladdened the heart of Thomas Jefferson. There also are evidences of a struggle between the followers of Jefferson and of Hamilton in the story of the 400-league grants and in later developments down to the present day. At the mid-point of the twentieth century, however, the "big business" element in Texas has a somewhat different complexion than its equivalent in the East. The typical Texas capitalist, plain of appearance and modest in demeanor when not aroused, resents attacks on his vast interests in oil or industry in exactly the same spirit in which the homespun early Texan fought off any attempt to prevent him from peaceably working his rightfully acquired league and labor of land. Thus the Hamiltonians in Texas today have a strong strain of Jeffersonian blood.

The fact that the liberal laws of Texas were developed under an absolute monarchy need occasion no surprise. Defenders of absolutism have pointed out with some justice that life under such a government may sometimes be freer than life under the tyranny of a majority.[94] The crude theory of divine right, which was developed as a defense for the English monarchs in the seventeenth century, never was accepted in Catholic countries like Spain. Rather, the King was made to feel that his right depended on his ruling justly, in accordance with the standards of his time. A disinterested examination of Spanish-American history will show that the King was generally more of a humanitarian than his *conquistadores*, and he was not entirely above the law. A subject who felt himself threatened with injustice could appeal to the King's judges, who referrred to the Siete Partidas and the Code of Justinian in much the same way that American judges now refer to the Constitution. It was the King who tried to enforce the laws or made new ones which had to be in harmony with the old, and it was the overseas officials who applied, misapplied, or ignored them.

During the prerevolutionary period in Texas, the desire to enjoy security on the land showed itself in a willingness to abide by the traditional laws and the Mexican Constitution of 1824—despite their grave denials of civil and religious liberty—as against the vagaries of successive revolutionary leaders. This feeling on the part of the colonists, explicitly described in their writings, explains both the loyalty of the Texans to Mexico for fifteen years and the final break in 1836.

"The general cause of the revolt," says Eugene C. Barker, "was the same [as in the American Revolution]—a sudden effort to extend imperial authority at the expense of local privilege."[95] The historian, of course, is here speaking of the immediate cause of the outbreak. In both the American and the Texan situations there were traditions of long growth which explained why the people rose in protest when they were threatened with the loss of rights or privileges which they had learned to expect. In the case of Texas, the general American tradition of democracy had been transplanted to Texas soil after taking on the characteristic coloration of the Jacksonian age. What was added under Mexican rule was the reality of free land and the expectation of personal independence to be gained therefrom under stable laws. Only when this personal independence was threatened by the recentralization of the Mexican government and other abuses, did the Texas colonists strike out for a change in sovereignty.

Thus is seen the double paradox in which a free-spirited people, who had found greater freedom under the laws developed by a despotic monarchy than under the democratic government of their own country, were then driven to rebellion by the semi-anarchy of contending revolutionary leaders in the Mexican republic which had taken over the functions of the monarchy. The Americans of 1776, on the other hand, had been driven to revolt by the actions of the same government under which most of them had been born. The Texans had no stable government against which to revolt. They merely moved aside from the confusion of contemporary Mexican politics. It hardly seems probable that the Texans, with the experience of more than a decade of change behind them, could have regarded the dictatorship of Antonio López de Santa Anna as a permanent state of affairs.

No doubt the movement for complete independence was strengthened by the influx of newcomers—largely adventurers—who had come from the United States soon after the first disorders and who had no feeling of obligation toward Mexico. Although these newcomers were of a more turbulent character than the original settlers brought in by the empresarios, their objectives were essentially the same, and it is probable that their presence accelerated the revolutionary process without materially changing its course.

When independence had been achieved, the security of the colonists still depended upon the maintenance of the rights they had acquired under the Spanish-Mexican laws. Hence, they set about establishing a new code which would confirm the existing rights and would secure for the future the peculiar advantages of both the Anglo-American and the Spanish legal systems strengthened with improvements derived from the advanced thinking of the time. A study of the laws adopted in early Texas provides a common denominator, a key to the motives of the people of Texas from the day when Moses Austin first walked across the plaza in San Antonio, through the early difficulties of the empresarios, the Texas Revolution, the organization of the Republic of Texas, annexation, secession, and many otherwise unrelated events in the history of the state.

Notes

1. Mattie Austin Hatcher, *The Opening of Texas to Foreign Settlement, 1801-1821* (Austin, 1927), 109.

2. Eugene C. Barker (ed.), *The Austin Papers* (I and II, Annual Report of the American Historical Association for the Years 1919 and 1922, Washington, 1924, 1928; III, University of Texas Press, Austin, 1926), I, 115.

3. Samuel Harman Lowrie, *Culture Conflict in Texas, 1821-1835* (New York, 1932), 10.

4. Frederick Jackson Turner, *The United States, 1830-1850: The Nation and Its Sections* (New York, 1935), 19.

5. *Ibid.*, 20.

6. *Ibid.*, 244-245.

7. Barker (ed.), *Austin Papers*, III, 19.

8. Arthur M. Schlesinger, Jr., *The Age of Jackson* (Boston, 1946), 283.

9. *Ibid.*, 22.

10. *Ibid.*, 16.

11. *Ibid.*, 139.

12. Schlesinger, *Age of Jackson*, 136-140.

13. H. Hale Bellot, *American History and American Historians* (Norman, 1952), 168.

14. Eugene C. Barker, *Mexico and Texas, 1821-1835* (Dallas, 1928), 17-18.

15. Schlesinger, *Age of Jackson,* 30-31.

16. Barker, *Mexico and Texas*, 18.

17. Walter Prescott Webb, *The Great Plains* (New York, 1931), 385-452.

18. Austin to James F. Perry in Eugene C. Barker, *Life of Stephen F. Austin* (2d. ed., Austin, 1949), 272.

19. Turner, *United States: 1830-1850*, 385.

20. Schlesinger, *Age of Jackson*, 190.

21. Barker, *Stephen F. Austin*, 21, 195-196.

22. Mary Austin Holley, *Texas*, (facs. ed., Austin, 1935), 138.

23. Schlesinger, *Age of Jackson*, 134.

24. Barker, *Stephen F. Austin,* 194-199; *Novisima Recopilación de las Leyes de la Espana* (Madrid, 1805), Tomo V, Libro XI, Titula XXXI, Leyes XII, XV, XVIII, XIX, 291-294; *Recopilación de Leyes de los Reynos de las Indias* (3d. ed., Madrid, 1774), Tomo I, Libro II, Titulo I, Ley II, 127.

25. *Ibid.*, 194.

26. *Ibid.*, 197; H. P. N. Gammel (comp.), *The Laws of Texas: 1822-1897* (10 vols.; Austin, 1898), I, 220; II, 126.

27. Act of February 5, 1840, in Gammel (comp.), *Laws of Texas*, II, 347. For later laws on the same subject see *ibid.*, V, 1078; VI, 301; X, 861.

28. See Constitution of 1876, Article XVI, Sections 28, 49, 50, in Gammel (comp.), *Laws of Texas,* VIII, 779-834.

29. Barker, *Stephen F. Austin*, 200.

30. Bellot, *American History*, 41-72.

31. On land grants and land policy in Mexico generally, see Wistano Luis Orozco, *Legislación y Jurisprudencia sobre Terrenos Baldiós* (2 vols.; Mexico, 1895) and Andrés Molina Enriquez, *Los Grandes Problemas Nacionales* (Mexico, 1909).

32. For compilations of the land laws of Texas under the Spanish and Mexican governments, see John and Henry Sayles, *Early Laws of Texas*, (3 vols.; 2d. ed., Kansas City, 1891), I, 17-191; Gammel (comp.), *Laws of Texas*, I, 272, 299, 357, 407, 420. The colonization laws of 1823 and 1824 are also printed in Holley, *Texas,* 196-204.

33. Webb, *Great Plains*, 385-452.

34. Barker, *Stephen F. Austin*, 119ff.

35. Harbert Davenport and J. T. Canales, *The Texas Law of Flowing Waters, with Special Reference to Irrigation from the Lower Rio Grande* (Brownsville, 1949), 20.

36. *Texas Almanac and State Industrial Guide* (Dallas, 1949), 613.

37. Dudley G. Wooten, *A Comprehensive History of Texas* (2 vols.; Dallas, 1898), I, 792.

38. Davenport and Canales, *Texas Law of Flowing Waters*, 20.

39. *Ibid;* see also F. W. Blackmar, *Spanish Institutions of the Southwest* (Baltimore, 1891), Chapter XV.

40. Henderson Yoakum, *History of Texas* (2 vols.; New York, 1855), II, 230.

41. John Locke, "An Essay Concerning the True Original, Extent and End of Civil Government" in Charles L. Sherman (ed.), *Treatise of Civil Government and a Letter Concerning Toleration* (New York, 1937), 32.

42. *Ibid.*, 24.

43. Holley, *Texas*, 273.

44. Yoakum, *History of Texas,* II, 234-235.

45. *Ibid.*, 239-240. The originals have been preserved in the General Land Office of the State of Texas.

46. Harbert Davenport to G. A., March 4, 1952 (MS. in writer's possession). The many constructive suggestions of Mr. Davenport, based on a combination of legal experience and historical knowledge, have been indispensable to the writer in finding and co-ordinating the widely-scattered information needed for this article.

47. Alleine Howren, "Causes and Origin of the Decree of April 6, 1830," *Southwestern Historical Quarterly*, XVI, 395-396.

48. Austin to [Edward Lovelace?], Mexico, November 22, 1822, in Barker (ed.), *Austin Papers*, I, 555.

49. Austin to J. E. B. Austin, Saltillo, May 10, 1823, in *ibid.*, 638-639.

50. *Ibid.*, 638.

51. Austin to Lucas Alaman, January 20, 1824, in *ibid.*, 725-727.

52. Austin to the Colonists, August 6, 1823, in *ibid.*, 679-680.

53. For more details on Austin's views on slavery see Barker, *Stephen F. Austin*, 201-225.

54. Petition Concerning Slavery, in Barker (ed.), *Austin Papers*, I, 827.

55. Memorial to the Legislature, in *ibid.*, 996-1002.

56. Austin to Colonists, June 7, 1825, in *ibid.,* 1125.

57. Barker, *Stephen F. Austin,* 168-174; Barker, *Mexico and Texas,* 44, 49-51.

58. B. W. Edwards and H. B. Mayo to Inhabitants of Pecan Point, Nacogdoches, December 25, 1826, in Barker (ed.), *Austin Papers,* I, 1544.

59. Resolutions of Loyalty, January 27, 1827, in *ibid.*, 1594.

60. Barker, *Mexico and Texas*, 147.

61. Austin to the People of Texas, in Barker (ed.), *Austin Papers*, III, 117-119.

62. Constitution of 1845, in Gammel (comp.), *Laws of Texas,* II, 1277.

63. Journal of the Consultation, Articles XV, XVIII, XIX, XX, in *ibid.*, I, 542.

64. Constitution of the Republic of Texas, in *ibid.*, 1084.

65. Constitution of 1845, in *ibid.*, II, 1277; William F. Weeks, *Debates of the Texas Convention*, (Houston, 1846), 168.

66. Sam A. Willson, *Texas Criminal Statutes* (2 vols.; St. Louis, 1888), I, i-v.

67. Blackmar, *Spanish Institutions*, 312; Walter Prescott Webb, *The Great Frontier* (Boston, 1952), 259-279.

68. Act of January 20, 1840, in Gammel (comp.), *Laws of Texas*, II, 177.

69. Wooten, *History of Texas*, I, 844.

70. Webb, *Great Plains*, 385-452.

71. L. W. Newton and H. P. Gambrell, *Social and Political History of Texas* (Dallas, 1935), 267.

72. Webb, *Great Plains*, 385-452.

73. William Ransom Hogan, *The Texas Republic* (Norman, 1946), 11-12.

74. McMullen *v.* Hodge, *Reports of Cases Argued and Decided in the Supreme Court of the State of Texas*, V, 34. Hereinafter cited *Texas Reports*.

75. Case of Juan Percheman in Richard Peters (ed.), *Report of Cases Argued and Adjudged in the Supreme Court of the United States*, January Term, 1833, VII, 51.

76. Kilpatrick *v.* Cisneros, *Texas Reports*, XXIII, 113.

77. Constitution of 1845, in Gammel (comp.), *Laws of Texas*, II, 1277; Constitution of 1876, in *ibid.*, VIII, 779-834.

78. McMullen *v.* Hodge, *Texas Reports*, V, 34.

79. State *v.* Balli *et al., South Western Reporter, Second Series*, CLXXIII, 522.

80. Davenport and Canales, *Texas Law of Flowing Waters*, 18.

81. Harbert Davenport to G. A., March 4, 1952 (MS.).

82. Constitution of 1876, in Gammel (comp.), *Laws of Texas*, VIII, 779-834, which cites the several Relinquishment Acts.

83. *Vernon's Annotated Revised Civil Statutes of the State of Texas, Revision of 1925*, XVI, Article 5730, effective June 17, 1919.

84. *Texas Almanac (1949-1950)*, 619.

85. Burr *v.* Wilson, *Texas Reports*, XVIII, 367.

86. Act of January 20, 1840, in Gammel (comp.), *Laws of Texas*, II, 180.

87. *Britannica Book of the Year* (Chicago, 1951), 664.

88. *Vernon's Civil Statutes, Revision of 1925*, III, Articles 1299-1300; *Bulletin, The League of Women Voters of Texas* (March, 1951), 1.

89. Act of January 28, 1840, in Gammel (comp.), *Laws of Texas*, II, 341ff.

90. Harbert Davenport to G. A., March 4, 1952 (MS.).

91. For discussions of ownership of mineral rights in Texas, see Walace Hawkins, *El Sal del Rey* (Austin, 1947); John A. Rockwell, *A Compilation of Spanish and Mexican Law* (New York, 1851); Gustavus Schmidt, *The Civil Law of Spain and Mexico* (New Orleans, 1851).

92. Curtis Bishop, *Lots of Land* (Austin, 1949), 296.

93. Newton and Gambrell, *Social History of Texas*, 248-252.

94. Erik von Kuehnelt-Leddihn, *Liberty and Democracy* (Caldwell, 1952).

95. Barker, *Mexico and Texas*, 147. For additional judicial decisions concerning the application of Spanish-Mexican law in Texas, see Lucas *v.* Strother in Peters (ed.), *Report of Cases Argued and Adjudged in the Supreme Court of the United States*, XII, 411; U.S. *v.* –, *ibid.*, X, 306; State *v.* Sais, *Texas Reports*, XLVII, 307; State *v.* Cardinas, *ibid.*, 250; State *v.* Cuellar, *ibid.*, 395; State *v.* Bustamente, *ibid.*, 320; State *v.* Sarnes, *ibid.*, 323; State *v.* Vela, *ibid.*, 325; Villareal *v.* State, *ibid.*, LXXIV, 370. Many other references to court decisions are given in the notes of Davenport and Canales, *Texas Law of Flowing Waters*. Other information of this type can be found in J. H. Davenport, *History of the Supreme Court of Texas: With Biographies of the Chief and Associate Justices* (Austin, 1917).

The British corn crisis of 1845-46 and the Oregon Treaty

Frederick Merk

The rise of the trans-Allegheny West as a major exporter of foodstuffs was one of the most important facts of nineteenth century American history. Although none dispute this, there has been intense disagreement on the timing. Ever since 1903, when Guy Callender wrote "The Early Transportation and Banking Enterprises of the States in Relation to the Growth of Corporations," some historians have argued for the early growth of economic interdependence between the three major sections—the East, the West, and the South. According to this thesis the regions specialized before 1850. The East concentrated on industrial products, which it sent to the South and West; the South specialized in staple crops, primarily cotton, but also tobacco and rice, which it sent to the North and abroad; and the West produced foodstuffs, which it sent to the cities of the North, overseas, and to the South to feed the plantation slaves. Douglass North stressed this pattern in his perceptive *Economic History of the United States 1790-1860* (1961).*

   While historians do not question the rise of manufacturing in the East or the importance of southern staple production, since the 1960s the role of the West has come under increasing scrutiny. A number of questions have been asked. When did the West begin to produce a surplus above its own needs? When did transportation become adequate to move bulky crops from the West to outside markets? What evidence do we have that the West actually exported a surplus of food before the 1850s? How do we know that the southern plantations were not able to feed themselves? Scholars discovered that Callender and North provided little hard statistical data about western agricultural production and distribution.

   Recently the "new economic historians," who are mostly economists trained in economic theory and the collection of statistics, have begun to throw fresh light on the problem. Particularly significant have been essays by Robert Fogel of the University of Chicago and Albert Fishlow of the University of California at Berkeley. By collecting statistics about the transportation of foodstuffs from the West, Fishlow has concluded that there was very little outflow of agricultural products from the West prior to 1850. Fogel has challenged some of Fishlow's findings, but an analysis of interregional trade by Diane Lindstrom of the University of Wisconsin has supported Fishlow's concepts. The

Reprinted with permission from *Agricultural History*, 8 (July 1934), 95-123.

controversy has wide significance for American history. As Frederick Merk, Professor Emeritus of History at Harvard University, points out in the following essay, historians writing about such issues as the Oregon Treaty have assumed the existence of a large surplus food supply in the West and have argued that this factor was crucial in shaping America's diplomatic relations with Britain.

For further reading: Guy Callender, "The Early Transportation and Banking Enterprises of the States in Relation to the Growth of Corporations," *Quarterly Journal of Economics,* XVII (1903), 114-131; Douglass North, *Economic History of the United States 1790-1860* (Englewood Cliffs, N.J.: Prentice-Hall, 1961);* Robert Fogel, "American Interregional Trade in the Nineteenth Century," in Ralph Andreano, ed., *New Views on American Economic Development* (Cambridge, Mass.: Schenkman Publishing, 1965);* Albert Fishlow, "Antebellum Interregional Trade Reconsidered," *ibid.* ; Albert Fishlow, *American Railroads and the Transformation of the Ante-Bellum Economy* (Cambridge, Mass.: Harvard University Press, 1965); Diane Lindstrom, "Southern Dependence upon Interregional Grain Supplies: A Review of Trade Flows, 1840-1860," *Agricultural History*, XLIV (January 1970), 101-113; Thomas P. Martin, "Free Trade and the Oregon Question, 1842-1846," in *Facts and Factors in Economic History: Articles by Former Students of Edwin Francis Gay* (Cambridge, Mass.: Harvard University Press, 1932), 470-491; Henry Commanger, "England and Oregon Treaty of 1846," *Oregon Historical Quarterly*, XXVIII (March 1927), 18-38; Robert Gallman, "Self-sufficiency in the Cotton Economy of the Antebellum South," *Agricultural History*, XLIV (January 1970), 5-23.

*Available in paperback.

Three major crises confronted the British government in the autumn of 1845: a harvest shortage of seemingly famine proportions; a Corn Law conflict revolutionary in intensity; and a controversy over the Oregon Country that imperilled Anglo-American peace. By the spring of 1846 all three had passed out of the crisis stage; the harvest reports proved overdrawn; the anti-Corn Law crusade triumphed in Peel's famous measure; and by Aberdeen's treaty *projet* of May, ratified by the American Senate in June, the Oregon controversy was brought to a peaceful close. In recent American historical writing the thesis has gained currency that these problems stood to each other in more than a mere temporal relationship, that the harvest shortage and the Corn Law repeal were actually important causative factors in the Oregon settlement.[1] This thesis it is my purpose to examine.

The harvest shortage took on the appearance of a national catastrophe in the autumn of 1845. By all reports the two most necessary British crops, potatoes and wheat, were appalling failures. Of potatoes the report was but too true. Throughout the United Kingdom and especially in Ireland the tuber lay in the fields stricken by a mysterious and uncontrollable fungus which caused a rot in the harvest. The ravages of the disease were widespread on the continent of Europe; they extended even to distant North America. The wheat harvest was reported failed both in the United Kingdom and in the Baltic provinces from which England was accustomed to supply her deficiencies of bread. In the free-trade press the extent of the losses and the danger of famine were magnified as part of the campaign against the Corn Laws. A panic swept the public. The government was caught in it, and England passed through a political and social upheaval which was one of the gravest in her history.

The international effect of the shortage, according to the newer writings, was to bring Great Britain and Ireland to dependence for food on the United States. From this, it is believed, flowed in part the pacific and conciliatory attitude of the British government in the Oregon negotiations which made possible the treaty of 1846.[2] This view is conservatively formulated by one writer as follows:

In October 1845, there had come the disheartening news of the destruction, by the potato blight, of one-half of the whole Irish crop of that year, which threatened famine for the winter, and no seed for the spring planting. Already, Peel has written, he had before this resolved to take the unusual step of purchasing on account of the Government a large quantity of Indian corn in the United States. The purchase was conducted by the Barings firm, who acted for the British Treasury. . . .

It is too much to conclude that under no conditions would England have gone to war with the United States [over Oregon], but it is certainly to be regarded as highly unlikely that with French relations in a delicate situation, with the abandonment of protectionism in mind, and with England buying sorely needed grain from the United States to meet a threatened famine, Sir Robert Peel would have risked a war with this country if it could be avoided in any honourable way.[3]

By another student the famine threat is described in its international aspects in more vivid terms.

During the summer [1845] came the terrible blight which destroyed the potato crops of western Europe as well as those of Great Britain and Ireland; and it became certain by the middle of October that the United States was the only considerable and dependable source for plentiful supplies of food. Indeed it seemed that the British Isles had suddenly been pushed off the continental shelf and anchored in the middle of the Atlantic, as dependent upon the United States for food supplies as they had ever been for raw cotton.[4]

The chief constituent of this dependence thesis is the Irish shortage. It is accordingly examined first. The shortage was of unquestioned gravity, producing misery on a wide scale in Ireland. Yet it led strangely enough to no net food imports into the island. The Irish flow of food, on the contrary, in the winter and spring of 1845-46 was the usual one of export. Ireland at this time exemplified a cruel economic paradox,—a land chronically in a state of starvation yet always sending quantities of food abroad. Of high-grade foods Ireland raised wheat, barley, and livestock. These she sent to England; from their sale she paid her rents. She even sent a portion of her plebeian potatoes and oats. Year after year that export went on impelled by the iron laws of supply and demand and the inexorable requirements of rent. It went on whether the Irish peasantry starved or survived. In the twelvemonth ending July 5, 1846, Ireland exported to England, of wheat, 354,058 quarters; of wheat flour, 1,166,111 cwts.; of oats, 1,202,854 quarters; of oatmeal, 845,162 cwts.; of barley, 116,270 quarters; and of sheep, lambs, swine, and beeves, numbers correspondingly large.[5]

Potatoes were Ireland's humble fare. According to Lord Devon's *Report* of 1845 they were in some areas practically her only fare.[6] They were varied in districts more prosperous by oatmeal, milk from the unsold produce of a family cow, and on holidays a slice of bacon. A failure of potatoes in any locality was followed promptly by starvation. That was not because of absence of other food. It was because the destitution of cottiers and laborers made the purchase of other food impossible or even the holding of their own.

In 1845 the failure of the potato was dramatic and widespread. In the early autumn, when the crop was nearly mature, the blight, a disease hitherto almost unknown, appeared. Its work was done with fearful swiftness. Fields which it found green were left black and decayed in a week. Potatoes on which its minute spores were washed became hills of putrefaction. The infection, favored by a wet autumn, spread throughout Ireland, ravaging especially the unhappy southern and eastern counties. Its total damage was difficult to estimate. Half the crop was the loss estimated to Peel.[7] Probably that was an exaggeration. Early maturing potatoes came through the harvest unscathed. The losses of the later varieties differed from district to district, but the yield, except for the blight, would have been everywhere exceptional, a third over the average, and this was reflected in the amounts saved. There were compensations for potato losses in the abundance of other crops. Wheat, oats, and barley were a full average. Hay was plentiful, and there was a good yield of turnips and carrots.[8] The harvest as a whole was not a tragic failure such as that of 1846 when nature made a general sweep of Irish fields. The 1845 crops would have sufficed for Ireland if only they could have been kept at home. Of scarcity in any national sense there was none; only poverty which forced the export of foods saved from the blight.

The British government took this view of the crisis. It directed all its energies of relief to the problem of a blight-deepened poverty. Its relief measures, in order of importance, were public works designed to provide employment for the destitute, coordination of the activities of local relief committees, and the prevention of profiteering. As a check to profiteering it accumulated in Ireland a quantity of cheap food of undisclosed amount which it held during the winter suspended over the produce markets. The food thus used was Indian corn meal purchased, to the amount of £100,000, through the house of Baring in the United States. This has been cited as proof of Irish national scarcity and British dependence on the United States. But proof of Irish national scarcity it is not. A government does not provide against scarcity in a population of eight million by one purchase to the amount of £100,000. The purchase was accounted for to Parliament by Sir James Graham, speaking for the ministry as follows:

They did not so order it for the purpose of meeting the entire wants of the Irish people, but for the purpose of checking the markets, of preventing the holding back of corn [grain] to enhance the price, and of arresting the progress of the very evil of which the hon. Gentleman complained—that, in midst of plenty, when the crops of oats had been unusually large, the supply of oatmeal was so limited that the price was raised one-third.[9]

The choice of American Indian corn meal as the medium of this control was made for reasons none of which support the theory that Britain was dependent on the United States. Peel preferred not to make government food purchases in British markets, more particularly purchases of ordinary European foods, lest the result be a raising of British prices. This objection was met by the purchase of corn meal in the United States. Corn meal was the cheapest of cereals; a government supply of it could be sold to Irish relief committees at less cost than oatmeal without burdening the British treasury. Peel hoped the purchase might result in the permanent addition to Irish diet of a cheap and whole-some food, correcting thus a dangerous dependence on potatoes.[10]

The experiment was a partial success. The purchase order placed in November was gradually and quietly filled, months incidentally before the Oregon negotiations of 1846 began. The meal was kept stored in Ireland; it was held in reserve until May, serving in the meantime as a curb on potato and oats speculators. In May when supplies of potatoes were nearly exhausted it was gradually sold in small lots to local relief committees at a price of £10 to £11 per ton. As a price regulator its purpose was achieved.[11]

But Ireland did not readily use corn meal. At first fear militated against its use. In Irish workhouses the meal was thought to be a poison; the serving of it led to riots.[12] In the credulous countryside women spread the dread news that to eat it was to have offspring that were yellow like mulattoes, or more terrifying still, that to feed it to the men was to render them impotent.[13] If objections of this kind were ultimately overcome, one other could not be. Corn meal is a food the taste for which has to be acquired. It has never been acquired in Ireland or anywhere else in Europe. The consumption of it was therefore limited to about what the government purchased. In the twelvemonth ending June 30, 1846, imports of corn and corn meal into Ireland from the United States amounted, according to the *Report* of the United States Secretary of the Treasury, to 425,960 bushels of the one and 33,750 barrels of the other,[14] truly not an impressive support for a dependence theory.

One considerable source of famine alarm in the autumn of 1845 was the reputed failure of the British and the European wheat harvest. This is the second constituent of the dependence thesis. The United Kingdom consumed of wheat, according to an 1846 estimate of J. R. McCulloch, the greatest of contemporary British statisticians, about 15,000,000 quarters a year.[15] Of this the bulk, in any year of normal harvest, was raised at home;[16] less than an eighth was imported. The average annual import of wheat and wheat flour for the five-year period prior to 1846 amounted to but 1,879,000 quarters.[17] Even in such a year of harvest calamity as 1847 no more than an eighth of the nation's total grain requirements, according to McCulloch, came from overseas.[18]

In 1845 the domestic wheat crop, notwithstanding early alarms, turned out to be little below the average in quantity. It was deficient in quality, but mixed with the carry-over of the excellent crop of 1844 it made satisfactory flour.[19] The United Kingdom was obliged to draw on the outside world for wheat and wheat flour in the year ending May 31, 1846 to the extent of only 1,932,000 quarters, which is but 53,000 quarters more than the average of the five years prior to 1846.[20] England had in bond in Febru-ary, 1846, waiting for the repeal of the Corn Laws, the extraordinary accumulation of 1,117,000 quarters of imported wheat and 703,961 cwts. of imported flour,[21] which in itself was little short of a year's importation.

A barometer of food scarcity is price. Price would have registered scarcity had any existed in England in the spring of 1846. When scarcity did exist in June, 1847, the price of wheat rose to a peak of 102s. 5d. per quarter and the average for the year was 69s. 9d. per quarter.[22] For the first six months of 1846 the average was 54s. 9d., which is exactly the average of the preceding five years. A height of 60s. was reached in the panic months of the autumn of 1845 but by March, 1846, the price had fallen to a low of 54s. 3d.,[23] a drop that meant ruin to many an unwary grain factor who had made heavy commitments abroad in the autumn in anticipation of famine prices in the spring. An epidemic of bankruptcies among grain factors gave evidence that the autumn wheat alarms had been groundless. [24]

Even in free trade circles the groundlessness of those alarms had to be admitted. It was acknowledged by Lord John Russell on January 22, 1846, when the government bill for the repeal of the Corn Laws was introduced into Parliament. [25] Free trade journals had to follow suit. The London *Economist* for instance, which had been a leader in spreading apprehension in the autumn, confessed in March, 1846, that British wheat losses had been overstated and that insufficient account had been taken of the heavy stocks held over from the preceding year. [26]

The ministry felt the same reassurance. It abandoned the famine argument in the debate on the Corn Laws, the Protectionist Opposition in the meantime questioning the sincerity of even the autumn fears and greeting references made to them with jeers. [27] Reassurance was evident in the weary length to which the debate on Corn Law repeal was allowed to run. Not until the end of June, 1846 was repeal enacted and not until February, 1849, did protective duties on grain altogether disappear.

If, however, the wheat harvest had been as calamitous as free traders at first reported, Britain would not have turned to America for rescue. From America she was accustomed to receive only a morsel of bread. Such imported wheat as she needed was bought in the basins of the Baltic and the Mediterranean. In the five-year period prior to 1846 she obtained there 80 percent of her wheat imports,—from the Baltic 61 percent, from the Mediterranean 19 percent. From the whole of North America she obtained 15½ percent or less than 3 percent of her consumption. [28] In the year ending June 30, 1846, the year of supposed dependence, she obtained from the United States 975,000 bushels of wheat and 1,005,000 barrels of flour. [29]

Such facts were common knowledge in the markets, ministry, and press. They were pointed out by government spokesmen in Parliament again and again during the debates on the repeal of the Corn Laws. [30] The London *Times* at the height of the November famine scare made a detailed survey of the world's surplus wheat areas, in which it observed as to the United States: "The growth of the population in the manufacturing and non-corn [non-grain]-growing districts is sufficiently rapid to consume all the additional corn-produce of the country, supposing 130,000 acres of new land per annum to be put under wheat culture alone, and three times that quantity under other crops and pasturage. The extension of agriculture barely keeps pace with the population; and the whole supply of wheat is hardly more than one month's consumption ahead of the demand in the Union." [31]

Thus dissolves the thesis that in the period of the Oregon crisis Britain felt herself dependent on the United States for food. No informed person in England so much as conceived of such a relation. The thesis is, in truth, an historical anachronism, an anticipation of conditions later, if ever, realized.

Another food question did, however, in British discussion relate itself to the Oregon crisis, the question of the repeal of the Corn Laws. British free traders stated the relationship in the form of the following argument. The American trans-Allegheny West is a center of surplus wheat production. It is also a center of ancient grudges against England and in particular of belligerence on the subject of Oregon. If the West by the repeal of the Corn Laws could be given a free entrance for its grain to the British market, its belligerence would yield to enlightened sectional interest. President Polk would be induced to bring the Oregon controversy to a prompt and amicable close, and Anglo-American relations would be permanently improved. Western wheat would intertwine with the Southern cotton and Eastern commerce to render forever secure the bonds of Anglo-American peace.[32]

This free-trade formula was a useful if incidental argument in the campaign against the Corn Laws. It was employed for a month or two while the Oregon crisis was acute on the hustings, in the free-trade press, and in Parliament. It was sanctioned by the ministry and by Whigs who were temporarily allied with the ministry in abolishing the Corn Laws. Lord Jim Russell stated it to a receptive audience in Glasgow on January 12, 1846, as follows:

There is another advantage, which I think would arise from the total abolition of the duties on the importation of grain—it would bind this country much more closely in the bonds of peace and amity with foreign states, and more especially with one—I mean the United States of America [cheers]. I think nothing of the questions which are at present in dispute [loud cheering] —questions of territory, in which, as they now stand, the honour of neither country is engaged [cheers] and, regarding which I think calm men representing the government of Her Majesty and the United States, might, by a calm and fair discussion come to an amicable agreement. I see no prospect of war or serious difference arising out of the circumstance. If we are determined on this side to import the products of the United States, and if the United States are equally satisfied to do the same with the manufactures of this kingdom, that they should feed us, and that we should clothe them, if no unhallowed legislation should stand in the way of these desirable results, then we should see two nations of the same race and speaking the same language united in the bonds of amity and peace.[33]

Lord Morpeth, a Liberal, linked the two issues in the same way in a public speech on his election to Parliament.

They may talk of a black cloud in the West, but the harvest sun has a ray warm enough to scatter it. [Renewed and enthusiastic cheering.] I know that on the other side of the Atlantic they are uttering big words about Oregon and we hear that the inhabitants of the Western States of the American Republic talk particularly loud on that subject, and that they are anxious to have a brush with us, while it seems that the inhabitants of the Eastern States are more pacific in their disposition. Why is this, gentlemen?. . . They [the Westerners] produce nothing but agricultural produce, and they know that if besides living five or six thousand miles away from us, the quarter of wheat which they might be inclined to send over shall have to pay a duty of 20s. when it arrives, they would not be able to get rid of a single bushel of it, and therefore they fling up their caps for war. But give them the same motives for peace which the inhabitants of the Eastern States have, and being sprung from the same stock as their brethren of Boston, New York and Philadelphia, being the sons of Puritans and broad brims themselves, they will be actuated by the same motives as their more sedate and sober fellow-citizens, and instead of wishing themselves to go a thousand miles further, where they would meet more new tribes of red Indians to contend against than draughts of water by the way, and when they arrived there, to go to war with us for a number of uninhabited pine swamps, they might think it were desirable to bestow a little more skill on their own rich clay bottoms if you would only give them the means of taking your cottons, your woolens, your worsted, your hardware, in exchange for what they can send us whether it be wheat or Indian corn. [34]

The same argument appeared repeatedly in the free-trade press. The leading Whig daily of London, the *Morning Chronicle*, presented it to the British public on January 17, 1846, as follows:

We must strengthen the bonds of the peace party in the American republic by reenforcing their pacific and patriotic counsels with the argument of commercial interest. We must disarm or neutralize the passions of the war party by presenting to it that which interests it as a free-trade party. We must subdue the hostility of the bellicose and ambitious Western States by addressing them in their other character of corn-growing States. And we must do this soon, at once, for time presses. [35]

Punch, a paper free-trade in sympathy, presented the argument in pictorial form. Sir Robert Peel was shown pelting a warlike Polk, who stood across the Atlantic, with a billet labeled "Free Corn," and knocking him off his legs. This British caricature needed considerable explanation. The explanation was as follows: "Peel's Free Trade must be victorious against Polk's firebrands. America may, if it pleases, pelt us with its corn, while we return the compliment by pitching into the United States some of our manufactured articles. This will be much better for both parties than an exchange of lead." [36]

The argument was used in Parliament as seasoning for the debate on Corn Law repeal. It appeared in the speeches of Lord John Russell, Lord Morpeth, Lord Clarendon, Sir James Graham, Charles Buller, and other free-trade notables. Granville Vernon's statement of it is a good sample:

Throughout America he had found but one feeling among the friends of peace, who said that if we would only interest, by prosperity, the Western States of America, which were invulnerable to our arms, and inaccessible to our commerce (for we had already the interests of the Eastern States in our favour) we should do more to promote the peace of America than all the concessions we should make in the Oregon or elsewhere. [37]

Protectionists replied to this formula by questioning the premise that repeal of the Corn Laws would benefit the American West. The only beneficiary of repeal, they maintained, would be continental Europe, which would inundate, with serf-produced grain, a British market made free. Such was the opinion of Lord Ashburton, who spoke out of the experience of many years in the international produce trade as former head of the house of Baring. Replying on January 19, 1846, to Lord John Russell's Glasgow speech Lord Ashburton observed that continental Europe currently supplied 90 percent of the grain imports of Britain. Cheap labor rendered this possible, and would continue to do so in a free British market. Against such a handicap the American West could not hope to compete. [38]

These opposing views, developed in the heat of political controversy, ought to be subjected to rigid testing before they are adopted for historical purposes. Yet without any testing the free-trade view has been adopted by historians who relate the Corn Law question to the Oregon question. A change in tense alone is made. Free-trade propagandists predicted that a repeal of the Corn Laws would mollify the American West. Historians of the problem assert that repeal, or rather the promise of it, did mollify the West.[39]

An analysis of this view is best begun by examining the record of the American wheat trade. The United States produced in the half-decade 1841-45 an annual average of from 90,000,000 to 105,000,000 bushels of wheat.[40] All of it, with the exception of seven or eight percent,[41] was consumed at home. The West was its own wheat market to a considerable extent, its incoming pioneers being in the first year or two of settlement chiefly grain consumers.

Exports were not only small but, relative to population, declining. In the first half-decade of the nation's life, when population was about 4,000,000, wheat exports averaged per year, reducing wheat flour to wheat, 5,118,000 bushels. In the quarter-century 1790-1814 the average was 4,642,000 bushels; in the next quarter-century 4,850,000 bushels; in the half-decade 1841-45 (when population was over 17,000,000), 7,165,000 bushels.[42] Of this 7,165,000 bushels, 73 percent went to areas adjacent to or near the United States, to Canada, to the Caribbean, and to Brazil, in the order of importance named.[43]

American wheat was exported to Europe in any quantity only in abnormal times. The European market was unprofitable to the American farmer except when crises such as the Napoleonic Wars, the famine of 1847, or the Crimean War lifted grain prices to exceptional heights. As Henry Clay pointed out in 1824,[44] Europe was an accidental market to the American grain grower. It was not more than that on account of the competitive handicaps of the United States. Farm labor in the United States was too costly as compared with tenant labor in the United Kingdom or serf labor in Prussia or Russia. American inland transport was too expensive whether by the roundabout highway of the Mississippi or by the Great Lakes and Erie Canal which necessitated transshipments. Cheap carriage, such as the Vistula, the Bug, or the Elbe gave grain growers in northern Europe, interior America did not provide. The ocean voyage from New York or New Orleans to England was too long compared with that from Hamburg or Danzig or other north European ports. These were the disabilities, not the Corn Laws, which had been restricting the American farmer's participation in the grain markets of Great Britain. Not until after the Civil War, when prairie labor costs had been reduced by the invention and wide-scale use of agricultural machinery, when costs of grain handling had been minimized by great economies in elevator operation such as the standardization of grades; and when handicaps of distance had been lessened by revolutionary changes in lake and rail and ocean transport could the United States export wheat successfully to European markets and make felt there the full weight of its cheap and fertile land.

Repeal of the Corn Laws in the meantime proved of little advantage to the American West. Britain imported after 1846 a considerably larger proportion of her bread than before. For the five-year period 1848-53, which avoids the famine year 1847, the annual average of imports of wheat and wheat flour into the United Kingdom was 4,442,000 quarters. Of this amount the Baltic provinces gave 45½ percent, the Mediterranean 30½ percent, and North America 19 percent.[45] North America gave about the same percentage in this period as in the period 1841-45, 19 percent as against 15½ percent. Repeal merely made clear that in a free British market the American farmer could not offer effective competition.

In one important respect repeal actually injured the wheat grower of the American West. He lost as a result of it a favored status in the British market as a participator in Canada's privileges of colonial preference. Canada enjoyed colonial preference in the British market under an imperial law of 1828, which was based on the ancient principles of the Navigation System. Whenever British wheat prices reached a point that indicated crop shortage in the United Kingdom colonial wheat and wheat flour were admitted at a purely nominal rate of duty. The colonial duty was only half a shilling a quarter at a price of 67s. or more. At less than 67s. the duty rose to 5s. On foreign wheat the duty at the price of 67s. was 18s. 8d. If prices declined below 67s., for every shilling of fall the duty on foreign wheat advanced a shilling until at a price of 40s. the duty reached the extravagant height of 46s. 8d. At a price of 40s. the colonial duty was less than a ninth of the foreign; at a price of 67s. the colonial duty was one thirty-seventh of the foreign. [46]

In 1842 this preference was somewhat reduced. Under the new law, whenever the price per quarter was 58s. or more, the duty on colonial wheat was one shilling. When the price fell below 58s., for every shilling of fall the duty advanced a shilling until it was 5s. at prices under 55s. On foreign wheat the shilling duty applied only when the price was as high as 73s. or above. When the price declined below 73s., for every shilling of fall the duty advanced a shilling until it was 20s. at a price under 51s. The colonial duty when the price was under 51s. was but one-fourth of the foreign; it was one-twelfth of the foreign at a price of 60s. [47]

In the year after this act was passed Canada was singled out for special Parliamentary favor. As an encouragement to her forwarding and milling interests, and as a concession to a growing anti-Corn Law sentiment in Britain, Parliament, by the Canada Corn Act of 1843, permitted Canadian wheat and wheat flour to be admitted into the United Kingdom after October, 1843, at the nominal duty of a shilling a quarter, regardless of British prices. [48]

In these Canadian privileges the United States shared. Wheat from the United States entered Canada free of duty under an imperial act of 1831 [49] which remained in force until October, 1843. After October, 1843, under a provincial act complementary to the Canada Corn Act, American wheat paid a duty at the Canadian border of 3s. a quarter. [50] Accordingly, American wheat, ground into Canadian flour, entered Britain after October, 1843, at the combined colonial and imperial duty of 4s. a quarter. That gave American wheat a preference as against other foreign wheat of from 10s. to 16s. a quarter, dependent on the state of British prices. Between October, 1843, and June, 1846, the actual preference was much of the time 16s. and seldom as little as 10s. [51]

Some part of this advantage was offset by the shortcomings of the St. Lawrence as an export route. Its channel was closed to commerce by ice for a considerable part of the year, some of its main improvements were completed only in 1848; the Gulf of St. Lawrence was beset by a number of perils which made insurance rates relatively high; the British navigation acts were a considerable restriction; and the varied means of assorting cargo and the assurance of return freights which New York and other American ports offered were lacking at Montreal. Gladstone in 1843 estimated these transit handicaps as equivalent to an added freight on wheat of 2s. a quarter [52] as compared with the route of the Erie Canal. But that cancelled only a fraction of the legislative advantage which Canadian preference gave American wheat moving into Britain.

The Corn Laws thus constituted a protection rather than a barrier to the West. [53] Western grain growers penetrated the barrier by means of the Canadian back door. Inside it they found protection against Prussian and Russian competitors. By the repeal of the

Corn Laws the barrier and the back door were both levelled. The competition of Europe had to be met in the open British market.

The loss thus suffered by the American West is measured in the shrinkage of the "back door trade." In the period just prior to repeal this trade had been growing rapidly. From October, 1843, to June, 1846, wheat and wheat flour flowed from Canada to Britain at the annual rate of 2,030,000 bushels.[54] A large part was American grain, for Canada had little surplus of her own to export.[55] The trade was cut in half by the Corn Law repeal; it fell in the years 1848-53 to an annual average of 1,036,000 bushels.[56] In irritation over the loss Canada talked secession from the Empire and annexation to the United States.[57] Canada's partner in the trade was her partner in its fall.

Of these facts the West was not ignorant. Whig politicians kept it informed. They had an interest in proving that a British market, even open at the back door, was to the West unimportant and unattractive. That was the Whig protective tariff argument; it was the complement to the home-market argument. Statistics showing the relative decline of American wheat exports to Europe during the preceding half-century supported it and were therefore perennially spread before the West. In 1839 Samuel Hazard compiled and published them with appropriate protectionist comments in his *United States Commercial and Statistical Register.*[58] In 1841 he republished them with new data concerning the Canada back-door trade, taken from the *Detroit Daily Advertiser.*[59] Joshua Leavitt in the same year presented an elaborate grain-trade memorial to Congress, and the next year another, supported by serried rows of figures, both of which a Whig Senate ordered to be printed.[60] C. G. Child, editor of the *Philadelphia Price Current and Commercial List*, in January, 1842, published in his paper a careful historical grain-trade review, which won wide notice, and in the succeeding autumn *Niles' Register* gave the statistics yet another airing.[61] Once more when Peel's Bill appeared Whigs paraded the figures before the West and this time supported the argument by dwelling on the prospective loss to the West of even the back-door trade.[62]

In America Peel's bill was awaited with intense interest. The outcome of the cabinet crisis in December had made clear that the Corn Laws would be changed, but the actual repeal measure was not published until January when Parliament reassembled, and it did not reach the United States until the 19th of February. So keen was public interest in it that a group of Eastern newspaper proprietors, to hasten its publication a few hours in New York, arranged to intercept the British mail steamer at Halifax and run the press despatches southward by special overland express.[63]

The measure chanced to arrive at the beginning of a heated American controversy over the Democratic low-tariff measure framed by Secretary Walker. To Walker's measure Peel's lent aid. It was received therefore by Democrats with delight, by Whigs with dismay. The two measures became identified in American tariff politics. Together they were gnawed and fought over as one bone of party and sectional contention.[64] This was a development which British free-trade propagandists had not taken sufficiently into account in predicting that the repeal of the Corn Laws would mollify the belligerent West.

In the East the bill had a favorable initial reception. The powerful commercial classes in the cities welcomed its promise of freer trade. Party Democrats and professional internationalists were delighted with it. Word was sent to Gladstone, who relayed it at once to Peel, that the bill had created "an immense sensation" and that there had been "illuminations."[65] Eastern Whigs and protectionists were consoled by the thought that the bill might appease the "Western Warriors" and facilitate a pacific adjustment of the Oregon controversy. Whig editors professed to discern British friendliness toward the United

States in the bill though contending in the same breath that the measure could not benefit American agriculture. Whig tolerance lessened as the bill became drawn into the Walker tariff controversy. Some editors of ultra-protectionist views reacted against it then by raising their tone on the Oregon question, which led William Cullen Bryant, the editor of the Democratic New York *Evening Post*, on March 3, 1846 to observe in an article entitled "War Rather Than Free Trade," that "the loudest cry for war with Great Britain seems just at present to come from the owners of the spindles."

The bill was received in the South with enthusiasm. It was a free-trade measure which was enough to commend it to a free-trade community. It was likely to hasten reform of the domestic tariff. It was conceived of in the South as in the East as an olive branch regarding Oregon and no section more earnestly desired the preservation of Anglo-American peace than the cotton South.

The bill seemed to offer least to the West. In Western produce markets its benefits were discouragingly appraised. In Baltic markets wheat prices advanced promptly two to three shillings a quarter on the publication of the bill.[66] In the West prices advanced not at all.[67] They declined, on the contrary, in harmony with British prices. Cincinnati markets tell the story for the whole section. Wheat in Cincinnati in the early winter of 1845 moved sharply upward in response to reports of harvest failure in Britain and northern Europe. The price was eighty-five cents a bushel on December 18, 1845.[68] Thereafter it declined as correct accounts arrived of the state of the British harvest. The decline continued throughout the spring of 1846. On July 17, 1846, wheat sold in Cincinnati at forty cents a bushel, which was its lowest level since the year 1830.[69] Flour in Cincinnati on December 18, 1845, was $4.85 to $5.00 a barrel.[70] From this peak it declined to $2.10 or $2.15 by September 18, 1846,[71] which was its lowest level since 1822. Mess pork on October 16, 1845, was $14.50 to $15.00 per barrel.[72] From this height it fell by September 18, 1846 to $7 a barrel,[73] its lowest level, except for the disastrous period 1841-43, since 1827. A descent so general and so steep could hardly have seemed a happy augury to the West of benefits to be derived from the repeal of the Corn Laws.

An intensification of party warfare over the protective tariff was the chief political effect of the bill in the West. Soon after the bill's appearance Whig editors throughout the section broadcast in excerpt or editorially a notable congressional speech by Charles Hudson, a Massachusetts protectionist, on "The Wheat Trade of the Country," in which the theory that a repeal of the Corn Laws could benefit Western agriculture was demolished.[74] A few weeks later the party press widely disseminated a public letter of Congressman E. D. Baker of the seventh Illinois congressional district to his constituents in which appeared an ordered demonstration of the following eight propositions:

1st. That the British wheat market has not required more than fourteen millions of bushels of wheat from abroad upon an average of any long series of years.

2nd. That a reduction of the duties will not materially diminish the amount produced by their own agriculture.

3rd. That the quantity consumed will not be largely increased.

4th. That the market, both as to quantity and price must be an unsteady, and therefore a poor one.

5th. That a reduction of the duty destroys the monopoly which we have enjoyed in consequence of the trade through Canada.

6th. That the reduction of duties gives a great advantage to the wheat-growing countries on the Mediterranean and in the North of Europe, beyond what they have previously enjoyed in competition with us.

7th. That as, notwithstanding the advantages in our favor, these countries have supplied Great Britain with the larger portion of wheat imported, so they will furnish a still larger proportion when the duties are reduced.

8th. That the market created by our domestic consumption is steadier, broader, and in every sense more profitable than any other. [75]

A discord of argument and counter-argument followed such Whig blasts. [76] Democratic editors sought to prove that on a basis of current costs of production and distribution the West could compete successfully in the markets of England. [77] Whigs in answer pointed to the insignificance of American exports to England even via Canada and the difference between Baltic and American price reactions to Peel's measure. [78] The Democratic press appealed to national pride, maintaining with feeling that the manly and enlightened freeman of the American Republic could hold his own in any competition with European serfs. The reply of *Niles' Register* was that the American freeman could indeed compete provided he was willing to reduce his wants to the serf level. [79] Some few Democratic editors of weak faith confessed that Western wheat could not sell to advantage in the open British market, but argued that maize could, if only prejudices in the British Isles could be overcome.

However disunited and unpersuasive the Western Democratic press was on the tariff issue, it was unanimous on one score,—that Peel's measure could have no effect on the Oregon question. A careful search has revealed not one Democratic journal in the whole section that had been aggressive on the Oregon question prior to the arrival of Peel's bill which subsequently changed its tone. Least mollified were the editorial "Western Warriors." Though some of them were pleased with Peel's measure they were loud in maintaining that the nation's birthright to the line of 54:40 must not be sold for a mess of pottage. Thus the editor of the *Illinois State Register*, though convinced that Peel's bill would benefit the West, warned all those who contemplated a partition of Oregon:

They may yet call upon the rocks and mountains to cover them from the wrath of an indignant people whose cherished Liberties will have received so terrible a blow: for what is it but a last final decision between those great principles of Monarchy and Democracy, as to which shall take the firmest, deepest, widest foothold on the long coast of the Pacific? Divide by 49, and Democracy must crouch before Monarchy forever, on the western side of this mighty continent because the despotic flag of the latter will hold sway over two degrees, while the glorious ensign of Freedom can float over but one. Will posterity—the sons of Freedom—ever forgive a policy leading to such terrible results as this? They never will. [80]

The editor of the *Ohio Statesman*, a free-trade Democrat rejoicing in repeal, was unreconciled as late as June 15, 1846, to any partition of Oregon. He wrote:

Withered be the hand that dismembers Oregon, and palsied the tongue that consents to an act so treasonable, foul and unnatural. Let Freedom's holy banner be planted upon the farthest ice-bound cliff, to which our title is clear and unquestionable, and our answer to our arrogant foe be given in the words of Vasa—'Here will we take our stand.' [81]

Similarly unappeased by Peel's bill were the "Western Warriors" in Congress. One of their leaders was Senator Hannegan, an Indiana free-trade Democrat, an ardent expansionist, and an aspirant to the mantle of President Polk. On March 5, 1846, in a speech which attracted national notice, he assailed with impartial violence Whigs who defended, on the ground of Peel's bill, a compromise solution of the Oregon question, and a Southern Senator, Haywood, a personal friend of Polk, who had caustically described Oregon extremists as small men seeking high places and had asserted that the President was in no way committed to the extravagant policy of 54:40. Hannegan declared:

Let me tell the Senator from North Carolina, that, . . . I would much sooner be found a small man seeking a high place, than the subservient, pliant, supple tool—the cringing flatterer, the fawning sycophant, who crouches before power, and hurries from its back stairs to bring before the Senate its becks, and nods, and wreathed smiles. The last steamer from Europe, it is said, puts this question in such a position, that for Oregon we can get free trade. Free trade I love dearly; but never will it be bought by me by the territory of my country. He who would entertain such an idea is a traitor to his country. I speak for myself, and my own section of the country. Free trade for a surrender of the ports and harbors on the Pacific? Never, sir; never. Whence this movement for free trade on the part of England? Does not every one know that she has been driven into this course by the outcries of starving millions? That she has been forced into this policy by the landowners, to save their lives from the knife of the midnight assassin, and their palaces from the torch of the prowling incendiary? But the West is to be provided for; it is to have a new and most profitable market. True it is, we in the west are born in the woods, but there are some among us who know a little, and, among other things, know that, long before our supplies could reach the British market, the granaries of the Baltic and the Black sea and the Mediterranean would have been poured into it to over-flowing. . . . I have only to add, that so far as the whole tone, spirit, and meaning of the remarks of the Senator from North Carolina are concerned, if they speak the language of James K. Polk, James K. Polk has spoken words of falsehood, and with the tongue of a serpent. [82]

Such intransigeance was voiced despite Peel's bill by the whole group of "Western Warriors" in Congress. A week after the arrival of the bill the Washington correspondent of the *Manchester Guardian* wrote home:

The news of Sir Robert Peel's great economical scheme has not tended to allay the zeal of the western members for war as much as might have been expected. The constituents of these gentlemen, it must be remembered, are about the most reckless and dangerous population under the sun, just civilized enough to read the paltry village newspaper, which panders to their vanity. . . . This very day . . . Mr. Breeze, senator from Illinois, Cass, from Michigan, Allen, from Ohio, and Hannegan, from Indiana, have addressed the senate in their usual strain, and endeavoured, as much as possible, to oppose the pacific views of the majority of that body. It would be impossible to name four states so likely to be benefited by Sir Robert Peel's measure as those which these persons represent; indeed, that measure seems to be framed expressly for them. [83]

When the Senate voted on June 18, 1846, to ratify the Oregon Treaty, the "Western Warriors" were still unrelenting. Though the country was then deep in the Mexican War, fourteen senators, all Democrats, reaffirmed their loyalty to 54:40 by voting against the Oregon Treaty. In the group were Allen of Ohio, Breeze and Semple of Illinois, Hannegan and Bright of Indiana, Cass of Michigan, Dickinson of western New York, Cameron and Sturgeon of Pennsylvania, and Atchison of Missouri.[84] Allen was so outraged by the Oregon Treaty that in protest against it he resigned his chairmanship of the Senate committee on foreign relations.[85]

Thus the British free-trade prediction that American belligerence on the Oregon question would be calmed by a repeal of the Corn Laws was belied. The repeal bill failed as an American soothing syrup. It was swallowed by the East and by the South, with relish even, but they did not need the medicine. The West, where the Oregon fever raged, rejected it and fumed and sputtered as before. The thesis of the beneficent intervention of the bill in the American crisis thus dissolves. It is, in truth, the serving up of contemporary propaganda as history.

But the free-trade movement did contribute, within the British Isles, to the quieting of the Oregon crisis. It did so by removing political obstacles to a policy of concession. In earlier negotiations British governments had rejected again and again the proposal made by the American government to divide Oregon by a line drawn along the 49th parallel to the sea. Lord Aberdeen, Peel's foreign secretary, regarded this line as a reasonable basis of partition. As early as March, 1844, he was personally willing to accept it, stopping it short only at the coast so as not to sever Vancouver Island.[86] The cabinet, however, was less pliant. The territory between the 49th parallel and the Columbia River, which British governments had held out for, had become steadily more British since the first negotiations, as a result of Hudson's Bay Company occupation. A government surrendering it to the United States under such circumstances exposed itself to the Opposition charge of having abandoned British pride and honor. The chief obstacle to an amicable adjustment of the Oregon controversy during the critical years 1845-46 was this political hazard.[87]

The anti-Corn Law crusade served to lessen this hazard. It did so by releasing in England a spirit of international conciliation. The free-trade doctrine was a gospel of peace. Its postulates were international good will and the dependence of nations on each other. The anti-Corn Law League was a peace society potent in England beyond any of the professional peace societies of the period.[88] Its leaders were conspicuous internationalists, friendly in particular toward the United States. They contended, as illustrated elsewhere in this paper, that if the Corn Laws were repealed, the resulting trade would unite England and America in permanent bonds of concord,—America would feed England, and England would clothe America. In the Oregon crisis the anti-Corn Law League turned the militant fervor of a triumphant crusade into channels of Anglo-American conciliation.

Louis McLane, American minister in London, wrote to his government early in February, 1846,

It is very obvious that the leading men of all parties uniting in favor of the [repeal] measure, regard it as destined to have great influence upon the intercourse with the United States; and in preserving and perpetuating amicable relations between the two

countries. They do not hesitate to speak of it, and on all occasions to advocate it, as the means of extending the interests of peace, and of making it more difficult to produce war; and, certainly, if the statesmen of England desire that the experiment of Free Trade should be successful, the surest, if not the only means of accomplishing that end, will be to cultivate peace with the United States. They would adopt the proposed scheme to very little purpose, if, for the sake of a degree of latitude on the Pacific, they should destroy the commercial intercourse of Great Britain with all the Atlantic States. [89]

But a more direct contribution of the anti-Corn Law crusade to the peaceful adjustment of the Oregon question was the realignment of British political parties it produced in the winter of 1845-46. The potato shortage and the famine scare lent to this change the drive of urgency. The shortage and the scare produced a crisis in the cabinet over the repeal of the Corn Laws, followed by the resignation of Peel. The formation of a Whig government was attempted by Lord John Russell. It failed as a result of dissension within the party over the nomination of Lord Palmerston to the Foreign Office. Sir Robert Peel was recalled. He reorganized his cabinet, and with the countenance of Lord John Russell proceeded to the abolition of the Corn Laws. Peelites and Whigs, neither strong enough to effect repeal alone, were thus brought, in the winter of 1845-46, into a temporary alliance against the embittered protectionists of the Conservative Party.'

That alliance rendered possible an Oregon treaty of renunciation. It assured the ministry of Whig protection, at least until the issue of the Corn Laws could be settled. In the cabinet crisis Whigs had themselves been won over to a policy of Oregon concession. Their failure to form a government had grown out of Lord Palmerston's belligerence, as a member of the Opposition, in matters of foreign policy, which had produced the impression that the party was in the hands of a war faction. It was necessary for the party leaders to erase that impression if they were to be successful in taking over the government on Peel's impending fall. Lord John Russell, therefore, in two speeches delivered in Glasgow on January 12, 1846, warmly advocated a settlement of the Oregon question by concession. [90] In these speeches he made of the free-trade issue a bridge over which to transport himself and party from earlier belligerence on the Oregon question to the new policy of peace. In response to an appeal from Edward Everett, former minister at the Court of St. James, for a party truce on the Oregon question, he gave Lord Aberdeen private assurance that he would make no objection to the ministry's surrendering to the United States the lower valley of the Columbia. [91] Lord John Russell bound his Whig associates by such a pledge, for they could not, without a party rift, publicly attack what he had privately approved.

As a result of these developments a settlement of the Oregon question became politically feasible. Early in January, 1846, Lord Aberdeen was actively preparing his public for a treaty of renunciation. By May the work was completed and the draft of the treaty was ready. Delay was occasioned by the difficulty of reopening negotiations which the American government had closed the preceding year. Lord Aberdeen chose to regard the reopening as accomplished by a notice from the American government announcing its decision to terminate the convention of joint occupation of Oregon at the end of a year. He despatched the completed draft of the treaty to Washington at once, which, without a single alteration, the American Senate accepted. Sir Robert Peel in his valedictory address to Parliament at the end of June, 1846, was able to announce triumphantly that the menacing Oregon problem had been solved.

By one of the accidents of history the crisis in the Oregon question was reached when England was in the midst of virtual revolution. The driving forces of the revolution were the anti-Corn Law crusade, the Irish potato failure and the threat of famine. The Corn Laws were denounced by British urban workers in the panic months of 1845-46 as a brutal exploitation of poor by rich, a generator of famine in the interests of a landed aristocracy. The landed aristocracy, on the other hand, conceived of the Corn Laws as the bulwark of the British Constitution, the removal of which meant the overturn of whatever was conservative in the British government. The free-trade agitation, the mass propaganda, the electioneering catchwords and phrases, the giant extra-legal organization of the League, the crusading temper of Leaguers and Radicals, the aligning of class against class, of city against country, of proletariat and bourgeoisie against aristocracy, seemed to British Tories the beginning of the end of orderly government. And the Corn Law repeal seemed actual revolution. A revolution, in truth, it was, but a revolution of peace. To England it brought quietly a changed order of society; to America it helped to bring, though only as a British political by-product, the Oregon Treaty of 1846.

Notes

1. See the references cited in footnotes 2 and 39.

2. For this view see St. George Leakin Sioussat, "James Buchanan," in Samuel Flagg Bemis, ed., *The American Secretaries of State and Their Diplomacy*, 5:260-261, 398-400 (New York, 1928); Thomas P. Martin, "Free Trade and the Oregon Question, 1842-1846," in *Facts and Factors in Economic History; Articles by Former Students of Edwin Francis Gay*, 470-491 (Cambridge, Mass., 1932); and "Influence of Trade on Anglo-American Relations," ch. 10 (MS., Ph.D. Thesis, Harvard University, 1922); Henry Commager, "England and Oregon Treaty of 1846," in the *Oregon Historical Quarterly*, 28:32-38 (March, 1927). See for a variant theory, Randolph Greenfield Adams, *A History of the Foreign Policy of the United States,* 228 (New York, 1924).

3. Sioussat, "James Buchanan," in *American Secretaries of State*, 5:260.

4. Martin, "Free Trade and the Oregon Question, 1842-1846," in *Facts and Factors in Economic History*, 485.

5. *Parliamentary Papers* (1846), 44 (16); *ibid.* (1847), 59 (32). The British imperial quarter equals 8¼ bushels. The hundredweight is 112 lbs.

6. *Parliamentary Papers* (1845), 11, Report of the Commissioners, 35.

7. *Memoirs by the Right Honourable Sir Robert Peel*, 2:171-172 (London, 1858); see also London *Times*, Feb. 5, 1846.

8. *Parliamentary Papers* (1846), 37 (735), *passim* (Correspondence explanatory of the measures adopted by Her Majesty's Government for the Relief of Distress arising from the failure of the Potato Crop in Ireland); W. P. O'Brien, *The Great Famine in Ireland*, 66 (London, 1896). Potato prices fell in Ireland in the spring of 1846.

9. *Hansard* (3d series), 85:712.

10. *Parliamentary Papers* (1846), 37 (735), *passim*.

11. *Ibid.*, p. 223, 247.

12. *Ibid.*, p. 84, 89; *Manchester Guardian*, Aprl 15, 1846; London *Spectator*, May 23, 1846. The government corn meal was referred to in Ireland as "Peel's Brimstone."

13. *Manchester Guardian*, Apr. 15, 1846; *Parliamentary Papers* (1846) 37 (735): 187; see also Monteagle to Peel, Sept. 27, 1845. Peel MSS., British Museum.

14. 29 Congress, 2 session, *Senate Document 7*, p. 16. Exports to the whole of the United Kingdom amounted to 1,192,000 bushels corn and 50,164 barrels corn meal.

15. J. R. McCulloch, *A Dictionary, Practical, Theoretical, and Historical, of Commerce and Commercial Navigation*, 425-449 (London, 1850).

16. Thomas Tooke, *A History of Prices*, 2:225-345 (London, 1838).

17. *Statistical Abstract for the United Kingdom*, 12 (1854).

18. McCulloch, *Dictionary of Commerce*, 427, note.

19. London *Times*, Jan. 3, 1846 (Brown and Co's. Circular); Apr. 8, 1846 (Letter of "A mealman" to the editor).

20. *Parliamentary Papers* (1846), 44 (130):4, *ibid.* (1847), 59 (259):4.

21. *Ibid.*, (1846), 44 (114):8.

22. *Statistical Abstract for the United Kingdom*, 22 (1854); T. Tooke and W. Newmarch, *A History of Prices*, 5:142-148 (London, 1857).

23. *Statistical Abstract for the United Kingdom*, 30 (1854); see also Hunt's *Merchants' Magazine*, 15:88-89.

24. London *Economist*, Feb. 21, 1846, p. 231; Feb. 28, 1846, p. 261, 271; Baring Brothers & Co. to Prime, Ward and King, Mar. 18, 1846. Baring MSS., Dominion Archives, Ottawa.

25. *Hansard* (3d series), 83:108.

26. London *Economist*, Feb. 28, 1846 (Body & Co's. Circular); and Mar. 14, 1846, p. 359.

27. *Hansard* (3d series), 83:281 (Peel); *ibid.*, 551 (Milnes); London *Times*, Jan. 17, 1846 (Speech of Sir J. Trollope); Jan. 19, 1846 (Speech of J. Bailey); Jan. 21, 1846 (Speech of Earl of Carnorvon).

28. *Statistical Abstract for the United Kingdom*, 12 (1854).

29. 29 Congress, 2 session, *Senate Documen 7*, p. 14,16.

30. *Hansard* (3d series), 86:629 (Sydney Herbert); *ibid.*, 606 (Lord John Russell); *ibid.*, 86:640-641. See also *post*, 106. The inability of American wheat growers to compete in the British market even under conditions of special favor is pointed out in the London *Economist*, Dec. 13, 1845.

31. London *Times*, Nov. 11, 1845.

32. See *post*, 103-106.

33. London *Chronicle*, Jan. 15, 1846.

34. *Ibid.*, Feb. 5, 1846. John Bright advanced the same argument in repeated speeches attacking the Corn Laws. See London *Times*, Dec. 6, 8, 10, 1845; Jan. 7, 1846; and *Louisville Democrat*, Mar. 12, 1846.

35. London *Chronicle*, Jan. 17, 1846.

36. *Punch*, 10:155.

37. *Hansard* (3d series), 84:1466. Lord Aberdeen, foreign secretary under Peel, made the same argument as applied however to maize. He concluded a letter written on December 3, 1845 to the British minister in Washington on the Oregon question by observing: "The access of Indian corn to our markets would go far to pacify the warriors of the Western States." Aberdeen to Pakenham, Dec. 3, 1845. Aberdeen MSS., British Museum. See also C. C. F. Greville, *A Journal of the Reign of Queen Victoria*, 2:312, 313.

38. London *Times*, Jan. 21, 1846.

39. Sioussat, "James Buchanan," in *American Secretaries of State*, 5:256-264; R. C. Clark, "British and American Tariff Policies and Their Influence on the Oregon Boundary Treaty," in the American Historical Association, Pacific Coast Branch, *Proceedings*, 1926, 32-49; Martin, "Free Trade and the Oregon Question, 1842-1846," in *Facts and Factors in Economic History*, 470-491; Henry Commager, "England and Oregon Treaty of 1846," in the *Oregon Historical Quarterly*, 28:32-38 (March, 1927). The question of the relation of the American tariff to the British politics of the Oregon question, which is dealt with in these writings, I intend to review elsewhere.

40. Crop estimates of each year are to be found for this period in the annual report of the United States Commissioner of Patents in the *Congressional Documents*.

41. See the statistics in the next paragraph.

42. *Hazard's Commercial and Statistical Register*, 4:242; see also the reference in the succeeding footnote.

43. 45 Congress, 3 session, *House Executive Document 15*, p. 106, 107.

44. 18 Congress, 1 session, *Annals of Congress*, 2:1962-1970.

45. *Statistical Abstract for the United Kingdom*, 12 (1854).

46. 9 Geo. IV, c. 60.

47. 5 and 6 Vict., c. 14.

48. 6 and 7 Vict., c. 29.

49. 1 William IV, c. 24.

50. *Provincial Statutes of Canada*, 6 Vict., c. 31. The terms of the measure are recited in the preamble to the Canada Corn Act.

51. *Statistical Abstract for the United Kingdom*, 22 (1854).

52. Gladstone Memorandum, Feb. 17, 1842, Peel MSS.; *Parliamentary Papers* (1843), 53 (218); *New York Journal of Commerce*, Feb. 17, 1846. The benefits of colonial preference to Canada are minimized—unduly in my opinion—in D. L. Burn, "Canada and the Repeal of the Corn Laws," in the *Cambridge Historical Journal*, 2:252-272 (1928).

53. Edward Everett, American minister to London, wrote to his government in 1844: "It is a matter of doubt whether the interest of the United States as a grain-growing region does not stand better under the present law with the Canada Corn bill as part of it than it would under a change either for a fixed duty or entire freedom of trade. Either of these measures would subject our corn to a competition with those ports in the North of Europe, from which it can generally be imported cheaper than from America, whereas under the present state of the law, although the transportation is monopolized by English bottoms, it would seem as if all the corn imported from abroad must come from the United States through Canada." Everett to Upshur, Mar. 2, 1844, no. 93, Everett MSS., Massachusetts Historical Society.

54. *Parliamentary Papers* (1847), 59 (259):9.

55. *Ibid.* (1843), 53 (218):4, 5. See also *Hansard* (3d series), 60:1235-1236 (Gladstone); Gillespie to Stanley, Jan. 10, 1842, C. O. 42:500; Stanley to Worsley, Apr. 17, 1843, Peel MSS., British Museum. The figures given by Mr. Burn in the *Cambridge Historical Journal*, 2:255, should be compared with those in *Statistical Abstract for the United Kingdom*, 12 (1854); 45 Congress, 3 session, *House Executive Document 15*, p. 106, 107. *Hazard's Commercial and Statistical Register*, 4:242.

56. *Statistical Abstract for the United Kingdom*, 12 (1854).

57. W. P. Morrell, *British Colonial Policy in the Age of Peel and Russell*, 197-198; Theodore Walrond, ed., *Letters and Journals of James, Eighth Earl of Elgin*, 99 ff. (London, 1872). Adam Shortt and A. G. Doughty, ed., *Canada and its Provinces*, 5:214-227. The loss to Canada was chiefly the flour milling and the transit trade.

58. *Hazard's Commercial and Statistical Register* (1839), 1:251-253.

59. *Ibid.*, 4:242.

60. 26 Congress, 2 session, *Senate Document 222*; 27 Congress, 2 session, *Senate Document 339*.

61. *Niles' Register*, 63:25.

62. See Edwin Williams, *The Wheat Trade of the United States* (New York, 1846); see also J. R. Williams, "Production of Wheat in the United States," in Hunt's *Merchants' Magazine*, 12:307-323; Charles Hudson, "Corn Trade of the United States," in *ibid.*, 12:421-432.

63. *New York Journal of Commerce*, Feb. 19, 1846.

64. Pakenham, the British minister at Washington, described the American reception of Peel's bill as follows:

"A great, and I think I may say, a very gratifying sensation has been produced in this Country by the news received by the last Packet of the intended alterations in the Commercial Policy of England. In the midst of a general expression of satisfaction some dissenting voices are of course to be heard. Amongst these may be classed that of the Manufacturing Interests who foresee in the example thus set by England the downfall of the protective system in this country, and those also of a mischievous and ungracious class of Politicans, who trade upon the agitation of questions of an anti-English tendency, and who cannot but perceive how much the measures now under discussion in England must tend to narrow the field of their operations.

"On the other hand the anti-tariff party seem to be in the highest degree elated by the adoption of a policy so much in consonance with their views, and to consider the success of the bill lately sent to Congress by the Secretary of the Treasury for the reduction in the existing scale of import duties, to be now almost certain." Pakenham to Aberdeen, Feb. 26, 1846. F. O. 5:446.

65. C. S. Parker, *Sir Robert Peel*, 3:374 (London, 1899).

66. London *Times*, Feb. 7, 14, 1846, citing Body & Co's. Circular. Baltic prices later declined,

however, in sympathy with British prices. For detailed statistics of wheat prices for the years 1844-49 in European and American ports, see *Parliamentary Papers* (1850), 52 (206).

67. J. E. Boyle, *Chicago Wheat Prices for Eighty-One Years*, 5, 6, 13 (Ithaca, N. Y., 1922); Hunt's *Merchants' Magazine*, 15:87, 214, 215, 411. See also the daily newspapers of the period.

68. *Cincinnati Atlas*, Dec. 18, 1845. For this and the succeeding Cincinnati citations I am indebted to the kindness of Mr. T. S. Berry of Cambridge.

69. *Cincinnati Chronicle*, July 17, 1846.

70. *Cincinnati Atlas*, Dec. 18, 1845.

71. *Cincinnati Chronicle*, Sept. 18, 1846.

72. *Cincinnati Atlas*, Oct. 16, 1845.

73. *Cincinnati Chronicle*, Sept. 18, 1846. See also G. F. Warren and F. A. Pearson, "Wholesale Prices in the United States . . . 1797 to 1932," in *Wholesale Prices for 213 Years, 1720 to 1932*, 113 (Ithaca, N. Y., 1932). Wholesale prices of farm foods in the United States as measured by an index number established in this volume rose to a height of 68 in December, 1845, from which they precipitously declined by September, 1846, to 48, the lowest level, except for the period August, 1842, to September, 1844, to which they had sunk since 1821.

74. 29 Congress, 1 session, *Congressional Globe*, App. 459-464. For a reply to this speech by a Virginia congressman, see *ibid.*, 402-411.

75. See *Rochester Daily American*, Mar. 11, 1846; Alton *Telegraph and Democratic Review*, Mar. 21, 1846. The *Chicago Daily Journal* (w. ed.) of Mar. 24, 1846 commented as follows on Peel's bill: "It is too well known that we cannot supply England with wheat so cheap as can the merchants of Dantzic and the grain growing regions of the southeast of Europe. It is true Sir R. Peel proposes to admit our corn meal and buckwheat duty free. But are we assured that the shipments of such articles will prove sources of permanent traffic? It is hard to change the diet of thirty millions of people—to uproot the prejudice even in favor of rotten potatoes; and even if we do break down these walls of brass, cannot all these things be secured with the tariff as it is? . . . "

76. This account rests on an examination of the following newspapers for the first half of 1846. Democratic: New York *Evening Post*, New York *Globe*, Buffalo *Courier*, Washington *Union*, Charleston *Mercury*, Pittsburgh *Democratic Union*, Columbus *Ohio Statesman*, *Cincinnati Enquirer*, *Cincinnati Herald*, *Indiana State Sentinel*, Springfield *Illinois State Register*, *Chicago Democrat*, *Louisville Daily Democrat*, *Nashville Union*, *Jefferson Inquirer*, St. Louis *Missourian*, St. Louis *Missouri Reporter*. Whig: New York *Courier and Enquirer*, New York *Tribune*, Buffalo *Commercial Advertiser*, *Rochester Daily American*, Philadelphia *North American*, *Baltimore American*, *Baltimore Patriot*, *National Intelligencer*, *Cincinnati Chronicle*, *Cincinnati Gazette*, Chillicothe *Scioto Gazette*, *Chicago Daily Journal*, Alton *Telegraph and Democratic Review*, *New Orleans Commercial Bulletin*.

77. See in addition to the above DeBow's *Commercial Review*, 1:33-44.

78. *National Intelligencer*, Mar. 10, 1846. See also London *Economist* for February and March, 1846.

79. *Niles' Register*, 68:162 (May 17, 1845).

80. Springfield *Illinois State Register*, May 15, 1846.

81. Columbus *Ohio Statesman*, June 15, 1846.

82. 29 Congress, 1 session, *Congressional Glove*, 458-460. I have restored to the speech the sentence,

"True it is, we in the West are borne in the woods . . . ," which does not appear in the revised statement published in the *Congressional Globe,* but was reported in press accounts. See *Niles' Register*, 70:23, Mar. 14, 1846.

83. *Manchester Guardian*, Mar. 18, 1846. The letter is dated Feb. 26, 1846.

84. 29 Congress, 1 session, *Senate Journal*, 555.

85. 29 Congress, 1 session, *Congressional Globe,* 972; see also Columbus *Ohio Statesman*, June 19, 1846.

86. Aberdeen to Pakenham, Mar. 4, 1844. Aberdeen MSS. See also my article on "The Oregon Pioneers and the Boundary," in the *American Historical Review*, 29:681-699 (July, 1924); and "British Party Politics and the Oregon Treaty," in *ibid.*, 37:653-677 (July, 1932).

87. *Ibid.*

88. New York *Evening Post*, Feb. 20, 1846. William Cullen Bryant commented in this issue on the League as follows:
   "We have already spoken of the prodigious strength of the League in England, and the very strong support it received from public opinion. The League is not merely a combination of the hungry against the full-fed; it is the wealth of the manufacturers organized against the wealth of the landholders; but the people are on the side of the manufacturers, or rather the manufacturers are on the side of the people. . . .
   "The influence which has wrought this great change [the bill abolishing the Corn Laws] is altogether an influence favorable to peace. The powerful association of which we have spoken is, in its tendencies and feelings, a kind of peace society, without peace its favorite theory cannot be put into practice; without peace it can make no perfect experiment of the benefits of free trade. Its object is to give the laboring classes of Britain the cheapest and most abundant sustenance, by drawing it directly from those parts of the world where the articles which form the food of mankind are produced in the greatest plenty and with the least cost. A war with the United States, to which the League looked for the principal supplies which are to feed the population of the United Kingdom, would wholly frustrate this object. We may trace in the language of Lord John Russell, who has so recently become a champion of free trade in corn, a def[er]ence to the views of the League on this very question of peace. He is no longer the belligerent Lord John Russell, inveighing against the weakness of the ministry in yielding to the claims of the United States. He finds, as he tells the House of Commons, that the state of the question has greatly changed, and reproves the haste with which the British minister rejected Mr. Polk's proposal for settling the boundary of Oregon by the forty-ninth parallel of latitude. He disapproves of putting by so unceremoniously the opportunity of peacefully adjusting the difference." See also J. C. Calhoun to G. Wilson, Mar. 24, 1845, in London *League*, May 3, 1845.

89. McLane to Buchanan, Feb. 3, 1846, no. 34. Department of State, *Despatches, England*, v. 56.

90. *Manchester Guardian*, Jan. 17, 1846.

91. Russell to Palmerston, Feb. 2, 1846. Palmerston MSS., Broadlands; see also my article "British Party Politics and the Oregon Treaty" in the *American Historical Review*, 37:653-677 (July, 1932).

The Southern expansionists of 1846

John Hope Franklin

After the Missouri Compromise of 1820 every push westward inflamed the growing sectional conflict between the North and South. Friction reached a peak during James K. Polk's push to fulfill America's "Manifest Destiny." Some historians have argued that the Democrats attempted to defuse trouble by balancing expansion in Texas and Mexico (potential slave territories) with the acquisition of all of Oregon (which would most certainly enter the Union as several free states). The Mexican War produced sharp opposition from Northern abolitionist groups, epitomized by Thoreau's *Essay on Civil Disobedience* and his brief stay in a Massachusetts jail for refusing to pay taxes to support an immoral war. Balancing northern hostility to expansion in Mexico was southern opposition by men of the stature of John C. Calhoun to Polk's claim to the Oregon country north of the forty-ninth parallel. These well-known stands by prominent men of both North and South raise important questions about American society in the mid-1840s.

How representative were their views when compared with those of the rank and file of each section? Did Manifest Destiny have a special meaning in each section, or was there a feeling of national identity that superseded regional peculiarities? Was one section more nationalistically inclined than the other? How did each section feel about the annexation of California and New Mexico which were the main fruits of the Mexican War? In the following essay, John Hope Franklin, Professor of History at the University of Chicago and an expert on Black history and southern life, analyzes southern expansionism. His work complements Professor Merk's studies of the diplomacy of the Oregon Question.

For further reading: George L. Rives, *The United States and Mexico, 1821-1848*, 2 vols. (New York: Scribner, 1913); Charles G. Sellers, *James K. Polk, Continentalist 1843-1846* (Princeton: Princeton University Press, 1966); Edwin A. Miles, "Fifty-four Forty or Fight—An American Political Legend," *Mississippi Valley Historical Review*, XLIV (September 1957), 291-309; Justin H. Smith, *The War with Mexico*, 2 vols. (New York: Macmillan, 1919); H. Donaldson Jordon, "A Politician of Expansion: Robert J. Walker," *Mississippi Valley Historical Review*, XIX (December 1932), 362-381;

From *Journal of Southern History*, XXV (August 1959), 323-338. Copyright 1959 by the Southern Historical Association. Reprinted by permission of the managing editor.

Richard R. Stenberg, "The Failure of Polk's Mexican War Intrigue of 1845," *Pacific Historical Review*, IV (March 1935), 38-68; William E. Dodd, "The West and the War with Mexico," *Journal of the Illinois Historical Society*, V (July 1919), 159-172; Chauncey S. Boucher, "In Re That Agressive Slavocracy," *Mississippi Valley Historical Review*, VIII (June-September 1921), 13-79; Clayton S. Ellsworth, "The American Churches and the Mexican War," *American Historical Review*, XLV (January 1940), 301-326; Frederick Merk, *Manifest Destiny and Mission in American History*, (New York: Knopf, 1963)*

*Available in paperback.

The decade of the 1840's witnessed a remarkable growth in expansionist sentiment in the United States.[1] For years restless Americans, their voracious appetite for land whetted by the acquisition of Louisiana, had hoped to extend their territorial possessions in many directions. But their efforts had fallen far short of the mark. They got nothing from the second war with England; the annexation of Florida was certainly not satisfying; and the long struggle to remove the Seminoles was humiliating to say the least. The numerous efforts to acquire Texas had ended in failure, while the hope of securing Canada and California had become little more than an idle dream. Prospects suddenly became brighter in the early 1840's. Texas gave clear indications that she preferred annexation to independence or to some subordinate arrangement with a European power. California and, perhaps, other parts of Mexico now seemed within reach. And if Canada could not be taken in one stroke, at least all of Oregon might be wrested from Britain upon the termination of the treaty of joint occupation.

The motivations for expansion had increased in number and complexity with the passing years. Among the principal ones was the desire to push Britain out of the Northwest and generally to frustrate the machinations of European powers. There was widespread fear of British designs in the New World; and an English foothold in Oregon could, in all probability, jeopardize American settlements there.[2] There was, moreover, the steady deterioration of the relations of the United States with Mexico. For years they had been unsatisfactory, and the entrance of the Republic of Texas into the picture merely aggravated the situation at a time when many Southerners were casting covetous eyes on the new republic and other territories still under the Mexican flag.[3] Then, too, there were the vague dreams of an empire of continental proportions, made more attractive by the desire to extend Protestant Christianity and Anglo-Saxon institutions and to enlarge the area of American commercial and industrial domination. To these must be added the feverish race between the slave states and free states to bring in new territories that would strengthen their respective positions. These were the major considerations that created an urgency regarding expansion in the middle forties.

Beneath the movement and giving it emotional and intellectual content was the agitation for expansion that came from many quarters, including the South. The expansionist views of many Southerners were represented by Richard Hawes, the Kentucky Whig, who told Calhoun in 1844 that it should be the policy of this country to own "all the cotton lands of North America if we can."[4] In the House of Representatives an Alabama Democrat, James Belser, asserted that it was impossible to limit the area of freedom, "the area of the Anglo-Saxon race." In the Senate William Merrick of Maryland declared that the question of the annexation of Texas was "a subject which concerned the fate of empires, and which was to effect, for weal or for wo, through ages yet to come, millions of the Anglo-Saxon race."[5] While visiting California in 1845 a Calhoun correspondent said, "We only want the Flag of the United States and a good lot of Yankees, and you would soon see the immense natural riches of the Country developed and her commerce in a flourishing condition. To see that Flag planted here would be most Acceptable to the Sons of Uncle Sam, and by no means repugnant to the native population."[6] The editor of the Richmond *Enquirer* rejoiced that the Whig *American Review* had come out boldly for California in 1846. He had no fear of extending the area of freedom, he asserted, for he was satisfied that "a federative system of free republics like our own, is capable of almost indefinite expansion, without disadvantage."[7]

The extent of the expansionist fever in 1846 can be seen in the resolution of Senator David Yulee of Florida proposing that the President open negotiations with Spain with a view to purchasing Cuba.[8] In the first weeks of the Mexican War a Charleston friend described to Calhoun a fantastic scheme launched by Southerners for the acquisition of all Mexico. Some years earlier, he said, an undisclosed number of Southerners had taken an oath to enlist in the conquest of Mexico. Each person was to do everything possible to bring into the cause every man who would make a good soldier, to hold himself in readiness, and to report to any place he was summoned for the purpose of carrying out the scheme.[9] Meanwhile, the sentiment for acquiring Oregon up to 54° 40′ had gained currency during the first year of Polk's administration. Views supporting the occupation of Oregon ranged from the lusty expansionist aims of the venerable John Quincy Adams to the noisy demands of young Andrew Johnson.[10]

There was, however, no unanimity regarding either the area into which the United States should expand or whether it should expand at all. Even in the South for instance, there was some sentiment against expansion. Meredith Gentry of Tennessee told the House of Representatives that he saw no reason for contaminating American institutions by expanding into new areas. "If England were to propose to cede Canada to this Government to-morrow in my humble judgment, it would be unwise to accept the cession," and if Mexico asked to be annexed, she, too, should be rebuffed.[11] Men like Alexander Stephens and John Calhoun had such grave doubts about the validity of the American title to Oregon that they felt it would be extremely rash to press any claims above 49°. Meanwhile, they frowned on any involvement with Mexico, even though victory there would surely lead to the acquisition of new territory.[12]

On the question of expansion, party considerations loomed important in 1846. The Democrats had won the Presidential election of 1844, and even if "Fifty-four Forty or Fight" was not their slogan, expansionist sentiment within the party was strong.[13] But conservative Southern members of the party, gratified over the annexation of Texas, were not as enthusiastic about "reannexing" Oregon as they might have been, and their Northern colleagues chided them for it. This led Jefferson Davis, among other Southerners, to speak for the section. He defended the South's desire to get Texas by declaring that this was in the national interest. While he did not want to do anything to precipitate a war with Britain, he wished to preserve the whole of Oregon for the United States.[14] As the Democrats argued among themselves about whether to demand all of

Oregon, Southern Whigs showed little enthusiasm for the project.[15] Many Northern Whigs, with their growing antislavery radicalism, hoped that Oregon would be acquired to offset the mounting strength of the slave power.[16]

The lukewarm-to-indifferent attitude of many Southerners toward Oregon in 1846 was enough to raise suspicions regarding their lack of interest in territories into which slavery could not expand. On December 18, 1845, Ohio's William Allen, chairman of the Senate Committee on Foreign Relations, introduced a resolution authorizing the President to give formal notice to England of the termination of the joint occupation of Oregon. This was the first of a number of resolutions, of varying degrees of bellicosity, hinting that if England did not withdraw from Oregon she would be driven out. Some expansionists were indeed rash in their statements and resolutions. And it is not surprising that resolutions for the occupation of Oregon were enthusiastically supported by the antislavery leaders in Congress.

Southern leaders in Congress who had little or no enthusiasm for Oregon were much too astute to oppose it on the obvious ground that eventually Oregon would enter the union as one or several free states. These men, to whom a duel was commonplace, who had fought Indians incessantly and bitterly, some of whom had agitated for war against England in 1812, suddenly became the leading peacemakers of the country. In his notable speech of March 16 against giving notice unless it proposed negotiation and compromise, Calhoun rather feebly asserted that he was for Oregon. He hastened to add, however, that because the time was improper to insist on all of it, he favored compromise to avert war. He painted a vivid picture of the terrible destruction that war would bring. He spoke of the great mission of the people of the United States to occupy the entire continent and asserted that war would impede this high mission. He insisted that he wanted Oregon as much as Texas, but the latter was being secured without endangering peace. The only possible way to obtain Oregon was through patient negotiation, which an "all or none" attitude would make impossible.[17]

Calhoun received generous support in his position from Southerners on both sides of the aisle. Alexander Barrow, the Whig senator from Louisiana, said he was certain war would result if the United States adopted an uncompromising position on Oregon. He was equally certain that public sentiment was not prepared for war with England. He hoped that the government would not be ashamed to do what the people demanded, and would enter into negotiations leading to an amicable settlement.[18] Whig Senator William Archer of Virginia asserted that he did not believe that the United States had a clear title to 54° 40', but he thought it would be unstatesmanlike and undiplomatic to be intransigent. Other Southerners followed Calhoun's lead, including men of great prestige like George McDuffie of South Carolina, Joseph Chalmers of Mississippi, and John Berrien of Georgia.[19]

Some of the leading Democratic and Whig organs of the South were as opposed to a firm stand for all of Oregon as were Calhoun and his supporters. Even in Polk's own state there was considerable opposition to an uncompromising position on Oregon. The Memphis *Enquirer* was highly critical of Senator Allen for introducing the resolution to give notice and expressed the fear that the administration policy might lead to war.[20] In January 1846, the Nashville *Republican Banner*, a Whig newspaper, warned the administration to be cautious about Oregon. It denounced John Quincy Adams and the others who insisted on 54° 40' and praised Calhoun for his moderation. Later in the year the

The Southern Expansionists of 1846   **249**

paper expressed the fear that the pressure to acquire Oregon was largely an abolitionist plot, since Adams, Joshua Giddings, and other abolitionist congressmen were so anxious for the territory.[21] In Charleston the *Mercury* asserted that "never was there a greater mistake than to suppose that the feeling of the nation is in favor of a war for Oregon, so long as our national honor is not involved. . . . " After most of the speeches for and against notice had been made in Congress the *Mercury* insisted that the 54° 40′ pretension was the result of "shallow ignorance. . . . Our just *claims* are limited by the latitude of 49; and with such a basis for adjustment, there can be neither war nor cause of war. Substantially we must have it; and we will have it."[22]

A partially neglected consideration that influenced some Southern opposition to drastic action in Oregon was the South's interest in a relaxed trade and antislavery policy for England. As early as 1841 Duff Green went to England to promote a policy of free trade, arguing that the American West's interest in Oregon would cool if England would be willing to negotiate a treaty for the admission of American grain. If England dropped her campaign against slavery *and* repealed her Corn Laws, the West would be more kindly disposed to England; and the South, which purchased a good deal of Western produce, would benefit from lower grain prices as well as from a softer British antislavery policy.[23] In his endeavors Green undoubtedly spoke for Calhoun, McDuffie, and other Southerners who supported a compromise with England on the Oregon question.

Still, despite the great prestige and the eloquent arguments for peace of men like Calhoun and papers like the *Mercury*, they did not speak for the entire South. Even while Senator Joseph Chalmers of Mississippi was declaring that the people of his state favored conciliation and compromise up to 49°, the legislators of his state were adopting a resolution supporting the claim of the United States up to 54° 40′ and praising the President's stand, which was "marked by a spirit of liberal concession, firmness, patriotism, and signal ability."[24] Nor did the equivocal position of Senators Berrien and Colquitt of Georgia represent the views of all their constituents. After Polk declared that the title of the United States to Oregon was "clear and unquestionable," one of Howell Cobb's friends wrote him that the message had stimulated the mountain folk around Clarksville, Georgia, to thought and discussion. "Every one understands, or thinks he understands, all about the Oregon question," he said. "I heard a crowd on Christmas, not one of whom knew on which side of the Rocky Mountains Oregon was, swear they would support and fight for Polk *all over the world*, that he was right, and we would have Oregon and thrash the British into the bargain."[25] Southerners like these, inured to the hard life, quick to defend themselves, and ever-willing to fight any nation large or small, would have rejected the olive branch that was being proffered so generously by their more conservative representatives in the Congress.

Southerners who favored unqualified expansion were not mere voices crying in the mountains and desolate countrysides of their section. They had an impressive group of able young men as their spokesmen in Congress—largely in the House. There were about twenty men in Congress who represented what may be termed the hard core of Southern expansionism. They came from every state of the South with the exception of South Carolina, where the Calhoun intransigence seemed pervasive. Twelve were serving their first terms in the Congress in 1846, and four had been elected for the second time. Thus only four can be regarded as veteran congressmen. Most of them were under forty years of age. The elder statesman of the group was Seaborn Jones, a fifty-eight-year-old lawyer from Columbus, Georgia. The other member beyond the half century mark was Sam Houston, who at fifty-three had just taken his seat as one of the first senators from Texas.

These Southern spokesmen for expansion seemed bound by neither the conservative traditions of Congress nor the vested interests of the section from which they came. Largely small-town lawyers and farmers, their only loyalties seemed to be to party and country. All of them except Henry Hilliard of Alabama were Democrats who took much more seriously than some of the older members the avowed expansionist commitments of the party. These older members irritated some of the "true" expansionists in the party like Howell Cobb, who went so far as to say that the Southerners who did not stand upon the great question of Oregon "as *some of us* did" were responsible for "alienating the good feelings of many of our northern and western democrats and thereby rendering the harmonious and united action of the party more difficult than it would have been...."[26] No voices in the country spoke out more clearly or vigorously in behalf of the fulfillment of the American dream of empire than these young "War Hawks" of 1846.

The Southern expansionists thought that President Polk's description of the American title to Oregon as "clear and unquestionable" was modest and conciliatory. They spoke with great familiarity of the American claims, based on discovery, exploration, and settlement; and none of them entertained the slightest doubt as to the validity of the American title. "Oregon is *ours*," thirty-four-year-old Representative Henry Bedinger of Virginia cried. "Every acre, every poor rood of it—and we must and *will* have it. . . . This great territory is of such immense value and importance to this Union, that we would deserve to be regarded as idiots by the civilized world, if we should suffer any portion of it to be wrested from us by any power upon earth."[27]

Lucien Chase of Clarksville, Tennessee, twenty-nine years old and serving his first term in the House, asserted that the United States had the "sole and indisputable right from 42° to 54° 40'." It would be humiliating as well as dangerous, he said, for the country to surrender any portion of it.[28] The young Greeneville, Tennessee, tailor, Andrew Johnson, said that he was for the whole of Oregon up to 54° 40' "and for enough on the other side to *deaden the timber* on beyond, that we may know where the line is."[29]

Several of the Southern expansionists insisted that the people of the country would not tolerate any concession on a matter so clear and unmistakable as America's claim to Oregon. Edmund Dargan from Mobile said that the people had been taught to believe "that the whole of Oregon is ours...." The people of Alabama, he declared, took the position that all of Oregon belonged to the United States, and they were determined to maintain their rights by not yielding one inch. Senator Ambrose Sevier of Arkansas also doubted that the people would accept a compromise short of 54° 40'. "They were words that had sunk deep into the hearts of the people, and before the summer was over, they would become so deeply impressed as not to be erased." They would, therefore, go to any lengths to save Oregon. Jacob Thompson, the former schoolmaster from Pontotoc, Mississippi, asserted that the claim of the United States was better than Britain's and that the people of this country were demanding action. It was idle for members of the Congress to say they were for Oregon "and yet do nothing towards asserting our rights...."[30]

The sentiments of "Manifest Destiny" uttered by these Southern expansionists were as strong as those of any expansionists of any period in the nation's history. The Southerners deftly coupled the historic mission of the nation with the immense economic and military importance of the territory they sought, thus appealing to the realists as well as the idealists. It was Robert M. T. Hunter, one of the few veteran congressmen among the Southern expansionists, who was sufficiently practical and astute to develop this argument. "There is no man with an American heart in his bosom," he declared, "who could be insensible to the prospect of planting our flag and our settlements upon the shores of the Pacific. There is no such bosom which would not swell . . . at the prospect of the influence, commercial, political, and military, which we should derive from a position on the shores of Oregon and California. . . ." The possession of Oregon would place the Union in a position of "impregnable strength and stable greatness, with one arm on the Atlantic sea and the other on the Pacific shore, ready to strike in either direction with a rapidity and an efficiency not to be rivalled by any nation on the earth."[31] Henry Hilliard predicted that after the nation had established her exclusive rights in Oregon, a profitable trade with China and numerous other benefits would accrue from such an acquisition; "then would be fulfilled that vision which had wrapt and filled the mind of Nunez as he gazed over the placid waves of the Pacific."[32]

Some Southern expansionists apparently thought it unnecessary to emphasize the great value of Oregon but merely to declare that it was the destiny of the United States to rule all of North America. Representative Seaborn Jones of Georgia declared that the flag of the United States must "ultimately float everywhere over this continent." In the same vein Henry Bedinger of Virginia said that he hoped that "the 'American eagle' would take its onward flight, unresisted and unopposed, to the rich regions of Oregon." Henry S. Clarke of Washington, North Carolina, regarded Oregon as "our own soil, our own patrimony," and thought that it would be wonderful to see the American flag float over the mountains of Oregon, for "mountainous countries are the nurseries of freemen."[33]

Insinuations by Northerners that the people of the South were not really interested in acquiring Oregon deeply wounded the feelings of the Southern expansionists. Although they came from a section whose animosity toward the North was mounting steadily, they spoke for expansion as nationalists, not sectionalists. The Northern jibes were directed at the Southern pacificators, of course, but the expansionists also took offense and were quick to defend their constituency. To those Northerners who said that the South did not want to risk war with England because of its disastrous consequences for the South, Jacob Thompson of Mississippi admitted that there was no section that would feel more heavily the weight of war.

Yet this indiscriminate assault upon the South was unworthy of the gentlemen; this assumption that it was a sectional question—that it was a noarthern question—was ridiculous and absurd. . . . Gentlemen should remember that there may be differences of opinion between individuals from different sections of the Union; but, as regards the South, they have never been actuated by any such narrow and contracted considerations. . . . [34]

This was, of course, an overstatement of the case. Likewise, Henry Bedinger objected to the gratuitous insults of the Northerners and assured them that Southern honor and Southern integrity would stand by them in the hour of need. Howell Cobb could never regard Oregon as a sectional question and looked forward to the day when "not a British flag floats on an American breeze; that not a British subject treads on American soil."[35]

Regarding the prospect of war with Britain over Oregon, the Southern expansionists thought it peculiarly unbecoming for some of their Southern colleagues to assume the role of peacemakers when national honor and integrity were involved. Young James C.

Dobbin of Fayetteville, North Carolina, refused to be frightened by the assertion that the resolution to terminate joint occupation was a war measure.

"This incessant alarm-shout of war, war, war, shall not deter me from voting to give this notice, when I entertain the sincere conviction that national honor demands it . . . good policy demands it . . . justice to our adventurous pioneers in Oregon demands it. . . . " He did not expect war, but if it did come, "our best fortifications will be found in the noble hearts of our patriotic countrymen; our best preparation, to let the people understand their rights."[36]

Andrew Johnson said that he was not afraid of the British lion.

Let him but growl, let him assume a menacing attitude, and on some lofty peak in Oregon . . . the armor-bearer of Jupiter will be found. . . . The British lion will be descried in the distance, if he shall dare approach, and if he shall moor to our shore, he will descend from his elevated position, and . . . strike terror to his heart, and cause him . . . to retreat, with the reeking blood dripping from his mane, from a soil that he has dared to pollute by his impious tread.[37]

The Southern expansionists tried to convince their opponents that the best way to avoid war was to take a firm stand against Britain.[38] Seaborn Jones insisted that England would not dare go to war to defend Oregon. If she did, Ireland would rebel, Canada would strike for her liberty, and British commerce would be ruined. If British leaders were short-sighted enough to start a war, the United States would be victorious. Archibald Yell of Arkansas could not see why anyone feared England. "We have whipped her twice, and we can whip her again," he exclaimed inaccurately but confidently. Yell's colleague from Arkansas, Senator Ambrose Sevier, said that the people of Arkansas would go to war rather than lose any of Oregon. They were a warlike people, he asserted, who gave guns to their children for playthings![39]

It was Sam Houston who topped off the argument for the "War Hawks." Deprecating the compromise as a position that would merely make Britain more aggressive and un-reasonable, Houston contended that the peacemakers had exaggerated the evils of war. War certainly had its virtues, such as "draining off the restless and dissatisfied portion of the population, who might be killed off with benefit to the remainder; and also the effect it had in disciplining the habits of men into subordination to the rules of order."[40]

When the Oregon treaty was ratified in June 1846, settling the boundary at 49°, the score of Southern expansionists who led the drive to place the boundary at 54° 40', could view with satisfaction their valiant struggle. There were some Southerners, such as Robert Toombs of Georgia and L. H. Sims of Missouri, who had spoken out for all of Oregon but who were finally won over to a policy of compromise. The "hard core" Southern expansionists stood their ground and seemed proud of what they had done. They had given about as much support for all of Oregon as any Southerners had given for Texas. Their consciences were clear, for they had acted as "Manifest Destiny" Americans, not as narrow-minded sectionalists. But they never seemed to realize that they had almost no chance for success. In the highest quarters there were always serious doubts about the validity of the American claim north of 49°, and the official contentions of the two governments never took serious cognizance of the American claim in that area. President Polk, moreover, doubtless took that into consideration when he offered in the spring of 1846 to settle at 49°.

There were other considerations that made it unthinkable to hold out for a more favorable settlement than 49°. The impending repeal of the Corn Laws indicated to the Washington government that it would be folly to risk alienating a country whose new trade policy would mean so much to the American farmers. Then, too, the deterioration of relations with Mexico made it highly desirable that the difficulties with England be settled promptly and amicably.[41] Certainly, experienced men like Calhoun and Mc-Duffie, despite their awkward position in the administration, exerted effective pressure on Polk not to pursue a course of action that would increase the complexities and difficulties of United States foreign relations and of the Southern cotton planters.[42] Finally, the Southern expansionists had joined their Northern and Western colleagues in contending for something in which not even the Oregon pioneers were interested. In 1846 there were only eight American settlers north of the Columbia River, and there seemed to be no immediate prospect of an increase. They preferred to remain in the Willamette Valley, by far the most attractive portion of Oregon. It was, therefore, inaccurate to declare that the Oregon settlers were merely waiting for American action before moving into the territory up to 54° 40'.

In participating in the unsuccessful struggle to secure Oregon up to 54° 40' the Southern expansionists of 1846 represented American "Manifest Destiny" at its best. Their Southern colleagues who had been enthusiastic for Texas revealed a strong sectional bias in dragging their feet so noticeably when the Oregon question arose. Some of them doubtless agreed with Robert Toombs who said that he did not care a "fig about *any* of Oregon. . . . I don't want a foot of Oregon or an acre of any other country, especially without 'niggers.' These are some of my reasons for my course which don't appear in print."[44] Many of the pro-Oregon Northerners indicated clearly that they regarded the Oregon question as a sectional matter when they castigated Southerners who did not support it and by declaring gleefully that it would be a new area of freedom. Only the Southern expansionists seemed to transcend sectional lines by contending for a territory whose acquisition they deemed to be in the national interest.

Too, the Southern expansionists described more accurately and honestly than did the Southern peacemakers the views of their constituents when they insisted that the Southern people did not deprecate war. And they were closer to the truth than their Northern critics when they declared that the Southern people would fight to extend the nation's possessions in any direction. They did not have the opportunity to prove the point in regard to Oregon, but they did when the Mexican crisis arose. Some Southern peacemakers like Calhoun and Berrien had no enthusiasm for the Mexican War, and some expansionists like Cobb thought that the United States should have been fighting England instead of Mexico.[45] But the Southern expansionists had done their job well. They filled the common people of the South with a desire to defend the national honor, and when Zachary Taylor's troops were fired on near Matamoros in early May 1846, Southerners felt the national honor had been impugned. They would do in Mexico what they did not have the chance to do in Oregon.

Notes

1. Albert K. Weinberg, *Manifest Destiny: a Study of Nationalist Expansionism in American History* (Baltimore, 1935), 100 ff.

2. This point was frequently made in the debates on the Oregon question in 1846. See *Congressional Globe*, 29 Cong., 1 Sess., Appendix, 72 ff.

3. John D. P. Fuller, *The Movement for the Acquisition of All Mexico, 1846-1848* (Baltimore, 1936), 15 ff.

4. Chauncey S. Boucher and Robert P. Brooks (eds.), *Correspondence Addressed to John C. Calhoun*, American Historical Association, *Annual Report, 1929* (Washington, 1930), 217.

5. *Congressional Globe*, 28 Cong., 2 Sess., 88, 321, 324.

6. Stephen Smith to John C. Calhoun, December 30, 1845, in J. Franklin Jameson (ed.), *Correspondence of John C. Calhoun*, American Historical Association, *Annual Report, 1899* (2 vols., Washington, 1900), II, 1068-69. 7. Richmond

7. Richmond *Enquirer*, January 26, 1846. In the same issue, see also the prediction of the Mobile *Register* that California would soon be a part of the United States.

8. *Congressional Globe*, 29 Cong., 1 Sess., 92. See also Fuller, *The Movement for the Acquisition of All Mexico*, 28 ff.

9. Jameson (ed), *Correspondence of John C. Calhoun*, 1883-84.

10. For the expansionist views of Adams and Johnson, see *Congressional Globe*, 29 Cong., 1 Sess., 143, 288, 324.

11. *Ibid.*, Appendix, 184.

12. See Jameson (ed.), *Correspondence of John C. Calhoun*, 691; *Congressional Globe*, 29 Cong., 1 Sess., 504 ff, 795; and Ulrich B. Phillips (ed.), *The Correspondence of Robert Toombs, Alexander H. Stephens, and Howell Cobb*, American Historical Association, *Annual Report, 1911* (2 vols., Washington, 1913), 11, 71-72.

13. A valuable corrective regarding the lack of emphasis on the drive for Oregon up to $54^\circ 40'$ in the campaign of 1844 has been made by Edwin A. Miles in " 'Fifty-four Forty or Fight'–An American Political Legend," *Mississippi Valley Historical Review*, XLIV (September 1957), 291-309, and by Hans Sperber, " 'Fifty-four Forty or Fight': Facts and Fictions," *American Speech*, XXXII (February 1957), 5-11.

14. *Congressional Globe*, 29 Cong., 1 Sess., 319.

15. Fuller, *The Movement for the Acquisition of All Mexico*, 58, and Weinberg, *Manifest Destiny*, 117 ff.

16. See Arthur Cole, *The Whig Party in the South* (Washington, 1913). For an illuminating and significant discussion of the interests and sources of strength of the Whig party in the South, see Charles Grier Sellers, Jr., "Who Were the Southern Whigs?" in *American Historical Review*, LIX (January 1954), 335-46.

17. [Richard K. Crallé (ed.)], *The Works of John C. Calhoun* (6 vols., New York, 1851-1856), IV, 258 ff. See also Charles M. Wiltse, *John C. Calhoun* (3 vols., Indianapolis, 1 4-1951), 111, 260 ff.

18. *Congressional Globe*, 29 Cong., 1 Sess., 570 ff.

19. *Ibid.*, 514, 540, 604.

20. Memphis *Enquirer*, February 24, 1846.

21. Nashville *Republican Banner*, January 16, April 22, 1846.

22. Charleston *Mercury*, April 9, 1846.

23. Thomas P. Martin, "Free Trade and the Oregon Question, 1842-1846" in *Facts and Factors in Economic History* (Cambridge, 1932), 470-91.

24. Reported in Richmond *Enquirer*, February 7, 1846. For Chalmers' views, see *Congressional Globe*, 29 Cong., 1 Sess., 540.

25. George D. Phillips to Howell Cobb, December 30, 1845, in Phillips (ed.), *The Correspondence of Robert Toombs*, 70. For examples of enthusiastic Southern endorsement of Senator Allen's resolution to give notice, see letters to him from Lloyd Selby, Warrenton, Mississippi, February 6, 1846; William Mims, Americus, Georgia, May 9, 1846; and Old Dominion, New Orleans, Louisiana, May 19, 1846, in William Allen Papers (Manuscripts Division, Library of Congress).

26. Howell Cobb to Mrs. Howell Cobb, June 14, 1846, in Phillips (ed.), *The Correspondence of Robert Toombs*, 81-82.

27. *Congressional Globe*, 29 Cong., 1 Sess., Appendix, 118.

28. *Ibid.*, 29 Cong., 1 Sess., 307. Chase said, too, that "surrender, on the part of any nation, was the signal for its downfall, and an invitation to all the nations of the earth to commence their aggressions upon her." For another discussion of Southern expansionists in the Twenty-ninth Congress, see Norman A. Graebner, *Empire on the Pacific*, (New York, 1955), 125 ff.

29. *Congressional Globe*, 29 Cong., 1 Sess., 288.

30. *Ibid.*, 315, 317, 548, 294-96.

31. *Ibid.*, Appendix, 89. In the end, however, Hunter did not stand with the ardent expansionists.

32. *Ibid.*, 29 Cong., 1 Sess., 150. See also Henry W. Hilliard, *Politics and Pen Pictures at Home and Abroad* (New York, 1892), 136 ff.

33. *Congressional Globe*, 29 Cong., 1 Sess., 308; *ibid.*, Appendix, 120, 243, 247.

34. *Ibid.*, 29 Cong., 1 Sess., 296-97.

35. *Ibid.*, Appendix, 120; *ibid.*, 29 Cong., 1 Sess., 165- 167.

36. *Ibid.*, Appendix, 107, 109.

37. *Ibid.*, 29 Cong., 1 Sess., 289. The Nashville *Republican Banner*, February 13, 1846, called the Johnson speech "intemperate, unkind, and inconsiderate." At the end of a long critique the editor said that the Johnson "rantings" were like those of Giddings and other abolitionists.

38. See Henry Hilliard's speech in which he emphasized this point. *Congressional Globe*, 29 Cong., 1 Sess., 148.

39. *Ibid.*, 308; *ibid.*, Appendix, 267; *ibid.*, 29 Cong., 1 Sess., 548-49.

40. *Ibid.*, 672-73. See also Marquis James, *The Raven, a Biography of Sam Houston* (New York, 1929), 361.

41. Justin Smith, *The War with Mexico* (2 vols., New York, 1919), 1, 82 ff.

42. See Wiltse, *John C. Calhoun*, III, 252, 278, for an account of the pressures Calhoun put on Polk to proceed cautiously in the Oregon negotiations.

43. Frederick Merk, "The Oregon Pioneers and the Boundary," *American Historical Review*, XXIX (July 1924), 681-99.

44. Robert Toombs to George W. Crawford, February 6, 1846, in Phillips (ed.), *The Correspondence of Robert Toombs*, 74.

45. Calhoun and Berrien abstained from voting on the war resolution when it was passed by the Senate. *Congressional Globe*, 29 Cong., 1 Sess., 804. See also Jameson (ed.), *Correspondence of John C. Calhoun*, 689-91. For Howell Cobb's attitude, see the letter to his wife, May 10, 1846, in Phillips (ed.), *The Correspondence of Robert Toombs*, 76.

Part V
Sectionalism and the West

The Mississippi valley and the Constitution, 1815-29

Curtis Nettels

Three great interrelated themes—the rise of sectionalism, the triumph of the loose constructionists over the strict constructionists in the interpretation of the federal constitution, and the creation of large-scale internal improvements—dominated the first five decades of nineteenth century American history. In all of these the westward movement played a vital part. Historians have long minimized the role of the federal government in supporting highway, railway, and waterway improvements prior to 1850. They have emphasized such landmarks as Madison's veto of the 1817 Bonus Bill (which New York State counted on to aid construction of its Erie Canal), Monroe's veto of laws providing for the maintenance of the National Road, and Jackson's veto in 1832 of federal funds for Kentucky's Maysville Road. All of these, it is true, restricted the national government's participation in works of internal improvement. In consequence many of the best studies of road, canal, and railway building during this period, such as those by Louis Hartz, Milton Heath, Nathan Miller, and Harry Scheiber, have focused on state rather than federal initiative in transportation development.

At the same time political historians, taking their cue from the constitutional storm set off by the admission of Missouri and Maine as states in 1820, have emphasized the growth of divisions between the North and South. Often lost in the shadows created by the rush toward Civil War was the rise of the West as a coherent sectional force. For a brief two or three decades after 1810 the Old Southwest (Alabama, Mississippi, Louisiana, Arkansas, and Missouri, together with the border states of Kentucky and Tennessee) had more in common with the Old Northwest (Ohio, Indiana, Michigan, Illinois, and Wisconsin) than it had with the older seaboard states. This formed the basis for a western political alliance that cut across the slavery issue.

In the following essay, Curtis Nettels, Professor Emeritus of History at Cornell University, analyzes how the West worked together as a section to undermine strict construction of the Constitution. His work also provides a needed corrective that underlines the significant role played by the federal government in road and canal construction prior to 1830.

Reprinted with permission from the *Mississippi Valley Historical Review*, XI (December 1924), 332-357.

For further reading: Frederick Jackson Turner, *The Rise of the New West* (New York: Harper & Brothers, 1906)*; George Rogers Taylor, *The Transportation Revolution, 1815-1860* (New York: Holt, Rinehart, and Winston, 1951)*; Louis Hartz, *Economic Policy and Democratic Thought: Pennsylvania 1776-1860* (Cambridge, Mass.: Harvard University Press, 1948); Milton Sydney Heath, *Constructive Liberalism: The Role of the State in Economic Development in Georgia to 1860* (Cambridge, Mass.: Harvard University Press, 1954); Nathan Miller, *Enterprise of a Free People: Aspects of Economic Development in New York State during the Canal Period* (Ithaca, N.Y.: Cornell University Press, 1962); Carter Goodrich, *Government Promotion of American Canals and Railroads 1800-1890* (New York: Columbia University Press, 1960); Harry N. Schieber, *Ohio Canal Era: A Case Study of Government and the Economy 1920-1861* (Athens: Ohio University Press, 1969); Robert A. Lively, "The American System: A Review Article," *Business History Review*, XXIX (March 1955), 81-96; Homer C. Hockett, *Western Influences on Political Parties to 1825* (Columbus: Ohio State University Press, 1917); R. B. Way, "The Mississippi Valley and Internal Improvements," Mississippi Valley Historical Association *Proceedings*, IV (1910-1911), 153-180; Charles S. Sydnor, *The Development of Southern Sectionalism, 1819-1848*, History of the South, Vol. 5 (Baton Rouge: Louisiana State University Press, 1948).

*Available in paperback.

A highly important fact in the history of the federal Union during the first half century of its existence was the admission between 1816 and 1821 of five new states situated in the Mississippi Valley. These five states, Indiana, Mississippi, Illinois, Alabama, and Missouri, were as many as had been admitted during the preceding twenty-seven years. Together with the other new states of Ohio, Kentucky, Tennessee, and Louisiana, they formed a compact body of territory, united by similar interests, and separated from the old states by the Allegheny Mountains. Their importance in the Union is illustrated partially by the following table showing the growth of their delegation in Congress.

		Senate	
		Members	*Relative strength*
	Total	*from West*	*of West*
Fourteenth Congress	38	10	.26
Eighteenth Congress	48	18	.37
	House of Representatives		
Fourteenth Congress	192	24	.12
Eighteenth Congress	213	47	.22

During the period when the new states were being created and were growing rapidly in population, the chief constitutional question before Congress was that involving the right of the federal government to construct roads and canals. The agitation for internal improvements inaugurated by Gallatin's report in 1807 was quieted by the War of 1812, only to break out with greater vigor after the cessation of hostilities. The chief obstacles in the way of those who urged that the general government build roads and canals were the Constitution and the views of it held by many representatives of the old states. When the Fourteenth Congress convened in December, 1815, it contained a group of members sharing the strict constructionist view of the Constitution which denied to the federal government the right of constructing roads and canals within the limits of a state. They reached this position by applying the familiar doctrines of a restricted government possessing a few positive powers which had been surrendered by the states and were enumerated in the Constitution. The Fourteenth Congress contained also an active party under the leadership of Clay which insisted that the time was ripe for federal legislation in behalf of internal improvements. The fifteen years following the opening of this Congress witnessed a bitter, and at times violent, controversy over the points involved in this question. In this controversy, the yearly-increasing delegation from the Mississippi Valley acted with all but unanimity and exerted an influence that finally determined the result.

The important conditions within the newly-settled areas which shaped the views of both voters and representatives in Congress on the subject of internal improvements were in clear contrast with conditions existing in many of the old states. The emigrants who swarmed into the Mississippi Valley after 1815 needed all at once a communication system such as the eastern settlements had acquired as the result of a century—or perhaps two centuries—of slow development. Hence the actual need for roads and canals in the Mississippi Valley was far more acute than in the East, not alone because of the newness of settlements, but also because distances were greater. Moreover, the state governments beyond the Alleghenies were weak and helpless in comparison with those on the seaboard. The new states were seriously restricted in taxing power, because the emigrants had but little personal property, and because their lands were for the most part controlled by Congress or subject to the taxation prohibition contained in the five percent agreements made between the new states and the federal government. The people who entered the western forests after 1815 no longer lived in regions where state traditions, power, and sovereignty were political facts of great vitality. Every adult newcomer was older than the infant state in which he resided. The general government was older than any of the new states, and more capable than they of conferring benefits upon the needy settlers. Thus, the states of the Mississippi Valley, during the early years of their history, were characterized by conditions which caused their residents to seek more eagerly for federal aid in supplying transportation facilities than did the people of the more compactly settled portions of the Union.

I

In addition to the consideration just mentioned, there were six constitutional sanctions for federal construction of roads and canals in the Mississippi Valley that did not apply to the old states. The representatives from the West, as a whole, considered that the provision in the Constitution which empowered Congress to make needful rules and regulations respecting the territories authorized the building of roads and canals within those areas. On January 23, 1824, the western senators voted 14-0 for a bill appropriating $15,000 for a road from Memphis to Little Rock.[1] The following year, January 26, 1825, they voted 16-2 on the third reading of a bill appropriating $10,000 for a road from the Missouri border to New Mexico.[2] Although the principle underlying appropriations for territorial roads was accepted by Monroe, it was opposed by the most severe of the strict constructionists—men like John Randolph of Virginia and Senator Chandler of Maine. However, only three territorial road bills in the Senate, and none in the House, during the period 1815-29—in which time were authorized eighteen separate appropriations, totalling $219,000—met formal opposition at the hands of the strict constructionists.

The constitutional warrant for these appropriations could not, of course, apply directly to grants of funds solicited by the new states. However, there were four cases peculiar to the Mississippi Valley in regard to which it was continually reasserted by the friends of internal improvements that Congress was empowered to act within the territory of a state. The first was the right of constructing a road in obedience to treaties concluded with the Indian tribes. This right proceeded from two clauses in the Constitution—one authorizing the making of treaties and the other empowering Congress "to make all laws which shall be necessary and proper for carrying into execution . . . all powers vested . . . in the Government of the United States." The two important cases of exercise of this power during the period under consideration were those arising from the treaty of Brownstown, concluded in 1808, and from the treaty of the Mississinewa in 1824. By the first treaty, the negotiating tribe ceded a strip of land to the United States for the construction of a road from the foot of the rapids of the Miami of the Lake to the western line of the Connecticut Reserve. Inasmuch as the road thus authorized was not constructed for a number of years after the treaty ratification, the General Assembly of Ohio passed a resolution, January 22, 1820, calling for congressional action. A bill in the Sixteenth Congress providing for the construction of the road by the federal government failed to pass, but in 1823 another bill, modified so as to allow the state of Ohio to build the road, passed the Senate without a division and was easily carried in the House, by a vote of 130-21, the western members voting 21-1 in its favor. The act granted to Ohio the land ceded by the tribes in 1808.[3]

Although this act did not provoke a prolonged discussion of the right of Congress to appropriate lands or money for the construction of a road within a state, the right to aid in state enterprise even when authorized by Indian treaties was denied by the strict constructionists in 1827. The bill then under consideration provided for a grant to the General Assembly of Indiana of land ceded to the United States by the Potawatomi, October 16, 1824, on the condition that the United States build a road from Lake Michigan to the Ohio River through the ceded territory. The bill further authorized the state of Indiana to sell the lands thus relinquished and to apply the proceeds to the construction of the road. This proposal was opposed in the Senate by such strict constructionists as Branch, Chandler, Cobb, Macon, Randolph, and Smith of South Carolina. The Senate accepted it, however, by a vote of 30-12, the Mississippi Valley senators voting 16-0 on the motion to engross.[4] Although the vote of the western senators was not needed to carry the bill, the result indicated that they were far more friendly to the principle than were the representatives of the old states. The House acquiesced in the measure without debate or a division.

A second class of grants of land and money made by Congress for the construction of roads within the new states was that embracing appropriations for building or repairing roads traversing territory to which the Indian title had not been extinguished. Obviously, in these cases, the states were not competent to act, inasmuch as the regulation of Indian affairs, under the Constitution, was an exclusive federal power. During the period between 1815 and 1820, Congress made six separate appropriations, totalling $57,920, which were based upon the assumption that the federal government was obliged, under the Constitution, to construct roads within the Indian country.[5] Most of these appropriations passed Congress without serious opposition. Only once, in 1818, was the principle contested to the extent of occasioning a division. The House then voted 83-55 for a bill appropriating $10,000 for repairing roads leading from Georgia and Tennessee to Alabama Territory and Louisiana respectively.[6] The Westerners who opposed the bill were strict constructionists, John Rhea, William G. Blount, and Thomas Hogg—all of Tennessee—and Anthony New of Kentucky, three of whom were soon overcome by the rising tide of internal improvement sentiment in the West. The vote on the measure again revealed a firmer faith among the Mississippi Valley representatives in the constitutionality of the power involved than among the congressmen from the old states.

A far more important group of congressional grants which were peculiar to the new states was that arising from the federal control of unsold lands lying within the confines of Ohio, Illinois, Alabama, and Indiana. Each of these states had large canal projects which it considered essential to its development: these included, in Ohio, canals connecting the Ohio River and Lake Erie; in Indiana, a canal between the Wabash and Lake Erie; in Illinois, a canal from Lake Michigan to the Illinois River; and in Alabama, a canal around Muscle Shoals in the Tennessee River. The right-of-way of the proposed canals in the three northwestern states had to run through lands owned by the federal government. Hence the state governments, before beginning construction, were obliged either to purchase the right-of-way or to secure a land grant from Congress. The second alternative was the logical one for the Westerners to pursue, because their state exchequers were usually exhausted and because they believed that the construction of the canals would be a great boon to the federal treasury, in that the United States' lands adjoining the canals would be enhanced in value after the work had been completed. For constitutional justification of cession of the lands to the states, they turned to the clause in the Constitution which stipulated that Congress might dispose of the property of the United States.

The first action on this question came in 1822, when a bill granting to Illinois a right-of-way 180 feet wide for the canal connecting the Illinois River with Lake Michigan was accepted by both houses.[7] A similar grant was proffered to Indiana for its canal in 1824.[8] These modest donations seemed so just and indispensable that they obtained their majorities without much opposition. But when the new states extended their requests, and asked for large donations of lands to be sold by the state in order to procure the funds for projecting the canals, a different principle came into action, and the right of Congress to appropriate funds or their equivalents for state aid to internal improvement was immediately involved. The issue was decided in 1827, when two acts were passed, one for Illinois and one for Indiana, making large grants to the general assemblies of the two states. A serious debate occurred in the Senate on the Indiana bill, in which Senators Harrison, Hendricks, Kane, McKinley, and R. M. Johnson—all from the Mississippi Valley—defended the grant, and Smith of Maryland and Chandler and Holmes of Maine, using the strict constructionist argument, spoke in opposition.[9] But for the affirmative vote of the western representatives the bill would have failed to pass.[10]

An act of no little political importance which was passed on the heels of the Indiana and Illinois bills was a land grant to Ohio for the purpose of aiding that state to construct canals designed to connect the Ohio River with Lake Erie.[11] Ohio had been seeking congressional assistance since 1825, in which year the General Assembly had unanimously voted that the work be undertaken. In the first session of the Twentieth Congress the supporters of both Adams and Jackson were vying with each other in efforts to secure the favor of those Mississippi Valley states which were so plainly committed to internal improvements. On May 19, 1828, the Adams men carried in the House a bill authorizing a grant of five sections of land to every mile along the route of the canal between Dayton and the Maumee river.[12] The bill of the Jackson party provided for an unlocated grant of 500,000 acres to be sold by the state to cover debts contracted for constructing the canals. This bill was voted on after the Adams measure had passed the House, and was defeated on the third reading.[13] The Adams bill passed the Senate May 24, the western vote being necessary to the result.[14] Thereupon the Senate, where the representatives of the new states and the Jacksonian forces were stronger than in the House, added the Jackson bill as an amendment to the Adams measure. This arrangement was agreed to by a conference committee, accepted by the House, and the bill signed by President Adams May 24.[15] Its passage affords a clear example of the new states successfully exerting their pressure at a strategic point when a presidential election was impending.

The fourth constitutional justification advanced by the spokesmen of the Mississippi Valley for the construction of roads within the territory of a state related to the westward extension of the Cumberland Road. When Ohio was admitted in 1802, the new state entered into an agreement with the United States by which the former should receive five percent of the proceeds of the public lands sold within the state, in return for a promise not to tax lands owned by the United States, or lands which had been purchased by individuals from the federal government until five years after sale. Forty percent of the fund set aside for the use of Ohio was to be devoted to the purpose of building roads, under the direction of Congress, leading to the new state. In compliance with this agreement, President Jefferson signed an act in 1806 which authorized the construction of the Cumberland Road, from Cumberland, Maryland, to the Ohio River.

When Indiana, Illinois, and Missouri were admitted in the years between 1816 and 1821, each entered into an agreement similar to that between the United States and Ohio. One of the early acts of the General Assembly of Illinois in its first cession was the passage of resolutions requesting that the National Road be extended to the Mississippi River, and urging the legislatures of Indiana and Ohio to cooperate in the effort to obtain favorable action in Congress.[16] The people of the new states did not feel that the completion of the road to the Ohio River satisfied the clauses in *their* agreements with the federal government, which provided that two percent of the public land sales be devoted to the construction of roads leading to *their* borders. The movement for the extension of the road was supported with practical unanimity in Missouri, Ohio, Illinois, Indiana, Kentucky, and Louisiana.[17] Federal appropriations were defended, constitutionally, on the ground that Congress possessed the right to make necessary rules for admitting new states and to pass laws necessary to the execution of the delegated powers.

The first move in the campaign for the extension of the road produced an appropriation for surveying the route from the Ohio River to the Mississippi.[18] The two-percent fund of the new states was pledged to reimburse the Government for the sum thus granted. A series of appropriations for the actual construction of the road followed in the train of this initial grant. A prolonged debate preceded the passage of the first act (March 31, 1825) appropriating $150,000 for carrying the road to Zanesville, Ohio. This measure, like all the acts on the subject of extending the National Road, assumed the constitutionality of the agreements between Congress and the new states. In both the House[19] and the Senate[20] the affirmative vote of the Mississippi Valley was indispensable to the passage the act. The seven Westerners who did not vote on the final roll call in the House were habitual supporters of the internal improvements.

Each of the three following sessions yielded an appropriation for the extension of the road, that of 1826 for $110,000,[21] that of 1827 for $170,000,[22] and that of 1828 for $175,000.[23] Analysis of the votes on these appropriations reveals not only that the Mississippi Valley was united in favor of extending the road, but also that its force was necessary in order to overcome the opposition of the strict constructionists representing at least half of the old states.

The sixth case peculiar to the Mississippi Valley in regard to which the Westerners insisted that Congress might appropriate, with due regard for the Constitution and to the benefit of the new states, was concerned with the problem of improving the navigation of the Ohio and Mississippi rivers. The reasoning on this subject ran as follows:" . . . the Constitutional difficulty is not at all involved in the present investigation. Let it be remembered that the Ohio and Mississippi are the boundaries of neighboring states; and with the exception of Louisiana, that they do not pass through the territorial limits of the states; that they . . . are justly regarded, not as the property of particular states, but as common stock—as national property."[24] The problem was peculiar to the new settlements in that there was no other river in the United States comparable with the Ohio-Mississippi, in respect either to its length or to its importance to a dozen states and two territories. It was entirely natural, therefore, that the first federal act appropriating funds for river improvement should apply to this mighty river system, so essential to the prosperity of all the western states.

The first important bill on this subject—an appropriation of $75,000 devoted principally to experiments in improving the navigation of the Ohio—was introduced in the first session of the Eighteenth Congress. It passed the House without encountering opposition on the score of constitutionality, the new states being almost solidly aligned in its support.[25] In the Senate, however, progress was less easy. The constitutionality of the bill was denied by Chandler and Holmes of Maine, Taylor of Virginia, and Macon of North Carolina.[26] The support of the Mississippi Valley states was essential to the success of the bill on the third reading, when it encountered a full array of twenty opponents, in a heavily attended session, and came through with but a slight majority.[27] The fourth section of the act (signed May 24, 1824) instructed the President to report on its execution in order that Congress might "be enabled to adopt such further measures as may from time to time be necessary . . . "—an indication that subsequent action was anticipated.[28]

The next step was taken in 1827 when the sum of $30,000 was appropriated to continue the work started by the act of 1824. The bill met the usual resistance from the strict constructionists, but passed both houses without serious difficulty.[29] An item in the rivers and harbors bill of 1828 granted an additional $50,000—the largest item in the list of appropriations and a recognition of the fact that the Ohio-Mississippi traffic route was the parent of the river improvement policy.[30]

From the preceding paragraphs it is clear that there were six classes of appropriations which Congress might, by one constitutional sanction or another, make for the benefit of the Mississippi Valley which did not apply to the old states of the Union. In all, between 1815 and 1829, forty appropriations gained their constitutional authority from conditions peculiar to the West. The result, expressed in tabular form is as follows:

Purpose of the grant	Number of appropriations	Total amount appropriated
1. For territorial roads	18	$219,465
2. For roads within states authorized by Indian treaties	2	land
3. For roads within states over land to which Indian title had not been extinguished	6	$57,920
4. For roads and canals traversing the public lands	6	land
5. For improving the navigation of the Ohio and Mississippi rivers	3	$155,000
6. For the National Road, authorized by the two percent contracts	5	$616,000
		$1,048,385
		Approximately 4,000,000 acres of public lands

Considered as a whole, these items constituted a formidable mass of precedents in favor of the right of the federal government to assist the new states in solving their transportation problems. By 1828 there were but few projects for which grants of land or money might not be solicited on the strength of one of the precedents established after 1815. Moreover, each of these forty grants made for the benefit of the new states had implications that extended to the larger problem of the right of Congress to undertake a comprehensive system of roads and canals within the states.

Practically, there was little difference between federal construction of a road in a territory and in the border region of a new state. The physical conditions of the two areas were identical. If a road might be built by congressional order from the Louisiana border to the Missouri border, it seemed to the western mind illogical to stop it in the wilderness when it might be continued to the nearest towns within the limits of the states. For this reason, when territorial road bills were before Congress, frequent attempts were made to locate the termini of the roads within state boundaries. An example of this occurred in 1827, when a bill was introduced for constructing a road from Fort Smith to Natchitoches. Naturally the project was opposed by strict constructionists. The vote of the western senators indicates that four out of five of them did not discriminate between the territorial status of the land on the northern side of the lower border of Arkansas Territory and that of the land adjacent in Louisiana.[31]

Furthermore, it was a rather anomalous condition which allowed Congress to build a road in a region one year when included within a territory, and which denied the same right a year later, when the same region had become part of a state. " . . . It is said we have now an absolute right to apply the funds for making a road through Alabama Territory; can it then be contended that, when it becomes a state, this right to apply our funds will cease. . . ?"[32] Thus argued Representative Tucker of Virginia in 1818. John Randolph expressed the logic of the situation effectively when he said that he could not "very well see the difference . . . of pouring out the money of the Treasury upon these projects, whether within the body of a state, or within the body of a Territory. He thanked God he was not so much of a political metaphysician as to think such nice distinctions of an importance." Continuing in the same vein, he declared that "he did not see the difference between Congress putting their hand into his pocket, for the purpose of cutting a canal in the state of Alabama, which was a territory yesterday; or in the territory of Florida, which will be a state tomorrow."[33]

The exercise of the right on the part of the federal government of constructing roads upon lands within states to which the Indian title was not extinquished involved the same sort of anomaly inherent in the right respecting the territories. It seemed illogical to Westerners that Congress might not construct a road through one unsettled part of a state when it might do so through another. The need of roads between frontier towns was too great to promote respect for technicality that prevented the federal government from constructing an important road merely because it crossed an imaginary line supposed to designate the lands not yet ceded to the United States by the local Indian tribes.

The argument for an extension of the principle upon which the land grants to the new states rested was implied in a speech by Senator Smith of Maryland. "What difference was there," he asked, "between giving lands and giving money from the Treasury? Congress, it was true, would not venture now to take money from the Treasury to give to the state of Indiana for the construction of a canal. He was against this donation . . . because . . . this plan of giving to the States was fast gaining ground; and thus a measure which he thought unconstitutional was wearing itself into constitutionality by frequent repitition."[34]

Although the appropriations for the Cumberland Road were based upon the five-percent clauses, the money was actually taken from the funds of the United States. The two-percent fund was exhausted about eight times by the grants that had been made to extend the road as far as the Ohio River. When the appropriation of 1826 was before the House, Representative Beecher of Ohio moved that the money be taken outright from the treasury, without pledging the two-percent fund for an eventual reimbursement of the Government.[35] Representative James Buchanan insisted that it was preposterous and deceitful to assume that the bill in reality was based upon the agreements with the new states.[36] There was, indeed, a tinge of the ludicrous in appropriating $606,000 (the total of the four appropriations made between 1825 and 1828) for a road from the Ohio River to Zanesville, on the theory that Congress was constructing a road leading to the borders of Illinois, Indiana, and Missouri—especially as the fund for carrying the road even as far as the eastern border of Indiana was already many times exhausted. The practical operation of the first five acts for the extension of the road served to draw upon the common funds of the Government for improving the transportation facilities of a single state. The claim that Congress was merely performing its contract with the new states was pretty much of a sham.

The funds which have been granted for river improvement since 1824 are sufficient evidence of the importance of the early western demand for improving the navigation of the Ohio and the Mississippi.

II

The influence of the Mississippi Valley on the construction of the Constitution was not confined to the enactment of laws applicable solely to the territories or to the new states. The larger aspect of the problem centered in the contention that Congress was authorized to construct a comprehensive system of roads and canals covering the entire country. The liberal constructionists deduced the authority for federal action from clauses in the Constitution which vested Congress with the right to provide for the general welfare and from the specific powers for regulating commerce among the states, establishing post roads, and declaring war. The strict constructionists denied that such authority was necessary or proper to the execution of any of the enumerated powers.

The Fouteenth,[37] Fifteenth,[38] and Sixteenth Congresses, 1815-21, were hampered in dealing with the subject of internal improvements by the constitutional scruples of Presidents Madison and Monroe, expressed by the former in his veto of Calhoun's famous bonus bill in 1817, and by the latter in his annual message to Congress in December of the same year. Consequently, no bill of general scope became law during these sessions. The change in Monroe's position, which brought him to accept the principle that Congress might appropriate money for the construction of roads and canals within states, was of such importance to later developments that a review of the steps involved in his reversal of opinion is necessary at this point.

The bill which wrung from Monroe this concession to loose construction was the one providing that toll houses, etc., be erected on the Cumberland Road for the collection of tolls to be used for the upkeep of the road. Its constitutional implications were, as stated by Monroe in his veto message:[39]

A power to establish turnpikes, with gates and tolls, and to enforce the collection of tolls by penalties, implies a power to adopt a complete system of internal improvements. A right to impose duties to be paid by all persons passing a certain road . . . involves the right to take the land from the proprietor on a valuation and to pass laws for the protection of the road from injuries, and if it exists as to one road, it exists as to . . . as many roads as Congress may think proper to establish. A right to legislate for one of these purposes is a right to legislate for the others. It is a complete right of jurisdiction and sovereignty for all the purposes of internal improvement.

The bill was suppressed during the Sixteenth Congress, but a well-formed plan to procure its passage marked the opening of the Seventeenth Congress in December, 1821. In the House, the strength of the Mississippi Valley at the time of the final vote was sufficient to break the deadlock resulting from the conflicting opinions of representatives of the old states.[40] Votes on other propositions indicated that the Mississippi Valley was united in favor of the right of the United States to retain title to,[41] and to appropriate money for, the repair[42] of the road. In every case, proportionately, the West was far more emphatic in support of the federal power than were the eastern states. The senate accepted the bill,[43] but in spite of large initial majorities neither house could muster the two-thirds vote requisite for passing it over the President's veto.

On the same day that Monroe sent his veto message to Congress he forwarded also an elaborate statement of the whole constitutional problem that had been raised. In this exposition he argued that Congress was empowered to appropriate money without limit for the constructing of roads and canals within states, although, according to his new view, it could not direct the work. The strict constructionists witnessed this surrender with dismay. Representative Alexander of Virginia voiced their fears, saying that "if any greater latitude were to be claimed or desired by the friends of power" he was "at loss to conceive where it could be more completely and satisfactorily sought for" than in Monroe's new position.[44]

Twenty years after this incident, when Benton spoke of Monroe's yielding to the "temper of the times" he no doubt had in mind, in part at least, the pressure from the Mississippi Valley which was being exerted on the Government in behalf of internal improvements. It has been noted that the vote of the western delegation in the House was necessary to the passage of the act. An analysis of the western vote reveals that Clay's supporters were united in upholding at all points the principle of federal power. With these facts in view, the testimony which Van Buren offers[45] in respect to the history of this bill merits serious consideration.

I have always thought that political rivalry was not without its influence in producing a result so remarkable and so much to be deprecated. . . . To compel Mr. Monroe, with the sanction of his Cabinet, not less than three of whose members were contestants . . . for the Presidency, to apply the general principle to which he had volunteered an avowal at the preceding session, of his continued adherence to the pet public work of the West, or, by omitting to do so, to admit its unsoundness, was a temptation too strong for a man like Mr. Clay to resist. . . . I am confident that Mr. Monroe and the principle members of the cabinet so understood the movement. In resisting it, Messrs. Adams, Crawford, and Calhoun acted as a unit, for although in regard to their political aspirations each engineered for himself, they were equally opposed to Mr. Clay's pretensions. . . . The movement was met . . . by an act of a strong stamp, the extent and bearing of which Mr. Clay can hardly have foreseen. The veto was promptly interposed, and so far the Administration was successful, but by the accompanying Presidential manifesto, Mr. Monroe, changing the opinions of his whole previous life, exposed the national treasury to appropriations to any extent for the construction of roads and canals and internal improvements of every description.

The increase in the population in the Mississippi Valley following the war was first officially recorded in the census of 1820. The first Congress to convene after the reapportionment of seats occasioned by the census was the Eighteenth, in December, 1823. The western delegation in the House was enlarged by additions as follows:

	Seventeenth Congress	*Eighteenth Congress*	
Ohio	6	14	
Kentucky	10	12	Increase of 1823
Tennessee	6	9	over 1821
Indiana	1	3	68%
Louisiana	1	3	
Mississippi	1	1	
Alabama	1	3	Total percent of House
Illinois	1	1	membership in 1823, 22
Missouri	1	1	
	28	47	

In 1823, therefore, the Mississippi Valley, for the first time, marshalled its full strength on the floor of Congress.

"From the Eighteenth Congress," declared Representative Holcombe of New Jersey, January 13, 1824,[46] "much is expected in relation to internal improvement. It represents a new era in our politics. It represents millions of freemen, who, for the first time have exercised their rights and realized their political existence upon this floor; and who, from peculiarity of their situation (being principally the inhabitants of frontier states) must necessarily feel the deepest interest in the consummation of a system, one of the first objects of which is to obviate the inconveniences of location and draw the extremities of the Union together within the immediate neighborhood of our great outlets and markets."

The measure which leaders of the internal improvement forces agreed on for this session was a bill authorizing surveys of national roads and canals and appropriating money therefor. A long debate ensued in the House which turned almost solely upon the constitutionality of the appropriation. Clay led off with a long speech in which he denied the validity of Monroe's new position, and defended the bill on the principle of broad construction of the powers of Congress to establish post roads, to regulate commerce among states, and to wage war. The measure drafted was certainly in consonance with Clay's views, for it authorized the survey of routes for postal, military, and commercial roads and canals. A group of strict constructionists, including Wood of New York, Foot of Connecticut, Mallory of Vermont, Randolph, Archer, Stevenson, P. P. Barbour, Tucker, Rives, and Smythe of Virginia, attacked the principle of the bill, maintaining that it meant a subversion of the Constitution and an immeasurable advance toward federal consolidation. "The power which many gentlemen have claimed," warned Representative Foot,[47] "and which some have declared 'they will not surrender' transcends the power claimed by a majority of the Congress during the dark days of '98-'99; and involves the right of the extension of the power of Congress, even to the omnipotence of a British Parliament."

Five members from the Mississippi Valley spoke in behalf of the bill. Clay proclaimed that a new world had "come into being since the Constitution was adopted" and asked if the "limited necessities" of parts of the old states "were forever to remain the rule of its interpretation."[48] Buckner of Kentucky denied that the passage of the bill would mean a usurpation of power.[49] Edward Livingston of Louisiana, in an elaborate argument,[50] urged a common-sense view of the Constitution, and discredited arguments drawn from the *Federalist* and the convention debates. "The instrument," he said, "was made by the people, and for their use; the popular, not the learned signification of the term 'regulate commerce' must therefore be sought." Gazlay of Ohio warned[51] against the dangers of strict construction and the effect which its application would have in cramping the activities of the federal government. Reynolds of Tennessee complained[52] that the "refinements" of the opposition were beyond his comprehension, particularly, he said, "when I look at the . . . end we ought to have in view." On the third reading in the House the vote stood:[53] Total vote, 114-82; vote of Mississippi Valley, 43-1; vote of East, 71-81.

In the Senate, as in the House, the weight of the Mississippi Valley was necessary to overcoming the opposition of the old states to the break with the past which the surveys entailed.[54] Whenever the Westerners in either house spoke in debate on the issue, they pled for an expanded construction of the Constitution. Among the sixty-five senators and representatives from the new states, only three, Cocke of Tennessee in the House, and Edwards of Illinois and King of Alabama in the Senate voted on the deciding divisions with the strict constructionists.

The success of the Survey Bill led to repeated efforts in subsequent sessions for continuing the appropriation. A grant of $28,567 was included in the military-appropriation bill of 1825. In the Senate, on a motion to strike out this item, Senators Cobb, Chandler, Macon, and Holmes spoke against the grant, the latter grounding his opposition on the assumption that "the money that was gathered in the East, would be expended in the West, and the southern states would get nothing."[55] The clause was defended by R. M. Johnson, Benton, J. S. Johnston and Talbot. But for the strength of the new states, the motion for striking out the appropriation would have been carried.[56] The House accepted the item without a division.

Each of the two appropriations of the first and second sessions of the Nineteenth Congress, for $50,000[57] and $30,000[58] respectively, required the influence of the Mississippi Valley for its acceptance. The final appropriation of the period under consideration was that included in the general internal improvement bill of 1828. The votes on the grant of $30,000 were similar to those which have been recorded above.[59] The appropriations authorized between 1824 and 1828, six items in all, amounted to $168,000. Whenever a division was required, the result revealed that the Mississippi Valley was united in support of the policy on trial and that its vote was indispensable to obtaining the particular grant in question.

The first bill applying to the improvement of river navigation has been considered. The three laws on the general subject of rivers and harbors which were enacted in 1826, in 1827, and in 1828, did not occasion divisions, and so the part played by the new states in securing their adoption cannot be determined from the *Debates*. The share of the grants to be expended on rivers in the Mississippi Valley, however, was considerable.[60] The influence of the new states in this connection is indicated indirectly by the fact that nearly two-fifths of the appropriations was directed to improvements for their benefit.

The principle of loose construction as applied to transportation problems obtained by the general internal improvement act of 1828 as full a recognition in Congress as it was ever destined to receive. This measure lumped together under one head thirteen different appropriations—one for the extension of the Cumberland Road, eight for improving rivers, creeks, and harbors in various parts of the country, two for territorial roads, and one for survey of roads and canals within states. All of these grants were based on principles which had been established before 1829. The significance of the law consisted in the fact that it was the first attempt at a comprehensive grouping of internal improvements projects for the purpose of future systematic action on the part of the federal government. Its importance to the Mississippi Valley is indicated by the fact that of the $295,000 appropriated, $217,000 were to be used for objects beneficial to western interests and conducive to the development of the new states.[61]

It appears from the foregoing review of internal improvement legislation that the influence of the Mississippi Valley was exerted as readily to secure the application of the principles of loose construction for the passage of general measu es as to enact laws peculiarly favorable to the West which did not necessitate extensive departures from strict construction. During the fourteen years after the close of the war, Congress almost completely reversed its constitutional position on the transportation issue. The period witnessed a series of appropriations which may be summarized in tabular form as follows:

	Grants authorized on principles peculiar to West	*Grants authorized on general principles*	*Total*
Number of acts and appropriations	40	77	117
Money appropriated	$1,048,384	$1,018,972	$2,067,357
Land granted	Approximately 4,000,000 acres	none	4,000,000 acres
Authorization for purchase of stock in private companies	none	$250,000 11,500 shares at price to be determined later	$250,000 11,500 shares

In 1828, sixty-nine surveys of roads and canals had officially been undertaken by the Government. In addition to these, Senator Smith of South Carolina reported that "he had collected from the documents recently laid on the tables of members, thirty-eight other reports for private turnpike companies, for canals, for harbors, for break-waters, for piers, for seawalls, for artificial harbors, for removing obstructions from creeks, for charitable institutions, for colleges, for schools, and for the public bounty to as many private citizens of the West as chose to ask for it."[62]

Lack of space precludes listing the names of representatives and senators as they voted on the various bills, but if such detailed information could be included it would show that among the seventy-four Westerners who sat in the House between 1823 and 1829, only one, James K. Polk of Tennessee, and among the twenty-nine senators, only one, Hugh White, also of Tennessee, held to strict construction throughout the entire period. But by 1829 a division was discernible in the ranks of the Westerners. The supporters of Adams and the Jackson men both declared for internal improvements, but the latter, and especially those from Tennessee, Alabama, Kentucky, and Missouri, were beginning to insist that federal appropriations be devoted to projects of national consequence. This position, of course, could be defended only by loose construction of the Constitution.

The apparent triumph of the nationalistic forces provoked in the South a spirited resistance, and especially in Georgia, Virginia, and South Carolina. The General Assembly of the state last named, in its famous resolutions of December, 1827, argued thus the case against internal improvements:[63] "If the United States government can construct one road or canal within the body of a State, it may construct a thousand; and thus draw within the vortex of its influence what properly belongs to the States. If Congress can expend one thousand dollars to purposes not enumerated in the Constitution, it may expend an hundred millions; and in this way, so increase its patronage . . . as to leave little or nothing for the subordinate authorities to do."

The resolutions were sent by the General Assembly to the other states for replies. Not all of these are accessible to the writer of this paper, but the attitude of the Mississippi Valley states may be gleaned from several sources. The representatives of Louisiana, Illinois, and Missouri in Congress were consistent, unbending supporters of internal improvements. After Jackson had voted for the Survey Bill in 1824, Tennessee regularly sent a delegation to Congress which voted almost as a unit for projects of national importance. The representatives of Mississippi never denied the principle that Congress might appropriate money for the construction of a road or canal, and did not deny it in 1828. The Kentucky Senate replied to South Carolina "without hesitation or doubt" that Congress did possess the power, if exercised with the consent of the states involved.[64] The General Assembly of Ohio expressed "its most solemn dissent" from the views of South Carolina.[65] On January 15, 1828 the Alabama legislature petitioned Congress for a land grant and expressed itself on the subject thus: "Feeling a laudable wish to participate in the great efforts of internal improvement, that so eminently distinguish the present age, your memorialists, finding the means of the State inadequate to the objects, look with confidence to the General government for assistance, in some shape. . . ."[66] The General Assembly of Indiana on January 24, 1828 instructed its senators "to give their united aid and cooperation with those of our sister states who encourage a national system . . . of internal improvements."[67]

"In less than thirty years from its adoption," lamented Senator Smith of South Carolina in April, 1828, "the Constitution has been thrown aside as rubbish, as not understood, or if understood at all, not by any two politicians in the same way. Gentlemen are weary of the Constitution. . . . Economy is now parsimony, and a regard for the Constitution is a want of patriotism."[68] To criticism such as this Senator Hendricks had replied in 1826,[69] "The solicitude of the western States on the subject of internal improvement is often spoken of on this floor as a matter of deep regret. This solicitude must, nevertheless, continue. It cannot be otherwise. . . . Do you say that on the subject of roads and canals we are undermining the Constitution? We reply—give us the soil of our country, and we will be as other states."

This request from Senator Hendricks repeated in different form an appeal made by Clay in the House as early as 1818.[70] " . . . Am I, who come from the interior . . . to be told that the Constitution was made for the Atlantic margin of the country only; that, in regard to the great power of regulating internal commerce, Indiana, Kentucky, Tennessee, and indeed, all parts of the interior are to be wholly denied the benefit of it?" "I ever have, [voted] and ever will vote for a reasonable appropriation," declared Richard M. Johnson in 1820,[71] "whether it is intended to improve the rivers of Maine or Georgia, or to fill up valleys or level mountains, or to remove natural and artificial obstructions in our navigable rivers or to unite them by canals."

Senator Talbot of Kentucky in 1823 expressed the view that the proper mode of interpreting the Constitution was that of referring disputed points to practical legislators for settlement, "and not to the recluse and retired scholar, issuing from his closet, covered with the dust and cobwebs of his study,"[72] Speaking for Ohio, Senator Ruggles proclaimed in 1825 that the constitutional issue respecting internal improvements had been disposed of, and that the only question remaining was "how can we best improve the condition of the country by a wise application of its resources.[73] "The power to improve the country," maintained Senator Reed of Mississippi, "could not well be deemed unconstitutional;"[74] and Senator Noble of Indiana seconded his views on the same day, asserting that "internal improvement was an object that ought at all times to be promoted, when it could be done without being burthensome to the people."[75] Governor James B. Ray of Indiana declared to the General Assembly of that state in 1827 that no other power could be found in the Constitution which would authorize legislation beneficial to the Mississippi Valley, and argued that "to give up this power is to break the staff into pieces which supports us."[76]

The views of the Westerners above mentioned, and those of scores of others in responsible places, were baldly and frankly summed up by Representative Vance of Ohio in 1827.[77] "Sir," he asked, "what is the situation of at least seven of the Western States, if they are to be bound by what a certain class of politicians . . . would class a legitimate construction of the Constitution? I mean Kentucky, Tennessee, Mississippi, Missouri, Illinois, Indiana, and Ohio. With the exception of the latter, which may have a lighthouse or two on the lake, there is not one object within the limits of those States, that would receive one dollar, if the power of constructing roads and canals is denied to the General Government; and sir, talk as we may about expanded and liberal views . . . there is much in the locality of members . . . If this fatal and limited construction of the constitution is to be the settled policy of this country, it will require but little arithmetic to demonstrate the fate of every state I have enumerated, ten years after they shall have reached their maximum in population. . . . The System of disbursements that now exists, must and will bankrupt the whole valley of the Mississippi."

Notes

1. *Annals of Congress*, 18 Cong., 1 Sess., 137.

2. *Ibid.*, 18 Cong., 2 Sess., 361.

3. Act signed February 28, 1823. *Ibid.*, 17 Cong., 2 Sess., 552-53; 1345-46.

4. *Congressional Debates*, 19 Cong., 2 Sess., 346.

5. Acts of April 27, 1816, March 3, 1817, March 27, 1818, March 3, 1823, April 20, 1826, and May 20, 1826.

6. *Annals*, 15 Cong., 1 Sess., 1400.

7. Act of March 30, 1822. *Ibid.*, 17 Cong., 1 Sess., 2586-87.

8. Act of May 26, 1824. *Ibid.*, 18 Cong., 1 Sess., 3252-53.

9. *Debates*, 19 Cong., 2 Sess., 310-18.

10. Total vote of Senate, 28-14; vote of Mississippi Valley, 15-0; vote of East, 13-14. *Ibid.*, 228. The House joined in the donations by a vote of 90-76, the yeas and nays not being recorded. *Ibid.*, 300-302.

11. The principle established in 1827 was acted upon again during the next session of Congress. Alabama was given 400,000 acres of land, the proceeds from the sale of which the General Assembly

should use for making the canal around Muscle Shoals, and for improving certain rivers within the state. This bill was resisted in the Senate by Senators Branch, Cobb, and Chandler, and opposed on the roll call by all of the strict constructionists. The strength of the Mississippi Valley was necessary to the success of the measure. Total vote of Senate, 22-13; of Mississippi Valley 15-0; vote of East 7-13. *Debates*, 20 Cong., 1 Sess., 453-58.

12. *Ibid.*, 2735.

13. Total vote of House, 86-87; vote of Mississippi Valley, 43-3; vote of East, 43-84. *Ibid.*, 2743.

14. Total vote of Senate, 24-14; vote of Mississippi Valley, 12-1; vote of East, 12-13. *Ibid.*, 809.

15. *Ibid., Appendix,* xxxiv.

16. Ohio *House Journal*, 1819-20, 203, 212.

17. *Annals*, 16 Cong., 1 Sess., 313, 365, 425.

18. The vote in the House on the passage of the bill was as follows: Total vote, 74-35; vote of Mississippi Valley, 41-1; vote of East, 60-34. *Ibid.*, 2244.

19. Total vote of House, 97-72; vote of Mississippi Valley, 39-1; vote of East, 58-71. *Debates*, 18 Cong., 2 Sess., 334.

20. Total vote of Senate, 28-16; vote of Mississippi Valley, 16-2; vote of East, 12-14. *Ibid.*, 671.

21. Appropriation for 1826. *Senate:* Total vote, 21-15; vote of Mississippi Valley, 11-2; vote of East, 10-13. *House:* No division. *Debates*, 19 Cong., 1 Sess., 864.

22. Appropriation for 1827. *Senate:* Total vote, 27-15; vote of Mississippi Valley, 14-2; vote of East, 13-13. *House:* Total vote, 107-55; vote of Mississippi Valley, 37-2; vote of East, 70-53. *Ibid.*, 19 Cong., 2 Sess., 490, 1266.

23. Appropriation for 1828. *Senate:* Total vote, 25-18; vote of Mississippi Valley, 13-3; vote of East, 12-15. *House:* No division. *Ibid.*, 20 Cong., 1 Sess., 125.

24. Representative Henry, Kentucky, May 5, 1824, *Annals*, 18 Cong., 1 Sess., 2579.

25. Total vote of House, 155-60; vote of Mississippi Valley, 41-2; vote of East, 114-58. *Ibid.*, 2596.

26. *Ibid.*, 764.

27. Total vote of Senate, 25-20; vote of Mississippi Valley, 16-1; vote of East, 9-19. *Ibid.*, 765.

28. *Ibid.*, 3227.

29. *Debates*, 19 Cong., 2 Sess., 497-98, *Appendix*, xxii.

30. *Ibid.*, 20 Cong., 1 Sess., *Appendix*, xxiv.

31. *Ibid.*, 18 Cong., 2 Sess., 174.

32. *Annals*, 15 Cong., 1 Sess., 1338.

33. *Debates*, 19 Cong., 1 Sess., 90, 91, 101.

34. *Ibid.*, 19 Cong., 2 Sess., 313-14.

35. This motion, however, was defeated by such a heavy majority that the yeas and nays were not recorded. *Ibid.*, 18 Cong., 2 Sess., 199.

36. *Ibid.*, 206-207.

37. The leading measure of the second session of the Fourteenth Congress was that incorporating Calhoun's plan for using the bonus from the charter, and the Government's share of the dividends of the United States Bank for federal construction of roads and canals. After the bill had passed the House by a narrow margin, it was amended in the Senate so as to secure a distribution of the fund among the states in proportion to population. President Madison vetoed it on the grounds of constitutionality. It was not passed over his veto. *Annals*, 14 Cong., 2 Sess., 934, 191.

38. The House, in March, 1818, debated a series of resolutions on the constitutionality of internal improvements: one resolution to the effect that Congress had power to construct post roads and military roads; one to the effect that Congress might construct roads and canals when necessary for commerce between states; and one declaring that Congress was authorized to construct canals for military purposes. Although the vote of the five Mississippi Valley states which participated in the decisions was neither solidly unified nor indispensable for committing the House to broad construction on any of the points raised by the resolutions, the balloting nevertheless indicated a higher degree of friendliness in the West towards the exercise of federal power than that which characterized the states east of the Alleghenies. *Annals*, 15 Cong., 1 Sess., 1375-89.

39. James D. Richardson, *Messages and Papers of the Presidents* (Washington, 1895-99), II, 142-43.

40. Total vote of House, 87-68; vote of Mississippi Valley, 23-2, vote of East, 64-66, *Annals*, 17 Cong., 1 Sess., 1734.

41. Vote on the Taylor amendment authorizing the President to cede to Maryland, Virginia, and Pennsylvania all right and title of the United States in the Cumberland road; total vote of House, 50-103; vote of Mississippi Valley, 2-20; vote of East, 48-83. *Ibid.*, 1691.

42. Vote in Committee of the Whole on amendment appropriating $9,000 for the initial work of erecting toll houses, etc.: Total vote of House, 84-71; vote of Mississippi Valley, 20-2; vote of East, 64-69. *Ibid.*, 1691-92.

43. Total vote of Senate, 29-7; vote of Mississippi Valley, 14-3; vote of East, 15-4. *Ibid.*, 444.

44. *Ibid.*, 17 Cong., 2 Sess., 1046.

45. *The Autobiography of Martin Van Buren*, edited by John C. Fitzpatrick (Washington, 1920), 305-307.

46. *Annals*, 18 Cong., 1 Sess., 1021.

47. *Ibid.*, 1464.

48. *Ibid.*, 1035.

49. *Ibid.*, 1361.

50. *Ibid.*, 1443-44.

51. *Ibid.*, 1420.

52. *Ibid.*, 1392.

53. *Ibid.*, 1041.

54. Total vote of Senate, 24-18; vote of Mississippi Valley, 16-2; vote of East, 8-16. *Ibid.*, 570-71.

55. *Debates*, 18 Cong., 2 Sess., 549-55.

56. Total vote of Senate, 19-21; vote of Mississippi Valley, 2-14; vote of East, 17-7. *Ibid.*, 558.

57. The Senate voted as follows on a motion to strike out the grant of $50,000 incorporated within the military appropriation act of 1826: Total vote, 13-19; vote of Mississippi Valley, 2-11; vote of East, 11-8. The House offered no formal resistance. *Debates*, 19 Cong., 1 Sess., 364-65.

58. The vote in the House on the acceptance of this appropriation yielded this result: Total vote, 101-67; vote of Mississippi Valley, 36-7; vote of East, 65-60. *Debates*, 18 Cong., 2 Sess., 1332. In the Senate, the West saved the day by throwing its weight in favor of the grant: Total vote, 26-19; vote of Mississippi Valley, 14-3; vote of East, 12-16. *Ibid.*, 491.

59. *Ibid.*, 20 Cong., 1 Sess., 1801-11, 608.

60.

	Total Appropriation	*For West*	*For East*
Act of 1826	$ 100,600	$ 35,200	$ 65,400
Act of 1827	82,175	22,177	59,998
Act of 1828	312,313	136,500	176,813
	495,088	193,877	302,211

Ibid., 19 Cong., 1 Sess., *Appendix*, xxv, xxvi; 19 Cong., 2 Sess., *Appendix*, xvi; 20 Cong., 1 Sess., *Appendix*, xxiv.

61. *Ibid.*, 20 Cong., 1 Sess., xvii, xviii.

62. *Ibid.*, 635.

63. Senate Document No. 29, 20 Cong., 1 Sess., p.17.

64. *Journal* of Kentucky Senate, 1827-28, 328-30.

65. Senate Document No. 123, 20 Cong., 1 Sess., p.5.

66. *Ibid.*, No. 82, p.2.

67. *Ibid.*, No. 113, p.3.

68. *Debates*, 20 Cong., 1 Sess., 634-46.

69. *Ibid.*, 19 Cong., 1 Sess., 596.

70. *Annals*, 15 Cong., 1 Sess., 1175-76.

71. *Ibid.*, 16 Cong., 1 Sess., 441.

72. *Ibid.*, 17 Cong., 2 Sess., 86-87.

73. *Debates*, 18 Cong., 2 Sess., 661.

74. *Ibid.*, 19 Cong., 1 Sess., 719.

75. *Ibid.*, 714.

76. Indiana *Senate Journal*, 1827-28, 18.

77. *Debates*, 19 Cong., 2 Sess., 1224-25; 1227-28.

Andrew Jackson and the rise of southwestern democracy

Thomas P. Abernethy

The election of Andrew Jackson has been portrayed as the triumph of the West over the East and of democracy over privilege. Beneath these assertions is the assumption, fueled by Frederick Jackson Turner and his followers, that American democracy has its roots in the frontier process. According to this belief, the old structures of civilization dissolved on the frontier and, for a brief time and while the "cake of custom" had been cut, something like equality reigned. Eventually, of course, the frontier moved westward; in its place remained some of the older settlers, whose vested interests became the germs of new economic, political, and social stratification. Can Jackson's career in any way be fitted into this analysis? Certainly there are elements of democratic rhetoric in Jackson's presidency. His Bank War rang with denunciation of monopoly and economic special privilege. But was there anything *western* in Jackson's fight against the Bank of the United States?

A good case can be made that Jackson acted for eastern interests, not western. After all Jackson's chief advisers in the matter were David Henshaw, a Boston banker on the periphery of the city's financial circle; Martin Van Buren, who was closely connected with Wall Street; and Roger B. Taney, who had interests in Maryland banks. Certainly there were westerners who opposed the bank, but there were many men of the West who followed Henry Clay of Kentucky and supported the institution. The conclusion seems clear; the Bank War was not based on controversy between the sections. Should one conclude, then, that there were no significant sectional disputes between East and West? This is not tenable either, because as Curtis Nettels demonstrated in his essay "The Mississippi Valley and the Constitution, 1815-29" certain issues such as internal improvements were viewed differently in the interior than they were in the seaboard states. The significant fact is the difference in the nature of western sectionalism as seen by the Turner school and that postulated in Nettels' essay.

Nettels saw differences arise largely out of the timing of settlement. In the 1820s the East had basic facilities such as turnpikes and canals that the West lacked, and the main interest of westerners was in the acquisition of these facilities. Turner, however, claimed that the East and West differed in fundamental political and social outlook. The westerner in power, therefore, tried to shape national policy to make the aristocratic East

Reprinted with permission from *American Historical Review*, XXXIII (October 1927), 64-77.

conform to the democratic West. Some questions that arise from this are: To what extent were Jacksonian reforms (abolition of imprisonment for debt, prison reform, banking changes, and so on) western? How did western political philosophy differ from eastern? What economic and political interests transcended the sections?

In the following essay, Thomas P. Abernethy, Professor Emeritus of History at the University of Virginia, examines the nature of Tennessee society and Jackson's place in it. His views are amplified in *From Frontier to Plantation in Tennessee* (1932).

For further reading: James Parton, *Life of Jackson*, 3 vols., (New York: Macmillan, 1911); John W. Ward, *Andrew Jackson, Symbol for an Age* (New York: Oxford University Press, 1955);* Charles G. Sellers, "Banking and Politics in Jackson's Tennessee, 1817-1827," *Mississippi Valley Historical Review*, XLI (June 1954), 61-84; Charles G. Sellers, *James K. Polk, Jacksonian, 1795-1843* (Princeton: Princeton University Press, 1957); Bray Hammond, *Banks and Politics in America from the Revolution to the Civil War* (Princeton: Princeton University Press, 1957); Peter Temin, *The Jacksonian Economy* (New York: Norton, 1969);* Harry R. Stevens, "Henry Clay, the Bank and the West in 1824," *American Historical Review*, LX (July 1955), 843-848; Edward Pessen, *Jacksonian America: Society, Personality, and Politics* (Homewood, Ill.: Dorsey Press, 1969);* Frank Otto Gatell, ed., *Essays on Jacksonian America* (New York: Holt, Rinehart and Winston, 1970);* Thomas P. Abernethy, *From Frontier to Plantation in Tennessee* (Chapel Hill: University of North Carolina Press, 1932).

*Available in paperback.

The name of Andrew Jackson is inseparably linked with the rise of Western democracy, but the biographers of the general have confined their attention largely to his military exploits and to his contest for the occupancy of the presidency. It is not these phases of his life, however, which connect him most intimately with the struggle of the pioneer and early Western farmer for political power. Before he was a general or a presidential possibility, he was a Tennessee politician. In this capacity he was closely associated with those events which constituted an integral part of the democratic movement of the West. A study of this phase of his career, and of the setting in which he worked, should give a better idea of the man and of the cause for which his name has come to stand.

In 1796 Tennessee adopted her first constitution. Jackson was a member of the committee which drafted it. For its day it was a liberal document, but among its provisions were two which later attracted much unfavorable attention. One provided that the justices of the peace should be chosen by the general assembly for life terms, and that the justices should choose, with a few exceptions, the other county officials;[1] the second stipulated that all acreage should be taxed at the same rate, regardless of value.[2]

These provisions make it clear that the democracy of the West had not grown to full stature by 1796. The peculiarities of the early frontier go far toward explaining this fact. The familiar portraits of John Sevier show him in military costume of the Continental type, such as officers of the line wore during the Revolutionary War, but in his fighting days he wore a hunting shirt as did the men who followed him as he tracked the elusive Indian through the forest.[3] Distinctions existed on the border, but they were not patent to the eye and the simple backwoodsman was not alive to them. The voters who elected delegates to the constitutional convention of 1796 did not realize to what extent they were smoothing the way for the selfaggrandizement of their leaders, the colonels, the legislators, and the land-grabbers—classifications which greatly overlapped.

The years which elapsed between 1796 and 1812 were years of relative peace and considerable growth for the Southwest, but frontier conditions persisted throughout the period. The settlers, whether in town or country, continued, in the main, to live in log cabins and wear homespun. The acquisition of Louisiana and the final opening of the Mississippi River to the trade of the West was a boon to the country. Such towns as Nashville began to emerge from the primitive and to take on the appearance of civilization. Yet it was only with great difficulty that the rivers could be ascended by keel boats, and the majority of the roads were mere trails through the woods. Money was scarce, and the interchange of goods was difficult and hazardous. Barter was still commonly employed in conducting commercial transactions.[4]

The War of 1812 ushered in a change. Tennessee troops saw considerable service in the campaigns against the Indians and the British, and the supplies necessary for their maintenance were secured largely in the West. This brought ready money into regions which had previously known little of its use,[5] and money meant purchasing power, and luxuries, and trade. Moccasins gave place to shoes, and log cabins to brick and frame houses. The Indians caused less trouble after Jackson's conquest of the Creeks in 1813, and large tracts of land were wrested from the natives. The depression suffered by our infant industries as a result of the dumping of British goods on the American market at the end of the long European wars, and the depleted condition of the soils of the South Atlantic states were conditions tending to force population westward.[6] The Cotton Kingdom of the Gulf region was planted in these years.[7] The high price of the staple, which reached thirty-four cents a pound in 1817,[8] hastened this movement, and the steamboat came just in time to facilitate the commercial side of the development.[9]

Specie payments had been suspended by the banks south of New England in 1814, and cheap paper money had been one of the elements conducive to the rapid exploitation of the West which followed the war.[10] In 1817 the Second Bank of the United States went into operation, and it was hoped that it would, by bringing pressure to bear upon doubtful state banks, be able to restore the currency of the country to a sound basis.[11] This meant the retirement of much worthless paper money issued by the state banks, and a consequent restraint on speculative operations.

In order to offset this curtailment of currency and credit, Tennessee chartered a "litter" of state banks in 1817.[12] Kentucky did likewise during the next year.[13] At the same time, the legislature of Tennessee prevented the establishment of a branch of the Bank of the United States within her borders by levying a tax of $50,000 a year upon any such institution.[14] This prohibitive measure was sponsored by Hugh Lawson White,[15] while the opposition was led by Felix Grundy[16] and supported by William Carroll and Andrew Jackson.[17] Its passage seems to indicate the jealousy felt by local financial interests rather than the influence of constitutional scruples on the subject.

The period of speculation was followed by the panic of 1819. East Tennessee had largely escaped the financial excesses of the post-war boom,[18] for her valleys were not suited to the culture of cotton, and transportation was so difficult as to make commercial expansion almost impossible. In Middle Tennessee, however, the growing of cotton was far more widespread during these years than it is at the present time. It was, for instance, Jackson's principal crop at the Hermitage, whereas one now has to travel many miles south of Nashville before reaching cotton country. The very high price which the staple commanded from 1815 to 1819 was the primary cause of this expansion, and the result was that thousands of farmers in this section were ruined when the price fell and the panic came on in 1819. Between five and six hundred suits for debt were entered at one term of the court of Davidson County [19] —the county of which Nashville is the seat of justice.

The indications are that the panic of 1819 hit the small farmers of the Southwest harder than has any succeeding financial disaster. After settled conditions are established and farms are paid for, economic crises do their worst only among the trading and speculating classes, but in new country the farmers are the speculators. The result in this case was that the democracy, for the first time, rose up to demand legislative relief.

In Tennessee the agitation was led by Felix Grundy, who piloted through the assembly a bill providing for the establishment of a loan office. [20] The state was to furnish the capital, the legislature was to elect the directors, and the loans were to be apportioned among the counties according to the taxes paid in each. A "stay" law was also enacted which provided that any creditor who refused to receive the notes issued by the loan office, or state bank, as it was called, would be required to wait two years before he could enforce collection of his debt. [21] These measures were passed by the votes of Middle Tennessee, East Tennessee being opposed. [22] For the first and last time, the debtors of the state were clearly in the saddle.

Within a few months Kentucky established a loan office similar to that of Tennessee, [23] and in 1823 Alabama launched a state-owned bank. [24] Relief legislation was quite general throughout the states south of New England. [25]

The only prominent men in Middle Tennessee who were conspicuous for their opposition to these measures were Edward Ward and Andrew Jackson. They addressed a memorial of protest to the assembly which that body refused to accept on the ground that its language was disrespectful to the law-makers. The memorial did, in fact, charge the members who voted for the loan office act with perjury since they had taken an oath to support the Constitution of the United States, and now assented to a law which made something beside gold and silver a tender in payment of debts. [26]

In 1821 Tennessee experienced one of her most exciting gubernatorial elections. The candidates were Edward Ward and William Carroll. The former was he who had, together with Jackson, protested against the loan office; he was a native of Virginia, a man of education and wealth, and a neighbor to General Jackson. [27] The latter was a merchant from Pennsylvania who had opened the first nail store in Nashville. He was a young man of energy and address, and Jackson had befriended him in his early days. As major-general of Tennessee militia he had served with signal distinction at the battle of New Orleans, but a break, the causes of which are obscure, developed between him and Jackson in 1816. [28]

In the contest of 1821 Jackson used his influence in support of Ward, and looked upon Carroll and his friends as a group of demagogues. [29] The press of the state entered heartily into the campaign and Carroll was touted as a man of the people—an unpretentious merchant, without wealth and without social prestige—whereas Ward's wealth, his slaves, and his education were held against him. He was pictured in the press as a snobbish representative of the aristocracy of the planters. [30]

Both candidates were opposed to the loan office of 1820. Ward advocated a centralized state-banking system in place of it, [31] whereas Carroll simply stressed a policy of retrenchment.[32] The people appear to have discovered that the legislative relief was no panacea for their financial ills, and they were ready to accept Carroll's harsher doctrine of economy. They were beginning to understand that farmers, whose profits did not often run above five per cent, could not afford to borrow from banks at six per cent. Carroll carried every county in the state except two,[33] and the mere magnitude of the victory indicates that his success was due to his reputation for democracy rather than to his merchant-class economic ideas.

With the exception of a one-term intermission made necessary by the state constitution, William Carroll presided over the government of Tennessee continuously until 1835. He was the most constructive governor who ever held office in the state, for, curiously enough, it was he who, staunchly opposed by Jackson, established "Jacksonian democracy" within her borders. He believed in government of, for, and by the people, but he also believed in a financial policy of specie payments and legislative non-interference between debtor and creditor. Under his leadership, Tennessee disavowed the kind of democracy which had mounted into the saddle on the heels of the panic of 1819, and of which Felix Grundy had been the protagonist.

In his first message to the general assembly, the new chief magistrate outlined his policy. He stuck tenaciously to his programme throughout his twelve years in office, and, though it was slow work, nearly every item of his platform was finally carried into effect. In 1821 he advocated the erection of a penitentiary and the abolition of the use of the whipping post, the pillory, and the branding iron. These changes were finally brought about in 1831.[34] Imprisonment for debt was abolished at the same time.[35] In 1821 the "stay" law of 1820 was held unconstitutional by the supreme court of the state.[36] In 1826 the law of 1817 which prevented the establishment of a branch of the Bank of the United States in Tennessee was repealed with few dissenting votes in the lower house of the legislature,[37] and accordingly that institution established an office in Nashville during the following year. In 1831 the loan office of 1820 was abolished upon Carroll's recommendation,[38] and in 1832 and 1833 several important privately owned banks of the usual commercial type were established.[39] The sales of the public lands belonging to the state, which had been put upon a credit basis in 1819, were put upon a cash basis in 1823,[40] and the prices were graduated according to the principle later advocated in Congress by Thomas H. Benton.[41] Finally, after several unsuccessful attempts had been made in the legislature to bring the question before the people, a referendum was held and a constitutional convention assembled in 1834.[42] The new instrument of government which was now drawn up and adopted provided for a revision of the judicial system which would facilitate the collection of debts, for popular election of county officials, and for the taxation of real estate according to its value. Thus democracy won its victory in Tennessee, and the guiding spirit was that of William Carroll.

Up to this time, the state had gone through three distinct political phases. The first, extending from 1796 until the panic of 1819, was a period during which the people gratefully and implicitly accepted the leadership of a group of outstanding citizens. The frontiersman was busy with his clearings and he gladly accepted the services of such energetic men as would organize governments and fight the Indians. The fact that these same men were usually land speculators did not disturb him even if he knew it. Land was cheap.

The second period was that of the panic of 1819 during which economic ills aroused the people to a consciousness of their political power. Felix Grundy was the first to see the possibilities of the situation and to organize the movement for his own advancement. He was the first, but by no means the last, demagogue of Tennessee. Carroll won the people away from him and inaugurated the third period, which was one of constructive social and conservative economic legislation. It is noteworthy that until 1829 both Carroll and the legislature favored federal as well as state banks, nor does anything in the history of the state indicate that there was any general feeling against such institutions before Jackson became President.

It was well for Tennessee that Carroll remained so long in office, for the demagogue was not dead. The people had been aroused and Grundy had taught a lesson to the politicians. Public office was eagerly sought by the young lawyers and others, and electioneering, unknown in the earlier days, grew rapidly in vogue during the period following 1819. Stump speaking came to be an art and cajolery a profession, while whiskey flowed freely at the hustings. The politicians could most easily attain their object by appealing to the prejudices of the masses. Colleges were said to exist for the rich, and the ignorant were asked to elect the ignorant because enlightenment and intelligence were not democratic.[43] America, to say nothing of Tennessee, has not out-lived this brand of democracy.

It was during the years of Carroll's supremacy that the Jackson presidential boom took shape and ran its course. The relation between this movement and the rise of Western democracy is of considerable interest for the reason that the two have ordinarily been considered as amounting to practically the same thing. The truth of the matter is that Jackson had little to do with the development of the democracy of the West. The movement made him President, but he contributed to it not one idea previously to his election in 1828. He rode into office upon a military reputation and the appeal which a self-made man can make so effectively to self-made men.

It did not take as astute a politician as Aaron Burr to see the possibility of making the Hero of New Orleans President of the United States. Not only Burr, but Edward Livingston and others saw it shortly after January 8, 1815.[44] In fact, the general himself probably saw it, but did not admit it. He at least began taking a keen interest in national politics and set himself the agreeable task of helping Monroe keep Crawford out of the chief magistracy,[45] for the enmity between the general and the secretary dates from 1816. It arose as a result of an agreement which Crawford negotiated with the Cherokees during that year, according to the terms of which the Indians were allowed to retain three million acres of land which the Creeks had claimed and which had been ceded to the government by Jackson's treaty of 1813. The Cherokees were also allowed damages for depredations alleged to have been committed by Jackson's troops during the course of the Creek campaign.[46] The general considered this a slur on his military reputation, and the author of it was duly condemned. It was also good political material, for Crawford was made to appear an enemy of the Western heroes and an opponent of westward expansion. It was only after the election of 1820, however, that the friends of Jackson could tactfully avow their intention to make him President, and the movement did not actually take shape until after his retirement from the governorship of Florida in 1821.

At the time when Jackson resigned this commission and returned to the Hermitage to spend his declining years "surrounded by the pleasures of domestic felicity," a little group of friends in Nashville was forming to make plans of campaign for their distinguished fellow-townsman. The leaders of this group were William B. Lewis, John Overton, and John H. Eaton.

The first-named was a planter and Jackson's neighbor. He was a close personal friend and adviser of long standing, but he was not a man of large affairs. Parton has over-estimated his importance because he obtained much of his information on the campaign from Lewis himself.[47] John Overton was a former member of the supreme court of Tennessee and one of the richest men in the state. At that time he and Jackson were partners in a large land deal: namely, the establishment of a trading-town on the Mississippi by the name of Memphis.[48] They were closely associated in Jackson's political venture, too, and Overton later burned the papers relating thereto so that the curious might not pry into its details.[49] In 1816 John H. Eaton, then comparatively unknown in Tennessee, undertook to complete a biography of Jackson.[50] In 1818 he was appointed to the United States Senate,[51] and in 1819 he defended the general when the Seminole campaign was before that body for investigation.[52] From his vantage-point in Washington he served as field agent for the little group of Nashville managers.

Both Overton and Eaton were accused of having entertained Federalist opinions in their early days.[53] There was certainly nothing in the background or the connections of the group to tie it up with the democratic movement which was in full tide about them. In 1823 a former judge who had sat with Overton in the supreme court of the state wrote to him: "True republicanism must supersede the Democracy of the present day before public employment will be suited to my taste. . . . There are too many who would prefer a directly contrary state of things."[54] At about this time Jackson himself was keenly interested in a legal scheme to throw open to question the titles to about half the occupied lands in Tennessee. This, of course, was in the interest of speculators like himself. The legislature however set itself against the plan and it failed miserably.[55]

The general had no personal dealings with either Grundy or Carroll during the early years of his candidacy, and though Grundy, with an eye to personal advancement, refused to break with him politically, and Carroll was later reconciled, it is significant that the latter is the only outstanding Tennessee Democrat who did not, sooner or later, receive federal recognition at the hands of Jackson's party.

Yet Jackson's political views were little known outside Tennessee at the time when he began to be looked upon as presidential timber. His strength lay in his military reputation, in his connection with the expansion of the West at the expense of the Spanish and Indians, and in the fact that he was not closely connected with the intrigue of Washington politics. A movement to turn out the "Virginia dynasty" and to forestall Crawford, the "heir apparent," was inevitable. The dissatisfied element in the Southern and Middle states instinctively turned to Jackson as the logical instrument for this purpose, and certainly no role could have been more congenial to the general than one which cast him in opposition to William H. Crawford.

The first statement that he was being definitely considered for the presidency came from Pennsylvania in 1821, where the leaders were said to have canvassed the situation and found that he was the logical man.[56] North Carolina followed the lead of Pennsylvania,[57] and word came from Virginia that the people were for Jackson, but that leadership was needed in order that the politicians be overthrown.[58]

The movement in Tennessee was brought to the surface in 1822 when it was proposed that the general assembly present the general's name to the nation as a suitable candidate for the presidency. The proposition was carried by that body without a dissenting vote.[59] This in the face of the fact that Jackson's candidate for the governorship had been defeated during the previous year by an overwhelming majority. This apparently conflicting vote merely shows that national and state politics were not closely related at that time. The general had been repudiated in no uncertain manner as a state politician, but as a national hero he was a success. Discredited because of his conservative stand in the state, he was chosen to lead the progressive movement in the nation.

A sidelight on the situation is afforded by an incident which occurred during the next year. Colonel John Williams, of Knoxville, had represented Tennessee in the United States Senate since 1815,· and had attacked Jackson during the Seminole investigation of 1819.[60] His term expired in 1823, and he was up for re-election with excellent prospects of success. Jackson's friends decided that his presidential prospects would be blighted by the election of one of his bitterest enemies to the Senate from his own state, and when no other candidate could develop sufficient strength to defeat Williams, the general himself was, at the last minute, induced to run.[61] A number of the members of the legislature had already pledged their votes to Williams and could not change, but the ballot, when counted, stood twenty-five to thirty-five in favor of Jackson. The names of those voting were not recorded in the journal—a significant omission. Tennesseans would not permit Jackson to dictate to them, but his personal prestige was great, and there were few who dared stand against him face to face.

Jackson went to the Senate against his will. Back in 1798 he had resigned from that body after a year of uncongenial service. He was now returned to the national forum at the behest of friends who had previously devoted their best efforts to keeping him quiet. Yet it was not because he was afraid to speak his mind that he shrank from the Senate. Above all things, save perhaps a good fight, the general liked to speak his mind. That he gave in so often to his advisers shows that he was not devoid of political discretion. His real objection to Washington, as he so often stated, was its partizan intrigue. There was too much competition in the capital.

There was no doubt but that, before the presidential election, Jackson's hand would be revealed in regard to the important questions which were agitating the country. It was a brave stand for a general in politics to take, but he took it unequivocally. He voted consistently for internal improvements and for the tariff of 1824.[62]

Jackson posed as a Jeffersonian, as did nearly all the Southern Republicans of his day, and in 1822 he had written to Monroe congratulating him upon the veto of the Cumberland Road bill.[63] Yet Tennessee needed internal improvements and ardently desired them. As late as 1825 James K. Polk advocated federal aid for such purposes.[64] In voting as he did in 1824, Jackson represented the interests of his constituents, but during the same year he expressed the opinion that the consent of the state should be secured before the national government should give assistance.[65] During 1827 his supporters in the Tennessee legislature were said to have opposed a federal aid project because of the effect that the agitation of such a question by them might have upon the presidential election in Pennsylvania and Virginia.[66] Finally, when the general became President, he vetoed the Maysville Road bill on the ground that the thoroughfare in question was one of only local importance. The fact was, however, that it was the main highway—an extension of the old Cumberland Road—along which the eastern mail was, at the very time, being carried to Nashville and the Southwest.[67]

In his stand on the tariff question in 1824, Jackson stressed the military importance of domestic manufactures, and also argued for the development of a home market for agricultural products.[68] In this matter he doubtless voiced his personal convictions. The homemarket argument had an appeal for the grain farmers of the West, and there were more grain farmers in Tennessee than there were cotton planters, yet Jackson himself belonged to the latter group and protection was not popular with them as a class. Furthermore, despite the rise of democracy, the wealthy cotton planters still had a large share in the creation of public opinion, and there were, in Tennessee, few active advocates of a high tariff before 1840.[69]

In regard to the Bank of the United States, Jackson's views were not developed until after the period of his senatorial services. He certainly did not take a stand against that institution before 1826. In 1827 he began making unfavorable comments on it, but public opposition did not develop until after his election to the presidency.[70] This was clearly not a question of long-standing prejudice with him, and the evidence seems to point to Van Buren as the source of his opinions on the subject.[71] In addition to this, Jackson knew that most of the branches of the bank were in the hands of his opponents and had good reason to believe that their influence was used against him during the election of 1828.[72] It was entirely Jacksonian for him to form his opinion upon such grounds.

Jackson had once been a merchant and he was still a man of business affairs. He had long been a believer in a sound currency and the rights of the creditor. His early economic ideas were in accord with those of William Carroll, and there was nothing here to bring him into conflict with the Bank of the United States. The motives of his opposition were political, not economic.

No historian has ever accused Jackson, the great Democrat, of having had a political philosophy. It is hard to see that he even had any political principles. He was a man of action, and the man of action is likely to be an opportunist. Politically speaking, Jackson was certainly an opportunist. If he gave any real help or encouragement before 1828 to any of the movements which, under men like Carroll, aimed at the amelioration of the condition of the masses, the fact has not been recorded. He belonged to the moneyed aristocracy of Nashville, yet he was a self-made man and devoid of snobbishness. He thought he was sincere when he spoke to the people, yet he never really championed their cause. He merely encouraged them to champion his.

It seems clear that Jackson's political habits were formed in the period of the early settlement of the Southwest when a few leaders were able to shape the public mind and use their official positions as an aid to their exploitation of the land. He never failed, for instance, to use the patronage of office for the promotion of the interests of his friends. The democratic awakening which took such hold upon the people of Tennessee after the panic of 1819 failed to enlist his sympathy. He was called upon to lead the national phase of this movement, but played no part in the formulation or promotion of its constructive programme. He did, however, in 1824, represent the needs of the West for improved commercial facilities, and he was a nationalist from early conviction. After 1824 he came under political influence—that of Van Buren, it seems, being paramount[73]—which caused him to change his earlier opinions in several respects. This accounts for the fact that his presidential policy favored the seaboard staple growers rather than the grain producers of the West. Yet he failed, in the main, to capture the support of the cotton planters of the South, for many of them either sympathized with nullification or desired a United States bank and internal improvements. He was a political hybrid—too strong a nationalist for some, too strong a state-rights man for others. On the other hand, he held to the end the loyalty of the small farmers, for the Jacksonian tradition was deeply rooted in them, and Jackson's bank policy looked to them like democracy. Banks often worked to their disadvantage, and they could manage without commercial facilities. They constituted the rank and file of the Democratic party in the South until the Whig organization went to pieces and the planters were thereby forced to accept, at a late date, the bait which Jackson had proffered them in vain.

Notes

1. Art. V., sec. 12; art. VI., sec. 1.

2. Art. I., sec. 26.

3. J. G. M. Ramsey, *Annals of Tennessee* (Kingsport, Tenn., 1926), p. 711.

4. Account book of H. Tatum, merchant, Nashville, 1793-1798, Tennessee Historical Society MSS., Box T-1, no. 5; *Correspondence of Andrew Jackson*, ed. J. S. Bassett (Washington, 1926), I. 89-90, 99-101.

5. Nashville *Gazette*, Oct. 29, 1820.

6. A. O. Craven, *Soil Exhaustion as a Factor in the Agricultural History of Virginia and Maryland* (Urbana, Ill., 1926), pp. 118-121.

7. T. P. Abernethy, *Formative Period in Alabama* (Montgomery, Ala., 1922), pp. 50-56.

8. U.S. Department of Agriculture, Office of Farm Management, *Atlas of American Agriculture* (Washington, 1918), pt. V., sec. A, 20.

9. Moore and Foster, *Tennessee, the Volunteer State* (Chicago, 1923), II. 85-86; Nashville *Banner*, Apr. 14, 1827.

10. D. R. Dewey, *Financial History of the United States* (New York, 1920), pp. 144-145.

11. *Ibid.*, pp. 145-151.

12. Tennessee, *Public Acts*, 1817, pp. 163-180.

13. McMaster, *History of the People of the United States* (New York, 1895), IV. 508.

14. Tennessee, *Public Acts*, 1817, pp. 138-139.

15. John Catron to Polk, June 17, 1837, Papers of James K. Polk in Library of Congress; *A Memoir of Hugh Lawson White*, ed. Nancy N. Scott (Philadelphia, 1856), pp. 19-23.

16. St. George L. Sioussat, "Some Phases of Tennessee Politics in the Jackson Period," in *Am. Hist. Rev.*, XIV. 60; Nashville *Whig*, Feb.7, 1818.

17. James Phelan, *History of Tennessee* (Boston, 1888), pp. 394-395; R. C. H. Catterall, *Second Bank of the United States*, p. 183.

18. Thos. Emmerson to John Overton, Oct. 24, 1820, John Overton Papers in Tennessee Historical Society library; P. M. Miller to Jackson, Aug. 9, 1820, Jackson Papers in Library of Congress; Nashville *Gazette*, June 20, 1820; Knoxville *Register*, June 20, 1820.

19. Jackson to Capt. James Gadsden, Aug. 1, 1819, *Correspondence of Andrew Jackson*, ed. J. S. Bassett, II. 421; Nashville *Clarion*, July 13, 1819.

20. Knoxville *Register*, July 18, 1820.

21. Tennessee, *Public Acts*, 1820, p. 13.

22. Tennessee Assembly, *Journal of the House*, 1820, p. 129.

23. Nashville *Gazette*, Dec. 9, 1820.

24. T. P. Abernethy, *Formative Period in Alabama*, p. 99.

25. Thos. H. Benton, *Thirty Years' View* (New York, 1854), I. 5.

26. Nashville *Clarion*, July 25, 1820; Knoxville *Register*, Aug. 15, 1820.

27. Hale and Merritt, *A History of Tennessee and Tennesseans* (Chicago, 1913), II. 267.

28. Jackson to Coffee, Feb. 2, 1816, Papers of John Coffee in Tenn. Hist. Soc. library.

29. Jackson to Coffee, July 26, 1821, *ibid.*; Jackson to Capt. John Donelson, Sept. 2, 1821, Jackson Papers.

30. Knoxville *Register*, July 17, 1821; Nashville *Clarion*, July 18, 1821.

31. Nashville *Gazette*, June 2, 1821; Nashville *Clarion*, June 13, 1821; Knoxville *Register*, June 16, 1821.

32. Nashville *Clarion*, June 27, 1821.

33. *Ibid.*, Aug. 15, 1821.

34. See messages of 1821 and 1823. Tennessee Assembly, *Journal of the Senate*, 1821, pp. 86-99, and *Journal of the House*, 1823, pp. 9-15.

35. Tennessee, *Public Acts*, 1831, p. 56.

36. Townsend *v.* Townsend *et al.*, *Tennessee Reports* (Peck), pp. 1-21.

37. Tennessee, *Public Acts*, 1826, p. 18; Tennessee Assembly, *Journal of the House*, 1826, pp. 173-174.

38. Tennessee Assembly, *Journal of the Senate*, 1831, pp. 6-9, *Journal of the House*, 1831, pp. 41 *et seq.*

39. Tennessee, *Public Acts*, 1832, pp. 2-13, and 1833, pp. 30-42; Phelan, *History of Tennessee*, pp. 267-268.

40. Whitney, *Land Laws of Tennessee* (Chattanooga, 1891), pp. 387-394.

41. *Ibid.*, pp. 398-400; see also Sioussat, "Tennessee Politics in the Jackson Period," *loc. cit.*, pp. 54-58.

42. The question of calling a convention was voted on by the assembly and defeated in 1821, 1823, and 1826. It was finally carried by the assembly and ratified by popular vote in 1833.

43. For suggestions on this topic, see J. W. M. Breazeale, "Satirical Burlesque upon the Practice of Electioneering," in *Life as It Is* (Knoxville, 1842), pp. 158-226; and "An Address to Farmers and Mechanics," in *Works of Philip Lindsley* (Philadelphia, 1866), III. 265-316.

44. J. S. Bassett, *Life of Andrew Jackson* (New York, 1925), p. 279; William Carroll to Jackson, Oct. 4, 1815, *id., Correspondence of Andrew Jackson*, II. 217-218; James Parton, *Life of Andrew Jackson* (Boston, 1887), II. 350.

45. A. P. Hayne to Jackson, Jan. 21, 1819, Jackson Papers; *id.* to *id.*, Mar. 6, 1819, Jackson to Governor Clark of Georgia, Apr. 20, 1819, *Correspondence of Andrew Jackson*, ed. J. S. Bassett, II. 412, 416; Address of Enoch Parson, Mar. 25, 1819, Jackson Papers; Jackson to Coffee, Apr. 3, 1819, Coffee Papers.

46. Parton, *Jackson*, II. 355-356; Bassett, *Jackson*, p. 281; Nashville *Whig*, July 31, 1819; Jackson to Monroe, Oct. 10, 1823, Jackson Papers; Jackson to Crawford, June 10, 13 ?, and 16, 1816, *Correspondence of Andrew Jackson*, ed. J. S. Bassett, II. 243-250.

47. Parton, *Jackson*, III. 17.

48. Phelan, *History of Tennessee*, p. 317.

49. W. W. Clayton, *History of Davidson County, Tennessee* (Philadelphia, 1880), p. 99.

50. Nashville *Whig*, June 4, 1816.

51. C. A. Miller, *Official and Political Manual of the State of Tennessee* (Nashville, 1890), p. 173.

52. Jackson to William Williams, Sept. 25, 1819, Bassett, *Correspondence of Andrew Jackson*, II. 430.

53. Nashville *Clarion*, Jan. 5, 1819; Phelan, *History of Tennessee*, p. 241.

54. Thos. Emmerson to John Overton, May 25, 1823; see also *id.* to *id.*, Dec. 26, 1823, and June 3, 1824, Overton Papers.

55. This had to do with a decision of the state supreme court which overruled former decisions and declared that titles to land, in order to be valid, must be connected by an unbroken chain with the original grant, and that occupiers might be ejected even though they held under color of title. The legislature added another justice to the court, and John Catron, afterward justice of the United States Supreme Court, was appointed to fill the place in order that this decision might be annulled. Jackson had a personal interest in the matter and denounced the action of the legislature. See Jackson to Coffee, April 15, and May 24, 1823, Coffee Papers. For the legal phase of the question, see Barton's Lessee *v.* Shall, *Tennessee Reports* (Peck), p. 172.

56. S. R. Overton to Jackson, Aug. 1, 1821, Jackson Papers.

57. A. D. Murphy to John H. Eaton, Jan. 16, 1824, Overton Papers.

58. Thos. G. Watkins to Jackson, Mar. 13, 1822, Jackson Papers.

59. Jackson to Dr. J. C. Bronaugh, Aug. 1, 1822, S. R. Overton to Jackson, Sept. 10, 1822, Jackson Papers; Nashville *Whig*, July 31, 1822. See also Grundy to Jackson, June 27, 1822, Jackson Papers.

60. Jackson to William Williams, Sept. 25, 1819, Bassett, *Correspondence of Andrew Jackson*, II. 430.

61. Thos. L. Williams to Overton, Sept. 10, 1823, Overton Papers. Wm. Brady and Thos. Williamson to Jackson, Sept. 20, 1823, Jackson to Brady and Williamson, Sept. 27, 1823, Jackson Papers; Jackson to Coffee, Oct. 5, 1823, Coffee Papers; Knoxville *Register*, Oct. 10, 1823.

62. Bassett, *Jackson*, pp. 344-345.

63. Jackson to Monroe, July 26, 1822, Jackson Papers.

64. Phelan, *History of Tennessee*, p. 396.

65. Jackson to James W. Lanier, May (?), 1824, Jackson Papers; Jackson to Polk, Dec. 4, 1826, Polk Papers.

66. Knoxville *Enquirer*, Jan. 9, 1828.

67. J. P. Bretz, "Early Land Communication with the Lower Mississippi Valley," in *Mississippi Valley Historical Review*, XIII. 27-29.

68. Jackson to Coffee, May 7, 1824, Jackson to John Overton, June 18, 1824, Coffee Papers; Parton, *Jackson*, III. 35-36.

69. Phelan, *History of Tennessee*, p. 425.

70. Catterall, *Second Bank of the United States*, pp. 183-184.

71. R. L. Colt to Biddle, Jan. 7, 1829, June 10, 1830, Henry Clay to Biddle, June 14, 1830, *The Correspondence of Nicholas Biddle*, ed. R. C. McGrane, pp. 66-67, 104, 105.

72. Wm. B. Lewis to Biddle, Oct. 16, 1829, pp. 79-80, Biddle to Geo. Hoffman, Nov. 22, 1829, *ibid.*, pp. 87-88.

73. Bassett, *Jackson*, pp. 484-489; *David Crockett's Circular*, pamphlet in Library of Congress (Washington, 1831), pp. 2-5.

The pattern of migration and settlement on the southern frontier

Frank L. Owsley

In the years immediately preceding the Civil War, Frederick Law Olmsted, a reporter for the New York *Times*, made a series of lengthy trips throughout the South. His articles became the basis for three books, which were condensed in 1861 into a single volume, *The Cotton Kingdom*. Olmsted's works are the most vivid and accurate firsthand descriptions we have of southern frontier life in the 1850s. Like most of his northern contemporaries, Olmsted had a deep interest in slavery. Olmsted's South was a region dominated by two classes, a wealthy slaveholding minority and a mass of poor whites. Olmsted's readers found little evidence of a strong and prosperous yeoman class. To the contrary, Olmsted implied that slavery, through its occupation of the best land and its degradation of free labor, inevitably created an indolent poor white mass.

Later historians adopted this thesis, and it became almost standard for explaining the poverty associated with the southern Piney Woods and Appalachia. That the Piney Woods and particularly Appalachia are depressed and have been so for many decades there can be no doubt. But what many have overlooked is that most of the South, including portions of the seaboard states, was a frontier area throughout the antebellum period.

In the following essay, Frank Lawrence Owsley, who taught southern history for many years at Vanderbilt University and the University of Alabama before his death in 1956, examines the nature of the southern frontier. This essay stresses both cultural and environmental factors in the emergence of southern society prior to 1860. It supports a major reinterpretation of southern history that Professor Owsley developed in his *Plain Folk of the Old South* (1949). In that book he produced significant evidence of a large nonslaveholding middle class in the antebellum South.

For further reading: Frank Lawrence Owsley, *Plain Folk of the Old South* (Baton Rouge: Louisiana State University Press, 1949);* Frederick Law Olmsted, *A Journey in the Seaboard Slave States* (New York: Sampson Low, Son & Co., 1856); Frederick Law Olmsted, *A Journey through Texas: Or a Saddle-Trip on the Southwestern Frontier* (New York: Dix, Edwards & Co., 1857); Frederick Law Olmsted, *A Journey in the Back Country* (New York: Mason Brothers, 1860); Frederick Law Olmsted, *The Cotton*

From *Journal of Southern History*, XI (May 1945), 147-176. Copyright 1945 by the Southern Historical Association. Reprinted by permission of the managing editor.

Kingdom (New York: Mason Brothers, 1861); Everett Dick, *The Dixie Frontier* (New York: Knopf, 1948);* Ulrich B. Phillips, "The Origin and Growth of the Southern Black Belts," *American Historical Review*, XI (July 1906), 798-816; William O. Lynch, "The Westward Flow of Southern Colonists before 1861," *Journal of Southern History*, IX (August 1943), 303-327; Lewis C. Gray, *History of Agriculture in the Southern United States to 1860*, 2 vols. (Washington, D.C.: Carnegie Institution, 1933); Avery O. Craven, *Soil Exhaustion as a Factor in the Agricultural History of Virginia and Maryland, 1606-1860* (Urbana: University of Illinois Press, 1926); Robert R. Russel, "General Effects of Slavery upon Southern Economic Progress," *Journal of Southern History*, IV (February 1938), 34-54; Robert R. Russel, "The Effects of Slavery upon Nonslaveholders in the Antebellum South," *Agricultural History*, XV (April 1941), 112-126; Fabian Linden, "Economic Democracy in the Slave South," *Journal of Negro History*, XXXI (April 1946), 140-189.

*Available in paperback.

The motives for migrating from the old, well-established communities of the United States into the fresh lands of the state and federal public domains varied with many individuals. A debtor might flee into the wilderness and divest himself of his debts as a cow rids herself of the swarms of tormenting insects by dashing through a thicket of bushes; the lawbreaker might thus get beyond the reach of the sheriff; the complexities of family and marital relations could be permanently simplified without wasting money on a lawyer and alimony by a move of a hundred miles in a well-chosen direction; old vices and old cronies could be left behind by the morally bankrupt who wished to begin life anew; tragedy might be put out of mind in a country so new and exciting. Thus sanctuary for all those desiring escape seemed to lie out beyond the fringe of settlement. Indeed, going from the old communities into the new country was, to many a migrant, like passing through a doorway, which closed behind him and through which he returned no more.

Others moved to the new country, not to seek escape but to be with their families and friends who were moving into the promised land. Love of adventure was often a powerful inducement to migrate. But the motive common to most immigrants was the desire to acquire the ownership or the free use of some portion of the public domain.

If one considers the landed resources that were available to the American people in the period between the Revolution and the Civil War, it would appear that the average American farmer, North and South, had ample opportunity of becoming a landowner; for a total of 1,309,591,680 acres had been federal lands during this time.[1] But there were also large bodies of state land on which immigrants might settle during the ante-bellum period. Much of the 22,400,000 acres that comprised the province of Maine was public land at the beginning of the period.[2] Perhaps 90 per cent of the 37,929,600 acres in Georgia was unsettled at the end of the Revolution.[3] Pennsylvania, New York, western Virginia, and western North and South Carolina contained large areas of lands yet to be disposed of by those states. Kentucky's 24,115,200 acres and Tennessee's 29,184,000 acres were just being pioneered at the close of the Revolution.[4] In 1845, Texas, having retained ownership of its public lands, possessed an imperial domain of 175,587,840 acres, about 100,000,000 acres of which were arable.[5]

The existence of these vast unsettled areas of public lands was an irresistible invitation to the land hungry to come and help themselves. And help themselves they did: speculators, land thieves, modest blackmailers who took only what the traffic would bear, squatters who wished to graze their hogs and cattle and to hunt, squatters who were carving out farmsteads and plantations, swarmed into what seemed a boundless empire.

During the interval between the Revolution and the Civil War the combined federal and state public domains in the South were greater than those in the North, while the population of the South was far less. In 1848, before the creation of Oregon as a territory, the area of the organized states and territories of the South was more than twice as great as that of the North, while the white population of the South was less than half of that of the North.[6] But the southern agricultural immigrants had another great advantage over the northern settlers, in that the grain and livestock farmers of the Upper South and the southern highlands could move into the public domain of the Northwest, while the northern farmers could not profitably move farther South.

With such great landed resources so cheap and available and such a relatively small population, it was inevitable that the majority of the agricultural population, and even those dependent upon a grazing economy, should become freeholders in the newer portions of the Old South. But the continued emigration of vast numbers from the older southern states caused a sharp decline in land values in those areas, so that those who were unable or unwilling to emigrate could purchase farms and plantations in their own community almost at frontier prices.[7]

In the settlement of the public domains of the South, there were usually two distinct waves of settlers rather than the three generally ascribed to the northern frontier. The first wave consisted of herdsmen, who subsisted primarily upon a grazing and hunting economy; and in the second wave were the agricultural immigrants, coming to possess the land. Though many families of the second wave moved regularly from one frontier to another in one generation, it seems to be true that the desire of most was to find a place for permanent settlement.

The herdsmen, who were the typical southern pioneers, resembled in many respects the pioneer settlers of the Northwest, whom John M. Peck described in his *A New Guide for Emigrants to the West*. "First," observes Peck, "comes the pioneer, who depends for the subsistence of his family chiefly upon the natural growth of vegetation, called the 'range,' and the proceeds of hunting. His implements of agriculture are rude, chiefly of his own make, and his efforts directed mainly to a crop of corn and a 'truck patch.' The last is a rude garden for growing cabbage, beans, corn for roasting ears, cucumbers and potatoes. A log cabin, and occasionally, a stable and corn crib, and a field of a dozen acres, the timber girdled of 'deadened' and fenced, are enough for his occupancy."[8] He occupies this place "till the range is somewhat subdued, and hunting a little precarious," and too many settlers come in; then he moves on to other frontiers.[9] But the pioneer whom Peck thus describes was usually a subsistence farmer and hunter, while the southern pioneer as a rule was a livestock grazier and hunter who cultivated small truck gardens and corn patches for subsistence.

That the southern pioneer should be a herdsman in a land which has not been noted for its livestock and the northern pioneer should not be a grazier in a country of fine pasture lands, may seem odd. The explanation, however, is simple. The southern pioneers were much nearer the markets than were the northern settlers west of the mountains; but, of more importance, cattle and swine could be grazed in the South without having to be fed and sheltered during the winter, whereas in the Northwest the cold weather necessitated both feeding and housing of livestock. Livestock feeding, in contrast to grazing, of course, is the occupation of a well-settled farming community that has fair access to market. It must be observed, however, that the frontier ranges in the South were all that man and beast could desire as long as they were not overgrazed. The trees were loaded with nuts and mast for the swine, and the savannas and open forests, which had been kept clear of underbrush by the annual burnings by the Indians, billowed with wild oats and grasses, vetch, and peavines "tall enough to reach the shoulder of a man on horseback"; and the swamps and valleys were covered with dense canebrakes that furnished winter pasturage and protection from the cold.[10]

The best pasture lands were always those most suited for agriculture, and the herdsmen in quest of fine pastures naturally drove their herds into those parts of the public domain which the immigrant farmers would soon occupy. The result was that all the way from the Atlantic coast to the arid regions of the Southwest and from colonial times till after the Civil War, these pastoral folk were continuously crowded from the arable lands by the agricultural folk.

Livestock grazing was a major occupation in the South as long as there were large bodies of public lands. In colonial times many fortunes were made from herding livestock upon the wild lands of the proprietors or the king. Men owned herds ranging from a few dozen into the thousands of head.[11] Alexander Gregg says that in South Carolina "the number owned by a single individual were very large, almost incredibly so."[12] A British official in the late colonial period has left a vivid picture of cattle grazing in South Carolina and Georgia. He observed great droves of cattle "under the auspices of cowpen keepers, which move (like unto the ancient patriarch or the modern Bedowin in Arabia) from forest to forest in a measure as the grass wears out or the planters approach them."[13]

In the first thirty-odd years of the nineteenth century, as the herdsmen were forced by the agricultural settlers—who cleared and fenced the land and brought along their own smaller herds—to drive their livestock farther westward into the rich prairie and canebrake lands of Alabama, Mississippi, and Louisiana, both the size and the profits of the business increased. Contemporary travelers and writers were always impressed with the great herds of cattle and swine that they observed feeding upon the luxuriant pasture lands of the public domain. Estwick Evans in traveling through the South during the year 1818 saw thousands of cattle feeding along the banks of the Mississippi in the state of Mississippi;[14] Thomas Nuttall at about the same time noted huge droves of livestock on the prairies of southwestern Louisiana and in the Red River district of Arkansas.[15] William Darby, who dwelt in the Southwest for some time and traveled extensively throughout the region in the preparation of his *Emigrant's Guide to the Western and Southern States*, also took note of the large droves of cattle along the lower Mississippi and in the western portions of Louisiana.[16] Tilly Buttrick during the same period saw the cattlemen of Kentucky pasturing their herds north of the Ohio,[17] and Fortescue Cuming, on a journey into Arkansas, found the Kentuckians grazing the lush pastures of the public domain in that territory.[18] As late as 1837 John M. Peck remarked that "much of the forest lands, in the Western [Mississippi] Valley produces a fine range for domestic animals and swine. Thousands are raised, and the emigrant, grows wealthy, from the bounties of nature, with but little labor."[19] In northern Florida cattle grazing was the chief occupation until late in the ante-bellum period. One observer wrote in 1850: "So numerous were the herds of cattle in Alachua . . . that from 7000 to 10,000 could be seen grazing at once on Payne's Prairie; and there was a single grazier on the Wacasassa whose stock had increased in the course of a few years to the number of 3000 without any other expense than that of herding them."[20]

The grazing of livestock on the agricultural lands and the lives of the herdsmen followed a regular pattern from colonial days to the Civil War. When a cattleman became wealthy he settled down in some well-selected spot, usually as a planter, and placed his livestock in charge of cowboys, who pastured them out past the fringe of settlement, along with the herds of the smaller owners living upon the frontier. William Darby describes in his *Guide*, this planter-cattleman combination in southern and western Louisiana, where the planters lived in the Teche country on their plantations, and employed cowboys, for one-fifth of the increase of the herd, to graze their livestock on the prairies far to the West. Many such cowboys acquired wealth, after which they in turn settled as planters and hired other cowboys to tend their herds out on the frontier. Frequently, too, the smaller herdsmen settled as farmers on land which they had purchased, and allowed their livestock to graze, along with those of neighboring farmers, on the unfenced farm and government lands of the community.[21]

By 1840 the better agricultural lands in the older states and in many parts of the newer ones had been sufficiently settled by farmers to interfere with grazing upon the open range, and the herdsmen had largely disappeared from such lands. Those who had not desired to settle as planters and farmers,[22] but preferred their occupation and the frontier with its plentiful game, fresh cattle ranges, and scarcity of neighbors, took up their abode in the pine forests and in the mountains where occasional graziers had already settled. Here, protected by the sterile, sandy soils of the piney woods and the rugged surface of the highlands, the herdsmen and hunters found sanctuary from the pursuing agricultural settlers. Thus it was agriculture rather than slavery that pressed these settlers into the less fertile and more rugged lands. This was an old phenomenon. From ancient times an agricultural economy has driven the livestock grazier into the deserts and the mountains, except in those states where the herdsmen control the government.[23]

The ante-bellum inhabitants of the pine belt and, to a lesser extent, of the mountains have been classified rather broadly as poor whites. While groups of the same type of people could be found scattered here and there in the rough, timbered areas that constituted numerous islands in the midst of the richer lands, the dwellers in the highlands and in the piney woods appeared to those who lived outside these regions to constitute the two chief bodies of poor whites. They lived in log cabins or hewn log houses. Their means of support visible to the usual traveler who made hasty detours through the edges of the great woods and mountains were meager indeed. There were usually a few acres of corn, patches of sweet potatoes, cabbage, collards, peas, beans, pumpkins, and turnips, and perhaps a few rows of cotton and tobacco in a "deadening" where blackened stumps of pitch pine or hardwood stood like a ghost forest. There would be a lean milk cow, two or three scrubby horses, a few razor-back hogs in a pole pen or roaming about the premises, and a pack of emaciated hounds. On the woodpile near-by would be a fine, bright bladed ax; and should the stranger peep into the cabin he would see homemade beds, tables, stools, and chairs, and the wall lined with pegs on which to hang things. Over the mantel and, if there was more than one male member of the family, on the wall in racks made of horns or pronged branches cut from trees would be the shiny, long-barreled "rifle guns." If the visitor were to go up in the "loft" he would probably find hanging from pegs numerous steel traps waiting to be set or repaired. The men seemed shiftless; for they would sit almost motionless for hours like a lizzard on a sunny log, whittling transparent shavings from a piece of pine or spruce and occasionally squirting a liberal quantity of tobacco "juice" into the eye of a pig or chicken that came too close. While the men were thus taking their ease, the women hoed the corn, cooked the dinner, or plied the loom, or even came out and took up the ax and cut wood with which to cook the dinner.[24]

Of course the great error that contemporary travelers and later writers have committed concerning the mountain and piney wood folk of the ante-bellum South has been to consider them agriculturists. Had they lived upon the plains, their livestock economy would have been apparent; but because of the great forests their herds of cows and droves of hogs were seldom to be seen by anyone passing hurriedly through the country. Nor could the economic importance of their subsidiary occupation of hunting and trapping be realized except by one who tarried long and learned the way of these taciturn folk. Another error that has helped develop the idea that the backwoodsmen and mountaineers as a class were poor whites has been the failure to regard them, during the period under consideration, in their true character as frontiersmen. Much of the mountain and pine areas was, except for the absence of the Indians, frontier country as truly as was the outer or western frontier; indeed these regions might be called the inner frontier. Great portions of the mountain country and the pine belt from Georgia to Texas were public domain until after the Civil War, and were sparsely settled and bountifully stocked with game.

Local historians, biographers, genealogists, and writers of autobiography and reminiscences, particularly lawyers, preachers, small town newspaper editors, and doctors, who have lived in and near the pine belt and mountains, possessed fuller knowledge and understanding of the life and character of the folk in these regions than did the casual traveler from the outside. A brief examination of some of their accounts will be useful in giving a more authentic view of backwoods and mountain life.

In 1840 John F. H. Claiborne of Natchez traveled slowly and systematically through the piney woods east of the Pearl River in Mississippi as a newspaper reporter in the company of a group of politicians on a political speaking tour. Claiborne's reports go right to the heart of the frontier economy of these people. It was quite obvious to him on his leisurely journey that the real business of the piney wood folk was the grazing of cattle and hogs. The beauty and abundance of the range impressed him. Much of the country, he observed, "is covered exclusively with the long leaf pine; not broken, but rolling like the waves in the middle of the great ocean. The grass grows three feet high and hill and valley are studded all over with flowers of every hue. . . . Thousands of cattle are grazed here for market."[25] "The people are for the most part pastoral, their herds furnishing their chief revenue."[26] "These cattle are permitted to run in the range or forest, subsisting in summer on the luxuriant grass with which the teeming earth is clothed, and in winter on green rushes or reeds, a tender species of cane that grow in the brakes or thickets in every swamp, hollow and ravine."[27] The trade in cattle, observed Claiborne, "has enriched many people."[28] He was amazed at the ease with which fish, wild turkeys, and other edible game were procured, and the great variety of food supplied the table on the shortest notice.[29] Only one agricultural product seems to have connected these people in his mind with farming: the incredible quantities of sweet potatoes used at all meals and between meals. He recounted with gusto one occasion on which his kindly hostess surpassed the usual hospitality in dispensing sweet potatoes. He ate sweet potatoes with wild turkey and various other meats, had a potato pie for dessert and roasted potatoes offered to him as a side dish, drank sweet potato coffee and sweet potato home brew, had his horse fed on sweet potatoes and sweet potato vines, and when he retired he slept on a mattress stuffed with sweet potato vines and dreamed that he was a sweet potato that someone was digging up.[30]

William H. Sparks, the jurist, who dwelt in the Natchez district, appears to have ridden the judicial circuit as lawyer and judge in the region described by Claiborne, where he had an opportunity of becoming closely acquainted with the piney wood folk. Later, in writing his memoirs, he devoted considerable space to a description of these people. Those settlements east of the Pearl River, he said:

. . . were constituted of a different people [from the agricultural population farther west]: most of them were from the poorer districts of Georgia and the Carolinas. True to the instincts of the people from whom they were descended, they sought as nearly as possible just such a country as that from which they came, and were really refugees from a growing civilization consequent upon a denser population and its necessities. They were not agriculturists in a proper sense of the term; true, they cultivated in some degree the soil, but it was not the prime pursuit of these people, nor was the location sought for this purpose. They desired an open, poor, pine country, which forbade a numerous population.

Here they reared immense herds of cattle, which subsisted exclusively upon coarse grass and reeds which grew abundantly among the tall, long-leafed pine, and along the small creeks and branches numerous in this section. Through these almost interminable pine-forests the deer were abundant, and the canebrakes full of bears. They combined the pursuits of hunting and stock-minding, and derived support and revenue almost exclusively from these.[31]

Sparks knew some of these people quite well and he records a significant interview with a man whose grandfather and grandmother had settled in the Mississippi backwoods—then the Indian country—a few years after the Revolutionary War. The grandfather, he told Sparks, migrated from Emanuel County, Georgia.

He carried with him a small one-horse cart pulled by an old gray mare, one feather bed, an oven, a frying-pan, two pewter dishes, six pewter plates, as many spoons, a rifle gun, and three deer-hounds. He worried through the Creek Nation, extending then from the Oconee River [in Georgia] to the Tombigbee River [flowing through parts of eastern Mississippi and western Alabama].

After four months of arduous travel he found his way to Leaf River, and there built his cabin; and with my grandmother, and my father, who was born on the trip in the heart of the Creek Nation, commenced to make a fortune. He found on a small creek of beautiful water a little bay land, and made his little field for corn and pumpkins upon that spot, all around was poor, barren woods, but he said it was a good range for stock; but he had not an ox or cow on the face of the earth. The truth is it looked like Emanuel County. The turpentine smell, the moan of the wind through the pine-trees, and nobody within fifty miles of him, was too captivating a concatenation to be resisted, and he rested here.

About five years after he came, a man from Pearl River was driving some cattle by to Mobile, and gave my grandfather two cows to help drive his cattle. It was over one hundred miles, and you would have supposed it a dear bargain; but it turned out well, for the old man in about six weeks got back with six other head of cattle [he had obviously been engaged in a bit of cattle rustling]. From these he commenced to rear a stock which in time became large [which indeed, according to Sparks' account, developed into a sizeable fortune]. [32]

The great pine belt of Alabama was primarily a cattle country. F. L. Cherry, writing in 1883, described one portion of the pine belt of that state, extending up into Russell County near which he had lived for fifty years:

There is a section of country about a hundred square miles or more, between the Chewakla and the Uchee Creeks, which fifty years ago [1833] would not number more than a dozen families and they were mostly cow "boys". This section was known as "Piney Woods" of Russell County, and as compared with the country on the creeks, was considered very poor, and profitably available only as a stock range. . . . As the land was nearly all public domain, and a market near at hand, the stock business was receiving considerable attention, and moderate fortunes soon accumulated. [33]

Cherry also said that piney woods people raised no corn the first few years, and "but little of anything else except stock which ran wild on the public domain." [34] In 1855 the pine lands of Alabama were still regarded as an unbroken forest affording "a fine stock range," practically undisturbed by the plowman; [35] indeed until after the Civil War little change had occurred and cattle grazing still prevailed. [36]

It is estimated that in the contiguous piney woods districts in northwestern Florida, southern Alabama, and southeastern Mississippi, there were 1,000,000 head of cattle in 1850. [37] This is probably too high, but there were certainly no less than 650,000 head of cattle in this area, and a proportionate number of sheep and swine. [38] The Alabama piney woods county of Covington may be taken as typical of this grazing region. With a population of 3,645 and with only 9,201 acres under cultivation in 1850, this county had 824 horses and mules, 10,617 head of cattle, 1,306 sheep, and 18,272 swine. [39]

In Georgia, and wherever there was a considerable area of sandy, pine-clad country, the story was the same. Simon Peter Richardson, a Methodist circuit rider and presiding elder on practically every circuit and district in northern Florida and southern Georgia during the late ante-bellum period, has left his impressions of the piney woods folk. In 1843 he was given the Irwin circuit, composed almost exclusively of the piney woods of southern Georgia. Richardson in his autobiography describes the country and the people of this circuit:

[It] . . . reached from Mobly Bluff to the Okenefenokee swamp; a round of about two hundred and fifty miles, to be traveled in three weeks. The most of the people then lived by raising stock. . . . There were many good, kind families on the circuit. Everybody was hospitable in those days, whether he had much or little. I went round the circuit. The congregations were meager. All the church houses were small log cabins, and the seats were benches without backs. The people were nearly all dressed homespun. . . . The whole country was a vast plain of long leaf pine forest. Sometimes the settlements were ten miles apart: but other parts were thickly settled. [40]

Richardson later occupied some of the richest charges in his conference, yet of the fifty charges he had held when he wrote his autobiography, he considered the Irwin circuit of the pine barrens one of the most satisfactory of them all.[41]

William P. Fleming, basing his account in part upon the testimony of surviving pioneers, gives a vivid picture of Crisp County, Georgia, and its grazing economy. The pine lands of Crisp, he said:

were by that very classification, adjudged not the best for farm purposes, and, besides, these lands were fearfully "cumbered" with primitive forests of immense pines. Their adaptation to pasturage purposes, however, was apparent. Much of these lands, especially low lands hereabouts, grew wild oats in profusion, and the more elevated lands were heavily carpeted with wire grass, succulent and desirable to a prospective cattleman. A few older people now living are familiar with the fact that droves of cattle and sheep, numbering thousands, might be hidden from sight in wild oats when only a short distance from someone searching for them.

Cattle, hog, and sheep raising, he continued, "was the principal business" until the sawmills cut the timber in the 1880's and 1890's.[42]

The importance of herding livestock in the Georgia pine belt and the almost exclusive devotion of its inhabitants to this business is shown in the census reports. In 1850, for example, the Georgia pine barrens, comprising about one-fourth of the area of the state and having about one-tenth of the population, produced over 400,000 head of cattle, 85,000 sheep, 356,000 swine, and 36,000 horses and mules.[43] This was nearly half the cattle, and about one-sixth of the sheep, swine, horses, and mules of the state. The huge county of Ware, with only 3,888 people and 11,316 acres under cultivation, had, according to the 1850 census, 781 horses and mules, 919 sheep, 20,993 head of cattle, and 26,054 swine.

The mountains were better ranges than the pine belt, for the soil was often fertile. In fact, more cattle, swine, and sheep per capita were raised in the Appalachians, the Cumberland Plateau, and the Ozarks than in the bluegrass basins of Kentucky and Tennessee.[44] But because of the difficulty of the terrain, cattle and herdsmen were unable to utilize as great a territory as could be grazed in the pine belt. Those who were fortunate enough, however, to gain control of the entrance of a high valley with ranges practically encircling it, had a natural pasture into which they might turn their cattle without danger of their straying. In May, cattle, horses, and sheep were turned into the mountains and allowed to remain there until October. The owners would visit their herds once a week and salt them to keep them gentle and prevent them from straying too far. In the fall they would drive them to market, usually on the coast. Through Buncombe County alone, high in the mountains of western North Carolina, 150,000 hogs and thousands of cattle passed annually on their way to market.[45] Unlike the pine belt, however, there were many rich valleys in which grain farmers raised huge quantities of corn to sell to the cattlemen to fatten the livestock for market or to feed them on their way to market. There were numerous "stock stands" along the French Broad River which fed 90,000 to 100,000 hogs a month while en route to market. Frequently, there would be 2,000 in one drove to be fed.[46] While cattle were grazed in large numbers just as in the piney woods, hogs were more important than cattle, for the hardwood growth produced immense crops of chestnuts, acorns, walnuts, and hickory nuts, and in the rich narrow valleys excellent corn could be grown. Not only did the mountains of North Carolina contribute to this stream of porkers and cattle; but many also came from those of Kentucky and Tennessee. In 1849-1850 at least 81,000 head of swine were driven to the east coast from the mountains in the two latter states.[47] The Cumberland Plateau was covered with grass "where an immense pasturage is afforded to the cattle," observed the British traveler, George W. Featherstonhaugh, in 1834.[48] Even the oak barrens on the highland rim in Tennessee to the west of the plateau was devoted primarily to grazing cattle and hogs.[49]

Frederick L. Olmsted has left what may be accepted as a very good generalized picture of mountain economy in the late ante-bellum period.

The hills generally afford an excellent range, and the mast is usually good, much being provided by the chestnut, as well as the oak, and smaller nut-bearing trees. The soil of the hills is a rich dark vegetable deposit, and they cultivate upon very steep slopes. It is said to wash and gully but little, being very absorbtive. The valleys, and gaps across the mountain ranges, are closely settled, and all the feasible level ground that I saw in three weeks was fenced, and either under tillage or producing grass for hay. . . . Horses, mules, cattle and swine, are raised extensively, and sheep and goats in smaller numbers throughout the mountains, and afford almost the only articles of agricultural export.[50]

Ashe and Buncombe counties of North Carolina, located high up in the Smoky Mountains, may be considered typical of the mountains. In 1850 Ashe had a population of 8,777 and had only 64,805 acres under cultivation. There were in the county 2,713 horses and mules, 14,675 head of cattle, 18,250 sheep, and 25,267 swine. Buncombe's population at this time was 13,425, and there were 75,360 acres under cultivation. The county had 3,708 horses and mules, 16,349 head of cattle, 14,000 sheep, and 28,608 swine.[51]

There are no adequate statistics for the livestock business prior to the census of 1840; but grazing as distinct from livestock feeding was of greater relative importance in the ante-bellum South than in any other part of the United States. Indeed, the South produced a larger number of mules, swine, and beef cattle in proportion to population than any section until 1860, when the sparsely settled Pacific states led in cattle raising.[52] This leading position was due largely to the presence of vast bodies of unimproved land, not only in the mountains and pine barrens, but interspersed all through the less fertile and swampy areas of the arable lands. The table below[53] gives the total area of each southern state with the improved acreage for 1850 and 1860, and it can be seen at a glance that the bulk of land in the South was unimproved.

The states of Arkansas, Texas, and Florida had scarcely been touched by the ax and the plow before the Civil War, and only a fraction of the land, ranging from about one-ninth of the total in Louisiana to nearly half in Maryland, had been put to agricultural uses in the other southern states.

A summary of livestock production in the southern states and in the Old Northwest, the section in the North that ranked next to the South, is presented in the following table.[54] This will show the comparative value of livestock production in the South which was so largely based upon grazing the open range.

The relative importance of livestock production in the Northwest and the South can be more easily seen from a comparison of the average per capita ownership of livestock in each state. The following table computed from the preceding table, gives the average ownership of each person in several states in terms of dollar evaluation.

States	Total Acreage	Improved Land	
		1850	*1860*
Arkansas	33,410,063	751,530	1,983,313
Florida	37,931,520	349,049	654,213
Texas	175,587,840	643,976	2,650,781
Kentucky	24,115,200	5,968,270	7,644,208
Tennessee	29,184,000	5,175,173	6,795,337
Missouri	41,836,931	2,938,425	6,246,871
Mississippi	30,179,840	3,444,358	5,065,755
Louisiana	26,461,440	1,590,025	2,707,108
Alabama	32,462,115	4,435,614	6,385,724
Georgia	37,120,000	6,378,479	8,062,758
South Carolina	21,760,000	4,072,051	4,572,060
North Carolina	32,450,560	5,453,975	6,517,284
Virginia	39,262,720	10,360,135	11,437,821
Maryland	7,119,360	2,797,905	3,002,257

Old Northwest

State	Population	Horses Mules	Cattle	Sheep	Swine	Value of Livestock
Ohio	1,757,556	466,820	1,358,947	3,942,929	1,964,770	44,121,741
Indiana	931,392	321,898	714,966	1,122,493	2,263,776	22,478,555
Illinois	736,931	278,226	912,036	894,043	1,915,907	24,209,258
Michigan	341,591	58,576	274,449	746,435	205,847	8,008,734
Wisconsin	197,912	30,335	183,433	124,896	159,276	4,897,385

The South

State	Population	Horses Mules	Cattle	Sheep	Swine	Value of Livestock
Virginia	1,421,666	293,886	1,076,269	1,310,004	1,829,843	33,658,659
North Carolina	869,039	173,952	693,510	595,249	1,812,813	17,717,647
South Carolina	668,507	134,654	777,686	285,551	1,065,503	15,060,015
Georgia	906,185	208,710	1,097,528	560,435	2,168,617	25,728,416
Alabama	771,622	187,896	728,015	371,880	1,904,540	21,690,122
Florida	87,444	15,850	261,085	23,315	209,453	2,880,058
Mississippi	606,526	170,007	733,970	304,929	1,582,734	19,887,580
Arkansas	209,897	71,756	292,710	91,256	836,727	6,647,969
Louisiana	517,762	134,363	575,342	116,110	597,301	11,152,275
Texas	212,592	89,223	330,114	100,530	692,022	10,412,927
Missouri	682,044	266,986	791,510	762,511	1,702,625	19,887,580
Kentucky	982,405	381,291	752,502	1,102,091	2,891,163	29,661,436
Tennessee	1,002,717	345,939	750,762	811,591	3,104,800	29,978,416
Maryland	583,034	81,328	219,586	177,902	352,911	7,997,634

The second wave of settlers to come into the public domain were, as previously observed, the farmers and planters who desired the ownership rather than the free use of some portion of the public domain. The migratory direction of an agricultural people is

The Old Northwest		The South	
State	*Per capita value of livestock*	*State*	*Per capita value of livestock*
Wisconsin	$24.74	Arkansas	$31.67
Michigan	23.44	Florida	32.93
Ohio	25.67	Texas	48.98
Indiana	24.13	Kentucky	30.19
Illinois	32.85	Tennessee	29.89
		Missouri	29.15
		Mississippi	32.75
		Louisiana	21.53
		Alabama	28.10
		Georgia	28.39
		South Carolina	22.52
		North Carolina	20.38
		Virginia	23.67
		Maryland	13.72

determined, where there is a choice, by several factors. The agricultural immigrant far more than the herdsman has a tendency to seek out a country as nearly as possible like the one in which he formerly lived, in the matter of soil, rainfall, temperature, and appearance—that is, having similar topography, streams, trees, and grasses. The similarity of appearance is of great importance for both psychological and practical reasons. The fact that the emigrant shakes from his feet the dust of his old community does not mean that he divests himself of the mental picture and love of the old countryside, of those rich limestone valleys, rolling hills, and sandy levels where the odor of the resinous pine scents the air and the tall trees moan in the wind, or of the rugged mountains with purple shadows and smoke hanging above the cove in the late afternoon, announcing the cheery news of supper a-cooking or the still making a run. A settler simply could never be entirely happy and at home unless he was surrounded by a landscape much like the one where he had spent his earlier years. Those accustomed to rugged country seldom debouched upon the plains, but migrated to a country where there were other hills and valleys—the Ozarks, for example, were largely settled by those from the Appalachians—while those who had inhabited level country usually avoided the hills unless they could settle in a wide valley with the hills in the distance. Those who had lived in a wooded country shunned the open prairies.

Aside from sentiment that grows into acute nostalgia in strange surroundings, the agricultural migrants—though to a much lesser degree the pastoral folk—have scientific and practical reasons for selecting a country similar to the one from which they emigrate. The basic and sound assumption of the farmer who seeks a country similar in appearance, climate, and soil to the old community in which he has lived is that he can continue in the new country to grow the field crops, fruits, and vegetables, the tillage, habits, and marketing of which are part of his mental furniture. "Men seldom change their climate," observed the superintendent of the Bureau of the Census in 1860, "because to do so they must change their habits."[55] William H. Sparks, who himself had migrated west, remarked that the emigrants were sure to select their new home, as nearly as possible, "in the same parallel, and with surroundings as nearly like those they had left as possible. With the North Carolinian, good springwater, and pine-knots for his fire, were the *sine qua non*." [56] Paul Vidal de La Blache, the geographer, applies this principle to the migratory movements of the Chinese into the unsettled areas within their own country. "How," he asks, "could such individuals contrive to get along there, if unable to live in customary ways, and with customary means?" They must "find an environment similar to the one which they have been obliged to leave." [57] Isaiah Bowman observes that the primary function of the individuals who went out upon the American frontier to locate a fit place for settlement for themselves and their neighbors usually "consisted merely in finding soils and slopes that resembled those back at home that were known to be good." [58] The letters and diaries of pioneers abound with reports to those in the East that the soil and climate of the new country were like those back at home. As a result of such reassuring knowledge, "one great bugbear of pulling up stakes and removing to a distant home was greatly neutralized by this comfortable feeling that, however great the distance and the consequent toil, men knew toward what kind of haven they were faring and that they would meet there conditions which they had mastered before."[59]

It was soon known by the average person in the eastern states that, outside the highlands, the temperature, rainfall, and soil of the country lying to the west, until the Great Plains were approached, were sufficiently like those in the East to permit the continuation of the same types of agriculture. This information was derived from land prospectors, and the emigrant guides prepared by such writers as William Darby, who made a careful study of these and related matters; but chiefly from the reports of the herdsmen, who had raised their little patches of corn, truck, tobacco, and cotton while hunting and grazing their livestock on the frontier. By 1860 the trend of migration had been scientifically examined by the Census Office on the basis of the nativity reports in the census tables of 1850 and 1860, and the superintendent of the census was able to state the fact that "the almost universal law of internal migration is, that it moves west on the same parallel of latitude."[60]

The necessity of continuing to grow the usual crops was not the sole practical motive that prompted the immigrant farmer to settle upon land like that which he had cultivated in the East. Of great importance was the need to continue to employ the methods and tools with which he was familiar. Those accustomed to the use of certain farm implements adapted to one kind of soil had great difficulty in changing to another type of soil, even though such a change did not entail any change in their farm economy. This was particularly true of those who, having cultivated sandy or loamy soils, moved into gummy clays and lime soils. Indeed there has been since ancient times a preference among agricultural folk for a soil with a sand or silt content because of the greater ease with which it can be cultivated.[61]

The implication of this prejudice in favor of a country similar in climate, surface appearance, streams and springs, soil, and the natural growth of grass, timber, and wild flowers, is this: the farmers making new homes in the West were, in the majority of cases, not in search of the richest lands of the public domain, but merely the richest of the particular type of land to which they were accustomed back in the East. Perhaps in most cases they were content with land almost identical with that left behind except that the new land was fresh.

Naturally, therefore, the rural folk of the Upper South dwelling in the limestone valleys and highlands, whose pattern of farm husbandry had been the growing of grain and livestock, did not erupt into the Lower South where climate and soil would force a radical change in farm economy and methods of cultivation. On the contrary, when they migrated it was usually into the highlands, limestone basins, and valleys of Tennessee, Kentucky, Missouri, and northern Arkansas and into the wooded lands across the Ohio River, where climate, soil, timber, and the grasses indicated that the new country would be hospitable to the familiar old crops. Both Darby and Peck, in their guides for emigrants, observed this westerly trend of the agricultural migrants,[62] and the federal censuses of 1850 and 1860 fully sustain their observations. In 1850 there were 142,102 free natives of Virginia living in the upper southern states of Missouri, Kentucky, and Tennessee, and 155,978 living in the Old Northwest; but in the lower southern states of Georgia, Florida, Alabama, Mississippi, Louisiana, Arkansas, and Texas there were only 38,311 such Virginians. The Virginians had settled chiefly in the tobacco, grain, and livestock regions. Maryland exemplifies better than Virginia the zonal trend of the migration of agricultural folk. In 1850 over 30,000 free natives of that state were living in Virginia and Pennsylvania—obviously the western portions—, 54,310 in the Old Northwest, 12,277 in Tennessee, Kentucky, and Missouri, and only 4,722 in the seven states of the Lower South mentioned above. Thus Maryland contributed little either to the upper or lower southern states west of the mountains. North Carolina which, outside of the highlands, is essentially a state of the Lower South, had 103,315 free natives living in Tennessee, Kentucky, and Missouri, 52,467 in the Old Northwest, and 107,912 in the newer states of the Lower South.[63]

The Carolinas settled Georgia, and, with considerable aid from Virginia, settled Tennessee. The remainder of the states of the Lower South were the children and grandchildren of the Carolinas, Georgia, and Tennessee. In 1850 there were 140,261 free native South Carolinians, 140,041 Georgians, 99,140 North Carolinians, and 79,640 Tennesseans living in the newer states of the Lower South compared with about 43,000 from Virginia and Maryland. Though Tennessee and North Carolina had contributed heavily to the upper slave states and to the Old Northwest, South Carolina and Georgia had only 12,000 free natives in that region in 1850.

The census of 1860 continues to show the westward trend of population in the South, the newer states such as Alabama, Mississippi, Tennessee, and Kentucky contributing heavily to the states in the same zones to the west.[64]

The first agricultural settlers in the new farm lands in the Southwest as a rule came from the piedmont of "up-country" of the Carolinas and Georgia where they had already been engaged in the cultivation of cotton, and where the soil was similar in its clay and sand contents to much of the soil of the new country. Local pioneer writers agree that the early settlers of the Southwest—especially Alabama and Mississippi—were up-country Carolinians or Tennesseans, many of whom had originally come from up-country South Carolina. For example, most of the South Carolinians, who moved into Blount, Jefferson, and Pickens counties, Alabama, were from the York, Abbeville, and Fairfield districts,[65] very similar both in soil and in topography to the country in which they settled. More recent studies show that in all parts of Alabama as late as 1828, most of those immigrants whose origin could be ascertained came not from the tidewater regions of the South Atlantic states, but from the piedmont, where they had been cultivating the short staple cotton. Few of the tidewater planters migrated into the Southwest during this period, probably because their heavy investments in land, the stability of their principal money crops—rice, tobacco, and long staple cotton—and their established social position tended to hold them where they were.[66] But it may well be that the climate of the Southwest, which was not hospitable to the culture of rice, tobacco, and long staple cotton, was a decisive factor in retarding the migration from the low country.

These up-country cotton farmers and planters who settled in the newer lands, as has been suggested, selected the lighter sandy loam and sand and clay soils in preference to the stiff clays and rich black prairie lands. A. J. Brown, in his history of Newton County, Mississippi, observed that the early settlers in that region preferred the poorer sandy lands to the richer prairies and clay soils. "The prairies of the county were very open; thousands of acres of this kind of land were entirely unobstructed by timber or undergrowth, and were very easily brought into a state of cultivation. The level, sandy and uplands were much more in demand, as the people much preferred the level uplands to the ridges or prairies."[67] Nettie Powell noted the same thing in Marion County, Georgia. "The section south of where Buena Vista now is and leading towards Draneville was known as 'turkey ridge,' and was not attractive to early settlers on account of the hard red clay soil [indicating rich soil] which was not easy to cultivate with the wooden plows that were then in use. The most of this region was left vacant until the middle thirties."[68]

The method of migration and settlement in the South was fairly uniform during the pioneer period. Friends and relatives living in the same or neighboring communities formed one or more parties and moved out together, and when they had reached the promised land they constituted a new community, which was called a "settle-ment"—and still is so called. Settlements were frequently miles apart, and the inhabitants of a single settlement would be more scattered than they had been in the old community in the East; and other settlers would come in after the first trek in smaller groups or in single families and fill in the interstices. These later comers would often be relatives or friends of those who had come first, or friends of their friends. Frequently church congregations would move in a body into the Southwest or an entire hamlet or community would simply evacuate and march together into the "land of milk and honey." In describing the settlement of Wilkinson County, Georgia, Victor Davidson observes that "frequently large tracts were purchased and whole communities [from the older parts of the state and the Upper South] would move and settle on them. There were instances where congregations would follow their pastors here."[69] One entire community from Virginia "came in a body from that State and purchased lands near each other."[70]

The migration of a family group from Abbeville, South Carolina, to Cherokee County in the Coosa River Valley of Alabama in 1835, has been described by one of the members of the group. "In November 1835," he says, "we bade adieu to friends and left the old homestead never to look upon it again. . . . Late in the afternoon of our first day's travel we were joined, as we rolled on, by my maternal grandparents and several other members of the family, the party thus numbering forty or fifty souls."[71] Similarly, the migration from Alabama into Louisiana and Texas about 1840 was made in groups. On one occasion, for example, "some thirty families, forming a single party, are said to have met near Clarksville, and started together in their wagons for Louisiana and Texas."[72] One of the most interesting group migrations into the wilderness was that of the Presbyterian congregation of Bethel Church which came in a body from Williamsburg district of Columbia, South Carolina, and settled in Maury County, Tennessee, in 1808, where they established their church, "Zion," and their Zion community—which has remained virtually intact until this day.[73] The settlements at Watauga and in neighboring valleys, the Cumberland settlements, and those of the Kentucky bluegrass basin, such as Harrodsburg and Boonesboro, are all too well known as group undertakings to need more than mention. Such examples might be endlessly repeated. Thus the early communities of the newer states and territories were essentially transplanted organisms rather than synthetic bodies.

These groups did not move into the public domain in ignorance of their exact location; but rather, like the children of Israel, they sent their Calebs and Joshuas ahead to spy out the land and prepare the way. An early description of Blount County, Alabama, relates how the plain folk chose their location and how they made ready for the families to settle in a new community. As they prepared to move into the wilderness, the prospective immigrants usually sent

> . . . *a few strong men, generally their sons, without families, deep into the then wilderness in the fall, to make corn and prepare for them. The father generally went with them and chose the place, and then went back to prepare for moving when the corn was made. A bushel of meal will suffice a man one month, and if he has no other than wild meat, he will require even less bread. In the fall season, place three or four men, one hundred miles in a wilderness, with proper tools and two horses, they will pack their bread stuff for the hundred miles—procure their meat—clear land—and produce corn sufficient to bread one hundred persons one year.*[74]

Blount County, which comprised much of northern and western Alabama at the time of the first settlement in 1816 and 1817, was settled in this fashion.

The same preparations made in the migration of families of wealth are easily traced in the case of the family of Judge Charles Tait. The Taits lived in Elbert County, Georgia, from which many of the early settlers of Alabama migrated. In January, 1817, Charles Tait commissioned his son, Captain James A. Tait, to go into the public domain of Alabama territory to select a future home for the family. The father gave careful specifications as to the type of place to select. There were certain characteristics that the place must possess, he said:

> . . . *such as a stream near at hand for a mill and machinery—a never failing spring at the foot of a hillock, on the summit of which a mansion house can be built in due time; that it have an extensive back range where our cattle and hogs can graze and fatten without the aid of corn houses, that on the right and left there is an extensive body of good land where will settle a number of good neighbors and from whom the pleasure and benefits of society will soon be realized.*[75]

In December of the same year Captain Tait wrote his father that he would go the next year to the Alabama territory, taking two or three Negroes with him, and would buy a few Negroes in Alabama, where they would make a corn crop. Later, when it was safe, the family was to be brought to the new home.[76] With several Negroes—and presumably several of his neighbors—he proceeded to the present Wilcox County and became a squatter on the public domain, where he raised a crop of corn just as had the small farmers who came to Blount County in northern Alabama in the same year. After a year on the public domain he purchased some land at two dollars an acre; but the government held most of the land off the market and he complained to his father that "we shall have to make another crop on the public land. The failure of the sale of all the townships advertised is a grievous and most mortifying disappointment to those generally settled on the land and to us in particular."[77]

In the meantime, the neighbors were moving into the Alabama territory, some of them to become neighbors of the Taits at their new home at Fort Claiborne—where a place on the bluffs of a river was selected with the requirements that met the elder Tait's specifications. The son's letters show that the trek from Elbert County had begun even before he himself set out to select a plantation. "Mr. Goode and family started yesterday for the Alabama territory," he reported in November, 1817. "Gov. Bibb will start on Thursday, I believe, Esquire Barnet was to have broke ground on Thursday last, his son-in-law Taliafero, follows in about three weeks, and I suppose his son Thomas in the course of the winter. Thus you see the present inhabitants are moving off."[78]

In the main outline, then, migration and settlement on the southern frontier followed a pattern. The herdsmen who combined livestock grazing with hunting pioneered the arable lands, and they were closely followed, if not pursued, by the agricultural settlers. When the best lands had been taken up by the farmers, the smaller herdsmen who had not become farmers and planters retreated with their droves of cattle and swine into the pine barrens and highlands, where they would be protected from the encroachment of agriculture by poor or rugged land.

The agricultural folk in migrating into the public domain sought a country as similar as possible to the country in which they had lived. The reasons for this were the natural love of familiar environment and the necessity of continuing the accustomed farm husbandry, which only a country similar to the old one in climate, soil, and natural growth could meet. The migrants thus found themselves moving in a westerly direction along those isothermal lines or temperature zones in which they had lived in the East. Grain and cattle farmers of the Upper South remained such and settled in the Upper South to the west of the mountains and in the lower portion of the Old Northwest. Tobacco and cotton farmers did likewise and moved into the middle and lower southern territories and states. Before migrating, one or more representatives of a group spied out the land, whereupon the group—which was frequently a congregation or neighborhood—moved out together and became neighbors in the new country.

This pattern of migration and settlement had a significant bearing upon the social and economic structure of the Old South and the New. The herdsmen, who withdrew to the rugged and sterile lands in order that they might continue the occupation that they preferred, placed drastic limitations upon their own future economic well-being. As long as the pine belt and highlands were not overcrowded by man and beast, the range remained good and these semi-pastoral folk lived well and possessed a strong sense of security. They were certainly not poor whites as a class; but neither were many of them wealthy. Eventually, when these regions began to be crowded—and this was happening in a few places prior to the Civil War—the people would be compelled to graze fewer cattle and cultivate more and more land until they would find themselves farmers cultivating poor soil without much knowledge of agriculture.

Those agricultural immigrants who had deliberately shunned the fertile but tough clay and lime soils and had settled upon inferior sandy-loam lands placed limitations—though not as severe—upon their future economic prosperity in a way similar to the piney wood and mountain folk. While many became well-to-do, few became rich, for the economic level of an agricultural people can rise but little above the level of the fertility of the soil.

On such lands were many large farmers and small planters with ten or fifteen slaves, but there were few if any large planters. Those agricultural migrants who moved into the rich lands were most fortunate; for, while most who settled in the black belt were possessed of only moderate means at the time of settlement, nearly all rose greatly in the economic scale and many who were poor in the beginning became immensely wealthy before 1860. There were thus several regions differing greatly in fertility of soil, and consequently in wealth. As between these regions there was segregation; but within each region there was very little. In the black belt, for example, the property of the non-slaveholders and the great planters lay intermingled, and the census and tax lists show that the values of their lands and their agricultural productions per acre were about the same.

Notes

1. Benjamin H. Hibbard, *A History of the Public Land Policies* (New York, 1924), 78; Thomas C. Donaldson, *The Public Domain; Its History, with Statistics* (Washington, 1884), table on p. 13.

2. Roy M. Robbins, *Our Landed Heritage; The Public Domain, 1776-1936* (Princeton, 1924), 9.

3. Samuel G. McLendon, *History of the Public Domain of Georgia* (Atlanta, 1924), *passim*.

4. Robbins, *Our Landed Heritage*, 9, 26-27; Donaldson, *Public Domain*, 202; Hibbard, *Public Land Policies*, 78.

5. *De Bow's Review* (New Orleans, 1846-1880), XIII (1852), 53. See Aldon S. Lang, *Financial History of the Public Lands in Texas* (Waco, 1932), and Reuben McKitrick, *The Public Land System of Texas, 1823-1910* (Madison, 1918), for detailed treatment of the landed resources of Texas.

6. See Donaldson, *Public Domain*, 28-29, for areas of states and territories.

7. Avery O. Craven, *Soil Exhaustion as a Factor in the Agricultural History of Virginia and Maryland, 1606-1860* (Urbana, 1926), 118, 120, 122-25; Avery O. Craven, *Edmund Ruffin, Southerner; A Study in Secession* (New York, 1932), 52, 53, 63; Luther P. Jackson, *Free Negro Labor and Property Holding in Virginia, 1830-1860* (New York, 1942), 35, 36.

8. John M. Peck, *A New Guide for Emigrants to the West* (Boston, 1837), 119-20.

9. *Ibid.*, 120.

10. Sallie W. Stockard, *The History of Guilford County, North Carolina* (Knoxville, 1902), 55-56; Hope S. Chamberlain, *History of Wake County, North Carolina* (Raleigh, 1922), 69; Victor Davidson, *History of Wilkinson County* [Georgia] (Macon, 1930), 107-108; William P. Fleming, *Crisp County, Georgia, Historical Sketches* (Cordele, Ga., 1932), 24-25; Jethro Rumple, *A History of Rowan County, North Carolina* (Salisbury, 1881), 28-29, 54; A. J. Brown, *History of Newton County, Mississippi, from 1834 to 1894* (Jackson, 1894), 40-44; George G. Smith, *The Life and Letters of James Osgood Andrew, Bishop of the Methodist Episcopal Church South* (Nashville, 1883), 23; George E. Brewer, History of Coosa County, Alabama (MS. in Alabama Department of Archives and History, Montgomery), 48, 49.

11. Joseph Schafer, *The Social History of American Agriculture* (New York, 1936), 93, 94, 95, 96; Lewis C. Gray; *History of Agriculture in the Southern United States to 1860*, 2 vols. (Washington, 1933), I, 148-51, 200-212; Bartholomew R. Carroll (ed.), *Historical Collections of South Carolina*, 2 vols. (New York, 1836), II, 129; Alexander Gregg, *History of the Old Cheraws* (Columbia, 1905), 109, 110; William A. Schaper, *Sectionalism and Representation in South Carolina*, in American Historical Association, *Annual Report*, 1900, I (Washington, 1901), 295, 318-19.

12. Gregg, *History of the Old Cheraws*, 109.

13. Quoted in Schaper, *Sectionalism in South Carolina*, 295, and Gray, *History of Agriculture in the Southern United States*, I, 148.

14. Estwick Evans, *A Pedestrious Tour*, in Reuben G. Thwaites (ed.), *Early Western Travels, 1748-1846*, 32 vols. (Cleveland, 1904-1907), VIII, 303.

15. Thomas Nuttall, *Journal of Travels into the Arkansas Territory*, in Thwaites (ed.), *Early Western Travels*, XIII, 311.

16. William Darby, *The Emigrant's Guide to the Western and Southwestern States and Territories* (New York, 1818), 76-77.

17. Tilly Buttrick, *Voyages, Travels, and Discoveries, 1812-1819*, in Thwaites (ed.), *Early Western Travels*, VIII, 78.

18. Fortescue Cuming, *Sketches of a Tour to the Western Country (1807-1809)*, in Thwaites (ed.), *Early Western Travels*, IV, 298.

19. Peck, *New Guide for Emigrants*, 41.

20. Quoted in Gray, *History of Agriculture in the Southern United States*, II, 834. Chapter XXXV of this work gives a sketch of the cattle business in the South for the post-revolutionary and ante-bellum period. See also, Brown, *History of Newton County*, 54, 55, 56; Simon P. Richardson, *The Lights and Shadows of Itinerant Life: An Autobiography* (Nashville, 1901), 86; Timothy H. Ball, *A Glance into the Great South-East; or Clarke County, Alabama, and Its Surroundings from 1540 to 1877* (Grove Hill, Ala., 1882), *passim*; Timothy Flint, *Recollections of the Last Ten Years* (Boston, 1826), 265.

21. Darby, *Emigrant's Guide*, 76-77. Cf. Schafer, *Social History of American Agriculture*, 93-97.

22. But it was no simple matter to change from a grazing economy to agriculture. Paul M. J. Vidal de La Blache, *Principles of Human Geography* (edited by Emmanuel de Martonne, translated from the French by Millicent T. Bingham, New York, 1926), 124, note 15, quotes a letter from M. Woeikof in support of the difficulty of changing from a grazing to an agricultural economy: "As far as I know the change from nomad [livestock grazing] to farmer does not occur except under the influence and in imitation of agricultural neighbors." See also, Norman S. B. Gras, *A History of Agriculture in Europe and America* (New York, 1925), 9-10.

23. Vidal de La Blache, *Principles of Human Geography*, 54, note 9, and 130-31. Invaders like the nomadic Mongols and Huns into weak agricultural states have imposed their economic system upon the country. In a mountainous country like Greece and much of the Balkans, livestock grazing has been more important than agriculture and has been able to push the farmer out of many a small valley.

24. Frederick L. Olmsted, *A Journey in the Seaboard Slave States, with Remarks on Their Economy* (New York, 1856), 348-51, gives a traditional picture of piney woods people. See also, *De Bow's Review*, XVIII (1855), 188-89.

25. John F. H. Claiborne, "A Trip through the Piney Woods," in *Mississippi Historical Society Publications* (Oxford-Jackson, 1898-1925), IX (1906), 514.

26. *Ibid.*, 515. Cf. *ibid.*, 523, 533.

27. *Ibid.*, 521. Cf. *ibid.*, 530.

28. *Ibid.*, 522. Cf. *ibid.*, 521.

29. *Ibid.*, 516, 522.

30. *Ibid.*, 532-33.

31. William H. Sparks, *The Memories of Fifty Years* (Philadelphia, 1870), 331.

32. *Ibid.*, 332-33.

33. F. L. Cherry, The History of Opelika and Her Agricultural Tributary Territory (MS. in Alabama Department of Archives and History), 160.

34. *Ibid.*, 163.

35. "On the Forests and Timber of South Alabama," in *De Bow's Review*, XIX (1855), 611-13. Cf. Lewis Troost, "Mobile and Ohio Railroad," *ibid.*, III (1847), 322.

36. Joseph Hodgson (ed.), *Alabama Manual and Statistical Register for 1869* (Montgomery, 1869), 18-19. Cf. *ibid.*, for 1868, pp. 148-49.

37. Gray, *History of Agriculture in the Southern United States*, II, 834.

38. See *Seventh Census of the United States: 1850* (Washington, 1853), Table XI, 407-409, 429-33, and 456-60, for livestock production by counties in Florida, Alabama, and Mississippi.

39. *Ibid.*, Table XI, 429-33.

40. Richardson, *Lights and Shadows of Itinerant Life*, 26-27. See Also, Smith, *Life and Letters of James O. Andrew*, 23.

41. Richardson, *Lights and Shadows of Itinerant Life*, 43.

42. Fleming, *Crisp County Historical Sketches*, 24-25. See also, Davidson, *History of Wilkinson County*, 107-108, for a similar description of the range in the piney woods of Georgia at an earlier time.

43. *Seventh Census*, Table XI, 377-84, for livestock, and Table I, 364-65, for population.

44. Gray, *History of Agriculture in the Southern United States*, II, 876, 884.

45. John P. Arthur, *Western North Carolina; A History* (Raleigh, 1914), 285.

46. *Ibid.*, 285-87.

47. "The Hog Business in the West," in *De Bow's Review*, XVI (1854), 539-40.

48. George W. Featherstonhaugh, *Excursion through the Slave States*, 2 vols. (London, 1844), I, 185.

49. William T. Hale, *History of De Kalb County, Tennessee* (Nashville, 1915), 49.

50. Frederick L. Olmsted, *A Journey in the Back Country* (New York, 1860), 222-23.

51. *Seventh Census*, Table XI, 318-24, for agricultural production, and Table I, 307-308 for population.

52. *Eighth Census of the United States, 1860: Agriculture* (Washington, 1864), cxii-cxiii, cxxv-cxxvii, and cxviii.

53. Donaldson, *Public Domain*, 28-29, gives areas of states; *Seventh Census*, Table LV, lxxxii-lxxxiii,

and *Eighth Census, Agriculture*, Table I, vii, give amount of improved land of states in 1850 and 1860, respectively.

54. *Seventh Census*, Table LV, lxxxii-lxxxiii.

55. *Eighth Census, Population*, xxxv.

56. Sparks, *Memories of Fifty Years*, 20.

57. Vidal de La Blache, *Principles of Human Geography*, 68. Cf. Timothy Flint, *The History and Geography of the Mississippi Valley* (Cincinnati, 1832), 217.

58. Isaiah Bowman, *The Pioneer Fringe* (New York, 1931), 6.

59. Archer B. Hulbert, *Soil: Its Influence on the History of the United States* (New Haven, 1930), 78. See also, *ibid.*, 21-23; Albert B. Faust, "German Americans," in Francis J. Brown and Joseph S. Roucek (eds.), *Our Racial and National Minorities; Their History, Contributions, and Present Problems* (New York, 1937), 171; and Laurence M. Larson, *The Changing West and Other Essays* (Northfield, Minn., 1937), 11-12, 69-70, 71, for settlement of the Northwest by Europeans from similar regions.

60. *Eighth Census, Population*, xxxv.

61. Vidal de La Blache, *Principles of Human Geography*, 62, observes that the early agricultural communities of Europe were located on "the most easily cultivated" and "not always the most fertile" soils. "Mellow friable lands forming a sort of band from southern Russia to northern France" were the early abode of agricultural settlers. "Men began to seek out certain localities because they were easy to cultivate." *Ibid.*, 65.

62. Darby, *Emigrant's Guide*, 121, 231; Peck, *New Guide for Emigrants*, 62, 63, 108.

63. *Seventh Census*, Table XV, xxxvi-xxxviii.

64. *Eighth Census, Population* xxxiv, and 616-23. See also, William O. Lynch, "The Westward Flow of Southern Colonists before 1861," in *Journal of Southern History* (Baton Rouge, 1935-), IX (1943), 303-27.

65. George Powell, "A Description of Blount County," in *Transactions of the Alabama Historical Society, July 9th and 10th, 1855* (Tuscaloosa, 1855), 37-41; Nelson F. Smith, *History of Pickens County, Alabama* (Carrollton, Ala., 1856), 37-49. See also, A. B. McEachin, History of Tuscaloosa (MS. copy in Alabama Department of Archives and History; also published in Tuscaloosa *Times*, 1880); and Ezekiel Abner Powell, Fifty Years in West Alabama (MS. copy in Alabama Department of Archives and History; also published in Tuscaloosa *Gazette*, August 12, 1886-September 5, 1889).

66. See, especially, Thomas P. Abernethy, *The Formative Period in Alabama, 1815-1828* (Montgomery, 1922), 25-26.

67. Brown, *History of Newton County*, 54.

68. Nettie Powell, *History of Marion County, Georgia* (Columbus, 1931), 21.

69. Davidson, *History of Wilkinson County*, 147.

70. *Ibid.*, 162.

71. J. D. Anthony, *Life and Times of Rev. J. D. Anthony: An Autobiography with a Few Original Sermons* (Atlanta, 1896), 14.

72. Ball, *Glance into the Great South-East*, 207. See also, Louis F. Hays, *History of Macon County, Georgia* (Atlanta, 1933), 112-13, 118-21, for an account of the settlement of that county, and particularly the town of Marshallville, by family and community groups from Orangeburg and Newberry, South Carolina.

73. Records of the Zion Church, Maury County, Tennessee (microfilm copies in Joint University Libraries, Nashville, Tennessee).

74. Powell, "Description of Blount County," *loc. cit.*, 42. See also, Brewer, History of Coosa County, 48, for the example of Joel Speigner "spying out the lands for a group back in South Carolina."

75. Charles Tait to James A. Tait, January 20, 1817, in Charles Tait Papers (Alabama Department of Archives and History). At the time this letter was written Charles Tait was a United States senator from Georgia. See sketch in Allen Johnson and Dumas Malone (eds.), *Dictionary of American Biography*, 20 vols. and index (New York, 1928-1937), XVIII, 274-75.

76. James A. Tait to Charles Tait, December 15, 1817, Tait Papers.

77. *Id.* to *id.*, January 17, 1819, *ibid.*

78. *Id.* to *id.*, November 10, 1817, *ibid.*

Part VI
Claiming the land

Origin of the land speculator as a frontier type

Ray Allen Billington

Of all frontier types none has been more universally condemned than the land speculator. One of the most thoughtful scholars to devote a lifetime of studying the public domain is Paul W. Gates, Professor Emeritus at Cornell University. One theme runs throughout Professor Gates' work—a sympathy for the actual settler, that is, the small farmer, and a suspicion of the motives and achievements of the moneyed class, the land speculators, bankers, railroad promoters, politicians, and merchants. In his essay "The Role of the Land Speculator in Western Development," Gates made sharp observations about the impact of land speculators. Among other things he asserted that they "forced widespread dispersion of population," encouraged the growth of farm tenancy, and increased the taxes paid by the actual settlers. Unfortunately, Professor Gates supplied very little hard analysis and practically no evidence to substantiate these claims. Like all influential historians, however, he raised questions and issues that have attracted the attention of other scholars.

Recently one of Professor Gates' own students, Leslie E. Decker, in *Railroads, Lands, and Politics: The Taxation of Railroad Land Grants, 1864-1897* (1964), subjected to rigorous analysis his mentor's argument that the land-grant railroads in Kansas and Nebraska kept their property off the tax rolls and forced the burden on the homesteaders. Decker's careful study, using the records of the various county registers of deeds, demonstrated that the opposite was true: railroad land found its way onto tax rolls ahead of land held by small holders. Another of Gates' students, Allan Bogue, has begun the reevaluation of the farm mortgage broker on the frontier. One fact is clear from Gates' own work. Many speculators met financial disaster in their western land ventures. Put another way, this means that easterners invested capital in the West and lost it. What has not emerged is a systematic study of this transfer of wealth to determine who were the beneficiaries. Westerners, particularly those who migrated to the frontier, were perennially short of capital. Further study may reveal that despite some spectacular individual success stories, on balance the speculators as a group lost money and the chief gainers were the small farmers. Whatever the truth, there is still much to be learned about this important aspect of western history.

Reprinted with permission from *Agricultural History*, XIX (October 1945), 204-212.

In the following essay Ray Allen Billington, Professor Emeritus of Western History at Northwestern University, analyzes the origin of the land speculator.

For further reading: Paul Wallace Gates, *Illinois Central Railroad and Its Colonization Work* (Cambridge, Mass.: Harvard University Press, 1934); Paul Wallace Gates, *Fifty Million Acres: Conflicts over Kansas Land Policy, 1854-1890* (Ithaca, N.Y.: Cornell University Press, 1954); Paul Wallace Gates, "The Homestead Act in an Incongruous Land System," *American Historical Review*, XLI (July 1936), 652-681; Paul Wallace Gates, "The Role of the Land Speculator in Western Development," *Pennsylvania Magazine of History and Biography*, LXVI, 3 (July 1942), 314-333; Leslie E. Decker, *Railroads, Lands, and Politics: The Taxation of Railroad Land Grants 1864-1890* (Providence, R.I.: Brown University Press, 1964); Allan G. Bogue, *Money at Interest: The Farm Mortgage on the Middle Border* (Ithaca, N.Y.: Cornell University Press, 1955); Roy H. Akagi, *The Town Proprietors of the New England Colonies* (Philadelphia: University of Pennsylvania Press, 1924).

When Frederick Jackson Turner pictured the westward movement of the American people in terms of a succession of pioneer types—traders, cattlemen, primitive farmers, and equipped farmers—all moving in orderly procession across the face of the continent, he omitted one individual who played a major role in the march of civilization, namely the land speculator.[1] Only during the past dozen years have historians become fully aware of the importance of Professor Turner's omission.[2] Their industrious spading over a previously uncultivated field has indicated both the extent of land-jobbing activity in the history of the frontier and the effect of that activity on the developing social patterns of the United States,[3] and yet much remains to be done. The rich returns waiting future investigators can be shown by examining the part played by speculators in the early colonial period. This examination will indicate both the many aspects of the subject needing further investigation and the importance of the land jobber in an era when he has generally been believed to have had little influence.

Students of land speculation have made clear the distinction between the various types of speculators who moved westward with the pioneers.[4] Some were ordinary farmers who, on reaching the frontier, engrossed far more land than they could use in hope of subsequent profitable resale to later arrivals. Others were businessmen and bankers who lived in the tiny western hamlets and supplemented their income by bartering lands as well as furs, whiskey, and merchandise. Still others were eastern merchants or planters who, as individuals, used their wealth or political influence to acquire large estates in the wilderness. More spectacular were the capitalists who organized into companies, large and small, and used their combined resources to secure vast frontier tracts which were then advertised widely and sold. All of these men, from the shabby farmer staking out his "tomahawk claim" to a hundred acres more than he could use in the Yadkin Valley to the wealthy Philadelphia merchant plotting to secure a royal grant for a new interior colony, were speculators.

The frontiersmen, however, made a clear distinction between two types of land jobbers, the amateurs and the professionals. In their eyes the amateurs—small farmers who simply purchased more land than they could use—were not objectionable, for the frontier never realized that the pioneer who held back land from settlement in this way separated himself from his neighbors, delayed the coming of schools and internal improvements, and hindered the development of social institutions that would have made life easier. Instead the westerners concentrated their attacks on the professional speculators, most of whom were absentee owners who, it was claimed, wrung an unearned profit from hard-working farmers while contributing nothing themselves to the advance of civilization. To understand the role of the speculator in colonial America it is necessary to follow this distinction and consider the amateurs and professionals separately.

The importance of the former group, even in colonial times, is today clearly recognized. The European peasants who swarmed across the Atlantic Ocean in the seventeenth century were land hungry. Most of them had never owned farms in the Old World, and the presence of so much land in the New, to be had cheaply, was more of a temptation than they could resist. But little is known of the effect of their speculations on the settlement process. How much land, in excess of the 40 or 50 acres that a pioneer farmer could clear and care for, did they take out? Did their purchases vary in periods of prosperity and depression, with a tendency to engross more in good times when prospects of resale were bright? Did this variance affect the speed with which the frontier advanced? These questions offer a tempting—if somewhat tedious—field of study for the frontier historian. Most of the answers can be found only by a minute study of county records, with their detailed listing of individual purchases and resales, which must be carried on by many scholars. Fortunately the careful listing of these important sources by the Historical Records Survey of the Works Progress Administration has made the task easier. It is to be hoped that college instructors throughout the country will awaken to the importance of this work (and to the happy prospect of as many masters' thesis subjects as there are counties in the United States) and direct their students into the many detailed studies needed to throw light on this vital subject.

An example of the possibilities awaiting investigators is provided by a recent survey of the amazingly complete county records of Virginia's Eastern Shore.[5] This study challenges the long-accepted belief that small-farm agriculture persisted in the tobacco colonies through the seventeenth century by proving that the average Accomac grants in the 1650s contained more than 900 acres.[6] By 1700, however, the fractional division of these great estates had reduced them to the size generally recognized by historians as typical of the whole century. These statistics in themselves prove little, for the area under study is too small to illustrate any general trend, but a similar study of the records for the rest of Virginia and Maryland would probably dovetail them into an important pattern illustrative of landownership in the Southern Tidewater. This might show that the large mid-century holdings were accumulated amidst the prosperity of that period primarily with the hope of resale. It might demonstrate that a rapid breaking up of the great estates accompanied the depression of the 1670s and 1680s, and that while these were being divided others were rising along the frontier. It might offer a sound reason for the conservatism of the Eastern Shore during Bacon's Rebellion by showing that planters there could sell off their excess holdings and thus escape the poverty that shaped discontent in the rest of the colony. Certainly such a study would give us a clearer picture of life in the tobacco provinces than we have today.

Moreover careful surveys of the records of these Southern Colonies would probably reveal a typical speculative pattern in landholding: a succession of zones distinguished by the varying size of farms—in the far west a band of small clearings tilled by squatters or restless pioneers, then a belt of large estates owned by reasonably well-equipped farmers who planted corn and tobacco on a few of their broad acres and held the rest for resale, then a zone of slightly smaller holdings in a higher stage of civilization where an initial division was taking place, and finally a settled region of small farms that could be cared for by the owners and indentured servants then available. The presence of this pattern was suggested by two laws passed by the Virginia burgesses in 1705, one limiting the size of patents and the other applying the law of entail. The former was an obvious attempt to check the growth of speculative holdings in the west, while the latter sought to end the rapid division of eastern estates then going on. Apparently the frontier process had reached a stage, even on the narrow strip of the Virginia Tidewater, that was causing alarm among the embryo planters of the seaboard who controlled the legislature.

Finally, a detailed examination of landholdings in the Southern Colonies might shed light on the relationship between speculation and the speed with which the frontier advanced. Speculative buying undoubtedly was greater in periods of prosperity than in times of depression, for purchases were encouraged both by the plentiful capital seeking investment and by the prospect of speedy resale. The one statistical study of this problem, dealing with a later period, shows an exact correlation between commodity prices and land sales.[7] This heavy buying would, in turn, hurry the westward movement of the population for the large holdings accumulated along the frontier would drive home seekers still farther inland in search of cheap sites. In periods of depression, on the other hand, newcomers to the west would no longer seek lands beyond the fringe of settlement, for they could buy up the excess holdings that the speculators could no longer afford to keep. In other words, a careful study of the relationship between land sales and the westward advance of pioneers would probably disclose two things: that the size of farms in the west varied with the region's prosperity, swelling in good times and shrinking in periods of depression, and that those extensions and contractions were primarily responsible for each westward surge of the frontier, rather than Indian wars, immigration, internal improvements, or distressing conditions at home. Thus the effect of speculation was to accentuate the cyclical nature of the westward movement, speeding pioneers toward the interior when times were good, and checking their advance in periods of depression.

These results, and the spirit of speculation responsible for them, are easily understandable in the Southern Colonies, for the encouragement to private initiative given by crown and proprietors created an atmosphere conducive to this form of activity. That the same speculative fever could develop in seventeenth-century New England was a better indication of the effect of the New World environment on transplanted Englishmen. Not even the staunch Puritans who built their homes along that stern and rock-bound coast could restrain the urge to accumulate lands, and within half a century after they planted their settlements their carefully-planned Wilderness Zion was threatened by forces that stemmed directly from speculation.

The founding fathers certainly envisaged no such development. Their ambition—a commonwealth of orthodox believers devoted to propagating the revealed word—led them to abandon the system of headrights and grants authorized by the royal charters and to vest in the legislatures sole authority over the "sitting down of men," with the understanding that lands were to be given free to groups of unquestioned faith. They viewed the public domain, not as a source of profit, but as a medium to be employed in spreading the true religion westward. Hence they authorized only two types of grants—to individuals and to groups—both to be made without charge to men of proper social and religious status.

The awards made to individuals deserve further study, for they apparently were sufficiently common to indicate that some of the leading colonists were not above engrossing land for profit purposes. Between 1630 and 1675 the Massachusetts General Court alone granted 130,000 acres to influential persons. About half of this went to favored officials; during these years thirty-two assistants and governors voted themselves nearly 60,000 acres in plots that varied from 1,000 to 9,000 acres each. The size of these holdings, in a region where the usual farms were only from 10 to 100 acres in extent, seems to indicate a speculative purpose. This was made even clearer by the fact that few awards were made to ministers—only eleven grants totalling 6,000 acres in the forty-five years—despite the repeated assertion that all allotments were made to reward meritorious service.[8] Although these individual grants were dwarfed by the more common group grants, they were sufficiently numerous to indicate that even the earliest Puritans were not completely disinterested in speculation or profits.

Even more important was the gradual development of a speculative spirit in the administration of town lands. Town sites in colonial New England were ordinarily awarded to any group of acceptable believers with the understanding that land was to be divided without charge among later comers until the village was settled. At first these proprietors lived up to their obligations cheerfully, but as time passed and thickening settlement brought home the value of their holdings, they showed an increasing tendency to retain control of the undivided lands and refuse grants even to men of proper religious views. Thus there grew up in each New England town two distinct classes, one consisting of the original proprietors and their heirs, the other of new arrivals who were landless or whose holdings were restricted to the farm plots originally granted them. The landless and the small holders wanted to divide the remaining town lands; the proprietors, sensing possible future profits, were reluctant to meet this demand. Thus were planted the seeds of conflict that racked nearly every village.

This conflict usually began in the town meetings where the newcomers, or freemen, had an equal political voice with the proprietors. It went on until the freemen, who were steadily increasing in numbers while the proprietory group remained stable, gained ascendency. At this point their clamor grew so great that arbitrators were often called in from neighboring towns, or the case carried into the law courts in an attempt to force a further division of the town property. The proprietors, when faced with this threat, attempted to protect their holdings by forming a separate corporation, distinct from the town meeting, with the sole purpose of guarding their holdings from popular attack. This step was legalized by Plymouth and Rhode Island in 1682, Massachusetts in 1698, New Hampshire in 1718, and Connecticut in 1723. Thus organized, the proprietory corporations were strong enough to triumph over their enemies, for the courts had no choice but to recognize the sole right of the original grantees to the town lands. Although these corporations made few attempts to sell the undivided fields for cash in the seventeenth century, their willingness to fight in courts and town meetings against further divisions certainly indicated the development of a speculative spirit, at least in embryo form.[9]

These conflicts between proprietors and freemen had much to do with the rapid expansion of the New England frontier, for each defeat left the nonproprietors dissatisfied and convinced that only by moving farther inland could they secure the larger fields that they wanted. Probably few of them went west as proprietors themselves; the aristocratic governors of New England would hesitate to assign the task of laying out new towns to men of such small property. Instead most of them moved as individuals to frontier communities whose proprietors had not yet caught the speculative fever and would be more generous in their allotments. Thus land grabbing, even in this rudimentary form, proved one of the powerful expelling forces sending New Englanders westward during the seventeenth century.

These speculators, in New England and the tobacco colonies, typified the amateurs who through the history of the frontier engrossed more land than they needed. Present among them, even in the early days of settlement, were other jobbers who made the buying and selling of land a major activity. These professional operators usually lived in seaboard cities or on the richer Tidewater plantations; some of them maintained agents to acquire and supervise their western holdings or organized companies to pool their resources for greater purchases. Their activities in the late eighteenth century have recently been recognized by historians, but the history of professional land speculation in the seventeenth century is still a virtually unexplored field.

The little research that has been done discloses the possibilities of the subject, for apparently professional speculators were operating from New England to the Carolinas within a few years after the first settlements. They were certainly at work in Maryland and Virginia well before the end of the seventeenth century, encouraged by the peculiar conditions that shaped the agricultural development of those tobacco colonies. Land suitable to the production of this staple was comparatively rare; only the rich river bottoms offered both the deep soil and the adequate water transportation necessary. Land jobbers who could secure these choice sites in advance of settlement were assured handsome profits, for new settlers were crowding in from Europe and old settlers were moving westward as soil exhaustion drove them from their barren fields. Here were conditions likely to breed speculative activity.

The speculators' first problem was to find some means of acquiring land, for none was sold in early Maryland or Virginia. Their ingenious methods demonstrate their eagerness. They soon found that ship captains and contractors who received headrights for transporting indentured servants to America were ready to sell for a small sum, and by the middle of the seventeenth century the jobbers were buying up these warrants, pushing up the river valleys, and patenting the richest fields. When this source proved inadequate, they turned to the indentured servants themselves. These laborers, after completing their seven years of bonded service, were given from 50 to 100 acres of land on which to make their homes. The speculators found that most of these freed workers did not have the capital needed to exploit their new possessions and were willing to sell. Frequently a land jobber would herd as many as fifty recently released servants into the office of the secretary of the province, supervise them while they secured their land patents, and purchase all the warrants then and there. These were then used, as were the headrights secured from ship masters and contractors, to engross choice river sites.[10]

These activities undoubtedly affected the ebb and flow of the advancing tide of settlement. By usurping the best lands and holding them for higher prices—prices in Maryland rose 130 percent between 1660 and the end of the century[11]—the speculators hurried the peopling of the less desirable regions that were either distant from rivers or beyond the protection of the older settlements. Most of the indentured servants who had sold their grants probably sought homes there, using the money obtained from land jobbers to buy needed materials, and either squatting on the land or purchasing the inferior sites cheaply. Thus here, as elsewhere, the speculators helped speed the westward advance by withholding from cultivation great tracts east of the frontier line.

Professional speculators also began to operate in New England during the seventeenth century. Most of them were wealthy seaboard businessmen who had accumulated modest fortunes through commercial or shipping ventures. With their money chests overflowing, they naturally cast about for profitable investments. These were difficult to find. Land offered the only outlet, yet speculative accumulations within their own colonies were impossible, for the legislatures would make no grants except to groups for religious purposes. Hence they were forced to turn to three other regions in their search for wealth: to Maine, the neighboring provinces of New York and New Jersey, and to Rhode Island.

Little is known of the activity of these New England businessmen in the first two sections. They certainly invested widely in Maine lands, for that northern province was only thinly settled and promised rich returns. The companies that sprang up to exploit its resources deserve study. Similarly Boston and New Haven capitalists, organized into trading and speculating corporations, played some part in the conquest of New Jersey. One important company, the Delaware Company, engaged in a three-cornered contest with Netherlands and Sweden for control of the Delaware Valley,[12] and others probably encouraged the settlement of New Englanders in New Jersey and on the eastern end of Long Island. Some such incentive must have been responsible for the large Puritan migration to those remote parts. Other organizations of speculators intruded into the Dutch domain along the Hudson Valley and helped precipitate the conflict that added New York to the British Empire. The attempt of a New Haven concern to establish a trading colony near Albany in 1645 so enraged bluff old Peter Stuyvesant that he visited Hartford to protest, and a Boston company that tried to plant itself near Poughkeepsie in 1659 might have plunged the two nations into a premature war had not unsettled conditions attending the Restoration ended the enterprise.[13] Probably a further study of these activities would lead to a rewriting of much of the diplomatic history of colonial America.

Something more is known of New England speculation in the third field open to Boston entrepreneurs—Rhode Island—yet this too deserves investigation. This tiny colony, scorned by the Puritans for its tolerance and liberalism, was considered a legitimate field for exploitation, for Massachusetts and Connecticut were willing to back their businessmen in any blow at Roger Williams' despised followers. At least three speculating companies operated there, all concentrating their activities in the fertile region west of Narragansett Bay occupied by an Indian tribe of the same name. Two of these, the Pettiquamscutt Company and the Misquamicutt Company, evidently were fairly unimportant, but a third, the Atherton Company, influenced New England affairs for some time. An examination of its brief career will illustrate the importance of these land-jobbing schemes in the life of the day.[14]

The Atherton Company was formed at Boston in 1659 with most of the leading capitalists of that city, Taunton, and Portsmouth included in its ranks, as well as Governor John Winthrop, Jr., of Connecticut. In the same year two large tracts adjoining Narragansett Bay were purchased from the Indians in open defiance of a Rhode Island law of 1658 forbidding such sales. A year later the company saw a chance to extend its operations when the colonial authorities imposed an impossible fine on the Narragansett tribe for one of its periodic outbursts. The company's leaders immediately offered to assume the debt in return for a mortgage on all the Narragansett lands, to be repaid within six months. Probably the sachems who made this agreement did not understand its terms; certainly they were unable to meet their payments, and in 1662 the speculators took over the whole Narragansett country. For the next dozen years their efforts to make good their claim over the protests of Rhode Island and the crown seriously affected colonial affairs.

Their first step was to solicit the aid of one of the company's members, Governor Winthrop of Connecticut, whose solution was to seek a new charter for his colony that would extend Connecticut's boundaries as far east as Narragansett Bay, thus bringing the whole disputed region under his jurisdiction. These efforts were temporarily crowned with success in May 1662, when a charter with the desired boundaries was issued by the king, but Rhode Island's outcry was so vigorous that the royal officials consented to take the whole question under advisement. The company, desperately afraid of losing its advantage, enlisted as a new member one John Scott, a court hanger-on well skilled in the use of bribes, who immediately sent in a bill for "a parcel of curiosityes to ye value of 60: to gratifye persons that are powerfull." These precautions were in vain, for a committee of arbitration eventually decided that the Rhode Island boundary extended west to the Pawcatuct River. Connecticut refused to accept this finding, and the dispute dragged on for a number of years. Its details can never be understood until the influence of the Atherton Company has been properly appraised.

Before this conflict was settled, another opportunity for the company presented itself in the form of King Philip's War. At first this promised to be only a minor rebellion, for King Philip was the chieftain of only one small tribe, the Wampanoags, whose few villages in the marshes east of Narragansett Bay could offer only feeble resistance. The strong force from Massachusetts and Plymouth that set out in pursuit of the marauders in the spring of 1675 easily drove them into a large swamp. Victory seemed certain, for the colonists needed only to wait until their savage foes were starved into surrender, when the Massachusetts officials took the one step needed to transform this war from a minor outbreak to a major conflict. They ordered the Massachusetts soldiers to march southward into the Narragansett country, supposedly to wring a treaty of peace from that already-peaceful tribe. The results were disastrous. With most of the guards removed, Philip and his warriors escaped into western Massachusetts, persuaded the Indians there to take to the warpath and swept against the interior settlements in a series of bloody raids that lasted for two years. At the same time the Narragansett Indians, who had shown every intention of remaining peaceful, were driven into the war by the invasion of their territory.

This foolish blunder on the part of the Massachusetts authorities could have been prompted by only two things. One was a desire to strike a blow at unpopular Rhode Island through an Indian tribe that was closely bound to Williams' colony by ties of trade and friendship. The other was the ambition of the Atherton Company. If the Narragansett Indians could be goaded into war and then decisively defeated, their lands, which were claimed by the company, would be open to settlement. The large company representation among the Massachusetts officials who ordered this ill-fated expedition seems to indicate that pressure from these speculators was at least partially responsible for a war that cost hundreds of lives and thousands of dollars.

Important as the speculators' role was in shaping the course of seventeenth-century history, the land-jobbing fever did not reach its height in America until well into the next century. This was a day of bold commercial enterprise, of a wild scramble after wealth, of the pyramiding of giddy paper fortunes, on both sides of the Atlantic. In the colonies this activity was confined largely to speculation in land, for other forms of investment were few, and both money and grandiose dreams were plentiful. Historians have recognized the importance of these speculators, but their scattered studies leave many gaps to be filled.

Thus far little attention has been paid to the first half of the eighteenth century. Speculation in the South during those years evidently took the form of vast individual grants to favored Tidewater planters by the legislatures of Virginia and the Carolinas. Hundreds of tracts in the Piedmont and the Great Valley, ranging from 10,000 to 50,000 acres, were parceled out free of charge or for a small fee, despite all the efforts of the crown and royal officials to check the practice. Thus Governor Alexander Spotswood of Virginia, after waging a brief but gallant battle against speculation, succumbed to the mania and began engrossing land himself, while a royal agent sent to North Carolina with specific instructions to end the granting of large estates proved such an easy victim that he built up nearly a million acres of speculative holdings. [15] The means by which the planters accumulated land, their methods of advertising and selling their estates, and the effect of their operations on the Scotch-Irish and German immigrants then crowding down the Great Valley, remain untold chapters in the history of the frontier. So also does the story of the speculation in New York and Pennsylvania that drove these new arrivals southward in search of cheap lands. [16]

The speculative fever also swept across New England in the first half of the eighteenth century, with devastating effects on the land systems of the colonies there. Wealthy business leaders of Boston and Salem caught the infection first and began buying up plots from proprietors of new towns or from old towns where undivided lands were still available. For a time the legislatures resisted this pressure and continued to grant land only to orthodox religious groups, but Connecticut succumbed in 1715, Massachusetts in 1727, and the others soon afterward. From that time on they openly sold their town sites to the highest bidders, with little thought of contiguous settlement by nonprofit-seeking true believers. This desire for profits changed the whole course of New England's westward advance by breaking down the emphasis on groups and preparing the descendents of the Puritans to move into the trans-Appalachian area as individuals. A study of the transition of this land system would not only shed light on the settlement of that region's upland country but would make clearer our understanding of the whole frontier process. [17]

Thorough investigations of these many activities, both amateur and professional, together with special studies to fill the gaps between the excellent monographs that have recently described the large-scale speculations of the late eighteenth century, [18] would not only illuminate the history of the colonial period but would help assign the land jobber to his proper place in the frontier process. Was he a worthless wretch who wrung unearned profits from helpless pioneers and spread suffering and poverty in his wake? Or did he contribute his mite to the settling of the American continent?

Such a survey would probably show that the amateur speculators and the small professionals did more harm than good. Their purchases forced a more rapid dispersal of population than was healthy for institutional development, delayed the coming of schools and churches, and slowed the transformation from wilderness to civilization. [19] Their frantic efforts to improve their properties corrupted politics and subordinated national to local interests in locating internal improvements, county seats, and colleges. Even the larger speculating companies, backed by rich reservoirs of European capital, apparently contributed little, for their lavish expenditures only deprived the frontiersmen of the quick profits normally awaiting the first pioneers, and their faulty advertising aroused false hopes among eastern innocents. Why, in the face of this imposing list of wrongs, did public opinion allow the land jobbers to endure?

The speculators probably survived popular wrath for two centuries only because they played a legitimate but unpopular role as middlemen between the original governmental owners of land and the ultimate purchasers. The average pioneer wanted two things when he moved west: good land adjacent to adequate transportation facilities, and credit extended over enough years to permit payment from the proceeds of his farm. The speculators could provide both and had a real reason for existence as long as they could do so.

The speculators had the facilities to spy out the best land. Most of the large companies, and many of the individual jobbers, maintained regular agents along the frontier, usually employing traders or hunters for this task. These experienced woodsmen sought out the rich soil regions, or the fertile areas near navigable rivers and preempted them for their employers. A pioneer farmer who purchased from a speculating company could be reasonably sure that his land was good and that he could count on the best transportation available in that area, while one who located his own lands might be misled by surface features to select a farm with poor soil and inadequate market outlets.

More important was the fact that the great companies, and even the larger individual speculators, could provide credit. Their resources allowed them to pay cash for large blocks of western land, which could then be parceled out among small purchasers on easy terms. Usually a frontiersman was allowed so much time to complete his payments that he was able, with any luck, to earn enough from his farm to buy the property and lay aside a comfortable nest egg as well. Few pioneers could have purchased land without the help of jobbers before the middle of the nineteenth century.

Proof of their valuable role can be found in the history of the national land laws. Each measure passed after the initial Ordinance of 1785 was in response to western pressure and was designed to eliminate speculators by depriving them of their functions. This was the purpose of the credit system that was introduced into government sales by the acts of 1796 and 1800, of the gradual reduction in the minimum amount purchasable, and of preemption. Yet none succeeded. The professional land jobbers could still seek out the most productive sites, and they could still offer smaller down payments and easier credit terms than the land office. Even after the Preemption Act of 1841 was passed, their activities continued, for few pioneers could accumulate sufficient cash to pay for their farms in the few years allowed them and were forced to borrow from speculators, serving now in the new role of "loan sharks," or lose their lands and improvements. Only the Homestead Act deprived the jobbers of their principal function and reduced them to the less valuable task of engrossing the railroad, mineral and forest lands for their own selfish ends.

Clearly the speculators played an important part in the conquest of the frontier and in the larger scene of the Nation's history. Forging steadily ahead to mark out the best lands, pleading always with purchasers for long-overdue payments, suffering risks that reduced their profits to a minimum,[20] and enduring the hatred that the frontiersmen reserved for tax collectors, absentee landlords, and others who tried to wring cash from flat western pocketbooks, they were as omnipresent along the cutting edge of civilization as the axe-swinging pioneers themselves. Their contribution to the frontier process deserves more attention than it has received.

Notes

1. The reading incident to the preparation of this article was made possible by a Guggenheim Memorial Foundation Fellowship during 1943-44. The article, in somewhat extended form, was delivered as the Schouler Lecture at Johns Hopkins University in April 1944.

2. Frederick J. Turner, *The Frontier in American History*, 12 (New York, 1920).

3. A number of scholars have exploited the rich materials on land speculation in the national period. Thomas P. Abernethy, *Western Lands and the American Revolution* (New York, 1937), is an excellent treatment of the speculator in the formative years of the Republic, while Merrill Jensen has shown the influence of speculation on the early national government in several brilliant studies: "The Cession of the Old Northwest," *Mississippi Valley Historical Review*, 23:27-48 (1936); "The Creation of the National Domain, 1781-1784," *ibid.*, 26:323-342 (1939); and *The Articles of Confederation* (Madison, Wis., 1940). Speculative activity in the southwest is the theme of Arthur P. Whitaker in "The Muscle Shoals Speculation, 1783-1789," *Mississippi Valley Historical Review*, 13:365-386 (1926), and "The South Carolina Yazoo Company," *ibid.*, 16:383-394 (1929). Paul D. Evans has studied the large companies that operated in New York at the turn of the nineteenth century in "The Pulteney Purchase," New York State Historical Association, *Quarterly Journal*, 3:83-104 (1922), and *The Holland Land Company* (Buffalo, N.Y., 1924). Helen I. Cowan, *Charles Williamson, Genesee Promoter* (Rochester, N.Y., 1941), is another study of the same area. A number of Middle Atlantic States companies operating at the same time, such as the Pennsylvania Population Company, still wait investigation. Speculative activity in the Ohio Valley just after the Revolution is traced in: Archer B. Hulbert, *The Records of the Original Proceedings of the Ohio Company* (Marietta, Ohio, 1917), "The Methods and Operations of the Scioto Group of Speculators," *Mississippi Valley Historical Review*, 1:502-515, 2:56-73 (1915), and "Andrew Craigie and the Scioto Associates," American Antiquarian Society, *Proceedings* (n.s.), 23:222-236 (1913); Joseph S. Davis, *Essays in the Earlier History of American Corporations* (Cambridge, Mass., 1917); and Helen M. Carpenter, "The Origin and Location of the Firelands of the Western Reserve," *Ohio State Archaeological and Historical Quarterly*, 44:163-203 (1935). The role of the railroads as land jobbers was first explored by James B. Hedges in "The Colonization Work of the Northern Pacific Railroad," *Mississippi Valley Historical Review*, 13:311-342 (1926); "Promotion of Immigration to the Pacific Northwest by the Railroads," *ibid.*, 15:183-203 (1928); *Henry Villard and the Railways of the Northwest* (New Haven, 1930); and *Building the Canadian West* (New York, 1939). His scholarship has inspired two similar studies: Paul Wallace Gates, *The Illinois Central Railroad and Its Colonization Work* (Cambridge, Mass., 1934), and Richard C. Overton, *Burlington West* (Cambridge, Mass., 1941). Gates has roamed far over the field with such stimulating studies as: "The Homestead Law in an Incongruous Land System," *American Historical Review*, 41:652-681 (1936); "Southern Investments in Northern Lands before the Civil War," *Journal of Southern History*, 5:155-185 (1939); "Land Policy and Tenancy in the Prairie Counties of Indiana," *Indiana Magazine of History*, 35:1-26 (1939); and "The Role of the Land Speculator in Western Development," *Pennsylvania Magazine of History and Biography*, 66:314-333 (1942).

4. Paul Wallace Gates, "The Disposal of the Public Domain in Illinois, 1848-1856," *Journal of Economic and Business History*, 3:216-240 (1931).

5. Susie M. Ames, *Studies of the Virginia Eastern Shore in the Seventeenth Century* (Richmond, Va., 1940).

6. Thomas J. Wertenbaker, *The Planters of Colonial Virginia* (Princeton, N.J., 1922).

7. Arthur H. Cole, "Cyclical and Sectional Variation in the Sale of Public Lands, 1816-60," *Review of Economic Statistics*, 9:41-53 (1927).

8. Statistics compiled by S. H. Brockunier from N. B. Shurtleff, ed., *Records of the Governor and Company of the Massachusetts Bay in New England*, vols. 1-4 (Boston, 1853-54).

9. Roy H. Akagi, *The Town Proprietors of the New England Colonies* (Philadelphia, 1924), and Florence M. Woodard, *The Town Proprietors in Vermont* (New York, 1936), contain the best account of the New England land system.

10. Abbot Emerson Smith, "The Indentured Servant and Land Speculation in Seventeenth Century Maryland," *American Historical Review*, 40:467-472 (1935); V. J. Wyckoff, "The Sizes of Plantations in Seventeenth-Century Maryland," *Maryland Historical Magazine*, 32:331-339 (1937).

11. V. J. Wyckoff, "Land Prices in Seventeenth-Century Maryland," *American Economic Review*, 28:82-88 (1938).

12. For a brief account of these activities, see Amandus Johnson, *The Swedish Settlements on the Delaware* (New York, 1911).

13. Arthur H. Buffinton, "New England and the Western Fur Trade, 1629-1675," Colonial Society of Massachusetts, *Publications*, 18:160-192 (Boston, 1917), emphasizes the trading aspect of these ventures, which were also speculative.

14. For a factual account of these companies, see Irving B. Richman, *Rhode Island* (New York, 1902).

15. These activities are mentioned in Herbert L. Osgood, *The American Colonies in the Eighteenth Century*, 4:116-135 (New York, 1924); Charles L. Raper, *North Carolina*, 101-124 (New York, 1904); and Leonidas Dodson, *Alexander Spotswood* (Philadelphia, 1932).

16. The importance of such a study for New York is indicated by the materials in Ruth L. Higgins, *Expansion in New York, with Especial Reference to the Eighteenth Century* (Columbus, Ohio, 1931).

17. For the best account of the transition, see Woodard, *The Town Proprietors in Vermont*.

18. Clarence W. Alvord, *The Mississippi Valley in British Politics* (Cleveland, 1917) was the pioneering work in this field. Recent important studies include: John R. Alden, *John Stuart and the Southern Colonial Frontier* (Ann Arbor, Mich., 1944); Clarence W. Alvord, ed., *The Illinois-Wabash Land Company Manuscript* (Chicago, 1915); Kenneth P. Bailey, *The Ohio Company of Virginia* (Glendale, Calif., 1939); Ray A. Billington, "The Fort Stanwix Treaty of 1768," *New York History*, 25:182-194 (1944); Julian P. Boyd, ed., *The Susquehanna Company Papers* (Wilkes-Barre, Pa., 1930-31); Archibald Henderson, "Dr. Thomas Walker and the Loyal Company of Virginia," American Antiquarian Society, *Proceedings* (n.s.) 41:77-178 (1931); William S. Lester, *The Transylvania Colony* (Spencer, Ind., 1935); George E. Lewis, *The Indiana Company, 1763-1798* (Glendale, Calif., 1941); Max Savelle, *George Morgan, Colony Builder* (New York, 1932).

19. Paul Wallace Gates, "The Role of the Land Speculator in Western Development," *Pennsylvania Magazine of History and Biography*, 66:314-333 (1942).

20. One careful study for a later period shows that the majority of a group of speculators averaged less than 5 percent profit. James W. Silver, "Land Speculation Profits in the Chickasaw Cession," *Journal of Southern History*, 10:84-92 (1944).

Preemption—a frontier triumph

Roy M. Robbins

The theme of the conservative, aristocratic East arrayed against a democratic West runs deeply throughout the literature of American history, especially in the accounts of the federal government's land policy. This traditional picture often obscures more than it explains. It assumes, for example, that the eastern moneyed elite unanimously fought land reforms such as preemption, graduation, and homesteads because easterners preferred that the government sell land in large blocs to speculators who would reap the profit of sales to individual farmers. Another variant is that the eastern states preferred to shift the financial burden of running the federal government to those who purchased western lands. While there is truth in both these notions, they ignore important factors. Not all eastern men of property were potential land speculators. Many invested in western internal improvements by the purchase of state canal bonds, turnpike bonds, or, after 1840, railroad securities. These projects, most built well ahead of traffic demands, depended upon a liberal land policy that attracted rapid settlement, for without intensive farming there would not be enough freight and passenger revenues to make internal improvements pay.

It would, therefore, have been to the interest of any substantial investor in transportation improvements to favor cheap land for actual settlers and oppose laws that would lock up large tracts in the hands of speculators who would keep land off the market while awaiting a rise in its value. Other easterners granted credit to western storekeepers, who profited from mass migration westward. Still other easterners, particularly those in New England, New York, and Pennsylvania, were manufacturers who catered to western farmers and who stood to gain from the growth of this market caused by an easy land policy.

The traditional viewpoint also errs in another respect. It places too much emphasis on *eastern* speculators and on the democratic nature of the West. It understates the propensity for *westerners* to speculate. How else can one explain the fact that preemption's chief opponent was that western idol Henry Clay of Kentucky? Or must he be regarded as merely a tool of eastern interests?

In the following essay, Roy M. Robbins, Professor of History at the University of

Reprinted with permission from *Mississippi Valley Historical Review* (December 1931), 331-349.

Omaha, explains the fight over preemption in traditional terms. His views are expanded in *Our Landed Heritage* (1942), which remains the standard one-volume survey of American land policies.

For further reading: Roy M. Robbins, *Our Landed Heritage: The Public Domain, 1776-1936* (Princeton: Princeton University Press, 1942);* Benjamin H. Hibbard, *A History of Public Land Policies* (New York: Macmillan, 1924); Raynor G. Wellington, *Politics and Sectional Influence of the Public Lands, 1828-1842* (Cambridge, Mass.: Riverside Press, 1914); George M. Stephenson, *The Political History of the Public Lands from 1840 to 1862: From Pre-emption to Homestead* (Boston: R. G. Badger, Gorham Press, 1917); Helen S. Zahler, *Eastern Workingmen and National Land Policy, 1829-1862* (New York: Columbia University Press, 1941); John S. Sanborn, "Some Political Aspects of Homestead Legislation," *American Historical Review*, VI (October 1900), 19-37; Vernon Carstensen, ed., *The Public Lands: Studies in the History of the Public Domain* (Madison: University of Wisconsin Press, 1962).

*Available in paperback.

From time immemorial land has been an important source of economic life. In the development of any people the treatment of the land question is a determining factor in the characteristics of their civilization. Problems pertaining to the soil have been most seriously neglected in the study of the evolution of American society, and consequently historians have had little basis for measuring the influence of these problems upon the better known forces of history. One important force emanating from the soil—that of agrarianism—has had an important effect upon the established American political and economic order. In at least one instance before the Civil War this force of agrarianism, in the form of the preemption movement, was successful in tearing down an old aristocratic land system and in dictating the democratic basis for a new system.

Ever since early colonial days the danger of frontier revolt was a menace to established society. The opening of vacant lands to the westward always stimulated a frontier spirit— a peculiar democratic leveling influence, likely to be arrogant, daring, dangerous, and even uncontrollable. All colonies, fearing destruction of what seemed to be the foundations of government, very early adopted iron-clad policies to control these peculiar leveling influences from the backwoods. So long as the movements of population were on a small scale, the dominant forces could control the frontier spirit. But once settlement began to spread beyond the reach of the colonial governments, danger was imminent. A frontier population of squatters and trespassers stood ready to defy the law of the land, and a clash between frontier agrarianism and the established order was certain to result.

Naturally, the frontiersman wanted free access to the soil. But free land would destroy the economic and political values upon which government was founded. A compromise was thus generally effected in the form of preemption—by which the government pardoned the squatter for his illegal settlement and in addition confirmed his title to the land on condition that he buy it at a much reduced price. The word "preemption" means "prior right of purchase" or "purchase before the sale." Preemption, in other words, was an expedient which a government was forced to adopt so as to make established law and order conform with the lawless and uncontrollable spirit of the American frontier. It was to become the means by which thousands of acres of land were to be settled by a sturdy and enterprising population.

Colonial records contain numerous instances of the squatting problem which at times became serious—as the case of the squatting population that nursed Bacon's Rebellion in Virginia,[1] or the numerous conflicts with the Scotch-Irish and German settlers in Pennsylvania. It was not, however, until after the French and Indian War that the problem became so unmanageable as to necessitate concessions to the frontier element. Unable to meet the question effectively, the mother country, herself, began to assume responsibility for some unified control, as was evidenced in the issuing of the Proclamation of 1763 and the various orders in council which followed.[2]

It was fear of the frontier that caused Governor Dunmore of Virginia, in 1770, to protest against the project of establishing a colony on the Ohio. "The scheme alarms all the settled parts of America, the people of property being justly apprehensive of consequences that must inevitably ensue," Dunmore declared, emphasizing the importance of maintaining the established values by refusing permission to colonists desiring to migrate westward since the withdrawal "of those Inhabitants will reduce the value of Lands in the provinces even to nothing," and such destruction of land values would in time have direct results upon the entire country.[3]

Notwithstanding the fear expressed by the conservative interests, a certain group thought it better to compromise with than to struggle against the agrarian forces. This included Thomas Jefferson, who, in 1776, wrote: "The people who will migrate to the Westward . . . will be a people little able to pay taxes. . . . By selling the lands to them, you will disgust them, and cause an avulsion of them from the common union. They will settle the lands in spite of everybody,—I am at the same time clear that they should be appropriated in small quantities."[4]

Had the central government, in 1785, when it established a land system for the newly created public domain, heeded the experience of the state governments or the thoughts of men like Jefferson, it would not have found itself later in the embarrassing position of being compelled to change its system. By 1785, the preemption principle was recognized as essential to the land policies of many of the state governments—especially in North Carolina, Virginia, and Pennsylvania with their far-flung frontiers.[5] But the natural rights philosophy of the Revolutionary period seemed to have been forgotten, and an aristocratic philosophy stressing propertied interests arose to take its place.

The land policy adopted in the Ordinance of 1785 was quite unfavorable to actual settlement. The land first of all had to be cleared of Indian title; secondly, it had to be surveyed—after which it was to be thrown open to sale. But the smallest amount of land that could be purchased from the government was 640 acres and this was priced at the minimum of one dollar per acre. The best land was to be put up at auction and would thus go to the highest bidder.[6]

The typical American settler had no opportunity under such a policy. If he wanted good land, he would have to compete with men of money at the auction sale. Even the poor land brought as much as $640 per section. Since this was beyond the means of the pioneer, and since he naturally hated the speculator who offered him smaller parcels of land—but at advanced prices, he often chose the uncertainties of unlawful settlement, hoping and praying for government sanction to establish the legality of his holding.

The brunt of the attack from the frontier settlers was borne by the large land companies for the next few years. Great tracts of land north of the Ohio River were sold to them on extended terms of credit; the companies then proceeded to employ strict measures in dealing with squatters on their lands. But even such stringent methods failed. While land companies were having their troubles with the squatters, the government was attempting to settle the same problem with no better success. In 1787, Colonel Harmar was sent to remove a group of squatters along the Ohio. His troops burned the settlers' cabins, tore down their fences, and destroyed their potato patches; but, no sooner had the soldiers left than the trespassers returned.[7]

Such was the problem inherited by the federal government when it began its operations in 1789. The new Congress sanctioned the land policy evolved by the Congress of the Confederation, and immediately the discussion of the land question assumed an extraordinary importance. Representatives from the frontier regions began agitating for a general preemption law and some even went so far as to demand free land.[8] A representative from western Pennsylvania voiced the typical frontier argument for a democratic policy when he put the following question to the conservative eastern interests:

What will these men think who have placed themselves on a vacant spot, anxiously waiting its disposition by the Government, to find their preemption right engrossed by the purchaser of a million acres? . . . They will do one of two things: either move into Spanish territory, or . . . move on United States territory, and take possession without leave. . . . They will not pay you money. Will you then raise a force to drive them off? . . . They are willing to pay an equitable price for those lands; and, if they may be indulged with a preemption to the purchase, no men will be better friends to the government. . . . The emigrants who reach the Western country will not stop till they find a place where they can securely seat themselves.[9]

At first, Congress listened attentively. But when the condition of the treasury was realized and Hamilton recommended that the public domain be retained as a source of revenue, all hope for the frontiersman was abandoned. A well balanced social structure was a national necessity to Hamiltonian interests. Since easterners thought that any inducement to settlement would rob them of their population a wide open public domain had its dangers. For one thing, there was much good land in the eastern states and preemption on the public domain would lessen the value of these state lands. Moreover, did not a too rapid expansion of the frontier threaten to involve the new republic in foreign difficulties? For the time being, then, the conservative eastern states held sway in Congress—the frontier plea was rebuffed.

Under the decision to retain the old policy many difficulties arose. The government found itself a creditor of land speculators who could neither fulfill their contracts nor successfully settle their own lands. The Symmes purchase especially caused the federal government a great deal of trouble. Much of the land of this purchase eventually reverted back to the government because of inability to pay. But Symmes had sold land that did not belong to him, and his purchasers held tracts under the impression that Congress would confirm their titles since they had bought of Symmes in good faith. At first unwilling to grant such confirmation of title, Congress finally yielded under pressure to the extent of granting preemption in the act of March 2, 1799.[10] The settlers who had made contracts with Symmes were to be given title to their disputed holdings on payment of the minimum price per acre. This was the first preemption law passed by the United States Congress. After 1799, several other relief preemptions followed in quick succession, all of them applying to the Symmes purchase.[11] These were the first of a long series of indulgences to the frontier which, though apparently small in the beginning, in time proved to aid materially in the liberalization of the land policy.

Realizing that the system of land sales to companies was not working to advantage, Congress revised its policy in the land act of 1796.[12] Unfortunately for the poor man, this act raised the minimum price per acre to $2.00. A year's credit was to be allowed and a ten per cent discount for cash payment but such terms did not appeal to the average settler.

The act naturally failed in its purpose. Speculators were too much interested in the values of state lands. As yet the government had refused to realize that its best customer was the actual settler, and that the system of selling land in large quantities to speculators was inexpedient. Only when the government should realize that a policy attractive to settlement must be adopted would it be possible to interest speculators or anyone else in buying public land.

Events, however, were rapidly making way for such a revision. The democratic forces under the leadership of Jefferson were determined on overthrowing the aristocratic tendencies in government. Under these new standards there were many men who were sympathetic with the West. This general revulsion against the Hamiltonian interests made possible the land act of 1800.

William Henry Harrison, elected in 1799 as the first delegate from the Northwest Territory, conspicuously brought the land question before Congress.[13] As chairman of the committee, he bore the main responsibility for breaking down the prevailing conservative standards. The new act of 1800 reduced the minimum amount of land that could be purchased to 320 acres.[14] But the greatest liberality in the act is found in the provision establishing a new credit system—a credit that was to extend over a period of four years, at the end of which time it was supposed that the settler would have made enough from his land to pay for it. W. C. Claiborne of Tennessee attempted to establish the principle of preemption in the act, but eastern interests prevented this indulgence.[15]

One might suppose that the era of Jeffersonian democracy would have inaugurated an even more liberal land policy. But when Jefferson became president his liberalism gave way to more pressing problems, as he realized that little would be gained by encouraging a rapid expansion of the frontier—a frontier that was already seething with discontent— where the danger of stirring up Indian wars and even a foreign war constantly threatened.

Meanwhile, the time-worn problem of intrusions on public lands was continually pressing upon Congress. Petition after petition begging relief through preemption was presented from western settlers only to be met with successive rebuffs. A committee of the House of Representatives reported in 1801 a typical petition of settlers who "with much labor and difficulty . . . have settled upon, cultivated, and improved certain lands, the property of the United States, between the waters of the Scioto and Muskingum rivers, and have thereby not only enhanced the value of the lands upon which they have respectively settled but of other lands in the vicinity of the same, to the great benefit of the United States, and pray for a pre-emption right to those lands at two dollars per acre, and such credit as Congress may think proper to extend to them, clear of interest." To this the committee offered sympathy, but feeling that there were many other settlers in the same predicament, it recommended that "granting the indulgence prayed for would operate as an encouragement to intrusions on public lands, and would be an unjustifiable sacrifice of the public interest . . . the prayer of the petition ought not be granted."[16] In 1806 another committee declared that "when it is considered that these individuals settled without authority, or any reasonable ground of expectation from Government, it is evident that any hardships to which they may be exposed are chargeable only to their own indiscretion."[17]

The credit system, provided for under the act of 1800, worked badly from the start. Settlers took advantage of it, but could rarely meet the terms of credit. As early as 1804, Gallatin advised its abolition, and in its place advocated the more liberal policy of reducing the minimum price per acre of land to $1.25 and selling it in small tracts of 160 acres.[18] When the question arose as to whether preemption might not be offered in order to quiet the frontier Gallatin replied: "The principle of granting them the right of preemption, exclusively of the abuses to which it is liable, appears irreconcilable with the idea of drawing revenue from the sale of lands."[19] Congress, however, refused to consider any of Gallatin's proposals.

Whether Congress desired to adopt preemption or not, it was forced to use the principle as a temporary expedient in granting relief to certain settlers and in quieting land titles in various territories, the latter function being necessary before the government could proceed with systematic land administration. The beneficiaries of this generosity were the many settlers of the frontier whose titles were based upon grants made by foreign countries before these regions became part of the United States. Because of the uncertain records in these cases, the government felt that it was making a concession in allowing a confirmation of title on the payment of the minimum price per acre. Between 1804 and 1830, there were sixteen such acts passed by Congress, granting preemption in a limited form to special groups in the various territories and states.[20]

Such a limited grant of preemption failed to satisfy the frontiersmen, many of whom were unable to take advantage of the acts. In order to cope with the lawlessness of these backwoodsmen, Congress adopted stringent legislation. As early as 1802 John Randolph introduced a bill to prevent intrusions on the public domain.[21] It was not, however, until 1807 that Congress seriously took up the matter and finally passed the Intrusion Act, which in itself admitted the inability of the government to administer the law. This act provided that unlawful settlers could become tenants-at-will until they were able to pay for their land or until someone else bought it. If the intruder on public land did not register his tenancy he was subject to a six months' imprisonment and a fine of $100. According to the act, the frontier army was to imprison the illegal settlers who did not conform to these regulations. Since most of the frontier army was made up of frontiersmen, many themselves squatters, it remains to be shown how Congress expected the law to be enforced. This act was but a typical example of eastern ignorance concerning frontier conditions. The act was partially repealed seven years later, though most of it remained on the statute books for many decades.[22]

In 1815, it could be said that the national government was persistently trying to maintain a conservative land policy, but had not been successful in enforcing it along a lawless frontier. Public land records made clear a situation which the frontiersmen were not slow to realize. An estimate submitted in 1816 to the House of Representatives showed that land sold at auction-sale, most of it to men of money, averaged only ten and a half cents more than the minimum price per acre.[23] Already over 212,000 acres of land had been sold under the special preemption laws. The question arose as to whether it would not be better to allow the settlers a general preemption and thus provide for actual settlement rather than to sell to speculators who merely held lands until they reached higher values. But again the conservative eastern interests in control of Congress refused to listen to argument.

Meanwhile, however, there was taking place a westward movement of population such as had never before been equalled in American history. Administrative problems accordingly multiplied rapidly, and with their increase the abuses of the land policy established in 1800 became more apparent. The panic of 1819 and its destructive results caused Congress once again to focus attention on the public land system. The answer was the land act of 1820.

Under this act the minimum amount of land that could be purchased was reduced to 160 acres and the price was lowered to $1.25 an acre.[24] This was a step in favor of the frontiersman. But coupled with these concessions was a provision which abolished the credit system. This latter proved to work untold hardships upon the West. From a settler's viewpoint, it seemed that the government was tightening its control of the frontier. In fact, the act of 1820 proved to be a greater boon to speculation than to actual settlement.

As when in the 1790's frontier interests had rallied under the banner of democracy to win concessions from the conservative eastern interests, so now the growing West once more mustered its strength in Congress to challenge the aristocratic tendencies in the government. In this new struggle there were prominent congressmen from Illinois, Mississippi, and Alabama; but perhaps most outstanding among the leaders was that "veritable champion of the West"—Thomas Hart Benton, Senator from Missouri.

Faced with the possibility of having to relinquish their holdings, many settlers frantically petitioned Congress for relief from their obligations under the new law. The problem was complex as well as embarrassing. If Congress refused relief these frontiersmen would become squatters. On the other hand, if some indulgence were granted, might not the return of prosperity enable them to pay their debts? In face of the circumstances, it was much better for Congress to compromise the issue than to antagonize a region where population and political strength was increasing from day to day.

In 1821, the first relief act was passed, granting an extension of time for payment to those settlers indebted to the government under the old credit system. As might have been expected, a temporary measure was not sufficient to satisfy the frontier element. Accordingly, in 1822, Congress extended the act of 1821. This policy of extended credit once begun was continued in one form or another until by 1832 eleven relief acts had been passed.[25] However, such a solution of the problem contained evil as well as virtue. It was the compromising attitude displayed by eastern leaders that in reality enabled the frontier forces to gather their strength into such form as to prove very threatening to the whole land policy. Having been successful in gaining numerous concessions along one line, there was all the reason to expect that similar concessions could be gained along other lines.

In 1826, Benton declared that it was better economy to sell the public lands in eight years for twenty millions, than to sell them in the distant future for three hundred millions.[26] Only a few eastern leaders who were well-versed in land matters were able to discern the meaning of such declarations. One of these leaders, Richard Rush, secretary of the treasury, in 1827, did not exaggerate the importance of the problem confronting the government when he declared:

The maxim is held to be a sound one, that the ratio of capital to population should if possible, be kept on the increase. . . . The manner in which the remote lands of the United States are selling and settling, whilst it may possibly tend to increase more quickly the aggregate population of the country . . . does not increase capital in the same proportion. It is a proposition too plain to require elucidation, that the creation of capital is retarded, rather than accelerated, by the diffusion of a thin population over a great surface of soil. Anything that may serve to hold back this tendency to diffusion from running too far and too long into an extreme can scarcely prove otherwise than salutary.[27]

No plainer words than these could have warned eastern interests of the crisis at hand, yet it was difficult for politicians in the East to realize that the time had come for the West to play a vital part in the solution of the nation's problems.

It was the victory of Andrew Jackson in 1828 that spelled the overthrow of more than one conservative eastern policy.[28] Jacksonian democracy was to mean much to the settlement of the public domain. Under his administration land policies were gradually altered from the conservative system evolved over a period of forty years to a more liberal one better suited to the West.

Much to the surprise of the East, western interests controlled the balance of power in the Congress which ushered in Jackson's administration. On December 29, 1829, Senator Samuel A. Foot of Connecticut introduced a resolution inquiring into the expediency of limiting the sale of public lands.[29] Benton challenged this resolution claiming it to be a direct attack upon the West. Senator Hayne of South Carolina came to Benton's aid and the land question was soon forgotten as the discussion settled down into a lengthy debate between Hayne and Webster on the question of the structure of the government. This debate showed that the South would ally itself temporarily with the West.[30]

In 1830, through such an alliance came the passage of the preemption act which gave the American frontier its first important concession and the conservative eastern interests their first blow.[31] By this act, any settler who had migrated to the public domain and had cultivated a tract of land in 1829, was authorized to enter any number of acres of this tract, not exceeding 160, by paying the minimum price of $1.25 per acre.[32] Although the act was only temporary in character it nevertheless provided a general pardon to all those inhabitants who had settled illegally. Once the government granted this concession it could not retract.

The act in reality encouraged illegal settlement, for settlers immediately took up the best lands they could find and then petitioned Congress for another general pardon. Why not pardon us, they queried, as well as the unlawful settlers of 1830? So again in 1832 another temporary preemption was granted in renewal of the act of 1830.[33] And in 1834 the act was once more renewed.[34]

By 1835 the rush for western lands was getting beyond the control of the government. Many persons who had good intentions of going west and settling permanently found it more profitable to become speculators. So, besides the regular eastern speculator who bought up lands, there was the western settler himself who purchased land, sold it to newcomers, and then proceeded to a new tract to repeat the process. The preemption laws of 1830, 1832, and 1834 were instrumental to many illegal operations. Both eastern and western speculators took out claims under these laws only to sell their claims as soon as possible for higher prices. There was much speculation in the rich cotton lands of

Alabama and Mississippi. In this region, it is said that speculators obtained the services of negroes, poor settlers, and Indians, to set up claims under the law and thus obtain these productive areas at the minimum price of $1.25 per acre.[35] Such speculative enterprise endangered the preemption principle—a principle which had been established to protect the actual and real settler.

As the wave of speculation in western lands reached its greatest height, glaring abuses and even scandalous frauds were brought to light.[36] Under such stress and strain, the preemption principle was challenged. In 1834 a very bitter fight occurred in the House before the preemption act of that year could be enacted. Representative Samuel F. Vinton, a member from the more settled parts of Ohio, declared that the only design of the bill was to aid the speculators.[37] On the subject of the rich cotton lands in Alabama and Mississippi Clement C. Clay of Alabama stated that "in sales which embraced three million acres of such cotton lands, the price realized was only $1.27, out of which was to be taken all the expenses of the sale."[38] Edward Everett, of Vermont, set forth that "if this bill passed, in a year or two we shall be called upon to pass another and another. If this is to be done, why not at once throw open all the public lands for a general scramble and abolish the auction system?" In his mind, "it seemed there were combinations of settlers as well as land speculators."[39]

The typical frontier defense with all its eloquence was voiced by Representative Balie Peyton of Tennessee who questioned the harm of giving a poor man the right to preempt.

That poor man who had blazed the trees and planted the potatoes had chosen that spot as the home of his children. He had toiled in hope. He had given it value, and he loved the spot. It was his all. When the public sales were proclaimed, if that poor man attended it, he might bid to the last cent he had in the world, and mortgage the bed he slept on to enable him to do it. He might have his wife and children around him to see him bid; and when he had bid his very last cent, one of these speculators would stand by his side and bid two dollars more. And thus he would see his little home, on which he had toiled for years, where he hoped to rear his children and to find a peaceful grave, pass into the hands of a rich moneyed company. . . . Such a policy would but teach the republic to alienate her children."[40]

The rage for speculation increased at such a rate that by 1836 Congress was seriously considering means of stemming the tide.[41] In this mad scramble for land the greedy speculators had small regard for settlers' claims, legal or otherwise. Finding that the government had little interest in preserving his rights, the western settler determined to take the duty upon himself. Accordingly, numerous claims clubs or settlers' associations,[42] began to spring up all along the frontier. Naturally, the western press and territorial legislatures sympathized with the settlers in their actions.[43] With rough and ready methods, the frontiersman not only protected his squatter rights but also got his land at a much lower figure, generally at the minimum price. Woe to the speculator who at the auction sale attempted to outbid a settler belonging to one of these frontier associations!

But the settler did not have to wait long for a solution of his difficulties. The Panic of 1837 proved to be a very effective force in stopping speculation. As soon as active speculation died down, leaders in Congress were willing to grant legal sanction to the claims of hundreds of pioneers who had encroached upon the public domain since 1834.

Such action was taken in 1838 when Congress again renewed the Act of 1830.[44] And two years later when the question came up once more, another renewal was the result.[45]

By 1840, the principle of preemption had been in use for more than forty years. But as yet the application of it was always in the form of a pardon for irregularities or for illegalities already committed. The agrarian West had reached the point where it did not like the idea of constantly being pardoned for illegal actions. It wanted the government to legalize trespassing. It wanted a permanent, prospective, preemption law—a law which would allow a person to go anywhere upon public land, select his claim to the exclusion of all other persons—especially speculators, and buy his land at the minimum price per acre. A new goal was thus established by the frontier West.

A certain prestige was now added to the cause when President Van Buren came out openly in favor of the preemption principle as a permanent feature of the land system and it became a plank in the Democratic platform.[46] On the other hand, the West could hardly mistake the principles of William Henry Harrison, proponent of the land act of 1800 and Whig candidate in the campaign of 1840. Though the latter was elected, no section of the country had direct control of the government. Yet by playing its cards carefully the frontier might now gain a complete victory over the conservative East. The ensuing fight in Congress in 1840 and 1841 was one of the most terrific in the history of the land question.

Evidence of the importance of this issue is found in the statement of John C. Calhoun, who on January 12, 1841 declared: "I regard the question of public lands, next to that of the currency, the most dangerous and difficult of all which demand the attention of the country and government at this important juncture of our affairs."[47] During the same period Senator Ambrose H. Sevier from the frontier state of Arkansas was insistent that the West considered it the most important question of the day.[48]

The Whigs had made promises to the frontiersmen in the campaign. It remained to be seen whether they could be relied upon when Senator Benton in December of that year introduced his Log-Cabin bill providing for permanent, prospective, preemption.[49] The Democrats who for the most part favored the principle, enjoyed the possibilities of Whig discomfiture. As ex-President Jackson remarked: "It places Clay in a position that he must vote for the Bill, or expose his hypocrisy."[50] Among the frontier leaders who pushed forward for victory and aided Benton materially were Senators Robert J. Walker of Mississippi and Clement C. Clay of Alabama. In support of the bill Clay very ably showed that the average from the sale of land varied only from $1.26 per acre in 1828 to $1.31 in 1834. In 1836, the year of the largest sales in land history, the price averaged scarcely more than $1.25 per acre.[51] If the expense of the auction sales is taken into consideration the average return per acre was probably considerably less than the established minimum. "Was not the question distinctly presented," asked the Senator, "whether the government was to sell the public domain in small quantities, to men of small capital, who would immediately occupy, improve, and render it productive, or whether it was the better policy to sell it at auction to bands of speculators and capitalists, in larger quantities, to lie idle and unprofitable till they could extort the desired profit from those whose necessities compel them to have it?"

A very tense fight ensued in the Senate over the provisions of the bill. Henry Clay visualized an exodus of the peoples of Europe to America, who he thought would in a short time take up the remainder of the public domain and establish alien governments. It was still the age-old fight of the interests of the established states against the agrarian interests of the frontier. Among the states whose representatives fought to block legislation were Kentucky, Vermont, Massachusetts, and Connecticut, whilst ardent champions of preemption spoke for Missouri, Alabama, Illinois, and Indiana.[52] Throughout the whole month of January, 1841, the Senators from the frontier states, especially Benton of Missouri, stood up against the fire from all sections of the country.[53]

A Whig Senator from Illinois introduced, as an amendment to the Log-Cabin bill, Clay's pet project—that of distributing the proceeds of the sales of public lands among the several states according to their population. On February 1, the Democrats rallied to vote down this amendment by the vote of 31 to 20.[54] The following day the Log-Cabin bill passed the Senate by vote of 31 to 19, fourteen Whigs and five Democrats from the Atlantic Coast states voting against it.[55] The bill was then presented to the House, but it was too late to gain consideration in that session of Congress.[56] The tardiness of its passage in the Senate had blasted the hopes of its success in the House. The frontier cause was in danger of losing ground; the next Congress contained an increased Whig representation.

President Tyler called a special session of the new Congress. Clay was quick to grasp the opportunity which the composition of its membership afforded. The increasing strength of the frontier forces caused him to decide that the West would have its preemption law, but only on the condition that distribution should pass along with it. Crittenden of Kentucky in January had promised the West that Clay's Whig following would go for preemption if the frontier would support distribution.[57] Without consulting the frontier interests, a combined distribution-preemption bill was introduced in the House. From the very beginning it was evident that not many of the frontier representatives would vote for the combined measure, but the Whigs needed to gain only a few votes.

The bill passed the House on July 13, by the close vote of 116 to 108.[58] The last stages of the struggle have been aptly described by an eye-witness:

> *The noise was now so great, and so many members were addressing the Chair at once, that it seemed as if "chaos were come again.". . . . The Chair exerted itself to the utmost to restore order, but in vain. The uproar continued, while the rain fell, and the thunder rolled in terrific peals, and the blue lightning glaring at intervals through the hall, appeared to be mocking the storm that raged within. . . . The House having been in session for ten hours, a proposition was made that adjournment take place. . . . This was rejected by the majority. So amidst a terrific storm of thunder and lightning and rain, which at intervals rendered voices inaudible, the bill was forced ahead.[59]*

In the Senate the bill met with even greater opposition. Benton fought the measure from start to finish, constantly demanding that preemption be passed separately from distribution. Before Clay could hope for success, he had to appease the fear of the southern Senators by agreeing to an amendment which provided that distribution should cease if the tariff were raised above the twenty per cent level. The Whig forces battered away at the Democratic defense until August 30, when the bill was voted through by the count of 25 to 18.[60] On September 4, 1841, the bill was approved by President Tyler.

The frontier interests "accepted the law as a concession wrung from a reluctant Congress whose sympathy for the West was far from cordial."[61] They never forgave Henry Clay for stealing Benton's thunder. For the last twenty years he had consistently sided with the East in its condemnation of the frontier spirit. Knowing him to have been the author of the hated principle of distribution, they branded him as insincere in his attempt to reconcile such diametrically opposed principles as distribution and preemption. They called him "the worst enemy of the squatter." An Arkansas newspaper in 1844 said that he had done all in his power "to oppress the poor and hardy settlers upon the public lands, striving to place them in the merciless hands of heartless speculators, and proposing to send a military force against them and force them out of their hard-earned homes at the point of the bayonet."[62] Certainly Clay could not be called the champion of the frontier West in 1841. The frontier denied any claim to him. Instead, it was over-joyous when in 1842 the tariff was raised above the twenty per cent level and Clay's distribution was discontinued. Only the preemption principle remained to carry on the memory of the bitter fight of 1841.

The East was slow in reconciling itself to preemption. In 1838, the New York *Courier and Enquirer* had declared that the preemption principle was one of "granting bounties to squatters engaged in cheating the government out of the best tracts of land."[63] This sentiment continued long after the passage of the distribution-preemption act of 1841. Even Horace Greeley, later one of the outstanding advocates of free land, had little sympathy with the principle.[64] In 1843, he declared: "We detest the whole business believing that nothing has wrought so fearful a woe to the industry, morals and prosperity of the West."[65] In the same year he gave the following advice to emigrants: "We counsel emigrants not to go beyond the bounds of civilization, but . . . to stop off this side of the jumping-off place, select land that is surveyed and pay for it; if you have not enough money, go to work and earn it, and buy your land manfully."[66]

Passing beyond the realm of contemporary estimates, Shosuke Sato, a foreign student, declared in 1886 that the preemption act of 1841 was the most important agrarian measure ever passed by Congress.[67] In light of the foregoing, his conclusion appears to have been accurate, for it is a well-known fact that this act marked the end of the old conservative land policy established in 1785, democratized the American land system, and placed the actual settler on an equal basis with the speculator in competition for land. An individual, henceforth, could legally venture forth upon public surveyed land and stake a claim to the exclusion of all others.[68] The policy inaugurated in 1841 lasted as long as the frontier itself—the repeal of the law in 1891 being symbolic of the disappearance of the frontier. The western frontiersmen well fulfilled Jefferson's prophecy: "They will settle the lands in spite of everybody." Preemption was truly a frontier triumph.

Notes

1. William E. Dodd, "Causes for Bacon's Rebellion," paper read at the American Historical Association annual meeting in Boston, December 29, 1930.

2. Archibald Henderson, "A Pre-Revolutionary Revolt in the Old Southwest," in *Mississippi Valley Historical Review*, XVII (1930), 191-213.

3. E. B. O'Callaghan (ed.), *Documents Relative to the Colonial History of the State of New York* (Albany, 1856-87), VIII, 253.

4. Jefferson to [Edmund Pendleton], August 13, 1776, in Paul L. Ford (ed.), *The Works of Thomas Jefferson* (New York, 1904), II, 239-40.

5. Amelia C. Ford, "Colonial Precedents of Our National Land System as It Existed in 1800," in University of Wisconsin, *Bulletin*, No. 352 (Madison, 1910), 123-43.

6. *Journals of the American Congress*, IV, Ordinance of May 20, 1785, p. 520.

7. *Annals of Congress*, 1 Cong., 1 Sess., 412.

8. *Ibid.*, 411-12, 624; 1 Cong., 3 Sess., 1841.

9. *Ibid.*, 1 Cong., 1 Sess., 411.

10. *Ibid.*, 4 Cong., 2 Sess., 2353; 5 Cong., 2 Sess., 3018; *Statutes at Large*, I, Act of March 2, 1799, p. 728.

11. Acts were passed in 1801, 1802, 1803, and 1804.

12. *Statutes at Large*, I, Act of May 18, 1796, p. 464.

13. *Annals of Cong.*, 6 Cong., 1 Sess., 209.

14. *Statutes at Large*, II, Act of May 10, 1800, p. 73.

15. Payson J. Treat, *The National Land System, 1785-1820* (New York, 1910), 94.

16. *American State Papers* (Washington, 1832-61), *Public Lands*, I, 111.

17. *Ibid.*, 261.

18. *Ibid.*, 183.

19. *Ibid.*, 184.

20. For a careful study of this subject see Treat, *op. cit.*, chap. IX.

21. *Annals of Cong.*, 7 Cong., 1 Sess., 421.

22. *Statutes at Large*, II, Act of May 3, 1807, p. 445. On failure of enforcement see *Niles' Register* (Philadelphia), XV (1819), 301; XXXVIII (1830), 99; *Official Opinions of the Attorneys General of the United States* (Washington, 1852-), I, 471, 475.

23. *American State Papers, Public Lands*, III, 170.

24. *Statutes at Large*, III, Act of April 24, 1820, p. 566.

25. The amount of indebtedness was considerably reduced by this series of relief acts which are outlined in Treat, *op. cit.*, 161.

26. *Congressional Debates*, 19 Cong., 1 Sess., 724.

27. Report of the Secretary of the Treasury on the State of the Finances, 1827, *American State Papers, Finance*, V, 638.

28. The era had at last been reached when the East was forced to recognize frontier values. The stabilization once begun of eastern policies and frontier policies would no doubt have been continued many decades had it not been for the advent of the slavery issue, an issue which divided the country into North and South sectionalism.

29. *Cong. Debates*, 21 Cong., 1 Sess., 3.

30. Raynor G. Wellington, *The Political and Sectional Influence of the Public Lands, 1828-1842* (Boston, 1914), 24-26.

31. The yea's and nay's of the House are not recorded, but on January 13, 1830, the vote in the Senate was as follows: *Yea's*: Mo., Ky., Ill., Ind., Ohio, Pa., Vt., Mass., N.C., S.C., Ga., Ala., La., Miss., Tenn.; *Nay's*: Del., N.J., Conn., Maine; *Divided*: N.H., N.Y., R.I., Md. *Vote*: 2 to 12. *Senate Journal*, 21 Cong., 1 Sess., 83.

32. *Statutes at Large*, IV, Act of May 29, 1830, p. 420.

33. *Ibid.*, IV, Act of July 14, 1832, p. 603.

34. *Ibid.*, IV, Act of June 19, 1834, p. 678.

35. *Cong. Debates*, 23 Cong., 1 Sess., 4477 ff.

36. *American State Papers, Public Lands*, VII, 732-77, VIII, No. 1507, p. 612; *Senate Documents*, 24 Cong., 2 Sess., no. 168; Reginald McGrane, *The Panic of 1837* (Chicago, 1924), 44-45.

37. *Cong. Debates*, 23 Cong., 1 Sess., 4469.

38. *Ibid.*, 4470.

39. *Ibid.*, 4473.

40. *Ibid.*, 4480.

41. Calhoun's cession idea gained consideration, and Robert J. Walker of Mississippi advocated the plan of limiting the sales of land to only actual settlers. *Ibid.*, 24 Cong., 2 Sess., 705, 419-28.

42. See Benjamin F. Shambaugh, "Frontier Land Clubs or Claims Associations," in American Historical Association *Report*, 1910, I, 67-85.

43. *Racine Argus* (Racine, Wisconsin Territory), March 9, 1838; *Wisconsin Territorial Gazette* (Burlington, Wisconsin Territory), September 7, 1838; *Wisconsin Territorial Democrat* (Chicago, Illinois), January 20, 1841; *La Crosse Independent Republican* (La Crosse, Wisconsin), December 20, 1854.

44. *Statutes at Large*, V, Act of June 22, 1838, p. 251.

45. *Ibid.*, V, Act of June 1, 1840, p. 382.

46. James D. Richardson, *Messages and Papers of the Presidents* (Washington, 1879-1903), III, 388.

47. *Cong. Globe*, Appendix, 26 Cong., 2 Sess., 52.

48. *Ibid.*, 64.

49. Wellington, *op. cit.*,, 75.

50. Jackson to Blair, January 5, 1841, Wellington, *op. cit.*, 87.

51. *Cong. Globe, Appendix*, 26 Cong., 2 Sess., 19.

52. *Ibid.*, 21, 22, 27, 29, 38, 48, 70.

53. *Ibid.*, 20, 58, 61, 78.

54. *Cong. Globe*, 26 Cong., 2 Sess., 138.

55. *Ibid.*, 138.

56. *Ibid.*, 230.

57. *Cong. Globe, Appendix*, 26 Cong., 2 Sess., 48.

58. *Cong. Globe*, 27 Cong., 1 Sess., 156.

59. *Ibid.*, 155-56.

60. *Ibid.*, 405-406. Three Whigs who had voted against the distribution amendment in February were brought in line; several Democrats who had opposed in February were brought over; which, together with the new Whigs elected in 1840, made for the sum of twenty-five votes. Of the eighteen votes opposed, all but one, Clayton of Delaware, were Democratic votes, mostly from the West and South.

61. George M. Stephenson, *The Political History of the Public Lands from 1840 to 1862* (Boston, 1917), 97.

62. *Arkansas Banner* (Little Rock), April 24, 1844.

63. New York *Courier and Enquirer*, January 27, 1838.

64. New York *Daily Tribune*, April 29, 1843; New York *Weekly Tribune*, May 4, 1843.

65. *Ibid.*, June 15, 1843.

66. *Ibid.*, July 29, 1843.

67. Shosuke Sato, "The History of the Land Question in the United States," in *Johns Hopkins University Studies* (Baltimore, 1886), IV, 159.

68. *Statutes at Large*, V, Act of September 4, 1841, p. 453-58.

The Iowa claims clubs: Symbol and substance

Allan G. Bogue

Prior to World War II most historians writing about the West shared a common bias. They favored the farmers as opposed to the speculators, and they looked with suspicion on eastern capital and the large corporation typified by the railroad and mining ventures. Many of these historians—like Frederick Jackson Turner, Charles Beard, and Frederick Merk—came from small-town, rural mid-America, and they were influenced by the traditions that permeated their home regions. While these historians castigated corporate and speculative misbehavior, they accepted many of the myths propagated by westerners about themselves. Some of these historians were close enough to the frontier to know original pioneers.

In recent decades this has changed. America has become urban, and most historians have never lived in a small town or on a farm. Even those who come from rural America are far enough away from the pioneer experience not to be captivated by its myths. Two of the most influential historians of recent years have been Richard Hofstadter and Oscar Handlin. Hofstadter's book *The Age of Reform* (1956) exposed the hard side of the family farm, pointing out that it, like the mainstreet hardware store, was a business and often represented a substantial capital investment. Oscar Handlin's immigrants peopled not the rural Midwest but the crowded industrial cities. This was but the beginning of a trend that has seen historians take a harsher view of farm subsidies. Aid to farmers, once portrayed as a liberal triumph, has now been attacked as special interest legislation often at variance with the interests of the urban workers. In tune with these trends the newer generation of western historians has begun a reevaluation of institutions developed on the frontier.

In the following essay Allan G. Bogue, Professor of History at the University of Wisconsin, systematically analyzes the workings of the Iowa claim clubs, once hailed as a spontaneous frontier democratic institution designed to protect the honest settler. In so doing he also throws light on the symbiotic relationship between the land speculator and the real settler.

For further reading: Richard Hofstadter, *The Age of Reform from Bryan to F.D.R.*

Reprinted with permission from *Mississippi Valley Historical Review* (September 1958), 231-253.

(New York: Knopf, 1956)* Benjamin F. Shambaugh, "Fronter Land Clubs or Claims Associations," American Historical Association *Annual Report,* 1900, 2 vols. (Washington, D.C.: Superintendent of Documents, 1901), I, 67-85.

*Available in paperback.

The claim club or squatters' association has long occupied a modest but secure place in western history. The presence of such extralegal organizations on the middle-western frontier led students of the federal land system to suggest that the land laws in effect when the Midle West was being settled were ill-adapted to frontier needs.[1] Frederick Jackson Turner and others, going further, saw the claim clubs as a manifestation of the frontiersmen's capacity for democratic action.[2] No social historian, however, has fully explored the possibilities of the frontier claim club as an illustration of social interaction in newly formed frontier groups. Further study of this frontier institution can perhaps illuminate not only our understanding of American democracy but also our knowledge of the federal land disposal system and of pioneer social behavior.

Although claim clubs existed elsewhere in the Middle West, the Iowa variety has occasioned particular comment. When historians have believed citation to be in order, Jesse Macy's early study of institutional beginnings in Iowa, the records of the claim club in Johnson County, Iowa, edited by Benjamin F. Shambaugh, and Shambaugh's article on "Frontier Land Clubs or Claim Associations" have been standard exhibits.[3] To Shambaugh, who built upon Macy's work, the claim club was an organization which the settlers used to protect their claims on the public domain until they could obtain title from the federal government. Squatters organized such clubs, he suggested, so that they might forestall the land speculator and the claim jumper. Although pointing out that the claim club did allow settlers to transfer claims to which they had not received legal title, and that technically the squatters were trespassing, Shambaugh emphasized that these squatters were "honest farmers," establishing homes and improving their claims. Representing "the beginnings of Western local political institutions," the clubs fostered "natural justice, equality, and democracy."[4] Land historians and the authors of widely used western history texts have not deviated to any extent from this general interpretation. One text writer modified Shambaugh somewhat by suggesting that the clubs died out in Iowa because "the Pre-emption Law in 1841 ended the difficulty."[5]

Neither the work of Macy nor that of Shambaugh is heavily documented. Macy discovered the manuscript records of the Johnson County club and printed its by-laws in his essay, as well as the brief regulations of a lead miners' association at Debuque. Although claiming that there were scores of these associations,[6] he referred specifically to only two. Shambaugh edited the complete record of the Johnson County club and transcribed the minutes of an association at Fort Dodge, drawing upon both of these sources for his article on frontier land clubs. He thought it "safe to say that over 100 of these extra-legal organizations existed in Territorial Iowa."[7] Old settlers who had observed club action still lived when Macy and Shambaugh investigated the claim clubs, and the former at least tapped the memories of some of these. Although they did not cite them, a number of contemporary descriptions and reminiscences substantiating the Macy and Shambaugh interpretation of the role of the squatters' club were also available.[8]

Histories of Iowa counties, most of which were unavailable or were ignored by Macy and Shambaugh, provide additional source material on the claim clubs.[9] They show clearly that Iowa settlers frequently held "claims" in the public domain for varying lengths of time before they tried to obtain title from the federal government. Organized claim clubs, however, definitely existed in only twenty-five counties, if, on the evidence in the county histories, we limit ourselves to those instances where the names of club members are given and to specific descriptions of local club activity in Cedar County, published in a local newspaper and later copied in two county histories, the number is raised to twenty-six.[10]

A few associations which did not quite conform to type were also described in the county histories. Settlers in Lee County, for example, banded together in opposition to the title of non-resident speculators in the Half Breed Tract during the 1830's and 1840's.[11] Along the Des Moines River to the north of the Raccoon Fork, settlers on lands claimed by the Des Moines Navigation and Railroad Company united to fight the title of the eastern grantees of the company in a struggle which continued from the 1860's to the 1890's.[12] In O'Brien and Monona counties, settlers organized to contest the title to lands which railroad corporations claimed as part of their land grants.[13] A number of homesteaders who had falsely certified that they were of legal age banded together in Sioux County to intimidate settlers who might wish to contest their titles.[14] Finally, the local historian of Sac County told of the residents of two townships who packed the land office at Sioux City when their claims were offered at auction to prevent speculators from bidding, because the settlers as yet lacked the means to purchase them.[15]

Of the twenty-six counties in which claim clubs of the usual type existed, nineteen lay contiguous one to the other—outliers running north, south, and east from a solid block of nine counties located in the third and fourth tiers of counties north from the Missouri border and lying in the east central portion of the state. Most of these counties were settled during the 1830's and 1840's, but they were not the only counties settled in that period. In general, also, considerable numbers of settlers of southern stock settled in these counties, although not to the same degree as in the counties in the two southern tiers. Those counties in which the southern stock mingled with Yankee or alien settlers made up the central block of claim club counties.[16] Whether the tensions generated by the mixing of cultural stocks stimulated the formation of organizations designed to deal with the basic problem of control of the land in these frontier settlements can only be conjectured. Very definitely, however, club activity was not linked to the absence of a pre-emption law. In the first place limited pre-emption laws applied to many of the settlers who moved to Iowa prior to 1841, and secondly the claim clubs in sixteen of the twenty-six counties were active considerably after the passage of the general pre-emption act of 1841.[17]

The county histories contain all or a portion of the club laws in nineteen cases, and in a few instances the original manuscript records are still available.[18] The manuscript records of the Johnson County and the Fort Dodge claim clubs give a much more accurate picture of squatter law in those counties than do the secondary accounts in the published histories of Johnson and Webster counties. The club laws ranged all the way from the general to the specific, depending in part, perhaps, on the degree of pressure to which the organizers believed themselves subject and in part on the predilections of those who drew up the regulations. Granted such local variations, the regulations covered the size of the claims allowed; directions for marking, registering, and transferring claims; and the procedure to be followed when club members contested each other's rights, when members were threatened by claim jumpers, and when the date of the land sale arrived.

In any re-evaluation of the role of the squatters' associations the responsibilities and the privileges of the members must be carefully considered in order to discover whether they were consistent with the avowed purpose of the clubs. The pioneers justified the organization of claim clubs on a variety of grounds. In some cases formal justification was given as a preamble to the club regulations. Most common was the wording, "Whereas it has become a custom in the western states, as soon as the Indian title to the public lands has been extinguished by the General Government for the citizens of the United States to settle upon and improve said lands, and heretofore the improvement and claim of the settler to the extent of 320 acres, has been respected by both the citizens and laws of Iowa. . . . "[19] Other clubs emphasized the need of protection against "reckless claim jumpers and invidious wolves in human form," or the need "for better security against foreign as well as domestic aggression."[20] In a number of cases the acquisition and peaceable possession of land were given in the preamble as objectives of the settlers. Improvement of the claims was usually stated as an obligation of the members. In no case did a preamble specifically mention preservation of the home.

The squatter could expect that his comrades in the club would come to his assistance if claim jumpers threatened his holding and that similarly his friends would intimidate speculators who might seek to outbid him at the land auction. The settlers who organized the Jackson and Mahaska county clubs agreed to protect each other in the enjoyment of their claims for a period of two years, if necessary, after the land sales.[21] The squatters usually placed an upper limit upon the size of the claim to be protected. In ten out of fourteen cases the maximum was set at 320 acres, but in two instances 480 acres was specified, and on one occasion 200 acres. Club members in another county limited themselves to 160 acres but allowed each other to reserve an additional 160 acres for a non-resident friend. In Poweshiek, Johnson, and Webster counties, where the manuscript claim records were preserved in rather complete form, one did not have to be a resident to enjoy the protection of the club. Nor was it necessary in some clubs for a settler to have attained his majority. In two cases the minimum age of members was set at sixteen years, in one instance at seventeen, and in two others at eighteen. None of the clubs forbade members to sell their claims; indeed the right to make such transfers was specifically guaranteed at times and the purchaser assured of the protection of the club.

If the squatters of a claim club expected to benefit from membership they also assumed responsibilities. They pledged that they would assist their officers in maintaining club law in their districts should it be challenged. They promised to co-operate with the other members in intimidatory action at the land auction if necessary. In some clubs members paid small sums to the recorder or other club officers for their services. Regulations prescribing the degree to which the member must improve his claim appear in the manuscript records of the Poweshiek, Johnson, and Webster county associations, but not in the selections of the club laws printed in the histories of other counties. The members of the Webster County or Fort Dodge club agreed to expend labor worth $10 on their claims each month after the first month. The members of the Poweshiek Protection Society pledged in their revised by-laws to put in $30 worth of labor on their claims within six months of registration and $30 additional labor for each succeeding six months the claim was held. In the Johnson County club, however, only non-residents were compelled to improve their claims to the extent of $50 worth of labor for each six months held. If the squatters actually envisioned developing their holdings into productive farms and homes it would seem reasonable to expect more frequent and more stringent improvement requirements in the club laws.

Questions might also be raised concerning the motives of the members in protecting the claims of minors, who were ineligible to purchase land under the pre-emption law. Allowing membership to minors was no doubt justified in the eyes of members on the grounds that the minor might well be of age by the time of the government land sales, but it might also have been used by squatters to acquire additional land through their children. The club laws also reveal that although all clubs regarded the public auction as the main reason for their existence, a number of them pledged themselves to maintain control of the claims beyond the date of the land sales. In addition, most club regulations provided that the squatters could claim an acreage which was much larger than needed for a farm unit in the mid-nineteenth-century Middle West.

Local historians often viewed club activities in the same light as did Shambaugh. Extra-legal though its activities might be, the claim club was justified, they said, because it protected the honest squatter against the claim jumper and the land speculator and allowed him to improve his claim and protect his home. As one local historian put it, "the thought was intolerable that speculators, or eleventh-hour newcomers who knew nothing of the burden and heat of the day should enter upon land which actual settlers had staked out and tilled, and upon which they had builded homes."[22] Some writers admitted that inequities perhaps resulted from club action, but they obviously believed that these were trifling in comparison to the beneficial achievements of the clubs. In nine of the twenty-six accounts, however, the authors introduced material which ran counter to the usual interpretation, some apparently not realizing the conflict. For example, a local historian of Cedar County wrote:

Early in the county's history, a ring of mercenary characters, anticipating immigration, claimed all the untaken groves and wooded tracts in the county, and when an actual settler—one who wanted land for a home and immediate occupancy . . . settled on a portion of the land rings' domain, he was immediately set upon by the bloodhounds, and it was demanded of him that he either abandon the claim or pay them for what they maintained was their right. If the settler expressed doubts of their having previously claimed their site, the "ring" always had one or more witnesses at hand to testify to the validity of the interest they asserted. The result was nearly always the same. These settlers, more to avoid difficulties than for any other reason, would purchase their pretended right for forty, fifty or one hundred dollars, more or less, according to value after which the ring was ready for operation in some other locality.[23]

Such activity, continued the writer, led the "settlers who came to find homes" to form mutual protection leagues to resist such bogus land claimants. Undoubtedly, however, the persons in the "ring" defended their behavior on the grounds that they were acting under claim law and as members of a squatters' association.

An incident in Clinton County reveals the possible inequities of claim club activity. David Hess and his family, late-comers to the county, wished to settle near the town of Lyons, where they had discovered former neighbors from the East, but they "found that the 'claim-makers' had ploughed their furrows and set their corner stakes around all the land near the river, leaving their agents to 'sell-out' while they had sought new fields for similar enterprise."[24] The Hesses decided to go elsewhere, but their old neighbors interceded with the other residents of the settlement and they were "informed that they were at liberty to settle upon any lands not occupied by an actual settler, and that the settlers would protect them against all claimants." Here, evidently, the early comers had banded together to sell government land to late-comers on the pretext that it was claimed land, although the claims they were selling had no substantial improvements on them and were not occupied. Daniel H. Pearce, one of the early settlers in Clinton, later wrote:

Some of the chivalry, or gentlemen of elegant leisure, followed the business of making claims and selling them to emigrants as they came through. As soon as a new settler arrived, the above named gentry would ascertain his "pile," by some means best known to themselves. They would then have a claim to suit the newcomer's purpose and purse, and, if he demurred paying anything to them, contending that his right to the public land was as good as theirs, they would very soon convince him of his error. He would be summoned to appear before a justice of the peace as a trespasser, or, as they called it, a "claim jumper." The magistrate issuing the summons belonged to the fraternity, and the poor settler would have to sell out or leave, and, even if he went, would have to go a poorer if not sadder man.[25]

Pearce may have been moved somewhat by resentment, since he admitted having himself contested title to a tract of land with the squatter element, but his account does corroborate the evidence given by Hess.

A similar situation existed in Appanoose County, where a claim club had been organized in 1845. There, the resident friends of a group of newly arrived settlers pointed out to the newcomers good farm locations which were unoccupied but claimed by other settlers. Although the club was called out in force as a result, the local residents who had tried to assist their friends stood fast, maintaining that they would not hesitate to point out surplus lands to inquirers in those instances where the ostensible claimant already held a quarter section plus a reasonable amount of timber land.[26] Some local historians make it clear that claim club action was often precipitated not by a threat to a squatter's occupied claim but rather by the effort of a squatter to defend an unoccupied second tract against the claim of late-comers. The historian of Harrison County tells in language more expressive than precise of a "claim jumper" who "thought that because the claimant held down a good hundred and sixty acre tract, that, having spread himself over this number of acres, that there was not enough left of the said claimant to amount to [as] much as the additional one hundred and sixty acre claim." Within an hour, according to this account, "a score of earnest, angry men," had brought the "claim jumper" before a settler jury. This same historian justified club action because the " 'home,' absolute right of all, was invaded."[27]

In his history of Marion County, William M. Donnel pointed out that the spirit of monopoly was not confined to speculators. He wrote: "Many settlers were not content with the amount of land the law entitled them to, but made pretended claims to so large a portion of the territory, that in some instances, it was difficult for a buyer to find an unclaimed lot. Of course such claims were without improvements, but the pretended claimants, by representing themselves as the real owners thereof, would frequently impose upon some unwary buyer, or, by threats extort from him sums, varying in proportion to the supposed value of the claim, or whatever sum could be obtained."[28] Donnel then told of a member of his family who had been forced by the local claim club to reimburse a club member for his rights in land which he had already entered at the land office in the belief that it was unoccupied. Donnel's account incidentally provides an illustration of the way in which the nature of club activities may have been transmuted with the passing of time. Although two subsequent historians of Marion County evidently drew upon Donnel's description of club activities, their narratives, dedicated to the glorification of the pioneer past, omitted the material which failed to show the claim club as the protector of the frontier hearth.[29]

The descriptions of claim club activities in some of the other local histories also show the clubs as protectors of greedy settlers as well as protectors of the home. James W. Merrill, for example, in his history of two townships in Des Moines County, climaxed his account of the claim system with a description of the land sale at Burlington. In general the settlers were not an extremely prosperous group, he said, but "Some sold claims on lands contiguous to their homestead for enough money to make their entry. Others borrowed money for that purpose. Many 'Barretted,'—a word coined to signify allowing a lender to take title till the settler could pay."[30] Here then is one explanation for the large holdings allowed by the claim club to its members. Such holdings represented not only a prospective farm but the means to purchase it, if all went well and a newcomer could be sold an unimproved claim. Many settlers, according to Merrill, did not even take the trouble to purchase the land they claimed from the government. As soon as an opportunity appeared they sold their claims and moved on, leaving the purchasers the problem of establishing their titles.

In writing of Kossuth County, Benjamin F. Reed candidly admitted that "Some made considerable easy money by constantly taking claims and then selling their rights to them," although Reed believed that the claim clubs did not countenance such methods.[31] In Madison County, an area which was "singularly free of molestation by land speculation," according to the local historian, a claim club was organized by a small group of settlers. "Half a dozen persons who, in a small and modest manner, were doing something in a legitimate way, at trading in claims to 'accommodate new settlers,' jumped aboard the proposition" to form a club.[32] This squatters' association seems therefore to have been organized as a means of protecting the trade in claims rather than as a device to protect the home from the speculator and the claim jumper. One unusual indication that the clubs were not always considered as desirable institutions appeared in Monroe County where the members of a local Presbyterian church declared outright defiance of the claim association and ultimately broke it up.[33]

Analysis of the variant accounts in the county histories would seem to cast doubt on the traditional assumption that claim clubs were always a wholesome manifestation of democracy at work on the frontier. Instead, another pattern of club activity seems to emerge, in which the clubs were organized by claim speculators rather than by settlers, and in many instances were actually used against the best interests of the very same settlers who have usually received the credit for creating and operating them. The soundness of this alternative interpretation can perhaps best be tested by a more detailed analysis of the information contained in the manuscript records of the Johnson, Poweshiek, and Fort Dodge clubs.

Professor Shambaugh argued that the Johnson County claim club was "in its organization and administration, one of the most perfect . . . in the West."[34] Actually, the detailed nature and length of the club's published records, which along with the editor's introduction and an index fill 215 pages, suggest the atypical. The size of the club and the activity of its members perhaps stemmed from the fact that the designation of Iowa City as the territorial capital in 1839 made claims more valuable in Johnson County than elsewhere. In all, 325 individuals either signed the compact of the claim club, filed claims, or participated in transactions noted by the recorder between March, 1838, and January, 1843.[35] The members of the group fell into at least nine discernible categories. Ninety-six settlers filed from one to three claims under the auspices of the association. Another seventy-three signed the compact but did not appear in the claim and deed record of the club. In contrast to the members of this group, forty-three individuals appeared in the record four or more times; Samuel Bumgardner, indeed, was a party in twenty-two entries. Although filing no original claims of their own, forty-two settlers purchased from one to three claims. Seventeen pioneers filed claims and also sold claims, not always the same ones. Three groups, each consisting of sixteen individuals, either filed original claims and also purchased claims, or purchased a claim and sold one, or merely sold claims not originally registered in the club records. Finally, a small group of six filed one claim, purchased one claim, and sold one claim.

Further analysis of the Johnson County club membership sheds light on the motivation of these pioneers. The settlers who merely filed claim entries made up only about 30 per cent of the group, although the simple filing of a claim supposedly characterized the Macy-Shambaugh stereotype of a claim club member. The fact that seventy-three names affixed to the club compact do not appear again in the record and that another sixteen club members sold claims which were not on record suggests also that the claim record is not the complete chronicle of membership activity that Shambaugh believed it to be. Some 13 per cent of the association members appeared in four or more entries on the claim record. Although a certain amount of trading in claims might be occasioned by the running of the congressional surveys, there seems little need for the actual settler to have been involved in more than three entries if he simply wished to make, hold, and improve his future home. Close examination of the transactions in which members with multiple entries were involved shows that many of them were dealing in claims—they were, in other words, claim speculators. Six of the first seven men who signed the club compact in Johnson County appeared in four or more entries on the club record and of the eighteen officers who served the club, thirteen fell into the same category. Although the members might describe their activities as "garding our rights against the speculator,"[36] the land dealer and the engrosser were actually in their midst.

Of course the claim dealer's operations were petty in comparison to those of land speculators who purchased large holdings at the land sale or entered considerable acreages at private entry after the auction. But in Johnson County even flagrant land speculators were not excluded from membership in the claim club, despite the worthy resolutions of the squatters. Morgan Reno, who entered one claim on the club record, proved to be anything but an impecunious settler when the land was offered by the federal government. In the townships subject to club law in Johnson County, Reno purchased 2,834 acres, enough land, probably, for thirty farm units. He also purchased land in at least one nearby county. Although it is difficult to be certain, some of his purchases may be illustrations of the time entry system, the practice known among the settlers at the Burlington sales as "Barretting."

Did the claim club insure that the member obtained his claim at the land sale? To this question the abstract of original entries and the deed indexes of Johnson County hold an answer.[37] Of the 325 individuals whose names appear in the club records, 115, or only 35 per cent, actually purchased land from the federal government in the townships where club law was in force. If the claim club in Johnson County was designed to insure that the claim holder purchased his claim, it was manifestly a very imperfect mechanism. What is more, those members who best fit the settlement pattern sketched by Macy and Shambaugh did least well: only twenty-five, or 26 per cent, of those who simply entered claims on the club record purchased land from the federal government at or immediately after the land sales. Conversely, those who most often followed through and purchased land came from the group which comprised the claim speculator element: twenty-two, or 51 per cent, of those individuals purchased federal land.

Not long after the land sales four squatters in Johnson County obtained deeds to part of their original claims from individuals who had purchased them from the federal government. Since many of the claims filed with the club cannot be identified because the congressional survey descriptions were not given, it is not possible to say how many other settlers may have acquired a portion of their claims in the same way. This was the type of purchase pattern found when settlers resorted to the time entry system. The settler allowed a capitalist to purchase his claim with the understanding that the settler might repurchase all or a portion of it as soon as possible after the government auction. In such an arrangement the capitalist might give a bond for a deed in return for the settler's note. Other squatters in the Johnson County club purchased holdings from land speculators, although they failed to obtain title to their original claims. Perhaps prior agreements between the parties had been reached in these cases as well.

Of the 210 club members who failed to purchase land from the federal government, 68 did obtain land in the community within ten years after the date of the last land sale. Since credit extended under the time entry system was ordinarily short-term in nature, anyone who had resorted to the money-lending speculator at the land sales would undoubtedly have completed his purchase in the ten-year time span. These findings change the picture somewhat: 35 per cent of the squatters purchased government land at the auction, another 21 per cent ultimately obtained land in the community, and 44 per cent did not obtain any holding at all. Perhaps some members of this last group did resort to the speculator but failed to meet their obligations and saw their claims fall into other hands. But among the sixty-eight settlers who ultimately purchased land in Johnson County from vendors other than the federal government, one major sub-category stands out. Thirty-one members of this group obtained title to lots within Iowa City, although often holding other land as well. Were these members squatters intent upon improving their claims and defending their homes, or were they businessmen hoping to profit from the increased value of land in the vicinity of the county seat and territorial capital?

In the case both of squatters who purchased land from the federal government and of those who, failing to do so, subsequently obtained land in the community from other sources, other qualifications must be made. Dealing first with the 115 federal land purchasers, thirty-one did not appear again in the club records except as signatories to the compact. If they had claims they either did not record them or they purchased them so late in the history of the club that it did not seem worth while to put them on record. The claims of another thirty-five federal land purchasers were described so loosely that it is impossible to locate them accurately, or to determine whether their original claims coincided with their later purchases from the federal government. In twenty-three other cases, however, the squatters bought land other than their own claims. Four squatters who owned several claims did not purchase the claims which they described in terms of the congressional survey, although they may have purchased claims which they had described less precisely. Only twenty-two of 115 purchasers from the federal government, therefore, ultimately and unquestionably gained possession of their original claims. Similarly, a sizable percentage of the sixty-eight squatters who did not purchase government land but who ultimately obtained land in the community did not acquire their original claims. Of thirty-five persons whose claims could be positively located, only fourteen, by the most generous of interpretations, ultimately obtained title to a portion of their claims, and the land acquired by the remaining twenty-one definitely was not a part of their claims. Where it was possible to check, therefore, fewer than half of the squatters who obtained land in Johnson County actually acquired their original claims—the "homes" which they were defending against the speculator.

Further light is shed upon the role of the Johnson County claim club by a close examination of one of the incidents in which the club exercised its punitive power. Shambaugh gave a detailed account of the incident, drawing upon an unfinished history of Johnson County, which was written by two former members of the association, Cyrus Sanders and Henry Felkner. These writers described the efforts of the club members in 1839 to drive "a man named Crawford" from a claim owned by William Sturgis. When Crawford refused to abandon the claim, even though Sturgis offered to pay for the improvements, some sixty members of the club under the leadership of its marshal tore down Crawford's substantial log and clapboard cabin. Crawford then rebuilt the cabin and moved his family into it. The club members returned to the claim, however, and this time Crawford "adjusted" the matter to the "full satisfaction" of Sturgis.[38]

To both Shambaugh and Roscoe Lokken, the historian of public land disposal in Iowa, the Sturgis-Crawford incident was illustrative of claim club action. Lokken cited it as an illustration of "pioneer justice."[39] The action of the aggrieved squatter Sturgis, however, did not conform to the pattern of squatter democracy sketched by Macy, Shambaugh, and those who have relied upon them. Sturgis apparently had not made any improvements on the claim, for if he had Sanders and Felkner would certainly have mentioned them. Between April 1, 1839, and March 9, 1843, the name of William Sturgis appeared repeatedly on the club record.[40] He filed three claims, purchased five additional claims for an outlay of $270, and sold five claims for sums totaling $400. The amount of the "adjustment" with Crawford does not appear in the claim record. At the land sales, Sturgis purchased 463 acres—much more than any pioneer farmer needed for farming operations. Patently he was no hard-pressed pioneer defending his home; and in the Crawford incident he was playing the role of a claim speculator who used the club for support in extorting tribute from late-comers to the community. That the club membership would twice mobilize to support Sturgis illuminates the sympathies and aspirations of his colleagues in the association.

Records of the Poweshiek County claim club show some patterns of activity similar to that of the Johnson County club. On February 22, 1851, the members of the Poweshiek club revised their claim laws. The reason for the change is not explicitly stated, but a reference to "actual settlers" in the first resolution of the amended rules suggests that the club members may have attempted to exclude claim speculators from the new organization.[41] If that was their aim they did not entirely succeed, as the following analysis of the club records shows.

Ninety-one settlers of Poweshiek County registered claims with the club after the revision of the rules.[42] Of this group, thirty, or 32 per cent, purchased land from the federal government in the sections in which they had reserved claims in the club records.[43] Fourteen of these settlers, however, did not purchase any of their original claim but purchased instead a tract or tracts adjoining. Although the thirty entrymen had originally laid claim to some 5,200 acres, their purchase of government land in the final analysis amounted to only 2,700 acres. Of the sixty-one members who did not purchase federal land, forty-five, or 49 per cent of the total registrants, did obtain title to land in Poweshiek County before the end of 1860. The club recorder preserved a complete description of the claims of all but two of this group of forty-five. Of those whose claims were adequately described on the club roll, sixteen obtained all or, more often, a portion of their claim. But the first deeds of record of twenty-seven, or 60 per cent, of this group embraced lands which had not been part of their claims. The purchasing patterns of three individuals placed them in a separate category. These three settlers bought government land outside the limits of the sections in which their claim was located. In one instance the purchase was considerably removed from the original claim; in the other two cases it lay in an adjacent section. In addition to these purchases from the government, each of these three men acquired tracts of land from private landholders. Of the forty-eight club members who purchased land from holders other than the federal government, fourteen— almost a third—purchased lots in Montezuma, the county seat. We may question, therefore, whether these were genuine pioneer farmers. One further category of claim club members remains to be mentioned. Thirteen, or 15 per cent of the membership, did not purchase land directly from the federal government, nor do they appear on the early deed registers of Poweshiek County as having acquired any landed estate whatsoever.

Evidence in Poweshiek County points to the time entry system more clearly than in Johnson County. In seventeen cases in which a settler subsequently acquired all or a portion of his claim subsequent to its original disposition by the federal government, the grantor could be easily identified as a speculator or land agent. Furthermore, a number of settlers acquired title to tracts lying outside their original claims from members of the speculator group—perhaps by the time entry system.

Although 85 per cent of the members of the reformed Poweshiek club did acquire land in the county, only one third of them were able to purchase a portion of their claims directly from the government; and their total purchases of government land amounted to only about 50 per cent of the area of their original claims. Quite possibly some of the group sold a portion of their claims before or at the land sale. Almost half of the settlers purchased their land after it had passed through the hands of an intermediary, who in many cases evidently provided a source of credit. For this group the claim club could have been important not because it protected the members from speculator bids but rather because it strengthened the settler's bargaining power when he arranged for the speculator to purchase his claim.

Between July, 1854, and June, 1856, a claim club was active in the district centering at Fort Dodge on the upper Des Moines River, where 255 squatters claimed land which today falls within the boundaries of Webster and Humboldt counties. A few other settlers filed claims to land in other nearby counties, but analysis of the behavior of the settlers in Webster and Humboldt adequately reveals the workings of this association.[44] Sixty-eight of the 255 club members actually purchased all or a portion of their claims from the federal government when the lands were offered for sale at Fort Dodge.[45] Another five settlers purchased land from the government which was not part of their original claims. The seventy-three settlers who thus acquired land directly from the government made up 29 per cent of the total group. These seventy-three purchasers claimed 23,873 acres of land, but they bought only 12,442 acres at the land office. Thirty of the seventy-three were not the original claimants to the tracts which they acquired but had purchased the claims from the squatters who had first filed descriptions.

Another fifty-four of the 255 claim club members in Webster and Humboldt counties, or 21 per cent, did acquire title to land in these counties before the end of 1866, although they did not purchase their claims from the federal government. In only two cases did the deeds recorded by the members of this group cover a portion of the claims which they had reserved on the club record. If members of this group had conformed to the Macy-Shambaugh stereotype the deeds should uniformly have covered their claims. Actually, thirty-one of the fifty-four members of this group recorded deeds to lots in Fort Dodge or, in two instances, in a nearby townsite.

In Humboldt and Webster counties, 128 of the squatters, or 50 per cent, fell into a third category—those who neither purchased land directly from the federal government nor acquired it from private parties. Seventy-two per cent of the squatters from Humboldt County and 41 per cent of those from Webster County fell into this group.[46] Of the group of 128 squatters who failed to acquire title in the two counties, twenty did transfer their claims to other parties; if the remainder did so the club records give no clue to the fact.

Although many claims were sold in Webster and Humboldt counties, there seems to have been much less dealing in claims than in Johnson County. Nor can we be certain that the time entry system was at work to any extent in the Fort Dodge area. Ultimately the Fort Dodge club was to be described as a tool of land speculators, but since the charges appeared in a hard-fought political campaign they should perhaps be discounted.[47]

Comparison of the percentages of entrymen, private land buyers, and non-landholders provides a foundation for generalizations upon the three clubs for which manuscript records exist. Strikingly similar percentages of entrymen were found in each club. About one third of the members of each club actually purchased land from the federal government. Not all of these purchases by any means, however, represented the purchase of the actual claims recorded with the claim club. In this last respect, however, the Fort Dodge club was exceptional; almost all of the entrymen did obtain a portion of their original claims. Whether their purchases were or were not part of the original claims, the entrymen in each club purchased only about half of the acreage which they had originally reserved on the club record. In both the Johnson and Fort Dodge clubs 21 per cent of the membership failed to buy federal land but did ultimately acquire a holding of some sort from other sources. These percentages contrast sharply with the 49 per cent who fell into this category in Poweshiek. In every case, however, a considerable number of settlers in this group, ranging from slightly less than a third in Poweshiek to more than half in the Fort Dodge area, were very probably town businessmen, since they acquired lots in the county seat. One can question whether such individuals ever seriously contemplated developing their claims as agricultural properties. In Johnson County 44 per cent of the squatters apparently never acquired land in the county, or at least obtained such land so many years after the land sales that the claim club cannot be said to have aided them. The corresponding proportion at Fort Dodge was 50 per cent. In Poweshiek County, however, only 15 per cent of the club members failed to acquire land.

The striking difference in the number of purchasers and nonpurchasers in Poweshiek County as compared to that of the other two clubs is puzzling. It is possible that earlier members of the Poweshiek association who had left the community were simply dropped from the rolls when the club reorganized in 1851, and that the claim register of the reorganized club, therefore, did not show all of those who at one time held claims. Possibly, also, more club members in Poweshiek County acquired land because fewer petty speculators were attracted to that area than to Iowa City and Fort Dodge, towns that aspired to become state and regional centers.

These details concerning the behavior of the squatters and the activities of the claim clubs in Johnson, Poweshiek, Webster, and Humboldt counties clearly reveal certain conditions which have not received adequate attention in the standard accounts of claim clubs in Iowa. One of the most striking oversights is the failure to take into account the fact that only a small percentage of the squatters actually purchased their land directly from the federal government. If the claim club was designed to insure that the squatter could purchase his claim from the government, "that practical, inventive turn of mind, quick to find expedients,"[48] which Turner saw as a characteristic of frontiersmen, had produced a highly inadequate solution to the problem. The standard accounts have also failed to show that the actual entrymen acquired only about half of the area claimed, and that even such purchases as they made were often not a portion of the original claim. In the light of the evidence that many settlers wanted to sell all or a portion of their claims, these discrepancies between squatters and entrymen and between claim and purchase become more readily understandable. Presumably the squatter might apply the revenue from such sales to the purchase of a clear title to other land—an unsold portion of his claim, perhaps, or unoccupied land elsewhere in the vicinity. This may explain why a large percentage of the Poweshiek entrymen purchased other land close-by instead of their own claims. When the squatter raised funds for buying land by selling his own claim, the club of course had in a way been of assistance to him since without his fellows at his back he might not have been able to extract anything from the late-coming settler or the speculator.

It was in Johnson County that the sale of claims was most striking. Although many settlers in Webster and Humboldt counties recorded sales or transfers, and some had claims totaling as much as a section and a half, none rivaled the Johnson County club member who participated in more than twenty claim transactions. Holdings in excess of the club rules were common in Johnson County. Ironically, the outstanding illustration of the club militant in Johnson County—the Crawford-Sturgis case—turned out on analysis to be a case of coercion of an actual settler at the behest of a claim dealer.

Neither Shambaugh nor Macy described the time entry system or connected it in any way with claim club activities. When squatters' claims were purchased from the federal government by a land agent or speculator who deeded a portion to the original claimant within a few years, the time entry system was apparently in use. Here the speculator benefited from interest charged on the investment which he made for the squatter, and he might also acquire outright possession of a portion of the claim. Particularly in Poweshiek County, but also in Johnson County, this was the case. The existence of the time entry system shows the hollowness of the squatters' criticism of the speculators. The speculator was a necessity to the squatter who desired to purchase land but who did not have the cash. Had there not been speculators some settlers would not have been able to acquire title. The claim club could have been of assistance to such a squatter by strengthening his bargaining position.

Thus much of the evidence derived from the records of three Iowa claim clubs and the appropriate county records supports the view of claim club activity given by the dissenting local historians rather than the Macy-Shambaugh interpretation. No doubt squatter associations did protect many an honest settler in the enjoyment of improvements and in the purchase of a home from the federal government, but the clubs also shielded the activities of others whose motives and procedures were far more complex. At times the squatters' association was the vehicle of men who sought simply to capitalize on priority or to meet the financial problem posed by a government minimum price of $1.25 per acre by deriving fictitious values from a cunning mixture of brute force and virgin land. If we are to understand the role of the claim club, therefore, we must not confuse the symbols of agrarian democracy with its substance.

Notes

1. Benjamin H. Hibbard, *A History of the Public Land Policies* (New York, 1924), 198-208; Roy M. Robbins, *Our Landed Heritage: The Public Domain, 1776-1936* (Princeton, 1942), 67-68; George M. Stephenson, *The Political History of the Public Lands from 1840 to 1862: From Pre-emption to Homestead* (Boston, 1917), 20-23.

2. Frederick J. Turner, *The Frontier in American History* (New York, 1920), 137, 212.

3. Jesse Macy, *Institutional Beginnings in a Western State* (*Johns Hopkins University Studies in Historical and Political Science*, Series II, No. 7: Baltimore, 1884); Benjamin F. Shambaugh (ed.), *Constitution and Records of the Claim Association of Johnson County, Iowa* (Iowa City, 1894); and Shambaugh, "Frontier Land Clubs or Claim Associations," American Historical Association, *Annual Report*, 1900 (2 vols., Washington, 1901), I, 67-85.

4. Shambaugh, "Frontier Land Clubs or Claim Associations," American Historical Association, *Annual Report*, 1900, I, 71, 83.

5. Ray A. Billington, *Westward Expansion: A History of the American Frontier* (New York, 1949), 476. See also Robert E. Riegel, *America Moves West* (3rd ed., New York, 1956), 410-11; Roscoe L. Lokken, *Iowa Public Land Disposal* (Iowa City, 1942), 69-75; and the general works by Hibbard, Robbins, and Stephenson cited in note 1 above.

6. Macy, *Institutional Beginnings*, 5.

7. Shambaugh, "Frontier Land Clubs or Claim Associations," American Historical Association, *Annual Report*, 1900, I, 72.

8. See Albert M. Lea, *Notes on the Wisconsin Territory; Particularly with Reference to the Iowa District or Black Hawk Purchase* (Philadelphia, 1836), reprinted by the State Historical Society of Iowa as *The Book that Gave Iowa Its Name* (Iowa City, n. d.), 18-21; John B. Newhall, *Sketches of Iowa, or the Emigrant's Guide* (New York, 1841), 54-58; Hawkins Taylor, "Squatters and Speculators at the First Land Sales," *Annals of Iowa* (Iowa City-Des Moines), First Series, VIII (July, 1870), 269-74; Charles A. White, "The Early Homes and Home-Makers of Iowa," *ibid.*, Third Series, IV (October, 1899), 179-95.

9. The writer checked all of the Iowa county histories available in the library of the Iowa State

Historical Society at Iowa City and in the extensive collection of the library at Iowa State College, Ames. For ninety-eight of the ninety-nine counties in Iowa he found at least one history available, and in some cases as many as four. Such histories are admittedly a treacherous type of source. A number of middle-western companies specialized in publishing these bulky catch-alls during the late nineteenth and early twentieth centuries. Several of the companies accumulated a supply of filler which the editors included in every history, while at the same time supplementing this material county by county with information compiled by anonymous local agents. The reader must take care, therefore, to distinguish between filler and information which bears specifically upon the county under study. The Union Historical Company included a passage of filler on claim clubs in its Iowa county histories, which was supplemented by seemingly authentic local information, when available, or was left to stand by itself at times in apparent but undocumented testimony to the presence of squatters' associations. On the other hand, no publisher could be too cavalier in handling the facts because the major market for the histories lay in the home county and flagrant inaccuracies might cause protest. Nor was the general approach in these histories one that the historian finds conducive to accuracy. Dedicated sometimes to the pioneers in the hope that their "virtues may be emulated and . . . [their] toils and sacrifices duly appreciated," they are unblushingly filiopietistic. No doubt the publishers found this formula to be remunerative, but it could hardly fail to influence both the selection and the interpretation of materials. This being the case we must give more weight to incidents which show a less flattering side to pioneer behavior than the frequency of their appearance in the county histories might seem to justify.

   Since most of the county histories have extremely long titles and since there is little danger of misleading the research student by doing so, shortened titles with ellipses are used in the first citation to each in the references which follow, and the ellipses are omitted in later citations to the same work.

10. Western Historical Company, *The History of Appanoose County, Iowa* . . . (Chicago, 1878), 364-66; Union Historical Company, *The History of Boone County, Iowa* . . . (Des Moines, 1880), 326-31; Western Historical Company, *The History of Cedar County, Iowa* . . . (Chicago, 1878), 325; Western Historical Company, *The History of Clinton County, Iowa* . . . (Chicago, 1879), 444-46; Union Historical Company, *The History of Dallas County, Iowa* . . . (Des Moines, 1879), 324-26; Western Historical Company, *The History of Des Moines County, Iowa* . . . (Chicago, 1879), 377-79; Franklin T. Oldt and Patrick J. Quigley, *History of Dubuque County, Iowa* . . . (Chicago, 1911), 480; Pioneer Publishing Company, *History of Emmet County and Dickinson County, Iowa* . . . (2 vols., Chicago, 1917), I, 256-57; Union Publishing Company, *History of Hardin County, Iowa* . . . (Springfield, Ill., 1883), 967; Joseph H. Smith, *History of Harrison County, Iowa* . . . (Des Moines, 1888), 80-83; Western Historical Company, *The History of Jackson County, Iowa* . . . (Chicago, 1879), 333-35; Western Historical Company, *The History of Jasper County, Iowa* . . . (Chicago, 1888), 350; *History of Johnson County, Iowa* . . . (Iowa City, 1883), 323-31; Union Historical Company, *The History of Keokuk County, Iowa* . . . (Des Moines, 1880), 317-25; Union Historical Company, *History of Kossuth, Hancock, and Winnebago Counties, Iowa* . . . (Springfield, Ill., 1884), 240; Western Historical Company, *The History of Lee County, Iowa* . . . (Chicago, 1879), 440-43; Herman A. Mueller, *History of Madison County, Iowa* . . . (2 vols., Chicago, 1915), I, 126-37; Union Historical Company, *The History of Mahaska County, Iowa* . . . (Des Moines, 1878), 293-97; William M. Donnel, *Pioneers of Marion County, Consisting of a General History of the County* . . . (Des Moines, 1872), 42-49; Western Historical Company, *The History of Monroe County, Iowa* . . . (Chicago, 1878), 376-77; Johnson Brigham, *Des Moines, The Pioneer of Municipal Progress and Reform of the Middle West, Together with the History of Polk County, Iowa* . . . (2 vols., Chicago, 1911), I, 662-67; Leonard F. Parker, *History of Poweshiek County, Iowa* . . . (2 vols., Chicago, 1911), I, 57-60; Union Historical Company, *The History of Warren County, Iowa* . . . (Des Moines, 1879), 304-305; Harlow M. Pratt, *History of Fort Dodge and Webster County, Iowa* (2 vols., Chicago, 1913), I, 76-78; W. E. Alexander, *History of Winneshiek and Allamakee Counties, Iowa* (Sioux City, 1882), 189-90; A. Warner & Co., *History of the Counties of Woodbury and Plymouth, Iowa* . . . (Chicago, 1890), 70-71.

11. Western Historical Company, *History of Lee County*, 529-31; Charles Mason to D. W. Kilbourne, December 22, 1869, Charles Mason Papers (Iowa State Department of History and Archives, Des Moines), Vol. 29.

12. Lokken, *Iowa Public Land Disposal*, 210-35; Nathan E. Goldthwait (ed.), *History of Boone*

County, Iowa (2 vols., Chicago, 1914), I, 145-51; *Hamilton Freeman* (Webster City), February 12 and May 6, 1868, May 11 and 25, 1870.

13. National Publishing Company, *History of Monona County, Iowa* . . . (Chicago, 1890), 202-203; John L. E. Peck, Otto H. Montzheimer, and William J. Miller, *Past and Present of O'Brien and Osceola Counties, Iowa* . . . (2 vols., Indianapolis, 1914), I, 84-107.

14. Charles L. Dyke, *The Story of Sioux County* (Orange City, Iowa, 1942), 99-101.

15. William H. Hart, *History of Sac County, Iowa* . . . (Indianapolis, 1914), 56. This story is not completely plausible since these lands ordinarily would have become subject to private entry in short order and available, therefore, to any speculator who desired to purchase them at the minimum government price.

16. For an intensive study of the diversity of origins of the population of Iowa between 1850 and 1860, see Morton Rosenberg, "The Democratic Party of Iowa, 1850-1860" (Ph.D. dissertation, State University of Iowa, 1957), 459-501.

17. The pre-emption laws may be found in *United States Statutes at Large*, IV (1845), 678, and V (1845), 251-52, 382, and 453-58. Lokken, *Iowa Public Land Disposal*, 80, is in error in stating that the pre-emption act of 1834 did not apply to Iowa. See, for instance, Records of the General Land Office, Dubuque Land Office Original Entries, Nos. 401 and 419 (National Archives, Washington).

18. The counties are Boone, Dallas, Des Moines, Dubuque, Dickinson, Jackson, Johnson, Keokuk, Kossuth, Madison, Mahaska, Marion, Monroe, Polk, Poweshiek, Warren, Webster, Winneshiek, and Woodbury. See note 10 above for references to published histories of these counties. A typescript copy of the Poweshiek County revised rules and the deed register is available in the Iowa State Historical Society at Iowa City but the location of the originals is unknown. The Society holds the original manuscript rules and claim register of the Johnson County club and a copy of the Fort Dodge club record. The original of the Fort Dodge record is in the Iowa State Department of History and Archives at Des Moines.

19. Union Historical Company, *History of Mahaska County*, 294-95. John W. Wright and William A. Young (eds.), *History of Marion County, Iowa, and Its People* (2 vols., Chicago, 1915), I, 61-62; Western Historical Company, *History of Jackson County*, 334.

20. Union Historical Company, *History of Dallas County*, 325-26; Mueller, *History of Madison County*, I, 127; Western Historical Company, *History of Monroe County*, 376-77; Union Historical Company, *History of Warren County*, 305.

21. Western Historical Company, *History of Jackson County*, 334; Union Historical Company, *History of Mahaska County*, 294.

22. Brigham, *Des Moines . . . Together with the History of Polk County*, I, 664.

23. Western Historical Company, *History of Cedar County*, 325.

24. Western Historical Company, *History of Clinton County*, 444-45.

25. Patrick B. Wolfe, *Wolfe's History of Clinton County, Iowa* . . . (2 Vols., Indianapolis, 1911), I, 51.

26. Western Historical Company, *History of Appanoose County*, 365-66.

27. Smith, *History of Harrison County*, 82.

28. Donnel, *Pioneers of Marion County*, 49.

29. Union Historical Company, *The History of Marion County, Iowa* . . . (Des Moines, 1881), 325-30; Wright and Young (eds.), *History of Marion County*, 59-62.

30. James W. Merrill, *Yellow Spring[s] and Huron: A Local History Containing Sketches of all the People, Institutions, and Events, from the Earliest Settlement to Date of Publication* (Mediapolis, Iowa, 1897), 43. The capitalist whose name became a verb was Richard Barrett of Springfield, Illinois.

31. Benjamin F. Reed, *History of Kossuth County, Iowa* . . . (2 vols., Chicago, 1913), I, 72.

32. Mueller, *History of Madison County*, I, 126.

33. Western Historical Company, *History of Monroe County*, 377.

34. Shambaugh (ed.), *Constitution and Records of the Claim Association of Johnson County*, xiv.

35. The following analysis of the transactions of the membership is based on a man-by-man study of the club membership, using the claim register and quitclaim deed record of the club.

36. Shambaugh (ed.), *Constitution and Records*, 21.

37. Johnson County, Book of Original Entries, and Index of Deeds, 1839-1854, consulted in the County Recorder's Office, Iowa City.

38. Shambaugh (ed.), *Constitution and Records*, xv-xvi.

39. Lokken, *Iowa Public Land Disposal*, 73, 75.

40. Shambaugh (ed.), *Constitution and Records*, 35, 39, 85, 113, 117, 119, 127, 133, 148, 161, 162, 169, 182.

41. Unfortunately the club recorder did not preserve the original by-laws of the Poweshiek association, and it is not possible to determine what changes were made in preparing the revised regulations.

42. Typewritten copy of the Poweshiek claim records, obtained through the agency of Professor Leonard F. Parker of Grinnell, Iowa, and now held by the Iowa State Historical Society. Parker had himself obtained the record from Joseph Satchell, who discovered the original manuscript while auditor of the county during the early 1880's. Joseph Satchell, Redlands, Calif., to Parker, January 17, 1906, filed with the Historical Society's copy of the claim compact and register.

43. Information concerning original entries and the purchase of land from grantees other than the federal government is based on an analysis of the Poweshiek County Book of Original Entries, and the Index of Deeds, 1849-1860, consulted in the County Recorder's Office, Montezuma, Iowa.

44. The writer used the copy of the Fort Dodge Claim Club records available in the library of the Iowa State Historical Society at Iowa City. The original is in the possession of the Iowa State Department of History and Archives at Des Moines.

45. Information concerning original entries and the purchase of land from grantees other than the federal government is based on an analysis of the Webster County Book of Original Entries, and the Index of Deeds, 1854-1866, consulted in the County Recorder's Office, Fort Dodge, Iowa, and the Humboldt County Book of Original Entries, and the Index of Deeds, 1855-1869, in the County Recorder's Office, Dakota City, Iowa.

46. So high a percentage of those in Humboldt County failed to acquire any title that the writer turned to the federal census records to corroborate his work in the county records. None of the settlers who failed to appear in the abstract of original entries or the deed indexes of Humboldt County greeted the census taker in that county in 1870.

47. *Hamilton Freeman* (Webster City), December 10, 1857, and October 5, 1859.

48. Turner, *Frontier in American History*, 37.

Part VII
Western types: Vigilante and cowboy

Pivot of American vigilantism: The San Francisco Vigilance Committee of 1856

Richard Maxwell Brown

There have been few more controversial subjects in frontier history than lynch law. The enforcers of this extralegal "popular justice" were generally called regulators prior to the 1850s, but became known as vigilantes after San Francisco's first vigilance committee in 1851 stamped that name indelibly upon American consciousness. Most nineteenth century writers looked with approval upon the vigilance movements, which they associated with the bringing of law and decency to the roughhewn frontier. Thus in 1877 Thomas C. Cary, writing an account of the San Francisco Vigilance Committee of 1856 for a very respectable eastern journal, *The Atlantic Monthly*, concluded that the committee had turned a wickedly corrupt gold rush boomtown into "one of the best-governed cities in the United States.

The progressive historians had a different emphasis. Like their nineteenth century counterparts, they approved of the "people's justice," but their reasons were different. Frederick Jackson Turner in his essay "The Old West," first published in 1908 in the *Proceedings of the State Historical Society of Wisconsin*, saw the South Carolina regulator movement arise out of inequities between the up-country frontier and the wealthy, long-settled coast. Turner saw the up-country "oppressed" by the lack of courts and by corrupt officials. This "led the South Carolina up-country men to take affairs in their own hands, and in 1764 to establish associations to administer lynch law under the name of 'regulators.'" Turner stressed that the regulation movement "alleviated" the difficulties until the Revolution. As the twentieth century wore on, historians began to associate lynch justice with the suppression of unpopular elements, such as labor leaders, and members of minority groups, such as Negros or Chinese. A staunch civil libertarian, U.C.L.A.'s Professor John W. Caughey, has condemned nearly all vigilance movements in his book *Their Majesties the Mob* (1960).

In the following essay, Richard Maxwell Brown, Professor of History at the College of William and Mary, analyzes the San Francisco Vigilance Committee of 1856, which he sees as a watershed separating the old vigilantism that righted social injustice from the new type that persecuted minorities.

Western Historical Studies, 1967, John Alexander Carroll, ed., *Reflections of Western Historians*, University of Arizona Press, 1969, pp. 105-109. Reprinted by permission.

For further reading: Richard Maxwell Brown, *The South Carolina Regulators* (Cambridge, Mass.: Harvard University Press, 1963) Frederick Jackson Turner, "The Old West," in *The Frontier in American History* (New York: Holt, Rinehart and Winston, 1920)* John W. Caughey, *Their Majesties the Mob* (Chicago: University of Chicago Press, 1960) Hubert H. Bancroft, *Popular Tribunals*, 2 vols. (San Francisco: History Company, 1887) Mary Floyd Williams, *History of the San Francisco Committee of Vigilance of 1851* (Berkeley: University of California Press, 1921) Stanton A. Coblentz, *Villains and Vigilantes* (orig. pub. 1936; New York: Thomas Yoseloff, 1957) Laurence Veysey, ed., *Law and Resistance: American Attitudes toward Authority* (New York: Harper Torchbooks, 1970), pp. 195-245.*

*Available in paperback.

October 1967 marked the two hundredth anniversary of American vigilantism.[1] The long history of this ancient if not honorable American institution divides into two major phases: the old vigilantism and the new vigilantism. The old vigilantism occurred mainly before the Civil War, was directed primarily against frontier lawlessness, and focused chiefly upon horse thieves and counterfeiters in the far-flung Mississippi Valley,[2] It was a frontier phenomenon of the agrarian era of American history. The new vigilantism was a much broader and more complex thing. Not confined to frontier or countryside, it was a function of the transition from a rural to an urban America. The new vigilantism found its victims among Catholics, Jews, immigrants, Negroes, laboring men and labor leaders, radicals, free thinkers, and defenders of civil liberties.[3]

The San Francisco committee of 1856 is pivotal in the history of American vigilantism because it signals the transition from the old to the new vigilantism. The two phases overlapped, but the change began to occur in the mid-nineteenth century. The San Francisco vigilantes blended the methods of the old with the objectives and victims of the new. Not only was the committee of 1856 the largest and best organized vigilante movement in American history, but it was by far the best known. It received publicity on a worldwide scale and attracted the editorial approval of the Eastern press.[4] The performance of the San Francisco vigilance committee was widely copied and even more widely admired[5] and had much to do with creating the favorable image of American vigilantism in the nineteenth century. It marked a turning point in American vigilantism from a concern with rural frontier disorder to a groping—and unsuccessful—quest for solutions to the problems of a new urban America.[6]

Ethnically, there was perhaps no more cosmopolitan city anywhere in the Western world of the 1850's than San Francisco. Virtually all strains were represented in the population. Old-stock Americans; English, Scotch, and Irish; French, Germans, Italians, and Scandinavians; Mexicans, South Americans, Polynesians, and Australians; Jews, Negroes, Chinese, and many more were present. Many ethnic and religious groups had their own special societies and newspapers.[7] The French had not merely one newspaper but four, and shortly after the height of the vigilante movement even a Negro newspaper hit the streets.[8]

In official pronouncements and editorials there was much ethnic tolerance and good will,[9] but under the surface ethnic hostility was rife. To a great extent, the political alignments of San Francisco represented the ethnic tensions of the fast-growing city. The

Democratic Party was split into two wings. One faction was Southern-oriented, but the dominant wing was the machine of David C. Broderick. Broderick was an aggressive political operator from New York City who introduced the system of New York ward politics into San Francisco.[10] The Broderick machine dominated the city by ballot-box stuffing, manipulation, and the strongarm election efforts of Irish Catholic "shoulder strikers" from the East.[11] It ran roughshod over the opposition of the Know Nothings who had inherited much of the old-stock appeal of the fading Whig Party. There is no doubt that the Broderick faction looked to the Irish and the Catholics, and to the black-leg and laboring elements of the population, for the nucleus of its strength.

San Francisco was a seething cauldron of social, ethnic, religious, and political tensions in an era of booming growth. In the short space of seven years—from 1849 to 1856—the City had ballooned to a population of 50,000.[12] Streets were built, municipal services established, the shoreline improved, and wharves constructed. But all this was done at the cost of enormous payments to the Broderick machine. Huge salaries, rampant graft, a soaring municipal debt, depreciating city scrip, and rising taxes were the signs of fast approaching municipal bankruptcy.[13] By 1855 the municipal budget had skyrocketed to $2,500,000.

It was against this background that the vigilance committee of 1856 arose. The story begins in October, 1855, with the launching of the San Francisco *Daily Evening Bulletin* under the excited editorship of James King of William.[14] King gave his readers one sensational editorial after another in which he blasted the alleged conditions of crime and corruption in the city.[15] Then, on November 17, 1855, an Italian Catholic gambler named Charles Cora fatally shot the U.S. Marshal, William Richardson.[16] When Cora's trial ended in a hung jury in January, 1856, King's flaming editorials in the *Bulletin* roused San Franciscans to a white heat. King had been a San Francisco vigilante in 1851, and the threat of vigilante justice frequently appeared in his columns.[17]

By the spring of 1856 King had created a near-panic psychology in San Francisco with his fulminations against the Broderick machine. Laying claim to a martyr's halo in advance, King predicted time and again that his enemies would get him. Finally on May 14, 1856, his prediction came true when he was shot and fatally wounded by James P. Casey, an Irish Catholic political manipulator and erstwhile inmate of Sing Sing prison.[18] The shooting of King hit San Francisco with sledge-hammer impact. The very next day the vigilance committee was organized by William T. Coleman and other leading merchants of the city, who were determined that Casey would not escape retribution as Cora had thus far.[19]

Within a matter of days the vigilantes tried and hanged both Casey and Cora. Two months later they hanged two more;[20] altogether they expelled twenty-eight men. Meanwhile, thousands of San Franciscans flocked to join the vigilance committee. Soon its membership was approaching its peak figure of 6,000 to 8,000.[21] It was well understood at the time, and cannot be emphasized too strongly, that the vigilance committee was dominated lock, stock, and barrel by the leading merchants of San Francisco who controlled it through an executive committee.[22] In this body, William T. Coleman, one of the leading importers of the city, had near-dictatorial powers as president of the organization.[23] The papers of the vigilance committee have survived today in the manuscript collection of the Huntington Library, and countless documents testify to its strongly mercantile ethos. It was a highly rationalized movement with everything organized to the last degree. Nothing was overlooked by the directing businessmen, who had the same passion for order and system in the running of a lynch-law movement as they had in their own commercial affairs.

It was this passion for order and system that caused the vigilantes to use printed forms for membership applications. Out of a total membership of 6,000 to 8,000 some 2,500 applications have survived in the Huntington Library collection.[24] These constitute an unique file in the history of American vigilantism and provide a rather complete picture of the make-up of the 1856 committee. In addition to his name, each applicant was required to state his age, occupation, where he was from, and where he lived in San Francisco. On the basis of the data in these applications, it can be said, in general, that the vigilance committee was composed of young men in their twenties and thirties. Virtually every ethnic strain, American state, and country of Europe was represented, but the American membership was predominantly from the northeastern United States from Maine to Maryland. There were also strong contingents from Germany and France. Significantly, few Irishmen were members. The fact that the bulk of the membership was drawn from the North Atlantic basin—that is, from the coastal states of the northeastern United States and from such western European countries as France, Germany, England, and Scotland—seems to reflect the maritime orientation and origin of so much of San Francisco's population. As to occupation, the vigilantes came largely from the ranks of the city's merchants, tradesmen, craftsmen, or their young employees. Laborers were in a scant minority, and gamblers were forbidden to join.[25]

The mercantile complexion of the vigilance committee is the key to its behavior. The merchants of San Francisco were dependent on Eastern connections for their credit.[26] Like most businessmen, the San Francisco merchants had a consuming interest in their own credit ratings and the local tax rate. In the eyes of Eastern businessmen, San Francisco economic stability was being jeopardized by the soaring municipal debt, rising taxes, and approaching bankruptcy under the Broderick machine. The spectre of municipal bankruptcy made Eastern creditors fearful that the city was on the verge of economic chaos. The restoration of confidence in San Francisco's municipal and financial stability was a *sine qua non*. It had to be accomplished—and in such a way that would let Easterners know that conservative, right-thinking men had definitely gained control.[27] Fiscal reform at the municipal level was thus basic to the vigilante movement. But in order to bring about fiscal reform it was first necessary to smash David C. Broderick's machine.

Vigilante violence was the means used to destroy the Broderick organization. Consider the hanging of James P. Casey: Casey had recently broken with Broderick, but he had formerly served him as a hard-hitting election bully and manipulator. The execution of Casey not only had done away with the assassin of James King of William, but it put Broderick's Irish Catholic political henchmen on notice of the sort of fate that might await them. Even more important was the banishment of the twenty-eight men, for it was their expulsion that really broke the back of Broderick's power. After the hangings of Casey and Cora, the vigilance committee organized sub-committees and methodically went about collecting evidence of ballot-box stuffing, election fraud, and municipal corruption.[28] The Irish Catholic "shoulder strikers" and bully boys who had bossed elections were rounded up, jailed, tried, and sentenced to expulsion from California. Broderick himself was called before the committee. There were rumors that he would be hanged or banished, but this the committee did not quite dare. Broderick was released, but he had the wisdom to leave quickly for sanctuary in the mountains.[29]

Broderick would come back to San Francisco another day, but when he returned his chief lieutenants would be gone—put aboard ships for foreign or Eastern ports with the warning never to re-appear. To understand what happened, it is only necessary to consider the names of those expelled. A Celtic tinge is unmistakable. Among the twenty-eight banished were Michael Brannegan, Billy Carr, John Cooney, John Crowe, T. B. Cunningham, Martin Gallagher, James Hennessey, Terrence Kelly, James R. Maloney, Billy Mulligan, and Thomas Mulloy.[30] The most famous of all—Broderick's trusted aide, Ned McGowan—ran for his life.[31] Thought to be implicated in the shooting of James King of William, McGowan was sought for hanging by the vigilantes. He escaped to Santa Barbara with neck unstretched but would no more turn out the vote for Broderick.[32]

With the Broderick machine in ruins, it was time to put something in its place. On August 11 the leaders of the vigilance committee initiated a political reform movement which they called the People's Party.[33] The People's Party represented the consummation of the movement that began with hangings and banishments. The violent, illegal phase of the vigilance committee lasted only three months, from its organization on May 15 to its disbanding with a grand review and parade on August 18.[34] The legal, political phase of the movement, on the other hand, lasted for ten years—until 1866—during which time the People's Party controlled the politics of San Francisco.

The call for the mass meeting that founded the People's Party and the resolutions adopted at it, although mentioning crime, put the emphasis on municipal financial reform. Great complaint was made of "heavy taxes filched from honest industry," of the near prostration of city and county credit, and of the vast sums that went into the pockets of office-holding drones. The plea was made that the best men of the city give their attention to levying taxes and making public appropriations. An "economical administration of the public funds" was demanded. Close control of salaries and fees was stipulated.[35]

The call for the meeting had been signed by virtually the entire corps of San Francisco merchants. The "Committee of 21," which was chosen to make People's Party nominations, was firmly dominated by merchants. On September 16 the committee published its slate of candidates. It was a large list but chosen very carefully so as to give full representation to the business enterprises, trades, and professions of San Francisco. The appeal of the slate was to the commercial occupations of the city rather than to religious or ethnic groups.[36]

It was unmistakably a vigilante-dominated ticket. In the first place, support of the vigilance committee was demanded of the entire list of People's Party candidates. Beyond that, some of the leading vigilantes were put at the head of the ticket. Charles Doane, the commander of the vigilance committee's 5,000-man military force, was nominated for sheriff. Other prominent vigilantes ran for chief of police and the state legislature.[37] The People's Party forbore making a choice in the Presidential race between Buchanan, Fremont, and Fillmore, but its sympathies were clearly Republican. In fact, the opportunistic young Republican Party of San Francisco made its support of the vigilance committee a principal appeal in the election. The Republicans endorsed all People's Party municipal and county candidates, and in return gained endorsement of their state and national candidates who greatly benefited from vigilante votes.[38] In time, most of the leading vigilantes became Republicans in state and national politics.

The result of all of this was a smashing victory for the People's Party in the November general election. It buried the weakened Democratic opposition by margins that often ran as high as two to one. Not a single People's Party candidate was defeated. The reformers carried the entire city with the exception of the waterfront first ward. Even the sixth ward—formerly a Broderick machine stronghold—went heavily into their column.[39]

In terms of a lower tax rate and lower municipal expenditures, the People's Party delivered on its promises. It drastically slashed municipal expenditures from a height of $2,500,000 in 1855 to $353,000 in 1857.[40] For ten years the People's Party held the government, mainly on the basis of its platform of keeping the tax rate down.[41] In proudly reviewing the history of the vigilance committee from the vantage point of 1891, William T. Coleman was in no doubt as to the significance of its offspring. The People's Party, he said, introduced a "new era" into San Francisco life by lowering taxation and introducing "economies" which "radically reduced" the municipal debt. "The credit of the city, State, and people, which before all was uncertain," wrote Coleman, "soon after took a foremost rank, which has since been finally held and maintained."[42] Coleman's statement emphasizes that vigilante action and People's Party fiscal reform raised the credit rating not only of the city but of the "people." By "people" Coleman meant San Francisco's businessmen—such as himself—who were crucially dependent on Eastern lenders and suppliers.

To what extent did conditions of crime lead the businessmen of San Francisco to employ the traditional penalties of hanging and banishment that were often used by frontier vigilantes? In their rhetoric both James King of William and the vigilantes in the early stages of their movement made much of a supposed crime problem. Did the reality support the rhetoric? The crime news in the San Francisco newspapers of 1855-1856 indicates that the regular organs of law and order had crime fully under control.[43] The main thrust of the vigilante movement was not against crime but was directed toward smashing the political machine of Broderick and the Irish Catholic Democrats and establishing one of its own.

This raises another question. If political reform was fundamentally the main concern of the vigilantes, why did they not try that in the first place? The answer of the vigilantes to contemporaries who asked that very question was that there was no possibility of political reform at the polls, since the corrupt element simply stuffed the ballot boxes and counted out the opposition. Hence, the vigilantes claimed, they were forced to take the law into their own hands.[44] That was their answer, but it is too simple. Implicitly, the reason why the reform-minded businessmen of San Francisco first resorted to vigilante violence rather than political action stemmed from the perennial problem of reformers: the difficulty of organizing apathetic and indifferent voters against an organized and entrenched political machine. Yet in the fall of 1856 the vigilantes did triumph at the polls by a two-to-one count. No amount of skullduggery by Broderick's henchmen could have overcome such an overwhelming majority.

The final question, then, is why did not the vigilantes invoke that overwhelming sentiment for reform in the first place and save themselves the trouble of the hangings and banishments? The answer, of course, is that it took the vigilance committee itself to break through the crust of apathy and bring about a mass movement for reform.

Before the founding of the vigilance committee there simply was no reform organization in San Francisco. In order to carry out the banishments and executions, the vigilance committee enrolled thousands of members. Since they had to control a large city and since they feared that the governor might raise a militia force against them,[45] the vigilante leaders felt it necessary to fashion a tightly organized movement with military discipline. Thus vigilantes were enrolled in military companies of fifty to one hundred members which, in turn, were organized into battalions and regiments. The companies, battalions, and regiments all had officers.[46] The rank and file of the vigilantes elected representatives to an Assembly of Delegates of about 150 members, and the president of the vigilance committee in turn named an executive committee of about forty members.[47] The military establishment was headed by a grand marshal,[48] the president and the executive committee exercised autocratic control over the movement, and the Assembly of Delegates functioned merely as an organ for voicing rank and file opinion.[49]

Thus the vigilance committee—organized in pyramidal, chain-of-command fashion and based on primary units of fifty to one hundred members—was ideally constituted for success in an election campaign. To win a smashing victory at the polls, all the People's Party leadership had to do was to draw upon the vigilante apparatus—and that is exactly what it did.

Seen superficially, the San Francisco vigilantes were faced with the familiar problem of a corrupt Irish Catholic Democratic political machine. Their solution was to crush it. But in Broderick's approach to government, and in his appeal to the voters and his concept of municipal life, there was something more basic than boodle. At issue in the San Francisco of the 1850's were the same unresolved questions that came to typify American cities. Could gigantic urban improvements be made only at the cost of wholesale corruption?[50] In ethnically mixed cities, would newcomers of minority-group status—Irish, Italians, Catholics, Jews, and others—be fully absorbed into American life, or would they be permanently condemned to economic degradation and social inferiority?[51]

To complex problems such as these the vigilance committee's starkly simple response of hanging and banishment was tragically inappropriate—tragic for the victims, of course, but tragic also for the vigilantes who thought they were solving something when they really were not. From his viewpoint of 1891 William T. Coleman complacently believed that the vigilance committee of 1856 had left San Francisco a permanent legacy of civic virtue and fiscal integrity. But he spoke too soon, for San Francisco was at that very time on the eve of the most turbulent period in its history: the era of the monumentally corrupt regime of Boss Ruef and Mayor Schmitz and the reform crusade of Fremont Older, Francis J. Heney, and Hiram Johnson.

The vigilantes of 1856 were on the right track when they abandoned the rope for the ballot box, but their People's Party reform movement was much too narrowly concerned with fiscal matters to achieve any lasting solutions to San Francisco's problems. The vigilantes never had a real understanding of the fundamental issues involved.

The new vigilantism, of which the vigilance committee of 1856 was a harbinger, was one of the birth pains of urban America. But for the problems of the new America it was a symptom rather than a solution.

Notes

Grateful acknowledgment is given to the Huntington Library for a grant-in-aid for July-August, 1966, which allowed research on this subject.

1. The first vigilante movement in American history was that of the South Carolina Regulators beginning in October, 1767. Richard Maxwell Brown, *The South Carolina Regulators* (Cambridge, Mass., 1963), 39.

2. Richard Maxwell Brown, "American Regulators and Vigilantes: An Hypothesis" (unpublished paper read at the annual meeting of the Mississippi Valley Historical Association, Cleveland, Ohio, May 1, 1964).

3. The terms "old" and "new" vigilantism are my own. On the new vigilantism see, for example, John W. Caughey, *Their Majesties the Mob* (Chicago [1960], 1-25, 100-205.

4. See Hubert H. Bancroft, *Popular Tribunals* (San Francisco, 1887), II, 548-559, where many Eastern and European editorials are reprinted, most of which (including such journals as the *Tribune, Herald,* and *Times* of New York and the Boston *Journal*) favored the vigilance committee. This second volume of Bancroft's massive two-volume *Popular Tribunals* is devoted entirely to the vigilance committee of 1856. Its 748-page text amounts to practically a primary source on the movement because of Bancroft's friendship with, and access to, many old vigilante leaders, including the greatest of them all, William T. Coleman. Despite Bancroft's strong and open bias in favor of the vigilantes, the book remains not only the largest but the best published treatment of the 1856 vigilance committee.

5. Perhaps the most notable example of a vigilance committee outside of California, which modeled itself on the San Francisco committee of 1856, was that of Virginia City, Montana in 1863-1864.

6. In San Francisco in the 1850's the contrast between the old and the new vigilantism is graphically revealed. The San Francisco vigilance committee of 1851 arose mainly in response to an orthodox crime problem stemming from Australian ex-convicts and other ne'er-do-wells. The vigilante movement of 1856 was in its objectives much more typical of the new vigilantism.

7. Harris, Bogardus, and Labatt (comps.), *San Francisco City Directory for the year commencing October, 1856* . . . (San Francisco, 1856), 129-132.

8. *The Daily Town Talk* (San Francisco), Sept. 13, 1856. The four French newspapers were *Bibliotheque Populaire, Echo du Pacifique, Le Phare,* and *De La Chapelle.* Harris, *Directory*, 127; *Town Talk*, May 22, 1856. The *Town Talk* was founded in the spring of 1856 shortly before the vigilante movement got underway. Contrary to the implication of its title, the *Town Talk* was not a scandal or gossip sheet. Instead, it was a regular four-page daily, similar to the other leading dailies of San Francisco of the era. The *Town Talk* gave excellent coverage to the vigilante movement. Its editorial policy, like that of all the dailies of the city except the *Herald*, favored the vigilance committee.

9. The vigilance committee itself gave lip-service to the ideal of brotherhood. Thus its motto was: "No creed. No party. No sectional issues." Bancroft was technically correct when he said that the vigilance committee was "composed of all classes and conditions of men" with every nationality, political and religious sentiment, trade, occupation, and profession represented. *Popular Tribunals*, II, 84-85, 110. This was true, not surprisingly, in a movement of from 6,000 to 8,000 members; but the important point is that the movement was strongly dominated by merchants and old-stock Americans of Northern origin and of Whig, Know Nothing, or Republican politics with relatively few Irish or Catholics among the membership.

10. John Myers Myers, *San Francisco's Reign of Terror* (New York, 1966), 35-36, 68-69.

11. Bancroft, *Popular Tribunals*, II, 1-21. Professor David A. Williams of Long Beach State College, who is preparing a badly needed biographical study of Broderick, has told me that he feels that Broderick had a good deal of social consciousness in regard to his Irish Catholic and mainly lower class adherents in San Francisco. From my own knowledge of Broderick I believe that this was probably so, and it is not incompatible with the sort of ward tactics Broderick used to dominate San Francisco politics in the 1850's.

12. Myers, *San Francisco's Reign of Terror*, 80. J. P. Young, *San Francisco: A History of the Pacific Metropolis* (San Francisco, [1913], I, 216.

13. See the expose´ in the form of a front-page, three-column report from the executive committee of

the vigilantes: "Official Corruption," San Francisco *Daily Evening Bulletin*, July 14, 1856. This is one of the key documents in the vigilante episode. See also Young, *San Francisco*, I, 216.

14. The Huntington Library has a complete file of the *Bulletin* for the years 1855-1856 which the writer used. The *Bulletin*, especially the editorials of King, are crucial for an understanding of the fears and anxieties which gave rise to the vigilance committee of 1856. Had his newspaper career not been cut short before it had fairly gotten started, I am confident that King would have become one of the famous journalists in American history. King had been a failure in business but had found his metier in journalism. He was a remarkably trenchant, even demagogic, editor, and he took San Francisco by storm in the months before his death. Although it is a favorable treatment, *Villains and Vigilantes: The Story of James King of William and Pioneer Justice in California* (New York, 1961) by Stanton A. Coblentz does not adequately explain the martyred editor.

15. For examples, see especially these issues of the *Bulletin*: Oct. 13, 16, and Dec. 27, 1855; Jan. 4, 8, 22, Feb. 2, and Apr. 1, 3, 1856.

16. *Bulletin*, Nov. 19, 1855.

17. See, for example, *Bulletin*, Nov. 20, 22, 24, and Dec. 12, 1855; Jan. 8, 17, 1856.

18. On Casey's background see *Bulletin*, Nov. 5, 1855.

19. Bancroft, *Popular Tribunals*, II, 69ff. *Bulletin* and *Town Talk*, May 15, 1856.

20. *Town Talk*, July 30, 1856.

21. In the *Century Magazine* of November, 1891, Coleman put the membership at about 8,000 (p. 145). The 1856 sources on the vigilance committee estimated its military force as being about 6,000. The file of applications for membership documents the frequent contemporary assertion that each vigilante was assigned a number. The highest number that I have seen in the Committee of Vigilance Papers in the Huntington Library is, 5,757.

22. Bancroft, *Popular Tribunals*, II, 80-81, 117-118, 121, 125-126, 418. Letter from "Cosmos" in *Bulletin*, June 6, 1856. All contemporary sources attest mercantile domination.

23. Bancroft, *Popular Tribunals*, II, 86-87 and *passim*. See also James A. B. Scherer, *"The Lion of the Vigilantes": William T. Coleman and the Life of Old San Francisco* (Indianapolis and New York, 1939).

24. Box labeled "Applications for Membership, 1856," Committee of Vigilance Papers, Huntington Library.

25. These generalizations are made upon the basis of my analysis of each one of the approximately 2,500 applications. Internal evidence indicates that virtually all of the applications were accepted. Only one was marked as rejected. It is likely that most of the rejected applications were not retained in this file. Thus the approximately 2,500 applications represent the same number of members or from about 30% to 40% of the entire membership, depending upon whether 6,000 or 8,000 is accepted as the figure for the total membership. For statistical purposes, the 2,500 applications represent a more than adequate sample of the vigilante membership.

26. For the anxieties which this could cause, see the article, "Steamer Day," in *Town Talk*, Oct. 5, 1856. Steamers left San Francisco every two weeks for the East with remittances for Eastern creditors. The attempt of San Francisco businessmen to raise money for the Steamer Day sailings had economic reverberations throughout the entire city.

27. Following the executions of Casey and Cora, the effects of further vigilante actions were anticipated in *Town Talk*, May 28, 1856: "The 'reign of terror' is working our redemption, and California stocks will rise in the market when this news reaches the Atlantic."

28. Extensive testimony and evidence are in "Papers relating to Ballot Box Stuffing and Fraudulent Elections, 1854-1856," a box of 112 pieces in Committee of Vigilance Papers.

29. [James O'Meara], *The Vigilance Committee of 1856* (San Francisco, 1887), 46-56.

30. *Town Talk*, Oct. 5, 1856; Bancroft, *Popular Tribunals*, II, 590-609.

31. The colorful story of Ned McGowan is ably told by John Myers Myers in *San Francisco's Reign of Terror* (New York, 1966) on the basis of good research. Despite the deceptive title, this book is really a biography of McGowan with heavy emphasis on the vigilante period. Myers grossly overrates McGowan as a writer and at times exaggerates his importance, but Myers' anti-vigilante interpretation, in contrast to that of the predominant pro-vigilante historians, is refreshing and realistic.

32. A prominent "shoulder striker" and election manipulator, Yankee Sullivan, would have undoubtedly been banished had he not died, allegedly by suicide, while in vigilante custody. *Town Talk*, May 31, 1856. Bancroft, *Popular Tribunals*, II, 649 states that it was "roughly estimated" that eight hundred of the "worst characters" voluntarily left San Francisco because of the vigilante action. Included were "thieves, murderers, corrupters of public morals, gamblers, prize-fighters, ballot-box stuffers, loafers, and vagabonds."

33. *Town Talk*, Aug. 9, 12, 1856.

34. *Bulletin*, Aug. 18, 19, 1856.

35. *Town Talk*, Aug. 9, 12, 1856.

36. *Daily Alta California* (San Francisco), Aug. 9, 1856; *Town Talk*, Aug. 12, Sept. 16, 1856.

37. *Town Talk*, Sept. 16, Nov. 4, 1856.

38. *Bulletin*, Oct. 9, 11, 1856.

39. *Bulletin*, Nov. 25, 1856.

40. Young, *San Francisco*, I, 216.

41. *Ibid*, 104.

42. *Century Magazine*, XLIII (November 1891), 145.

43. Despite King's fulminations in the editorial columns, my survey of the police news columns in the *Bulletin* and *Town Talk* during the fall, winter, and spring of 1855-1856 has convinced me that the San Francisco crime problem was under control. King was outraged at the hung jury in the murder trial of Charles Cora, but the circumstances surrounding Cora's killing of Richardson leave the real possibility that it could have been in self-defense. That Cora went free does not seem to be a reflection on San Francisco justice. At another level, King's crusade against wide-open houses of prostitution in San Francisco showed a commendable regard on his part for the general conditions of morality in the city, but the news of arrests and convictions indicate that any overt crime stemming from the latitude of life in a wide-open city was kept well under control. Vigilante leaders had sufficient confidence in the regular system that in the summer of 1856, while the vigilance committee had an iron grip on the city, they allowed the police officers and courts to enforce law in a regular way. The vigilance committee restricted itself to four hangings, investigation of the Broderick machine, and banishment of its leading operatives. For some examples of regular law enforcement in San Francisco during the height of the vigilante period, see *Town Talk*, May 28, 29, 30, 31, 1856. See also Joseph L. King, "The Vigilance Committee of '56," *Overland Monthly*, LXVIII (July-December 1918), 519.

44. *Town Talk*, June 10, 15, 1856. The vigilantes made much of their discovery of a ballot box with

false bottom which had been used for stuffing purposes by Yankee Sullivan in the interest of Ned McGowan, Charles Duane, and other Broderick stalwarts. See Bancroft, *Popular Tribunals*, II, 6-8 where the false ballot box is described and sketched.

45. *Town Talk*, June 4, 5, 1856.

46. Bancroft, *Popular Tribunals*, II, 87-111. The names of vigilante officers were printed in the newspapers. A convenient listing of the officers, down to the level of the captains who commanded the companies, is in Samuel Colville, *Colville's 1856-1857 San Francisco Directory: Volume I: for the year commencing October, 1856 . . . (San Francisco, 1856), 226-227.*

47. Bancroft, *Popular Tribunals*, II, 113.

48. *Colville's Directory for 1856*, 226-227.

49. Bancroft, *Popular Tribunals*, II, 109-113; *Town Talk*, Aug. 8, 1856.

50. Seymour J. Mandelbaum in *Boss Tweed's New York* (New York, [1965]), 46-47, has pointed out that this was a major problem in New York City after the Civil War. The similarities between the problems of San Francisco in the 1850's and New York after the Civil War are striking. The Tammany machine in New York, like the Broderick machine in San Francisco, produced similar reactions although in New York incipient vigilante movements never got to the point of taking the law into their own hands.

51. This problem has been of major concern in important studies by Oscar Handlin, John Higham, Barbara Miller Solomon, Stephan Thernstrom, Moses Rischin, David Brody, Gunther Barth, and others.

The evolution of the cow-puncher

Owen Wister

Of all the colorful figures produced by the American West, none has been more enduring or more popular than the cowboy. As a frontier character, however, the cowboy arrived late, appearing first in post-Civil War Texas and then spreading North in the 1870s and 1880s to the great cattle country of Colorado, Wyoming, Montana, and the Dakotas. The cowboy's actual span was brief. As Owen Wister has pointed out it was over by the first decade of the twentieth century. With a reign so short and so geographically limited it is surprising that the cowboy has achieved such lasting popularity. That he has is in no small measure due to three Ivy League easterners—the politician Theodore Roosevelt, the artist Frederic Remington, and the novelist Owen Wister—who discovered and popularized the cowboy in the late nineteenth century. Wister and Roosevelt were good friends, having met while attending Harvard in 1880. Remington, a Yale man, met Wister and Roosevelt by illustrating their writings. All three became ardent progressives. Each saw great threats to America from undesirable immigration by "racially inferior" southern and eastern Europeans, from misbehavior by Wall Street capitalists, and from the rising radicalism of the working class.

Roosevelt discovered the West through his sojourn as a "gentleman cowboy" in Dakota Territory, and romanticised the cowboy in his essays and in his three volume *Winning of the West*. It was Wister, however, who really focused the attention of educated America on the cowboy. Initially he wrote short stories, the first two of which ("Hank's Woman" and "How Lin McLean went East") appeared in the early 1890s. Finally, in April 1902, he published his best-selling novel, *The Virginian*.

Wister's "Evolution of the Cow-Puncher" resulted largely from the urging of Remington. "Say Wister," wrote Remington, "Go ahead please make me an article on the evolution of the puncher—'the passing' as it were—I want to make some pictures of the ponies going over the hill rearing after a steer on the jump." Wister's article, appearing in the September 1895 edition of *Harper's*, purported to be factual. In reality it was highly interpretive. Wister's assumptions were deeply racist, but they were not original with him. For Wister the cowboy represented much of the best of a simple, uncorrupted, and vanishing American way of life. In portraying the cowboy as an Anglo-Saxon throwback to the English cavalier and the Germanic teutonic knight, Remington and

Reprinted from *Harper's New Monthly Magazine* (September 1895), 602-617.

Wister amplified a theme about the origins of American institutions made popular by scholars such as Herbert Baxter Adams of Johns Hopkins University. Wister's article is significant because its basic tenets went unchallenged by his own age. Wister's view of history emerged in his short stories and in turn influenced for several decades the writers of cowboy novels and the makers of "western" movies.

For further reading: N. Orwin Rush, *Frederic Remington and Owen Wister–The Story of a Friendship 1893-1909* (Tallahassee: Florida State University, 1961); Andy Adams, *The Log of a Cowboy* (orig. pub. 1903; Lincoln: University of Nebraska Press, 1964);* Ernest Staples Osgood, *The Day of the Cattleman* (Minneapolis: University of Minnesota Press, 1929);* J. Frank Dobie, *The Longhorns* (Boston: Little, Brown, 1941);* Edward E. Dale, *The Range Cattle Industry: Ranching on the Great Plains from 1865 to 1925* (Norman: University of Oklahoma Press, 1930); Louis Pelzer, *The Cattleman's Frontier* (Glendale, Calif.: Arthur H. Clark, 1936); Wayne Gard, *The Chisholm Trail* (Norman: University of Oklahoma Press, 1954).

*Available in paperback.

Two men sat opposite me once, despising each other so heartily that I am unlikely to forget them. They had never met before–if they can be said to have met this time–and they were both unknown to me. It happened in a train by which we journeyed together from Leamington to London. The cause of their mutual disesteem was appearance; neither liked the other's outward man, and told him so silently for three hours; that is all they ever knew of each other. This object-lesson afterward gained greatly by my learning the name and estate of one of these gentlemen. He was a peer. He had good rugs, a good umbrella, several newspapers–but read only the pink one–and a leather and silver thing which I took to be a travelling-bag beside him. He opened it between Banbury and Oxford, and I saw, not handkerchiefs and ivory, but cut-glass bottles with stoppers. I noticed further the strong sumptuous monogram engraved here and there. The peer leisurely took brandy, and was not aware of our presence. But the point of him is that he garnished those miles of railroad with incomparably greater comfort than we did who had no rugs, no cut glass, no sandwich-box, no monogram. He had understood life's upholstery and trappings for several hundred years, getting the best to be had in each generation of his noble descent.

The enemy that he had made, as a dog makes an enemy of a cat by the mere preliminary of being a dog, sat in the other corner. He wore a shiny silk hat, smooth new lean black trousers, with high boots stiff and swelling to stove-pipe symmetry beneath, and a tie devoid of interest. I did not ascertain if the pistol was in his hip pocket, but at stated intervals he spit out of his window. By his hawk nose and eye and the lank strength of his chin he was a male who could take care of himself, and had done so. One could be sure he had wrested success from this world somehow, somewhere; and here he was, in a first-class carriage, on a first-class train, come for a first-class time, with a mind as complacently shut against being taught by foreign travel as any American patriot of to-day can attain or recommend, or any Englishman can reveal in his ten-day book about our continent and people. Charles Dickens and Mark Twain have immortalized their own blindness almost equally; and the sad truth is that enlightenment is mostly a stay-at-home creature, who crosses neither ocean nor frontier. This stranger was of course going to have a bad time, and feel relieved to get home and tell of the absence of baggage-checks and of the effete despot who had not set up the drinks. Once he addressed the despot, who was serenely smoking.

"I'll trouble you for a light," said he; and in his drawl I heard plainly his poor opinion of feudalism.

His lordship returned the drawl—not audibly, but with his eye, which he ran slowly up and down the stranger. His was the Piccadilly drawl; the other made use of the trans-Missouri variety; and both these are at bottom one and the same—the Anglo-Saxon's note of eternal contempt for whatever lies outside the beat of his personal experience. So I took an observation of these two Anglo-Saxons drawling at each other across the prejudice of a hundred years, and I thought it might come to a row. For the American was, on the quiet face of him, a "bad man," and so, to any save the provincial eye, was the nobleman. Fine feathers had deceived trans-Missouri, whose list of "bad men" was limited to specimens of the cut of his own jib, who know nothing of cut-glass bottles. But John gave Jonathan the light he asked, and for the remainder of our journey ceased to know that such a person existed.

Though we three never met again, my object-lesson did not end when we parted at Paddington. Before many seasons were sped the fortunes of the nobleman took a turn for the scandalous. He left cut glass behind him and went to Texas. I wish I could veraciously tell that he saw the stranger there—the traveller between whose bird-of-freedom nostrils and the wind his luxurious nobility had passed so offensively. But I do know that his second and more general skirmish with democracy left both sides amicable. In fact, the nobleman won the Western heart forthwith. Took it by surprise: democracy had read in the papers so often about the despot and his effeteness. This despot vaulted into the saddle and stuck to the remarkably ingenious ponies that had been chosen with care to disconcert him. When they showed him pistols, he was found to be already acquainted with that weapon. He quickly learned how to rope a steer. The card habit ran in his noble blood as it did in the cowboy's. He could sleep on the ground and rough it with the best of them, and with the best of them he could drink and help make a town clamorous. Deep in him lay virtues and vices coarse and elemental as theirs. Doubtless the windows of St. James Street sometimes opened in his memory, and he looked into them and desired to speak with those whom he saw inside. And the whiskey was not like the old stuff in the cut-glass bottles; but he never said so; and in time he died, widely esteemed. Texas found no count against him save his pronunciation of such words as bath and fancy—a misfortune laid to the accident of his birth; and you will hear to-day in that flannel-shirted democracy only good concerning this aristocrat born and bred.

Now, besides several morals which no pious person will find difficult to draw from the decline and fall of this aristocrat, there is something more germane to my democratic contemplation: after all, when driven to flock with Texas, he was a bird of that wild feather. That is the object-lesson; that is the gist of the matter. Directly the English nobleman smelt Texas, the slumbering untamed Saxon awoke in him, and mindful of the tournament, mindful of the hunting-field, galloped howling after wild cattle, a born horseman, a perfect athlete, and spite of the peerage and gules and argent, fundamentally kin with the drifting vagabonds who swore and galloped by his side. The man's outcome typifies the way of his race from the beginning. Hundreds like him have gone to Australia, Canada, India and have done likewise, and in our own continent you may see the thing plainer than anywhere else. No rood of modern ground is more debased and mongrel with its hordes of encroaching alien vermin, that turn our cities to Babels and our citizenship to a hybrid farce, who degrade our commonwealth from a nation into something half pawn-shop, half broker's office. But to survive in the clean cattle country requires spirit of adventure, courage, and self-sufficiency; you will not find many Poles or Huns or Russian Jews in that district; it stands as yet untainted by the benevolence of Baron Hirsch. Even in the cattle country the respectable Swedes settle chiefly to farming, and are seldom horsemen. The community of which the aristocrat appropriately made one speaks English. The Frenchman to-day is seen at his best inside a house; he can paint and he can play comedy, but he seldom climbs a new mountain. The Italian has forgotten Columbus, and sells fruit. Among the Spaniards and the Portuguese no Cortez or Magellan is found to-day. Except in Prussia, the Teuton is too often a tame, slippered animal, with his pedantic mind swaddled in a dressing-gown. But the Anglo-Saxon is still forever homesick for out-of-doors.

Throughout his career it has been his love to push further into the wilderness, and his fate thereby to serve larger causes than his own. In following his native bent he furthers unwittingly a design outside himself; he cuts the way for the common law and self-government, and new creeds, polities, and nations arise in his wake; in his own immense commonwealth this planless rover is obliterated. Roving took him (the Viking portion of him) from his Norse crags across to Albion. From that hearth of Albion the footprints of his sons lead to the corners of the earth; beside that hearth how inveterate remains his flavor! At Hastings he tasted defeat, but was not vanquished; to the Invincible Armada he proved a grievous surprise; one way or another he came through Waterloo—possibly because he is inveterately dull at perceiving himself beaten; when not otherwise busy at Balaklava or by the Alma, he was getting up horse-races, ready for sport or killing, and all with that silver and cut-glass finish which so offends our whistling, vacant-minded democracy. Greatest triumph and glory of all, because spiritual, his shoulders bore the Reformation when its own originators had tottered. Away from the hearth the cut-glass stage will not generally have been attained by him, and in Maine or Kentucky you can recognize at sight the chip of the old rough block. But if you meet him upon his island, in the shape of a peer, and find him particular to dress for dinner seven days of the week, do not on that account imagine that his white tie has throttled the man in him. That is a whistling Fourth-of-July misconception. It's no symptom of patriotism to be unable to see a man through cut glass, and if it comes to an appraisement of the stranger and the peer, I should say, put each in the other's place, and let us see if the stranger could play the peer as completely as the nobleman played the cowboy. Sir Francis Drake was such a one; and Raleigh, the fine essence of Anglo-Saxon, with his fashionable gallant cloak, his adventure upon new seas, and his immediate appreciation of tobacco. The rover may return with looted treasure or incidentally stolen corners of territory to clap in his strong-box (this Angle is no angel), but it is not the dollars that played first fiddle with him, else our Hebrew friends would pioneer the whole of us. Adventure, to be out-of-doors, to find some new place far away from the postman, to enjoy independence of spirit or mind or body (according to his high or low standards)—this is the cardinal surviving fittest instinct that makes the Saxon through the centuries conqueror, invader, navigator, buccaneer, explorer, colonist, tiger-shooter; lifts him a pilgrim among the immortals at Plymouth Rock, dangles him a pirate from the gallows on the docks of Bristol. At all times when historic conditions or private stress have burst his domestic crust and let him fly out naturally, there he is, on Darien's peak, or through Magellan, or across the Missouri, or up the Columbia, a Hawkins, a Boone, a Grey, or a nameless vagrant, the same Saxon, ploughing the seas and canning the forests in every shape of man, from preacher to thief, and in each shape changelessly untamed. And as he has ruled the waves with his ship from that Viking time until yesterday at Samoa, when approaching death could extract no sound from him save American cheers and music, so upon land has the horse been his foster-brother, his ally, his playfellow, from the tournament at Camelot to the round-up at Abilene. The blood and the sweat of his jousting, and all the dirt and stains, have faded in the long sunlight of tradition, and in the chronicles of romance we hear none of his curses or obscenity; the clash of his armor rings mellow and heroic down the ages into our modern ears. But his direct lineal offspring among our Western mountains has had no poet to connect him with the eternal, no distance to lend him enchantment; though he has fought single-handed with savages, and through skill and daring prevailed, though he has made his nightly bed in a thousand miles of snow and loneliness, he has not, and never will have, the "consecration of memory." No doubt Sir Launcelot bore himself with a grace and breeding of which our unpolished fellow of the cattle trail has only the latent possibility; but in personal daring and in skill as to the horse, the knight and the cowboy are nothing but the same Saxon of different environments, the nobleman in London and the nobleman in Texas; and no hoof in Sir Thomas Mallory shakes the crumbling plains with quadruped sound more valiant than the galloping that has echoed from the Rio Grande to the Big Horn Mountains. But we have no Sir Thomas Mallory! Since Hawthorne, Longfellow, and Cooper were taken from us, our flippant and impoverished imagination has ceased to be national, and the rider among Indians and cattle, the frontiersman, the American who replaces Miles Standish and the Pathfinder, is now beneath the notice of polite writers.

From the tournament to the round-up! Deprive the Saxon of his horse, and put him to forest-clearing or in a counting-house for a couple of generations, and you may pass him by without ever seeing that his legs are designed for the gripping of saddles. Our first hundred years afforded his horsemanship but little opportunity. Though his out-of-door spirit, most at home when at large, sported free in the elbow-room granted by the surrender of Cornwallis, it was on foot and with an axe that he chiefly enjoyed himself. He moved his log cabin slowly inward from the Atlantic, slowly over the wooded knolls of Cumberland and Allegheny, down and across the valley beyond, until the infrequent news of him ceased, and his kinsfolk who had staid by the sea, and were merchanting themselves upwards to the level of family portraits and the cut-glass finish, forgot that the prodigal in the backwoods belonged to them, and was part of their United States, bone of their bone. And thus did our wide country become as a man whose East hand knoweth not what his West hand doeth.

Mr. Herndon, in telling of Lincoln's early days in Illinois, gives us a complete picture of the roving Saxon upon our continent in 1830. "The boys . . . . were a terror to the entire region—seemingly a necessary product of frontier civilization. They were friendly and good-natured. . . . They would do almost anything for sport or fun, love or necessity. Though rude and rough, though life's forces ran over the edge of their bowl, foaming and sparkling in pure deviltry for deviltry's sake, . . . yet place before them a poor man who needed their aid, . . . a defenceless woman, . . . they melted into sympathy and charity at once. They gave all they had, and willingly toiled or played cards for more. . . . A stranger's introduction was likely to be the most unpleasant part of his acquaintance. . . . They were in the habit of 'cleaning out' New Salem." Friendly and good-natured, and in the habit of cleaning out New Salem! Quite so. There you have him. Here is the American variety of the Saxon set down for you as accurately as if Audubon himself had done it. A colored plate of Robin Hood and the Sheriff of Nottingham should go on the opposite page. Nothing but the horse is left out of the description, and that is because the Saxon and his horse seldom met during the rail-splitting era of our growth. But the man of 1830 would give away all that he had and play cards for more. Decidedly nothing was missing except the horse—and the horse was waiting in another part of our large map until the man should arrive and jump on his back again.

A few words about this horse—the horse of the plains. Whether or no his forefathers looked on when Montezuma fell, they certainly hailed from Spain. And whether it was missionaries or thieves who carried them northward from Mexico, until the Sioux heard of the new animal, certain it also is that this pony ran wild for a century or two, either alone or with various red-skinned owners; and as he gathered the sundry experiences of war and peace, of being stolen, and of being abandoned in the snow at inconvenient distances from home, of being ridden by two women and a baby at once, and of being eaten by a bear, his wide range of contretemps brought him a wit sharper than the street Arab's, and an attitude towards life more blasé than in the united capitals of Europe. I have frequently caught him watching me with an eye of such sardonic depreciation that I felt it quite vain to attempt any hiding from him of my incompetence; and as for surprising him, a locomotive cannot do it, for I have tried this. He relishes putting a man in absurd positions, and will wait many days in patience to compass this uncharitable thing; and when he cannot bring a man to derision, he contents himself with a steer or a buffalo, helping the man to rope and throw these animals with an ingenuity surpassing any circus, to my thinking. A number of delighted passengers on the Kansas Pacific Railway passed by a Mexican vaquero, who had been sent out from Kansas City to rope a buffalo as an advertisement for the stock-yards. The train stopped to take a look at the solitary horseman fast to a buffalo in the midst of the plains. José, who had his bull safely roped, shouted to ask if they had water on the train. "We'll bring you some," said they. "Oh, I come get," said he; and jumping off, he left his accomplished pony in sole charge of the buffalo. Whenever the huge beast struggled for freedom, the clever pony stiffened his legs and leaned back as in a tug of war, by jumps and dodges so anticipating each move of the enemy that escape was entirely hopeless. The boy got his drink, and his employer sent out a car for the buffalo, which was taken in triumph into Kansas City behind the passenger train. The Mexican narrated the exploit to his employer thus: "Oh, Shirley, when the train start they all give three greata big cheers for me, and then they give three mucha bigger cheers for the little gray hoss!"

Ah, progress is truly a wonder! and admirable beyond all doubt it is to behold the rapid new square miles of brick, and the stream rich with the contributions of an increased population, and tall factories that have stopped dividends just for the present, and long empty railroads in the hands of the receiver; but I prefer that unenlightened day when we had plenty of money and cheered for the little gray hoss. Such was the animal that awaited the coming of the rail-splitter. The meeting was a long way off in 1830. Not the Mexican war, not the gold on the Pacific in '49 (though this, except for the horse, revealed the whole Saxon at his best and worst, and for a brief and beautiful moment waked once more the American muse), not any national event until the war of the rebellion was over and we had a railroad from coast to coast, brought the man and his horse together. It was in the late sixties that this happened in Texas. The adventurous sons of Kentucky and Tennessee, forever following the native bent to roam, and having no longer a war to give them the life they preferred, came into a new country full of grass and cattle. Here they found Mexicans by the hundred, all on horses and at large over the flat of the world. This sight must have stirred memories in the rail-splitter's blood, for he joined the sport upon the instant. I do not think he rode with bolder skill than the Mexican's, but he brought other and grittier qualities to bear upon that wild life, and also the Saxon contempt for the foreigner. Soon he had taken what was good from this small, deceitful alien, including his name, *Vaquero*, which he translated into Cowboy. He took his saddle, his bridle, his spurs, his rope, his methods of branding and herding—indeed, most of his customs and accoutrements—and with them he went rioting over the hills. His play-ground was two thousand miles long and a thousand wide. The hoofs of his horse were tough as iron, and the pony waged the joyous battle of self-preservation as stoutly as did his rider. When the man lay rolled in his blankets sleeping, warm and unconcerned beneath a driving storm of snow, the beast pawed through to the sage-brush and subsisted; so that it came to be said of such an animal, "A meal a day is enough for a man who gets to ride that horse."

The cow-puncher's play-ground in those first glorious days of his prosperity included battle and murder and sudden death as every-day matters. From 1865 to 1878 in Texas he fought his way with knife and gun, and any hour of the twenty-four might see him flattened behind the rocks among the whiz of bullets and the flight of arrows, or dragged bloody and folded together from some adobe hovel. Seventy-five dollars a month and absolute health and strength were his wages; and when the news of all this excellence drifted from Texas eastward, they came in shoals—Saxon boys of picked courage (none but plucky ones could survive) from South and North, from town and country. Every sort and degree of home tradition came with them from their far birthplaces. Some had known the evening hymn at one time, others could remember no parent or teacher earlier than the street; some spoke with the gentle accent of Virginia, others in the dialect of baked beans and codfish; here and there was the baccalaureate, already beginning to forget his Greek alphabet, but still able to repeat the two notable words with which Xenophon always marches upon the next stage of his journey. Hither to the cattle country they flocked from forty kinds of home, each bringing a deadly weapon.

What motlier tribe, what heap of cards shuffled from more various unmatched packs, could be found? Yet this tribe did not remain motley, but soon grew into a unit. To begin with, the old spirit burned alike in all, the unextinguished fire of adventure and independence. And then, the same stress of shifting for self, the same vigorous and peculiar habits of life, were forced upon each one: watching for Indians, guarding huge herds at night, chasing cattle, wild as deer, over rocks and counties, sleeping in the dust and waking in the snow, cooking in the open, swimming the swollen rivers. Such gymnasium for mind and body develops a like pattern in the unlike. Thus, late in the nineteenth century, was the race once again subjected to battles and darkness, rain and shine, to the fierceness and generosity of the desert. Destiny tried her latest experiment upon the Saxon, and plucking him from the library, the haystack, and the gutter, set him upon his horse; then it was that, face to face with the eternal simplicity of death, his modern guise fell away and showed once again the medieval man. It was no new type, no product of the frontier, but just the original kernel of the nut with the shell broken.

This bottom bond of race unified the divers young men, who came riding from various points of the compass, speaking university and gutter English simultaneously; and as the knights of Camelot prized their armor and were particular about their swords, so these dusty successors had an extreme pride of equipment, and put aside their jeans and New York suits for the tribal dress. Though each particle of gearing for man and horse was evoked from daily necessity, gold and silver instantly stepped in to play their customary ornamental part, as with all primitive races. The cow-puncher's legs must be fended from the thorny miles of the Rio Grande, the thousand mongrel shrubs that lace their bristles together stiff over the country—the mesquite, the shin-oak, the cat's-claw, the Spanish-dagger; widespreading, from six inches to ten feet high, every vegetable vicious with an embroidery of teeth and nails; a continent of peevish thicket called *chaparral*, as we indiscriminately call a dog with too many sorts of grandfathers a cur. Into this saw-mill dives the wild steer through paths and passages known to himself, and after him the pursuing man must also dive at a rate that would tear his flesh to ribbons if the blades and points could get hold of him. But he cases his leg against the hostile *chaparral* from thigh to ankle in chaps—leathern breeches, next door to armor: his daily bread is scarcely more needful to him. Soon his barbaric pleasure in finery sews tough leather fringe along their sides, and the leather flap of the pocket becomes stamped with a heavy rose. Sagging in a slant upon his hips leans his leather belt of cartridges buckled with jaunty arrogance, and though he uses his pistol with murderous skill, it is pretty, with ivory or mother-of-pearl for a handle. His arm must be loose to swing his looped rope free and drop its noose over the neck of the animal that bounds in front of his rushing pony. Therefore he rides in a loose flannel shirt that will not cramp him as he whirls the coils; but the handkerchief knotted at his throat, though it is there to prevent sunburn, will in time of prosperity be chosen for its color and soft texture, a scarf to draw the eye of woman. His heavy splendid saddle is, in its shape and luxury of straps and leather thongs, the completest instrument for night and day travel, and the freighting along with you of board and lodging, that any nomad has so far devised. With its trappings and stamped leather, its horn and high cantle, we are well acquainted. It must stand the strain of eight hundred sudden pounds of live beef tearing at it for freedom; it must be the anchor that shall not drag during the furious rages of such a typhoon. For the cattle of the wilderness have often run wild for three, four, and five years, through rocks and forests, never seeing the face of man from the day when as little calves they were branded. And some were never branded at all. They have grown up in company with the deer, and like the deer they fly at the approach of the horseman. Then, if he has ridden out to gather these waifs from their remote untenanted pastures and bring them in to be counted and driven to sale, he must abandon himself to the headlong pursuit. The open easy plain with its harmless footing lies behind, the steep valley narrows up to an entering wedge among the rocks, and into these untoward regions rush the beeves. The shale and detritus of shelving landslides, the slippery knobs in the beds of brooks, the uncertain edges of the jumping-off place, all lie in the road of the day's necessity, and where the steer goes, goes the cow-puncher too—balancing, swaying, doubling upon his shrewd pony. The noose un-coiling flies swinging through the air and closes round the throat—or perhaps only the hind leg—of the quarry. In the shock of stopping short or of leaning to circle, the rider's stirrups must be long, and his seat a forked pliant poise on the horse's back; no grip of the knee will answer in these contortions; his leg must have its straight length, a lever of muscle and sinew to yield or close viselike on the pony's ribs; and when the steer feels that he is taken and the rope tightens from the saddle horn, then must the gearing be solid, else, like a fisherman floundering with snapped rod and tangled line, the cow-puncher will have misfortunes to repair and nothing to repair them with. Such a thing as this has happened in New Mexico: The steer, pursued and frantic at feeling the throttle of the flung rope, ran blindly over a cliff, one end of the line fast to him, the other to the rider's saddle horn, and no time to think once, much less twice, about anything in this or the next world. The pony braced his legs at the edge, but his gait swept him onward, as with the fast skater whose skate has stuck upon a frozen chip. The horse fell over the mountain, and with him his rider; but the sixty-foot rope was new, and it hooked over a stump. Steer and horse swung like scales gently above the man, who lay at the bottom, hurt nearly to death, but not enough to dull his appreciation of the unusual arrangement.

It is well, then, to wear leathern armor and sit in a stout saddle if you would thrive among the thorns and rocks; and without any such casualty as falling over a mountain, the day's common events call for uncommon strength of gear. Not otherwise can the steer be hooked and landed safely, and not otherwise is the man to hoist resisting beeves up a hill somewhat as safes are conducted to the sixth story, nor could the rider plunge galloping from the sixth story to the ground, or swerve and heavily lean to keep from flying into space, were his stirrup leathers not laced, and every other crucial spot of strain independent of so weak a thing as a buckle. To go up where you have come down is another and easier process for man and straps and everything except the horse. His breath and legs are not immortal. And in order that each day the man may be hardily borne over rough and smooth he must own several mounts—a "string"; sometimes six and more, either his own property, or allotted to him by the foreman of the outfit for which he rides. The unused animals run in a herd—the *ramuda*; and to get a fresh mount from the ramuda means not seldom the ceremony of catching your hare. The ponies walk sedately together in the pasture, good as gold, and eying you without concern until they perceive that you are come with an object. They then put forth against you all the circus knowledge you have bestowed upon them so painfully. They comprehend ropes and loops and the law of gravity; they have observed the errors of steers in similar cases, and the unattractive result of running inside any enclosure, such as a corral, they strategize to keep at large, and altogether chasing a steer is tortoise play to the game they can set up for you. They relish the sight of you whirling impotent among them, rejoice in the smoking pace and the doublings they perpetrate; and with one eye attentive to you and your poised rope, and the other dexterously commanding the universe, they will intertangle as in cross-tag, pushing between your design and its victim, mingling confusedly like a driven mist, and all this with nostrils leaning level to the wind and bellies close to the speeding ground. But when the desired one is at last taken and your successful rope is on his neck, you would not dream he had ever wished for anything else. He stands, submitting absent-mindedly to bit and blanket, mild as any unconscious lamb, while placidity descends once more upon the herd; again they pasture good as gold, and butter would not melt in the mouth of one of these conscientious creatures. I have known a number of dogs, one crow, and two monkeys, but these combined have seemed to me less fertile in expedient than the cow-pony, the sardonic cayuse. The bit his master gave him, and the bridle and spurs, have the same origin from necessity and the same history as to ornament. If stopping and starting and turning must be like flashes of light, the apparatus is accordingly severe; and as for the spurs, those wheels with long spikes cease to seem grotesque when you learn that with shorter and sharper rowels they would catch in the corded meshes of the girth, and bring the rider to ruin. Silver and gold, when he could pay for them, went into the make and decoration of this smaller machinery; and his hat would cost him fifteen dollars, and he wore fringed gloves. His boots often cost twenty-five dollars in his brief hour of opulence. Come to town for his holiday, he wore his careful finery, and from his wide hat-brim to his jingling heels made something of a figure—as self-conscious and deliberate a show as any painted buck in council or bull-elk among his aspiring cows; and out of town in the mountains, as wild and lean and dangerous as buck or bull knows how to be.

As with his get-up, so it went with his vocabulary; for any manner of life with a rule and flavor of its own strong enough to put a new kind of dress on a man's body will put new speech in his mouth, and an idiom derived from the exigencies of his days and nights was soon spoken by the cow-puncher. Like all creators, he not only built, but borrowed his own wherever he found it. *Chaps*, from *chapparajos*, is only one of many transfers from the Mexican, one out of (I should suppose) several hundred; and in *lover-wolf* is a singular instance of half-baked translation. *Lobo*, pronounced *lovo*, being the Spanish for wolf, and the coyote being a sort of wolf, the dialect of the southern border has slid into this name for a wolf that is larger, and a worse enemy to steers than the small coward coyote. Lover-wolf is a word anchored to its district. In the Northwest, though the same animal roams there as dangerously, his Texas name would be an unknown as the Northwest's word for Indian, *siwash*, from *sauvage*, would be along the Rio Grande. Thus at the top and bottom of our map do French and Spanish trickle across the frontier, and with English melt into two separate amalgams which are wholly distinct, and which remain near the spot where they were moulded; while other compounds, having the same Northern and Southern starting-point, drift far and wide, and become established in the cow-puncher's dialect over his whole country. No better French specimen can be instanced than *cache*, verb and noun, from the verb *cacher*, to conceal. In our Eastern life words such as these are of no pertinent avail; and as it is only universal pertinence which can lift a fragment of dialect into the dictionary's good society, most of them must pass with the transient generation that spoke them. Certain ones there are deserving to survive; *cinch*, for instance, from *cincha*, the Mexican girth. From its narrow office under the horse's belly it has come to perform in metaphor a hundred services. In cinching somebody or something you may mean that you hold four aces, or the key of a political crisis; and when a man is very much indeed upper-dog, then he is said to have an air-tight cinch; and this phrase is to me so pleasantly eloquent that I am withheld from using it in polite gatherings only by that prudery which we carry as a burden along with the benefits of academic training. Besides the foreign importations, such as *arroyo* and *riata*, that stand unchanged, and those others which under the action of our own speech have sloughed their native shape and come out something new, like quirt—once *cuerta*, Mexican for rawhide—is the third large class of words which the cowboy has taken from our sober old dictionary stock and made over for himself. Pie-biter refers not to those hailing from our pie belt, but to a cow-pony who secretly forages in a camp kitchen to indulge his acquired tastes. Western whiskey, besides being known as tonsil varnish and a hundred different things, goes as benzine, not unjustly. The same knack of imagery that upon our Eastern slope gave visitors from the country the brief, sure name of hayseed, calls their Western equivalents junipers. Hay grows scant upon the Rocky Mountains, but those seclusions are filled with evergreens. No one has accounted to me for *hobo*. A hobo is a wandering unemployed person, a stealer of rides on freight-trains, a diner at the back door, eternally seeking honest work, and when brought face to face with it eternally retreating. The hobo is he against whom we have all sinned by earning our living. Perhaps some cowboy saw an

Italian playing a pipe to the accompaniment of the harp, and made the generalization: oboe may have given us hobo. Hobo-ken has been suggested by an ingenious friend; but the word seems of purely Western origin, and I heard it in the West several years before it became used in the East. The cow-puncher's talent for making a useful verb out of anything shows his individuality. Any young strong race will always lay firm hands on language and squeeze juice from it; and you instantly comprehend the man who tells you of his acquaintances, whom you know to be drunk at the moment, that they are *helling* around town. Unsleeping need for quick thinking and doing gave these nomads the pith of utterance. They say, for instance, that they intend *camping on a man's trail*, meaning, concisely, "So-and-so has injured us, and we are going to follow him day and night until we are quits." Thus do these ordinary words and phrases, freshened to novelty by the cow-puncher's wits, show his unpremeditated art of brevity, varying in aptness, but in imagination constant; and with one last example of his fancy I shall leave his craft of word-making.

It is to be noted in all peoples that for whatever particular thing in life is of frequent and familiar practice among them they will devise many gradations of epithet. *To go* is in the cattle country a common act, and a man may go for different reasons, in several manners, at various speeds. For example:

"Do I understand you went up the tree with the bear just behind you?"

"The bear was not in front of me."

Here the cowboy made ordinary words suffice for showing the way he went, but his goings can be of many sorts besides in front of and behind something, and his rich choice of synonyms embodies a latent chapter of life and habits. To the several phrases of going known to the pioneer as vamoose, skip, light out, dust, and git, the cowboy adds, burn the earth, hit, hit the breeze, pull your freight, jog, amble, move, pack, rattle your hocks, brindle, and more, very likely, if I knew or could recall them; I think that the observer who caught the shifting flicker of a race or a pursuit, and said brindle first, had a mind of liveliness and arts.

It may be that some of these words I have named as home-bred natives of our wilderness are really of long standing and archaic repute, and that the scholar can point to them in the sonnets of Shakespeare, but I, at least, first learned them west of the Missouri.

With a speech and dress of his own, then, the cow-puncher drove his herds to Abilene or Westport Landing in the Texas times, and the easy abundant dollars came, and left him for spurs and bridles of barbaric decoration. Let it be remembered that the Mexican was the original cowboy, and that the American improved on him. Those were the days in which he was long in advance of settlers, and when he literally fought his right of way. Along the waste hundreds of miles that he had to journey, three sorts of inveterate enemies infested the road—the thief (the cattle-thief, I mean), who was as daring as himself; the supplanted Mexican, who hated the new encroaching Northern race; and the Indian, whose hand was against all races but his own immediate tribe, and who flayed the feet of his captives, and made them walk so through the mountain passes to the fires in which he slowly burned them. Among these perils the cow-puncher took wild pleasure in existing. No soldier of fortune ever adventured with bolder carelessness, no fiercer blood ever stained a border. If his raids, his triumphs, and his reverses have inspired no minstrel to sing of him who rode by the Pecos River and the hills of San Andreas, it is not so much the Rob Roy as the Walter Scott who is lacking. And the Flora McIvor! Alas! the stability of the clan, the blessing of the home background, was not there. These wild men sprang from the loins of no similar father, and begot no sons to continue their hardihood. War they made in plenty, but not love; for the woman they saw was not the woman a man can take into his heart. That their fighting Saxon ancestors awoke in them for a moment and made them figures for poetry and romance is due to the strange accidents of a young country, where, while cities flourish by the coast and in the direct paths of trade, the herd-trading interior remains medieval in its simplicity and violence. And yet this transient generation deserves more chronicling than it will ever have. Deeds in plenty were done that are all and more than imagination should require. One high noon upon the plains by the Rio Grande the long irons lay hot in the fire. The young cattle were being branded, and the gathered herd covered the plain. Two owners claimed one animal. They talked at first quietly round the fire, then the dispute quickened. One roped the animal, throwing it to the ground to burn his mark upon it. A third came, saying the steer was his. The friends of each drew close to hear, and a claimant thrust his red-hot iron against the hide of the animal tied on the ground. Another seized it from him, and as they fell struggling, their adherents flung themselves upon their horses, and massing into clans, volleyed with their guns across the fire. In a few minutes fourteen riders lay dead on the plain, and the tied animal over which they had quarrelled bawled and bleated in the silence. Here is skirmishing enough for a ballad. And there was a certain tireless man in northern New Mexico whose war upon cattle-thieves made his life so shining a mark that he had in bank five thousand dollars to go to the man who killed the man who killed him. A neighborhood where one looks so far beyond his own assassination as to provide a competence for his avenger is discouraging to family life, but a promising field for literature.

Such existence soon makes a strange man of any one, and the early cow-punchers rapidly grew unlike all people but each other and the wild superstitious ancestors whose blood was in their veins. Their hair became long, and their glance rested with serene penetration upon the stranger; they laughed seldom, and their spirit was in the permanent attitude of war. Grim lean men of few topics, and not many words concerning these; comprehending no middle between the poles of brutality and tenderness; indifferent to death, but disconcerted by a good woman; some with violent Old Testament religion, some avowing none, and all of them uneasy about corpses and the dark. These hermited horsemen would dismout in camp at nightfall and lie looking at the stars, or else squat about the fire conversing with crude sombreness of brands and horses and cows, speaking of *humans* when they referred to men.

To-day they are still to be found in New Mexico, their last domain. The extreme barrenness of those mountains has held tamer people at a distance. That next stage of Western progress—that unparalleled compound of new hotels, electric lights, and invincible ignorance which has given us the Populist—has been retarded, and the civilization of Colorado and silver does not yet redeem New Mexico. But in these shrunk days the cow-puncher no longer can earn money to spend on ornament; he dresses poorly and wears his chaps very wide and ungainly. But he still has three mounts, with seven horses to each mount, and his life is in the saddle among vast solitudes. In the North he was a later comer, and never quite so formidable a person. By the time he had ridden up into Wyoming and Montana the Indian was mostly gone, the locomotive upon the scene, and going West far less an exploration than in the Texas days. Into these new pastures drifted youths from town and country whose grit would scarcely have lasted them to Abilene, and who were not the grim long-haired type, but a sort of glorified farm hand. They too wore their pistols, and rode gallantly, and out of them nature and simplicity did undoubtedly forge manlier, cleaner men than what our streets breed of no worse material. They galloped by the side of the older hands, and caught something of the swing and tradition of the first years. They developed heartiness and honesty in virtue and in vice alike. Their evil deeds were not of the sneaking kind, but had always the saving grace of courage. Their code had no place for the man who steals a pocket-book or stabs in the back.

And what has become of them? Where is this latest outcropping of the Saxon gone? Except where he lingers in the mountains of New Mexico he has been dispersed, as the elk, as the buffalo, as all wild animals must inevitably be dispersed. Three things swept him away—the exhausting of the virgin pastures, the coming of the wire fence, and Mr. Armour of Chicago, who set the price of beef to suit himself. But all this may be summed up in the word Progress. When the bankrupt cow-puncher felt Progress dispersing him, he seized whatever plank floated nearest him in the wreck. He went to town for a job; he got a position on the railroad; he set up a saloon; he married, and fenced in a little farm; and he turned "rustler," and stole the cattle from the men for whom he had once worked. In these capacities will you find him to-day. The ex-cowboy who set himself to some new way of wage-earning is all over the West, and his old courage and frankness still stick to him, but his peculiar independence is of necessity dimmed. The only man who has retained that wholly is the outlaw, the horse and cattle thief, on whose grim face hostility to Progress forever sits. He has had a checkered career. He has been often hanged, often shot; he is generally "wanted" in several widely scattered districts. I know one who used to play the banjo to me on Powder River as he swung his long boots over the side of his bunk. I have never listened to any man's talk with more interest and diversion. Once he has been to Paris on the proceeds of a lengthy well-conducted theft; once he has been in prison for murder. He has the bluest eye, the longest nose, and the coldest face I ever saw. This stripe of gentleman still lives and thrives through the cattle country, occasionally goes out into the waste of land in the most delicate way, and presently cows and steers are missed. But he has driven them many miles to avoid live-stock inspectors, and it may be that if you know him by sight and happen to be in a town where cattle are brought, such as Kansas City, you will meet him at the best hotel there, full of geniality and affluence.

Such is the story of the cow-puncher, the American descendant of Saxon ancestors, who for thirty years flourished upon our part of the earth, and, because he was not compatible with Progress, is now departed, never to return. But because Progress has just now given us the Populist and silver in exchange for him, is no ground for lament. He has never made a good citizen, but only a good soldier, from his tournament days down. And if our nation in its growth have no worse distemper than the Populist to weather through, there is hope for us, even though present signs disincline us to make much noise upon the Fourth of July.

Negro labor in the Western cattle industry, 1866-1900

Kenneth W. Porter

For the last two or three decades, historians have been laboring to undo many of the cowboy myths created by the Wisters and the Roosevelts and their followers. Among the most successful of these efforts has been Joe B. Frantz and Julian E. Choate, Jr.'s perceptive *The American Cowboy* (1955). Until recently, however, the role of the black man on the frontier has been largely overlooked.

Fortunately, Kenneth Wiggins Porter, Professor of History at the University of Oregon, has undertaken to fill this void. His many authoritative essays published in various scholarly journals have now been collected under one cover, *The Negro on the American Frontier*. It is fascinating to compare Porter's cowhand with Wister's. Unfortunately there has been no similarly painstaking study of the Mexican-American cowhand.

For further reading: Joe B. Frantz and Julian E. Choate, Jr., *The American Cowboy: The Myth and Reality* (Norman: University of Oklahoma Press, 1955); Kenneth Wiggins Porter, *The Negro on the American Frontier* (New York: Arno Press, 1971); Philip Durham and Everett L. Jones, *The Negro Cowboys* (New York: Dodd, Mead, 1965); J. Frank Dobie, *Cow People* (Boston: Little, Brown, 1964); William H. Leckie, *The Buffalo Soldiers* (Norman: University of Oklahoma Press, 1967); Clifford P. Westermeier, *Trailing of the Cowboy: His Life and Lore as Told by Frontier Journalists* (Caldwell, Idaho: Caxton, 1955).

The range-cattle industry in its various aspects, and in its importance to the United States and particularly to the Great Plains for the post-Civil War generation, has been the subject of numerous studies. This industry was rendered possible by such factors as vast expanses of grazing land, projected railroad lines across the Missouri and onto the Great Plains, the rise of heavy industry and the consequent demand for beef of less-than-high quality by the meat-hungry industrial population. But like the steel, mining, packing, and other industries, it also needed a labor force—workers with special abilities and qualities—for although the cowhand or cowboy possibly was no more than a "hired man on horseback,"[1] he was a hired man with skills in riding, roping, and branding which could not be easily acquired. Most of his working hours were spent in such routine tasks as riding the range and turning back drifting steers; rounding up, branding, and castrating calves; selecting beeves for the market; and, even on the "long drive," jogging along and daily "eating dirt" on the flanks or in the rear of a few thousand "cow critters." But he also needed the inborn courage and quick thinking to use these skills effectively while confronting an enraged bull, swimming a milling herd across a flooded river, or trying to turn a stampede of fear-crazed steers.

But the general public, under the influence of decades of "Western" movies and, more recently, television shows has come to regard the cowboy's workaday activities as altogether secondary to fighting off hostile Indians, pursuing rustlers and holding "necktie parties" for them, saving the rancher's daughter from Mexican raiders, and engaging in quick-draw gunfights in dusty streets. From similar sources this same public has also learned that cowboys, with the exception of an occasional low-browed villain or exotic and comic-accented *vaquero*, were all of the purest and noblest Anglo-Saxon type, as in Owen Wister's *The Virginian*.

In reality, as George W. Saunders of the Texas Trail Drivers Association has authoritatively estimated, of the fully 35,000 men who went up the trail from Texas with herds during the heroic age of the cattle industry, 1866-1895, "about one-third were Negroes and Mexicans."[2] This estimate is closely confirmed by extant lists of trail-herd outfits which identify their members racially. These lists also demonstrate that Negroes outnumbered Mexicans by more than two to one—slightly more than 63 percent whites, 25 percent Negroes, and slightly under 12 percent Mexicans.

The racial breakdown of individual outfits, of course, varied widely. Some were nearly all of one race, such as the 1874 outfit which was all-Negro, except for a white boss, or the 1872 outfit which consisted of a white trail-boss, eight Mexicans, and a Negro; but more typical were the two 1877 outfits composed, respectively, of seven whites and two Negro cowboys, and a Negro cook; and seven whites, two Negroes, and a Mexican hostler. Many outfits had no Mexicans at all, but it was an exceptional outfit that did not have at least one Negro and enough outfits were nearly all Negro, or a third or more Negro, to bring the number up to the estimated twenty-five percent of the total.[3] A trail-herd outfit of about a dozen men would on the average consist of seven or eight whites, including the trail boss, three Negroes—one of whom was probably the cook, while another might be the horse wrangler, and the third would simply be a trail hand—and one or two Mexicans; if a Negro was not the wrangler, then a Mexican often was. Needless to say, this is not the typical trail outfit of popular literature and drama.

The racial make-up of ranch outfits, with their seasonal and day-by-day fluctuations, was not so well recorded as that of the trail-herd outfits, but available information indicates that ranch hands, in Texas at least, were white, Negro, and Mexican in proportions varying according to locality and to ranchowner tastes; probably the overall proportions differed little from those of trail outfits. A ranch in the Indian Territory during the late 1890s, for example, was staffed by eight cowhands, two of whom were Negroes.[4] Negro cowhands were particularly numerous on the Texas Gulf Coast, in the coastal brush east of the Nueces and at the mouth of the Brazos and south of Houston, and parts of the Indian Territory; in some sections they were in the majority, and some ranches worked Negroes almost exclusively.[5]

Negro trail drivers swarmed west and north with herds from the Texas "hive" and, though most returned, a few remained as ranch hands as far north as Wyoming, the Dakotas, and even Canada and as far west as New Mexico, Arizona, and even California and Oregon.[6]

Wranglers

Negroes occupied all the positions among cattle-industry employees, from the usually lowly wrangler through ordinary hand to top hand and lofty cook. But they were almost never, except in the highly infrequent case of an all-Negro outfit, to be found as ranch or trail boss.

Negroes and also Mexicans were frequently wranglers, or *remuderos*[7]—in charge of the saddle horses not immediately in use—usually regarded as the lowliest job in the cattle industry, except for the boy who sometimes served as wrangler's assistant.[8] There were exceptions, however, including some Negro wranglers who became "second in authority to the foreman" in a few camps.[9] Such wranglers were "horse men" in the highest sense: capable of detecting and treating illness and injury, selecting the proper horse for each job, and taking the ginger out of unruly animals. Among these wranglers-extraordinary were Nigger Jim Kelly, the horsebreaker, horsetrainer, handyman, and gunman of the notorious Print Olive; and the famous John Chisum's "Nigger Frank," "who spent a lifetime wrangling Long I horses" and whom a white cattleman declared "the best line rider and horsewrangler I ever saw."[10]

Cowboys

The majority of Negroes on the ranch or "long drive" were neither wranglers nor yet authoritative cooks (of whom more later). They were top hands or ordinary hands who, on the long drive, rode the point, the swing, the flank, or the drag, according to their experience and ability. The point—the position of honor—was at the front of the herd where the steers were strongest, most restless, and most likely to try to break away. There the most experienced top hands rode. Farther back, the cattle were somewhat less troublesome, while in the rear, where the tired beasts were comparatively easy to manage, could be found the fledgling cowboys of the drag, "eating the dust" of the entire herd. Negroes rode in all these positions.[11]

These Negro cowboys, whether on ranch or trail, were generally regarded as good workers, who got along well with others and who took pride in their work. A white Texan, a former cowboy and rancher, went so far as to write that "there was no better cowman on earth than the Negro."[12]

Old, experienced Negro cowhands frequently served as unofficial, one-man apprentice systems to white greenhorns. This was particularly true, of course, when the fledgling was the employer's son or relative. Will Rogers, for example, got his first lessons in riding and roping from a Cherokee Negro employee of his father.[13] Almost any young would-be cowboy who showed the proper spirit, however, might have the good fortune to be "adopted" and "showed the ropes" by one of these black veterans, who would sometimes take on the inexperienced boy as partner when white cowboys were unwilling to do so.[14] Charles Siringo, later famous as a cowboy-detective-author, recalled that Negro cowboys again and again came to his rescue when, in his reckless cowboy youth, his life was threatened by a mad steer, a wild bronc, and even a hired assassin.[15]

Negro cowhands confronted all the dangers and met all the tests of the long trail. One poorly clad cowboy froze to death in his saddle during a "norther" rather than give up and go in to the chuckwagon.[16] Stampedes were an ever-present danger, and experienced Negroes were frequently prominent in attempting to prevent or control them. Indeed they were also often among the few cowboys who stayed with the herd when others threw in their hands.[17]

Crossing the wide, deep, frequently flooded rivers was even more dangerous than stampedes. According to a white ex-cowboy, "it was the Negro hand who usually tried out the swimming water when a trailing herd came to a swollen stream"[18] —either because of his superior ability or because he was regarded as expendable. But whether or not this statement is valid, it probably would not have been made had not Negroes frequently demonstrated their ability to cope with the problems of river crossings. Numerous anecdotes about such crossings tell of Negro cowhands saving themselves by their own efforts, being assisted to dry land by white cattlemen[19] and, on more than one occasion, saving their lives.

Negroes not only often showed courage and quick thinking in extricating themselves and others from the danger of swollen rivers, but in at least one case also displayed ingenuity superior to that of a great trail boss. In 1877 Ab Blocker, "the fastest driver on the trail," had reached the Platte River, which was spanned by a bridge of sorts, but the wild longhorns had never seen a bridge and refused to cross it. It looked as if, after all, they would have to swim the herd when a Negro hand suggested—and his suggestion was adopted—that they should drive the chuckwagon slowly across, followed by old Bully, an ox; the lead steers would follow Bully and the rest of the herd would trail them.[20]

Riders and Ropers

Although every top hand had to be a skillful rider and roper, some were so outstanding as to be considered "bronco busters" and/or ropers *par excellence* rather than as merely uncommonly able cowboys. Numerous references suggest that Negroes and Mexicans were widely regarded as particularly expert in both these capacities—the Mexicans especially noted for their prowess with the *reata* (or lasso). Mexicans were also, correctly or not, blamed for cruelty toward animals and consequently fell in disrepute as horse-breakers,[21] whereas the Negroes maintained and even advanced a reputation which went back to ante-bellum days.

A white ex-cowpuncher-writer states that Negroes were hired largely for their ability to cope with bad horses which the white cowhands did not want to tackle. "The Negro cow hands of the middle 1880s . . . were usually called on to do the hardest work around an outfit. . . . This most often took the form of 'topping' or taking the first pitch out of the rough horses of the outfit. . . . It was not unusual for one young Negro to 'top' a half dozen hard-pitching horses before breakfast." Andy Adams, the cowboy-author and a man who was far from being a Negrophile, declared that the "greatest bit of bad horse riding" he ever saw was performed by a dozen Negro cowboys who were assigned to ride a dozen horses which the white cowpunchers of their outfit were afraid to tackle. But each of the Negroes stayed on his horse till the animal was conquered.[22]

The list of Negro bronc riders—the comparatively few whose names have survived—is still a long one. A few of the better known, partly because they attracted the attention of published writers, were the following: Isam, Isom, or Isham Dart of Brown's Hole, "where Colorado, Wyoming, and Utah cornered," who, although now remembered principally as a reputed rustler, was also "numbered among the top bronc stompers of the Old West";[23] Nigger Jim Kelly, whom oldtime cowboys considered the peer of any rider they had seen in the United States, Canada, or the Argentine;[24] a mulatto named Williams in the Badlands of South Dakota, who was a horse-trainer rather than a horsebreaker and whose methods won the admiration of Theodore Roosevelt;[25] and Jim Perry, the famous XIT cook, who was even better known as "one of the best riders and roper ever to hit the West."[26]

While most of the famous riders were bronco busters only as one aspect of their work as cowhands, some, including a number of Negroes, were officially recognized as ranch horsebreakers, and a few were full-time or nearly full-time professionals. Perhaps the most famous of the professionals was Matthew (Bones) Hoods of the Panhandle—remembered, after his retirement from horsebreaking to Pullman-portering, for having once taken off his jacket and cap and laid aside his clothes brush, to mount and break an outlaw which no one had been able to ride, while his train stood in the station.[27]

Other Negro cowhands were particularly renowned as ropers, such as Ab Blocker's Frank, who was, according to a white cowboy, "the best hand with a rope I ever saw," and whose roping skill once saved his employer from an angry steer;[28] Ike Word, according to Charles Siringo, "the best roper"[29] on his part of the Wyoming range;[30] and, more recently, the Negro rancher Jess Pickett who, according to a white neighbor, was "the world's best roper."[31]

Naturally enough, many of the famous Negro riders, such as Isom Dart and Jim Perry, were almost or quite as renowned as ropers. Once of the most spectacular at both riding and roping was "Nigger Add," "one of the best hands on the Pecos," who would as a matter of course "top off" several bad horses of a morning. Walking into a corral full of tough broncs, he would seize any one he chose by the ear and nose, lead him out of the bunch, and then show him who was boss. As a roper he was even more sensational, and had the unusual technique of roping on foot, a practice which would have killed an ordinary man. He would tie a rope around his hips, work up to a horse in the corral or in the open pasture, rope him around the neck as he dashed by at full speed, and then, by sheer strength and skill, flatten the horse out on the ground where a lesser man would have been dragged to death.[32] Indeed, the prowess of such Negro riders, horsebreakers, and horse-trainers was so outstanding as to contribute to the commonly held belief of the time that there was some natural affinity between Negroes and horses.[33]

Singing to the Cattle

Riding, roping, and branding were not the only skills required of a top cowhand. Singing to the cattle, particularly on night herd but sometimes during the day's march, was not only a practical necessity for calming the animals and reducing the danger of a stampede, it also had recreational and esthetic values for the drivers. Negro trail hands were conspicuous in this practice, although Negro chuckwagon cooks were the most noted cow-country musicians, singers, and composers. "Nigger" Jim Kelly, the Olives' versatile horse-breaker and gunman, is also credited with composing a humorous song, "Willie the Cook," which he sang to accordion accompaniment furnished by a white trail hand. "Teddy Blue," a white cowhand whose autobiography is a cow-country classic, tells movingly of his first memory of the "Ogallaly song," which had a verse for every river on the trail, beginning with the Nueces and ending in 1881, when he first heard it, with Ogallala.

There were [he recalled] thirteen herds camped on the Cimarron that night and you could count their fires. A Blocker herd was bedded close to ours; it was bright starlight, and John Henry was riding around the herd singing the Ogallaly song. John Henry was the Blocker's [sic] top nigger. . . .

'We left Nueces River in April eighty-one

With three thousand horned cattle and all they knowed was run

O-o-o-o-oh!'

and so on.[34]

The special quality which these Negro cowhands gave to the cattle country is epitomized in an episode at Doan's store on the Red River, which was the last place where a trail herd hand could receive mail and purchase supplies before reaching the Kansas cattle towns. One night a crowd sitting around the little adobe store heard the strains of "a lively air on a French harp." The door opened and in sailed a hat, closely followed by a big Negro who began to dance to his own accompaniment. "It was one of Ab Blocker's niggers"—perhaps John Henry himself—"who had been sent up for the mail, giving first notice of the herd's arrival."[35] The ranch or cattle trail, without its many Negroes, would not only have suffered from a lack of expert riders, ropers, and cooks, but would also have lacked much of its vitality and vivacity and spontaneous gaiety, and ranching and trail-driving would have been duller occupations.

Cowboy Cooks—Men of Parts

High in the hierarchy of cow-country employees was the ranch or trail cook,[36] who ranked next to the foreman or trail boss and, in camp, ruled supreme over an area of sixty feet around the chuckwagon. In addition to culinary skill—including the ability to prepare a meal in a blizzard, cloudburst, or high wind—the cook also had to be an expert mule-skinner or bullwhacker, capable of driving two or three yoke of oxen or a four-mule team attached to the chuckwagon over the most difficult terrain, including flooded rivers. He could do more than anyone else to make life pleasant and many a cowboy selected an outfit because of the reputation of its cook. In compensation for duties which few men could satisfactorily perform, the cook normally was paid from $5 per month more than the ordinary cowhand up to even twice as much.

The cowboy cook was also commonly credited with other qualities less essential and certainly less endearing than the ability to cook and drive the chuckwagon. He was frequently something of a despot; bad-tempered, hard-featured, and unlovely. "As tetchy as a cook" is still a ranch byword. He was often an old "stove-up" cowpuncher who resented having to "wait on" cowboys still in their prime, "just kids" in his opinion. He often was also a "hard character," and frequently had a drinking problem. Finally, as one authority has stated, cooks were seldom good riders.

The above description of the cowboy-cook is synthesized from the reports of numerous observers on cooks of all races and backgrounds in all parts of the cow-country. Some of these qualities doubtless applied to most of them, and all to some of them. But numerous accounts of Negro cow-country cooks suggest that the traditional "hard character" pattern fitted them much less than it did whites. The cow-country cook of the Texas and Texas-influenced range, if not typically a Negro, was at least very frequently one.[37] To be sure, the historian of the cowboy-cook writes: "Most bosses preferred a native white cook. . . . Some Negroes were good cooks, but were usually lazy, and, too, white cowboys refused to take orders from them." This statement, however, is not confirmed by the literature of the cattle country, which strongly suggests that many if not most cattlemen were in agreement with the trail boss who wrote: "For cooks I always preferred darkies."[38]

The primary reason for this preference is probably that Negroes simply were on the average better workers than the available whites. They could, of course, occasionally be lazy, stupid, careless, dishonest, and many whites were excellent cooks, but the cow-camp menus on record seem to have been disproportionately the work of Negro cooks. Good cooks occasionally supplemented the filling but somewhat monotonous diet of biscuits, "sowbelly," beef, molasses, and coffee by carying a gun in the wagon and, between dishwashing and starting the next meal, hunted deer, turkey, and other game. An extra-ordinary cook who took full advantage of such opportunities was a thirty-year-old Negro named Sam who, in 1878, prepared for an outfit on Pease River what one of its members years later described as "about the most luscious eating. . . . I have every enjoyed . . . an oven of buffalo steaks, another . . . of roast bear meat, better than pork, a frying pan full of the breast of wild turkey in gravy of flour, water, and grease, . . . antelope ribs barbe-cued on a stick over the coals." Sometimes he would roast a turkey in its feathers in a pit. He also cooked wild plums, stewing them or making them into a cobbler. Small wonder that the cowboys of his outfit always saw to it that he had plenty of wood.[39] Sam was merely one of a galaxy of Negro cow-country cooks, each with his speciality—Dutch oven-baked peach pies, "cathead biscuits," "son-of-a-gun stew," etc.

The cook was frequently in sole charge not merely of the kitchen but of the ranch house itself, and on the long drive was of course frequently left alone to protect the chuck-wagon and its contents in any emergency, whether crossing a river or encountering Indians. A Negro cook distinguished himself in an episode of 1877 in which the other members of his outfit played no very heroic roles. Four white men and three Negroes were working cattle in Coleman County, Texas, when Indians suddenly swooped down upon them. All took refuge in a cave except "old Negro Andy, the cook," who stayed by the wagon, fought off the Indians, and saved the supplies.[40]

By and large, Negro cooks managed their kitchens or chuckwagon, dealt with Indians, and accomplished their culinary feats without the "crankiness" which was almost as much standard equipment for cow-country cooks as was their "starter" for salt-rising bread. Some white cooks manifested such behavior to an almost psychopathic extent, and some Negro cooks lived up to the tradition, to be sure, but more typical were those remembered for opposite qualities.[41] Jim Perry was not only a fine cook but also "the best Negro who ever lived"; Sam "always had a cheerful word or a cheerful song"; etc. Frank Dobie believes that Negro and Mexican cooks were notably above average in their tendency to be "providers by nature" and in their readiness to go out of their way to furnish extra services, from medicinal supplies to home-made remedies. When, for exam-ple, a young cowboy drank alkali water, and "wasn't feeling too good," Jim Simpson, the Negro cook, told him to roll a can of tomatoes in his slicker for both food and drink; the acid from the tomatoes would help neutralize the alkali.[42]

The Negro cook often possessed other skills beyond the culinary. So many Negro cooks, in fact, were noted riders and ropers that something of a pattern emerges. The wild-game cook extraordinary, Black Sam, was such a good rider that "frequently one of the boys would get him to 'top' a bad horse." Jim Perry of the XIT was not only the best cook that ever lived, according to a white hand, but he was also the best rider as well. Jim Simpson, roundup cook and fiddler, who had come up from Texas in the 1880s with a herd of longhorns, was at one time also "about the best roper" in that part of the Wyoming range.[43] When an associate of one of the famous Blockers expressed some doubt about his roping ability, Blocker told his Negro cook, "Goat," to wipe the dough off his hands and get a rope and a horse. Blocker swung a regular "Blocker loop" on the first cow, which picked up her front feet, and the cow pony did the rest. "Goat" similarly roped and threw the next cow, Blocker the third, and so on, until they had roped about twenty, never missing.[44]

Negro cooks often left the chuckwagon for the saddle in an emergency. "Doc" Little, who had risen from cowboy to volunteer cook's assistant to full-time cook, "always remained the good cowboy" and in the event of a stampede was usually the first on a horse. The same was said of the Slaughter cook, "Old Bat." When a drove of 500 horses stampeded, taking the *remuda* with them, including the *remudero's* own picketed horse, the Negro cook threw himself on the trailing rope and "went bumping along for about a hundred yards" before he could stop the animal. He then mounted and took the lead in rounding up the herd.[45]

All cowboys, we have noted, were expected to be able to "sing" in order to soothe the restless cattle. Just as they were expert riders and ropers, Negro cooks were frequently singers, musicians, and even composers. Although hard-worked, they were about the only men in an outfit with the opportunity to carry and play a musical instrument. "The Zebra Dun," a song about a supposed greenhorn who surprised everyone by riding an outlaw horse, is said to have been composed by Jake, who worked for a Pecos River ranch.[46] One chuckwagon cook who supplemented his menu with deer and turkey which he shot himself, also sang and played the guitar.[47] Another, Old Bat, the Slaughter cook, played both the fiddle and the fife. Jim Perry, the XIT cook, was not only the best cook, the best rider, and the best Negro in the world, but also the best fiddler. Jim Simpson, Negro cook and roper of the Wyoming range, was also the regular fiddler for the Saturday night dances. Big Sam, cook and rider, played the banjo and sang until someone stepped on the instrument, whereupon the bunch bought him a fiddle on which he would play such songs as "Green corn, green corn, bring along the demijohn."[48] But the Negro cook-musician who made the most spectacular appearance on the cow-country stage was Gordon Davis, who led Ab Blocker's trail herd through Dodge City while mounted on his left wheel ox, fiddle in hand, playing "Buffalo Gals."[49]

Negro cooks, in addition to riding and roping, singing and playing, sometimes possessed skills so various as to be unclassifiable. The Negro cook, "Old Lee," was "handy as a pocket shirt, ready to do anything, and with the 'know-how' for almost anything that showed up, from cooking to horsewrangling to mending saddle leathers and boots." One of the most versatile of Negro cooks was John Battavia Hinnaut ("Old Bat"), probably the most useful man on the Slaughter spread. Although primarily and officially a roundup cook, he was a first-class ranch-hand, a musician, an expert teamster and coachman, an Indian fighter, a mighty hunter, and also served as the boss's valet, practical nurse, and bodyguard.[50]

That the Negro cow-country cook frequently possessed unusual abilities was due in part to limitations imposed because of racial discrimination. He was much more likely than the average white man to have been brought up about the kitchen and stables of a plantation or ranch and there, at an early age, to have become acquainted with cooking and horses. He was less likely to regard kitchen chores as somehow beneath him. The unusually able and ambitious white cowboy could look forward to possible promotion to foreman or trail boss; the Negro of equal ability knew he had little chance of attaining such a position. To become a ranch or roundup cook was about as much as could be expected. Age, inexperience, or physical handicap might preclude a white man from any ranch job outside of the kitchen; but for the superior Negro cowboy to preside over a chuckwagon or ranch kitchen meant an increase in pay or prestige.

Foremen and Trail Bosses

The Negro cowhand, however able, could, as we have seen, rarely rise to a position higher than chuckwagon or ranch-house cook. The principal obstacle to his becoming a ranch foreman or trail boss was a general belief that a Negro simply did not possess the qualities necessary for such a position. But even if a ranch owner or group of cattlemen were confident that a Negro had the necessary intelligence, initiative, and general capacity, there was always the practical consideration that such a man, even if in charge of an all-Negro outfit, would on occasion have to deal with white foremen and trail bosses who might refuse to recognize his authority, and that expensive trouble might ensue. A Negro, however great his ability, thus had difficulty in attaining greater authority than could be exercised over a chuckwagon or kitchen. The phenomenal success of Ora Haley, who for three decades was the dominant figure in the range-cattle business of Northwestern Colorado, is said to have been partly due to his Negro top hand Thornton Biggs, who although he "taught a whole generation of future range managers, wagon bosses, and all-round cowpunchers the finer points of the range-cattle business," himself "never became a range manager or even a foreman." The fairer-minded recognized the handicaps under which their Negro cowhands labored. Jim Perry, redoubtable cook, rider, and fiddler of the XIT ranch, once wryly remarked: "If it weren't for my damned old black face I'd have been boss of one of these divisions long ago."[51] "And no doubt he would have," a white employee commented.

And yet a very few Negroes of exceptional ability, and sometimes under unusual circumstances, did make the grade. There was the master West Texas rider and roper, "Nigger Add" or "Old Add" who, by 1889 if not earlier, was the LFD's range boss, working "South Texas colored hands almost entirely." One of his qualifications was that he was a "dictionary of earmarks and brands" but probably more important was his universal popularity among cattlemen from Toyah, Texas, to Las Vegas, New Mexico.[52] Nigger Add's outfit consisted "almost entirely" of Negroes—and one wonders who the exceptions were. Probably they were Mexicans.

But did any Negro break through the color line to direct outfits including at least some whites? A leading authority on the cow country doubts that it could have happened.[53] Nevertheless at least one Negro, it seems, through sheer ability and force of character was able to defy the tradition that the white man always gives the orders and the black man obeys. Al Jones was a six-footer with a proud carriage and finely chiseled features of a somewhat "Indian" type. He went up the trail no less than thirteen times, and four times—once was in 1884—he was trail boss, directing Negroes, Mexicans, and sometimes white men. As a trail boss he was resourceful and decisive, but probably needed an abundance of tact to get the job done.[54]

Paradoxically, the race prejudice which prevented more than a very few Negro cow-hands from rising to the status of foreman or trail boss may have spurred able and ambitious Negroes into taking up land, acquiring cattle, and setting up as independent small ranchers, whereas, lacking the incentive such an obstacle provided, they might have remained satisfied with a position as ranch foreman. But the story of the Negro rancher belongs to the history of petty capitalism rather than to labor history.

Henchmen, Bodyguards, "Bankers," and Factotums

Some especially able and trustworthy cow-country Negroes fulfilled roles for which there was no equivalent among white cowhands; as confidential assistants, factotums and, when it was necessary to transport large sums of money, bodyguards and "bankers."

Colonel Charles Goodnight wrote of Bose Ikard, his right hand man: "I have trusted him farther than any living man. He was my detective, banker, and everything else." Bose would sometimes have on his person proceeds from his employer's cattle sales amounting to as much as $20,000, since it was reasoned that a thief would be unlikely to search a Negro's belongings.[55]

John Slaughter's "Old Bat" played a similar role. Officially a roundup cook, he could also do almost any ranch work, but his major importance was as a general factotum in anything connected with Slaughter's personal needs—valet, practical nurse, and, above all, bodyguard. When Slaughter was on a cattle-buying trip, Bat always went along to guard the approximately $10,000 in gold which Slaughter usually carried in his money belt, watching while his employer slept. When Slaughter went into Mexico, where silver was preferable, Bat had charge of a mule loaded with "dobe" dollars. His fitness as bodyguard was demonstrated in action against the Apache and when, with another Negro, he stood at Slaughter's side and helped beat off an attack by Mexican bandits.[56]

Print Olive's handyman and bodyguard was Nigger Jim Kelly—wrangler, horsebreaker, gunman—who in the fall of 1869 accompanied his boss back from Fort Kearney, Nebraska, their saddlebags stuffed with currency and gold, and who in 1872, with a quick well-aimed bullet, saved Print's life after he had been shot three times and was about to be killed.[57]

Still another formidable Negro Henchman was Zeke, a giant "two-knife" Negro, who in 1879 accompanied Colonel Draper to Dodge City on a cattle-buying trip with a paper-wrapped bundle of $5,000 in currency.[58] Finally, there was "Old Nep." The famous "Shanghai" Pierce may have thought more of him, according to Frank Dobie, than of anyone else; for thirty five years Neptune Holmes used to accompany Shanghai on his cattle-buying expeditions, leading a mule loaded with saddlebags which bulged with gold and silver and on which he would pillow his head at night.[59]

Where large sums of money were involved, and courage and loyalty in protecting and defending it was needed, prominent cattlemen such as Goodnight, Slaughter, Olive, and Pierce, characteristically preferred to depend on Negro bodyguards.

Wages

For a generation and more, cow-country Negroes distinguished themselves as riders and ropers, cooks and bodyguards, as well as in the more common and still highly necessary positions of wranglers, ordinary cowboys, and top hands. What compensation, financial and psychological, did they receive for their services? And how did their wages, working, and living conditions, and opportunities for advancement and a "good life," compare with those of white hands of corresponding abilities and of Negroes outside the cattle country?

In view of the racial situation which then prevailed throughout the United States, particularly in the South and West, it can be assumed that Negro cowmen encountered discrimination and segregation. The question therefore is not: Did discrimination and segregation exist? But rather: What was their extent and character? And how uniform were they? For although racism was general, it did vary from region to region, from state to state, and even from community to community. It also varied from period to period, probably increasing rather than diminishing during the years in question.

Racial discrimination in the cattle country falls into several categories: wages and working conditions on the job; personal and social relations on the ranch or on cattle trails; and in town or at the end of the cattle trail.

Discrimination was probably least evident on the job. As to wages, cow-punching was, of course, by no means a highly paid occupation, regardless of race. Wages of various categories of cowhands varied widely not only from year to year and from region to region, but even within the same year and region and sometimes within the same outfit as well. Wages were generally low, but increased somewhat from the 1860s into the 1890s and were higher on the Northern Range than in Texas and Kansas. An ordinary hand in the South received from a minimum $15 per month immediately after the Civil War, to $20-$30 through the late 1860s, 1870s, and into the 1880s, to as much as $45 in the 1890s. An experienced top hand would receive $5 or $10 per month more than a less experienced man, and trail hands were paid somewhat more than ordinary ranch hands. Especially experienced trail hands, below the rank of trail boss, occasionally drew double wages of as much as $60 or even $75; but a "green" boy would receive half-wages of $10-$15. The wages of trail bosses and foreman normally ranged during this period from $100 to $150. Cooks' salaries, as we have seen, might be as little as that of a top hand or as much as double an ordinary cowhand's, but customarily were $5 or $10 more than those of the best-paid cowhand in the outfit. In the North, cowhands usually got about $10 a month more than those in the South. In all cases compensation included food and, in the case of ranch hands, sleeping accommodations, such as they were.[60]

Strange though it may seem, there is no clear-cut evidence that Negro cowhands were generally or seriously discriminated against in the matter of wages, though this was obviously so with Mexicans, who sometimes received one half to one third that of white cowboys earning $20-25.[61] "Teddy Blue," to be sure, says of the Olive outfit, for which he worked in 1879, that they hated Mexicans and "niggers" but "hired them because they worked cheaper than white men." He gives no details, however, and the notoriously violent Olives may have been no more typical in their wage policy than in their conduct generally. On the other hand, one trail boss stated: "I have worked white Americans, Mexicans, and Negroes and they all got just the same salary."[62] Wages were so much under the control of the individual employer that no doubt Negroes were sometimes discriminated against; but such discrimination seems not to have been characteristic and, when it occurred, was never nearly as serious as that to which Mexicans were subjected.

Cowboy Strikes

The question of wages naturally brings up the further question: Did cowboys, through united action, ever endeavor to raise their low wages? The general impression is that the happy, carefree, independent-spirited cowboy could not have cared less about wages, so long as they were sufficient to keep him in smoking tobacco and to finance a spree on pay day at the trail's end. The late Stanley Vestal—a better authority on the Northern Plains Indians than on the cattle industry—was writing in this spirit when he enquired, rhetorically and contemptuously, "What cowboy ever wished to join a union?"[63] The answer could have been supplied by anyone acquainted with the cattle industry of the Texas Panhandle and of the Powder River region of Wyoming during the 1880s.

In 1883, just before the spring roundup, cowboys on a number of big Panhandle ranches issued an ultimatum to their bosses demanding higher wages—$50 per month instead of the $25-35 they were then receiving. Better food, particularly more vegetables, is said to have been another objective, but there was apparently no demand for shorter hours than the usual 105 for a seven-day week—15 hours a day! According to the official record of the Federal Bureau of Labor Statistics, the strike was a prompt and unequivocal success, but all other evidence indicates that, though from five to seven large ranches and over 300 cowboys were involved, the strike dragged on for over a year and finally "petered out." Texas Rangers, hired gunmen, and dancehall girls, who soon consumed the strikers' savings, are all credited with responsibility for the failure of this first cowboy strike.[64]

The Panhandle cowboy strike, though the first, was not the last. The Wyoming cattle industry was largely in the hands of absentee ranch owners from Great Britain and the Eastern states, and early in 1886 they ordered a general cut of at least $5 in the prevailing monthly wage of $35-40. Just before the spring roundup the cowboys on the south fork of Powder River struck for $40 a month all around; the strike was led by men who were themselves getting $40, but who objected to working beside men who were getting only $35 and even $30. The strike, which spread to the Sweetwater-Platte area, was generally successful, though its leader was later blackballed.[65]

Negro cowboys could hardly have played any important part in these strikes, as there were not many in the Panhandle and very few in Wyoming. The only Negro cow-country employee in the Panhandle strike about whom we have clear-cut evidence was loyal to his employer rather than to his fellow workers. When it was rumored that a delegation of strikers was descending on the T-Anchor ranch, its owner planted a black-powder mine in an outbuilding—in case strikers should attempt to use the structure as cover for an attack on the ranch house. He commissioned "Gus Lee, the faithful and later famous Negro cook," in the event of such an attack, to crawl out and light the fuse. But the strikers, after a few bullets had kicked up dirt about their horses, advanced no farther and thus relieved Lee of this responsibility.[66]

A Negro or two may, however, have been among the Panhandle strikers. Both in the Panhandle and on Powder River the cowboy strike against the big ranches was followed within a few years by a bloody feud between the big ranchers and the "nester ranchers and little men," with the big ranchers hiring cowboy-gunmen and their opponents drawing support from disgruntled and sometimes blackballed cowboys. The little town of Tascosa in the Panhandle was headquarters for both the striking cowboys in 1883, and for the "nester ranchers" and their supporters in 1886. Among the cowboy partisans of the "little men" was "Nigger Bob" who, when cowboy-gunmen about 2 a.m. on March 21 invaded Tascosa, was "sleepin' on a hot roll" between a woodpile and a small adobe. As the gunmen advanced, firing, rifle shots apparently from the woodpile, drilled one of them through the chest. "Nigger Bob" claimed that, when the bullets got too close, he prudently left the scene, but his "tough hombre" reputation raised the suspicion that he might have done more shooting than he was willing to admit. If "Nigger Bob" and others like him were around during the strike, they probably supported it.[67]

Working Conditions

Negroes were not discriminated against in the work permitted them—below the rank of foreman and trail boss. An experienced Negro would not be told to help the wrangler or to "eat dust" on the drag while a white greenhorn rode at point. On the other hand, Negroes may have been worked harder and longer than whites. John M. Hendrix, a white former cowpuncher and ranger, writing in the middle 1930s, approvingly presented the most extreme picture of discrimination. Negroes, he says, "were usually called on to do the hardest work around an outfit," such as "taking the first pitch out of the rough horses," while the whites were eating breakfast. "It was the Negro hand who usually tried out the swimming water when a trailing herd came to a swollen stream, or if a fighting bull or steer was to be handled, he knew without being told that it was his job." On cold rainy nights, moreover, Negroes would stand "a double guard rather than call the white folks" and would even launder everyone's clothes when the opportunity offered. "These Negroes knew their place, and were careful to stay in it."[68]

Their "place," according to this white Texan, was to do the most dangerous and difficult work, and more of it than any white hand, and in addition to serve as *valets de chambre* to the white hands.

But such a picture cannot be accepted as generally valid. There may have been some outfits to which this description applied and some Negro hands who endeavored to win favor by such works of superogation, but firsthand accounts of the cattle industry in its heyday—Hendrix's own experiences belonged entirely to the twentieth century—hardly seem to confirm this picture. Negroes were frequently expert riders and did "top" horses for less able wranglers, but contemporaries indicate that such work was regarded as a favor, not as a duty, and its beneficiaries were grateful for it. That Negroes were usually sent to test a swollen stream or handle a dangerous animal cannot be confirmed. There is a similar lack of information about Negroes gratuitously acting as valets. The only Negro trail hand so described did it exclusively for the trail boss and even this was regarded as unprecedented.[69]

The Negro, to be sure, was occasionally given unpleasant chores, but due to individual unfairness rather than to accepted custom. They might be given jobs which no one else would do—such as killing the calves dropped during the night on a cattle drive.[70] They were sometimes tricked or bullied into doing more than their share of work.[71] But there is no evidence that Negroes were normally expected to do double night-herding duty or guard the cattle while the whites went on a spree—merely that some cowboys were cheats or bullies who were ready to take advantage of Negroes or, for that matter, of inexperienced white cowhands.

Living Conditions

Discrimination and segregation off the job, whether on the ranch or the cattle trail, would have been difficult. Hendrix insists on at least partially segregated eating facilities when he describes the Negroes as "topping" the white hands' horses while the whites ate breakfast—presumably the Negroes ate at the "second table"—and he also states that the Negroes "had their own dishes"! But one can hardly imagine the independent and even cranky chuckwagon cook actually taking the trouble to segregate the dishes! Hendrix may have been reading back into the 1870s and 1880s the pattern of race relationships which he considered proper in his own times.[72]

Actually, firsthand accounts of ranch and cattle-trail life indicate about as much segregation as prevailed on Huckleberry Finn's and the "Nigger Jim's" raft before the appearance of "The King" and "The Duke." The sleeping arrangements were usually such as to defy any idea of racial segregation. Ranchowner, trail boss, Negro and white cowhands—particularly in bad weather—frequently not only slept in the same shack or tent but also shared the same blankets.[73] The one case of such segregation I have encountered occurred on a Wyoming ranch in 1885 when an Irish cook (sex not specified) refused to allow a Negro bronc buster to sleep in the bunkhouse.[74] But when white women began to appear, those extreme manifestations of racial "integration" belonging to the womanless world of the cattle trail and the wintering camp yielded to a more formal and conventional pattern of conduct. When a highly respected Negro cowboy, in the midst of a blizzard, was permitted to sleep on the kitchen floor of a shack in which a camp manager was living with his wife was regarded by the Negro as an example of extreme condescension or of humanity or both.[75]

Hazing and Ill Treatment

A good deal of hazing and practical joking is inevitable in a community made up largely of rough and uneducated men. Negro hands, particularly those who were young, inexperienced, or timid, probably were subjected to more than their share of such horseplay. But no one in the cattle country—Negro or white, tenderfoot or old timer—was entirely immune to such treatment.[76] In the case of rough treatment which went beyond hazing and became grossly insulting or physically injurious, the Negro cowhand—nearly always a minority member of an outfit composed principally of whites—was in a difficult position. He was almost never a gunslinger. If he were, and if he succeeded in shooting a white opponent in a quarrel, it might have had very serious consequences for him. Negro cowhands rarely used, or attempted to use, a gun in a quarrel within their own outfit. One exception occurred in 1872, when Jim Kelly got the drop on a white cowboy with whom he had had words; but the boss, Print Olive, finally intervened on behalf of the threatened man.[77] Kelly, however, was not only a gunman; he was Print Olive's gunman as well, so nothing happened to him. In 1880 a Negro cowhand, who also served as the trail boss's flunky, attempted to draw on a recently-hired white cowboy who had "cussed him out" for taking his horse's hobbles after repeated warnings, but fell dead with three bullets through the heart.[78] In both these cases the Negro had a special relationship with his employer which encouraged him to brook no nonsense from a white man.

Cowboys seldom engaged in fisticuffs and I have found only one case of a fist fight between a Negro cowhand and a white: this involved the later famous "80 John" Wallace, then a youthful wrangler, and a white boy from another outfit, during a roundup. Wallace claimed the victory. But both participants were mere boys, who were encouraged by the older cowhands;[79] an inter-racial fight between adults probably would not have been so favorably regarded.

Negro cowhands normally depended for protection against insult or injury—whether from members of their own outfits or outsiders—not on fists or weapons but on good conduct, tactful behavior, and their standing among the better element of whites. Negro cooks, though supported by their traditional prestige and real power, were always in danger of encountering violently prejudiced white cowhands who would challenge their authority. For the most part, Negro cooks avoided such a challenge (or insured that, should it materialize, they would have the support of other white cowhands) by a policy of tact and good management—by means of their excellent cookery and, when they were exceptionally good riders, as they often were, by occasionally "topping" a difficult horse. Black Sam of Pease River was particularly skillful in maintaining his prestige without causing ill-feelings. He was an exceptional cook and rider and a popular musician, as well as the biggest and most powerful man in camp. One day when a cowboy jokingly said that he was "too big for a man but not big enough for a horse," he promptly replied that he *was* a horse and would give a dollar to any man who could ride him without spurs. Sam then stripped, with only a bandanna around his neck to hold on by, and one by one he hurled his would-be riders to the ground—thereby demonstrating, but in a friendly and tactful fashion, his ability to take care of himself. He never had any trouble.[80]

White cowhands repeatedly came to the support of Negro members of their outfits. When a drunken cowpuncher in Dodge City began to abuse a Negro cook, for no reason except that he was colored, a sixteen-year-old boy belonging to the Negro's outfit promptly sailed in—carrying guns was banned in Dodge at this time—and soon had the best of the fight. Potentially, a much more serious occasion arose in 1879. It involved the Olive brothers' trail boss, Ira Olive, who had killed a Mexican cowhand a year or so before and who for some reason now began to abuse Jim Kelly—with the aim, E. C. Abbott believed, of getting Kelly to go for his gun so that he could kill him. Kelly, himself a gunman, later claimed that he would have drawn and killed Ira except for the knowledge that he would have to reckon with his brother Print if he did; this he wished to avoid, since Print was his friend. So he took the abuse until Ira struck him in the mouth with his gun, knocking out two teeth. What might have happened next will never be known for at this point the nineteen-year-old Abbott brashly intervened. "If you hit that boy again," he warned ("that boy" was forty years old) "I'll shoot your damn eyes out."[81]

But such protection was not always available. In 1878 a Negro was hired to work on the 22 Ranch, but a member of the outfit—a "nigger killer" type—set out to run him off and one morning began shooting at him. In desperation, the Negro scrambled onto a horse and fled, with the white man in pursuit. Only the white man returned to camp and the Negro's horse showed up the next day with the saddle still on; a few years later a human skeleton, believed to be the Negro's, was found in the neighborhood. The Negro, during this fracas, apparently never attempted to defend himself nor did any member of the outfit lift a finger or even his voice on behalf of the man, or venture to question the white man's conduct. Possibly, had the Negro been with the outfit long enough to establish himself, someone would have intervened, but this is speculation: the outfit stands condemned, with not a single man of the calibre of young Abbott or the sixteen-year-old boy in Dodge City.[82]

Recreation and Social Life

The Negro cowboy engaged in the same amusements as the white—on a basis ranging from apparently complete integration to rigid separation. The extent of this segregation depended upon how well the parties knew one another and, more important, upon whether or not the whites included women.

To understand the character and degree of this segregation, and the way in which it was regarded by both whites and blacks, one must remember that the white men and women of the cow country were largely Southerners or Westerners with a Southern exposure, while the Negroes, if not former slaves, were usually the children of ex-slaves. Both whites and Negroes were thus acquainted, by personal experience or recent tradition, with racial *discrimination* far more severe than anything practiced in the post-bellum cow country, even though racial *segregation* under slavery was less rigid than it became during the late nineteenth century.

When ranch work was slack, particularly in the winter, the hands sometimes held a dance, either a "bunkhouse 'shindig' " in which the participants were all males or a "regular dance" with girls from neighboring ranches or from town if one was close enough. On these occasions the Negro hands had the opportunity to shine, as musicians or dancers or both. Although serving as musicians at either type of dance, they were more conspicuous as dancers in the womanless bunkhouse affairs. Indeed, they might not appear on the dance floor with white women, though, singly or in groups, they might present dancing exhibitions as part of the entertainment.[83]

Segregation in a cattle town, where the Negro cowhand was more of a stranger and white women were present, was much more clearcut than on the familiar ranch. But even here the restrictions were not always as rigid as one might perhaps expect. On the town's streets and among members of the same outfit, segregation might be non-existent. A French baron, returning in 1883 from a visit to the Black Hills, was astonished to see a group of cowboys throwing the lasso and wrestling in front of the door to the hotel bar, with a Negro participating "on a footing of perfect equality." Consequently, he naively assumed that race prejudice had disappeared,"[84] but had the cowboys *entered* the bar this illusion would probably have vanished, even though the region was the Northern Range, not Gulf Coast Texas.

Even in Texas, however, segregation in the saloons was apparently informal. Whites, it seems, were served at one end of the bar, Negroes at the other. But should a white man and a Negro choose to drink and converse together in the "neutral zone" between the two sections probably no objection would be raised. The gunman and gambler Ben Thompson once undertook to "integrate" a San Antonio saloon at the point of a revolver, forcing the bartender to permit the Negroes to "spread out" from their crowded corner into the vacant space at the "white" end of the bar. His friends charitably assumed that he was suffering from a nervous breakdown, but since, upon an earlier occasion, Thompson had shot a white bully who was trying to force a Cherokee-Negro cowboy to down a beer mug full of whiskey, he may actually have been in part influenced by a fleeting impulse to defend the underdog.[85]

If the Negro, however, moved from the saloon to a restaurant, he would encounter a completely segregated situation, partly because of the symbolic value attached to sitting down and eating together—as opposed to standing up at the same bar[86] —but principally because women might be guests in the dining room or cafe. In a town without a colored restaurant, the Negro might have food handed to him at the back door of a cafe—perhaps he might even be permitted to eat in the kitchen—but more probably would, like many white cowboys, prefer to purchase groceries and eat sitting on a hitching rail.[87]

Negroes, of course, were not lodged in "white" hotels—unless they were in attendance on prominent white cattlemen—but cowboys, black and white, usually felt that they had better use for their money than to spend it on hotel rooms. They preferred to spread their "hot rolls" in a livery stable or some other sheltered spot.[88]

The most rigorously segregated cow-town establishments, at least so far as Negro cow-hands were concerned, were brothels staffed with white prostitutes. However, the larger cow-towns at least, such as Dodge City, were also equipped with *bagnios* occupied by "soiled doves of color," while smaller communities usually had a few "public women" of color who operated independently. The rule that Negroes must not patronize white prostitutes did not of course bar relations between white cowhands and colored women.[89]

The cow-town gambling-house, on the other hand, was apparently entirely unsegregated. A gambler who intended to separate a Negro trail hand from his wages through the more than expert use of cards and dice could hardly do so without sitting down with him at the same card or crap table.[90]

The Negro cowhand was accustomed to a degree of segregation and apparently did not resent it—at least not to the extent of risking his life in defiance of the practice. Clashes between Negro cowhands and whites were exceedingly rare. When racial encounters occurred in cattle towns, the Negroes involved were almost always colored soldiers.

Conclusion

Without the services of the eight or nine thousand Negroes—a quarter of the total number of trail drivers—who during the generation after the Civil War helped to move herds up the cattle trails to shipping points, Indian reservations, and fattening grounds and who, between drives, worked on the ranches of Texas and the Indian Territory, the cattle industry would have been seriously handicapped. For apart from their considerable numbers, many of them were especially well-qualified top hands, riders, ropers, and cooks. Of the comparatively few Negroes on the Northern Range, a good many were also men of conspicuous abilities who notably contributed to the industry in that region. These cowhands, in their turn, benefitted from their participation in the industry, even if not to the extent that they deserved. That a degree of discrimination and segregation existed in the cattle country should not obscure the fact that, during the halcyon days of the cattle range, Negroes there frequently enjoyed greater opportunities for a dignified life than anywhere else in the United States. They worked, ate slept, played, and on occasion fought, side by side with their white comrades, and their ability and courage won respect, even admiration. They were often paid the same wages as white cowboys and, in the case of certain horsebreakers, ropers, and cooks, occupied positions of considerable prestige. In a region and period characterized by violence, their lives were probably safer than they would have been in the Southern cotton regions where between 1,500 and 1,600 Negroes were lynched in the two decades after 1882.[91] The skilled and handy Negro probably had a more enjoyable, if a rougher, existence as a cowhand than he would have had as a sharecropper or laborer. Bose Ikard, for example, had a rich, full, and dignified life on the West Texas frontier—as trail driver, as Indian fighter, and as Colonel Goodnight's right-hand man—more so undoubtedly than he could ever have known on a plantation in his native Mississippi.

Negro cowhands, to be sure, were not treated as "equals," except in the rude quasi-equality of the round-up, roping-pen, stampede, and river-crossing—where they were sometimes tacitly recognized even as superiors—but where else in post-Civil War America, at a time of the Negro's nadir, did so many adult Negroes and whites attain even this degree of fraternity? The cow country was no utopia for Negroes, but it did demonstrate that under some circumstances and for at least brief periods white and black in significant numbers could live and work together on more nearly equal terms than had been possible in the United States for two hundred years or would be possible again for nearly another century.

Notes

1. May Davison Rhodes, *The Hired Man on Horseback: A Biography of Eugene Manlove Rhodes* (Boston, 1938), ix-xiii.

2. John Marvin Hunter (ed.), *The Trail Drivers of Texas* (Nashville, 1925), 453.

3. *Ibid.*, 987, 255, 717, 157, 505, 472, 817, 138-139, 805, 718-719; R. J. (Bob) Lauderdale and John M. Doak, *Life on the Range and on the Trail*, Lela Neal Pirtle, editor (San Antonio, 1936), 169.

4. John Hendrix, *If I Can Do It Horseback* (Austin, 1963), 205.

5. John M. Hendrix, "Tribute Paid to Negro Cowmen," *The Cattleman*, XXII (Feb., 1936), 24. See also J. Frank Dobie to KWP, Jan. 30, 1953, J. Frank Dobie, *The Longhorns* (Boston, 1941), 309.

6. William A. Keleher, *The Fabulous Frontier: Twelve New Mexico Items* (Albuquerque, 1962), 162-163, 245, 271; Theodore Roosevelt, *Ranch Life and the Hunting Trail* (N.Y., 1920; 1st ed., 1888), 10-11. See also Floyd C. Bard as told to Agnes Wright Spring, in *Horse Wrangler: Sixty Years in the Saddle in Wyoming and Montana* (Norman, 1960), 12-13; Sir Cecil E. Denny, *The Law Marches West* (Toronto, 1939), 187.

7. J. Frank Dobie, *A Vaquero of the Brush Country* (Dallas, 1929), 12-13; Lauderdale and Doak, *op. cit.*, 11; Hunter, *op. cit.*, 679, 204.

8. Douglas Branch, *The Cowboy and His Interpreters* (N. Y., 1926), 42-43; Ross Santee, *Men and Horses* (N. Y., 1926); Agnes Morley Cleaveland, *No Life for a Lady* (Boston, 1941), 111; William T. Hornaday, "The Cowboys of the Northwest," *Cosmopolitan*, II (Dec., 1886), 226; Edward Everett Dale, *Cow Country* (Norman, 1942), 46-47.

9. Branch, *op. cit.*, 42-43. "For my money he [the wrangler] was one of the most capable fellows around an outfit." Hendrix, *If I Can Do It Horseback*, 185-186.

10. Harry E. Chrisman, *The Ladder of Rivers: The Story of I. P. (Print) Olive* (Denver, 1962), 34-35, 77, 102, 147, 217, 378; Dane Coolidge, *Fighting Men of the West* (Bantam Books, 1952; 1st ed., 1932), 14, 32, 41; Frank Collinson, *Life in the Saddle*, Mary Whatley Clarke, editor, (Norman, 1963), 145.

11. Charles A. Siringo, *Riata and Spurs: The Story of a Lifetime Spent in the Saddle as Cowboy and Ranger* (Boston, 1931; 1st ed., 1927), 27.

12. Ramon F. Adams to KWP, Feb. 6, 1953; Roosevelt, *op. cit.*, 10-11; Ellsworth Collings, "The Hook Nine Ranch in the Indian Territory," *Chronicles of Oklahoma*, XXXIII (Winter, 1955-56), 462; Angie Debo, editor, *The Cowman's Southwest, being the Reminiscences of Oliver Nelson, Freighter, Camp Cook, Frontiersman, in Kansas, Indian Territory, Texas, and Oklahoma, 1876-1893* (Glendale, 1963), 98-99, 107-108; Hendrix, *If I Can Do It Horseback*, 161,205.

13. Homer Croy, *Our Will Rogers* (N. Y. and Boston, 1953), 19-20, 250, 334; Donald Day, *Will*

Rogers: A Biography (N. Y., 1962), 11-16, Chrisman, 77; John Rolfe Burroughs, *Where the West Stayed Young: The Remarkable History of Brown's Park . . .* (N.Y., 1962), 109.

14. Collinson, *op. cit.*, 25-26; James Emmit McCauley, *A Stove-Up Cowboy's Story*, with an introduction by John A. Lomax (Dallas, 1956; 1st ed., 1943), 12.

15. Siringo, *A Texas Cowboy* (Signet Books, 1955; 1st ed., 1886), 38; Siringo, *Riata and Spurs* 17, 18.

16. Dobie *Vaquero*, 100-101.

17. Hunter, *op. cit.*, 112, 417-418; James C. Shaw, *North from Texas: Incidents in the Early Life of a Range Cowman in Texas, Dakota, and Wyoming 1852-1882*, Herbert O. Brayer, editor (Evanston, 1952), 46-47.

18. Hendrix, "Negro Cowmen," 24.

19. Hunter, *op. cit.*, 47-48, 987-988; A. J. Sowell, *Early Settlers and Indian Fighters of Southwest Texas* (Austin, 1900), 757-758; J. Frank Dobie, interview with Joe McCloud, Beeville, Texas, *ca.* 1928, in a letter to KWP, Feb. 16, 1953.

20. Dobie, *Longhorns*, 246-247; E. C. Abbott ("Teddy Blue") and Helena Huntington Smith, *We Pointed Them North: Recollections of a Cowpuncher* (N. Y., 1939), 263.

21. Emerson Hough, *The Story of the Cowboy* (N. Y., 1934; 1st ed., 1897), 91; James W. Freeman (ed.), *Poetry and Prose of the Live Stock Industry* (Denver and Kansas City, 1905), I, 13; Louis Pelzer, *The Cattleman's Frontier . . . 1850-1890* (Glendale, 1936), 48; Roosevelt, *op. cit.*, 10-11; Stanley Walker, "Decline and Fall of the Hired Man," *The New Yorker*, Sept. 12, 1953, p. 110; Clifford P. Westermeier, *Man, Beast, Dust: The Story of Rodeo* (n.p., 1947), 173.

22. Hendrix, "Negro Cowmen," 24; Elmo S. Watson, "Tales of the Trail," probably in a Colorado Springs newspaper in 1916, and Arthur Chapman, interview with Andy Adams, *Denver Times*, Aug. 18, 1915, p. 2. See also Wilson M. Hudson, *Andy Adams: His Life and Writings* (Dallas, 1964), 184, 251. To Professor Hudson's kindness I owe copies of the two newspaper items, *supra*.

23. Burroughs, *op. cit.*, 192-195; Coolidge, *op. cit.*, 79; Dean Krakel, *The Saga of Tom Horn: The Story of a Cattlemen's War* (Laramie, 1954), 9-12.

24. Chrisman, *op. cit.*, 34-35, 77, 217, 378; Harry E. Chrisman, Denver, to KWP, Oct. 23, 1965.

25. Lincoln A. Lang, *Ranching with Roosevelt* (Philadelphia, 1926), 286.

26. Lewis Nordyke, *Cattle Empire: The Fabulous Story of the 3,000,000 Acre XIT* (N. Y., 1949), 138.

27. Jean Ehly, " 'Bones' Hooks of the Panhandle," *Frontier Times*, XXXVI (June-July, 1963), 20-22, 54-55 (illustrated).

28. Edward Seymour Nichols, *Ed Nichols Rode a Horse*, as told to Ruby Nichols Cutbirth (Dallas, 1943), 8-9.

29. Siringo, *Texas Cowboy*, 82-83.

30. Bard, *op. cit.*, 67.

31. Fred Herring, Lometa, Texas, to KWP, July 20, 1965.

32. J. Evetts Haley, *George W. Littlefield, Texan* (Norman, 1943), 181-186.

33. Frederic Remington, "Vagabonding with the Tenth Horse," *The Cosmopolitan*, XXII (Feb., 1897), 352.

34. Abbott and Smith, *op. cit.*, 261-264.

35. Hunter, *op. cit.*, 778.

36. The standard work on the cow-country cook is, of course, Ramon F. Adams, *Come an' Get It: The Story of the Old Cowboy Cook* (Norman, 1952). Almost every general work on the cowboy or the cattle country, and many reminiscences and special studies also contain useful information.

37. Rufus Rockwell Wilson, *Out of the West* (N. Y., 1933), 377; Hough, *op. cit.*, 138-139; J. Frank Dobie, *Cow People* (Boston, 1964), 132; Hunter, *op. cit.*, 485, 43, 307, 535, 295-303, 416-417, 981, 688, 231, 606-607, 81, 679.

38. R. F. Adams, *op. cit.*, 21-22; Lauderdale and Doak, *op. cit.*, 183-185.

39. Dobie, *Vaquero*, 137-139; Dobie, *Cow People*, 140.

40. J. S. Hart, "Jesse Hart, Callahan County Pioneer," *Frontier Times* (Jan., 1953), 86.

41. Cordia Sloan Duke and Joe B. Frantz, *6,000 Miles of Fence: Life on the XIT Ranch of Texas* (Austin, 1961), 172n.; Dobie, *Vaquero*, 137-139; Frazier Hunt, *The Long Trail from Texas: The Story of Ad Spaugh, Cattleman* (N. Y., 1940), 141-145; Bard, *op. cit.*, 145-146.

42. Dobie, *Cow People* 139-140; Bard, *op. cit.*, 82.

43. Dobie, *Vaquero*, 137-139; Duke and Frantz, *op. cit.*, 172n, 84; Bard, *op. cit.*, 67.

44. J. Evetts Haley, *The XIT Ranch of Texas and the Early Days of the Llano Estacado* (Norman, 1953), 77-78.

45. Lauderdale and Doak, 183-185; Allen A. Erwin, *The Southwest of John H. Slaughter* (Glendale, 1965), 147-149; Hunter, *op. cit.*, 272.

46. John A. and Alan Lomax, *Cowboy Songs* (N. Y., 1938), 78-81, xvii-xix.

47. Max Krueger, *Pioneer Life in Texas* (San Antonio, 1930), 58-71.

48. Erwin, *op. cit.*, 147-149, 159; Dobie and Frantz, bet. 102 and 103; Bard, *op. cit.*, 102; Dobie, *Vaquero*, 137-139.

49. Colonel Jack Potter, *Cattle Trails of the Old West* (Clayton, N. M., 1939), 75.

50. Potter, *op. cit.*, 79-80; Erwin, *op. cit.*, 102, 147, 150, 159, 307-308, 317, 323.

51. Burroughs, *op. cit.*, 71; Duke and Frantz, *op. cit.*, 171-172.

52. N. Howard (Jack) Thorp, *Songs of the Cowboys* (Boston, 1921), 166-168; Thorp, "Banjo in the Cow Camps," *Atlantic*, CLXVI (Aug., 1940), 195-196; Thorp, *Pardner of the Wind* (Caldwell, Ida., 1945), 22, 285.

53. Ramon F. Adams, Dallas, to KWP, Feb. 6, 1953.

54. Frank Dobie, "Notes on Meeting of Trail Drivers of Texas, San Antonio, *ca.* October 1924";

Dobie, "The Old Trail Drivers," *Country Gentleman,* XC (Feb., 14, 1925), 8, 28 (photograph); Dobie to KWP, Feb. 16, 1953; Dobie, *Cow People,* 222-223 (photograph); Hunter, *op. cit.,* 378.

55. J. Evetts Haley, *Charles Goodnight: Cowman & Plainsman* (Boston and N. Y., 1936), 166-167; 207, 215, 242-243; *The West Texas Historical Association Year Book* (Oct., 1942), 127.

56. Erwin, *op. cit.,* 102, 147-150, 159, 307-308, 317, 323.

57. Chrisman, *op. cit.,* 93, 124, 321, 358-359, 401.

58. George Bolds, *Across the Cimarron: The Adventures of "Cimarron" George Bolds, Last of the Frontiersmen,* as he related his life story to James D. Horan (N. Y., 1956), 48-49.

59. Dobie, *Cow People,* 47; Chris Emmett, *Shanghai Pierce: A Fair Likeness* (Norman, 1953), viii, 4, 10, 47, 51-52, 101, 127, 130, 133, 265-266.

60. All the general works on the cattle industry and most of the personal reminiscences give more or less attention to wages. Perhaps most generally useful is Louis Pelzer, *op. cit.,* 166, 246.

61. Freeman, I *op. cit.,* 559; James Henry Cook, *Fifty Years on the Old Frontier as Cowboy, Hunter, Guide, Scout, and Ranchman* (New Haven, 1925; 1st ed., 1923), 8-9.

62. Abbott and Smith, *op. cit.,* 39; Lauderdale and Doak, *op. cit.,* 183-185.

63. Stanley Vestal, *The Missouri* (N. Y., 1945), 163.

64. The only treatment of this strike in any detail is by Ruth Allen, *Chapters in the History of Organized Labor in Texas* (Austin, 1941), 33-42. Excellent as is this pioneer study, the "cowboy strike" deserves still further attention. Other accounts of, or references to, this strike—not mentioned in the Allen article—are in Charles A. Siringo, *A Lone Star Cowboy* (Sante Fe, 1919), 268-269; and Lewis Nordyke, *Great Roundup: The Story of Texas and Southwestern Cowmen* (N. Y., 1955), 109-111.

65. Helena Huntington Smith, *The War on Powder River* (N. Y., 1966), 31-33, 289; John Clay, *My Life on the Range* (Chicago, 1924), 123, 125 (Clay mistakenly places this strike in 1884 rather than 1886; he also mentions another strike in the fall).

66. John L. McCarty, *Maverick Town: The Story of Old Tascosa* (Norman, 1946), 112-113; Boone McClure, "A Review of the T Anchor Ranch," *Panhandle Plains Historical Review,* III (1930), 68-69.

67. McCarty, *op. cit.,* 141-149, esp. 144 and 149.

68. Hendrix, "Negro Cowmen," 24.

69. Dobie, *Cow People,* 233.

70. Haley, *Goodnight,* 136.

71. Dobie, *Vaquero,* 97, 34-36, 46-47; Shaw, *op. cit.,* 34-36, 46-47.

72. C. Vann Woodward, *The Strange Career of Jim Crow* (N. Y., 1955), presents the thesis that segregation in the extreme form which it had assumed by the early 1900s was a comparatively recent development.

73. Siringo, *Riata and Spurs,* 27; Haley, *Littlefield,* 55, 90, 93, 100-101, 114, 134; J. Evetts Haley, *Jeff Milton: A Good Man with a Gun* (Norman, 1948), 19.

74. Amanda Wardin Brown," "A Pioneer in Colorado and Wyoming," *The Colorado Magazine*, XXXV (Oct., 1958), 274.

75. Duke and Frantz, *op. cit.*, 163-164.

76. Debo, *op. cit.*, 108; Dobie, *Longhorns*, 107-108; Hunter, *op. cit.*, 205; Ray M. Beauchamp, "The Town That Died Laughing," *Frontier Times* (Summer, 1960), 30-31, 50-52; Westermeier, *Trailing the Cowboy*, 202-203.

77. Chrisman, *op. cit.*, 104, 201; Harry E. Chrisman, Denver, to KWP, Oct. 23, 1965.

78. Dobie, *Cow People*, 233-237.

79. Hettye Wallace Branch, *The Story of "80 John": A Biography of the Most Respected Negro Ranchmen in the Old West* (N. Y., 1960), 17-18.

80. Dobie, *Vaquero*, 137-139.

81. Hendrix, "Negro Cowmen," 24; Ross Santee, *Lost Pony Tracks* (Bantam Books, 1956; 1st ed., 1953), 202-203; Abbott and Smith, *op. cit.*, 38-40; Chrisman, 201.

82. William Joseph Alexander Elliot, *The Spurs* (Spur, Texas, 1939), 209-210.

83. Duke and Frantz, *op. cit.*, 102-103, 189-190; Santee, *op. cit.*, 158-159.

84. Edmond Mandat-Gracey, *Cow-Boys and Colonels: Narrative of a Journey across the Prairie and over the Black Hills of Dakota*, translated by William Conn (Philadelphia and N. Y., 1963), 325-326.

85. J. H. Plenn, *Texas Hellion: The True Story of Ben Thompson* (n. Y., 1955), 60, 142; Hendrix, "Negro Cowmen," 24; O. C. Fisher with J. C. Dykes, *King Fisher: His Life and Times* (Norman, 1966), 124-126.

86. Harry Golden, *Only in America* (Permabooks, 1959; 1st ed., 1958), 105-107, presenting his "Vertical Negro Plan" for abolishing segregation, advances the theory that no Southerner objected to mingling with Negroes so long as neither party sat down!

87. See Rhodes, *op. cit*, 86-88, for the attempt of a Negro to eat in a white restaurant in a New Mexico cowtown.

88. Bolds, *op. cit.*, 48-49; McCarty, *op. cit.*, 149.

89. Nyle E. Miller and Joseph W. Snell, *Why the West Was Wild* (Topeka, 1963), 614-615, 127, 453; Burroughs, *op. cit.*, 71; William R. Cox, *Luke Short and His Era* (Garden City, N. Y., 1961), 54-55; Westermeier, *Trailing the Cowboy*, 209, 213; Walker D. Wyman and Bruce Sibert, *Nothing But Prairie and Sky: Life on the Dakota Range in the Early Days* (Norman, 1954), 142-143.

90. Lauderdale and Doak, *op. cit.*, 161; Haley, *Jeff Milton*, 95; Rhodes, *op. cit.*, 86-88; W. M. Hutchinson, editor, *A Bar Cross Man: The Life & Personal Writings of Eugene Manlove Rhodes* (Norman, 1956), 3-5.

91. Walter White, *Rope & Faggot: A Biography of Judge Lynch* (N. Y., 1929), *passim*; Jessie Parkhurst Guzman, editor, *Negro Year Book, 1941-1946* (Tuskegee, Ala., 1947), 306-307.